Shareholder Activism

Schriftenreihe zum Gesellschafts- und Kapitalmarktrecht

Herausgegeben von Lutz Michalski (†), Axel Jäger
und Klaus-Rudolf Wagner

Band 43

PL ACADEMIC RESEARCH

Marion D. Hartmann

Shareholder Activism

Benefits and Drawbacks

PL ACADEMIC RESEARCH

Bibliographic Information published by the Deutsche Nationalbibliothek
The Deutsche Nationalbibliothek lists this publication
in the Deutsche Nationalbibliografie; detailed bibliographic
data is available in the internet at http://dnb.d-nb.de.

Zugl.: Berlin, Humboldt-Univ., Diss., 2012

Library of Congress Cataloging-in-Publication Data

Hartmann, Marion D., 1980- author.
Shareholder activism : benefits and drawbacks / Marion D. Hartmann.
pages cm. -- (Schriftenreihe zum gesellschafts- und kapitalmarktrecht ; Band 43)
Doctoral Humboldt-Universit?t, Berlin 2012.
Includes bibliographical references.
ISBN 978-3-631-64293-1
1. Stockholders--Legal status, laws, etc.--United States. 2. Stockholders--Legal status, laws, etc.--Germany. 3. Corporate governance--Law and legislation--United States. 4. Corporate governance--Law and legislation--Germany. I. Title.
K1338.H37 2014
346.73'0666--dc23

2013042902

11
ISSN 1619-117X
ISBN 978-3-631-64293-1 (Print)
E-ISBN 978-3-653-03159-1 (E-Book)
DOI 10.3726/ 978-3-653-03159-1

PKL Academic Research is an Imprint of Peter Lang GmbH.

Peter Lang – Frankfurt am Main · Bern · Bruxelles · New York · Oxford · Warszawa · Wien

This book is part of an editor's series of PL Academic Research and was peer reviewed prior to publication.

www.peterlang.com

To my parents

Acknowledgements

This thesis was accepted as a dissertation by the Faculty of Law of Humboldt-Universität zu Berlin during the winter semester 2011/12. The print version has been updated and is at the level of end of December 2012.

First and foremost, my heartfelt thanks go to my supervisor, Prof. Dr. Christine Windbichler, LL.M. (Berkeley), for her wise and committed supervision of my work. I am very grateful for her valuable and farsighted advice characterized by her international understanding of corporate governance, for the very friendly, willing and open dialogue and her pragmatic approach. Further, I want to thank her for the suggestion to write this thesis in English and her commitment with regard to Duke Law School; both eased the co-supervision of the U.S.-American part of my thesis by Prof. James D. Cox, Brainerd Currie Professor of Duke Law School.

I very much want to thank Prof. Cox for his research suggestion on shareholder proposals and the insight on shareholder activism he provided me with during my LL.M. year at Duke; it was the reason why I decided to make it the topic of this thesis. I greatly appreciate his advice and hints on the most recent developments on the topic and his engagement from my time as an LL.M. student on to the defense of this work.

I would also like to acknowledge the assistance of Judy Horowitz and Jennifer Mayer of the International Office of Duke Law School which enabled me to participate in the LL.M. program of Duke Law School and to return as a visiting scholar using fantastic research conditions to advance my dissertation.

The State of Berlin has provided me with the generous Elsa-Neumann-Scholarship, which has made it possible for me to write this thesis. During my stay as a visiting scholar at Duke Law School, the German Academic Exchange Service increased this scholarship.

I am very grateful for the support of my family. This work would not have been possible without the understanding and assistance of my boyfriend Oliver. My heartfelt thanks go to my parents, who took it for granted to always encourage and support me during my education. This thesis is dedicated to them.

Summary of Contents

Table of Contents

List of Abbreviations

Abbreviation	For German Term/Translation	For English Term/Translation
A		
A.2d	–	Second Series of the Atlantic Reporter (regional case reporter containing selected opinions of state supreme and lower appellate courts, from 1939 until present)
a.D.	**Außer Dienst**	off duty
a.F.	**Alte Fassung**	old version
ABA	–	American Bar Association
ACAD. MGMT. REV.	–	Academic Management Review
AcP	Allgemeine Civilrechtliche Praxis	–
aff'd	–	affirmed
AFM	Authorité des Marchés Financiers	
AFSCME	–	American Federation of State, County and Municipal Employees
AG	**Aktiengesellschaft**	corporation
AG	Die Aktiengesellschaft	–
AKRON L. REV.	–	Akron Law Review
AktG	**Aktiengesetz**	(German) Stock Corporation Act
Ala.	–	Alabama
AM. ECON. REV.	–	American Economic Review
AM. J. COMP. L.	–	American Journal of Comparative Law
AMER. ECON. REV.	–	American Economic Review
Annot.	Kommentiert/Anmerkung	**annotated/annotation**
app.	Anhang	**appendix**
Apr.	April	**April**
ArbHdb	**Arbeitshandbuch**	handbook
Art.	**Artikel**	article
ARUG	**Gesetz zur Umsetzung der Aktionärsrechterichtlinie**	Act Implementing the Shareholder Rights Directive
Austl. J. Corp. L.	–	Australian Journal of Corporate Law

B		
B.C.	–	Bankruptcy Code

BaFin	**Bundesanstalt für Finanzdienstleistungsaufsicht**	(Germany's) Federal Financial Supervisory Authority
BAI	Bundesverband Alternative Investments e.V.	–
Bankr. N.D. Cal.	–	Bankruptcy Court Northern District of California
BayObLG	**Bayrisches Oberlandesgericht**	Court of appeals for selected matters in Bavaria
BB	Der Betriebsberater	–
Begr.	**Begründung**	reasoning
Begr. RegE	**Begründung des Regierungsentwurfs**	reasoning of the government draft
BEHG	**Bundesgesetz über die Börsen und den Effektenhandel (Schweiz)**	Federal Act on Stock Exchanges and Securities Trading (Switzerland)
Bell J. Econ.	–	The Bell Journal of Economics
BFH	**Bundesfinanzhof**	Federal Fiscal Court
BGB	**Bürgerliches Gesetzbuch**	German Civil Code
BGBl.	**Bundesgesetzblatt**	Federal Law Gazette
BGH	**Bundesgerichtshof**	Civil Court of Justice
BGHZ	**Entscheidungen des Bundesgerichtshofs in Zivilsachen**	decisions of the (German) Federal Court of Justice in civil matters
BKR	Zeitschrift für Bank– und Kapitalmarktrecht	–
BMF	**Bundesministerium für Finanzen**	Federal Ministry of Finance
BR–Drucks	**Bundesrat–Drucksache**	printed matter of the Bundesrat (German Federal Council)
BRT	–	Business Roundtable
BT–Drucks	**Bundestag–Drucksache**	printed matter of the Bundestag (German Federal Diet)
Bus. Law.	–	Business Lawyer
BVH	Bundesverband der Börsenvereine an deutschen Hochschulen e.V.	–

C		
C.F.R.	–	Code of Federal Regulations
CA. D.C.	–	California District Court
Cal.	–	California
CalPERS	–	California Public Employees Retirement System
Cardozo L. Rev.	–	Cardozo Law Review

CDU / CSU	**Christlich Demokratische Union / Christlich Soziale Union**	Christian Democratic Union / Christian Social Union
CEO	–	Chief Executive Officer
CESR	–	Committee of the European Securities Regulators
CFO	–	Chief Financial Officer
ch.	Kapitel	**chapter**
CII	–	Council of Institutional Investors
Cir.	–	Circuit Court
CLO	–	Chief Legal Officer
Co.	–	Company
COLUM. L. REV.	–	Columbia Law Review
Cong.	–	Congress
Conn.	–	Connecticut
CONN. L. REV.	–	Connecticut Law Review
COO	–	Chief Operating Officer
Corp.	–	Corporation

D		
D.	–	Democrat
D.C.	Amtsgericht	**District Court**
D.C. Cir.	–	United States Court of Appeals for the District of Columbia Circuit
D.C. Mass.	–	United States District Court for the District of Massachusetts
D.C. N.Y.	–	United States District Court for the District of New York
D.C. Nev.	–	United States District Court for the District of Nevada
D.D.C.	–	United States District Court for the District of Columbia
D.Nev.	–	United States District Court for the District of Nevada
DAI	Deutsches Aktieninstitut	–
DAV	**Deutscher Anwaltsverein**	German Lawyers' Association
DAX	Deutscher Aktien Index	German stock index
DB	Der Betrieb	–
DCGK	**Deutscher Corporate Governance Kodex**	German Corporate Governance Codex
Dec.	Dezember	**December**
Del. C.	–	Delaware Code
Del. Ch.	–	Delaware Chancery Court

Del. Code Ann.	–	Delaware Code Annotated
DEL. J. CORP. L.	–	Delaware Journal of Corporate Law
DGCL	–	Delaware General Corporation Law
DGCL	–	Delaware General Corporation Act
Div.	–	Division
Div. of Corp. Fin.	–	Division of Corporate Finance (of the SEC)
DNotZ	Deutsche Notar–Zeitschrift	–
DStR	Deutsches Steuerrecht	–
DSW	Deutsche Schutzvereinigung für Wertpapierbesitz	–
DTR	–	Disclosure Rules and Transparency Rules
DUKE L.J.	–	Duke Law Journal
DZWIR	Deutsche Zeitschrift für Wirtschafts– und Insolvenzrecht	–

E		
e.g.	**exempli gratia** – for example	
eBanz	**Elektronischer Bundesanzeiger**	Electronic Federal Gazette
ed.	Herausgeber/Auflage	**editor/edition**
eds.	Herausgeber (Plural)	**editors**
EEC	Europäische Wirtschaftsunion	**European Economic Community**
ERISA	–	Employee Retirement Income Security Act (1974)
ESMA	–	European Securities and Market Authority
ESME	–	European Market Expert Group
et al.	**et alii** – and others	
et seq.	**et sequentes** – and the following	
etc.	**et cetera** – and so on	
EuZW	Europäische Zeitschrift für Wirtschaftsrecht	–

F		
F.	–	Federal Reporter (covering cases from 1880 – 1924 of different U.S. courts)
F.2d	–	Federal Reporter, Second Series (cases from 1924 – 1993 of different courts)
F.3d	–	Federal Reporter, Third Series (cases after from 1993 on, of the United States Courts of Federal Claims or Appeals)
F. App'x	–	Federal Appendix (covering federal Courts of Appeals' cases since 2001)

F. Supp.	–	Federal Supplement (Case Law Reporter by West Publishing in the U.S. including selected opinions of the District Courts from 1933 – 1998)
F. Supp. 2d	–	Federal Supplement Second (District Court cases from 1998 and past)
FAZ	Frankfurter Allgemeine Zeitung	–
FCD		Fundamental Corporate Decision
FDP	**Freie Demokratische Partei**	Liberal Democratic Party
Feb.	Februar	**February**
Fed. Reg.	–	Federal Register
Fed. Sec. L. Rep.	–	Federal Securities Law Reporter
FIN. MKTS. PORTFOLIO MGMT.	–	Financial Markets Portfolio Management
FORDHAM L. REV.	–	Fordham Law Review
Frhr.	**Freiherr**	Baron
FS	**Festschrift**	commemorative publication
FSA	–	Financial Service Authority
FTD	Financial Times Deutschland	commemorative publication

G		
GA. L. REV.	–	Georgia Law Review
Gen. Assem.	–	General Assembly
GEO. L.J.	–	The Georgetown Law Journal
GA. L. REV.	–	Georgia Law Review
GG	**Grundgesetz**	German Constitution
GO	**Geschäftsordnung**	bylaw
Großkomm	Großkommentar	–
GWR	Gesellschafts- und Wirtschafts-recht	–

H		
HASTINGS L.J.	–	Hastings Law Journal
HAZ	Hannoversche Allgemeine Zeitung	–
HARV. BUS. REV.	–	Harvard Business Review
HARV. L. REV.	–	Harvard Law Review
Hdb.	Handbuch	Handbook
HGB	**Handelsgesetzbuch**	German Commercial Code
H.R.	–	House of Representatives

I		
id.	–	refers to single reference in immediately preceding footnote
Ill.	–	Illinois
Inc.	–	Incorporation
Indus.	–	Industries
InsO	**Insolvenzordnung**	German Insolvency Code
Int'l	–	International
InvG	**Investmentgesetz**	Investment Act
IRRC	–	The Investor Responsibility Research Center Institute
ISDA	–	International Swap and Derivatives Association Inc.
ISS		(former) Institutional Shareholder Services (past acquisition: RiskMetrics Group)

J		
J. Bus.	–	The Journal of Business
J. Corp. Fin.	–	Journal of Corporate Finance
J. Corp. L.	–	Journal of Corporation Law
J. Econ. Bus.	–	Journal of Economics & Business
J. Econ. Persp.	–	Journal of Economic Perspectives
J. Fin.	–	Journal of Finance
J. Fin. Econ.	–	Journal of Financial Economics
J. Fin. Research	–	The Journal of Financial Research
J. L. & Econ.	–	Journal of Law & Economics
J. Int'l L.	–	Journal of International Law
J. Political Econ.	–	The Journal of Political Economy
J. Portfolio Mmgt.	–	Journal of Portfolio Management
JZ	Juristische Zeitung	–

K		
KG	**Kammergericht (Berlin)**	Superior Court of Justice (of Berlin)
KöKo	Kölner Kommentar	–
KonTraG	**Gesetz zur Kontrolle und Transparenz im Unternehmensbereich**	Act for Control and Transparency in Business

L		
Law & Contemp. Probs.	–	Law and Contemporary Problems (Journal)
LBO	–	Leveraged Buy–out
LG	**Landgericht**	Regional Court

Litig.	Prozessführung	**Litigation**
LLC	–	Limited Liability Company
LLP	–	Limited Liability Partnership
LSE	Londoner Börse	**London Stock Exchange**

M		
Mar.	März	**March**
M&A	–	Mergers & Acquisitions
MaKonV	Marktmanipulations–Konkretisierungsverordnung	Market Manipulation Definition Regulation
Mass.	–	Massachusetts
Mass. App. Ct.	–	Massachusetts Appeals Court
MBCAA		Model Business Corporation Act Annotated
MBO	–	Management Buy-out
M.D.N.C.	–	U.S. District Court for the Middle District of North Carolina
Mich.	–	Michigan
MICH. L. REV.	–	Michigan Law Review
Minn.	–	Minnesota
Minn. Ct. App.		Minnesota Court of Appeals
MitBestG	**Gesetz über die Mitbestimmung der Arbeitnehmer (Mitbestimmungsgesetz)**	German Codetermination Act
mn(n).	Randnummer(n)	**marginal note(s)**
Mo.	–	Missouri
MPIfG	**Max Planck Institut für Gesellschaftsforschung**	Max Planck Institute for the Study of Societies
MR	**Ministerialrat**	Undersecretary
MüKo	Münchener Kommentar	–
Münch. Hdb.	Münchener Handbuch des Gesellschaftsrechts	–

N		
n./nn.	Fußnote/-en	**footnote/-s**
NASDAQ	–	National Association of Securities Dealers Automated Quotations
NaStraG	**Namensaktiengesetz**	Act on Registered Shares
NAL	–	No-Action Letter (of the Securities Exchange Commission)
NATP	–	National Association of Tax Professionals
N.C. L. REV.	–	North Carolina Law Review
N.E.2d		North Eastern Reporter Second (contains published U.S. state appellate courts case decisions for the according region)
N.D. Ill.	–	Northern District of Illinois
N.J.	–	New Jersey
N.J. Ch.	–	New Jersey Court of Chancery, now Superior Court

NJW	Neue Juristische Wochenschrift	–
no./nos.	Nummer(n)	**number(s)**
Nw. U. L. Rev.	–	Northwestern University Law Review
N.Y.L.J.	–	The New York Law Journal
NYSE	–	New York Stock Exchange
N.Y.S.2d	–	New York Supplement Second (opinions and decisions of state courts of New York, from 1938 on)
NZG	Neue Zeitschrift für Gesellschaftsrecht	–

O		
Oct.	Oktober	**October**
Ohio St. L.J.	–	Ohio State Law Journal
O.J.	–	Official Journal of the European Community
Okla.	–	Oklahoma
OLG	**Oberlandesgericht**	Higher Regional Court
OPEC	Organisation erdölexportierender Länder	**Organization of the Petroleum Exporting Countries**
Or.	Oregon	Oregon
OTC	außerbörslich (Finanztermingeschäfte)	**over the counter** (not exchange traded)
OWiG	**Das Gesetz über Ordnungswidrigkeiten**	Act of Administrative Offences

P		
P.2d	–	Pacific Reporter Second (1931 – 2000, Appellate Court Cases from certain states)
Pa.	–	Pennsylvania
Para.	–	Paragraph
PR	Öffentlichkeitsarbeit	**Public Relations**
pt.	Teil	part
Pub. L. No.	–	Public Law Number

R		
R&D	–	Research and Development
RabelsZ	**Rabels Zeitschrift für ausländisches und internationales Privatrecht**	The Rabel Journal of Comparative and International Private Law
RegBegr	**Regierungsbegründung**	governmental reasoning
RegE	**Regierungsentwurf**	government draft
Reg. Sess.	–	Regular Session
Regulation FD	–	Fair Disclosure regulation
Rep. No.	–	Report Number
Rev. Acc. Stud.	–	Review of Accounting Studies
RisikoBegrG	**Risikobegrenzungsgesetz**	Risk Limitation Act
RMBCA	–	Revised Model Business Corporation Act

S		
S.	Senate	**Senate**
SBSR	–	Security-Based Swap Reporting
S.C. L. Rev.	–	South Carolina Law Review
S. Cal. L. Rev.	–	Southern California Law Review
S. Ct.	–	Supreme Court Reporter
S.D.Fla.		U.S. District Court of the Southern District of Florida
SDR	–	Security-Based Data Repositories
S.D.N.Y.	–	U.S. District Court of the Southern District of New York
SEA	–	Securities Exchange Act 1934
SEC	U.S. Börsenaufsichtskontrolle für die Kontrolle des Wertpapierhandels	**Securities Exchange Commission**
SEC-NAL	–	Securities Exchange Commission – No-Action Letter
sec.	Paragraph	**section**
Servs.	–	**Services**
Sess.	Sitzung	**Session**
S'holders	Aktionäre	**Shareholders**
S.C. L. Rev.	–	South Carolina Law Review
SdK	**Schutzgemeinschaft der Kapitalanleger**	Society for the Protection of Small Investors
S.D.N.Y.	–	United States District Court of the Southern District of New York
Seattle U. L. Rev.	–	Seattle University Law Review
sent.	Satz	**sentence**
SIFM	–	Securities Industry and Financial Market Association
SOA	–	Sarbanes-Oxley-Act
S&P	–	Standard & Poor
SSRN	–	Social Science Research Network
SSRN-id	–	Social Science Research Network-identification number
Stan. J.L. Bus. & Fin.	–	Stanford Journal of Law, Business & Finance
Stan. L. Rev.	–	Stanford Law Review
StGB	**Strafgesetzbuch**	Penal Code
Sup. Ct.	–	Supreme Court (regional)
Supp.[1]	– Beilage (Zeitschrift) – Ergänzungslieferung (Loseblattsammlung)	**Supplement**
Sys.	–	System(s)

1 Please consider the different significance of the term supplement. In Germany, supplements are integrated into a binder by exchanging the corresponding old pages with new pages. In the United States, single pages of supplements are not integrated into the older version to update it, but a supplement as such that is added either in the back of a book or as a separate volume.

T		
TCI	–	The Children Investment Fund
TENN. J. BUS. L.	–	Tennessee Journal of Business Law
TEX. L. REV.	–	Texas Law Review
TIAA-CREF	–	Teachers Insurance and Annuity Association – College Retirement Equities Fund
tit.	Abschnitt	**title**
TransPuG	**Transparenz- und Publizitätsgesetz**	Law for Transparency and Publicity
TUL. L. REV.	–	Tulane Law Review

U		
U. CIN. L. REV.	–	University of Cincinnati Law Review
UCLA	–	University of California, Los Angeles
UCLA L. REV.	–	UCLA Law Review
UFTA	–	Uniform Fraudulent Transfer Act
U. ILL. L. REV.	–	University of Illinois Law Review
U.K.	–	United Kingdom
U. MIAMI L. REV.	–	University of Miami Law Review
UMAG	**Gesetz zur Unternehmensintegrität und Modernisierung des Anfechtungsrechts**	Act on Corporate Integrity and Modernization of the Right of Rescission
UmwG	**Umwandlungsgesetz**	German Reorganization Act
UmwStG	**Umwandlungssteuergesetz**	German Reorganization Tax Act
U. PA. L. REV.	–	University of Pennsylvania Law Review
U.S.	–	United States
U.S.C.	–	United States Code

V		
v.	gegen	**versus**
VA. L. REV.	–	Virginia Law Review
VAND. L. REV.	–	Vanderbilt University Law Review
VG	**Verwaltungsgericht**	Administrative trial court
VGR	Wissenschaftliche Vereinigung für Unternehmens- und Gesellschaftsrecht	–
VILL. L. REV.	–	Villanova Law Review
Vol.	Band	**Volume**
Vorb	**Vorbemerkung**	preliminary note
Vors.	**Vorsitzender**	presiding
VorstAG	**Gesetz zur Angemessenheit der Vorstandsvergütung**	Act on the Appropriateness of Management Board Compensation
VW	**Volkswagen**	Volkswagen

W		
Wall St. J.	–	The Wall Street Journal
WASH. & LEE L. REV.	–	Washington & Lee Law Review

Wash. U. L. Q.	–	Washington University Law Quarterly
Wis. L. Rev.	–	Wisconsin Law Review
WM	Wertpapiermitteilung	–
WpHG	**Wertpapierhandelsgesetz**	Securities Trading Act
WpÜG	**Wertpapiererwerbs- und übernahmegesetz**	Securities Acquisition and Takeover Act

Y		
Yale L. J.	–	Yale Law Journal
Yale J. On Reg.	–	The Yale Journal on Regulation

Z		
ZBB	Zeitschrift für Bankrecht und Bankwirtschaft	–
ZCG	Zeitschrift für Corporate Governance	–
ZGR	Zeitschrift für Unternehmens- und Gesellschaftsrecht	–
ZHR	Zeitschrift für das gesamte Handels- und Wirtschaftsrecht	–
ZIP	Zeitschrift für Wirtschaftsrecht	–
ZRP	Zeitschrift für Rechtspolitik	–

Bibliography

A

- Michael Adams, Aktienoptionspläne und Vorstandsvergütungen, ZIP 2002, 1323 et seq.
- Michael Adams, Eigentum, Kontrolle und Beschränkte Haftung, 1st Edition 1991, Baden-Baden.
- Michael Adams, Höchststimmrechte, Mehrfachstimmrechte und sonstige wundersame Hindernisse auf dem Markt für Unternehmenskontrolle, AG 1990, 63 et seq.
- Edward Adams/Arijit Mukherji, Spin-Offs, Fiduciary Duty, and the Law, 68 FORDHAM L. REV. 15 (1999).
- Frederick H. Alexander/James D. Honaker, Power to the Franchise or The Fiduciaries?: An Analysis of the Limits on Stockholder Activists Bylaws, 33 DEL. J. CORP. L. 749 (2008).
- Franklin Allen/Antonio E. Bernardo/Ivo Welch, A Theory of Dividends Based on Tax Clienteles, 1999, http://citeseerx.ist.psu.edu/viewdoc/download?doi=10.1.1.35.8843&rep=rep1&type=pdf.
- Holger Altmeppen, Arbeitnehmerbeteiligung im Personalausschuss des Aufsichtsrats, in: Gerd Pfeiffer/Joachim Kummer/Silke Scheuch (eds.), Festschrift für Hans Erich Brandner, 1996, Köln.
- Holger Altmeppen, Ausgliederung zwecks Organschaftsbildung gegen die Sperrminorität?, DB 1998, 49 et seq.
- American Bar Association – Section of Business Law – Committee on Corporate Laws, Changes in the Model Business Corporation Act – Proposed Amendments To Chapter 8 And 10 Relating To Voting By Shareholder For The Election of Directors, 61 BUS. LAW. 399 (2005).
- American Bar Association – Section of Business Law – Committee on Corporate Laws, Model Business Corporation Act Annotated, 4th Edition 2008, Chicago.
- American Bar Association – Section of Business Law – Corporate Governance Committee, Report of the Task Force of the ABA Section of Business Law Corporation Governance Committee on Delineation of Governance Roes and Responsibilities, 65 BUS. LAW. 107 (2009).
- Iman Anabtawi, Some Scepticism About Increasing Shareholder Power, 53 UCLA L. REV. 561 (2006).

- Iman Anabtawi/Lynn Stout, Fiduciary Duties for Activist Shareholders, 60 Stan. L. Rev. 1255 (2008).
- Gregor Andrade/Mark Mitchell/Erik Stafford, New Evidence and Perspectives on Mergers, 15 J. Econ. Persp. 103 (2001).
- Georg Annuß/Ingo Theusinger, Das VorstAG – Praktische Hinweise zum Umgang mit dem neuen Recht, BB 2009, 2434 et seq.
- Arnd Arnold, Aktive Aktionäre – Fluch oder Segen für die Corporate Governance? Zur Notwendigkeit einer Regulierung, ZCG 2008, 221 et seq.
- Heinz Dieter Assmann/Thorsten Pötzsch/Uwe H. Schneider (eds.) Wertpapiererwerbs- und Übernahmegesetz, 2005, Köln.
- Heinz-Dieter Assmann/Uwe H. Schneider (eds.), Wertpapierhandelsgesetz, 4th Edition 2006, Köln.

B

- Gregor Bachmann, Private Ordnung, 2006, Tübingen.
- Gregor Bachmann, Rechtsfragen der Wertpapierleihe, ZHR 173 (1999), 596 et seq.
- R. Franklin Balotti/Jesse A. Finkelstein, The Delaware Law of Corporations and Business Organizations, Volume 1, 3rd Edition (2010), Austin, Boston, Chicago, New York, The Netherlands.
- R. Franklin Balotti/Jesse A. Finkelstein, The Delaware Law of Corporations & Business Organizations, Statutory Deskbook, 2010, Austin, Boston, Chicago, New York, The Netherlands.
- Stephen M. Bainbridge, Constraints on Shareholder Activism in the United States and Slovenia, 2000, http://ssrn.com/abstract=228780.
- Stephen Bainbridge, Directors Primacy and Shareholder Disempowerment, 119 Harv. L. Rev. 1735 (2006).
- Stephen Bainbridge, Director Primacy: The Means and Ends of Corporate Governance, 97 Nw. U. L. Rev. 547 (2003).
- Stephen Bainbridge, Corporate Law and Economics, 2002, New York.
- H. Kent Baker, Dividends and Dividend Policy, 2009, Hoboken, New Jersey.
- Heinz Georg Bamberger/Herbert Roth (eds.), Beck'scher Online-Kommentar BGB, 17th Edition 2010, München.
- Alexander Bassen, Einflußnahme institutioneller Investoren auf Corporate Governance und Unternehmensführung – Ergebnisse einer empirischen Untersuchung, DtA-Stiftungslehrstuhl für Entrepreneurial Finance, 2001.

- Thomas W. Bates/David A. Becher/Michael L. Lemmon, Board Classification and Managerial Entrenchment: Evidence from the market of corporate control, 87 J. Fin. Econ. 646 (2008).
- Jobst-Hubertus Bauer/Christian Arnold, Festsetzung und Herabsetzung der Vorstandsvergütung nach dem VorstAG, AG 2009, 717 et seq.
- Adolf Baumbach/Alfred Hueck, GmbHG, 19th Edition 2010, München.
- Theodor Baums, Der Aufsichtsrat – Aufgaben und Reformfragen, ZIP 1995, 11 et seq.
- Baums, Stellungnahme zur Aktienrechtsreform 1997 von Prof. Dr. Theodor Baums, in: Die Aktienrechtsreform 1997, AG special issue 1997, 26 et seq.
- Theodor Baums/Christian Fraune, Institutionelle Anleger und Publikumsgesellschaft: Eine empirische Untersuchung, AG 1995, 97 et seq.
- Theodor Baums/Maike Sauter, Anschleichen an Übernahmeziele mit Hilfe von Aktienderivaten, ZHR 173 (2009), 454 et seq.
- Barry Baysinger/Robert E. Hoskisson, The Composition of Boards of Directors and Strategic Control: Effects on Corporate Strategy, 15 Acad. Mgmt. Rev. 72 (1990).
- Franz Xaver Bea/Jürgen Haas, Strategisches Management, 4th Edition 2005, Stuttgart.
- Lucian Ayre Bebchuk, Federalism and the Corporation: The Desirable Limits On State Competition in Corporate Law, 105 Harv. L. Rev. 1443 (1992).
- Lucian Ayre Bebchuk, Letting Shareholders Set the Rules, 119 Harv. L. Rev. 1784 (2006).
- Lucian Ayre Bebchuk, The Case for increasing Shareholder Power, 118 Harv. L. Rev. 833 (2005).
- Lucian Arye Bebchuk, The Case for Shareholder Access to the Ballot, 59 Bus. Law. 43 (2003).
- Lucian Bebchuk, The Myth of Shareholder Franchise, 93 VA. L. Rev. 102 (2007).
- Lucian Arye Bebchuk/Assaf Hamdani, Optimal Defaults for Corporate Law Evolution, 96 Nw. U. L. Rev. 489 (2002).
- Lucian Arye Bebchuk/Assaf Hamdani, Vigorous Race or Leisurely Walk: Reconsidering The Competition over Corporate Charters, 112 Yale L.J. 553 (2002).
- Lucian Arye Bebchuk/Scott Hirst, Private Ordering and the Proxy Access Debate, 65 Bus. Law. 329 (2010), *available at* http://ssrn.com/abstract=1513408.
- Marco Becht/Julian R. Franks/Jeremy Grant, Hedge Fund Activism in Europe, 2010, www.ssrn.com/abstract=1616340.
- Michael Becker, Verwaltungskontrolle durch Gesellschafterrechte, 1997, Tübingen.
- Daniel Beisel/Hans-Hermann Klumpp, Der Unternehmenskauf – Gesamtdarstellung der zivil- und steuerrechtlichen Vorgänge einschließlich gesellschafts-, arbeits- und

kartellrechtlicher Fragen bei der Übertragung eines Unternehmens, 6th Edition 2009, München.

- Adolf A. Berle, Jr., "Control" in Corporate Law, 58 Colum. L. Rev. 1212 (1958).
- Adolf A. Berle, Jr., For Whom Corporate Managers are Trustees: A Note, 45 Harv. L. Rev. 1365 (1932).
- Adolf A. Berle/Gardiner C. Means, The Modern Corporation And Private Property, 1st Edition 1933 / 2nd Edition 1968, New York.
- Markus Berndt, Global Differences in Corporate Governance Systems – Theory and Implications for Reforms, 2002, Wiesbaden.
- Wolfgang Bernhardt, Aufsichtsrat – die schönste Nebensache der Welt? ZHR 159 (1995), 310 et seq.
- Carsten Berrar, Zur Reform des AR nach den Vorschlägen der Regierungskommission "Corporate Governance", NZG 2001, 1113 et seq.
- Daniel Bertuccini, To Disclose or Not to Disclose? CSX Corp., Total Return Swaps, and Their Implications for Schedule 13D Filing Purposes, 31 Cardozo L. Rev. 267 (2009).
- Petra Dorothee Beyer, Minderheitsvertreter im Aufsichtsrat, 1st Edition 2001, Baden-Baden.
- Gerold Bezzenberger, Die Geschäftsordnung der Hauptversammlung, ZGR 1998, 352 et seq.
- Tilman Bezzenberger, Erwerb eigener Aktien durch die AG, 2002, Köln.
- Amar Bhide, The Hidden Costs of Stock Market Liquidity, 34 J. Fin. Econ. 31 (1993).
- Carter G. Bishop/Daniel S. Kleinberger, Limited Liability Companies: Tax and Business Law Current Through 2009, 2009, New York.
- Bernard Black, Shareholder Activism and Corporate Governance in the United States, 3 The New Palgrave Dictionary of Econ. L. 459 (1998), *available at* http://www.ssrn.com/abstract=45100.
- Bernard Black, Shareholder Passivity Reexamined, 89 Mich. L. Rev. 519 (1990), *available at* http://www.ssrn.com/abstract=366820.
- Fischer Black, The Dividend Puzzle, J. Portfolio Mgmt., Special Issue 1996, 8 et seq. (originally 1976).
- Margaret Blair/Lynn Stout, A Team Production Theory, 85 Va. L. Rev. 247 (1999).
- Margaret Blair/Lynn Stout, Director Accountability and the Mediating Rule of the Corporate Board, 79 Wash. U. L. Q. 403 (2001), *available at* www.ssrn.com/abstract=266622.

- Johannes Blome-Drees/Reiner Rang-Hans Böckler Stiftung, Die Aktivitäten von Finanzinvestoren in Deutschland am Beispiel der CeWe Color AG, 2009, www.boeckler.de/pdf/mbf_finanzinvestoren_cewecolor.pdf.
- Harold S. Bloomenthal, Securities Law Handbook, Volume 1, 2009-2010 Edition, Eagan, Minnesota.
- Peter Böckli, Konvergenz: Annäherung des monoistischen und des dualistischen Führungs- und Aufsichtssystems, 201 et seq., in: Peter Hommelhoff/Klaus J. Hopt/Axel von Werder, Handbuch Corporate Governance, 2003, Köln, Stuttgart.
- Oliver Böhm/Michael H. Grothe, Hedgefonds-Aktivismus in Deutschland, BVAI Newsletter IV 2009, 14 et seq., www.bvai.de/newsletter (Chose BAI Newsletter IV/2009).
- Hans Bollweg, Die Wahl des Aufsichtsrates in der Hauptversammlung der Aktiengesellschaft, 1997, Köln, Berlin, Bonn, München.
- Patrick Bolton/José Scheinkman/Wei Xiong, Pay for Short-Term Performance: Executive Compensation in Speculative Markets, 30 J. Corp. L. 721 (2005).
- Reinhard Bork, Materiell-rechtliche und prozeßrechtliche Probleme des Organstreits zwischen Vorstand und Aufsichtsrat einer Aktiengesellschaft, ZGR 1989, 1 et seq.
- Christian Bosse, Zulässigkeit des individuell ausgehandelten Rückkaufs eigener Aktien ("Negotiated repurchase") in Deutschland, NZG 2000, 16 et seq.
- Nicole Boyson/Robert Mooradian, Hedge Funds as Shareholder Activists from 1994 – 2005, 2007, http://ssrn.com/abstract=992739.
- Michael Bradley/L. Macdonald Wakeman, The Wealth Effects of Targeted Share Repurchases, 11 J. Fin. Econ. 301 (1983).
- William W. Bratton, Enron and the Dark Side of Shareholder Value, 76 Tul. L. Rev. 1275 (2002).
- William W. Bratton, Hedge Funds and Governance Targets, 95 Geo. L.J. 1375 (2007), *available at* http://ssnr.com/abstract=962347.
- William W. Bratton, Hedge Funds and Governance Targets: Long-Term Results, 2010, www.ssrn.com/abstract=1677517.
- William W. Bratton, The New Dividend Puzzle, 93 Geo. L.J. 845 (2005), *available at* http://ssrn.com/abstract=535462.
- Alon Brav/J.B. Heaton III, Did ERISA's Prudent Man Rule Change the Pricing or Dividend Omitting Firms? 1998, http://ssrn.com/abstract=98568.
- Alon Brav/Wei Jiang/Hyonseob Kim, Hedge Fund Activism: A Review, 2010 http://ssrn.com/abstract=1551953.
- Alon Brav/Wei Jiang/Randall Thomas/Frank Partnoy, Hedge Fund Activism, Corporate Governance, and Firm Performance, 2008, http://ssrn.com/abstract=948907.

- Alon Brav/Wei Jiang/Randall Thomas/Frank Partnoy, The Returns to Hedge Fund Activism, 2008, http://ssrn.com/abstract=1111778.
- Richard A. Brealey/Stewart C. Myers/Franklin Allen, Principles of Corporate Finance, 8th Edition 2006, New York.
- Michael J. Brennan/Anjan V. Thakor, Shareholders Preferences and Dividend Policy, 45 J. Fin. 993 (1990).
- Thomas W. Briggs, Corporate Governance and the New Hedge Fund Activism: An Empirical Analysis, 32 J. Corp. L. 681 (2007).
- Thomas W. Briggs, Shareholder Activism and Insurgency under the new Proxy Rules, 50 Bus. Law. 99 (1994).
- Samuel Brothwell/Angela Ho, Back to the Future: The new Corporate Raiders, Public Utilities Fortnightly, 2006, 24 et seq., http://www.fortnightly.com/pubs/09012006_BusinessMoney.pdf.
- Gert Brüggemeier, Die Einflussnahme auf die Verwaltung einer Aktiengesellschaft – Zur Struktur und zum Verhältnis der §§ 117 und 317 AktG, AG 1988, 93 et seq.
- Christopher M. Bruner, Shareholder Bylaws and the Delaware Corporation, 11 Tenn. J. Bus. L. 66 (2009), *available at* http://ssrn.com/abstract=1555716.
- Christoph von Bülow/Markus Stephanblome, Acting in Concert und neue Offenlegungspflichten nach dem Risikobegrenzungsgesetz, ZIP 2008, 1797 et seq.
- Tobias Bürgers/Torsten Körber (eds.), Heidelberger Kommentar zum Aktiengesetz, 2008, Heidelberg.
- Jeremy Bulow/Ming Huang/Paul Klemperer, Toeholds and Takeovers, 107 J. Political Econ. 427 (1999).
- Ulrich Burgard, Die Berechnung des Stimmrechtsanteils nach §§ 21 – 23 Wertpapierhandelsgesetz, BB 1995, 2069 et seq.
- Torsten Busch, Bedingungen in Übernahmeangeboten, AG 2002, 145 et seq.
- Volker Butzke, Stimmrechtsvertretung und –ausübung – Heute und in Zukunft, in: Rüdiger von Rosen-DAI (ed.), Die Hauptversammlung vor neuen Herausforderungen, Dokumentation des Seminars des Deutschen Aktieninstitutes vom 25 September 2008, 66 et seq.

C

- David Campbell, The Role of Monitoring and Morality in Corporate Law: A Criticism of the Direction of Present Regulation, 7 Austl. J. Corp. L. 343 (1997).
- Steffen Carl, Conflicts with Active Investors? Recommendations for Executive and Supervisory Boards, Finanzplatz March 2009, Volume 2, 13 et seq.

- Karl-Burkard Caspari, Die geplante Insiderregelung in der Praxis, ZGR 1994, 530 et seq.
- John J. Castellani/Amy L. Goodman, The Case against the SEC Director Election Proposal, in: Lucian Bebchuk (Eed.), Shareholder Access to the Corporate Ballot, 2004, http://www.law.harvard.edu/faculty/hjackson/alumnipapers/SEC_Director_Election.Castellani.and.Goodman.pdf.
- William B. Chandler, On the Instructiveness of Insiders, Independents, and Institutional Investors, 67 U. CIN. L. REV. 1083 (1999).
- Brian Cheffins, Company Law, 1997, Oxford.
- Brian Cheffins, Does Law Matter?: The Separation Of Ownership And Control In The United Kingdom, 2000, www.ssnr.com/abstract=245560.
- Stephen Choi/Andrew Guzman, Choice and Federal Intervention in Corporate Law, 87 VA L. REV. 961 (2001).
- Robert Charles Clark, Corporate Law, 1986, Boston, Toronto.
- Christopher P. Clifford, Value Creation or Destruction? Hedge Funds as Shareholder Activists, 14 J. CORP. FIN. 323 (2008), *available at* http://ssrn.com/abstract=971018.
- Ronald Coase, The Nature of the Firm, 4 ECONOMICA 385 (1937).
- John C. Coffee, The Bylaw Battlefield: Can Institutions Change the Outcome of Corporate Control Contests?, 51 U. MIAMI L. REV. 605 (1997).
- John C. Coffee, The Future as History: The Prospects for Global Convergence in Corporate Governance and its Implications, 93 NW. U. L. REV. 641 (1999).
- Robert Cooter/Thomas Ulen, Law and Economics, 2004, Boston.
- James D. Cox/Thomas Lee Hazen, Corporations, 2nd Edition 2003, 3rd Edition, 2010 (regarding the treaties chapter), New York.
- James D. Cox/Thomas Lee Hazen, Cox & Hazen on Corporations: Including Unincorporated Forms of Doing, Volume 3, 2nd Edition 2003, New York.
- James D. Cox/Robert W. Hillman/Donald C. Langevoort, Securities Regulation – Cases and Materials, 4th Edition 2004, New York.

D

- Gerhard Dannemann, Comparative Law: Study of Similarities or Differences?, in: Mathias Reiman/Reinhard Zimmermann (eds.), The Oxford Handbook of Comparative Law, 2006, Oxford, etc.
- DAV-Handelsrechtsausschuss, Stellungnahme zum Entwurf einer Überarbeitung und Ergänzung des Emittentenleitfadens der Bundesanstalt für Finanzdienstleistungsaufsicht (BaFin), NZG 2009, 175 et seq.

- DAV-Handelsrechtsausschuss, Stellungnahme zum Referentenentwurf eines Gesetzes zur Unternehmensintegrität und Modernisierung des Anfechtungsrechts (UMAG), NZG 2004, 555 et seq.
- Paul Davies, The Board of Directors: Composition, Structure, Duties and Powers, 2001, http://www.oecd.org/dataoecd/21/30/1857291.pdf.
- Paul Davies, Unternehmensführung in Großbritannien und Deutschland, ZGR 2001, 268 et seq.
- E. Philip Davis/Benn Steil, Institutional Investors, 2001, Cambridge, Massachusetts.
- Diane Del Guercio/Laura Seery/Tracie Woidke, Do Boards Pay Attention when Institutional Investor Activists 'Just Vote No', 2008, http://ssrn.com/abstract=575242.
- David J. Denis/Diane K. Denis, Performance Changes Following Top Management Dismissals, 50 J. Fin. 1029 (1995).
- George W. Dent, The Essential Unity of Shareholders and The Myth of Investor Short-Termism, 35 Del. J. Corp. L. 97 (2010).
- George W. Dent, Toward Unifying Ownership and Control in the Public Corporation, 1989 Wis. L. Rev. 881 (1989).
- Deutsches Aktieninstitut e.V., Der Erwerb eigener Aktien in Deutschland – Ergebnisse einer Untersuchung des Deutschen Aktieninstituts zum Rückkauf eigener Aktien durch die Gesellschaft, 1999, Frankfurt a.M.
- Deutsches Aktieninstitut e.V./McKinsey&Company Inc., Investorendialog im Umbruch – Zum Umgang börsennotierter Unternehmen mit aktiven Unternehmen, 1st Edition March 2009, Frankfurt.
- Hans Diekmann, Acting in concert: Absprachen zur Besetzung des Aufsichtsrats, Besprechung des BGH-Urteils vom 18.9.2006, DStR 2007, 445 et seq.
- Christian Dietrich, Voraussetzungen und Inhalte einer Geschäftsordnung der Hauptversammlung* – - zugleich eine Besprechung des Art. 1 Nr. 16 (§ 129 I 1 AktG neu) des Gesetzes zur Kontrolle und Transparenz im Unternehmensbereich (KonTraG), NZG 1998, 921 et seq.
- David Donald, Die Entwicklung der US-amerikanischen Corporate Governance nach Enron, WM 2003, 705 et seq.
- Meinrad Dreher, Treuepflichten zwischen Aktionären und Verhaltenspflichten bei der Stimmrechtsbündelung – Gesellschaftsrechtliche und zivilrechtliche Grundlagen, ZHR 159 (1993), 150 et seq.
- Michael R. Drill, Deutschlands Konzerne setzen erneut zur Portfoliooptimierung an, Jahrbuch 2009 Investmentbank Lincoln International, 60 et seq., http://pdf.lincolninternational.com/Articles/DE/Jahrbuch2009.pdf.

- Henrik Drinkuth, Gegen den Gleichlauf des Acting in Concert nach § 22 WpHG und § 30 WpÜG, ZIP 2008, 676 et seq.
- Ying Duan, The Role of Mutual Funds in Corporate Governance: Evidence from Mutual Funds' Proxy Voting and Trading Behaviour, 2008, (unpublished Ph.D. dissertation, Boston College), http://ssrn.com/abstract=1028367.
- Christian Duve/Denis Basak, Ungeahnte Unterstützung für aktive Aktionäre – wie das UMAG Finanzinvestoren hilft, BB 2006, 1345 et seq.

E

- Frank H. Easterbook, Two Agency-Cost Explanations of Dividends, 74 Am. Econ. Rev. 650 (1984).
- Frank H. Easterbrook/Daniel R. Fischel, The Economic Structure of Corporate Law, 1991, Cambridge/Massachusetts, London.
- Frank H. Easterbrook/Daniel R. Fischel, Voting in Corporate Law, 26 J.L. & Econ. 395 (1983).
- Carsten Thomas Ebenroth, Das Auskunftsrecht des Aktionärs und seine Durchsetzung im Prozess, 1970, Bielefeld.
- Carsten Thomas Ebenroth/Karlheinz Boujong/Detlev Joost/Lutz Strohn, Handelsgesetzbuch: HGB, Volume 2, 2nd Edition 2009, München.
- Carsten Thomas Ebenroth/Thomas Daum, Die Kompetenzen des Vorstands einer Aktiengesellschaft bei der Durchführung und Abwehr unkoordinierter Übernahmen (Teil I), DB 1991, 1105 et seq.
- Moritz Peter Eichner, Anschleichen bei Unternehmensübernahmen – Perfides taktisches Manöver oder achtbare strategische Entscheidung, ZRP 2010, 5 et seq.
- Horst Eidenmüller (ed.), Ausländische Kapitalgesellschaften, 1st Edition 2004, München.
- Horst Eidenmüller, Kapitalgesellschaftsrecht im Spiegel der ökonomischen Theorie, JZ 2001, 1041 et seq.
- Horst Eidenmüller, Regulierung von Finanzinvestoren, DStR 2007, 2116 et seq.
- Melvin Aron Eisenberg, Access to the Corporate Proxy Machinery, 83 Harv. L. Rev. 1489 (1970).
- Melvin Aron Eisenberg, Corporations and Other Business Organizations, 8th Edition 2000, 9th Edition 2005 (Chapter 5 – Proxy Regulation) New York, New York.
- Melvin Aron Eisenberg, The Conception that the Corporation is a Nexus of Contracts, and the Dual Nature of the Firm, 24 J. Corp. L. 819 (1998-1999).

- Melvin Aron Eisenberg, The Structure of Corporation Law, 89 COLUM. L. REV. 1461 (1989).
- Melvin Aron Eisenberg, The Structure of the Corporation – A Legal Analysis, 1976, Boston Toronto.
- Volker Emmerich/Mathias Habersack, Aktien- und GmbH Konzernrecht, Kommentar, 6th Edition 2010, München.
- Martin Empt, Corporate Social Responsibility, 2004, Berlin.
- Antonius Engberding, Pensionsfonds in den USA – Betriebsrente durch Shareholder Value?, in: Wirtschafts- und sozialpolitisches Forschungs- und Beratungszentrum der Friedrich-Ebert-Stiftung (ed.), Die Rolle von Pensionsfonds in Europa und den Vereinigten Staaten von Amerika, 63 et seq., 2002, Bonn.
- Alexander Engelhardt, Activist Investing aus Unternehmenssicht, M&A Review 4/2008, 194 et seq.
- Andreas Engert, Hedgefonds als aktivistische Aktionäre – Die Einflussnahme auf Publikumsgesellschaften als Anlagestrategie von Hedgefonds und ihre Eingrenzung durch Insiderrecht, Anteilstransparenz und übernahmerechtliches Pflichtangebot, ZIP 2006, 2105 seq.
- Andreas Engert, Kapitalgesellschaften ohne gesetzliches Kapital: Lehren aus dem U.S.-amerikanischen Recht, in: Lutter (ed.), Das Kapital der Aktiengesellschaft in Europa, ZGR special issue 17, 2006, Berlin.
- Josef Eßer, Gliederungsvorschriften, Bewertung, Gewinnverwendung und Pflichtangaben nach dem Aktiengesetz 1965, AG 1966, 24 et seq.

F

- Lisa Fairfax, Making the Corporation Safe for Shareholder Democracy, 69 Ohio ST. L.J. 53 (2008).
- Joachim Frhr. von Falkenhausen, Ausschüttungssperren für die Kapitalrücklage- Eine rechtspolitische Betrachtung von § 150 III und IV AktG, NZG 2009, 1096 et seq.
- Eugene F. Fama/Michael C. Jensen, Separation of Ownership and Control, 26 J.L. & ECON. 301 (1983), *available at* www.ssrn.com/abstract=94034.
- Eugene F. Fama/Kenneth R. French, Disappearing Dividends: Changing Firm Characteristics or Lower Propensity to Pay?, 2000, http://ssrn.com/abstract=203092.
- Martin Feldstein/Jerry Green, Why Do Companies Pay Dividends?, 73 AM. ECON. REV. 17 (1983), available at http://links.jstor.org/sici?sici=0002-8282%28198303%2973%3A1%3C17%3AWDCPD%3E2.0.CO%3B2-T.
- David Finch/Robert Long, The Fiduciary Relation of the Dominant Shareholder to the Minority Shareholders, 9 HASTINGS L.J. 306 (1957 – 1958)

- Jill E. Fisch, Securities Intermediaries and the Separation of Ownership and Control, 33 Seattle U. L. Rev. 877 (2010).
- Daniel R. Fischel, Efficient Capital Market Theory, The Market for Corporate Control, and the Regulation of Cash Tender Offers, 57 Tex. L. Rev. 1 (1978).
- Arthur Fleischer, Securities Trading and Corporate Information Practices: The Implications of the Texas Gulf Sulphur Proceeding, 51 Va. L. Rev. 1271 (1965).
- Holger Fleischer, Bestellungsdauer und Wiederruf der Bestellung von Vorstandsmitgliedern im in- und ausländischen Aktienrecht, AG 2006, 429 et seq.
- Holger Fleischer, Das Gesetz zur Angemessenheit der Vorstandsvergütung (VorstAG), NZG 2009, 801 et seq.
- Holger Fleischer, Finanzinvestoren im ordnungspolitischen Gesamtgefüge von Aktien-, Bankaufsichts- und Kapitalmarktrecht, ZGR 2008, 185 et seq.
- Holger Fleischer, Grundfragen der ökonomischen Theorie im Gesellschafts- und Kapitalmarktrecht, ZGR 2001, 1 et seq.
- Holger Fleischer (ed.), Handbuch des Vorstandsrechts, 1st Edition 2006, München.
- Holger Fleischer, Shareholders vs. Stakeholders: Aktien- und übernahmerechtliche Fragen, 129 et seq., in: Peter Hommelhoff/Klaus J. Hopt/Axel v. Werder/ Handbuch Corporate Governance, 2003, Köln, Stuttgart.
- Holger Fleischer, Ungeschriebene Hauptversammlungszuständigkeiten im Aktienrecht: Von „ Holzmüller“ zu „Gelatine“, NJW 2004, 2335 et seq.
- Holger Fleischer, Zur Abberufung von Vorstandsmitgliedern auf Druck Dritter, DStR 2006, 1507 et seq.
- Holger Fleischer, Zur aktienrechtlichen Verantwortlichkeit faktischer Organe, AG 2004, 517 et seq.
- Holger Fleischer/Klaus Ulrich Schmolke, Das Anschleichen an eine börsennotierte Aktiengesellschaft – Überlegungen zur Beteiligungstransparenz de lege lata und de lege ferenda-, NZG 2009, 401 et seq.
- Holger Fleischer/Klaus Ulrich Schmolke, Kapitalmarktrechtliche Beteiligungstransparenz nach § 21 ff. WpHG and „Hidden Ownership“, ZIP 2008, 1501 et seq.
- Holger Fleischer/Klaus Ulrich Schmolke, Zum beabsichtigten Ausbau der kapitalmarktrechtlichen Beteiligungstransparenz bei modernen Finanzinstrumenten (§§ 25, 25a DiskE-WpHG), NZG 2010, 846.
- William Meade Fletcher, Fletcher Cyclopedia of the Law of Corporations (2010), St. Paul, Minnesota.
- Thomas Martin Fojcik, Übernahmeschlacht um ABN Amro – Corporate Governance als Spielball institutioneller Anleger?, 1st Edition 2008, Norderstedt.

- R. Edward Freeman/John McVea, A Stakeholder Approach to Strategic Management, in: Michael A. Hitt/R. Edward Freeman/Jeffrey S. Harrison, The Blackwell handbook of strategic management, 2001, Oxford, Malden, Massachusetts.
- Tobias Freudenberg, Aktienrecht in Zahlen – Anzahl der Aktiengesellschaften in Deutschland, AG-Report 2007, R 375.

G

- Andreas Gätsch/Frank Schäfer, Abgestimmtes Verhalten nach § 22 II WpHG und § 30 II WpÜG in der Fassung des Risikobegrenzungsgesetzes, NZG 2008, 846 et seq.
- Nickolay M. Gantchev, The Costs of Shareholder Activism: Evidence from a Sequential Decision Model, 2009, http://fisher.osu.edu/supplements/10/9861/01222010-Nickolay%20Gantchev.pdf.
- José M. Garrido, Optimism and Pessimism: Complementary Views on the Institutional Investors' Role in Corporate Governance, 449 et seq., in: Klaus Hopt/Eddy Wymeersch (eds.), Capital Markets and Company Law, 2003, Oxford, New York.
- José M. Garrido/Angel Rojo, Institutional Investors and Corporate Governance: Solution or Problem, 427 et seq., in: Klaus Hopt/Eddy Wymeersch (eds.), Capital Markets and Company Law, 2003, Oxford, New York.
- José-Miguel Gaspar/Massimo Massa/Pedro Matos, Shareholder Investment Horizons and the Market for Corporate Control, 76 J. Fin. Econ. 135 (2005).
- Günther Gebhardt/Wolfgang Gerke/Manfred Steiner, Handbuch des Finanzmanagements – Instrumente und Märkte der Unternehmensfinanzierung, 1993, München.
- Stephan Geibel/Rainer Süßmann (eds.), Wertpapiererwerbs- und Übernahmegesetz, 2nd Edition 2008, München.
- Wolfgang Gerke/Matthias Bank/Max Steiger, The Changing Role of Institutional Investors – A German Perspective, 357 et seq., in: Klaus Hopt/Eddy Wymeersch (eds.), Capital Market and Company Law, 2003, Oxford New York.
- Harald Gesell, Wertpapierleihe und Repurchase Agreement im deutschen Recht, 1995, Köln.
- Ernst Geßler, Einberufung und ungeschriebene Hauptversammlungszuständigkeiten, 771 et seq., in: Marcus Lutter/Walter Stimpel/Hans-Joachim Mertens, Peter Ulmer (eds.), Festschrift für Walter Stimpel zum 68. Geburtstag am 29. November 1985, 1985, Berlin, New York.
- Ernst Geßler/Wolfgang Hefermehl/Ulrich Eckardt/Bruno Kropff, Aktiengesetz,
  1. Volume 1, §§ 1 – 75, 1973, 1983, 1984, München.
  2. Volume 2, §§ 76 -147, 1973, 1974, München.
- Jörg Geßler/Markus Käppler, Aktiengesetz, [Supp. 55, 2007], Köln.

- Otto Gierke, Das Wesen der menschlichen Verbände, 1902, Leipzig.
- Stuart L. Gillan/John W. Kensinger/John D. Martin, Value Creation and Corporate Diversification: The Case of Sears, Roebuck & Co., 55 J. Fin. Econ. 103 (2000).
- Stuart L. Gillan/Laura Starks, A Survey of Shareholder Activism: Motivation and Empirical Evidence, 1998, http://ssrn.com/abstract=663523.
- Stuart L. Gillan/Laura Starks, The Evolution of Shareholder Activism in the United States, 2007, http://ssrn.com/abstract=959670.
- Ronal J. Gilson, Globalizing Corporate Governance: Convergence of Form or Function, 49 Am. J. Comp. L. 329 (2001).
- Heinrich Götz, Rechte der Aktionäre der Konzernobergesellschaft, AG 1984, 85 et seq.
- Heinrich Götz, Rechte und Pflichten des Aufsichtsrats nach dem Transparenz- und Publizitätsgesetz, NZG 2002, 599 et seq.
- Cornelius Götze, Rechtliche Grenzen des Shareholder Activism, 119 et seq., in: Rüdiger von Rosen (ed.), Die Hauptversammlung vor neuen Herausforderungen – Dokumentation des Seminars vom 25. September 2008, DAI studies issue 41, 1st Edition 2008, Frankfurt a.M.
- Freiherr von Godin/Hans Wilhelmi, Aktiengesetz, Volume 1 §§ 1 – 178, 4th Edition 1971, Berlin, New York.
- Jeffrey Gordon, Institutions as Relational Investors: A New Look at Cumulative Voting, 94 Colum. L. Rev. 124 (1994).
- Jeffrey Gordon, Shareholders Initiative: A Social Choice and Game Theoretic Approach to Corporate Law, 60 U. Cin. L. Rev. 347 (1991).
- Jeffrey Gordon, The Rise of Independent Directors in the United States, 1950 – 2005: Of Shareholder Value and Stock Market Prices, 59 Stan. L. Rev. 1465 (2007).
- Peter Alexis Gourevitch/James J. Shinn, Political Power and Corporate Control, The New Global Politics Of Corporate Governance, 2005, Princeton and Oxfordshire.
- Christine Graeff, Reden mit den Rebellen, Shareholder Activism – Herausforderungen für die Kommunikation, Finanzplatz March 2009, Volume 2, 16 et seq.
- Kent Greenfield, Democracy and the Dominance of Delaware in Corporate Law, 67 Law & Contemp. Probs. 135 (2004).
- Yaniv Grinstein/Roni Michaely, Institutional Holdings and Payout Policy, 60 J. Fin. 1389 (2006), *available at* http://www3.interscience.wiley.com/cgi-bin/fulltext/118686374/PDFSTART.
- Manfred Groh, Shareholder Value und Aktienrecht, DB 2000, 2153 et seq.
- Wolfgang Groß, Zuständigkeit der Hauptversammlung bei Erwerb und Veräußerung von Unternehmensbeteiligungen, AG 1994, 266 et seq.

- Sanford J. Grossman/Oliver D. Hart, Takeover Bids, the Free-rider Problem, and the Theory of the Corporation, 11 Bell J. Econ. 42 (1980).
- Michael Grüner, Zeitliche Einschränkung des Rede- und Fragerechts auf Hauptversammlungen – zugleich Besprechung der BVerfG-Entscheidung „Wengler/Daimler-Benz", NZG 2000, 770 et seq.
- Joseph A. Grundfest, Advice and Consent: An Alternative Mechanism for Shareholder Participation in the Nomination and Election of Corporate Directors, 2003, http://papers.ssrn.com/abstract=481021.
- Joseph A. Grundfest, Just Vote No: A Minimalist Strategy for Dealing with Barbarians Inside the Gates, 45 Stan. L. Rev. 857 (1993).
- Joseph A. Grundfest, Measurement Issues in the Proxy Access Debate, 2010, http://ssrn.com/abstract=1538630.
- Barbara Grunewald, Rechtswidrigkeit und Verschulden bei der Haftung von Aktionären und Personengesellschaften, in: Karl-Heinz Forster/Barbara Grunewald/Marcus Lutter/Johannes Semler (eds.), Festschrift für Bruno Kropff, Aktien- und Bilanzrecht, 1997, Düsseldorf.
- Peter Guntz, Treubindungen von Minderheitsaktionären, 1997, Berlin.

H

- Mathias Habersack, Beteiligungstransparenz adieu? – Lehren aus dem Fall Continental/Schaeffler –, AG 2008, 817 et seq.
- Andreas Hackethal/Alexandre Zdantchouk, Signaling Power of Open Market Share Repurchases in Germany, 20 Fin. Mkts. Portfolio Mgmt. 123 (2006), *available at* http://ssrn.com/abstract=920815.
- Robert J. Haft, Analysis of Key SEC No-Action Letters, 2005-2006, St. Paul, Minnesota.
- Thomas Halberkamp/Olaf Gierke, Das Recht der Aktionäre auf Einberufung einer Hauptversammlung, NZG 2004, 494 et seq.
- Robert W. Hamilton, Corporations, 3rd Edition 1992, St. Paul.
- Hammermesh, Corporate Democracy and Stockholder-Adopted By-Laws: Tacking Back the Street?, 73 Tul. L. Rev. 409 (1998), *available at* www.ssrn.com/abstract=156308.
- James P. Hawley/Andrew T. Williams, The Rise of Fiduciary Capitalism: How Institutional Investors Can Make Corporate America More Democratic, 2000, Philadelphia, Pennsylvania.
- Thomas Lee Hazen, The Corporate Persona, Contract (and Market) Failure, and Moral Values, 69 N.C. L. Rev. 273 (1991).

- Thomas Lee Hazen, Transfer of Corporate Control and Duties of Controlling Shareholders – Common Law, Tender Offers, Investment Companies – And a Proposal for Reform, 125 U. Pa. L. Rev. 1023 (1977).
- Thomas Heidel, Aktienrecht und Kapitalmarktrecht, 2nd Edition 2007, Baden-Baden.
- Jan Von Hein, Die Rezeption US-amerikanischen Gesellschaftsrechts in Deutschland, 2008, Tübingen.
- Günter Henn/Jürgen Frodermann/Dirk Jannott (eds.), Handbuch des Aktienrechts, 8th Edition 2009, Heidelberg.
- Harry G. Henn/John R. Alexander, Laws of Corporations, 1983, St. Paul, Minn.
- Hartwig Henze, Die Treuepflicht im Aktienrecht, BB 1996, 489 et seq.
- Hartwig Henze, Entscheidungen Kompetenzen der Organe der AG: Vorgaben der höchstrichterlichen Rechtsprechung, BB 2001, 53 et seq.
- Hartwig Henze, Holzmüller vollendet das 21. Lebensjahr, in: Mathias Habersack/Peter Hommelhoff/Uwe Hüffer/Karsten Schmidt, Festschrift für Peter Ulmer zum 70. Geburtstag am 2. Januar 2003, 211 et seq., 2003, Berlin.
- Hartwig Henze, Leitungsverantwortung des Vorstands – Überwachungspflicht des Aufsichtsrats, BB 2000, 209 et seq.
- Hartwig Henze, Treuepflichten der Gesellschafter im Kapitalmarktrecht, ZHR 162 (1998) 186 et seq.
- J.A.C. Hetherington, The Minority's Duty of Loyalty in Close Corporations, 1972 Duke L.J. 921 (1972).
- Joseph Hinsey, Corporate Governance Activists are Headed in the Wrong Direction, Harvard Business School Working Knowledge, 2006, http://hbswk.hbs.edu/item/5442.html.
- Hendrik Hirsch, Der Erwerb eigener Aktien nach dem KonTraG Unter besonderer Berücksichtigung der Bilanzierung eigener Aktien, 2004, Köln.
- Albert O. Hirschmann, Exit, Voice, and Loyalty: Responses to Decline in Firms, Organizations, and States, 1970, Cambridge, Mass.
- Heribert Hirte, Bezugsrechtsausschluß und Konzernbildung, 1986, Köln, Berlin, Bonn, München.
- Heribert Hirte/Thomas M.J. Möllers (eds.), Kölner Kommentar zum WpHG, 2007, München.
- Wolfgang Hölters (ed.), Aktiengesetz, 2011, München.
- Dietrich Hoffmann/Jürgen Lehmann/Heinz Weinmann, Mitbestimmungsgesetz, 1987, München.

- Michael Hoffmann-Becking (ed.), Münchener Handbuch des Gesellschaftsrechts, Volume 4, 3rd Edition 2007, München.
- Michael Hoffmann-Becking/Gerd Krieger, Leitfaden zur Anwendung des Gesetzes zur Angemessenheit der Vorstandsvergütung (VorstAG), NZG 2009, Supp. Issue 26.
- Karl Hofstetter, Von der Landsgemeinde zur proxy Generalversammlung: Vorschläge für den Paradigmenwechsel in der Schweiz, ZGR 2008, 560 et seq.
- Klaus Hopt/Herbert Wiedemann (eds.), Aktiengesetz Großkommentar, 4th Edition, Berlin
  1. §§ 1 – 53, Volume 1, 2004,
  2. §§ 53a – 75, Volume 2, 2008,
  3. §§ 76 – 94, Volume 3, 2008,
  4. §§ 95 – 117, Volume 4, 2006,
  5. §§ 118 – 149, Volume 5, 2008,
  6. §§ 241 – 255, Volume 6, 1996
- Karl Barz/Herbert Brönner/Ulrich Klug/Konrad Mellerowicz/Joachim Meyer-Landrut/Wolfgang Schilling/Herbert Wiedemann/Hans Würdinger, Aktiengesetz Großkommentar, 3rd Edition, Berlin, New York
  §§ 1- 75, Volume 1, 1973.
- Henry Hu/Bernard Black, Empty Voting and Hidden (Morphable) Ownership: Taxonomy, Implications, and Reforms, 61 Bus. Law. 1011 (2006).
- Henry Hu/Bernard Black, Equity and Debt Decoupling and Empty Voting II: Importance and Extensions, 156 U. Pa. L. Rev. 625 (2008).
- Henry Hu/Bernard Black, Hedge Funds, Insiders, and the Decoupling of Economic and Voting Ownership: Empty Voting and Hidden (Morphable) Ownership, 2007, http://ssnr.com/abstract=976950.
- Henry Hu/Bernard Black, The New Vote Buying: Empty Voting and Hidden (Morphable) Ownership, 79 S. Cal. L. Rev. 811 (2006).
- Ulrich Hübner, Die Ausgliederung von Unternehmensteilen in aktien- und aufsichtsrechtlicher Sicht, in: Marcus Lutter/Hans-Joachim Mertens/Peter Ulmer (eds.), Festschrift für Walter Stimpel zum 68. Geburtstag am 29. November 1985, 791 et seq., 1985, Berlin, New York.
- Uwe Hüffer, Aktiengesetz, 9th Edition 2010, München.
- Uwe Hüffer, Zur Holzmüller-Problematik: Reduktion des Vorstandsermessens oder Grundlagenkompetenz der Hauptversammlung, 279 et seq., in: Matthias Habersack/Peter Hommelhoff/Uwe Hüffer/Karsten Schmidt (eds.), Festschrift für Peter Ulmer zum 70. Geburtstag, 2003, Berlin.

- Hanns F. Hügel, Verschmelzung und Einbringung – Unternehmensübertragung auf verbandrechtlicher Grundlage im österreichischen und deutschen Gesellschafts-, Bilanz-, Ertragssteuerrecht der Kapitalgesellschaften, 1993, Wien, Köln.
- James D. Hutchinson, The Federal Prudent Man Rule under ERISA, 22 Vill. L. Rev. 15 (1977).

I

- Ulrich Immenga, Die personalistische Kapitalgesellschaft – Eine rechtsvergleichende Untersuchung nach deutschem GmbH-Recht und dem Recht der Corporations in den Vereinigten Staaten, 1970, Bad Hamburg.
- IRRC/GMIRATINGS, The Election of Corporate Directors: What Happens When Shareowners Withhold a Majority of Votes from Director Nominees? (2012), http://www.irrcinstitute.org/pdf/Final%20Election%20of%20Directors%20GMI%20Aug%202012.pdf.

J

- Walter Jagenburg, Aktienrecht als Organisationsrecht, AG 1965, 156 et seq.
- Ravi Jain, Institutional and Individual Investor Preferences for Dividends and Share Repurchases, 59 J. Econ. Bus. 406 (2007), *available at* http://bschool.nus.edu.sg/staff-profile/bizrj/Inst%20and%20Indiv%20Pref%20for%20Div%20and%20Rep.pdf.
- Ronny Jänig, Die aktienrechtliche Sonderprüfung – Eine rechtsvergleichende Untersuchung zur außerordentlichen Kontrolle der Verwaltung im deutschen, schweizerischen, französischen, englischen und niederländischen Aktienrecht, 1st Edition 2005, Baden – Baden.
- Michael C. Jensen, Agency Costs of Free Cash Flow, Corporate Finance, and Takeovers, 76 Am. Econ. Rev. 323 (1986), *available at* http://ssrn.com/abstract=99580.
- Michael C. Jensen, The Takeover Controversy: Analysis and Evidence, 1986, www.ssrn.com/abstract=173452.
- Michael C. Jensen/William H. Meckling, Theory of the Firm: Managerial Behavior, Agency Costs and Ownership Structure, 3 J. Fin. Econ. 305 (1976), *available at* http://ssrn.com/abstract=94043.
- Uwe Jirjahn – Hans Böckler Stiftung, Ökonomische Wirkungen der Mitbestimmung in Deutschland: Ein Update, Arbeitspapier 186, 2010, Berlin, *available at* http://www.boeckler.de/pdf/p_arbp_186.pdf.
- Klose John/April Klein, Shareholder Proposals und Corporate Governance, 1995, www.ssrn.com/abstract=1297750.

- Detlev Joost, „Holzmüller 2000" vor dem Hintergrund des Umwandlungsgesetzes, ZHR 163 (1999), 164 et seq.

K

- Marcel Kahan/Edward Rock, Embattled CEOs, 2008, http://ssrn.com/abstract=1281516.
- Marcel Kahan/Edward Rock, Hedge Funds in Corporate Governance and Corporate Control, 155 U. Pa. L. Rev. 1021 (2007), *available at* http://ssnr.com/abstract=919881.
- Marcel Kahan/Edward Rock, The Hanging Chads of Corporate Voting, 96 Geo. L.J. 1227 (2008).
- Kallmeyer, Umwandlungsgesetz Kommentar – Verschmelzung, Spaltung und Formwechsel bei Handelsgesellschaften, 4th Edition 2010, Köln.
- Ehud Kamar, Does Shareholder Voting on Acquisitions Matter?, American Law & Economics Association Annual Meetings, 2006, http://law.bepress.com/cgi/viewcontent.cgi?article=1799&context=alea.
- Lothar Kamp/Alexandra Krieger – Hans Böckler Stiftung, Die Aktivitäten von Finanzinvestoren in Deutschland, Arbeitspapier 103, 2005, Düsseldorf, *available at* http://www.boeckler.de/pdf/p_arbp_103.pdf.
- Jonathan M. Karpoff, The Impact of Shareholder Activism on Target Companies: A Survey of Empirical Findings, 2001, http://ssrn.com/abstract=885365.
- David A. Katz/Laura A. McIntosh, Advance Notice Bylaws: Lessons From Recent Cases, New York Law Journal, May 23, 2008.
- David A. Katz/Laura A. McIntosh, Director Elections and Majority Voting, New York Law Journal, December 29, 2005.
- David A. Katz/Laura A. McIntosh, Majority Election of Directors, New York Law Journal, March 24, 2005.
- B. Philipp Kellerhals/Elmar Rausch, Die Liberalisierung von Aktienrückkäufen: Bundesdeutsche Erfahrungen, AG 2000, 222 et seq.
- Wolfgang Kessler/Stefan Köhler/Michael Kröner (eds.), Konzernsteuerrecht, Nation – International, 2008, München.
- Alexander Kitanoff, Der Erwerb eigener Aktien – Aktienrückkäufe und Interessen der Gläubiger, Aktionäre und des Kapitalmarkts, 2009, Frankfurt a.M.
- Tobias Klass, Der Buyout von Aktiengesellschaften, 1st Edition 2000, Baden-Baden.
- William Klein/John Coffee, Business Organization and Finance, 10th Edition 2008.
- April Klein/Emanuel Zur, Entrepreneurial Shareholder Activism: Hedge Funds and Other Private Investors, 64 J. Fin. 187 (2009).

- April Klein/Emanuel Zur, Entrepreneurial Shareholder Activism: Hedge Funds and Other Private Investors, 2006, http://www.ssrn.com/abstract=913362.
- Rolf Jürgen König, Ausschüttungsverhalten von Aktiengesellschaften, Besteuerung und Kapitalmarktgleichgewicht, 1990, Hamburg.
- Michael Kort, Die Haftung des Einflussnehmers auf Kapitalgesellschaften in ausländischen Rechtsordnungen – Vorbild für ein neues Verständnis von § 117 AktG?, AG 2005, 453 et seq.
- Renier Kraakman/(John Armour)/Paul Davies/(Luca Enriques)/Henry Hansmann/ Gerard Hertig/Klaus Hopt/Hideki Kanda/Edward Rock, The Anatomy of Corporate Law: A Comparative and Functional Approach, 1st Edition 2004, (2nd Edition 2009), Oxford, New York, etc.
- Lars Klöhn, Interessenkonflikte zwischen Aktionären und Gläubigern der Aktiengesellschaft im Spiegel der Vorstandspflichten – Ein Beitrag zur Leitungsaufgrabe des Vorstands gemäß § 76 AktG, ZGR 2008, 110 et seq.
- Gerhard Kraft/Christian Altvater, Die zivilrechtliche, bilanzielle und steuerliche Behandlung des Rückkaufs eigener Aktien, NZG 1998, 448 et seq.
- Bruno Kropff, Aktiengesetz 1965 mit Begründung des Regierungsentwurfs, Bericht des Rechtsausschusses des Deutschen Bundestages, 1965, Düsseldorf.
- Bruno Kropff/Johannes Semler, Münchener Kommentar zum Aktiengesetz, München:
  7. Volume 1 §§ 1 – 75 AktG, 3rd Edition 2008,
  8. Volume 2 §§ 53a – 75 AktG, 2nd Edition 2003,
  9. Volume 2 §§ 76 – 117 AktG, 3rd Edition 2008,
  10. Volume 3 §§ 76 – 117 AktG, 2nd Edition 2004,
  11. Volume 4 §§ 118 – 147 AktG, 2nd Edition 2004,
  12. Volume 5a, §§ 148-151, 161-178 AktG, §§ 238-264c, 342, 342a HGB, 2nd Edition, 2003,
  13. Volume 6, §§ 179 – 221 AktG, 2nd Edition 2005,
  14. Volume 7, §§ 222- 277 AktG, 2nd Edition 2001.
- Friedrich Kübler/Heinz-Dieter Assmann, Gesellschaftsrecht – Die privatrechtlichen Ordnungsstrukturen und Regelungsprobleme von Verbänden und Unternehmen, 6th Edition 2006, Heidelberg, München, Landsberg, Berlin.
- Manfred Kühn, Der Minderheitenschutz nach dem neuen Aktiengesetz, Der Betriebsberater, 1965, 1170 et seq.
- Christoph Kuhner, Unternehmensinteresse vs. Shareholder Value als Leitmaxime kapitalmarktorientierter Aktiengesellschaften, ZGR 2004, 244 et seq.
- Christoph Kumpan, Börsenmacht Hedge-Fonds _ Die Regelungen in den USA und mögliche Implikationen für Deutschland, ZHR 170 (2006), 39 et seq.

- Christoph Kumpan, Private Equity und der Schutz deutscher Unternehmen, AG 2007, 461 et seq.
- Christoph Kumpan/Martin Mittermeier, Risikoentleerte Stimmrechte – Auswirkungen von Wertpapierdarlehen im Gesellschaftsrecht, ZIP 2009, 404 et seq.

L

- Karl Lackner/Kristian Kühl, StGB, 27th Edition 2011, München.
- Brigitte Lammers, Verhaltenspflichten von Verwaltungsorganen in Übernahmeauseinandersetzungen – Eine rechtsvergleichende Untersuchung des US-amerikanischen, deutschen und europäischen Rechts, 1994, Frankfurt am Main.
- Jens Last, Der Erwerb eigener Aktien als Ausschüttungsinstrument, 2006, Berlin.
- Susanne Lenz, Steigerung der Hauptversammlungsteilnahme durch monetäre Anreize?, NZG 2006, 534 et seq.
- Franz-Josef Leven/Leonard Helm, Der Erwerb eigner Aktien – Ein notwendiges Instrument der Unternehmensfinanzierung, BHV-News & Aktienkultur, 3/1996, 5 et seq., *available at* http://www.dai.de/internet/dai/dai-2-0.nsf/webmaskenformeln/2A936D25BBEF1040C125747C0053B0EE?OpenDocument.
- Patrick C. Leyens, Deutscher Aufsichtsrat und U.S.-Board: ein- oder zweistufiges Verwaltungssystem? Zum Stand der rechtsvergleichenden Corporate Governance-Debatte, 67 RabelsZ 57 (2003).
- Thomas Liebscher, Konzernbildungskontrolle – Rechtsformspezifische und rechtsformunabhängige Aspekte der Problematik eines konzernrechtlichen Präventivschutzes im Rahmen des Konzernierungsprozesses, 1995, Berlin.
- Peter Limmer, Handbuch der Unternehmensumwandlung, 3rd Edition 2007, Münster.
- John Lintner, Distributions of Incomes of Corporations Among Dividends, Retained Earnings, and Taxes, 46 Am. Econ. Rev. 97 (1956).
- Martin Lipton/Steven A. Rosenblum, Election Contest in the Company's Proxy: An idea whose time has not come, 59 Bus. Law. 67 (2003).
- Martin Lipton/William Savitt, The Many Myths of Lucian Bebchuk, 93 Va. L. Rev. 733 (2007).
- Louis Loss/Joel Seligmann, Fundamentals of Securities Regulation, 4th Edition 2001, Gaithersburg, New York.
- Marcus Lutter, Das Girmes-Urteil, JZ 1995, 1053 et seq.
- Marcus Lutter, Defizite für eine effiziente Aufsichtsratstätigkeit und gesetzliche Möglichkeiten der Verbesserung, ZHR 159 (1995), 287 et seq.

- Marcus Lutter, Die Empfehlungen der Kommission vom 14. 12. 2004 und vom 15. 2. 2005 und ihre Umsetzung in Deutschland, EuZW 2009, 799 et seq.
- Marcus Lutter, Organzuständigkeiten im Konzern, in: Marcus Lutter/Hans-Joachim Mertens/Peter Ulmer (eds.), Festschrift für Walter Stimpel zum 68. Geburtstag am 29. November 1985, 825 et seq., 1985, Berlin, New York.
- Marcus Lutter, Stellungnahme zur Aktienrechtsreform 1997 von Prof. Dr. Dr. h.c. Marcus Lutter, in: Die Aktienrechtsreform 1997, AG special issue 1997, 52 et seq.
- Marcus Lutter, Treupflichten und aktuelle Anwendungsprobleme, ZHR 162 (1998), 164 et seq.
- Marcus Lutter, Zur inhaltlichen Besprechung von Mehrheitsentscheidungen – Besprechung der Entscheidung BGH WM 1980, 378 –, ZGR 1981, 171 et seq.
- Marcus Lutter, Zur Treupflicht des Großaktionärs, JZ 1976, 225 et seq.
- Marcus Lutter/Gerd Krieger, Rechte und Pflichten des Aufsichtsrats, 4th Edition 2002, Köln.
- Marcus Lutter/Rolf Leinekugel, Kompetenzen von Hauptversammlung und Gesellschafterversammlung beim Verkauf von Unternehmensteilen, ZIP 1998, 225 et seq.
- Marcus Lutter/Martin Winter (eds.), Umwandlungsgesetz Kommentar, Volume 1 §§ 1 – 137, 3rd Edition 2004, Köln.

M

- Rene Maatman/Geert T.M.J. Raaijmakers, Hedge Funds in Company Law: Virus or Vaccine?, Ondernemingsrecht 2006, 256-262, *available at* http://ssrn.com/abstract=931884.
- Jonathan R. Macey/Fred S. McChesney, A Theoretical Analysis of Corporate Greenmail, 95 Yale L.J. 13 (1985).
- Petri Mäntysaari, The Law of Corporate Finance: General Principles and EU Law, Volume 3: Funding, Exit, Takeovers, 2010, Berlin, Heidelberg.
- David Manry/David Stangeland, Greenmail: A Brief History, 6 Stan. J.L. Bus & Fin. 217 (2001).
- Reinhard Marsch-Barner, Treuepflichten zwischen Aktionären und Verhaltenspflichten bei der Stimmrechtsbündelung, ZHR 157 (1993), 172 et seq.
- Reinhard Marsch-Barner/Frank Schäfer (eds.), Handbuch börsennotierte AG, 2005, Köln.
- Klaus-Peter Martens, Das Bundesverfassungsgericht und das Gesellschaftsrecht, ZGR 1979, 493 et seq.

- Klaus-Peter Martens, Die Entscheidungsautonomie des Vorstands und die „Basisdemokratie“ in der Aktiengesellschaft – Anmerkungen zu BGHZ 83, S. 122 („Holzmüller“), ZHR 147 (1983), 377 et seq.
- Klaus-Peter Martens, Erwerb und Veräußerung eigener Aktien im Börsenhandel, Überlegungen de lege ferenda , AG 1996, 337 et seq.
- Philip Marx, Der Solvenztest zur Regulierung von Ausschüttungen im amerikanischen Recht, DZWIR 2006, 401 et seq.
- Therese Maynard, Mergers and Acquisitions: Cases, Materials, and Problems, 2005, New York.
- Brett H. McDonnell, Shareholder Bylaws, Shareholders Nominations, and Poison Pills, Minnesota Legal Studies Research Paper No. 05-06, http://ssrn.com/abstract=659322.
- Thomas Mecke, Konzernstruktur und Aktionärsbescheid, 1st Edition 1992, Baden-Baden.
- Manuel Meder, Die Mitwirkung des Vorstands am Kandidatenauswahlverfahren für Aufsichtsratswahlen, DStR 2008, 1242 et seq.
- Alan J. Meese, The Team Production Theory of Corporate Law: A Critical Assessment, 43 WM & MARY L. REV. 1626 (2002), *available at* www.ssrn.com/abstract=373783.
- Heinz Meilicke/Thomas Heidel, Das Auskunftsrecht des Aktionärs in der Hauptversammlung (Teil II), DStR 1992, 113 et seq.
- Andreas Merkner/Marco Sustmann, Vorbei mit dem unbemerkten Anschleichen an börsennotierte Unternehmen? NZG 2010, 681 et seq.
- Andreas Merkner/Marco Sustmann, Wertpapierleihe und Empty Voting – Weitergehender Transparenzbedarf im WpHG?, NZG 2010, 1170 et seq.
- Hanno Merkt/Stephan Göthel, US-amerikanisches Gesellschaftsrecht, 2nd Edition 2006, Frankfurt a.M.
- Hans-Joachim Mertens, Das Minderheitsrecht nach § 122 Abs. 2 AktG und seine Grenzen, AG 1997, 481 et seq.
- Hans-Joachim Mertens, Verfahrensfragen bei Personalentscheidungen des mitbestimmten Aufsichtsrats, ZGR 1983, 189 et seq.
- Herbert Messer, Die Abberufung des Vorstandes der AG wegen Vertrauensentzugs durch die Hauptversammlung, 681 et seq., in: Karl Bruchhausen/Wolfgang Hefermehl/Peter Hommelhoff/Herbert Messer (eds.), Festschrift für Rudolf Nirk zum 70. Geburtstag, 1992, München.
- Ernst-Joachim Mestmäcker, Verwaltung, Konzerngewalt und Rechte der Aktionäre, Eine rechtsvergleichende Untersuchung nach deutschem Aktienrecht und dem Recht der Corporations in den Vereinigten Staaten, 1958, Karlsruhe.

- Joachim Meyer-Landrut, Der “Mißbrauch” aktienrechtlicher Minderheits- oder Individualrechte, insbesondere des Auskunftsrechts, in: Robert Fischer/Wolfgang Hefermehl, Gesellschaftsrecht und Unternehmensrecht, Festschrift für Wolfgang Schilling zum 65. Geburtstag am 5. Juni 1973, 1973, Berlin, New York.
- Ralf Michaels, The Functional Method of Comparative Law, in: Mathias Reimann/Reinhard Zimmermann, The Oxford Handbook of Comparative Law, 2006, Oxford, etc.
- Mark Mietzner/Denis Schweizer, Hedge Funds versus Private Equity Funds as Shareholder Activists – Differences in Value Creation, 2008, www.ssrn.com/abstract=1100945.
- Merton H. Miller/Franco Modigliani, Dividend Policy, Growth, and the Valuation of Shares, 34 J. Bus. 411 (1961).
- David Millon, New Directions in Corporate Law: Communitarians, Contractarians, and the Crisis in Corporate Law, 50 Wash.& Lee L. Rev. 1373 (1993).
- Sara B. Moeller/Frederick P. Schlingemann/René M. Stulz, Wealth Destruction on a Massive Scale? A Study of Acquiring-Firm Returns in the Recent Merger Wave, 60 J. Fin. 757 (2005).
- Peter O. Mülbert, Aktiengesellschaft, Unternehmensgruppe und Kapitalmarkt – Die Aktionärsrechte bei der Bildung und Umbildung einer Unternehmensgruppe zwischen Verbands- und Anlegerschutz, 2nd Edition 1996, München.
- Peter O. Mülbert, Shareholder Value aus rechtlicher Sicht, ZGR 1997, 129 et seq.

N

- Dr. Günter Niedernhuber, Ausschüttungsregelungen für Aktiengesellschaften - Eine ökonomische Analyse-, 1988, Hamburg.
- Rudolf Nirk/Hildegard Ziemons/Burkhard Binnewies, Handbuch der Aktiengesellschaft, Band 1, 1994/2007, Köln.
- Ulricht Noack, Hauptversammlung der Aktiengesellschaft und moderne Kommunikationstechnik – aktuelle Bestandsaufnahme und Ausblick, NZG 2003, 241 et seq.
- Oyvind Norli/Charlotte Ostergaard/Ibolya Schindele, Liquidity and Shareholder Activism, 2010, www.ssrn.com/abstract=1344407.
- Martin Notthoff, Vorzeitiges Ausscheiden von Aufsichtsratsmitgliedern durch Mandatsaufhebung, WiB 1997, 848 et seq.

O

- Walter Obermüller/Windfried Werner/Kurt Winden/Volker Butzke, Die Hauptversammlung der Aktiengesellschaft, 4th Edition 2001, Stuttgart.

- Brent A. Olson, Publicly Traded Corporations: Governance & Regulation, 2nd Edition 2009, St. Paul, Minnesota.
- John F. Olson, A Practical Guide to SEC Proxy and Compensation Rules, 3rd Edition 2001, New York.

P

- Alexandre Padilla, The Regulation of Insider Trading as an Agency Problem, bepress Legal Series, Working Paper 641, 2005 http://law.bepress.com/expresso/eps/641.
- Walter G. Paefgen, Eigenkapitalrendite bei Aktienrückkäufen und Managementbeteiligungsmodellen – Zugleich ein Beitrag zur Entwicklung einer allgemeinen Systematik für die aktienrechtliche Beurteilung von Calls und Puts als Instrument der Unternehmensfinanzierung, AG 1999, 67 et seq.
- Otto Palandt, Bürgerliches Gesetzbuch, 69th Edition 2010, München.
- Alan Palmiter, Corporations, 4th Edition 2003, New York.
- Ulrich Pape, Kapitalmarktorientierte Ausschüttungspolitik am Beispiel der Daimler-Benz AG: Sonderausschüttung und Kapitalerhöhung, BB 1998, 1783 et seq.
- Tido Park (ed.), Kapitalmarktstrafrecht Handkommentar, 2nd Edition 2008, Baden-Baden.
- Frank S. Partnoy, Adding Derivatives to the Corporate Law Mix, 34 GA. L. REV. 599 (2000).
- Frank S. Partnoy/Randall S. Thomas, Gap Filling, Hedge Funds, and Financial Innovation, 2006, http://ssrn.com/abstract=931254.
- Oliver Peltzer, Die Neuregelung des Erwerbs eigener Aktien im Lichte der historischen Erfahrungen, WM 1998, 322 et seq.
- Udo Pfeifer, Schutzmechanismen bei der Umwandlung von Kapitalgesellschaften, 2001, Recklinhausen.
- David Porter, Competing with Delaware: Recent Amendments to Ohio's Corporate Statutes, 40 AKRON L. REV., 175 (2007).
- Dirk Posner, Der Erwerb eigener Aktien in der US-amerikanischen Unternehmenspraxis, AG 1994, 312 et seq.
- Richard A. Posner, Economic Analysis of Law, 2007, New York.
- James E. Post/Lee E. Preston/Sybille Sachs, Redefining the Corporation – Stakeholder Management and Organizational Wealth, 2002.
- Hans-Joachim Priester, Die klassische Ausgliederung – ein Opfer des Umwandlungsgesetzes 1994?, ZHR 163 (199), 187 et seq.

- Paul Pütz/Hans Willgerodt, Gleiches Recht für Beteiligungskapital – Vorschläge zur Reform von Unternehmensrecht und Kapitalmarkt, 1st Edition 1985, Baden-Baden.

R

- Peter Raisch, Unternehmensrecht-Aktien- und Konzernrecht, Mitbestimmung und Fusionskontrolle, Volume 2, 1974, Hamburg.
- Thomas Raiser/Rüdiger Veil, Recht der Kapitalgesellschaften, 5th Edition 2010, München.
- Alfred Rappaport, Shareholder Value, 1995, Stuttgart.
- Kurt Rebmann/Franz Jürgen Säcker/Roland Rixecker (eds.), Münchener Kommentar zum Bürgerlichen Gesetzbuch, Volume 5, §§ 705 – 853, 2009, München.
- Lee S. Redding, Firm Size and Dividend Payouts, 6 J. Fin. Intermediation 224 (1997), *available at* http://bbs.cenet.org.cn/uploadimages/200310231557139919.pdf.
- Wolfgang Renner, Holzmüller-Kompetenz der Hauptversammlung beim Erwerb einer Unternehmensbeteiligung?, NZG 2002, 1091 et seq .
- Scott Richardson, Overinvestment of Free Cash Flow, 11 Rev. Acc. Stud. 159 (2006).
- Rudolf Richter/Eirik G. Furubotn, Neue Institutionenökonomik, Eine Einführung und kritische Würdigung, 3rd Edition 2003, Tübingen.
- Larry E. Ribstein, Market vs. Regulatory Responses to Corporate Fraud: A Critique of the Sarbanes-Oxley Act of 2002, 28 J. Corp. L. 1 (2002), *available at* http://papers.ssrn.com/abstract=332681.
- Henrik-Michael Ringleb/Thomas Kremer/Marcus Lutter/Axel v. Werder, Deutscher Corporate Governance Kodex, 3rd Edition 2008, München.
- Edward B. Rock, The Logic and (Uncertain) Significance of Institutional Shareholder Activism, 79 Geo. L.J. 445 (1991).
- Mark J. Roe, Legal Origins and Modern Stock Markets, 120 Harv. L. Rev. 460, 495 (2006), *available at* http://www.ssrn.com/abstract=908972.
- Mark J. Roe, Political and Legal Restraints on Ownership and Control of Public Companies, 27 J. Fin. Econ. 7 (1990).
- Mark Roe, Political Preconditions to Separating Ownership from Corporate Control, 53 Stan. L. Rev. 539 (2000).
- Mark J. Roe, Strong Managers, Weak Owners: The Political Roots of American Corporate Finance, 2nd Edition 1996, Princeton, New Jersey.
- Broc Romanek/Cynthia M. Krus, Mergers & Acquisitions, 2002, Oxford.
- Broc Romanek/Beth Young/William Morley, Shareholder Proposal Handbook, 2001, New York, New York.

- Roberta Romano, Less is More: Making Shareholder Activism a Valued Mechanism of Corporate Governance 18 Yale J. On Reg. 174, (2000), *available at* http://ssnr.com/abstract=218650.
- Rüdiger von Rosen (ed.), Verhalten und Präferenzen deutscher Aktionäre, Eine Befragung von privaten und institutionellen Anlegern zum Informationsverhalten, zur Dividendenpräferenz und zur Wahrnehmung von Stimmrechten, DAI studies issue 42, 1st Edition 2009, Frankfurt a.M., *available at* http://www.dai.de/internet/dai/dai-2-0.nsf/0/399114E7707378DBC125757700344874/$FILE/B3540D04291E953FC125757700344721.pdf?openelement&cb_content_name_utf=2009-01_DAI-Studie-42_Post.pdf.
- Rüdiger von Rosen/Leohnard Held, Der Erwerb eigener Aktien durch die Gesellschaft – Plädoyer für ein neues Instrument der Unternehmensfinanzierung in Deutschland und einen wichtigen Impuls für den deutschen Kapitalmarkt, AG 1996, 434 et seq.
- Rüdiger von Rosen/Carl Wieandt, Activist Shareholders: Consensus Instead of Confrontation, Finanzplatz 3/2009, 22 et seq.
- Günter H. Roth/Ulrike Wörle, Die Unabhängigkeit des Aufsichtsrats – Recht und Wirklichkeit, ZGR 2004, 565 et seq.
- Michael S. Rozeff, Growth, Beta and Agency Costs as Determinants of Dividend Payout Ratios, 5 J. Fin. Research 249 (1982), *available at* http://ssrn.com/abstract=82031.
- Markus Ruffner, Die ökonomischen Grundlagen eines Rechts der Publikumsgesellschaft, 2000, Zürich.

S

- Franz-Jürgen Säcker, Rechtsprobleme beim Widerruf der Bestellung von Organmitgliedern und Ansprüche aus fehlerhaften Anstellungsverträgen, 745 et seq., in: Theo Mayer-Maly/Reinhard Richardi/Herbert Schambeck/Wolfgang Zöllner, Festschrift Gerhard Müller, Arbeitsleben und Rechtspflege, 1981, Berlin.
- Friedrich Carl von Savigny, System des heutigen Römischen Rechts, Volume 2, 1840, Berlin.
- Andreas Schaaf, Die Praxis der Hauptversammlung, 2nd Edition 1999, Köln.
- Carsten Schäfer, Diskussionsbericht – zu den Referaten Dreher und Marsch-Barner, ZHR 157 (1993) 192 et seq.
- Hans-Bernd Schäfer, Shareholder Activism und Corporate Governance, NZG 2007, 900 et seq.
- Frank A. Schäfer/Uwe Hamann (eds.), Kapitalmarktgesetze, Volume 1, 2nd Edition [Supp. 4 2009], Stuttgart, Berlin, Köln.

- Hans-Bernd Schäfer/Claus Ott, Lehrbuch der ökonomischen Analyse des Zivilrechts, 4th Edition 2005, Berlin.
- Kay-Michael Schanz, Schaeffler/Continental: Umgehung von Meldepflichten bei öffentlichen Übernahmen durch Einsatz von derivaten Finanzinstrumenten, DB 2008, 1899 et seq.
- Kay-Michael Schanz/Christoph Schalast (eds.), Schaeffler KG/Continental Ag im Lichte der CSX Corp.-Entscheidung des US District Court for the Southern District of New York – Meldepflichten bei öffentlichen Übernahmen und deren Umgehung durch Einsatz von derivativen Finanzinstrumenten-, Frankfurt-School working paper No. 100, 2008, www.frankfurt-school.de/dms/Arbeitsberichte/Arbeits100/Arbeits100.pdf.
- Maximilian Schiessl, Beteiligungsaufbau mittels Cash-Settled Total Return Equity Swaps – neue Modelle und Einführung von Meldepflichten, Der Konzern 2009, 291 et seq.
- Maximilian Schiessl, Die Kontrollfunktion der aktienrechtlichen Anfechtungsklage – Erwiderung aus Sicht der Praxis –, in: VGR (ed.), Gesellschaftsrecht in der Diskussion 1999, VGR Volume 2 (2000), 57 et seq.
- Karsten Schmidt, Gesellschaftsrecht, 4th Edition 2002, Köln.
- Karsten Schmidt/Marcus Lutter, Aktiengesetz Kommentar, Volume 1, 2nd Edition 2010, Köln.
- Joachim Schmitt/Robert Hörtnagel/Rolf-Christian Stratz, Umwandlungsgesetz, Umwandlungssteuergesetz, 5th Edition 2009, München.
- Klaus Ulrich Schmolke, Institutionelle Anleger und Corporate Governance – Traditionelle institutionelle Investoren vs. Hedgefonds, ZGR 2007, 701 et seq.
- Uwe H. Schneider, Acting in Concert: Vereinbarung oder Abstimmung über Ausübung von Stimmrechten? Zugleich Besprechung der Entscheidung BGH AG 2006, 883, ZGR 2007, 440 et seq .
- Uwe H. Schneider, Alternative Geldgeber oder Eigenkapitalräuber? – Die sieben Halbwahrheiten über die „neuen Investoren" – , AG 2006, 577 et seq.
- Uwe H. Schneider/Heribert M. Anzinger, Umgehung und missbräuchliche Gestaltung im Kapitalmarktrecht oder: Brauchen wir eine § 42 AO entsprechende Vorschrift im Kapitalmarktrecht?, ZIP 2009, 1 et seq.
- Uwe H. Schneider/Tobias Brouwer, Kapitalmarktrechtliche Meldepflichten bei Finanzinstrumenten, AG 2008, 557 et seq.
- Martin Schockenhoff/Eric Wagner, Zum Begriff des „acting in concert" – Das Verhältnis zwischen §§ 2 V und 30 II WpÜG und die Auswirkungen der geplanten Änderungen durch das Risikobegrenzungsgesetz, NZG 2008, 361 et seq.

- Ralf Schremper, Aktienrückkauf und Kapitalmarkt – Eine theoretischen und empirische Analyse deutscher Aktienrückkaufprogramme, 2002, Frankfurt a.M.
- Anja Schulz, Der Einfluss von Dividenden auf Aktienrenditen, 1st Edition 2006, Wiesbaden.
- Jan Schumacher, Das Informationssystem der Verschmelzung unter Beteiligung von Aktiengesellschaften, 2004, Köln.
- Stewart Schwab/Randall Thomas, Realigning Corporate Governance: Shareholder Activism by Labor Unions, 96 MICH. L. REV. 1018 (1998).
- Eberhard Schwark/Daniel Zimmer (eds.), Kapitalmarktrechts-Kommentar, 4th Edition 2010, München.
- Ulrich Seibert, Aktienrechtsreform in Permanenz?, AG 2002, 417 et seq.
- Ulrich Seibert, Das VorstAG – Regelungen zur Angemessenheit der Vorstandsvergütung und zum Aufsichtsrat, WM 2009, 1489 et seq.
- Ulrich Seibert, UMAG und Hauptversammlung – Der Regierungsentwurf eines Gesetzes zur Unternehmensintegrität und Modernisierung des Anfechtungsrechts (UMAG), WM 2005, 157 et seq.
- Christoph H. Seibt, Verbandssouveränität und Abspaltungsverbot, Aktien und Kapitalmarktrecht – Revisited: Hidden Ownership, Empty Voting und andere Kleinigkeiten, ZGR 2010, 795 et seq.
- Werner G. Seifert, Invasion der Heuschrecken – Intrigen – Machtkämpfe – Marktmanipulation, 2006, Berlin.
- Johannes Semler, The Practice of the German Aufsichtsrat, in: Klaus J. Hopt/Hideki Kanda/Mark J. Roe/Eddy Wymeersch/Stefan Prigge (eds.), Comparative Corporate Governance, 267 et seq., 1998, Oxford.
- Semler, Rechtsvorgabe und Realität der Organzusammenarbeit in der Aktiengesellschaft, 721 et seq., in: Uwe H. Schneider/Peter Hommelhoff/Karsten Schmidt, Festschrift Marcus Lutter, 2000, Köln.
- Johannes Semler/Kersten v. Schenck, Arbeitshandbuch für Aufsichtsratsmitglieder, 2nd Edition 2004, München.
- Johannes Semler/Arndt Stengel (eds.), Umwandlungsgesetz mit Spruchverfahrensgesetz, 3rd Edition 2012, München.
- Johannes Semler/Rüdiger Volhard (eds.), Arbeitshandbuch für die Hauptversammlung, 1999, München.
- Frederich O. Sewe, The Sarbanes Oxley Act and its Impacts on Corporate Finance and Corporate Governance Behavior, 2012, http://com/abstract=21111505.
- H. Nejat Seyhun, Investment Intelligence from Insider Trading, 1998, Cambridge, Mass., London.

- Andrei Shleifer/Robert W. Vishny, Large Shareholders and Corporate Control, 94 J. POLITICAL ECON. 461 (1986).
- William K. Sjostrom, Jr./Young Sang Kim, Majority Voting for the Election of Directors, 40 CONN. L. REV. 459 (2007).
- Markus Skrzipek, Shareholder Value versus Stakeholder Value: Ein Vergleich des des US-amerikanischen Raums mit Österreich, 1st Edition 2005, Wiesbaden.
- Axel Smend, Aktive Aktionäre, Zeitschrift für Corporate Governance (ZCG), 2/2008, 53 et seq.
- Gordon Smith, The Shareholder Primacy Norm, 23 J. CORP. L. 277 (1998), *available at* http://papers.ssrn.com/sol3/papers.cfm?abstract_id=10571.
- Michael P. Smith, Shareholder Activism by Institutional Investors: Evidence from CalPers, 51 J. FIN. 227 (1996), *available at* www.ssrn.com/abstract=7230.
- Gerald Spindler, Acting in Concert–Begrenzung von Risiken durch Finanzinvestoren?–Der Regierungsentwurf eines Risikobegrenzungsgesetzes–, WM 2007, 2357 et seq.
- Gerald Spindler/Eberhard Stilz (eds.), Kommentar zum Aktiengesetz, München, 2007
  15. Volume 1, §§ 1- 178 AktG,
  16. Volume 2, §§ 179 – 410 AktG.
- Statistisches Bundesamt/Federal Statistical Office (ed.), Statistisches Jahrbuch 2008 – Für die Bundesrepublik Deutschland/Statistical Yearbook 2008 – For the Federal Republic of Germany, 2008, Wiesbaden.
- Ursula Stein, Das faktische Organ, 1984, Köln, Berlin, Bonn, München.
- Roland Steinmeyer/Michael Häger, Wertpapiererwerbs- und Übernahmegesetz Kommentar, 2nd Edition 2007, Berlin.
- Nick W.A. Stokman, Influences of Hedge Fund Activism on the Medium Term Target Firm Value, 2008, www.ssrn.com/1019968.
- Lynn A. Stout, Why Carl Icahn is Bad for Investors, Wall Street Journal, August 1, 2008, A 11.
- Christian Strenger, Corporate Governance und Anteilseigner, insbesondere institutionelle Anleger, 697 et seq. in: Peter Hommelhoff/ Klaus J. Hopt/Axel von Werder, Handbuch Corporate Governance, 2003, Köln.
- Leo E. Strine, Toward a True Corporate Republic: A Traditionalist Response to Bebchuk's Solution for Improving Corporate America, 119 HARV. L. REV. 1759 (2006).
- Eckart Sünner, Aktionärsschutz und Aktienrecht, AG 1983, 169 et seq.
- Peter Swoboda, Betriebswirtschaftliche Finanzierung, 2nd Edition 1991, Heidelberg.

T

- Ralf Thaeter/Roman Gurski, Shareholder Activism: Gesellschaftsrechtliche Schranken aktiven Aktionärsverhaltens, AG 2007, 301 et seq.
- Ingo Theusinger/Daniel Möritz, Empty Voting als moderner Stimmrechtskauf?, NZG 2010, 607 et seq.
- Robert Thompson, The Limits of Hedge Fund Activism, 2006, UC Berkeley: Berkeley Program in Law and Economics, http://escholarship.org/uc/item/5jq9d71m.
- Robert B. Thompson/Randall S. Thomas, The New Look of Shareholder Litigation: Acquisition-Oriented Class Actions, 57 Vand. L. Rev. 133 (2004).
- Gregor Thüsing, Das Gesetz zur Angemessenheit der Vorstandsvergütung, AG 2009, 517 et seq.
- Wolfram Timm, Anmerkung zur Entscheidung des OLG Köln, Az.: 22 U 72/92, in ZIP 1993, 110 et seq.
- Wolfram Timm, Die Aktiengesellschaft als Konzernspitze, Köln, Berlin Bonn, München, 1980.
- Wolfram Timm, Die Mitwirkung des Aufsichtsrats bei unternehmensstrukturellen Entscheidungen – Grenzen der Aufsichtsrats- und Verwaltungszuständigkeiten in der Aktiengesellschaft, DB 1980, 1201 et seq.
- Wolfram Timm, Grundfragen des „qualifizierten" faktischen Konzerns im Aktienrecht – Bemerkungen zur „Banning"-Entscheidung des OLG Hamm vom 3. 11. 1986, NJW 1987, 977 et seq.
- Wolfram Timm, Zur Sachkontrolle von Mehrheitsentscheidungen im Kapitalgesellschaftsrecht – dargestellt am Beispiel „strukturverändernder Entscheidungen", ZGR 1987, 403 et seq.
- Stefanie Trost, Determinanten der Ausschüttungspolitik, 2009, http://www.opus.ub.uni-erlangen.de/opus/volltexte/2009/1408/pdf/diss_trost.pdf.
- Gerson Trüg, Ist der Leerverkauf von Wertpapieren strafbar?, NJW 2009, 3202 et seq.

U

- Peter Ulmer, Aktienrecht im Wandel – Entwicklungslinien und Diskussionsschwerpunkte, AcP 202 (2002), 143 et seq.
- Peter Ulmer (ed.), Max Hachenburg, GmbHG-Gesetz betreffend die Gesellschaften mit beschränkter Haftung, Kommentar, Volume 2, 8th Edition 1997, Berlin.

V

- Julian Velasco, Shareholder Ownership and Primacy, 2010 U. Ill. L. Rev. 897, *available at* http://ssrn.com/abstract=1274244.
- Jay W. Verret, Pandora's Ballot Box, Or a Proxy with Moxies? Majority Voting, Corporate Ballot Access and the Legend of Martin Lipton Re-Examined, 62 Bus. Law. 1 (2007).
- Sigurt Vitols, Ökonomische Auswirkungen der paritätischen Mitbestimmung: Eine ökonometrische Analyse, 2006, Berlin.
- Hans-Christoph Voigt, Haftung aus Einfluss auf die Aktiengesellschaft (§§ 117, 309, 317 AktG), 2003, München.
- Hans-Joachim Voth, Transparenz und Fairness auf einem einheitlichen europäischen Kapitalmarkt, Studie im Auftrag der Hans-Böckler-Stiftung, 2007, http://www.boeckler.de/pdf/gutachten_voth_2007.pdf.

W

- Jens Wagner, Beteiligungserwerb ohne „Holzmüller-Hauptversammlung", DStR 2004, 141 et seq.
- Rainer Walz, Ökonomische und soziologische Unternehmensleitbilder vor den Toren des Gesellschaftsrechts – Ein Plädoyer für interdisziplinäre Neugier, AG 1996, 161 et seq.
- Robert Weber, Activist Shareholders – Freedom of Action and Limits, Der Finanzplatz, Volume 2 March 2009, 10 et seq.
- Christoph Weber/Anne Meckbach, Finanzielle Differenzgeschäfte – Ein legaler Weg zum "Anschleichen" an die Zielgesellschaft bei Übernahmen?, BB 2008, 2022 et seq.
- Robert Weber/Christoph Schalast, Handlungsspielräume von Staatsfonds in Deutschland – Außenwirtschafts- und Gesellschaftsrecht, Studien des Deutschen Aktieninstituts, issue 45, 2009, Frankfurt a.M., *available at* http://www.frankfurt-school.de/dms/publications-cfe/Studie45/Studie45/Studie%2045%20-%20Staatsfonds.pdf.
- Martin Weber, Scalping-Erfindung und Folgen eines Insiderdelikts, NJW 2000, 562 et seq.
- Daniela Weber-Rey, Risikobegrenzung – Gratwanderung im Dienste der Transparenz, DStR 2008, 1967 et seq.
- Edward P. Welch/Andrew J. Turezyn/Robert S. Saunders, Folk on the Delaware General Corporation Law, Volume 1, 5th Edition 2010, Austin, Boston, Chicago, New York, The Netherlands.
- Ekkehard Wenger/Christoph Kaserer, Kursreaktionen auf steuerlich veranlasste Sonderausschüttungen – Die Auskehrung von EK 56 im Jahre 1994, ZBB 2005, 1 et seq.

- Axel v. Werder, Ökonomische Grundfragen der Corporate Governance, 3 et seq. in: Peter Hommelhoff/Klaus J. Hopt/Axel von Werder, Corporate Governance Handbuch, 2003, Köln Stuttgart.
- Windfried Werner, Ausgewählte Fragen zum Aktienrecht, AG 1972, 93 et seq.
- Winfried Werner, Zur Treupflicht des Kleinaktionärs, 419 et seq., in: Marcus Bierich/Peter Hommelhoff/Bruno Kropff (eds.), Festschrift für Johannes Semler zum 70. Geburtstag, 1993, Berlin, New York.
- Winfried Werner, Zuständigkeiten in der Aktiengesellschaft, ZHR 147 (1983), 429 et seq.
- Winfried Werner, Zuständigkeitsverschiebungen in der Aktiengesellschaft durch Richterrecht? Besprechung der Entscheidung BGHZ 83, 122, ZHR 147 (1983), 429 et seq.
- Stefanie C. Wettberg, Der Rückkauf eigener Anteile im deutschen Finanzsystem, 2003, Heidelberg, *available at* http://archiv.ub.uni-heidelberg.de/volltextserver/volltexte/2003/3555/pdf/Diss_wett.pdf.
- Siegfried Widmann/Dieter Mayer, Umwandlungsrecht: Umwandlungsgesetz, Umwandlungssteuergesetz, 3rd Edition [January 2009], Bonn.
- Herbert Wiedemann, Gesellschaftsrecht, Volume 1, 1980, München.
- Herbert Wiedemann, Organverantwortung und Gesellschafterklagen in der Aktiengesellschaft, 1989, Opladen.
- Herbert Wiedemann, Rechtsethische Maßstäbe im Unternehmensrecht, ZGR 1980, 147 et seq.
- Christian Wilde, Informationsrechte und Informationspflichten im Gefüge der Gesellschaftsorgane, ZGR 1998, 423 et seq.
- Charles M. Williams, Cumulative Voting, 33 Harv. Bus. Rev. 108 (1955).
- Oliver E. Williamson, Die ökonomischen Institutionen des Kapitalismus: Unternehmen, Märkte, Kooperationen, 1990, Tübingen.
- Hans-Ulrich Wilsing/Markus Ogorek, Der Minderheitsantrag auf gerichtliche Einsetzung eines Sonderprüfers gemäß § 142 Abs. 2 AktG – ein neues Betätigungsfeld für professionelle Minderheitsaktionäre, GWR 2009, 281217 (= GWR 2009, 75).
- Christine Windbichler, Zur Trennung von Geschäftsführung und Kontrolle bei amerikanischen Großgesellschaften – Eine „neue“ Entwicklung und europäische Regelungen im Vergleich, ZGR 1985, 50 et seq.
- Christine Windbichler/Alfred Hueck, Gesellschaftsrecht, 22nd Edition 2009, München.
- Sylko Winkler, Die Verantwortung institutioneller Anleger als Aktionäre in Publikumsgesellschaften in Deutschland und den USA, 2008, Gottmadingen.

- Günter Wöhe/Ulrich Döring, Einführung in die allgemeine Betriebswirtschaftslehre, 23rd Edition 2008, München.
- Daniel F. Wolcott/Bruce A. Rogers, Corporations and Business Organizations, Delaware Code Annotated – Revised 1974, Volume 4 2001 Replacement, 2008, Charlottesville, Virginia.
- Ralph Wollburg/Christian Gehling, Umgestaltung des Konzerns – Wer entscheidet über die Veräußerung von Beteiligungen einer Aktiengesellschaft?, 133 et seq., in: Ernst Niederleithinger, Rosemarie Werner, Gerhard Wiedemann (eds.), Festschrift für Otfried Lieberknecht, 1997, München.
- Jeffrey R. Wolters/James D. Honaker, Analysis of the 2008 Amendments to the Delaware General Corporation Law, 2008, Frederick, Maryland.

Y

- Joseph W. Yockey, On the Role and Regulation of Private Negotiations in Governance, 61 S.C. L. Rev. 171 (2009).
- Beth Young/The Corporate Library for the Council of Institutional Investors, The Limits of Private Ordering: Restrictions on Shareholders' Ability to Initiate Governance Change and Distortion of the Shareholder Voting Process, 2009, http://www.cii.org/UserFiles/file/The%20Limits%20of%20Private%20Ordering%20UPDATED%2011-17-09.pdf.

Z

- Andrea Zanoni, Hedge Funds' Empty Voting in Mergers and Acquisitions: A Fiduciary Duties Perspective, 2009, http://ssrn.com/abstract=1285589.
- Dirk Zetsche, Die Europäische Regulierung von Hedge Fonds und Private Equity – ein Zwischenstand –, NZG 2009, 692 et seq.
- Klaus Zimmermann, Vertrauensentzug durch die Hauptversammlung und Stimmrechtsausübung, in: Gerd Pfeiffer/Günther Wiese/Klaus Zimmermann (eds.), Festschrift für Heinz Rowedder zum 75. Geburtstag, 1994, München.
- Wolfgang Zöllner, Die Schranken mitgliedschaftlicher Stimmrechtsmacht bei den privatrechtlichen Personenverbänden, 1963, München, Berlin.
- Wolfgang Zöllner (ed.), Kölner Kommentar zum Aktiengesetz, Köln, Berlin, Bonn, München

  1st Edition

  Introductory Volume, 1984,

  Volume 1, §§ 1 – 147 AktG, 1985,

  2nd Edition

Volume 1, §§ 1 – 75 AktG, 1988, Köln, Berlin, Bonn, München,
Volume 2, §§ 76 – 117 AktG, 1996, Köln, Berlin, Bonn, München,
Volume 5/1, §§ 179 – 240 AktG, 1994, Köln, Berlin, Bonn, München,
Volume 6, §§ 291 – 338 AktG, 2004, Köln, Berlin, München,

- Wolfgang Zöllner/Ulrich Noack (eds.), Kölner Kommentar zum Aktiengesetz, 3rd Edition
  Volume 2/1, §§ 76 – 94, 2010, Köln.
- Wolfgang Zöllner, Unternehmensinnenrecht: Gibt es das?, AG 2003, 2 et seq.
- Konrad Zweigert/Hein Kötz, Die Einführung in die Rechtsvergleichung, 3rd Edition 1996, Tübingen.

A) The thesis

I) Motivation

According to the well-known U.S.-American financial investor Wyser-Pratte, who has been active since the 1970s, there are not only good active investors. There are also bad ones who trample the practices of local cultures, fire people, and enrich themselves at the expense of others, as some U.S.-American Funds have done. In Germany, the "Locust Debate," a discussion about the benefits and drawbacks related to active investors, began in 2005. Franz Müntefering, at that time head of the Social Democratic Party in Germany, used active investors, whose presence in Germany was rather new, as scapegoats to win the 2005 election.[2]

In both Germany and the United States, the debate about the benefits and drawbacks of active shareholders is closely related to the question of the adequacy of existing provisions in restricting destructive activism, the necessity of additional statutory provisions to restrict active shareholders in negatively affecting targeted corporations, or the need to lift current legal limitations that apply to (active) shareholders. Recent data on the long-term effects of shareholder activism applied to U.S. firms relating closely to short-termism as the sharpest charge active shareholders in both countries have been confronted with has fueled the debate again.

II) Aim, scope, and method

1) Aim

This study seeks to answer the following question: to what extent do the benefits and drawbacks of shareholder activism require the amendment of the current law? This question includes determining the necessary legal means and limitations in maximizing the positive function of shareholder activism in improving corporate governance. Such means and limitations could reduce agency issues and costs resulting from the separation of ownership and control while minimizing the potential for shareholder activism to be abused by opportunistic shareholders. This thesis will examine the current opportunities for shareholder activism and determine whether these should be maintained, legally restricted or increased in the light of their potential for abuse by those with vested interests that drastically deviate from the interest of the corporation. The aim regarding

2 Martin Dowideit/Anette Dowideit, *„Je mehr ein Fisch zappelt, desto größer ist er"*, DIE WELT, Dec. 20, 2005, *available at* http://www.welt.de/print-welt/article185389/Je_mehr_ein_Fisch_zappelt_desto_groesser_ist_er.html.

the latter two scenarios is to propose legal amendments necessary to support the function of shareholder activism while at the same time preventing abuse that could harm the corporation and its investors.

2) Scope

This work will compare the U.S.-American corporate and securities law and the German corporate and capital market law relevant to determining the opportunities and restrictions for shareholders to actively influence publicly listed corporations. Because of the multiplicity of corporate laws at the state level in the United States, this work will concentrate on the corporate law of the State of Delaware, which is in practice the most significant among the different states in terms of laws governing corporations.[3] Despite Delaware's small size and population, a disproportionate number of corporations have incorporated there, including half of the publicly traded corporations and the majority of the large publicly traded corporations.[4] Delaware's popularity stems from its extraordinary flexibility regarding the arrangement of the articles of incorporation of corporations as well as the state legislators' restrain in passing regulations.[5]

After a general introduction on shareholder activism and the underlying theories and relevant practical differences in the United States and Germany, this work will focus on three strategies repeatedly applied by active shareholders. The analysis will consider the means of active shareholders as well as the limitations they confront. Furthermore, it will take into account the controversies each strategy triggers.

3) Method

This work is a comparative analysis of the current opportunities and restrictions on active investors in public corporations imposed by American corporate and securities laws and the German corporate and capital-market regime that are pertinent to increasing control of corporate management as well as to the concerns confronting active shareholders.[6]

This study makes use of a functional approach[7] that considers economic models of the firm, particularly the modeled assumptions and analytical methods of the New Insti-

---

3 Becker, Verwaltungskontrolle durch Gesellschafterrechte, 1997, 105 et seq.; Greenfield, 67 LAW & CONTEMP. PROBS. 135, 135–37 (2004).

4 Bebchuk & Hamdani, 112 YALE L.J. 553, 554 n.3 (2002): "Delaware is the state of incorporation for 51 percent of U.S. public companies and for 63 percent of Fortune 500 companies."; Greenfield, *supra* note 4, at 135.

5 Leyens, RabelZ 67, 57 (69 et seq.).

6 Dannemann, *Comparative Law: Study of Similarities or Differences? in* Reimann/Zimmermann, THE OXFORD HANDBOOK OF COMPARATIVE LAW 383, 399 (2006).

7 Michaels, *The Functional Method of Comparative Law in* Reimann/Zimmermann, THE OXFORD HANDBOOK OF COMPARATIVE LAW 339, 340 et seq (2006).

tutional Economics[8] regarding public corporations. These methods include complementary used-agency[9] and transaction-cost[10] theories of the firm[11] as well as of nonlegal institutions. Transaction costs may result from trading relations between contractual partners and may be reduced in an organization like a firm. Agency costs, on the other hand, evolve in hierarchies based on incomplete information, permitting opportunism and different risk tolerances, among others. The aim of these approaches is to maximize the overall economic benefit of the involved parties by reducing the use of resources, including transaction or agency costs.

8 Fleischer, ZGR 2001, 1 (3 et seq.).

9 Jensen & Meckling, 3 J. FIN. ECON. 305 (1976).

10 Coase, 4 ECONOMICA 386, 390 et seq. (1937): according to whom the market may be led by an invisible hand, so Adam Smith, but there is a cost of using this price mechanism; Williamson, Die ökonomischen Institutionen des Kapitalismus: Unternehmen, Märkte, Kooperationen, 1990, 17 et seq.

11 POSNER, ECONOMIC ANALYSIS OF LAW 419 et seq. (420), 440 et seq. (2007); Ruffner, Die ökonomischen Grundlagen eines Rechts der Publikumsgesellschaft, 2000, 131; Schäfer/Ott, Lehrbuch der ökonomischen Analyse des Zivilrechts, 2005, 645.

B) Introduction to shareholder activism

I) What is shareholder activism?

1) Definition of shareholder activism

Shareholders dissatisfied with the management of a corporation or corporate performance may decide for the "exit" and adopt the "Wall-street-rule" by selling their shares. They may also continue to hold their shares without doing anything, better known as "loyalty."[12] Shareholders who aim to express their dissatisfaction employ a wide range of means lying between the sale of shares and the initiation of takeovers or LBOs.[13] In 1972, *Hirschmann* defined this "voice" option as any attempt to change rather than to escape from an objectionable state of affairs through individual or collective positions to the management directly in charge, appeals to a higher authority with the intention of forcing a change in management, or various types of actions and protests, including those meant to mobilize public opinion.[14] Its function is to alert a firm or organization to its failings while giving it some time and the choice to respond to the pressures that have been brought to bear on it,[15] depending on the costs of alternatives.[16] Nowadays, shareholder activism refers to the interest of shareholders in shaping the direction of their company through their participation in the normal processes that shape the company, such as voting through proxies during a shareholder meeting. At the other extreme lies the popular hedge fund practice of accumulating shareholder minority positions in public companies large enough to move the companies single-handedly in one direction or the other or in whatever form the activist practice may take. As a consequence, it is clear that the term refers to attempts by different types of shareholders to use whatever power they have as owners to influence the company's behavior regarding a wide range of topics from corporate governance issues to pure management decisions.[17] Despite this broad interpretation, active shareholders need to be distinguished from the German

12 Gillan & Starks, *The Evolution of Shareholder Activism in the United States* 6, www.ssrn.com/abstract=959670 (2007); *but see* Ruffner, Die ökonomischen Grundlagen eines Rechts der Publikumsgesellschaft, 2000, 441 et seq.: distinguishes Exit, Passivity and Control.

13 Gillan & Starks, *The Evolution of Shareholder Activism in the United States*, 5 et seq., www.ssrn.com/abstract=959670 (2007); Gillan & Starks, A Survey of Shareholder Activism: Motivation and Empirical Evidence 4, www.ssrn.com/abstract=663523 (1998).

14 Hirschmann, Exit, Voice and Loyalty: Responses to Decline in Firms, Organizations, and States 30 (1970).

15 *Id.* at 33.

16 *Id.* at 136.

17 Bassen, Einflußnahme institutioneller Investoren auf Corporate Governance und Unternehmensführung, 2001, 4 et seq., 7 et seq.; Bertaccini, 31 Cardozo L. Rev. 267, 267 (2009); Gillan & Starks, *The Evolution of Shareholder Activism in the United States* 5 et seq. www.ssrn.com/

phenomenon of professional opponents, whose goal is obstruction when they file legal suits against corporations to extract personal benefits. In contrast, active shareholders generally aim to exercise constructive control over the corporate administration[18].[19] This introductory section on shareholder activism will therefore consider the varieties of shareholder activism regarding the actors and the strategies and means they apply to pursue them.

2) Motivation to become active[20]

There may be good reasons for shareholders of large public corporations to remain passive instead of exerting their rights. These reasons include shareholder confidence in managerial expertise, limited returns from potential corporate value increase for individual shareholders with minimal stakes, and free-riding issues[21].[22] Additional reasons are the dispersed ownership amongst many shareholders–requiring complicated and costly efforts to realize joint decisions (collective-action issue[23])[24]–the quicker and less costly "exit" solution, the limited liability of shareholders,[25] and legal obstacles preventing them from using formal accountability mechanisms[26].[27]

Nevertheless, increasing numbers of shareholders decide to become active. "The main motive for active participation of institutional investors in the monitoring of cor-

---

abstract=959670 (2007); Kahan & Rock, 155 U. Pa. L. Rev. 1021 (2007); Schneider, AG 2006, 577 (577).

18 For practical reasons, this work will refer, where possible, to the "administration" when referring to supervisory board and/or management board and/or board of directors and/or executive officers.

19 Dreher, ZHR 157 (1993), 151 (167); Götze, in: Von Rosen, Die Hauptversammlung vor neuen Herausforderungen, DAI studies issue 41, 2008, 119 (120): Thaeter/Guski, AG 2007, 301 (301 n.3); Werner, Zur Treupflicht des Kleinaktionärs, in: Bierich et al., FS Semler, 1993, 419 (420 et seq.).

20 Arnold, ZCG 2008, 221 (225); Gillan & Starks, *A Survey of Shareholder Activism: Motivation and Empirical Evidence* 13, www.ssrn.com/abstract=663523 (1998); Winkler, Die Verantwortung institutioneller Anleger als Aktionäre in Publikumsgesellschaften in Deutschland und den USA, 2008, 90 et seq.

21 Clark, Corporate Law 94 (1986): "[F]reerider problem – the temptation faced by each individual member of a large group, like the shareholders of a public corporation, to fail to make the effort needed to contribute to a group action, because he hopes that the other will do the work and he will benefit anyway."

22 Garrido & Rojo, *Institutional Investors and Corporate Governance: Solution or Problem in* Hopt & Wymeersch, Capital Market and Company Law 427, 428 (2003).

23 Easterbrook & Fischel, The Economic Structure of Corporate Law 66 et seq. (1991); Ruffner, Die ökonomischen Grundzüge eines Rechts der Publikumsgesellschaft, 2000, 174 et seq., for more details *see* note 306.

24 Black, 89 Mich. L. Rev. 520, 525 (1990): noting that shareholder passivity is less a problem of collective action than of legal barriers.

25 Fleischer, ZGR 2001, 1 (17).

26 Black, 89 Mich. L. Rev. 520, 530–66 (1990): summarizing legal obstacles; Briggs, 32 J. Corp. L. 681, 701 (2007).

27 Cheffins, Company Law 62 (1997).

porations has been the potential to *enhance the value of their personal investments*."[28] The rationale for shareholder activism arises from the need to *resolve agency conflicts* inherent in a public corporation. Shareholders, as the (economic) owners of the corporation, delegate the decision-making to managers. The board of directors, bound by fiduciary duties towards the shareholders, is supposed to control management. This structure is intended to avoid possible agency problems such as managerial opportunism, in which managers make decisions in their own interest, rather than seeking to benefit shareholders by maximizing shareholder value. Using their delegated responsibility of hiring, firing, compensating, and monitoring the managers, the board of directors can ensure that managers act for the benefit of shareholders.[29] A need for shareholder activism arises when the board is not exercising its control task,[30] and, therefore, the organizational structure cannot fulfill its task in reducing agency issues resulting from the opportunistic decisions and actions of the managers. Besides the stock market and the market for corporate control, shareholder activism is a means of a *non-control related monitoring* by active investors that can reduce or eliminate these agency issues.[31]

Shareholders, such as the decreasing number of blockholders in the case of German corporations and institutional shareholders in U.S. and German corporations, are a less diversified group. Due to the size of their shareholdings they have the opportunity to overcome *rational apathy* problems based on *free-rider* issues. The larger sizes of their stakes may allow them to be compensated for their efforts to become active. Furthermore, their large total investments reduce *collective action* problems, while access to greater amounts of capital allows them to circumvent legal obstacles. The size of their stakes provides them with *stronger incentives* to become active, since it is usually difficult to choose the "exit" option by selling their stake without giving a significant discount.[32]

---

28 Gillan & Starks, *The Evolution of Shareholder Activism in the United States* 34, www.ssrn.com/abstract=959670 (2007); Götze, in: Von Rosen, Die Hauptversammlung vor neuen Herausforderungen, DAI studies issue 41, 2008, 119 (123).

29 Jensen & Meckling, 5 J. Fin. Econ. 305 (1976), *available at* www.ssrn.com/abstract=94043, 5: referring to an agency relationship as a contract under which one or more persons (the principals) engage another person (the agent) to perform some service on their behalf, which involves delegating some decision-making authority to the agent, but despite monitoring and bonding expenditures, the decisions of the agent will still diverge from the decisions that would maximize the welfare of the principal; Gillan & Starks, *The Evolution of Shareholder Activism in the United States* 13, www.ssrn.com/abstract=959670 (2007).

30 Gillan & Starks, *A Survey of Shareholder Activism: Motivation and Empirical Evidence* 13 www.ssrn.com/abstract=663523 (1998).

31 Fama & Jensen, 26 J. L. & Econ. 301, 313 (1983), *available at* www.ssrn.com/abstract=94034: referring to the stock market, the market for takeovers, expert boards as methods to control the agency problems of common stock; Arnold, ZCG 2008, 221 (225).

32 Cheffins, Company Law 63 (1997).

3) History of shareholder activism

Shareholder activism has a longer history in the United States than in Germany. In the United States, shareholder activism has existed since the first half of the past century. After the adoption of the predecessor to Rule 14a-8 of the Securities Exchange Act of 1934,[33] individual shareholders began to submit proposals that aimed to improve corporate governance as well as corporate performance.[34] Several decades later, shareholders increasingly used these measures to focus not only on corporate governance, but also on social issues.[35] Beginning in the mid-eighties, several groups of active shareholders emerged using shareholder proposals that generally aimed to raise awareness of the directors' accountability to shareholders.[36] During the mid-eighties and onward, the steadily growing amount of investments held by institutional investors[37] led to their growing stakes in and impact on corporations and resulted in their active involvement, marked by the formation of the Council of Institutional Investors (***"CII"***). The CII started as a lobbying group for shareholder rights. Later it began to focus on advancing the perspectives of institutional investors. The CII initially focused on proxy proposals, but by the early 1990s it increasingly made use of its access to the administrations and the media. With the decline of the takeover market and the repeated amendment of securities rules beginning in the 1990s, communication among shareholders on matters of voting as well as with the administration was improved.[38] The increasing

33 The Securities Exchange Act of 1934 (hereinafter „SEA") refers to §§ 78a and following of title 15 of the United States Code (15 U.S.C. §§ 78a et seq.).

34 Gillan & Starks, *The Evolution of Shareholder Activism in the United States* 34, www.ssrn.com/abstract=959670 (2007).

35 Gillan & Starks, *A Survey of Shareholder Activism: Motivation and Empirical Evidence* 6 et seq., www.ssrn.com/abstract=663523 (1998).

36 Gillan & Starks, *The Evolution of Shareholder Activism in the United States* 7 et seq., www.ssrn.com/abstract=959670 (2007).

37 ABA/Section of Business Law, 65 Bus. Law. 107, 135 (2009): estimating that in 2006 private stock ownership had fallen to 33 percent of U.S. equity, in 2007 76,9 percent of the largest 1000 companies were already owned by institutional investors; Kahan & Rock, *Embattled CEOs* 11, http://ssrn.com/abstract=1281516 (2008).

38 Anabtawi & Stout, 60 Stan. L. Rev. 1255, 1279 (2008); David Ben-Ur/Corbin Capital Partners, *Shareholder Activism* 2, http://www.pionline.com/assets/docs/CO19344522.PDF (2007): Besides comparably strong liquidity of corporations in the middle of the first decade of the new millennium, the corporate scandals of the early 2000's spurred substantial regulatory reform, like the Regulation Fair Disclosure and Sarbanes-Oxley Act, which enhanced the powers of shareholders at the expense of management teams and corporate boards, and more general the malfeasance at major corporations like WorldCom, Enron, and Tyco reduced the reputations of executives and boards and increased the public acceptance of activist programs. More importantly, traditional investors have come out strongly in favor of improved governance practices and their presence has substantially strengthened the hand of activist funds, efficiency enhancing technologies improving the activist tool-kit, and finally slimmer profit opportunities, resulting in many managers gravitating towards activist approaches.; Black, *Shareholder Activism and Corporate Governance in the United States* 1, www.ssrn.com/abstract=45100 (1997): pointing out the modest success of the 1992 amendments of the proxy rules in reducing barriers to coalition building amongst institutions; Briggs, 32 J. Corp. L. 681, 686 (2007); Briggs, 50 Bus. Law. 99, 99, 147 (1994): Even though only intended to improve communication amongst passive shareholders, active investors have also reaped many of the benefits. But

impact of commercial shareholder advisory firms, especially of the former Institutional Shareholder Services Inc. (***"ISS"***),[39] reduced collective action problems[40] and brought the activism of institutional investors to the fore. In recent years, lightly regulated hedge funds in particular have demonstrated growing interest in participating more directly in the decision-making process of their targeted companies, thereby contributing to a partial redefinition of the activism phenomenon.[41]

In contrast, the phenomenon of shareholder activism in Germany is still a relatively recent one. Prominent cases involving Deutsche Börse AG, TUI AG, or CeWe Color Holding AG, which will be analyzed *infra*, occurred during the second half of the first decade of the new millennium.[42] During the last seasons of shareholder meetings, shareholder activism became a reliable part. The number of active shareholders constantly increased in the last years, as indicated by the participation of active shareholders regarding the share capital.[43] This development is based, amongst many reasons, on *reforms of corporate law*. These included the introduction of the record date through the UMAG[44] in 2005, § 123 (3) sent. 3 AktG, making the deposit of shares superfluous while allowing even shareholders from abroad to register for participation. Other developments include the introduction of the shareholder forum, § 127a AktG, allowing shareholders to prepare common motions such as those according to §§ 122, 142 (2), 148 (2) AktG, and so on, seeking to increase ownership-based control in times of increasing freefloat and internationalization.[45] Another contribution to this phenomenon is the recently enacted

---

the 1992 amendments did not go far enough. Free speech continued to be chilled by the Proxy Rules and Rule 13(d) SEA; DAVIS & STEIL, INSTITUTIONAL INVESTORS 312 (2001); HAWLEY & WILLIAMS, THE RISE OF FIDUCIARY CAPITALISM 123 (2000): regarding the 1992 reforms to Rule 14a-2 SEA, *id.* at 149: regarding the 1992 reforms of Rule 13 (d) SEA; Winkler, Die Verantwortung institutioneller Anleger als Aktionäre in Publikumsgesellschaften in Deutschland und den USA, 2008, 123.

39 ISS exercised its impact from the late 1980s until 2007, profiting from a regulation of the Department of Labor requiring that pension funds and of the SEC that mutual funds hired someone to vote their shares. According to a Memorandum of the BRT in 2003, 28 et seq., http://www.sec.gov/rules/proposed/s71903/brt122203.pdf, 40 percent of its companies were voted by ISS, making the support of ISS essential to the success of a vote on an (corporate governance) issue.

40 Anabtawi & Stout, 60 STAN. L. REV. 1255, 1277, 1279 (2008); Briggs, 32 J. CORP. L. 681, 692 (2007); Kahan & Rock, *Embattled CEOs* 18 et seq., www.ssrn.com/abstract=1281516 (2008).

41 Anabtawi & Stout, 60 STAN. L. REV. 1255, 1278 (2008); Gillan & Starks, *The Evolution of Shareholder Activism in the United States* 4, 30 et seq., www.ssrn.com/abstract=959670 (2007); Park & Tonello, *Avoiding Shareholder Activism*, THE CONFERENCE BOARD – EXECUTIVE ACTION SERIES, 1, 8, www.srcibd.com (search "avoiding shareholder activism") (2009).

42 Götze, in: Von Rosen, Die Hauptversammlung vor neuen Herausforderungen, DAI studies issue 41, 2008, 119 (121).

43 DAI/McKinsey, Investorendialog im Umbruch, 2009, 9, 17.

44 Gesetz zur Unternehmensintegrität und Modernisierung des Anfechtungsrechs [UMAG] [Act on Corporate Integrity and Modernization of the Rescission Right] Sept. 22, 2005, BGBl I at 2802 (F.R.G.).

45 Stellungnahme des Bundesrates zum RegE eines Gesetzes zur Unternehmensintegrität und Modernisierung des Anfechtungsrechts [UMAG] [Statement of the Federal Council on the Draft Law of the Federal Government on an Act on Corporate Integrity and Modernization of the Rescission Right], Jan. 7, 2005, BR-Drucks 3/05, 28; Schmolke, ZGR 2007, 701 (727); Seibert WM 2005, 157 (158 et seq.).

legislation permitting corporations to opt into a regime allowing shareholders to participate at a shareholder meeting and vote, both online, through amendments in their articles of incorporation, § 118 (1) sent. 2, (2) AktG. Further contributions include the *increasing impact of proxy advisory firms*.[46] Beyond this, *market prerequisites* have been amended especially through the *divestiture of the "Deutschland AG*."[47] Many of the banks,[48] insurance companies, and industrial enterprises held share packages that became fragmented, leading to *increased freefloat* and *decreasing presence rates* during shareholder meetings. This made it easier for active shareholders to accumulate significant voting stakes.[49] Furthermore, the resulting increase in the number of international institutional investors[50] contributed to this movement. Among these were active shareholders, including particularly aggressive hedge funds,[51] with relatively small shareholdings who approached management with specific requests regarding corporate policy,[52] leading a change from management rule to shareholder rule.

As a consequence of the comparably short history of shareholder activism in German corporations, empirical data and experiences on the effect of shareholder activism on German corporations are correspondingly restricted. Therefore, this thesis will have to fall back on the use of data primarily from U.S. corporations' experiences with shareholder activism, in few parts only allowing careful inferences to Germany.

---

46 Duve/Basak, BB 2006, 1345 (1345 et seq.): The UMAG helps institutional investors by decreasing requirements regarding extraordinary audits as laid down in §§ 142 (2), 148 AktG, from 10 percent to 1 percent, therefore increasing the available measures for shareholders to pressure the administration; Götze, in: Von Rosen, Die Hauptversammlung vor neuen Herausforderungen, DAI studies issue 41, 2008, 119 (122 et seq.); Heinemann et al., Shareholders Activism-Aktiver Umgang mit aktiven Aktionären, Deutsches Eigenkapitalforum, Nov. 10 – 12, 2008, 12, http://www.eigenkapitalforum.com/082/presentations/f1/IR%20Seminar%20II%20Shareholder%20Activism.pdf; Schaefer, NZG 2007, 900 (900): The record date introduction, the in practice lowered significance of the „Depot" proxy, the availability of professional proxy advisors supporting institutional investors, the statutory squeeze out provisions, delisting case law, and so on have contributed to the movement.

47 DAI/McKinsey, Investorendialog im Umbruch, 2009, 3; *Der stille Ausverkauf*, HANDELSBLATT, Jan. 20, 2011, 6: pointing out a tax reform liberating the sales of participations from tax consequences as the main reason for the dissolution of the *Deutschland AG*; MartinHöpner/Böckler Stiftung, *Ende der Deutschland AG?*, DIE MITBESTIMMUNG 46 (2000), 11 et seq.

48 Interview with Reinhard Schmidt, Boeckler foundation, *Und wer kontrolliert die Manager?*, MAGAZIN MITBESTIMMUNG 06/2006, *available* at http://www.boeckler.de/163_82195.html: "This was mainly enforced by the state secretary of the Federal Chancellery Hans Martin Bury, who agreed with some business attorneys of law like Michael Adams that something needed to be done against the power of the banks, which has been successful. All the laws in support of the capital market are, bank authority hindering laws. For me, the lack of bank authority results in a lack of management control."

49 Götze, in: Von Rosen, Die Hauptversammlung vor neuen Herausforderungen, DAI studies issue 41, 2008, 119 (119 set seq.).

50 *Der stille Ausverkauf*, HANDELSBLATT, Jan. 20, 2011, 6: The participation of German shareholders in German DAX corporations has decreased from 64,5 percent in 2001, to 44,5 percent in 2011. Accordingly, the number of international investors has increased to 55,5 percent.

51 Götze, in: Von Rosen, Die Hauptversammlung vor neuen Herausforderungen, DAI studies issue 41, 2008, 119 (122).

52 DAI/McKinsey, Investorendialog im Umbruch, 2009, 3.

4) Actors of shareholder activism

The actors of shareholder activism vary according to the goals, strategies, and means employed. Shareholder associations such as the CII in the United States or the *Deutsche Schutzvereinigung für Wertpapierbesitz ("**DSW**")* and the *Schutzgemeinschaft der Kapitalanleger ("**SdK**")*[53] in Germany may exercise shareholder activism. Single minority shareholders and institutional investors can pursue it; the latter concentrate mainly on financial and sometimes strategic goals.[54] The significant and steady growth of the stakes in public corporations held by institutional investors—currently representing about three-fourths of the investments in the 1000 largest firms in the United States[55]—has made them the most important active investors. In Germany, the most active shareholders are domestic and international traditional investment funds, followed by hedge funds and other funds, including private equity funds.[56] International investors represent 79 percent of the active investors in Germany.[57]

A generally acknowledged definition of institutional investors does not exist. They may be comprised of independent legal entities whose core business is the professional management of assets on behalf of their clients and who manage a significant amount of funds that they tend to invest in a highly diversified manner.[58] Institutional investors include pension funds, mutual funds, banks, insurance companies, broker/dealers, and hedge funds.[59]

In the United States, hedge funds (which become active[60]) have proven to be the preeminent activist shareholders.[61] The funds they manage have increased rapidly to about $1.7

---

53 Smend, ZCG 2008, 53 (53).

54 Smend, ZCG 2008, 53 (53 et seq.).

55 ABA/Section of Business Law, 65 Bus. Law. 107, 135 (2009).

56 DAI/McKinsey, Investorendialog im Umbruch, 2009, 9; Von Rosen & Wieandt, *Activist Shareholders: Consensus Instead of Confrontation*, Finanzplatz 3/2009, 22 et seq.

57 DAI/McKinsey, Investorendialog im Umbruch, 2009, 16.

58 Garrido, *Optimism and Pessimism: Complementary Views on the Institutional Investors' Role in Corporate Governance in* Hopt & Wymeersch, Capital Markets and Company Law 449, 452 (2003): Pointing out that the unsolved question of a definition of the term institutional investors underlines different perceptions of institutional investors between Germans and U.S.-Americans, with Germans thinking of banks and Americans thinking of pension and investment funds, proposing pension funds, investment funds, and investment companies; Gerke et al., *The Changing Role of Institutional Investors – A German Perspective in* Hopt & Wymeersch, Capital Market and Company Law 357, 359 (2003); Pozen, *Institutional Perspective on Shareholder Nominations of Corporate Directors* 1, http://ssrn.com/abstract=437160 (2003); Ruffner, Die ökonomischen Grundlagen eines Rechts der Publikumsgesellschaft, 2000, 436 et seq.; Schmolke, ZGR 2007, 701 (704 et seq.): abstaining from a more specific definition of institutional shareholders as it depends strongly on the regulatory context.

59 Kahan & Rock, 155 U. Pa. L. Rev 1021, 1028 (2007); Kahan & Rock, *Embattled CEO's* 9, 11, 14, www.ssrn.com/abstract=1281516 (2008); Schmolke, ZGR 2007, 701 (734, n.98).

60 Kahan & Rock, 155 U. Pa. L. Rev 1021, 1026, 1046 (2007): referring to J.P. Morgan, Global Mergers and Acquisitions Review, 2006, 89; Kahan & Rock, *Embattled CEO's* 13, www.ssrn.com/abstract=1281516 (2008): only 5 percent of all hedge funds.

61 Kahan & Rock, 155 U. Pa. L. Rev 1021, 1028 (2007); Kahan & Rock, *Embattled CEO's* 13, www.ssrn.com/abstract=1281516 (2008); Klein & Zur, 64 J. Fin. 187, 214 (2009): noting that 65 percent of the initially stated purposes of hedge funds are aggressive as compared to 46 percent of the initially stated purposes of other entrepreneurial activists.

trillion in 2008.[62] Instead of concentrating on corporate governance, they have targeted specific aspects of the corporate business or management such as transaction decisions as shareholders of the acquirer or target[63] or the amendments of the financial and capital structure of the targeted corporation. Soft forms of shareholder activism have been applied by public pension funds and mutual funds. They are mainly related to corporate governance issues and make use initially of precatory shareholder proposals and resolutions later complemented by private negotiations with the boards.[64] However, in recent years, mutual funds particularly have gone beyond such a soft form of activism. For instance, they prevented the sale of the targeted corporation before a substantial rise in price, often teaming up with hedge funds, who took the lead.[65] *Mutual funds* are legally restricted by semiannual disclosure obligations regarding their securities ownership, tax-based diversification requirements, and potential redemption requests at short notice requiring liquidity in their investments. Furthermore, regulations hinder performance-based payments to the fund management company and a lack of incentives regarding shareholder activism results from their being indexed. This is complemented by the costs related to more active activism as well as conflicts of interest resulting from their affiliation with other financial institutions.[66] *Public pension funds*, in contrast, are not subject to diversification requirements or restraints on performance-based fees, nor do they have business ties possibly jeopardized by activism. However, they are confronted with political constraints and conflicts of interest, and their executives face low pay, making them less effective and less supported by other investors.[67] *Hedge funds*, on the other hand, are not confronted by the legal constraints facing mutual funds,[68] but only by the constraints confronting regular investors.[69] The conflicts of interest they are involved in are not as strong, as they are not affiliated with other financial institutions. Furthermore, management fees based on absolute return and proportionally larger investments per corporation have dramatically increased throughout the 2000s, providing hedge funds with stronger incentives to activism. This was made possible through debt-equity ratios beyond two in larger corporations as the financial resources available to hedge funds increased. Moreover, hedge funds make use of financial instruments, which allow

---

62 Hovanesian, *Attack of the Hungry Hedge Funds*, Business Week, Feb. 20, 2006, http://www.businessweek.com/magazine/content/06_08/b3972103.htm; Kahan & Rock, *Embattled CEO's* 9, 11 14, www.ssrn.com/abstract=1281516 (2008).

63 Kahan & Rock, *Embattled CEO's* 11, www.ssrn.com/abstract=1281516 (2008).

64 Kahan & Rock, 155 U. Pa. L. Rev 1021, 1042 (2007); Kahan & Rock, *Embattled CEOs* 13 et seq., http://ssrn.com/abstract=1281516 (2008).

65 Kahan & Rock, *Embattled CEOs* 13 et seq., http://ssrn.com/abstract=1281516 (2008).

66 Kahan & Rock, 155 U. Pa. L. Rev 1021, 1049 et seq. (2007).

67 *Id.* at 1057 et seq.

68 Schmolke, ZGR 2007, 701 (725): In Germany, in addition to non-specific restrictions, hedge funds are confronted with a limited number of specific restrictions, which are not able to hinder them from proceeding as active shareholders, however. According to § 112 InvG, they constitute "Sondervermögen mit zusätzlichen Risiken", which requires them to obey the principle of diversifying risks *(see* § 112 (1) InvG). Their ability to invest in illiquid financial means is further restricted by the quarterly obligation to repurchase, § 116 sent. 1 InvG.

69 Kahan & Rock, 155 U. Pa. L. Rev. 1021, 1049 (2007).

them to reduce costs and strengthen their incentives to pursue activism.[70] Finally, their proceedings are very sophisticated regarding their choice of targets, their strategies, and the means they use, including going public with their demands.[71] There is hope that hedge funds will finally resolve the issue regarding "who will be responsible for monitoring the managers when there is a separation of ownership and control in the public corporations that dominate our economy?"[72] But their precise procedures also provoke concerns.[73]

Active shareholders usually hold minority positions between 5 and 10 percent, the latter particularly pertaining to the United States.[74] A growing stake not only increases the impact of active shareholders, but it also results in economies of scale regarding the control of management. Furthermore, larger stakes make an active shareholder more credible. In case of friction he will scarcely be able to exit the corporation quickly.[75] Applicable rules have the consequence that active shareholders usually keep their shareholdings below 10 percent, particularly under the U.S. securities regulator's short-swing profit rules, as well as additional disclosure obligations.

5) Targeted firms

Targeted firms include all industry sectors, but specialized firms seem to be preferred.[76] Until recently, U.S. firms targeted by active shareholders were characterized as poor

---

70 Anabtawi& Stout, 60 STAN. L. REV. 1255, 1280 (2008).

71 Bratton, 95 GEO. L.J. 1375, 1384 (2006); Briggs, 32 J. CORP. L. 681, 711 et seq. (2007); Clifford, 14 J. CORP. FIN. 323, 325 (2008); Engelhardt, Activist Investing aus Unternehmenssicht, M&A Review 4/2008, 194 (195); Kahan & Rock, 155 U. PA. L. REV. 1021, 1062 et seq. (2007); Klein & Zur, 64 J. FIN. 187, 190 (2009); Mayer Brown Rowe & Maw, *Securities Update – Hedge Fund and Institutional Shareholder Activism*, Apr. 21, 2006, http://www.mayerbrown.com/publications/article.asp?id=2703&nid=6; Partnoy & Thomas, *Gap Filling, Hedge Funds, and Financial Innovation* 3, 24, 25 http://ssrn.com/abstract=931254 (2006); Schmolke, ZGR 2007, 701 (724 et seq.); Seifert, Invasion der Heuschrecken, 2006, 115 et seq.; Thompson, *The Limits of Hedge Fund Activism* 1 et seq., http://escholarship.org/uc/item/5jq9d71m (2006).

72 Thompson, *The Limits of Hedge Fund Activism* 1, http://escholarship.org/uc/item/5jq9d71m (2006).

73 Gillan & Starks, *The Evolution of Shareholder Activism in the United States* 34, www.ssrn.com/abstract=959670 (2007): referring to empty voting, hidden ownership and short-termism; For a discussion of empty voting and hidden ownership, see generally Hu & Black, *Hedge Funds, Insiders, and the Decoupling of Economic and Voting Ownership: Empty Voting and Hidden (Morphable) Ownership*, www.ssrn.com/abstract=353611 (2007); Hu & Black, 79 S. CAL. L. REV. 811 (2006); Hu & Black, 61. BUS. LAW. 1011 (2006); For an argument that the sharpest accusation against activist funds is a focus on short-termism at the expense of long-term profitability, see Kahan & Rock, 155 U. PA. L. REV. 1021, 1022 (2006): determining short-termism at the cost of long-term profitability as the sharpest accusation against activist funds.

74 Active shareholders hold typically less than 10 percent. DAI/McKinsey, Investorendialog im Umbruch, 2009, 14; HAWLEY & WILLIAMS, THE RISE OF FIDUCIARY CAPITALISM 128 (2000); Kahan & Rock, 155 U. PA. L. REV. 1021, 1088 (2007): noting that hedge funds acquire "rarely more than 5 to 10 percent."

75 Ruffner, Die ökonomischen Grundlagen eines Rechts der Publikumsgesellschaft, 2000, 459.

76 Böhm/Grothe, *Hedgefonds-Aktivismus in Deutschland*, BVAI NEWSLETTER IV 2009, 14 (15), WWW.BVAI.DE/NEWSLETTER (choose BAI Newsletter IV/2009): noting that no specific industries are preferred; Clifford, 14 J. FIN. 323, 328 (2008).

performing corporations, whose shares were held by many institutional investors with low inside ownership and whose governance structures were evaluated as comparably poor.[77] Meanwhile, the increase in experience and data about shareholder activism in U.S. firms and the altered strategies of active shareholders have changed the overall picture of target firms. Targets still have significantly higher institutional ownership, explainable by the need to rely on the expertise and the support from fellow shareholders to implement the changes given their minority stakes in the target firms.[78] Stock market liquidity possibly increases the likelihood of becoming a target because liquidity allows active investors to easily accumulate their stake and monitoring costs may be quickly compensated through trading profits.[79] Targets of hedge funds[80] are particularly characterized as having comparably low market to book ratio as compared to firms targeted by passive shareholders.[81] However, they are characteristically profitable firms with sound operating cash flows and return on assets.[82] Views on market capitalization,[83] payout

---

77 Gillan & Starks, *The Evolution of Shareholder Activism in the United States* 15, www.ssrn.com/abstract=959670 (2007); John & Klein, *Shareholder Proposals and Corporate Governance* 4, www.ssrn.com/abstract=1297750 (1995): data relating to shareholder proposals concerning corporate governance; Karpoff, *The Impact of Shareholder Activism on Target Companies: A Survey of Empirical Findings* 23 et seq., 26, www.ssrn.com/abstract=885365 (2001); Karpoff et al., 42 J. FIN. ECON. 365 (1996), *available* at www.ssrn.com/abstract=7551, abstract: Shareholder-initiated corporate governance resolutions tend to target poorly performing firms, as measured by market-to-book ratio, operating return, and recent sales growth.; Smith, 51 J. FIN. 227 (1996), *available at* www.ssrn.com/abstract=7230, abstract: Firm size and level of institutional holdings are found to positively related to the probability of being targeted.

78 Brav et al., *Hedge Fund Activism: A Review* 22, www.ssrn.com/abstract=1551953 (2010).

79 *Id.* at 22 et seq. n.7: pointing out models concluding with the opposite result; Norli et al., *Liquidity and Shareholder Activism passim*, www.ssrn.com/abstract=1344407 (2010).

80 Klein & Zur, 64 J. Fin. 187, 204 (2009): pointing out the difference between targets of other entrepreneurial activists, which resemble rather the historic opinion of activist targets, and those of hedge funds, which are significantly better performing.

81 Boyson & Mooradian, *Hedge funds as shareholder activists from 1994–2005* 3, www.ssrn.com/abstract=992739 (2007); Bratton, 95 GEO. L.J. 1375, 1390 (2007); Brav et al., *Hedge Fund Activism: A Review* 20, www.ssrn.com/abstract=1551953 (2010); Brav et al., *The Returns to Hedge Fund Activism* 2, www.ssrn.com/abstract=1111778 (2008); Clifford, 14 J. FIN. 323, 328 (2008); Greenwood & Schor, *Investor Activism and Takeovers* 9, www.ssrn.com/abstract=1003792 (2009).

82 Boyson & Mooradian, *Hedge funds as shareholder activists from 1994–2005* 3, www.ssrn.com/abstract=992739 (2007); Brav et al., *Hedge Fund Activism: A Review* 20, www.ssrn.com/abstract=1551953 (2010); Brav et al., *The Returns to Hedge Fund Activism* 2, www.ssrn.com/abstract=1111778 (2008); Clifford, 14 J. FIN. 323, 328 (2008): pointing out large returns on equity and assets and that in addition targets of hedge funds have better operating performance prior to the intervention of blockholders.

83 Bratton, 95 GEO. L.J. 1375, 1415 et seq. (2007): the market capitalization and the size of targets of active shareholders tends to be mid to large; Klein & Zur, 64 J. FIN. 187, 205 (2009): the market capitalization of hedge fund targets tends to be larger compared to the one of targets of other entrepreneurial investors; Brav et al., *Hedge Fund Activism: A Review* 20, www.ssrn.com/abstract=1551953 (2010): target firms are generally smaller than non-target firms and larger firms are less likely to be targeted by hedge funds possibly because of the large amount of capital a hedge fund would need to invest in order to amass a meaningful stake; Brav et al., *The Returns to Hedge Fund Activism*

ratios,[84] and cash level[85] prior to intervention diverge among legal scholars. But data increasingly support the idea of a preference for small targets,[86] which can be explained by the lower amount needed for substantial minority stakes and by the ability to avoid an excessive amount of idiosyncratic risk[87] with low payout ratios[88]. They invest after judging that their input by itself can cause the value to register. They are pursuing primarily one of three strategies: to get the target to sell itself at a premium (especially when merger waves apply to the concerned industry), to get the target to sell or spin off a significant asset, so-called "unbundling" (when a discount of around 15 percent applies), or to get the target to pay out spare cash.[89]

Data regarding firms outside the United States seem to confirm these characteristics.[90] Available data on German targets are still comparably limited. Active shareholders seem to prefer corporations possessing several of the following characteristics: strong freefloat, low shareholder presence, undervalued assets, heterogeneous fields of business, unspecified strategic position, and/or controversial management.[91]

2, www.ssrn.com/abstract=1111778 (2008): Relatively few targeted companies are large-cap firms, which is not surprising given the relatively high cost of amassing a meaningful stake in such a target.

84 Clifford, 14 J. FIN. 323, 328 (2008): indistinguishable pay-out ratio; Brav et al., *The Returns to Hedge Fund Activism* 2, www.ssrn.com/abstract=1111778 (2008): payout by companies targeted by hedge funds before intervention is lower than that of a matched sample.

85 Boyson & Mooradian, *Hedge funds as shareholder activists from 1994–2005* 11, www.ssrn.com/abstract=992739 (2007): firms with excess cash; Bratton, 95 GEO. L.J. 1375, 1415 et seq. (2007): only 61 percent of the *small* pay-out targets were cash rich; Clifford, 14 J. FIN. 323, 328 (2008): noting that firms targeted by activist have lower cash levels; More carefully Klein & Zur, 64 J. FIN. 187, 205 (2009): The targets of active shareholders have more cash on their balance sheets (even though there may be some basis to the argument that hedge funds target cash-rich companies, they also note that none of the activist samples' cash ratios are significantly different from their control samples' ratios, nor are there discernible differences in debt between the activist groups and control samples) when compared to the targets of other entrepreneurial activists.

86 Böhm/Grothe, *Hedgefonds-Aktivismus in Deutschland*, BVAI NEWSLETTER IV 2009, 14 (15), www.bvai.de/newsletter (choose BAI Newsletter IV/2009): arguing that the targets of hedge funds are primarily Prime Standard Mid-Cap corporations (68 percent), while a few are listed MDAX and SDAX corporations (each 8 percent), and very few are DAX corporations (5 percent), the average market capitalization being €981 million; Boyson & Mooradian, *Hedge funds as shareholder activists from 1994–2005* 2, 3, 10, 11, 23 www.ssrn.com/abstract=992739 (2007); Brav et al., *Hedge Fund Activism: A Review* 20, www.ssrn.com/abstract=1551953 (2010); Greenwood & Schor, *Investor Activism and Takeovers* 9, www.ssrn.com/abstract=1003792 (2009=; Klein & Zur, 64 J. FIN. 187, 205 (2009); Mietzner & Schweizer, *Hedge Funds versus Private Equity Funds as Shareholder Activists – Differences in Value Creation* 18, www.ssrn.com/abstract=1100945 (2008).

87 Brav et al., *Hedge Fund Activism: A Review* 20, www.ssrn.com/abstract=1551953 (2010).

88 *Id.* at 20 et seq.

89 Bratton, 95 GEO. L.J. 1375, 1390 et seq. (2007).

90 *See* Brav et al., *Hedge Fund Activism: A Review* 23 et seq., www.ssrn.com/abstract=1551953 (2010): referring to the results regarding shareholder activism in Japan and the U.K.

91 Götze, in: Von Rosen, Die Hauptversammlung vor neuen Herausforderungen, DAI studies issue 41, 2008, 119 (125).

6) Strategies and means used by active shareholders

The goals pursued by active shareholders today are, based on the numbers of institutional investors among the active shareholders, mainly financial in nature and aim to increase the value of their personal investment by raising the stock price or realizing the distribution of corporate capital to the shareholders. Sole strategic goals, such as the aim to improve the general corporate governance and social aims, have become rather secondary.

Active shareholders pursue several *strategies* to attain these objectives that vary according to the type of active shareholders.[92] These range from influence on corporate governance issues to strategic operative issues. The former refer to strategies applied by traditional active investors that aim to amend the corporate rules-of-the-game, while the latter involve corporate transaction decisions or financial and capital structure related decisions of the corporate management. The latter are preferred strategies of hedge funds[93] usually based on a careful prior analysis of the targeted corporation.[94] In general, active shareholders concentrate on the implementation of generalized strategies related to agency issues, like changes in corporate governance or payout policies on free cash flows, rather than on issues specific to a limited number of targeted firms.[95] This approach allows active investors to significantly lower costs when launching a new campaign because they can shift to the use of publicly available information while increasing the likelihood that the strategies are appreciated by market participants, resulting in inflated stock prices and support from fellow shareholders.[96] Several investors often act jointly to produce the necessary impact for pursuing a corresponding strategy.

Active shareholders who have decided to raise their "voice" against management and to pursue one or several of the mentioned strategies have a wide array of specific *means* at their disposal. On an abstract level, active shareholders employ several means to pursue their strategies. These can range from means exercised during the shareholder meeting, such as electing directors in U.S. corporations or supervisory board members of German corporations, respectively, to those exercised at all other times, such as personal talks between active shareholders and members of the administration. These comprise means exercised prior to the formation of the corporate decision as well as those

---

92 Klein & Zur, 64 J. Fin. 187, 189 (2009).

93 Gillan & Starks, *The Evolution of Shareholder Activism in the United States* 30, www.ssrn.com/abstract=959670 (2007).

94 Kahan & Rock, 155 U. Pa. L. Rev. 1021, 1022 (2007): hedge funds focusing on corporate governance and control; DAI/McKinsey, Investorendialog im Umbruch, 2009, 23: Active investors focus on four different strategies: corporate governance, M&A, capital structure, and strategic-operational changes; Götze, in: Von Rosen, Die Hauptversammlung vor neuen Herausforderungen, DAI studies issue 41, 2008, 119 (123 et seq.).

95 Bratton, *Hedge Funds and Governance Targets: Long-Term Results* 2, www.ssrn.com/abstract=1677517 (2010); Brav et al., *Hedge Funds Activism – A Review* 23, http://ssrn.com/abstract=1551953 (2010).

96 Bratton, *Hedge Funds and Governance Targets: Long-Term Results* 2, www.ssrn.com/abstract=1677517 (2010); Brav et al., *The returns to hedge fund activism* 7 et seq., http://ssrn.com/abstract=1111778 (2008).

exercised during its formation. Others range from means explicitly mentioned by statute (shareholder approval of a merger) or precedent (approval of a fundamental corporate decision according to the *Holzmüller/Gelatine* jurisprudence*)* to means not explicitly provided by either (***"Vote-no campaigns"***). Finally, the means of communication may be private or public. The former can simply be a phone call or personal talk to a member of the administration while the latter can involve such means as using media campaigns addressing personal or issue-related critiques.[97] Traditional active shareholders as well as hedge funds use an array of divergent means.[98]

The analysis will focus on three of the most relevant strategies of active shareholders that impact on the corporate governance, corporate M&A decisions, and financial structure of targeted corporations. As a corollary, the different means used by active shareholders to pursue these strategies will be analyzed.

7) Criticism regarding active shareholders

Despite pinning hope on active shareholders, especially hedge funds, to reduce agency issues and resulting costs that would consequently raise shareholder value in targeted corporations,[99] their impact has often been tainted with issues concerning opportunistic behavior motivated by vested interests at the expense of the other shareholders of the target. Concerns relate to hedging strategies based on the use of new financial instruments that can lead to decoupling the financial interests of shareholders from their control rights[100] as well as larger stakes in third corporations. The "sharpest" accusation

97 Davis & Steil, Institutional Investors 312, 314 (2001): distinguishing between *formal* means taking usually place during the annual shareholder meeting as opposed to *informal* means that may be used at all other times, as well as between *private* and *public* communication with members of the administration; Gillan & Starks, *A Survey of Shareholder Activism: Motivation and Empirical Evidence* 4, www.ssrn.com/abstract=663523 (1998); Pozen, *Institutional perspective on shareholder nominations of corporate directors* 3, http://ssrn.com/abstract=437160 (2003).

98 Gillan & Starks, *The Evolution of Shareholder Activism in the United States* 30, www.ssrn.com/abstract=959670 (2007); Kahan & Rock, 155 U. Pa. L. Rev. 2021, 2042 et seq. (2007): pointing out the *traditional active institutional investors* focus on precatory shareholder proposals or in following more active shareholders in their strategies; Brav mentions *hedge funds* as active shareholders with the widest array of means. He categorizes tactics of hedge funds in categories of increasing aggressiveness, from communication with the administration, to seeking board representation without proxy contest or confrontation, to formal shareholder proposals or public critique, to threats to wage a proxy fight to gain board representation, or to suing the company for a breach of duty. The most aggressive means is an actual proxy fight to replace board members, the hedge funds suing the company and finally the hedge funds intending to take control of the company. Brav et al., *Hedge Fund Activism, Corporate Governance, and Firm Performance* 43, http://ssrn.com/abstract=948907 (2008).

99 Arnold, ZCG 2008, 221 (225); Clifford, 14 J. Fin. 323, 323 (2008); Kahan & Rock, 155 U. Pa. L. Rev. 1021, 1028 et seq. (2007).

100 A similar effect results from the increasing involvement of intermediaries (like mutual funds, pension funds, insurance companies, and foundations) who hold publicly traded equity securities for their investors and who may pursue interests apart from increasing the shareholder value of the targeted corporations. Fisch, 34 Seattle U. L. Rev. 877, 878 (2010), *available* at www.lsr.

against active shareholders is that they are only acting to realize short-term benefits to the detriment of long-term corporate performance.[101] Other concerns are related to the sophistication of some of the active shareholders who may use their strategies to attain personal benefits that are not accorded to the rest of the shareholders.[102]

II) Theoretical background of shareholder activism – legal and microeconomic

The functional comparison of shareholder activism under U.S.-American and German law requires an understanding of the relevant theories underlying both legal systems of corporate law.

1) The concept of the firm

The theoretical understanding of the corporation as a firm is helpful regarding questions concerning the internal environment of the corporation and the parties involved who are subject to the relevant corporate law.[103] It is the first step in understanding the purpose of the internal authority distribution according to both jurisdictions at stake.

The U.S.-American and German understandings of the corporation differ significantly. Under German legal theory, corporations are a legal entity. On the other hand, economically oriented scholars of corporate law who consider the firm as a nexus of contracts have influenced the U.S.-American perspective.[104]

The German legal theory is determined by the conception of the firm as a separate legal entity independent of its members, having its own separate objective apart from the interests of its shareholders as well as its own rights and duties.[105] This conception allows a strict separation between the internal relations of shareholders amongst each other or towards the corporation and the external relations of the corporation with third persons.[106] Disputes about the nature of the corporation as a legal person awarded by the

---

nellco.org/upenn_wps/341/. However, this issue relates specifically to institutional investors and not to active shareholders in general and has been analyzed by the comparative thesis of *Sylko Winkler*, Die Verantwortung institutioneller Anleger als Aktionäre in Publikumsgesellschaften in Deutschland und den USA, 2008, who focuses on the responsibility of institutional investors as shareholders of public corporations in Germany and the United States.

101 Kahan & Rock, 155 U. Pa. L. Rev. 1021, 1083 et seq. (2007).

102 Anabtawi & Stout, 60 Stan. L. Rev. 1255, 1283 et seq. (2008); Briggs, 32 J. Corp. L. 681, 701 et seq. (2007); Kahan & Rock, 155 U. Pa. L. Rev. 1021, 1070 et seq. (2007).

103 Bachmann, Private Ordnung, 2006, 112.

104 Gillan & Starks, *A Survey of Shareholder Activism* 5, http://ssrn.com/abstract=663523 (1998); Walz, AG 1996, 161 (165).

105 Eidenmüller, JZ 2001, 1041 (1042); Hueck/Winbichler, Gesellschaftsrecht, 2003, § 20 mn.1; Schmidt, Gesellschaftsrecht, 4, 176; Raiser, Recht der Kapitalgesellschaften, 2001, § 3 mn.8.

106 Wiedemann, Gesellschaftsrecht, Vol. 1, 1980, § 1 V 1 a, 83.

legal system[107] or a real social organization with its own body, organs, spirit and soul[108] happened in the past due to its relevance for the external relations of corporations.[109] Meanwhile, legislation and court rulings have made the decision superfluous.[110]

In the Anglo-Saxon literature, the debate has been of little relevance in the past decades.[111] The growing acceptance of microeconomic approaches and knowledge of corporate law by German corporate scholars,[112] a long tradition for U.S.-American scholars, seems to have rekindled this old German dispute.[113] The U.S.-American understanding of the firm, introduced by the landmark paper of *Ronald Coase*,[114] is based on the understanding that the firm constitutes an alternative to the market. While it is the price mechanism that directs the resource allocation via exchange transactions in the market, authority and directions by an entrepreneur, similar to a relation between employer and employee, accomplish the allocation of factors of production in the firm.[115] Consequently, the use of the firm for the allocation of resources allows for the reduction of transaction costs under certain circumstances as compared to the use of the market mechanism.[116]

Jensen and Meckling objected to *Coase*'s understanding of the firm as an entity in which activities were governed by authority.[117] According to their conception, the firm is "simply a legal fiction which serves as a nexus for a set of contract relationships among individuals."[118] This individualistic conception[119] leads to a new order that allows concentrating on voluntary exchanges and occurring transaction costs as well as work-sharing delegation and delegation costs.[120] The nexus of contracts of a firm comprises several agency relationships, as they exist in numerous other contractual relationships with the focus on the relationship between shareholders and management.[121] Contracts are not to be understood as contracts in the sense of civil law, but rather as wholly legal relationships based on the will of the involved actors, whether directly or indirectly.[122] A separate corporate interest apart from the interest of the involved individuals is not justifiable under this concept.[123]

---

107 Savigny, System des heutigen römischen Rechts, Vol. 2, 1840, 236, 239.
108 Gierke, Das Wesen der menschlichen Verbände, 1902, 33.
109 Bachmann, Private Ordnung, 2006, 114.
110 *Id.*; Hueck/Windbichler, Gesellschaftsrecht, § 2 mn.8.
111 Bachmann, Private Ordnung, 2006, 114.
112 Adams, Eigentum, Kontrolle und Beschränkte Haftung, 14 et seq., Zöllner, AG 2003, 2 (12); Eidenmüller, JZ 2001, 1041 (1041); Walz, AG 1996, 161 (168 et seq.).
113 Bachmann, Private Ordnung, 2006, 114.
114 Coase, 4 Economica 386, 404 (1937).
115 *Id.*
116 Eisenberg, 24 J. Corp. L. 819, 821 (1999).
117 *Id.* at 822.
118 Jensen & Meckling, 3 J. Fin. Econ. 305, 312 (1976), *available at* www.ssrn.com/abstract=94043.
119 Eidenmüller, JZ 2001, 1040 (1042).
120 Walz, AG 1996, 161 (165).
121 Ruffner, Die ökonomischen Grundlagen eines Rechts der Publikumsgesellschaft, 2000, 131.
122 Zöllner, AG 2003, 2 (10).
123 Adams, Eigentum, Kontrolle und Beschränkte Haftung, 14 et seq.; Ruffner, Die ökonomischen Grundlagen eines Rechts der Publikumsgesellschaft, 2000, 168; Walz, AG 1996, 161 (165), Zöllner, AG 2003, 2 (8).

Concentrating on the individualistic character[124] of the involved actors allows a shift in focus to the contractual relationship between the fiction of the firm and the reciprocity of the firm's inputs and outputs. In this case, the question regarding what belongs to the firm and what lies outside of it loses its significance[125].[126] The central feature of this approach is that the consequent hypothetical market from which it cannot be distinguished may govern the company.

Even though the nexus of contracts theory appears similar to the fictional conceptions based on *Savigny*'s understanding of the corporation,[127] it is at odds with the legal understanding of the corporation. First, it is not a legal but an *economic* theory.[128] The significance of the term contract under this conception is far wider than the legal terminus,[129] thus preventing legal scholars from drawing any direct conclusions.[130] Further, it is a conception of the *firm,* which is not identical with the conceptions of the legal person. The former includes also business owners of companies without entrepreneurial purpose.[131] Regarding its content, the conception contradicts the legal understanding of the corporation as a distinct entity and artificial person.[132] This is so because a corporation not only owns the assets of the company, but it may also take action to enforce its legal rights and is responsible for its own debts apart from the rights and debts of its shareholders.[133] This latter principle constitutes the basis for the concept of limited liability, allowing investors to minimize their personal risk by offsetting any risk incurred by their investment in a single corporation through diversification.[134] Finally, experts have cast doubt on the consistency of the conception of the firm as a nexus of contracts.[135]

Despite these provisos, the contractual approach should not be completely abandoned. By deconstructing the corporate entity, it sheds light on the internal perspective of a corporation.[136] It helps to focus on the relationships between the relevant actors of the firm, such as shareholders and management, who act based on reciprocal expectations and behavior.[137]

---

124 Eidenmüller, JZ 2001, 1040 (1042).
125 Zöllner, AG 2003, 2 (11).
126 Ruffner, Die ökonomischen Grundlagen eines Rechts der Publikumsgesellschaft, 2000, 130.
127 Walz, AG 1996, 161 (165).
128 Bachmann, Private Ordnung, 2006, 115.
129 *Id.* at 115; Hueck/Windbichler, Gesellschaftsrecht, 2003, § 1 mn.28, n.48.
130 Hueck/Windbichler, Gesellschaftsrecht, 2003, § 1 mn.28 n.48.
131 *Id.* at § 1 mn.1.
132 Cheffins, Company Law 32 (1997).
133 *Id.*
134 Posner, Economic Analysis of Law 424 et seq (2007).
135 Eisenberg, 24 J. Corp. L. 819, 836 (1999).
136 Bachmann, Private Ordnung, 2006, 118.
137 Cheffins, Company Law 32 (1997).

2) Authority allocation in the corporation

Views about the allocation of corporate authority, particularly in the relationship between administration and shareholders, diverge, even on the question of ultimate control.

The economic foundation of the concept of shareholder primacy, which favors the maximization of wealth of the shareholders as residual claimants,[138] represents the understanding that the ultimate power rests with the shareholders as the (economic[139]) owners of the corporation[140].[141] Therefore, the relationship between shareholders and directors is a *principal-agent relationship*[142] in which corporate directors have the fiduciary duty to make decisions in the best interest of the shareholders.[143]

Those in favor of the team production theory provide another approach.[144] This concept forms the counterpart of the contractual approach[145] and is aligned with the communitarian understanding that aims to maximize stakeholder wealth analyzed *infra.*[146] Proponents assert that the main economic function of the public corporation is to provide a vehicle through which shareholders, creditors, executives, rank-and-file employees, and other potential corporate stakeholders can, for their own benefit, jointly relinquish control over the resources to a board of directors.[147] In this regard, the directors, as a mediating hierarchy, are seen as trustees of the corporation who balance the interests of competing team members rather than acting as agents.[148]

The main argument of the team production theory is that corporate productive activity requires contributions from multiple parties such as creditors, employees, managers, and local government, who in return expect to be compensated according to the contracts.[149] Strict shareholder primacy would discourage groups from making firm-spe-

138 EASTERBROOK & FISCHEL, THE ECONOMIC STRUCTURE OF CORPORATE LAW 35 -39 (1991).

139 Spindler, in: MüKo AktG, 2008, preliminary comment § 76 mn.2; Winkler, Die Verantwortung institutioneller Anleger als Aktionäre in Publikumsgesellschaften in Deutschland und den USA, 2008, 91 n.210.

140 Jensen & Meckling, 3 J. FIN. ECON. 305 (1976), *available* at www.ssrn.com/abstract=94043; Richter/Furubotn, Neue Institutionenökonomik, 2003, 173 et seq., 224 et. seq.; Ruffner, Die ökonomischen Grundlagen eines Rechts der Publikumsgesellschaft, 2000, 135 et seq.

141 Fleischer, Hdb Vorstandsrecht, 2006, § 1 mn.30.

142 This is also referred to, in a broader sense, as the shareholder primacy approach.

143 Bebchuk, 105 HARV. L. REV. 1435 (1992); Black, 89 MICH. L. REV. 520 (1990); EASTERBROOK & FISCHEL, THE ECONOMIC STRUCUTURE OF CORPORATE LAW (1991); Fama & Jensen, 26 J.L. & ECON. 301 (1983); Fleischer, ZGR 2001, 1 (7 et seq.); Jensen & Meckling, 3 J. FIN. ECON. 305 (1976), *available at* www.ssrn.com/abstract=94043, 5 et seq.; POSNER, ECONOMIC ANALYSIS OF LAW § 4.7, 420 n.3 (2007); Semler/Spindler, in: MüKo AktG, 2004, Vor § 76 mnn.90 et seq.; Smith, 23 J. Corp. L. 277 (1998), *available at* http://papers.ssrn.com/sol3/papers.cfm?abstract_id=10571.

144 Blair & Stout, 85 VA. L. REV. 247, 248 (1999).

145 *Id.* at 254: pointing out their approach as more consistent with the way a corporation actually works than are prominent contractarian interpretations; Klöhn, ZGR 2008, 110 (139).

146 Blair & Stout, *supra* note 144, at 253.

147 *Id.* at 255.

148 *Id.* at 280 et seq.

149 Blair & Stout, 85 VA. L. REV. 247 (1999); Blair & Stout, 79 WASH. U. L. Q. 403, 411-14 (2001), *available at* www.ssrn.com/abstract=266622.

cific investments that can be essential to the firm's success, leading ex ante or ex post to inefficient results. Therefore, from an efficiency standpoint, corporate directors should be required to maximize the sum of all returns to the groups participating in the firm. Public corporations would then be empowered to refrain from opportunistic exploitation of non-shareholder constituents, reducing the transaction costs associated with obtaining relationship-specific investments.[150] This approach represents an alternative to the principal-agent approach[151] which is not able to explain problems such as the exclusion of shareholders from the board, the meaning and function of the corporation's "legal personality," derivative action procedures, the structure of director fiduciary duties, and the limited number of shareholder voting rights.[152]

This approach is limited to public corporations, assuming that non-shareholder constituents are particularly vulnerable to opportunism.[153] However, supporters of the approach have not shown why non-shareholder participants in publicly held corporations are more vulnerable to opportunism than in private corporations, especially since certain facets of public corporations, such as the separation of ownership and control, render shareholders themselves more vulnerable than in private firms. Furthermore, this approach undermines the shareholder's role as the primary monitor and severely constrains the incentive of directors to maximize anything but their own welfare, leading to increased transaction costs.

The final approach is that of *director primacy*.[154] It is aligned with the contractual theory as well as the shareholder value approach analyzed *infra*. Under this approach, the authority to make decisions is vested in the board of directors, which represents not agents, but rather the embodiment of the corporate principal,[155] serving as the nexus of the several contracts that make up the corporation. Since the corporation is seen as something that cannot be owned, the shareholders merely hold a contractual entitlement to a residual claim on corporate assets and profits. Even though shareholder wealth properly controls decision-making, decisions are centralized through the board, which is an essential attribute of efficient corporate governance.

The different theoretical approaches regarding the allocation of authority in a corporation are relevant to an analysis of shareholder authority regarding certain actions. Shareholder actions regarding the corporate decision-making process may be evaluated differently depending on the underlying theoretical framework and the allocation of authority in

---

150 *See* Meese, 43 Wm & Mary L. Rev. 1629 (2002), *available at* www.ssrn.com/abstract=373783, 5.

151 Blair & Stout, 85 Va. L. Rev. 247, 253 (1999); *see also* Meese, 43 Wm & Mary L. Rev. 1629 (2002), *available at* www.ssrn.com/abstract=373783, 5.

152 Blair & Stout, 85 Va. L. Rev. 247, 253 (1999); *see also* Meese, 43 Wm & Mary L. Rev. 1629 (2002), *available at* www.ssrn.com/abstract=373783, 5.

153 Blair & Stout, 85 Va. L. Rev. 247, 281 (1999).

154 Anabtawi, 53 UCLA L. Rev. 561, 598 (2006): arguing that while shareholders have widely divering interests that may give them incentives to pursue their private objectives, directors are best suited to manage corporations as they, unlike individual shareholders, owe fiduciary duties to all shareholders; Bainbridge, 97 Nw. U. L. Rev. 547, 563 (2003).

155 Bainbridge, *Director Primacy: The Means and Ends of Corporate Governance*, UCLA, School of Law Research Paper No. 02-06 (2002).

the corporation. Under the *principal-agent–approach*[156] prevailing under U.S.- American law, the final authority rests with the shareholders; the *director primacy theory* identifies the board of directors as the principal; and finally, the *team production theory* focuses on the interests of all corporate stakeholders as the reason why authority is handed to a third party.

3) The purpose of the corporation

Another closely related theoretical approach relevant to the analysis of shareholder activism concerns the general purpose of the corporation that determines the actions of the administration. Two perceptions of the purpose of a corporation generally prevail. Advocates of the *shareholder value*[157] theory or the *shareholder primacy rule*[158] hold that the corporation's sole purpose is to serve its *shareholders* and to maximize their residual claims.[159] *Communitarians* or adherents of the *stakeholder theories*[160] assert that the responsibilities of the corporation are not only to its shareholders but also to other stakeholders, such as creditors, employees, management, clients, suppliers, and the public.[161] Correspondingly, corporate law ought to require directors to serve not only the shareholders' interests, but also those of employees, consumers, creditors, and other corporate *stakeholders*.[162] It does not come as a surprise that supporters of both approaches have widely divergent views on the use of corporate law to promote corporate social responsibility.[163] Under the first concept, limits on corporate behavior are set through external regulations or contracts between the relevant constituencies and the corporation. Within corporate law itself, profit maximization is *sacrosanct*. Communitarians, on the other hand, argue that external regulations and contracts are insufficient to protect the interests of non-shareholders so that those interests should be protected through corporate law, making managers fiduciaries of all stakeholders.[164] Concerning shareholders,

---

156 Adams, AG 1990, 63 et seq.; Adams, ZIP 2002, 1325 (1330); Richter/Furubotn, Neue Institutionenökonomik, 2003, 173 et seq.

157 RAPPAPORT, SHAREHOLDER VALUE 12 (1995); Eidenmüller, JZ 2001, 1041 (1044); Fleischer, Shareholders vs. Stakeholders: Aktien- und übernahmerechtliche Fragen, in: Hommelhoff et al., Hdb Corporate Governance, 2003, 129 (135); Wiedemann, Gesellschaftsrecht, Vol. 1, 1980, § 1 V 1 b, 84.

158 Berle, 45 HARV. L. REV. 1365, 1367 (1932); Smith, 23 J. CORP. L., 277, 278 (1998), *available at* www.ssrn.com/abstract= 10571; EASTERBROOK & FISCHEL, THE ECONOMIC STRUCTURE OF CORPORATE LAW 36 et seq. (1991).

159 Wöhe/Döring, Einführung in die allgemeine Betriebswirtschaftslehre, 2008, 55, 75.

160 Freeman & McVEA, *A Stakeholder Approach to Strategic Management*, *in* HITT ET AL., THE BLACKWELL HANDBOOK OF STRATEGIC MANAGEMENT 189, 192 et seq.; Hazen, 69 N.C. L. REV. 273 (1991); Millon, 50 WASH. & LEE L. REV. 1373 (1993); MITCHELL, PROGRESSIVE CORPORATE LAW (1995); V. Werder, Ökonomische Grundfragen der Corporate Governance, in: Hommelhoff et al., Hdb Corporate Governance, 2003, 3 (8 et seq.).

161 Wöhe/Döring, Einführung in die allgemeine Betriebswirtschaftslehre, 2008, 55 et seq., 75.

162 *See* Blair & Stout, 85 VA L. Rev. 247, 253 (1999).

163 Gordon Smith, *God, Mammon & Corporate Law*, THE CONGLOMERATE, Nov. 8, 2003, http://theconglomerate.org/2003/11/god_mammon_corp.html.

164 *Id.*

communitarians put great emphasis on corporate law as a means to regulate managerial opportunism. They also urge greater shareholder voting power, broad disclosure rights, and strong fiduciary protection.[165]

Both views have influential supporters.[166] Adherents of the communitarian approach argue that the firm constitutes several groups of stakeholders including shareholders, creditors, management, employees, clients, suppliers, and the general public.[167] Each of these groups contributes to operational performance, thereby justifying their participation in the management of the firm.[168] An economic advantage of this approach is that it binds employees and creditors to the corporation by making it worthwhile for them to be loyal to the corporation. Loyalty is seen as a means of diminishing friction losses.[169] Failure to consider their interests in corporate decisions and actions would, in contrast, expose them to the danger of exploitation.[170]

Opponents of the shareholder primacy concept argue that remuneration of different factor contributions below market value would lead to the migration of the different factors avoiding exploitation.[171] Furthermore, the shareholder primacy concept is said to result in management having a short-term focus, sacrificing long-term investments—particularly in research and development to assure product quality and human capital such as loyal employees—in order to maximize profit.[172]

Taking into account that shareholder value concerns all payment flows during all time periods, including residual value, these concerns are unconvincing.[173] Furthermore,

---

165 PALMITER, CORPORATIONS, 6 (2003).

166 For arguments in favor of shareholder primacy, see RAPPAPORT, SHAREHOLDER VALUE, 12 et seq. (1995); Bebchuk, 119 HARV. L. REV. 1784, 1813 (2006); Bebchuk, 118 HARV. L. REV. 833, 835 (2005); Bebchuk, 59 BUS. LAW. 43, (2003); Eisenberg, 24 J. CORP. L. 819, 832 (1999); Mülbert, ZGR 1997, 129 (156); For arguments in support of the communitarian or stakeholder view, see POST ET AL., REDEFINING THE CORPORATION – STAKEHOLDER MANAGEMENT AND ORGANIZATIONAL WEALTH 17 (2002); Raiser, Recht der Kapitalgesellschaften, 2001, § 7 mnn.14 et seq.; Windbichler/Hueck, Gesellschaftsrecht, 2009, § 20 mn.15, § 23 mn.15.

167 Freeman & McVEA, *A Stakeholder Approach to Strategic Management in* HITT ET AL., THE BLACKWELL HANDBOOK OF STRATEGIC MANAGEMENT 189, 192 (2001).

168 Fleischer, Hdb Vorstandsrecht, 2006, § 1 mn.26, Wöhe/Döring, Einführung in die allgemeine Betriebswirtschaftslehre, 2008, 55–57.

169 Interview with Reinhard Schmidt, Boeckler foundation, *Und wer kontrolliert die Manager?*, MAGAZIN MITBESTIMMUNG 06/2006, *available at* http://www.boeckler.de/163_82195.html.

170 Fleischer, Shareholders vs. Stakeholders: Aktien- und übernahmerechtliche Fragen, in: Hommelhoff et al., Hdb Corporate Governance, 2003, 129 (133).

171 *See* Fleischer, Shareholders vs. Stakeholders: Aktien- und übernahmerechtliche Fragen, in: Hommelhoff et al., Hdb Corporate Governance, 2003, 129 (133), who counters that a remuneration below market value would result in migration of the concerned groups; Fleischer, Hdb Vorstandsrecht, 2006, § 1 mn.27; Wöhe/Döring, Einführung in die allgemeine Betriebswirtschaftslehre, 2008, 78 et seq.

172 Bea/Haas, Strategisches Management, 2005, 84; Bodie, *Final Thoughts on the Progressive Dilema*, Dec. 9, 2005, THE CONGLOMERATE, http://theconglomerate.org/2005/12/final_thoughts_.html.

173 Fleischer, Shareholders vs. Stakeholders: Aktien- und übernahmerechtliche Fragen, in: Hommelhoff et al., Hdb Corporate Governance, 2003, 129 (134); Fleischer, Hdb Vorstandsrecht, 2006, § 1 mn.27; Rappaport, Shareholder Value, 54 et seq. (1995).

the corporation is primarily a performance of the shareholders, which justifies the primary consideration of their interests.[174] In contrast, management's attempt to serve the *corporate interest* is complicated because that term is comparably diffuse and hard to define with precision.[175] It requires not only additional effort for management to consider the consequences to all stakeholders and to balance their interests, but it can also lead to legal uncertainty as prognoses depend on the premises of management.[176]

American corporate law generally supports the shareholder primacy approach, as reflected in several important decisions of U.S. courts underlining shareholder wealth as the main focus of a public corporation.[177]

In contrast, *German* corporate law appears open to both approaches, leaving supporters of both sides enough leeway to argue for either one.[178] The case law of the German Federal Court of Justice refers to the interests of several stakeholders that have to be equally considered when determining the interest of the firm or corporation as the aim of management actions.[179] The prevailing approach of legal scholars[180] supports the stakeholder value concept as well.[181] Similarly, the German Corporate Governance Codex[182] demands management to act in the *interest of the firm*.

Again, it is economic analysis that brings more clarity into the jungle of legal arguments, as it can provide the determining arguments in favor of shareholder primacy.[183] Shareholders as residual claimants bear a comparably larger risk than the rest of the stakeholders since they only obtain what remains after the fixed claims of employees, creditors, suppliers, and others have been met.[184] Correspondingly, they are the only group of stake-

---

174 Fleischer, Shareholders vs. Stakeholders: Aktien- und übernahmerechtliche Fragen, in: Hommelhoff et al., Hdb Corporate Governance, 2003, 129 (135); Fleischer, Hdb Vorstandsrecht, 2006, § 1 mn.30; Wiedemann, Organverantwortung und Gesellschafterklagen in der Aktiengesellschaft, 1989, 33.

175 Hüffer, AktG, § 76 mn.15.

176 Klöhn, ZGR 2008, 110 (141).

177 Revlon, Inc. v. Mac Andrews & Forbes Holdings, Inc. 506 A.2d 179, 181–184 (Del. 1986); Dodge v. Ford Motor Co., 170, N.W. 668 (684) (Mich. 1919).

178 Fleischer, Hdb Vorstandsrecht, 2006, § 1 mn.29; Groh, DB 2000, 2153 (2158); Klöhn, ZGR 2008, 110 (136); K. Schmidt, Gesellschaftsrecht, § 28 II 1, 812 et seq.; Raiser, Kapitalgesellschaftsrecht, § 14 mn.13; Spindler, in: MüKo AktG, 2008, § 76 mn.77; Zöllner, AG 2003, 2 (7 et seq.); For restrictions in the case of paretetic codetermination Ulmer, AcP 202 (2002), 143 (159); *more in detail* EMPT, CORPORATE SOCIAL RESPONSIBILITY, 2004, 119 et seq., 138 et seq.

179 BGH, Urt. v. 23.06.1997, Az.: II Z 132/93, NJW 1997, 2815 (2816); BGH, Urt. v. 07.03.1994, Az. II ZR 52/93, NJW 1994, 1410 (1411); BGH, Urt. v. 05.05.1975, Az.: II ZR 156/73; NJW 1975, 1412 (1413); Henze, BB 2000, 209 (212).

180 Hüffer, Aktiengesetz, § 76 mn.12; K. Schmidt, Gesellschaftsrecht, § 28 II 1a, 813 et seq.

181 Klöhn, ZGR 2008, 110 (111).

182 Nos. 4.1.1., 4.3.3., 5.5.1. DCGK: Obligation of the members of the management and supervisory board to act in the interests of the enterprise, which according to the Codex's preamble is the "obligation of the Management Board and the Supervisory Board to ensure the continued existence of the enterprise and its sustainable creation of value in conformity with the principles of the social market economy".

183 Fleischer, Hdb des Vorstandsrechts, § 1 mn.25.

184 EASTERBROOK & FISCHEL, THE ECONOMIC STRUCTURE OF CORPORATE LAW 36 (1991); Fleischer, Hdb des Vorstandsrechts, § 1 mn.28.

holders with the appropriate incentives.[185] This circumstance has to be distinguished from the fact that all stakeholders of a corporation generally bear risks resulting from incomplete contracts, such as those resulting from hold-ups.[186] Furthermore, it is the diffuse character of the shareholder's investment that has a long-term aim. Its success depends on the right actions and omissions of the management and the economic efforts of the corporation;[187] shareholders have fewer opportunities to protect themselves contractually.[188] Consequently, they are the ones who most appreciate a gap-filling standard in favor of their interests.[189] While other stakeholders' interests are protected by specific rules outside of corporate law,[190] shareholders depend solely on corporate law for the protection of their interests.[191] Finally, a singular aim eases the control of management by diminishing management's discretion and giving it a clear goal. In contrast, the stakeholder concept leaves management with two masters: equity holders and the community. As a consequence, management is accountable to neither group and transaction costs rise.[192] Accordingly, the stakeholder approach becomes a formula of justification for almost any management action.[193]

Considering the stakeholder-friendly rules outside corporate law mentioned before that favor employees, creditors, consumers, and others, the necessity for management to take into account conditions set up by stakeholders to ensure their participation, and the need to satisfy the social expectation to consider interests apart from legal standards, recent German legislation models a moderate preference for shareholder interests.[194] It confirms that management may pursue actions to increase shareholder value[195] and may be best compared with the new, enlightened shareholder value model of the U.K. Companies Act.[196]

185 Ruffner, Die ökonomischen Grundlagen eines Rechts der Publikumsgesellschaft, 2000, 166.

186 V. Werder, Ökonomische Grundfragen der Corporate Governance, in: Hommelhoff et al., Hdb Corporate Governance, 2003, 3 (8).

187 Klöhn, ZGR 2008, 110 (152 et seq.).

188 Fleischer, Hdb des Vorstandsrechts, § 1 mn.28; Klöhn, ZGR 2008, 110 (152 et seq.); Ruffner, Die ökonomischen Grundlagen eines Rechts der Publikumsgesellschaft, 2000, 169.

189 Ruffner, Die ökonomischen Grundlagen eines Rechts der Publikumsgesellschaft, 2000, 167.

190 Fleischer, Shareholders vs. Stakeholders: Aktien- und übernahmerechtliche Fragen, in: Hommelhoff et al., Hdb Corporate Governance, 2003, 129 (134).

191 Fleischer, Hdb Vorstandsrecht, 2006, § 1 mn.28.

192 Easterbrook & Fischel, The Eonomic Structure of Corporate Law 38 et seq. (1991).

193 Eidenmüller, JZ 2001, 1041 (1044); Fleischer, Hdb Vorstandsrecht, 2006, § 1 mn.28; Klöhn, ZGR 2008, 110 (146).

194 Fleischer, Shareholders vs. Stakeholders: Aktien- und übernahmerechtliche Fragen, in: Hommelhoff et al., Hdb Corporate Governance, 2003, 129 (136 et seq.); Fleischer, Hdb Vorstandsrecht, 2006, § 1 mn.31; Seibt, in: Schmidt/Lutter, AktG, 2010, § 76 mn.12; Semler/Spindler, in: MüKo AktG, 2004, Vor § 76 mn.91: supports a moderate shareholder value approach; Weber, in: Hölters, AktG, 2011, § 76 mn.22.

195 Several rules have been implemented recently that favor a shareholder value oriented approach by the management board: a corporation may acquire own shares (§ 71 (1) No. 8 AktG), management may be granted share options (§ 192 (2) No. 3 AktG), and international accounting standards may be applied (§ 315 a HGB); Ulmer, AcP 2002, 143 (158 et seq.).

196 Fleischer, Shareholders vs. Stakeholders: Aktien- und übernahmerechtliche Fragen, in: Hommelhoff et al., Hdb Corporate Governance, 2003, 129 (136); Fleischer, Hdb Vorstandsrecht, 2006, § 1 mn.31.

The theory of the purpose of a corporation is particularly relevant for active shareholders, as they aim to enhance the shareholder value of the targeted corporation in order to privately benefit by having their efforts compensated accordingly. Under a system of shareholder primacy, this aligns the interests of the shareholders with those the administration is obliged to pursue as an agent of the shareholders. This would not be the case under a system of stakeholder preference, as the administration would be obliged not only to pursue shareholder interests but also those of other stakeholders. Accordingly, controlling the administration would not provide as strong an incentive for shareholders and would make shareholder activism less desirable. As the United States has historically followed the shareholder primacy approach, active shareholders have always been provided with the necessary incentives to engage in corporations. For German corporations, the growing acceptance of the enlightened shareholder value model has provided shareholders with the necessary incentives to become active. Under both legal systems, shareholder activism may therefore be evaluated as a potentially desirable corporate governance mechanism that aims to enhance corporate shareholder value of the targeted corporation.

4) The corporate decision-making process

The general decision-making process in public corporations may roughly be described as having four steps: the *initiation* of a decision, the *ratification* of the initiative to be implemented, the *implementation*—meaning the executing of the ratified decision—and finally the *monitoring*, which measures the performance of decision agents as well as the implementation of possible rewards. As the same agents usually initiate and implement corporate decisions, it may be summarized as *decision management*, while *decision control* summarizes ratification and monitoring.[197]

Public corporations may be characterized by a separation of residual risk bearing and decision management as well as of decision management and decision control. The specific knowledge spread throughout the corporation necessary to make an informed corporate decision as well as diffused residual claims require that corporate decisions are made by diffuse agents throughout the corporation as opposed to residual risk bearers. For cost reasons decision control and residual risk are also separated. The latter of the initially mentioned separations is intended to mitigate the resulting agency problems.[198]

5) The separation of ownership and control in the corporation

The separation of residual risk and decision management is also known as the separation of ownership and control introduced by *Berle and Means* in *The Modern Corporation and Private Property* (1932). Besides external monitoring via stock prices and

197 Fama & Jensen, 26 J. L. & Econ. 301, 303 et seq. (1983).
198 *Id.* at 322 et seq.

the market for corporate control, organizational mechanisms are intended to control the resulting agency issues. Accordingly, internal control in a corporation is delegated by residual claimants to a board of directors, the former retaining approval rights on matters such as board membership, auditor choice, and mergers. Furthermore, management and control functions are also delegated to the board, which in turn delegates most of the decision management functions and many decision control functions to internal agents over which it retains ultimate control. The latter comprise the ratification or monitoring of major policy initiatives as well as the right to hire, fire, and to set the compensation for top-level decision managers.[199] However, the latter mechanisms particularly have not always worked efficiently. Retained control rights by residual risk bearers regarding the board of directors under current corporate and securities law have been exercised inefficiently. Members of the board of directors failed to exercise their control rights unselfishly and independently. These agency issues resulted in agency costs as corporate decisions deviated from those which would have maximized shareholder value.[200] This provoked the question, "Who monitors the monitors?"

According to *Thompson*[201], shareholder activism by institutional investors, more recently that of hedge funds, represents the final of four attempts under U.S. law to deal with the issue of separation of ownership and control. After the Great Depression, the United States attempted to *empower shareholders* to make use of their retained control rights regarding the board of directors through the adoption of the securities regulation regime, which provided shareholders with comprehensive disclosure as well as the precatory shareholders proposal rule. The effects of securities laws in empowering shareholders to overcome the separation of ownership and control remained limited, however. Due to changes in shareholder census granting more shareholders a sufficient size and sophistication to counter traditional rational apathy barriers and the eased access to financing allowing shareholders to sell their shares when dissatisfied with corporate performance rather than voting, the *market for corporate control* grew in the 1980s.[202] However, the growing effectiveness of defense measures like poison pills and staggered boards increasingly prevented the quick exchange of boards and left the agency issues related to the separation of ownership and control unsolved. A third attempt that took place parallel to the takeovers represented the proceedings of financial entrepreneurs who assembled the necessary financial means to *buy out* the entire public ownership of a company. As a consequence, this overcame the separation of ownership and control. Whenever management submitted substantial investments, these provided strong incentives to produce positive payouts. However, since many of those investments involved substantial amounts of debt, the slowdown of the business cycle made many of them

199 *Id.* at 312 et seq.; Cheffins, Company Law 44 (1997); Cooter & Ulen, Law & Economics 139 et seq. (2004); Posner, Economic Analysis of Law 441 (2007).

200 Clifford, 14 J. Corp. Fin. 323 (2008); Jensen & Meckling, 3 J. Fin. Econ. 305, 312 (1976), *available at* www.ssrn.com/abstract=94043, 5 et seq.

201 Thompson, *The Limits of Hedge Fund Activism* 4, http://escholarship.org/uc/item/5jq9d71m (2006).

202 *Id.* at 7.

fall.[203] The substantial growth of *institutional investors* replacing individual shareholders seems, however, to overcome issues traditional *shareholder activism* had faced. The larger stake in the targeted corporations increases the benefits active shareholders reap from a successful campaign. Furthermore, the efforts and related costs necessary to convince and coordinate a reduced number of supportive shareholders may be attributed to a larger investment.[204] Economies of scale could further support an active approach. Institutional investors have the necessary financial sophistication on questions of corporate governance and have the opportunity to access necessary information. Both result in lower costs. Moreover, the percentage of shares held by a relatively small number of institutional shareholders, each of them being a repetitive player and possibly involved in a number of similar procedures, reduces costs further.[205] As a consequence, issues facing active shareholders from free-riding and rational apathy in controlling the board of directors are reduced. However, several concerns about the effectiveness of shareholder activism in reducing agency conflicts based on the separation of ownership and control that are related to potentially deviating interests have been raised. The remaining question is therefore whether these concerns are justified and, therefore, prevent in practice what has in theory been recognized as the potential of active shareholders to reduce agency issues and costs and increase shareholder value.

III) Systemic differences for shareholder activism in the United States and Germany

A functional legal comparison also needs to consider the systemic differences based on which shareholder activism has developed. These include different underlying legal approaches, but also characteristics of the market, politics, and related matters. Even though systemic differences may limit the ability to draw conclusions about the effect of certain legal rules, they may also be used to explain why different means may have the same function or vice versa.[206]

1) Organizational authority allocation within the administration

At first sight, a significant difference between the U.S.-American and German corporate governance systems lies in the organizational implementation of the allocation of authority within a corporation. Under the U.S.-American one-tier governance system, both management and control tasks are concentrated in one single organ, the board

203 *Id.* at 9.

204 Schmolke, ZGR 2007, 701 (708).

205 Black, 89 Mich. L. Rev. 519, 580 (1990); Schmolke, ZGR 2007, 701 (708); Thompson, *The Limits of Hedge Fund Activism* 10 et seq., http://escholarship.org/uc/item/5jq9d71m (2006).

206 Dannemann, *Comparative Law: Study of Similarities or Differences? in* The Oxford Handbook of Comparative Law 383, 398 (2006).

of directors.[207] It is the board of directors that is responsible for the core management of the corporation, including the determination of medium- and long-term corporate policy and the hiring, firing, and compensation of the executive officers. Especially in public corporations, the board has delegated its principal repository of inherent power to conduct the business and affairs of the corporation[208] to hired executive (officers on the highest level) and non-executive officers (the remainder of employees in accentuated positions).[209] Accordingly, corporate officers have relatively little inherent power by virtue of their offices.[210] While officers are directly determined by the board on the basis of the articles of incorporation or bylaws, which give them restricted authority by virtue of their office and task, the other employees only exercise contractual authority.[211] The articles of incorporation usually determine whether it is necessary for the corporation to have a president or chief executive officer (***"CEO"***), one or more vice presidents, a treasurer, and a secretary, while the bylaws may provide for a chief financial officer (***"CFO"***), a chief legal officer (***"CLO"***), or a chief operating officer (***"COO"***).[212] The board may consist of members who simultaneously hold an executive officer position (so-called inside directors) and persons that hold solely a board position (outside directors).

German corporate law, in contrast, requires a two-tier board structure for public corporations.[213] It provides for two separate and independent bodies in which the tasks of management and control are distributed, the management and the supervisory board.[214] The top corporate officers, who are usually absent from the first supervisory tier,[215] make up the board's second tier, while the first tier, in the case of corporations with more than 500 or more employees, also includes codetermination.[216] The management board is empowered to represent the corporation and is authorized to direct the corporation and manage the daily affairs of the corporation.[217] The supervisory board is generally responsible for controlling and directing the function of the management,[218] including the appointment and removal of members of the management board. The control of the management board by the supervisory board is not only *ex post*. This is particularly the case with regard to the annual financial statements, management's report on the corporate situation, and current reports of the management to the supervisory board, as well as the general control of the management board.[219] The supervisory board also exercises *ex ante* control of management at different levels of intensity. These include ongoing

207 Leyens, RabelZ 67, 57 (69).
208 HAMILTON, CORPORATIONS, 350 (1992).
209 Merkt/Göthel, US-amerikanisches Gesellschaftsrecht, 2006, mn.543, 575, 605, n.102.
210 HAMILTON, CORPORATIONS 350 (1992).
211 Windbichler, ZGR 1985, 50 (65).
212 Merkt/Göthel, US-amerikanisches Gesellschaftsrecht, 2006, mn.605.
213 KRAAKMAN ET AL., THE ANATOMY OF CORPORATE LAW 56 (2009).
214 Leyens, RabelsZ 67, 57 (70).
215 § 105 AktG; Kraakman et al., The Anatomy of Corporate Law 13 (2009).
216 KRAAKMAN ET AL., THE ANATOMY OF CORPORATE LAW 100 n.49 (2009).
217 §§ 76 (1), 78 (1) AktG; Hueck/Windbichler, Gesellschaftsrecht, § 23 mn.2.
218 Drygalla, in: Schmidt/Lutter, AktG, 2010, § 111 mn.11.
219 Leyens, RabelZ 67 (2003), 57, 86.

discussions and consultation about the formulation of an underlying corporate policy,[220] setting-up and increasing approval reserves in favor of the supervisory board, and personnel consequences.[221]

Nevertheless, this formal and functional distinction between the German two-tier and the U.S.-American one-tier system has started to fade.[222] Under Anglo-Saxon practice, there is a tendency to increasingly differentiate between inside and outside directors[223] in order to separate management and control tasks of the board between both groups. Daily business and important operational questions are transferred to a so-called management board while control is shifted to outside directors.[224] Prejudices regarding the effectiveness of independent directors seem to have disappeared. Since the ratification of the Sarbanes-Oxley-Act (***"SOA"***), which requires independent directors to be free of any dependence on the company, there exists a tendency of personal separation to ensure the effective control of the remaining members of the board.[225] Similarly, the New York Stock Exchange generally requires the independence of the majority of the board members in order to be listed.[226] Further, the SOA introduced the requirement that members of the audit committee be independent.[227] Under the German system, there is a parallel tendency of loosening the strict division between the responsibilities of the management board to direct and manage the affairs of the corporation and the supervisory board to control the management board. There is an increasing overlap of both functions. For instance, the supervisory board may consult the management board intensively as part of its task of *ex ante* management control[228] or former members of the management board may become a member of the supervisory board.[229] Furthermore, the *Societate Europae* allows the choice between a one-tier and two-tier corporate governance system.[230]

220 BGH, Urt. v. 25.03.1991, Az.: II ZR 188/89; BGHZ 114, 127 (132); Hueck/Windbichler, Gesellschaftsrecht, § 20 mn.26.

221 Henze, BB 2001, 53, 59.

222 Böckli, Konvergenz: Annäherung des monoistischen und des dualistischen Führungs- und Aufsichtssystems, in: Hommelhoff et al., in: Hommelhoff et al., Hdb Corporate Governance, 2003, 201 (212 et seq.); Spindler, in: MüKo AktG, 2008, Vor § 76 mn.74.

223 Besides functional convergence, the Sarbanes Oxley Act also leads to a formal convergence, Donald WM 2003, 705 (712 et seq.); An increasing functional convergence of the corporate governance systems is also confirmed by: Coffee 93 Nw. U. L. Rev. 641, 657 (1999); Gilson, 49, Am. J. Comp. L. 329, 337 et seq. (2001); *Leyens* RabelsZ 67 (2003), 57, 76 and 88; and Baums, ZIP 1995, 11 (15).

224 Spindler, in: MüKo AktG, 2008, § 76, mn.2; Windbichler, ZGR 1985, 50 (71): autonomization of management to fulfill daily management happens in a formalized way with legal reactions being the adaptation of boards duties including the duty of care regarding its task of election and control.

225 *See* H.R. 3763, sec. 301, 3; Spindler, in: MüKo AktG, 2008, Vor § 76, mn.74.

226 *See* §§ 303 A.01, 303A.00 New York Stock Exchange Listed Company Manual (2004).

227 *See* H.R. 3763, sec. 301.

228 BGH, Urt. v. 25.03.1991, Az.: II ZR 188/89; NJW 1991, 1830 (1831); Drygalla, in: Schmidt/Lutter, AktG, 2010, § 111 mn.5.

229 Spindler, in: MüKo AktG, 2008, Vor § 76 mn.74.

230 Since December 2004, a public corporation may be incorporated as a Societas Europaea in Germany according to European law and German implementing law, and it may be set up with a one-tier or two-tier structure.

This tendency of convergence[231] on both sides confirms the fact that the goal of either corporate governance system is to achieve the right balance between informed, but unbiased, control. The former is maximized under the one-tier system. Due to the partial identity of managing executive officers and board members, the controlling body is usually well informed about the daily operations of the corporation, which is an important background for efficient control. On the other hand, personal identity leads to a lack of objectivity.[232] The two-tier system, in contrast, grants the necessary objectivity for efficient control by providing personal diversity among members of the management and supervisory board, while members of the latter have comparably little information regarding daily corporate operations.[233]

2) Markets

a) Number of corporations

In contrast to the U.S.-American market, which has more than 12,000 publicly traded corporations,[234] the German market has only 3263,[235] compared to 80,277 closed corporations[236].[237] Of these public corporations, only 1100[238] are listed on a German exchange, while a significant number is part of a group.[239] This impacts the market for corporate control, which in the United States is still an important alternative means of management control. Takeovers in the United States are a frequent phenomenon that force management to produce increasing share prices to avoid being replaced. In comparison, the German corporate landscape allows only a comparably restricted number of takeovers.

b) Corporate finance

In the Anglo-Saxon system of corporate governance, the main source of finance for corporations is the stock market. The well-developed stock market and its underlying rules assure efficient protection for widely dispersed shareowners. They ensure that

231 V. Werder, Ökonomische Grundfragen der Corporate Governance, in: Hommelhoff et al., Hdb Corporate Governance, 2003, 3, 20, n.87.

232 Donald, WM 2003, 705 (713).

233 *Id.*: Davies, ZGR 2001, 268 (284 et seq.).

234 As of 2006, 11,898 companies filed annual reports with the SEC under the SEA. *See* Smaller Reporting Company Regulatory Relief and Simplification Act, Securities Act Release No. 8819, Exchange Act Release No. 56,013, 73 Fed. Reg. 934, 935 (Jan. 4, 2008), *available at* http://www.sec.gov/rules/final/2008/33-8876fr.pdf.

235 Statistisches Bundesamt, Statistisches Jahrbuch 2008, 497.

236 *Id.*

237 Lammers, Verhaltenspflichten von Verwaltungsorganen in Übernahmeauseinandersetzungen – Eine rechtsvergleichende Untersuchung des US-amerikanischen, deutschen und europäischen Rechts, 1994, 103 et seq.

238 Freudenberg, AG Report 2007, R 375.

239 Lammers, Verhaltenspflichten von Verwaltungsorganen in Übernahmeauseinandersetzungen, 1994, 104.

even investors with comparably small investments do not have to fear disadvantages and assure them a very high level of liquidity.[240]

The Continental system of corporate finance was in the past characterized by the predominance of banks not only as major blockholders of German corporations, but also as major creditors of most corporations. Thus, banks were able to impact corporations both as shareholders and creditors. The German capital market's relatively low liquidity, in contrast, played in the past only a secondary role regarding corporate finance. The significance of bank loans decreased, especially for large corporations, when the German capital markets became internationally integrated, allowing them to be emancipated more and more from national debt financing by banks. Banks, on the other hand, faced increasing competition from international capital markets and foreign banks.[241]

The German stock market's catching up with the global capital market has contributed a great deal to the emergence of international institutional investors under the German corporate governance system.[242] International institutional investors are often well acquainted with the phenomenon of shareholder activism and are generally more active than the remaining shareholders, making them a possible catalyst for shareholder activism in German corporations. However, the increasing significance of the capital markets and their control mechanism of takeovers increases the pressure on the corporate management to assure steadily increasing share prices to avoid being replaced. This may be in the interest of shareholders but not necessarily for the remainder of stakeholders. The growing impact of the capital markets for corporate finance therefore requires thinking about corresponding amendments.[243]

c) Shareholder structures

A proper analysis of the significance of shareholder activism for U.S.-American and German corporations requires consideration of the significantly different shareholder structures in both countries: while freefloat in U.S. corporations usually represents the largest stake, the average shareholdings of German corporations are significantly more concentrated with few significant blockholders and comparably low freefloat.[244] The shareholder structure remains not without impact on principal-agent issues. In U.S. corporations with significant freefloat, the conflict centers on the relationship of manage-

240 Garrido & Rojo, *Institutional Investors and Corporate Governance: Solution or Problem in* Hopt & Wymeersch, Capital Market and Company Law 427, 431 (2003).

241 Von Hein, Die Rezeption US-amerikanischen Gesellschaftsrechts in Deutschland, 2008, 383 et seq.; Garrido & Rojo, *Institutional Investors and Corporate Governance: Solution or Problem in* Hopt & Wymeersch, Capital Market and Company Law 427, 432 (2003).

242 Garrido & Rojo, *Institutional Investors and Corporate Governance: Solution or Problem in* Hopt & Wymeersch, Capital Market and Company Law 427, 437 (2003).

243 Interview with Reinhard Schmidt, Boeckler foundation, *Und wer kontrolliert die Manager?*, Magazin Mitbestimmung 06/2006, *available at* http://www.boeckler.de/163_82195.html.

244 Cheffins, *Does Law Matter?: The Separation of Ownership and Control in the United Kingdom* 2, www.ssrn.com/abstract=245560 (2000); Gourevitch & Shinn, Political Power and Corporate Control 160 (2005); Roe, 120 Harv. L. Rev. 460, 495 (2006), *available* at www.ssrn.com/abstract=908972.

ment and the shareholders. In German corporations with strong blockholders, agency issues shift to the relationship between minority and majority shareholders.[245] To understand the development of different shareholder structures requires analyzing the relevant background.

As discussed previously, the *Anglo-Saxon* system of corporate governance depends on the stock market as its main source of financing. The stock market is accordingly well developed, highly liquid, and has widely spread share ownership. As far as corporate governance is concerned, management of corporations with significant freefloat lies mainly in the hands of the board of directors, while control through dispersed shareholder meetings remains relatively weak.[246]

In the *Continental* system, the stock market was mainly a secondary source of finance, since most of the companies were financed through bank loans. The stock market was thus correspondingly less developed. Major shareholdings were in the hands of few economic actors (a network of families, insurance companies, banks, and industrial companies, collectively referred to as *Deutschland AG*), while corporate freefloat was insignificantly low. Banks not only provided the major portion of corporate financing via loans, but they also played a paramount role by holding significant stakes in most large companies.[247] This combination of strong shareholder meeting majorities, delegation of supervisory board representatives, the exercise of proxy voting rights for minor shareholders (the impact of which was reduced by the KonTraG[248],[249] while the ARUG[250] enhanced it in order to increase presence during shareholder assemblies[251]), and their influence as creditors[252] allowed banks to function as a strong control mechanism of management. There was little need to protect them against management opportunism. The German legislator issued regulations corresponding to the underlying circumstances of blockholding shareholders and little freefloat, concentrating on the protection of minority shareholders. As an example, the German group law (*Konzernrecht*) contains rules that guarantee compensation to minority shareholders for the disadvantages they may suffer at the hands of dominant shareholders.[253]

However, the dual impact of banks in the German corporate governance system has faded. The increasing impact of the global capital market as a financial source to German corporations has not only dislodged banks from their positions as corporate creditors but

245 Schäfer/Ott, Lehrbuch der ökonomischen Analyse des Zivilrechts, 2005, 645.

246 Garrido & Rojo, *Institutional Investors and Corporate Governance: Solution or Problem*, *in* Hopt & Wymeersch, Capital Market and Company Law 427, 431 (2003).

247 *Id.* at 432.

248 Gesetz zur Kontrolle und Transparenz im Unternehmensbereicht [Law for Control and Transparency in Business], Mar. 5, 1998, BGBl. I, at 768.

249 Gourevitch & Shinn, Political Power and Corporate Control, 163 (2005).

250 Gesetz zur Umsetzung der Aktionärsrechterichtlinie [Act Implementing the Shareholder Rights Directive], Jul. 30, 2009, BGBl. I at. 2479.

251 Freshfields Bruckhaus Deringer, *Das ARUG tritt in Kraft*, Aug. 2009, 3, http://www.freshfields.de/publications/pdfs/2009/aug09/26347.pdf.

252 Klöhn, ZGR 2008, 110 (151 et seq.); Von Hein, Die Rezeption US-amerikanischen Gesellschaftsrechts in Deutschland, 2008, 383.

253 Arnold, ZCG 2008, 221 (224).

has also started to erode their control positions as major shareholders. This development has occurred not only because the banks have aimed to increase their share price and market capitalization in order to prevent being taken over, but also because they have attempted to make themselves capable of acquiring third banks. Preferring to increase their own share price and based on tax law amendments allowing them to do so with significantly less costs, banks decided to give up their long-term industrial participations. They have become increasingly like typical investors who concentrate on areas of business and accounting with strict separation of business areas, allowing transparent capital market communications. Furthermore, a withdrawal from large industrial participations has allowed banks to improve their reputation and to concentrate on higher-profit activities such as investment banking. Banks had suffered from several scandals involving house banks that held significant stakes and control positions in corporations. Finally, agency costs to obtain reliable information on debtors, which were previously available primarily to house banks, have been reduced by increased corporate transparency rules.[254] As a consequence, banks have withdrawn from their historical role as corporate controllers for the entire German corporate landscape.[255]

The increasing withdrawal of banks from their positions as corporate blockholders represents only an example of an entire movement of disentanglement of long-term reciprocal blockholdings by participants of "*Deutschland AG*", caused mainly by the effort to catch up with the global capital market.[256]

These changes relating to the access of German corporations to the global capital market have impacted the shareholder structure of German corporations. Besides the internationalization and institutionalization of shareholders, freefloat has increased as blockholdings have decreased. The tendency of increasing freefloat is still ongoing and has not been stopped by the financial crisis[257]. Data provided by the daily press, the Max Planck Institute for the Study of Society, and the Monopoly Commission indicate a correlation between high freefloat and international shareholders, strong added value, and high market capitalization.[258] According to data collected and evaluated by the author regarding freefloat in German corporations as of 2008, freefloat in DAX[259] corporations amounts to 66 percent, compared to a lower average of 51 percent freefloat in German M-DAX[260] corporations.[261] The leading corporations united in the DAX increasingly

254 Von Hein, Die Rezeption US-amerikanischen Gesellschaftsrechts in Deutschland, 2008, 385–395.

255 *Id.* at 395.

256 Seibert, AG 2002, 417 (418).

257 Bundeszentrale für politische Bildung [Federal Agency for Civil Education], Aktionärsstruktur von DAX Unternehmen, 3 et seq., http://www.bpb.de/nachschlagen/zahlen-und-fakten/globalisierung/52598/aktionaersstruktur-von-dax-unternehmen : data for freefloat (stakes below 5 %) in DAX corporations, from year 2001 till 2009: rise from 64,5 % to 82,5 %.

258 Von Hein, Die Rezeption US-amerikanischen Gesellschaftsrechts in Deutschland, 2008, 380.

259 DAX evaluates the performance of Germany's 30 strongest corporations of the prime-standard measured by market capitalization, stock exchange turnover, and freefloat (blue-chips).

260 M-DAX contains the next 50 corporations in market capitalization, freefloat, and stock exchange turnover which also belong to the prime standard of German corporations.

261 Freefloat refers to shareholdings below three percent. The data have been collected between January and June 2008. The collected data are based on information provided by the FAZ as well as

resemble U.S.-American corporations in their shareholder structure. This trend makes it easier to apply data derived from the application of U.S.-American securities and corporate rules to German corporations, since the German and the U.S. models of corporate governance are becoming increasingly similar.[262] However, the remarkable difference in freefloat between the largest 30 and the next 50 largest prime standard corporations in Germany demonstrates the unique characteristics of DAX corporations and the time the general trend toward greater freefloat takes.

The evolving freefloat in German corporations results in increased management power due to the decrease in blockholders among rationally passive minority shareholders and a corresponding shift of agency conflicts from majority-minority shareholder relations to management-shareholder relations.[263] The declining prevalence[264] of blockholders therefore makes new control structures regarding the agency conflict between management and shareholders necessary.[265] One way to overcome the resulting control gap may be through shareholder activism. Shareholder activism may help overcome rational passivity of shareholders and therefore increase the control of management while reducing agency costs resulting from agency issues between management and shareholder authority. The catching up of the German stock market with the global capital market has contributed significantly to the emergence of international institutional investors under the German corporate governance system.[266] International institutional investors are often well acquainted with the phenomenon of shareholder activism and are generally more active than the remaining shareholders. They therefore play an important role in filling the control gap through shareholder activism. The reform policy of the German government in amending corporate law stepwise may therefore be understood, among other reasons, as a reaction to the corporate governance shift caused by increasing freefloat[267]. The question to be raised in this context is whether additional amendments are necessary to respond to this shift and the growing relevance of shareholder activism.

The shareholder structure has an impact on active shareholders. In U.S.-American corporations involving a high ratio of freefloat, the small stakes make the majority of

---

the BaFin as far as the DAX corporations are concerned, and on information from the BaFin and the Unternehmensregister as far as the M-DAX corporations are concerned.

262 Garrido & Rojo, *Institutional Investors and Corporate Governance: Solution or Problem in* HOPT & WYMEERSCH, CAPITAL MARKET AND COMPANY LAW 427, 432 (2003).

263 Their efforts under a system with several blockholders may allow them to "counterpower" the impact of the blockholders, but may as well give them no impact on the blockholders at all, since institutional investors due to their diversification strategy only invest relatively small stakes. Furthermore, the institutional investors may even be impacted by financial institutes, which additionally hold significant stakes resulting in even higher impact of the blockholders on the minority shareholders, *id.* at 437.

264 Schmolke, ZGR 2007, 701 (722).

265 Schäfer/Ott, Lehrbuch der ökonomischen Analyse des Zivilrechts, 2005, 633 et seq.; Seibert, AG 2002, 417 (418).

266 Garrido & Rojo, *Institutional Investors and Corporate Governance: Solution or Problem in* HOPT & WYMEERSCH, CAPITAL MARKET AND COMPANY LAW 427, 437 (2003).

267 Seibert, AG 2002, 417 (418).

shareholders rationally passive. As a consequence, active shareholders have to make more intense efforts to convince the relevant quorum of shareholders to support them in their strategy. In addition, corporate management has fewer anchor shareholders it may convince to support its strategy against the impact of active shareholders. On the contrary, the historic shareholder structures of German corporations had the potential to allow blockholding shareholders to exercise comparably intense control on the administration. This made active shareholders with minority positions insignificant in controlling the administration and less successful in the presence of blockholding shareholders who used their influence to reach agreement with the administration upon amendments informally. However, since the shareholder structure of larger listed corporations is changing toward more and more freefloat, the strategies of active shareholders are becoming more efficient.

3) Decision-making practice of the shareholder meeting

Closely related to the different shareholder structures of U.S.-American and German corporations are the different mechanisms for shareholders to participate in the corporate decision-making process.

In the *United States*, proxy voting is the dominant mode of corporate decision-making in publicly held corporations. The corporate management and sometimes shareholder groups solicit shareholder votes in annual or special shareholder meetings held for the election of directors and the approval of other corporate actions. This is governed by the SEA, while the compliance, particularly the necessary disclosure to shareholders, is assured by the SEC.[268] High freefloat is one of the reasons for the currency of proxy voting. This implies that the investment per corporation in relation to the diversified investments of typical U.S. investors is comparably small. In addition, U.S. shareholders, even though investing in U.S. firms, are very dispersed due to the geographic size of the country. For them, it is therefore not worth the effort to visit each shareholder meeting of the many corporations they have invested in. Physical attendance at a shareholder meeting often represents an "uneconomical use of a shareholder's time" if he can vote by proxy.[269] A proxy is a written instrument embodying the authority to vote shares on a shareholder's behalf. In order to obtain a proxy, the person seeking the proxy must systematically contact shareholders and urge them to execute and return the proxy forms authorizing the proxy holder to cast the shareholder's votes as designated in the proxy form or according to the proxy holder's discretion. Section 14(a) SEA authorizes the SEC to promulgate *Proxy Rules*[270] that govern the private conduct of proxy voting, primarily

268 Eisenberg, Corporations and other Business Organizations ch. 5, § 2 (b) (2005).

269 *Id.*, at § 3.

270 This is established in the Exchange Act Rules 14a-1 to 14a-20 (17 C.F.R. §§ 240.14a-1-14a-20), of which the most fundamental are the following: Rules 14a-4 and 5 addressing the proxy's format, Rule 14a-3 and Schedule 14A laying down the disclosure requirements in relation to transactions that demand shareholder approval as well as proxies for the election of the directors solicited on behalf of the corporation, backed up by Rule 14a-9, prohibiting false or misleading statements

for disclosure purposes.[271] As a consequence of the U.S.-American proxy system, the outcome of the shareholder meeting is usually determined even before it has begun.[272]

Under *German* corporate law, the general formation of shareholder opinion takes place during the shareholder meeting through the vote of the present shareholders[273]. The differences between the systems have been lessened, however, by changes in German law.[274] Besides admitting that shareholders grant proxy authority to banks, the German legislator has restricted the limitations on administrational proxy authority. This was initially aimed at preventing corporate organs from exercising voting rights for their shareholders resulting in a self-stabilizing system.[275] In 2001, the NaStraG[276] amended § 134 (3) sent. 3 AktG a.F. Even if it did not explicitly refer to the admissibility of an authorization of a corporate representative, its admissibility was implied through the underlying legislative materials[277] determining it constituted admissible proxy voting.[278] The legislative intent was to compensate the increasing withdrawal of banks from proxy voting.[279] Similarly, the DCGK recommends that a corporation select a representative who must exercise voting rights according to the directions of the concerned shareholders. The installation of an appropriate corporate representative may be considered a partial reception of the U.S.-American system of proxy voting. Its adoption, however, was limited to material law, and the provisions especially on disclosure and enforcement are not comparable to U.S. securities law and the SEC[280]. The recent adoption of the ARUG followed the general trend of relaxing the requirement of personal presence during shareholder meetings. Besides introducing online participation and online voting, it supports proxy voting through banks as compared to proxy voting through the administration. By increasing its flexibility through a total make-over of § 135 AktG, it intends to increase

---

in relation to the solicitation of proxies, Rule 14a-6 governs the filing requirements of the proxy materials with the SEC, while Rule 14a-2 concerns the coverage of solicitations to which the subsequent rules apply. The latter two will be analyzed *infra* in more detail. Rules 14a-7 and 8 provide shareholders with means to communicate with each other, the former through access to a list of shareholders or the circulation of the requesting holder's materials, the latter through shareholder proposals to be added to the corporate ballot.

271 Eisenberg, Corporations and Other Business Organizations ch. 5, sec. 3 (2005).

272 Eisenberg, 83 Harv. L. Rev. 1489, 1494 (1970); Hofstetter, ZGR 2008, 560 (572).

273 Marsch-Barner, in Marsch-Barner/Schäfer, Hdb börsennotierte AG, Aktien- und Kapitalmarktrecht, 2005, 1077 et seq.

274 Butzke, in: Von Rosen, Die Hauptversammlung vor neuen Herausforderungen, DAI studies issue 41, 2008, 66 (70).

275 Hüffer, AktG, § 134 mn.26.

276 Namensaktiengesetz [Law on Registered Shares], Jan. 18, 2001, BGBl. I at 123.

277 Beschlussempfehlung und Bericht des Rechtsausschusses zum Entwurf eines Gesetzes zur Namensaktie und zur Erleichterung der Stimmrechtsausübung [NaStraG] [Recommendation and Report of the Legal Committee regarding the Draft Law of an Act on Registered Shares], Nov. 15, 2000, BT-Drucks 14/4618, 14 left col.

278 Hüffer, AktG, § 134 mn.26a.

279 Von Hein, Die Rezeption US-amerikanischen Gesellschaftsrechts in Deutschland, 2008, 252: opposing opinion: Hüffer, AktG, § 134 mn.26a; Spindler, in: Schmidt/Lutter, AktG, 2010, § 134 mn.55.

280 Von Hein, Die Rezeption US-amerikanischen Gesellschaftsrechts in Deutschland, 2008, 254.

shareholder presence during shareholder meetings to increase shareholder control, since the latter has so far not proven to be a useful alternative[281].

4) Politics

The impact of politics on legislation, especially regarding the balance of authority between shareholders and the administration of the company, should not be underestimated. The United States, especially Delaware,[282] pursued for many years a policy in favor of a strong corporate management.[283] Necessary amendments on the legislative or administrative level in favor of increased shareholder power were repeatedly blocked or delayed. The tide seemed to turn with the inauguration of President Obama. In 2009, he declared giving shareholders increased power in the financial system a key goal, including authorizing the SEC to grant shareholders more voice in corporate elections.[284] Changes have not only affected the composition of the SEC. In Germany, Christian- and Social-Democratic governments[285] took care of the interests of the established industries and those of the trade unions.[286] However, the European policy of strengthening shareholder rights has substantially impacted German corporate and capital market law. This is reflected in the Shareholders' Rights Directive,[287] implemented in German corporate law through the ARUG, as well as past[288] and expected amendments to the Transparency Directive[289]. In the United States, resentments against strong banks were very popular, leading to restrictions against strong financial institutions (the Glass-Steagall-Act of 1933), which may represent only one reason for the comparably high freefloat in U.S. corporations.[290] Some argue that former German political support for, in contrast, strong banks has led to soft financial regulations that in the past resulted in concentrated ownership in German corporations.[291]

281 Hüffer, AktG, 2010, § 135 mn.3.

282 Becker, Verwaltungskontrolle durch Gesellschafterrechte, 1997, 16 mn.24.

283 *Id.* at 394; Kraakman et al., The Anatomy of Corporate Law 61, 269 (2009).

284 *See* Remarks by President Obama on Wall Street Reform, New York, Apr. 22, 2010, http://www.whitehouse.gov/the-press-office/remarks-president-wall-street-reform.

285 Gourevitch & Shinn, Political Power and Corporate Control 160 et seq. (2005).

286 Kraakman et al., The Anatomy of Corporate Law 191 (2004).

287 European Parliament and Council Directive, 2007 O.J. (L 184) 17.

288 Berndt, Global Differences in Corporate Governance Systems 11 (2002).

289 European Parliament and Council Directive, 2004 O.J. (L 290) 38.

290 Berndt, Global Differences in Corporate Governance Systems 5 (2002); Roe, Strong Managers, Weak Owners *passim* (1996).

291 Roe, Strong Managers, Weak Owners *passim* (1996); Berndt, Global Differences in Corporate Governance Systems 15 et seq. (2002).

5) Labor interests according to German law

Closely related to the impact of politics on corporate governance is their impact on the representation of labor interests in corporate governance. Social-Democratic governments in Germany have assured that corporate management respects employee interests, not only through co-determination. At the same time, the control allocation in favor of labor under German corporate law weakens the ability of investors to control management. Because of the mandatory representation of labor interests in the supervisory board of private and public corporations, the extent to which the controlling organ represents the interests of the economic owners of the corporation may be reduced to as little as the half. This is of particular significance, as the interests of employees and management run rather parallel and in tension with the interests of the capital providers, who aim primarily for increased shareholder value. Accordingly, management aims for an expansion of the firm for reasons of authority, prestige, and pay. Employees prefer an increase in size for better promotion opportunities while downsizing may leave them unemployed. Shareholders, in contrast, aim for efficient firms with good shareholder value. Managers as well as employees are risk averse, as both have tied up their human capital in one firm aiming to prevent risks to their jobs and careers. Shareholders, in contrast, have usually diversified their risk externally, aiming to maximize their shareholder value and preferring high-risk investments as long as the elevated risk is offset by correspondingly elevated return potential. Managers and employees prefer making use of available equity, before restructuring, while shareholders prefer the opposite. Finally, employees prefer high wages and shareholders lower wages, while management with substantial discretion on wages is not likely to fight as strongly for the interests of the shareholders.[292] Besides the coherence of interests between managers and employees, the representation of labor on the supervisory board restrains the impact of the economic owners on the composition of the management board; the two-tier system requires impact on the supervisory board before doing so. This is particularly important because the threat to or the actual impact on the management board composition represents one of the means for active shareholders to impact pure management decisions. This control allocation weakens the ability of investors to control management because the interests of labor may capture management's interests more easily. To make up for this deficiency, investors need to form larger control blocks in the corporation. As a consequence, managers would be monitored more, but not necessarily in the shareholders' interests.[293] This is also reflected in a usual discount on the value of the firm.[294]

292 Roe, 53 Stan. L. Rev. 539, 550 et seq. (2000).

293 Berndt, Global Differences in Corporate Governance Systems 18 (2002); *Id.* at 550.

294 Controversial: For a negative impact: Eidenmüller, Ausländische Kapitalgesellschaften, 2004, § 1 mn.20; more careful with regard to the efficiency effects of codetermination: Oetker, in: Großkomm AktG, 2008, Vor Mitbest mn. 32-34; Roe, 53 Stan. L. Rev. 539, 550 n.18 (2000): proposing a discout of 10 – 20 %; no negative impact: Vitols, Ökonomische Auswirkungen der paritätischen Mitbestimmung – Eine ökonometrische Analyse, 2006, 11; more differentiated: Jirjahn/Boeckler, Ökonomische Wirkungen der Mitbestimmung in Deutschland: Ein Update, 2010, 39 et seq., 51: in contrast to older studies, more recent studies increase evidence that codetermination positively

6) Relevant law levels

Finally, it is necessary to keep in mind the different levels of law relevant to the legal analysis of means and limits of shareholder activism that exist under U.S.-American and German jurisdiction. In the United States, securities laws,[295] the common law of corporations,[296] and listing rules[297] need to be considered as relevant law on the prevailing federal level. Corporate law provided on the state law level (this thesis will concentrate on Delaware Corporation Law) represents an additional and secondary rule level.[298] Even though corporate law is generally regulated at the state level, the federal legislator has imposed a distinct system of securities law which covers part of the corporate governance rules regarding listed corporations. The federal proxy rules contained in the Securities Exchange Act of 1934 are of particular relevance for this work.

In Germany, European law, the federal corporate, capital market, and co-determination law, and the DCGK are the relevant legislation. European law enjoys primacy and has significantly impacted German corporate and capital market law. The administrations of listed corporations are obliged to state whether or not they have followed the recommendations of the DCGK, § 161 AktG.

IV) Structure and initial thesis

The following analysis will concentrate on the comparison of three of the most frequently applied strategies by active shareholders to actively exercise control over the administration under U.S. and German law.

The *first part* concentrates on the comparably less active strategy of traditional active shareholders impacting the corporate governance of a targeted corporation by amending the underlying corporate rules-of-the-game. The nomination and election rules regarding directors and supervisory board members, respectively, are the rules-of-the-game that relate most closely to the corporate accountability mechanism of the shareholder franchise. Accordingly, the first part of the analysis will focus on the admissibility of four rule-of-the-game provisions which are important for the effectiveness of this mechanism and therefore for the responsiveness of the agents to the interests of their principals. The admissibility of their implementation has involved many controversies. The *second and third part* concern more active strategies that are mainly used by hedge funds, which tend to be supported by other active shareholders. Instead of relating to abstract rules-of-the-game, their impact targets the control of specific corporate management decisions. The second part analyses the impact of active shareholders on three specific types of

impacts productivity and provide more differentiated evidence with regard to the impact of co-determination upon profitability and evaluation on the capital market.

295 Especially the Securities Act 1933 and the Securities Exchange Act 1934, as well as rules adopted on their basis.

296 Especially the Sarbanes-Oxley Act adopted in 2002.

297 Especially the Listed Company Manual of the New York Stock Exchange.

298 Becker, Verwaltungskontrolle durch Gesellschafterrechte, 1997, 105 et seq.; Merkt/Göthel, US-amerikanisches Gesellschaftsrecht, 2006, mn.182 et seq.

corporate transaction decisions that have a large impact on the corporation and its shareholders, therefore frequently providing active shareholders with sufficient incentives to become active. The third part of the work focuses on how active shareholders facilitate three different measures relating to the corporate capital structure. The analysis of both the second and third strategy will concentrate on the means and limitations active shareholders are provided and confronted with as well as the effectiveness of the latter to restrict potential opportunistic behavior of active shareholders.

Each of the following three parts will consist of five subparts. After an introduction and initial thesis on each of the three strategies, each part will continue with the analysis of the relevant U.S. law for the strategy analyzed before drawing a conclusion regarding its impact on the thesis. The fourth subpart will continue with the analysis of the relevant German law and the final subpart will then conclude on the initial thesis of the part.

The answer this thesis intends to provide through the analysis of the three frequently applied strategies of active shareholders is, "What are the benefits and drawbacks of shareholder activism?" The question is to be understood in terms of whether current legal regimes need to be amended by, for instance, loosening the requirements for active shareholders to have more access to *means* granting them the opportunity to create impact. On the other hand, the question is also directed at the effectiveness of the *legal limitations* under current legal regimes relevant to restricting active shareholders, especially considering accusations of opportunistic behavior often leveled at active shareholders as they pursue their strategies, and, therefore, whether there is need to increase the currently applicable legal limitations.

C) Part I: Shareholder impact on nomination and election procedures

I) Introduction

The following Part will analyze the most influential formal means of shareholder impact on a corporation: the right to nominate and elect members of the board of directors under U.S.-American law and supervisory board members under German law. More specifically, it will focus on the opportunities for active shareholders to impact corporate nomination and election *procedure* to increase shareholder influence on nominations and elections and therefore make the administration more responsive to shareholder interests. This Part will concentrate on four issues in this context. First, this Part will examine the mandatory initiation right of shareholders to generally amend relevant rules-of-the-game for the nomination and election procedure. Next, it will analyze the admissibility (of the implementation) of the first nomination and election rule, the proxy access rule or nomination right. This rule grants shareholders the right to propose a nominee for a vacant director or supervisory board position via the corporate ballot. The second specific rule concerns the majority-voting rule, which makes the election of a director dependent on the support of a majority of the votes cast. Finally, this Part will analyze the cumulative-voting rule. It allows shareholders, in the case of several vacant director or supervisory board positions, to cast all of their votes for the different positions in favor of fewer or only one candidate.

1) Significance of nomination and election rights and procedures

The shareholder's *right to vote* represents his most important formal means of participation in the corporate decision-making process. It enables the shareholder to exert some influence on corporate decisions and to exercise control over the board of directors or the supervisory board. As residual claimants,[299] shareholders are allowed to vote in order to specify what has been left to their discretion by explicit contracts, whether expressly, by legal rule, or by the fiduciary principle.[300] Accordingly, shareholders may be required to approve important decisions leading to fundamental corporate transformations. Beyond this, the right to vote gives shareholders the opportunity to exercise control over the board of directors or the supervisory board, respectively, and to hold its members accountable for its decisions and actions, making them responsible to the interests of the voting shareholders, who also seek to have the board of directors or the supervisory

299 *See* the introductory chapter B (B II 2).
300 EASTERBROOK & FISCHEL, THE ECONOMIC STRUCTURE OF CORPORATE LAW 66 (1991).

board, respectively, control corporate management.[301] As a means of control, the right to vote can potentially reduce agency costs that result from the separation of ownership—vested in the shareholders—and control—given to the corporate management.

The right to vote is not a perfect control mechanism, however. Due to the *collective action problem*[302] resulting from information and transaction costs and leading to *rational apathy*[303] and *free rider problems,*[304] it is not guaranteed that shareholder resolutions will be value-enhancing or that value will not be reallocated at the expense of some shareholders. Even though those who have larger stakes in the corporation do not face the collective action problem to the same extent as small investors, the one who holds 100 percent has optimal incentives.[305] In addition to the collective action problem, management may use the rational apathy of the shareholders strategically to produce shareholder resolutions in its own favor. The effectiveness of the voting right as a gap-filling and disciplining instrument is therefore limited when the shares lack concentration.[306] Concentrated ownership of active shareholders may help overcome the problems of collective action and strategic management behavior. It allows shareholders to obtain a greater part of the benefits of an informed vote while the effort necessary for an informed and coherent vote are comparably lower for institutional shareholders. Accordingly, institutional shareholders are more likely to use the shareholder vote to their advantage because of the greater potential benefits and reduced costs, even if the remaining shareholders will also benefit.

In helping to reduce negotiation costs between shareholders and management, corporate law also provides the most important of those rights: the *right to cast votes for membership in a corporation's board of directors*[307] or the supervisory board. As discussed earlier, the

301 Ruffner, Die ökonomischen Grundlagen eines Rechts der Publikumsgesellschaft, 2000, 173.

302 Easterbrook & Fischel, The Economic Structure of Corporate Law 66 et seq. (1991): resulting from the fact that shareholders in large public corporations are convinced that their vote does not impact the result and the fact that the trivial part of any entire potential return for the corporation is not worth the effort for shareholders to study the firm's affairs and vote intelligently; *Id.* at 174 et seq.: The collective action issue results when a coporation has more than one shareholder. It is based on the information and transaction costs applying to shareholder votes on complex issues. Especially small shareholders have few incentives to inform themselves about a critical shareholder vote and tend to follow, for instance, the proposals of the administration. The same may apply to larger shareholders or blockholders who try to coordinate the shareholder votes. As all shareholders profit proportionally to their stake, even larger shareholders may not have optimal incentives. As a consequence, a majority of the shareholders tends to act rationally apathic in order not to have to incur substantial information costs. Furthermore, it seems worth to freeride on the efforts of other shareholders.

303 Clark, Corporate Law 390 (1986): Often, the aggregate costs for shareholders to inform themselves of potential corporate actions, independently assessing the wisdom of such actions, and casting their votes will greatly exceed the expected or actual benefits garnered from informed voting.

304 *Id.* at 94; Ruffner, Die ökonomischen Grundlagen eines Rechts der Publikumsgesellschaft, 2000, 176.

305 Easterbrook & Fischel, The Economic Structure of Corporate Law 67 (1991).

306 Ruffner, Die ökonomischen Grundlagen eines Rechts der Publikumsgesellschaft, 2000, 177.

307 Posner, Economic Analysis of Law, 441 et seq. (2007).

general influence of shareholders during the corporation's decision-making process is limited to a few decisions on particular to matters resulting in a fundamental transformation of the corporation, while management takes most of the decisions and acts for the corporation. It is the board of directors or the supervisory board that ratifies the actions of management and selects and replaces the corporation's chief executive officers or management board members. Accordingly, it is mainly the board of directors or the supervisory board who exercises control over the decisions and actions of management. The election by the firm's shareholders assures that the board remains responsive to the interests of the firm's owners, who bear the costs and benefits of the firm's decisions and whose interests are not strongly protected by contract.[308] However, the board of directors or the supervisory board may become responsive to the interests of management, thereby reducing its control responsibility.[309] Under such circumstances, shareholders may need to oust the responsible board member and replace it according to the corporate nomination and election procedures and therefore take the role of monitoring the monitors.[310] This role gives shareholders the opportunity to exercise indirect influence on the corporation's decisionmaking by influencing who will decide corporate matters in the future.[311] Nomination and election rights are therefore key strategies to address agency problems resulting from the separation of ownership and control. The nomination and election procedures govern their effectiveness. It is therefore important for active shareholders to get involved once this organizational mechanism to reduce agency issues is not functioning effectively and to set up nomination and election procedures that will ensure the effectiveness of this accountability mechanism.

2) Shareholder influence on the amendment of and design of rules-of-the-game decisions and rule design

Rules-of-the-game decisions concern the choice of the rules by which corporate actors play.[312] They also include provisions regarding the nomination and election process of the directors or members of the supervisory board.

a) Shareholder means to influence rule-of-the-game decisions

i) Under U.S.-American corporate law

Means for shareholders to influence *rule-of-the-game* decisions are very limited. Under U.S.-American corporate law, such means include precatory proposals, veto rights, and

308 Kraakman et al., The Anatomy of Corporate Law 14 (2009).

309 Baysinger & Hoskisson, 15 Acad. Mgmt. Rev. 72, 72–73 (1990): noting that "managers dominate the boards by using their de facto power to select and compensate directors and by exploiting personal ties with them".

310 Bainbridge, Corporate Law and Economics 37 (2002).

311 Kraakman et al., The Anatomy of Corporate Law 56 (2009); Ruffner, Die ökonomischen Grundlagen eines Rechts der Publikumsgesellschaft, 2000, 188.

312 Bebchuk, 118 Harv. L. Rev. 833, 844 (2005).

the mandatory initiation of changes. These different means of shareholder influence need to be matched at the different rule-setting levels of a corporation, which are the bylaws, articles of incorporation and corporate law of the state of incorporation.[313] The following table displays the means by which shareholders participate in amending the rules-of-the-game according to current U.S. corporate law:

Display I: Shareholder impact rule-of-the-game amendments, current U.S. corporate law

Rule level/Impact level:	Precatory proposals →	Veto rights →	Mandatory proposals
1. Bylaws	X	X	X (long time debate)
2. Articles of incorporation	X	X	-
3. State of incorporation	X	X	-

This model has often been criticized with regard to the U.S.-American understanding of the purpose of the corporation as well as the distribution of authority between directors and shareholders. Supporters of the director primacy rule argue that the power of shareholders to initiate the amendment of bylaws should be interpreted as rather limited.[314] Others, particularly the supporters of the shareholder primacy rule, see an even further extension of the shareholder power as the right approach. Accordingly, shareholders should not only be allowed to mandate certain bylaw amendments, but they should also be allowed to initiate rule-of-the-game decisions on the articles of incorporation level as well as the state of incorporation level. An increased right for shareholders to initiate changes in a corporation would avoid the need for the highly imperfect means of replacing the directors with a rival team[315] in order to implement shareholder-value-increasing rule-of-the-game amendments.[316] The following displays these increased means of shareholder influence.

Display II: Increase of shareholder initiation rights, shareholder value proponents

Rule level/Impact level:	Precatory proposals →	Veto rights →	Mandatory proposals
1. Bylaws	X	X	X
2. Articles of incorporation	X	X	X
3. State of incorporation	X	X	X

Both displays demonstrate the significance of single impact positions of shareholders in the corporate decision-making process to amend the rules-of-the-game within the entire range of given means. In this context, the right of shareholders to mandate bylaw amendments under current U.S. corporate law (Display I) is easily recognizable as the only means for shareholders to mandate the initiation of an amendment to a rule-of-the-

313 *Id.* at 844 et seq.

314 BAINBRIDGE, CORPORATION LAW AND ECONOMICS 45- 48 (2002); Hammermesh, 73 TUL. L. REV. 409, 479 (1998).

315 Bebchuk, 118 HARV. L. REV. 833, 857 (2005): Due to the fact that the risk of a proxy challenge is very low, and its success even less likely since the access to the corporate ballot is restricted and the reimbursement of campaign expenses as well.

316 *Id.* at 857 et seq. (2005).

game. It is the key to increased shareholder influence at the level of mandatory initiation and the later analyzed type of rules laid down on this level explains why it is of particular importance for active shareholders. Display II shows the significance of the right to mandate bylaw amendments from a shareholder primacy viewpoint as the first of the three mandatory shareholder initiation rights on the lowest of the three rule levels.

ii) Under German corporate law

The German system of the rules-of-the-game systematically differs in several ways from the one under U.S.-American law. Regarding the rule-setting levels, Germany provides only one uniform federal corporate law. Accordingly, rule-setting levels are reduced to the level of the articles of incorporation and bylaws. At the bylaw level, a further difference is that German law provides for separate bylaws (*Geschäftsordnungen "**GO**")* for all three organs of a corporation, including the management board, the supervisory board, and the shareholder meeting.

The following table displays the means by which shareholders participate in rule-of-the-game decisions according to current German corporate law:

<u>Display III: Shareholder impact rule-of-the-game amendments, German corporate law</u>

Rule level/Impact level:	Veto rights	→Mandatory proposal
1. Shareholder meeting-*GO*	X	X
2. Supervisory board-*GO*	-	-
3. Management board–*GO*	-	-
4. Articles of incorporation	X	X

Display III demonstrates the shareholders' initiation and veto right on the rule-of-the-game level of the shareholder meeting's *Geschäftsordnung* and the articles of incorporation.

b) Designing corporate rules

Another relevant aspect for the shareholder impact upon the corporate decision-making process is the design of the rules-of-the-game. Besides the opportunity to set up *mandatory* or *default* rules, it is also necessary for a rule-setter to consciously distinguish between the different types of private ordering. For instance, under a system of *opting in*, the default rule does not provide for a certain arrangement such as shareholder proxy access, but the corporation may decide to opt into the arrangement by deciding (initiation and approval) in favor of such an amendment of the rules-of-the-game on the relevant rule level. *Opting out*, in contrast, allows a corporation to decide against a certain corporate governance default rule as long as the amendment is initiated and approved as provided for in the decision-making process on the concerned rule level.[317]

317 Young/The Corporate Library for the CII, *The Limits of Private Ordering: Restrictions on Shareholders' Ability to Initiate Governance Change and Distortion of the Shareholder Voting*

Lawmakers under U.S. law usually approach two alternative arrangements by asking which one a fully informed and rational shareholder would have most likely have chosen as the one more likely to serve shareholder value,[318] according to the hypothetical bargain approach.[319] They usually take into account the choice between mandatory and default rules, but usually not the asymmetries of available means to impact the corporate decision-making process to amend a rule-of-the-game between shareholders and administration. These are not only important for the choice of the proper default rule[320] but also for the proper choice between mandatory and default rules.[321] In designing rules, lawmakers must particularly take into account the restricted shareholder impact on the corporate decision-making process, including the amendments of the rules-of-the-game requiring initiation and approval.

In the *United States*, shareholders are currently not able to initiate amendments of the *articles of incorporation*; only the administration is able to do so, while shareholders need to approve corresponding amendments.[322] The articles of incorporation may determine the "shares entitled to vote upon" an amendment of the articles of incorporation as well as the number of affirmative votes required for its approval, §§ 151(a), 102(b)(4) DGCL[323]. Approval requires at least a majority of the outstanding shares entitled to vote thereon, § 242(b)(1). In practice, many corporations have hindered approvals by adopting even stricter approval requirements which may also vary from one share/one vote, such as supermajority requirements, use of the denominator of shares outstanding instead of the votes cast, and capital structure amendments.[324] Similar restrictions apply on the *bylaw* level. Shareholders were for a long time not able to securely mandate the initiation of an amendment of governance arrangements through a bylaw amendment

Process, http://www.cii.org/UserFiles/file/The%20Limits%20of%20Private%20Ordering%20UPDATED%2011-17-09.pdf (2009).

318 EASTERBROOK & FISCHEL, THE ECONOMIC STRUCTURE OF CORPORATE LAW 15 (1991).

319 Bebchuk & Hamdani, 96 NW. U. L. REV. 489, 491 (2002).

320 *Id.* at 492.

321 Young/The Corporate Library for the CII, *The Limits of Private Ordering: Restrictions on Shareholders' Ability to Initiate Governance Change and Distortion of the Shareholder Voting Process*, http://www.cii.org/UserFiles/file/The%20Limits%20of%20Private%20Ordering%20UPDATED%2011-17-09.pdf (2009): Stating in the context of proxy access and private ordering that due to governance arrangements restricting the shareholder initiation right (mandatory initiation rights of shareholders aiming to amend the corporate bylaws face supermajority requirements) as well as the proportional expression of opinion of a shareholder majority (deviations from one share one vote) through a confirming majority resolution, private ordering may not be the right choice for certain arrangements.

322 § 242 (b)(1) DGCL; SEC STAFF LEGAL BULLETIN NO. 14D (CF), SHAREHOLDER PROPOSALS (2008); BALOTTI & FINKELSTEIN, THE DELAWARE LAW OF CORPORATIONS AND BUSINESS ORGANIZATIONS, Vol. 1, § 8.1 (2010); Bebchuk & Hamdani, 96 NW. U. L. REV. 489, 492 (2002).

323 *See* introductory remarks for limitation to Delaware corporate law (A.II.2.). Any sections in subpart two of this Part I (C.II.) without further determination refer to the DGCL.

324 Young/The Corporate Library for the CII, *The Limits of Private Ordering: Restrictions on Shareholders' Ability to Initiate Governance Change and Distortion of the Shareholder Voting Process* 8, http://www.cii.org/UserFiles/file/The%20Limits%20of%20Private%20Ordering%20UPDATED%2011-17-09.pdf (2009).

with regard to Rule 14a-8(i)(1) SEA as long as state law did not explicitly permit its use[325]. Furthermore, the approval requirements are often hard to achieve, as it often does not suffice to have the support of the majority of the votes cast for the amendment. If corporations have not prohibited the amendment of bylaws through shareholders, as few corporations have done, they may have imposed supermajority requirements, as many corporations have done, or installed two or more classes of voting stock and disparate voting rights, as in some corporations.[326]

In *Germany*, shareholder impact on the corporate decision-making process, including the amendment of rules-of-the-game, is different. Shareholders may initiate amendments of the *articles of incorporation* even by minority demand according to § 122. Since the implementation of the KonTraG in 1998, German corporate law has prohibited multiple votes per share, § 12 (2).[327] However, the approval of an amendment to the articles of incorporation generally requires a supermajority vote of three-fourths of the capital present during the shareholder meeting. But the articles of incorporation can go down to 50 % + 1, § 179 (2). The same applies to the *Geschäftsordnung* of the shareholder meeting, where shareholders may initiate an amendment but generally need to have the amendment approved by three-fourths of the represented capital, § 129 (1) sent. 1. An exception applies to an amendment cancelling the *Geschäftsordnung*, for which a simple majority of the votes cast suffices.[328]

The demonstrated limitations of shareholder impact resulting from certain rule designs should therefore be kept in mind by rule designers when deciding between mandatory and default rules as well as the different kinds of default rules.

3) Introducing hypothesis regarding the impact of active shareholders on nomination and election procedures

Active shareholders aim to increase their control over the administration to reduce agency costs. The shareholders' right to nominate and elect members of the administration represents their most influential formal means to assure that members of the administration remain responsive to their interests. The impact of active shareholders on the nomination and election procedures is therefore decisive for the degree of responsiveness of the administration, as it determines about their potential to improve the effectiveness of the nomination and election process. While weak nomination and election provisions may grant shareholders hardly any impact on the composition of the members of the administration, more effective nomination and election rules may grant shareholders

325 As it is now the case with proxy access in Delaware according to § 112 DGCL, see *infra* in the section on the proxy access rule.

326 Young/The Corporate Library for the CII, *The Limits of Private Ordering: Restrictions on Shareholders' Ability to Initiate Governance Change and Distortion of the Shareholder Voting Process* 6-8, http://www.cii.org/UserFiles/file/The%20Limits%20of%20Private%20Ordering%20UPDATED%2011-17-09.pdf (2009).

327 Heider, in: MüKo, AktG, § 12 mn.10.

328 *Id.*

greater influence while simultaneously restricting the administration's influence on its composition. The initiation and approval right of shareholders during the corporate decision-making process on the amendment of the rules-of-the-game on the relevant level is determinative of shareholder impact on the nomination and election procedures, unless protected by minority standards by law. Therefore, the stronger the shareholder impact on the decision process to amend rules on the relevant level, the better active shareholders may assure that the agents become increasingly responsive to the interests of the principals. This structure allows shareholders to implement a procedure justified by the theory of shareholder primacy and an enlightened shareholder approach. It assures that agents will be kept accountable for opportunistic behavior, reducing agency costs significantly.

It should therefore be assumed that the U.S. legal system of corporate governance, which is held to be one of shareholder primacy, either mandates corporate governance rules that assure a corresponding responsiveness or allows (active) shareholders to amend these accordingly. A system with a shareholder structure historically characterized mainly by freefloat justifies the assumption that the existing corporate governance rules have focused on balancing the interests of the administration and widely dispersed shareholders. Accordingly, shareholders should be provided with efficient means to bundle their votes, allowing them to keep the administration responsive to their interests by an accountability mechanism with effective nomination and election rules. However, as already indicated by shareholder influence on the corporate decision process to amend rules-of-the-game, shareholders' ability to facilitate accountability-enhancing rule changes seems to be rather limited. Though one could assume that the nomination and election rules in place already assure the necessary accountability, past management-orientated U.S. politics justify a different expectation.

The German corporate governance system, with its historic stakeholder approach, raises the expectation that statutory corporate governance rules restrict the impact of (active) shareholders on the nomination and election of administrative members as well as the means employed to amend the procedures to keep the interests of shareholders and stakeholders balanced. Even though proponents of the (modified) shareholder primacy approach have become increasingly numerous and the growing impact of the capital market will support this development, it can be assumed that rules in favor of increased directorial accountability will only increase over time. These assumptions are supported by the still prevailing blockholder structure, which shifted agency issues to the relationship between minority and majority shareholders with the expectation that corporate governance rules tend to focus on minority protection rather than on shareholder primacy. A parallel process represents the shift in from a blockholder structure to one with increasing freefloat. This development underscores the assumption that the German corporate governance system may need to react to the related shift in agency issues to the relationship between shareholders and management. By introducing provisions that grant shareholders more impact on the nomination and election of directors, this would reduce resulting agency costs. With regards to these assumptions, the results of the general impact of shareholders on the amendments of the corporate rules-of-the-game appear contradictory. This leads rather to the notion that shareholder impact under the current nomination and election regime may be comparably larger than under U.S. corporate law.

In this context, it may be further assumed that active shareholders can raise consciousness about the need for increasing shareholder impact regarding the current nomination and election regime in specific and the amendment of rules-of-the-game in general. They have the financial means to overcome given legal or practical barriers.

II) Shareholder impact on the nomination and election procedures under U.S.-American law

1) Introduction

The following analysis on U.S. law will focus on four issues related to shareholder impact in the context of the accountability mechanism of the nomination and election of directors: the general shareholder impact on the initiation of amendments of rules-of-the-game at the relevant rule level as well as the status quo and, where necessary, the permissibility of the shareholder-initiated implementation of proxy access, majority voting, and the cumulative-voting rule. All four issues have been subjects of ongoing debates involving several SEC no-action letters, court proceedings, and SEC rule proposals and releases.

2) Context of directorial nomination and election process

In order to ease the understanding of the matter and to permit easier comparison with German corporate law, the analysis will briefly focus on the context of the nomination and election rules, including the removal of directors and the impact of the board of directors on executive officer positions.

a) Removal of directors

The significance of increased shareholder impact on the nomination and election of directors depends on the removal strategy. It refers to removal from office at the end of the term as well as early removal opportunities. Regarding the former, the default rule for the length of the term of office under U.S. corporate law is one year, while the maximum length for staggered terms is three years.[329] According to the default rule for early removal, directors may be removed with or without cause by holders of a majority of shares entitled to vote during the election of directors, § 141 (k). Due to the short default

329 § 141 (b) DGCL for staggered boards, only a fraction of its members is elected each year with the total office term lasting three years; KRAAKMAN ET AL., THE ANATOMY OF CORPORATE LAW 61 n.28 (2009).

term length, early removals are of little practical significance. Of greater significance is therefore the annual nomination and election of directors.

b) Appointment and removal of executive officers

While the executive officers formulate and implement the corporate business policy, § 141(a), the board determines the larger medium- and long-term guidelines for the business and corporate policy and controls the decisions and actions of the executive officers via appointment and removal.[330]

The board of directors enjoys great liberty regarding the appointment and removal of corporate executive officers.[331] Usually, corporate bylaws specify the details of the lengths of the term of office and the prerequisites for a removal. Terms of office usually last for one year. Even though some states, excluding Delaware, require that executive officers stay in office for one year, the board of directors may prolong their term. Bylaws often determine that the board may remove an officer whenever it is in the best interest of the corporation.[332] In practice, the board of directors may therefore remove officers at any time, with or without delay and with or without reason regardless of the employment contract.[333]

Due to the great flexibility given to the board of directors regarding the appointment and removal of executive officers, the influence of (active) shareholders on the composition of the board of directors may result in the board using flexible control mechanism more efficiently to reduce agency issues and related costs. Depending on the exact arrangement of the targeted corporation, the boards of large public corporations may meet only a few times a year to make fundamental strategic corporate decisions, while most management tasks are delegated to the executive officers.[334] The influence on the composition of the (executive) officers therefore represents an increasingly important mechanism to control the management of large public corporations, who make the majority of corporate decisions.

The limited presence of the directors, however, allows reasonable doubts about the effectiveness of the board's control of the managing executive officers.[335] Shareholder activism aiming to increase the effectiveness of accountability mechanisms applying to the monitors should therefore be welcome as a means to make the monitors' control of the increasingly more influential executive officers more efficient.

---

330 Gillan & Starks, *The Evolution of Shareholder Activism in the United States* 11, www.ssrn.com/abstract=959670 (2007).

331 Merkt/Göthel, US-amerikanisches Gesellschaftsrecht, 2006, mn.606.

332 Hamilton, Corporations 1218 (1992).

333 Merkt/Göthel, US-amerikanisches Gesellschaftsrecht, 2006, mn.606.

334 *Id.* at mn.568.

335 Merkt/Göthel, US-Amerikanisches Gesellschaftsrecht, 2006, mn.568.

c) Practical relevance of nominating committees

Many large corporations have installed nominating committees. These are responsible for evaluating the performance of incumbent directors to determine whether they should be retained or replaced.[336] Furthermore, they control the work of officers and determine successors for top management positions.[337] Today, an increasingly accepted view is that independent, non-managing directors should occupy nominating committees.[338] NYSE[339] and NASDAQ[340] even require that the entire committee or at least a majority of it consist of independent directors. Accordingly, active shareholders in large public corporations who succeed in obtaining board representation will not necessarily be able to influence the determination of successors for officer positions. Doing so may require pressure from a broad basis of shareholders or even holding a seat on the nominating committee. Usually, representatives of or active shareholders on the board are independent and therefore represent potential candidates for the nominating committee.

3) Legal analysis of the four issues related to nomination and election procedures

a) A closer look at the four issues

The first and more general issue is whether shareholders should be generally allowed to mandate the initiation of bylaws amendments according to state law, as nomination and election procedures are mainly laid down on the bylaw level. This first issue represents at the same time a key for the implementation of the other three issues. It is a controversial issue, as granting shareholders this power calls into question the authority of the directors of a corporation to manage the business and affairs of the corporation. Its importance results from the fact that amending the bylaws is the most significant method under U.S. corporate law for shareholders to initiate a change in corporate policy without the board's concurrence.[341]

The second legal issue is whether shareholders should be allowed to implement a proxy access rule, which would provide certain shareholders under specific preconditions with a relevant and practical means of nominating candidates for a director position. This issue is significant because it would allow concerned shareholders to include information about their nominees in the corporation's proxy materials distributed to the shareholders before the shareholder meeting without having to pay the significant costs

336 Cox & Hazen, Corporations § 9.16 (2003).
337 *Id.*; Merkt/Göthel, US-Amerikanisches Gesellschaftsrecht, 2006, mn.602.
338 Cox & Hazen, Corporations § 9. 16 (2003); Merkt/Göthel, US-Amerikanisches Gesellschaftsrecht, 2006, mn.602.
339 § 303A.04(a) NYSE Listed Company Manual.
340 NASDAQ Stock Market Rule 4350(c)(4)(A).
341 Bloomenthal, Securities Law Handbook, Vol. 1, § 18.76 (2009-2010).

usually required when shareholders launch a proxy contest using their own proxy materials.

The third issue is whether shareholders should be allowed to implement a majority-voting rule for director elections. Such a rule would conflict with the prevailing default standard of plurality voting in the United States, under which the candidate to be elected is required to obtain votes in favor or, in the rare case of a contested election, more votes than the competing candidate(s). The majority-voting rule demands that the nominee receives the majority of the votes cast in order to be elected. Its introduction is closely related to efforts to increase the responsiveness of elected directors to the interests of voting shareholders.

Finally, the fourth issue relates to the cumulative-voting rule, which enables shareholders electing candidates for several vacant director positions to concentrate all of their votes on one candidate. In contrast to the prevailing direct voting rule, it assures a more proportional representation of the ownership structure on the board of directors. Such proportional board representation provides stronger minorities among shareholders the opportunity to assure that their interests are represented on the board.

b) Starting point mandatory shareholder proposals

The most important and efficient way for active shareholders under U.S.-American corporate law to initiate changes to the rules-of-the-game in a public corporation is the shareholder proposal according to Rule 14a-8 SEA. The purpose of Rule 14a-8 SEA is to prevent management from using discretionary voting authority to effectively shut down shareholders from being able to propose alternative courses of corporate action. Furthermore, Rule 14a-8 SEA provides a vehicle for shareholders to inform management of their concerns and for shareholders to communicate with each other.[342] It "addresses when a company must include a shareholder's proposal in its proxy statement and identify the proposal in its form of proxy when the company holds an annual or special meeting of shareholders. In summary, in order to have [a] shareholder['s] proposal included on a company's proxy card, and included along with any supporting statement in its proxy statement, [he] must be eligible and follow certain procedures. Under a few specific circumstances, the company is permitted to exclude [a shareholder's] proposal, but only after submitting its reasons to the Commission. ... In order to be eligible to submit a proposal [a shareholder] must have continuously held at least $2,000 in market value, or 1%, of the company's securities entitled to be voted on the proposal at the meeting for at least one year by the date [the shareholder] submit[s] the proposal. [The shareholder] must continue to hold those securities through the date of the meeting." Procedural requirements comprise the shareholder's "written statement that [he] continuously held the required number of shares for the one-year period as of the date of the statement; and ... [t]he proposal, including any accompanying supporting statement, may not exceed 500 words. ... If [the shareholder] ha[s] complied with the procedural requirements, ... [the] company [may] rely [on 13 substantive grounds] to exclude [the shareholder's proposal. One of

342 ROMANEK ET AL., SHAREHOLDER PROPOSALS HANDBOOK § 1-3 (2001).

them is worded as follows:] (i) ... (1) ... If the proposal is not a proper subject for action by shareholders under the laws of the jurisdiction of the company's organization; ... ." Rule 14a-8 SEA is mainly used by shareholders to raise questions of social or political importance concerning the corporation. More recently, it has been often used for matters of corporate governance,[343] such as takeover defenses, the board of directors, executive compensation, corporate responsibility, voting issues, and the sale of the company. Rule 14a-8 SEA allows a shareholder to include a proposal in the corporation's proxy materials at the issuer's expense. The company and therefore indirectly all other shareholders rather than the proponent have to bear the costs of the proposal.[344]

A shareholder proposal is usually precatory, but in the context of bylaw amendments state law grants shareholders the opportunity to *mandate* the initiation of an amendment, § 109. It is the mandatory character of this initiation right to amend the bylaws that makes it so important for active shareholders.

Issues related to the use of this *mandatory* shareholder initiation right usually become relevant at the level of the substantial exclusions contained in Rule 14a-8(i) SEA. The substantial exclusions under Rule 14a-8(i)(1) and (8) SEA, relating to the "legality under state law" and the "election of directors," are particularly relevant to the analysis of the issues discussed in this work. Regarding the possible exclusion of shareholder proposals based on one of the substantial exclusions, the Commission has almost completely delegated the interpretation of Rule 14a-8 SEA to its staff, as reasoned in *Committee for Human Rights v. SEC*[345]. The interpretation and application of Rule 14a-8 SEA is therefore almost exclusively the preserve of the staff; only the many staff letters each year have given the Rule its substantive meaning. The company has the burden to demonstrate that it is entitled to exclude the proposal for substantial reasons.[346] An appeals court review of the staff decisions is only possible if the Commission allowed it; therefore, few court decisions on Rule 14a-8 SEA exist.[347]

c) Exclusion under Rule 14a-8(i)(1) SEA

The substantial exclusion of Rule 14a-8(i)(1) SEA is relevant to the analysis of the first legal issue at stake, the validity of a mandatory bylaw amendment shareholder proposal to change nomination and election procedures. According to Rule 14a-8(i)(1) SEA, a company may exclude a proposal "if the proposal is not a proper subject for action by shareholders under the laws of the jurisdiction of the company's organization."

343 *Id.* at § 1-5; Cox et al., Securities Regulation 908 (2004).

344 Commissioner Paul S. Atkins/SEC, *Shareholder Rights, the 2008 Proxy Season, and the Impact of Shareholder Activism*, July 22, 2008, http://www.sec.gov/news/speech/2008/spch072208psa.htm#P26_5116.

345 Haft, Analysis of Key SEC No-Action Letters 220 (2005-2006).

346 Rule 14a-8(g) SEA; as initially stated by the Commission in Exchange Act Release 4979, 1954, http://content.lawyerlinks.com/default.htm#http://content.lawyerlinks.com/library/sec/sec_releases/34-4979.htm, later repeated by the courts, amongst others, by Medical Comm. for Human Rights v. SEC, 432 F.2d 659, 674 (D.C. Cir. 1970).

347 Med. Comm. for Human Rights v. SEC, 432 F.2d 659 (D.C. Cir. 1970).

i) *Rule 14a-8(i)(1) SEA in general*

The purpose of the exclusion is to prevent shareholders from proposing actions that represent an improper subject for a shareholder vote.[348] The intention is to allow the corporation to omit proposals involving acts that under state law may only be decided by the board of directors. The direct adoption of such an action by shareholder proposal would therefore ignore the statutory role of directors.[349] Three issues are relevant under this exclusion. The most controversial point is the evaluation of the appropriate division of corporate power between directors and shareholders according to the law of the state of incorporation. Since there is little state law precedent on the question of whether an action is proper for shareholders apart from the director's authority, there is very little guidance for the SEC staff on this legal issue.[350] Closely related is the conflict between state laws, which regulate substantive corporate matters such as the issues shareholders may present at a shareholder meeting, and federal law, which regulates procedural matters such as disclosure.[351] Finally, a third related issue concerns the more specific distinction between precatory shareholder proposals that ask the board to take a certain action and mandatory shareholder proposals that mandate the board to take a certain action. It is the staff's assumption that precatory proposals are proper under state law, whereas mandatory proposals are generally treated as improper. Consequently, in practice proponents formulate their proposals in a precatory manner.[352] The main holdings under this exclusion therefore concern mandatory bylaw proposals.

ii) *Mandatory bylaw amendment proposals under Rule 14a-8(i)(1) SEA*

Under state law, substantially all corporate decisions need to be initiated by the board of directors and those that involve fundamental changes need to be approved by the shareholders.[353] An important exception to the general rule that shareholders lack authority to initiate corporate decisions is their authority to launch shareholder proposals, including mandating additions, repeals, or amendments of bylaws.[354] Recently, shareholder-adopted bylaws have been discovered as a means to limit director authority. As mandatory initiation of bylaw amendments, these proposals represent the only means for shareholders to mandate the initiation of rules-of-the-game amendments that are of particular importance to active shareholders pursuing their "voice" strategy. In addition, bylaws may cover a very broad range of topics, such as the business of the corporation, the con-

348 Romanek & Krus, Mergers & Acquisitions § 14-5 (2002).
349 *Id.*
350 *Id.* at § 14-6.
351 *Id.* at § 14-7.
352 *Id.* at § 14-10.
353 Haft, Analysis of Key SEC No-Action Letters 264 (2005-2006).
354 *Id.*

duct of its affairs, the shareholder's, director's, officer's, and employee's affairs, as long as they conform to the certificate of incorporation, § 109(b).[355]

Most states allow shareholders to adopt, amend, or repeal bylaws without board agreement.[356] To restrict this power, the articles of incorporation may require a supermajority quorum of seventy-five percent of the outstanding shares to approve a new bylaw.[357] Many states place the bylaw amendment beyond repeal or amendment of the board, § 10.20(a)(2) RMBCA; other states allow the board to amend the bylaws if the certificate of incorporation provides for it, as long as shareholders are not divested of their right to amend the bylaws, § 109(a)[358].[359] The board of directors, on the other hand, is authorized to manage the business and affairs of the corporation according to § 141(a).[360] The existence of both provisions allows two interpretations regarding the admissibility of mandatory bylaws: either the board is the ultimate repository of all corporate power and authority or any deviation from that may be expressed in the certificate of incorporation and the cross-reference to other provisions may be read with reference to § 109(b).[361] As a consequence, it was for a long time highly controversial whether state law permitted shareholders to submit mandatory bylaw amendments concerning procedures relating to the directors. The following will analyze the main movements regarding this essential debate before analyzing the status quo.

(1) SEC staff decisions

Since there were few state court decisions on the conflict of shareholder bylaw authority and administrative authority, it was the duty of the SEC staff to make its own evaluation on the issue.[362] Several SEC no-action letters[363] in the 1990s signaled increased shareholder interest in using mandatory bylaw amendments to limit the authority of the board of directors. It was the obligation of the corporation to establish the ground for the exclusion of such a proposal. This is best exemplified by the *SEC-NAL of PLM International Inc.*[364] It involved a later slightly amended mandatory shareholder proposal

---

355 "The bylaws may contain any provision, not inconsistent with law or with the certificate of incorporation, relating to the business of the corporation, the conduct of its affairs, and its rights or powers or the rights or powers of its stockholders, directors, officers and employees."

356 Haft, Analysis of Key SEC No-Action Letters 246 (2005/2006).

357 *Id.*

358 "[T]he power to adopt, amend or repeal bylaws shall be in the stockholders entitled to vote . . . provided, however, any corporation may, in its certificate of incorporation, confer, the power to adopt, amend or repeal bylaws upon the directors . . . . The fact that such power has been so conferred upon the directors . . . shall not divest the stockholders . . . of the power, nor limit the power to adopt, amend or repeal bylaws."

359 Hammermesh, 73 Tul. L. Rev. 409, 415 et seq.

360 "The business and affairs of every corporation organized under this chapter shall be managed by or under the direction of a board of directors, except as may be otherwise provided in the chapter or in its certificate of incorporation."

361 Coffee, 51 U. Miami L. Rev. 605 (1997).

362 Romanek & Krus, Mergers & Acquisitions § 14-21 (2002).

363 From now on abbreviated as SEC-NAL.

364 SEC No-Action Letter, 1997 WL 219918 (Apr. 28, 1997).

relating to a bylaw amendment to terminate defensive measures under certain circumstances unless the majority of shareholders approved of such measures. The company in this case objected to the amended proposal on (c)(1) grounds.[365] It argued that the proposal would lead to an impermissible restriction of the statutory and fiduciary duties of the board under section 141(a), which vests in the board of directors the authority to manage the corporate enterprise. This provision has been interpreted in Delaware court decisions[366] to mean that corporate power may not be delegated to others or substantially restricted unless such measures are provided for in the certificate of incorporation. Furthermore, the counsel of the issuer pointed out that the proposal was not authorized by section 109(b) either. He determined it as inconsistent with section 141(a) and the board's fiduciary duty to act in connection with matters at the heart of the business and affairs of the corporation, such as the duty to evaluate and respond to takeover bids.[367] He therefore argued that section 141(a) prevails over section 109(b). The proponent's counsel, after illustrating the right of shareholders to amend bylaws as long as consistent with the law, pointed out a different interpretation of section 141(a).[368] Focusing on the interpretation of "business and affairs" of the corporation in section 141(a), the proponent's counsel underlined the very breadth of this phrase, which would also cover the takeover defenses at stake in the case. His main argument was that section 141(a) was not intended to prevent the adoption of bylaws that give stockholders decision-making power over the business and affairs of the corporation, since otherwise section 109(b) would have little meaning due to the enumerated areas shareholder-initiated bylaws relate to. Concerning the case law pointed out by the issuer's counsel, the proponent's counsel argued that such cases never addressed the validity of shareholder-amended bylaws but rather the transfer of the board's power (managerial function) to others, including shareholder attempts to determine the result of a board vote through a voting agreement.[369] The proponent's counsel concluded that the authority of the board according to section 141(a) does not preclude the adoption of a shareholder bylaw relating to the company's business and affairs.[370] Further, the legal counsel of the corporation admitted that neither the proponent nor the company could be sure of the interpretation of § 141(a) until the issue was resolved by the Delaware courts.[371] The proponent's counsel stated he had not found any Delaware case that invalidated a bylaw because of its inconsistency with § 141(a).[372] The staff did not agree with the company's view to exclude the proposal under Rule 14a-8(c)(1) SEA as an improper subject for shareholder action under applicable state law. It emphasized that the inappropriateness of a shareholder action appeared to be an unset-

365 Equals the current Rule 14a-8 (i)(1) SEA, letters (c) and (i) were exchanged without consequence in the substance of the exclusions.

366 For many: Grimes v. Donald, 673 A.2d 1207, 1214 (Del. 1996); Paramount Commc'ns, Inc. v. OVC Network Inc., 637 A.2d 34, 51 (Del. 1994).

367 PLM International, Inc., SEC No-Action Letter, 1997 WL 219918, at 14 (Apr. 28, 1997).

368 *Id.* at 17.

369 *Id.* at 18.

370 *Id.* at 18, 30.

371 France Braun & Martel LLP, Apr. 14, 1997, at 2 (incoming letter).

372 PLM International, Inc., SEC No-Action Letter, 1997 WL 219918, at 18, 30 (Apr. 28, 1997).

tled point under Delaware law and that the corporation was consequently not able to rely on Rule 14a-8(i)(1) SEA to exclude the proposal.[373]

In a major change of position in 1999, the staff repeatedly issued *"no-opinion" letters*[374] if neither counsel provided compelling state law precedent or legal authority, based on the fact that the interpretation of the law was unclear. The staff's uncertainty about the issue was also reflected in different positions it took in subsequent years. In 2000, the staff seemed to be inclined to evaluate bylaw amendments restricting board authority as improper under state law.[375] Shortly after the staff tried to get around the issue again[376] and during the 2002 proxy season issued three no-action letters to Atlas Air Worldwide,[377] Toys "R" Us,[378] and Mattel,[379] allowing them to exclude shareholder bylaw proposals. A 2007 proposal requiring shareholder approval for severance agreements in excess of 2.99 times the sum of the executive's base salary plus bonus presented to Halliburton by Amalgamated Bank Long View Collective Investment Fund gave hope to active shareholders, as the SEC was unable to concur on whether the proposal should be excluded.[380] Their hope was based on the fact that in all other cases where the staff declined to state an opinion or even issued a no-action letter, the only recourse for proponents had been to take the issue to the courts in order to compel the inclusion or to drop the mandatory aspect of the proposal.[381] The staff's initial change of position, however, resulted in a change of the burden of proof towards the proponent, since the proponent as plaintiff before court has to prove the grounds of his claim. Consequently, mandatory proposals brought before courts tended to be excluded rather than included.[382]

(2) Court decisions

Unfortunately, Delaware courts had left this important issue of state law unsolved. Before the *PLM International, Inc. SEC-NAL* was decided, the Oklahoma Supreme Court, whose decision was of particular importance since Oklahoma and Delaware have substantially similar corporate statutes, held in *Brotherhood of Teamster General Fund v. Fleming Co., Inc.*[383] that shareholders could propose mandatory bylaw amendments as

---

373 *Id.* at 32.

374 Community Bancshares, Inc., SEC No-Action Letter, 1999 WL 166982 (Mar. 15, 1999): Concerned bylaw proposals on director/president qualification, SEC decided not to express a view, because of a lack of legal authority; Union Carbide Corp., SEC No-Action Letter, 1999 WL 58519 (Feb. 5, 1999): Concerned a bylaw amendment introducing the requirement of a shareholder approval in order to adopt/amend a shareholder rights plan, SEC issued "no-view" letter because of lack of any legal authority.

375 Novell, Inc., SEC No-Action Letter, 2000 WL 223715 (Feb. 14, 2000).

376 Emcor Group, Inc., SEC No-Action Letter, 2000 WL 631012 (May 16, 2000).

377 Atlas Air Worldwide Holdings, Inc., SEC No-Action Letter, 2002 WL 1058533 (Apr. 5, 2002).

378 Toys "R" Us, Inc., SEC No-Action Letter, 2002 WL 1058521 (Apr. 9, 2002).

379 Mattel Inc., SEC No-Action Letter, 2002 WL 833515 (Mar. 25, 2002).

380 Halliburton Co., SEC No-Action Letter, 2007 WL 754961 (Mar. 15, 2007).

381 Haft, Analysis of Key SEC No-Action Letters 265 (2005/2006).

382 *Id.*

383 975 P.2d 907 (Okla. 1999).

long as the certificate of incorporation did not provide otherwise. The case concerned a bylaw that made the implementation or maintenance of a shareholder rights plan dependent on a majority shareholder vote. The board of directors argued that it was within its authority to create and issue a shareholder rights plan that could not be restricted by a shareholder-initiated bylaw amendment. The shareholders, on the other hand, argued that they had authority under Oklahoma state law to adopt bylaws addressing a broad range of topics concerning the corporation's business, corporate affairs, and the rights and powers of shareholders and directors according to 18 O.S. 1991 § 1013 OGCA.[384] The court reasoned that even though shareholders' direct authority was limited in order to allow large corporations to function in their day-by-day work, the work of the board of directors was not without oversight.[385] Shareholders did have the right to amend bylaws concerning a wide range of matters; only the articles of incorporation could restrict this authority. But the court could find neither Oklahoma law, which gave exclusive authority to a corporation's board of directors for the formulation of shareholder rights plans, nor any other authority that precluded shareholders from proposing bylaw amendments.[386] Furthermore, the court pointed out that the board's argument was based on the equivalent interpretation of the term "corporation" and "board of directors" in the relevant provision.[387] But the General Corporation Act and the relevant provision § 1038 OGCA distinguished both terms, and the court declined to transfer the power of the corporation automatically to the authority of the board.[388] It cited authority[389] in favor of shareholder ratification of stock option plans, which neither the OGCA nor the silence of the articles of incorporations on the issue contradicted,[390] and the failure to the legislator to adopt a shareholder rights plan endorsement statute. The court held that corporate boards could well be subject to general procedures of corporate governance imposed by means of bylaw amendment.[391]

Later, in Quickturn Design Systems, Inc. v. Mentor Graphics,[392] a case that involved a bylaw amendment implementing a delayed redemption provision, the Delaware Supreme Court held such a procedure to be invalid. The judges reasoned that, even though the exercise of business judgment by the board of directors is not absolute and is constrained by the fiduciary duties of board members, "[o]ne of the most basic tenets of Delaware corporation law is that the board of directors has the ultimate responsibility for managing the business and affairs of a corporation. Section 141(a) requires that any limitation

384 *Id.* at 910.

385 *Id.* at 911.

386 *Id.* at 908.

387 18 O.S. 1991 § 1038 concerns the issue of stock options. It also applies to shareholder rights plans.

388 Bhd. of Teamster Gen. Fund v. Fleming, 975 P.2d 907, 911 (Okla. 1999).

389 Michelson v. Duncan, 407 A. 2d 211, 218-20 (Del. 1979): pointing out that stock option plans can be subject to shareholder approval; Robert A. Wachsler, Inc., v. Florafax Int'l, 778 F.2d 547 (10th Cir. 1985): shareholders can ratify an interested director's contract if fully informed; 26 U.S.C. §§ 422 (b)(1) & 423 (b)(2): authority for shareholder approval of stock option plans.

390 Bhd. of Teamster v. Flemmings, 975 P.2d 907, 912 (Okla. 1999).

391 *Id.* at 913.

392 Quickturn Design Sys., Inc. v. Shapiro, 721 A.2d 1281 (Del. 1998).

on the board's authority has to be set out in the certificate of incorporation."[393] This could be interpreted to mean that mandatory bylaw amendments cannot restrict the ability of the board to carry out its fiduciary duty to manage the business and affairs of the corporation unless the amendment is set out in the certificate of incorporation.[394] However, the proposal related to the implementation of a *specific* delayed redemption provision.

General DataComm v. State of Wisconsin Investment Board[395] concerned a mandatory bylaw proposal of shareholders that would have restricted the ability of the board to re-price its stock options without shareholder approval. The Chancery Court had the opportunity to decide whether a mandatory shareholder bylaw was valid, but it did not rule on this issue. Instead, it pointed out that the shareholders had not adopted the proposal and declared the matter not ripe for consideration.[396] This outcome was repeated years later in Bebchuk v. CA, Inc.[397] Vice Chancellor Lamb refused plaintiff's claim for declaratory judgment on a shareholder bylaw proposal concerning the introduction of an approval requirement for the adoption or extension of poison pills on grounds of ripeness,[398] though he indicated that such a bylaw could potentially be valid[399].

Consequently, the interpretation of the relationship between section 109(a) and section 141(a), and therefore the legality of mandatory bylaw proposals, remained open. In combination with the SEC's long-term policy to issue "no-view" letters, it resulted in a high burden for shareholders trying to amend bylaws via mandatory proposals.

(3) Legal scholars

Legal arguments for and against shareholder-mandated bylaw amendments presented to the SEC and courts provide strong support for both sides. A third and distinct approach was provided by academics, which distinguished valid shareholder-mandated bylaw amendments from invalid ones. The most recognized and elaborated of these approaches is that of *Coffee*,[400] who proposed four different ways to distinguish valid from excludable proposals. According to his *first* approach, proposals concerning ordinary matters have to be distinguished from proposals concerning fundamental matters. Coffee determined that only the latter category is proper for a mandatory bylaw amendment proposal. This approach allows shareholders to exert greater control over managers when managers' conflicting personal interests may influence the efficacy of other legal and market controls. Still, fundamental decisions would be carved out from the manager's routine function, which courts call "the business and affairs of the corporation." Coffee's *second* approach distinguishes bylaws that contain affirmative orders from bylaws that comprise negative constraints on the board. Coffee determined only the latter ones to be valid. Even though at first glance

393 *Id.* at 1291.
394 Richards & Stearns, 54 Bus. Law 607 (1999).
395 731 A.2d 818 (Del. Ch. 1999).
396 *Id.*
397 902 A.2d 737 (Del. Ch. 2006).
398 Bebchuk v. CA, Inc., 902 A.2d 737, 738-42 (Del. Ch. 2006).
399 *Id.* at 742-743.
400 Coffee, 51 U. Miami L. Rev. 605 (1997).

this approach seems justified, it does not consider that the denial of options in a specific field can be much more intrusive on a decision maker's authority than compelling him to perform a specific action. Coffee's *third* approach in distinguishing admissible from inadmissible subjects for mandatory bylaw amendments is to admit bylaws that contain procedural regulations, whereas bylaws that contain a substantial regulation would not be admissible. This approach is appealing, since it takes into account the acknowledged function of bylaws to define rules of internal corporate procedure. On the other hand, the procedural character of a bylaw insufficiently insulates management from having the bylaw violate the board's authority to manage the business and affairs of the corporation. *Finally*, Coffee distinguishes valid corporate governance proposals from invalid bylaws concerning business decisions. The fact that bylaws are rules of general understanding supports this distinction, but once again it does not prevent management from having its exclusive managerial authority constrained. Coffee's four approaches underscore the difficulty of developing a bright line rule that clearly distinguishes valid shareholder-mandated bylaws from invalid ones. Even though Coffee's third proposal is often judged as the soundest approach, it faces practical restrictions as well. Therefore, Coffee's four different attempts may be jointly considered while taking a case-by-case-approach. In contrast to a bright line rule, it appears to be the more appropriate approach regarding the varieties of shareholder proposals to amend bylaws and their impact on the authority of the board of directors.[401]

(4) Functional counter arguments

The main counterarguments relate to rational apathy issues based on the lack of incentives for shareholders to come up with and win approval of successful proposals, the high costs of possible nuisance proposals, resulting in incorrect decisions, opportunistic behavior, and a social theory-related issue.[402]

Shareholder initiation faces *collective action* problems because of the costs of making informed proposals as generally imperfectly informed shareholders,[403] as well as the minimal participation of the average shareholder, leading to rational apathy and free-rider problems among the majority of shareholders in public corporations.[404] However, the alleged lack of shareholder incentives[405] is not convincing[406] regarding the *initiation* of well-known value-enhancing governance proposals. A preliminary consideration is that even if sharehold-

401 Hammermesh, 73 Tul. L. Rev. 409 (1998).

402 Bebchuk, 118 Harv. L. Rev., 833, 875 et seq. (2005); Choi & Guzman, 87 Va. L. Rev. 961, 985 (2001).

403 Clark, Corporate Law 24, 94-95; similar 803 (1986): according to whom it should depend on the amount, quality and range of information that an individual normally receives in order to determine how often an individual should make decisions.

404 Bainbridge, 119 Harv. L. Rev. 1735, 1745 (2006); Clark, Corporate Law 94 (1986); Ruffner, Die ökonomischen Grundlagen eines Rechts der Publikumsgesellschaft, 2000, 174 et seq.

405 *Similar* Letter from Robert Todd Lang & Charles Nathan/ABA Section of Business Law, Individually and on behalf of the other members of Task Force on Shareholder Proposals, to the SEC Division of Corporate Finance, at I F (June 13, 2003), http://www.sec.gov/rules/other/s71003/aba061303.htm.

406 Bebchuk, 118 Harv. L. Rev. 833, 875 (2005).

ers would be mainly subordinated under the *passivity rule*, it would only mean that bylaw proposals would be infrequent, but not mean that they would do any harm to the corporate governance system.[407] Furthermore, certain shareholders such as institutional investors holding block stakes in the corporation are not subordinated under the passivity rule.[408] On the contrary, they actively use their control rights as shareholders, since their block stakes lead to a larger stake in returns, allowing for a better effort-return ratio and for other reasons discussed *supra*. In fact, shareholder proposals have become more frequent, especially concerning corporate governance issues.[409] And the incentives to use shareholder proposals would be strengthened through the increased effectiveness of *mandatory* proposals encouraging stronger shareholder involvement.[410] Even though shareholder proposals do not lead to any direct benefits for the involved shareholders, the costs for these proposals are comparably low since not much informational effort and campaigning is necessary for well-known, value enhancing corporate governance rules. Those may as well be a legal fall-back rule. The costs required to file proxy statements and to solicit proxies would be limited, as Rule 14a-8 SEA allows the proposal to be placed on the corporate ballot.[411] Finally, even relatively low quotas of actual shareholder intervention do not automatically signal that shareholder initiation rights are insignificant. Rather, the indirect benefits of possible shareholder proposals need to be considered as well. These induce management to implement governance amendments in order to prevent successful shareholder intervention.[412]

Arguments that there are *collective action problems* relating to the required shareholder *approval* of bylaw-amending shareholder proposals are also unconvincing. As far as the necessity of costly information for the voting shareholders is concerned, value-enhancing governance arrangements usually require no firm-specific knowledge, but rather a general understanding of corporate governance that most shareholders possess.[413] This allows shareholders to become well-informed without having to incur substantial transaction costs to vote contrary to management's (potentially opportunistic) recommendation and in favor of a value-enhancing proposal.[414] The same argument counters the allegation that shareholders have the strong tendency to follow management's recommendations, which will likely be contrary to the proposal.[415] In contrast, management, which might have superior information,[416] might not necessarily have the incentives to

407 McDonnel, *Shareholder Bylaws, Shareholder Nominations, and Poison Pills*, Minnesota Legal Studies Research Paper No. 05-06, 53, www.ssrn.com/abstract=659322 (2005).

408 Leyens, 67 RabelsZ 57, 66 (2003).

409 Bebchuk, 118 Harv. L. Rev. 833, 877 (2005).

410 McDonnel, *Shareholder Bylaws, Shareholder Nominations, and Poison Pills*, Minnesota Legal Studies Research Paper No. 05-06, 53, www.ssrn.com/abstract=659322 (2005).

411 Bebchuk, 93 Va. L. Rev. 102, 134 (2007).

412 Bebchuk, 118 Harv. L. Rev. 833, 878 (2005).

413 McDonnell, *Shareholder Bylaws, Shareholder Nominations, and Poison Pills*, Minnesota Legal Studies Research Paper No. 05-06, 44, www.ssrn.com/abstract=659322 (2005).

414 Bebchuk, 118 Harv. L. Rev. 833, 877 (2005).

415 Choi & Guzman, 87 Va. L. Rev. 961, 985 (2001), Clark, Corporate Law 94 (1986).

416 Paramount Commc'ns, Inc. v. Time, Inc., [1989 Transfer Binder] Fed. Sec. L. Rep. ¶ 94,514, at 93, 277 (Del. Ch. July 14, 1989).

optimize corporate governance.[417] Relevant but inaccessible information may also be included in management's statement regarding the proposal on which it can base its corresponding recommendation, Rule 14a-8(m)(1) SEA.[418]

Neither do costs resulting from potential *nuisance proposals*[419] justify keeping shareholders from initiating governance amendments. Even though it is hard to deny that mandatory shareholder initiation may lead to additional costs apart from the question of its success, it is the task of the applicable regime to keep possibly resulting costs low. An ownership requirement is able to assure that the proposing shareholder has a relevant economic interest in the well-being of the concerned corporation[420] and has been involved as shareholder for a significant period of time before the shareholder meeting takes place.[421] It ensures not only a certain degree of identification with and knowledge about the corporation but also prevents spontaneous issue-related involvement. Additional tools are conceivable as well, such as Bebchuk's suggestion that two confirming resolutions be required in order to avoid unnecessary lobbying by management against possibly successful proposals.

Another objection is that shareholder-initiated governance amendments allow proposing shareholders to pursue *special interests or short-term goals*[422] as well as costly *inconsistencies* with management's corporate decisions[423]. Those concerns need to be distinguished from concerns that relate to the use of mandatory shareholder initiation rights as a bargaining chip to promote special interests. These are unrelated to the consequences of the implemented procedural rule and result from the fact that shareholders are given an effective place from which to negotiate with the board.[424] They may be countered by pointing out that the administration would have little reason not to follow the proposed mandatory governance amendment. While value-decreasing proposals will lack the necessary majority support, value-increasing proposals prevent blackmail of management since these are most likely to be initiated by other shareholders.[425] However, shareholder proposals directly promulgating special interests also depend on the approval of a majority of the outstanding shares. These proposals will hardly achieve

417 Bebchuk, 118 HARV. L. REV. 833, 881 (2005).

418 Bebchuk, 118 HARV. L. REV. 833, 881 (2005); McDonnell, *Shareholder Bylaws, Shareholder Nominations, and Poison Pills*, Minnesota Legal Studies Research Paper No. 05-06, 52, www.ssrn.com/abstract=659322 (2005).

419 Lipton & Rosenblum, 59 BUS. LAW. 67, 83 et seq. (2003).

420 Under current Rule 14a-8 SEA, the proponent has to hold 1 percent of the outstanding shares which are worth more than $2000.

421 Under current Rule 14a-8 SEA, the proponent has to hold the participation for a minimum of 1 year before submitting the proposal.

422 Anabtawi, 53 UCLA L. REV. 561, 564–65 (2006); Bainbridge, 119 HARV. L. REV. 1735, 1754–55 (2006); Lipton & Rosenblum, 59 BUS. LAW. 67, 78 and 82 (2003).

423 CLARK, CORPORATE LAW Appendix A, 801 et seq. (1986): pointing out the significance of coordination by corporate management.

424 *See* Bebchuk, 118 HARV. L. REV. 833, 884 et seq. (2005); Castellani & Goodman, *The Case Against the SEC Director Election Proposal in* BEBCHUK, SHAREHOLDER ACCESS TO THE CORPORATE BALLOT 9 – 10 (2004): in the context of the proxy access rule.

425 Bebchuk, 118 HARV. L. REV. 833, 885 et seq. (2005).

the necessary majority support when serving solely special interests and harming shareholder value by misleading the remaining shareholders.[426] Furthermore, as the debate on mandatory shareholder proposals concentrates on the amendment of rules-of-the-game, the risk of the realization of a short-term benefit for the shareholder is less likely compared to the shareholder impact on specific material decisions of the corporations. Therefore, the share price's reflection of short-term focused shareholder-initiated corporate decisions[427] will be analyzed *infra* where it is relevant. Regarding the argument of costly inconsistencies caused by shareholder proposals, shareholders as residual owners are most likely to choose means of interference that outweigh possible adverse effects.[428]

Finally, Gordon's *social choice implications of cycling* that lead to the disruption or paralysis of the corporate decision-making process[429] cannot act as a deterrent. Most shareholders agree on maximizing shareholder value, which makes conflicting goals that plague political choices far less present among shareholders.[430] Shareholder choice may, even if resulting in cycling, prevent management from reinforcing inferior choices, which would not be possible without the means of shareholder initiation. Management intervention via countermotions would allow the necessary stabilization if several equal value arrangements find support from shareholders.[431] Alternative suggestions are the inclusion of advance notice bylaws[432] limiting competing proposals and constraining the ability of shareholders to call special meetings.[433]

Having considered the several counterarguments, it is evident that, even though shareholder initiation may have some problems, these are not reason enough to refuse it. Rather, within the described limits, mandatory shareholder initiation of rules-of-the-

426 *Id.* at 884.

427 *Id.*

428 *Id.* At 883.

429 Gordon, 60 U. Cin. L. Rev. 347, 359 et seq. (1991); Choi & Guzman, 87 Va. L. Rev., 961, 986 (2001); Ruffner, Die ökonomischen Grundlagen eines Rechts der Publikumsgesellschaft, 2000, 183 et seq.

430 McDonnell, *Shareholder Bylaws, Shareholder Nominations, and Poison Pills*, Minnesota Legal Studies Research Paper No. 05-06, 54 et seq., www.ssrn.com/abstract=659322 (2005).

431 Bebchuk, 118 Harv. L. Rev. 833, 887 (2005).

432 An advance notice bylaw requires that a stockholder submit advance notice of his intention to introduce business at a stockholder meeting, such as the nomination of director candidates or the introduction of a shareholder proposal. It informs a company of stockholder business to be brought at the stockholder meeting an adequate time in advance of the meeting, provides an opportunity for all stockholders to be fully informed at such matters an adequate time in advance of the meeting, and enables a company's board to make informed recommendations or present alternatives to stockholders regarding such matters. Katz & McIntosh, *Advance Notice Bylaws: Lessons From Recent Cases*, New York Law Journal, May 23, 2008, *available at* www.law.com (search title).

433 McDonnell, *Shareholder Bylaws, Shareholder Nominations, and Poison Pills*, Minnesota Legal Studies Research Paper No. 05-06, 55, www.ssrn.com/abstract=659322 (2005): Since special meetings of stockholders may only be convened by the board of directors or by such person or persons as may be authorized by the certificate of incorporation or by the bylaws, § 211 (d) DGCL, a corresponding restriction requires that initially shareholders were allowed via provision of the articles of incorporation or the bylaws to convene a special meeting.

game amendments on the bylaw level constitutes a useful means for (active) shareholders to increase control of the board of directors. Therefore, it has the potential to reduce agency issues related to the separation of ownership and control in public corporations.

(5) Recent developments

A 2007 amendment to the Delaware Constitution paved the way for the decision of Delaware's highest court on the issue. New Article IV, Section 11(8) of the Delaware Constitution expanded the Delaware Supreme Court's jurisdiction by permitting it to decide questions of law certified to it by the SEC. In 2008, the supreme court first used its extended jurisdiction in the context of a shareholder bylaw proposal in *CA, Inc. v. AFSCME Employees Pension Plan*[434].[435] The proposal mandated the reimbursement of shareholders' proxy expenses under specified circumstances. The court held that the proposed bylaw was generally a proper subject for shareholder action under the DGCL, which means that a bylaw may be proposed and enacted by shareholders without the concurrence of the company's board of directors.[436] The court construed the § 141(a) exceptions as not including § 109(b), taking into account the extent of management power allocated to the board in contrast to the shareholders. Rather, for a bylaw to be consistent under the law pursuant to § 109(b), it needs to take into account § 141.[437] The remaining question on the scope of the shareholder power to adopt, alter, or repeal bylaws could not, therefore, be answered with a bright line approach, as the text of the statutory language was only "marginally helpful."[438] Rather, the court relied on decisions of the court of chancery[439] as well as different examples of procedural bylaws under DGCL[440] and case law[441]. These allow the court to endorse one of the factors advocated by *Coffee:* the distinction between procedure and substance. It is based on the well-established tenet of Delaware law that the proper function of bylaws is not specific business decisions, but rather the definition of process and procedure[442]. It is determined not primarily by the wording of the specific bylaw, but rather through its context and purpose.[443]

434 953 A.2d 227 (Del. 2008).
435 BLOOMENTHAL, SECURITIES LAW HANDBOOK, Vol. 1, § 18.86 (2009-2010); WOLTERS & HONAKER, ANALYSIS OF THE 2008 AMENDMENTS TO THE DELAWARE GENERAL CORPORATION LAW 3 (2008).
436 CA, Inc. v. AFSCME, 953 A.2d 227, 231, 237 (Del. 2008).
437 *Id.* at 232.
438 *Id.* at 234.
439 Hollinger Intern. Inc. v. Black, 844 A.2d 1022, 1079 (Del. Ch. 2004): "There is a general consensus that bylaws that regulate the *process* by which the board acts are statutorily authorized."; *id.* at 1080 n.136: "For similar reasons, I reject International's argument that that provision in the Bylaw Amendments impermissibly interferes with the board's authority under § 141(a) to manage the business and affairs of the corporation. Secs. 109 and 141 taken in totality, and red in light of Frantz, make clear that bylaws may pervasively and strictly regulate the process by which boards act, subject to the constraints of equity."
440 §§ 141 (b), (f) DGCL.
441 Frantz Mfg. Co. v. EAC Indus., 501 A.2d 401 (Del. 1985): concerning a shareholder enacted bylaw requiring unanimous board attendance and board approval for any board action.
442 C.A., Inc. v. AFSCME, 953 A.2d 227, 234 – 235 (Del. 2008).
443 *Id.* at 15 – 16.

Even though the final holding affirmed that the specific bylaw violated Delaware law because it impermissibly limited board power and responsibility in accordance with fiduciary duties requiring that the board be able to decline reimbursement, the holding still delighted activist shareholders.[444] Nomination and election procedures may also be theoretically mandated by a shareholder-initiated bylaw proposal. The affirmation in favor of such a shareholder initiation right is therefore the key for the adoption of other (active) shareholders' friendly corporate governance amendments, leading to a reduction of agency costs relating to the separation of ownership and control.

d) Exclusions under Rule 14a-8(i)(8) SEA

A further significant substantial exclusion in the context of bylaw proposals aiming to amend the director nomination and election procedure is laid down in Rule 14a-8(i)(8) SEA. Until December 2007, it permitted the omission of a shareholder proposal "[i]f the proposal relate[d] to an election for membership on the company's board of directors or analogous governing body." This led to the question whether the implementation of procedural voting rules concerning the election of directors, such as the proxy access, majority-voting, or cumulative-voting rule related to an election in the sense of Rule 14a-8(i)(8) SEA and was therefore subject to exclusion by the issuer.

The predecessor of this former Rule 14a-8(i)(8) SEA was first placed among the substantive exclusions in 1976 and the proposing release[445] explained that Rule 14a-8 SEA was not the proper means for conducting campaigns or effecting reforms in election, since other proxy rules applied to this scenario.[446] This was to ensure that the shareholder proposal process was not used to circumvent more elaborate rules governing election contests, such as the disclosure rules under Rule 14a-12 SEA.[447] The SEC issued no-action letters as long as a shareholder proposal concerned the nomination of a specific person or a specific group.[448] But if the proposal related to voting procedures in general, the SEC refused a no-action letter in favor of the corporation.[449] The analysis was whether the proposal affected the election that was taking place at the meeting at which the proposal was presented.[450] The proposal prevailed if it was prospective and left the

---

444 Bruner, 11 Tenn. J. Bus. L. 66, 67 (2009).

445 Proposed Amendments to Rule 14a-8 Under the Securities Exchange Act of 1934 Relating to Proposals by Security Holders, Exchange Act Release No. 12,598, 1976 SEC LEXIS 1290 (proposed July 7, 1976).

446 Haft, Analysis of Key SEC No-Action Letters 259 et seq. (2005/2006).

447 Proposed Amendments to Rule 14a-8 Under the Securities Exchange Act of 1934 Relating to Proposals by Security Holders, Exchange Act Release No. 12,598, 1976 SEC LEXIS 1290 (proposed July 7, 1976); Romanek & Krus, Mergers & Acquisitions § 21-4 (2002).

448 As it was the case in the later by courts confirmed case of Rauchman v. Mobil Corp., 739 F.2d 205 (6th Cir. 1984), where the seemingly general obligation required by the amended bylaw for directors not to be from a country that belongs to the OPEC aimed against the re-election of a Saudi Arabian citizen running for re-election.

449 Romanek & Krus, Mergers & Acquisitions § 21-4 to 20 (2002).

450 *Id.* at § 21-6.

board with enough space to select its own nominees for the upcoming meeting.[451] Therefore, proposals that were of particular interest for active shareholders, as they related to procedures of nomination and election of directors or to the general qualification of directors, were initially considered not to be excludable under Rule 14a-8(i)(8) SEA as long as these did not affect the current nominees/directors.[452]

i) The proxy access rule

The question whether shareholders have the right to mandate a bylaw amendment according to which they may propose their own nominees for a director position has remained one of the most highly controversial issues of U.S. corporate law. Institutional investors are increasingly interested in electing their own nominees to corporate boards. For this reason, several institutions filed proposals to implement a rule that allowed owners of a significant portion of outstanding shares to nominate their own candidates for a board position.[453] Corporations, in contrast, repeatedly asked the SEC to issue no-action letters. The legal basis expected to provide the answer to the question whether shareholders may mandate the initiation of such a proxy access rule has remained in flux over the last several years.

(1) Significance of proxy access rule

(a) Theoretical alternatives

Theoretically, there are three ways for shareholders to propose a nominee for a director position.[454] The *first* possible strategy is to engage in an election-related proxy contest requiring the proponents to solicit proxy authority from fellow shareholders via a proxy statement. The solicitation has to target either all or the most important shareholders in order to convince more shareholders to vote in favor of the shareholder nominee than for the administrative candidate. However, a proxy contest is tremendously expensive, if the proposal cannot be included in the proxy materials of the corporation, as is the case under Rule 14a-8 SEA. As a practical consequence, the solicitation of proxies to elect a new director is in practice left to the board, which may do so at the expense of the corporation[455]. Shareholders sometimes, albeit rarely, use this method. The *second* method is the proposal of a candidate at the annual shareholder meeting, if state law and the certificate of incorporation permit. This has, however, little practical relevance, as the

---

451 *Id.*

452 Int'l Banknote Co., SEC No-Action Letter, 1986 WL 65141 (Jan. 31, 1986); Green Mountain Power Corp., SEC No-Action Letter, 1985 WL 54069 (Apr. 3, 1985); Middle South Utilities, Inc., SEC No-Action Letter, 1984 WL 45010 (Mar. 14, 1984).

453 ROMANEK & KRUS, MERGERS & ACQUISITIONS, § 21-10 (2002).

454 SEC, Briefing Paper For Roundtable Discussion on the Proposed Security Holder Director Nominations Rules, Feb. 25, 2004, http://www.sec.gov/spotlight/dir-nominations/dir-nom-briefing.htm.

455 Bebchuk, 93 VA. L. REV. 102, 116 (2007); EISENBERG, THE STRUCTURE OF THE CORPORATION 97 et seq. (1976); Windbichler, ZGR 1985, 50 (61).

decision process of shareholders in a proxy dominated corporate governance system like the United States usually takes place before the shareholder meeting. Accordingly, management has already solicited sufficient proxies in advance of the meeting and, hence, has the discretion to match these proxies against any person nominated at the meeting. Finally, the *third* strategy for shareholders to nominate a candidate for a director position is to make a proposal to the nominating committee of the corporation. Such a proposal is not binding on the committee and usually fails. Consequently, the shareholders' ability to nominate a candidate is practically quite restricted under these approaches. Therefore it is the board that usually determines the nominees, usually only one nominee per vacant position, thus preventing contested elections.

The implementation of a proxy access rule via mandatory bylaw amendment would therefore represent a *fourth* and, for most of the shareholders, the only practical way to propose their own nominee. It would enable them under certain circumstances to include their nominees in the proxy materials of the corporation. They would neither have to incur costs for inclusion on the corporate ballot, nor would the board have any discretion on whether to integrate or not to integrate the nominee. Finally, it would allow them to influence the decision-making process of the electing shareholders at the right time. The fellow shareholders would obtain the information on the shareholder nominee and the administrative candidate simultaneously long before the shareholder meeting takes place. As a consequence, the shareholder nominee would have a chance to be elected.

(b) Significance of the shareholder nomination right

According to the *Unocal* decision,[456] shareholders may put their democratic tools to good use if they are dissatisfied with the actions of their elected representatives. Shareholders, as economic owners of the corporation, retain only some influence over the fundamental decisions of a corporation (incorporation, amendment of the articles of incorporation, mergers, dissolution) that have been transferred to the board of directors. Therefore, the shareholder's rights of election and removal of directors are particularly intended to assure that directors remain responsive to the shareholder's interests.[457] However, election implies nomination.[458] Under the system of Delaware state law and U.S. federal law, with shareholder access via costly proxy statements and solicitation, the impact of shareholder's choice is practically limited. According to Bebchuk,[459] the shareholder franchise in this system is a myth, as it is unable to establish the necessary responsiveness to shareholder interests.

The proxy access rule may represent a means to overcome this deficit. The opportunity for shareholders to propose their own nominees alongside those proposed by the board of directors is beneficial for corporate governance. According to the present prac-

456 Unocal Corp. v. Mesa Petroleum Co., 493 A.2d 946, 959 (Del. 1985).

457 Bebchuk, 93 Va. L. Rev. 102, 106 et seq. (2007).

458 Eisenberg, 83 Harv. L. Rev. 1489, 1505 (1970).

459 Bebchuk, 93 Va. L. Rev. 102, 136 (2007).

tice of de-facto cooptation,[460] the nominating directors usually determine only one candidate per vacant director position. This prevents contested elections and makes a candidate for a vacant director position dependent on the support of the nominating directors. A shareholder nomination right would increase the likelihood of contested elections. As a consequence, the election of directors would potentially depend on more numerous shareholder votes for a candidate than a competing individual. As a result, incumbent directors would be conscious that their re-election could depend on the number of shareholders who vote in their favor as compared to co-optation. Incumbent directors aiming to be re-elected and conscious that their re-election may potentially depend on a certain quorum of shareholder support will face an effective accountability mechanism and become more responsive to the interests of the shareholders. Accordingly, they will be increasingly inclined to fulfill their control function towards the executive officers and to focus more on shareholder value when pursuing decision management functions. In addition, the actual election of a generally independent shareholder nominee on the board of directors increases the information of the shareholders to a certain extent.

Considering the significance of credible threats or actual proxy fights for *active* shareholders to convince administrations of shareholder value enhancing decisions, its implementation may immensely lower their campaign costs.

(c) Counterarguments

Arguments against the admissibility of the implementation of a proxy access rule are numerous. They relate not only to the implementation of a proxy access rule via shareholder bylaw proposals involving similar concerns of collective action issues and the pursuit of special interests.[461] They also relate to the process of determining a nominee, the amendments to the election process, and the consequences once a shareholder nominee is elected.

Once a proxy access rule has been adopted, alleged *collective action issues* regarding the nomination of a candidate would be reduced due to the fact that shareholders may insert their nominee on the corporate ballot and therefore have comparably lower costs for placing proxy cards and soliciting proxies. Furthermore, it is usually the institutional investors who face fewer collective action issues relating from missing information, lack of financial means, and minimal return participation.

As far as concerns relate to shareholders tendency to *follow management suggestions* on specific corporate decisions, it may be countered that shareholders vote contrary to administrative recommendations where they have sufficient information to form a reasoned opinion. Apart from general and widely discussed corporate governance issues,

460 Chiapetta et al., *Board Elections in Europe: Transatlantic and Internal Market Perspectives*, Preliminary Summary prepared for the Sept. 27, 2005 Transatlantic Corporate Governance Dialogue Conference, http://209.85.135.132/search?q=cache%3AuhFSkfXSgAoJ%3Awww.law.yale.edu%2Fdocuments%2Fpdf%2FCBL_Symposium10_05%2FS3-1A%2520Board_Europe_Summary_NY_Meeting_2005.pdf+de+facto+cooptation+delaware&hl=de&gl=de.

461 Castellani & Goodman, *The Case Against the SEC Director Election Proposal in* BEBCHUK, SHAREHOLDER ACCESS TO THE CORPORATE BALLOT 9–10 (2004).

this is most likely the case for contested director elections. Accordingly, crucial votes tend to involve information on the candidates that is provided to the electing shareholders with sufficient time for them to digest it. Moreover, *incentives* of average shareholders to replace board members by voting for a shareholder nominee will be significantly stronger than the incentives for the implementation of general corporate governance issues. The reason is its potential for a strong positive impact on shareholder value.[462]

As far as the argument of *better information* of management or the nomination committee is concerned,[463] it does not solve the issue at hand. Even though they may have the appropriate information, the directors may not have the right incentives to remove their fellow directors or themselves[464]. The divergence of interests of shareholders aiming at maximizing shareholder value and the opportunism of directors to ensure their fellow's position makes it necessary to restore accountability in order to align director interests with those of the shareholders.[465]

The main counterargument relates to the concern of a significant *increase of election contests* and its consequences.[466] It is argued that the more contests would lead not only to the disruption of management in taking care of its usual business, but also to additional costs resulting from the contests.[467] The fact is that the proposed rule is not expected to lead to election contests becoming the norm. Rather, an election contest requires nominating shareholders to provide sufficient assurances that their nominee can be successful, which will likely be forthcoming only during times of mass dissatisfaction, since shareholders usually tend to be passive. The main effect of the implementation of a direct shareholder access rule lies in its indirect success in amending the incentives of incumbents, since they become subject to an exchange and therefore more accountable.[468] This circumstance runs counter to the argument that shareholder access will not be worth its costs since it will only lead to few successfully elected sharehold-

462 *See* McDonnel, *Shareholder Bylaws, Shareholder Nominations, and Poison Pills*, Minnesota Legal Studies Research Paper No. 05-06, 52, www.ssrn.com/abstract=659322 (2005).

463 Lipton & Rosenblum, 59 Bus. Law. 67, 92 et seq. (2003): noting the better position of a nomination committee to ensure that productive shareholder proposals become successful and to prevent successful suggestions of not sufficiently qualified candidates; McDonnell, *Shareholder Bylaws, Shareholder Nominations, and Poison Pills*, Minnesota Legal Studies Research Paper No. 05-06, 43-44, www.ssrn.com/abstract=659322 (2005).

464 Bebchuk, 118 Harv. L. Rev. 833, 881 (2005).

465 Bebchuk, 93 Va. L. Rev. 102, 147 (2007).

466 Letter from Wachtell, Lipton, Rosen & Katz, to Nancy M. Morris, Secretary, SEC (Sept. 19, 2007) at 10, 12 http://www.sec.gov/comments/s7-16-07/s71607-190.pdf; Letter from the BRT, to Jonathan G. Katz, Secretary, SEC (June 13, 2003) http://www.sec.gov/rules/other/s71003/brt061303.htm.

467 Castellani & Goodman, *The Case Against the SEC Director Election Proposal in* Bebchuk, Shareholder Access to the Corporate Ballot 19 (2004); Letter from the BRT, to Jonathan G. Katz, Secretary, SEC (June 13, 2003) http://www.sec.gov/rules/other/s71003/brt061303.htm; Letter from Wachtell, Lipton, Rosen & Katz, to Nancy M. Morris, Secretary, SEC (Sept. 19, 2007) at 11, http://www.sec.gov/comments/s7-16-07/s71607-190.pdf; Lipton & Rosenblum, 59 Bus. Law. 67, 83 et seq. (2003).

468 Bebchuk, 93 Va. L. Rev. 102, 143 (2007).

er-nominated directors.[469] In addition, the adjustment of ownership and reimbursement requirements may be used to influence the number of shareholder nominations.[470]

There are additional arguments relating to the *special interests* of shareholders. Apart from the argument of leverage of special interests based on the shareholder's right to nominate a director, countered *supra*, the allegation is that shareholders may choose a nominee to pursue a special interest apart from promoting long-term shareholder value.[471] The board in choosing candidates, in contrast, is obliged by its fiduciary duties to act in the best interest of the corporation.[472] It can be countered that even though the implementation of the proxy access rule would lower the effort necessary to propose a candidate, broad shareholder support has to be assured before spending a significant amount of (campaign) costs to assure his actual election.[473] Additionally, management may point out flaws of the competing candidates or disadvantages resulting from the election of shareholder-proposed candidates, making the pursuit of special interests difficult.

Closely related is the concern that increased election contests may lead to *divisive boards* due to the pursuit of special interests by shareholder-nominated directors. As a consequence, the board may experience difficulties functioning well as a team and communication breakdowns.[474] As far as the concern relates to the different origin of shareholder-nominated directors, it may, comparable to the position of independent directors, not justify the restriction. Rather, it is an argument in favor of it, since it may lead away from unchallenged conformity toward a more critical internal debate on more important decisions. And even if a certain tendency exists, there is no certainty that the extreme will occur. As far as opponents are afraid of the counterproductive influence of special interest representatives regarding long-term shareholder value, the above arguments may be referred to.

Another argument concerns a *shortsightedness* of incumbents seeking to please shareholders in order to remain on the board.[475] Allowing longer election periods than the usual one-year office periods under U.S.-American practice could reduce it. How-

469 Letter from Robert Todd Lang & Charles Nathan/ABA Section of Business Law, Individually and on behalf of the members of Task Force on Shareholder Proposals, to the SEC Division of Corporate Finance (June 13, 2003) at I, http://www.sec.gov/rules/other/s71003/aba061303.htm.

470 Bebchuk, 93 VA. L. REV. 102, 144 (2007).

471 Anabtawi, 53 UCLA L. REV. 561, 564–65 (2006); Bainbridge, 119 HARV. L. REV. 1735, 1754–55 (2006); *see* Bebchuk, 93 VA. L. REV. 102, 145 (2007); Grundfest, *Advice and Consent* 6, www.ssnr.com/abstract=481021 (2003); Lipton & Rosenblum, 59 BUS. LAW. 67, 82 et seq. (2003); Letter from Wachtell, Lipton, Rosen & Katz, to Nancy M. Morris, Secretary, SEC (Sept. 19, 2007) at 4, http://www.sec.gov/comments/s7-16-07/s71607-190.pdf.

472 Letter from the BRT, to Jonathan G. Katz, Secretary, SEC (June 13, 2003) http://sec.gov/rules/other/s71003/brt061303.htm; Lipton & Rosenblum, 59 Bus. Law. 67, 93 (2003).

473 Bebchuk, 93 VA. L. REV. 102, 145 (2007).

474 Castellani & Goodman, *The Case Against the SEC Director Election Proposal in* BEBCHUK, SHAREHOLDER ACCESS TO THE CORPORATE BALLOT 18, 19 (2004); Grundfest, *Advice and Consent* 7 et seq., www.ssnr.com/abstract=481021 (2003); Lipton & Rosenblum, 59 Bus. Law. 67, 82 et seq. (2003); Letter from from Wachtell, Lipton, Rosen & Katz, to Nancy M. Morris, Secretary, SEC (Sept. 19, 2007) at 12, http://www.sec.gov/comments/s7-16-07/s71607-190.pdf.

475 Bebchuk, 93 VA. L. Rev. 102, 147 et seq. (2007).

ever, it does not justify abandoning the demand for the responsiveness to shareholder interests.[476]

The final objection concerns the exacerbation of the issue of finding and retaining the most skillful candidates for a director position. Accordingly, opponents are afraid that potential candidates *may refuse a nominee position* if they face the risk of a contested election[477] in addition to issues like the decline of public prestige of a director positions, increased procedural burdens on directors, and the perception of personal liability.[478] Even though it is easy to understand that candidates prefer to have no competitor, there are many other business positions that are far less secure than a director position.[479] Besides, the most skilled candidates are the ones who should have the least fear of being removed from a board position as long as they use their skills in favor of the corporation and its shareholder value. Moreover, the benefits to a corporation from the opportunity to consider additional candidates in contested elections outweigh the costs resulting from the fact that some potential candidates may refuse to compete with other candidates.[480]

As a consequence, the functional arguments against the proxy access rule may not be convincing. Rather, from a functional perspective, the admissibility of a proxy access rule appears to be an important means to reduce the agency costs resulting from the separation of ownership and control by providing shareholders with a more effective accountability mechanism. Further, it is able to ease the work of active shareholders. The practical significance of a proxy access rule in overcoming the practice of de-facto cooptation is relative, however, as it depends on a number of closely related rules determining the *election* process.

(2) Chronological legal evaluation of proxy access proposals

In the United States, the proxy access rule has been for decades at the center of corporate governance debates involving federal and state legislation as well as the SEC's regulatory action and jurisdiction. The issue continues to be affected by the ongoing debate and recent political change.

Based on former Rule 14a-8(i)(8) SEA,[481] the SEC staff applied the "specific election vs. nomination process" interpretation in many of its decisions from the 1980s to the mid-1990s. Shareholder proposals concerning the nomination process of directors in general, such as the proposal to allow shareholders with a qualified holding to nominate

476 *Id.* at 148.

477 Letter from the BRT, to Jonathan G. Katz, Secretary, SEC (June 13, 2003) http://sec.gov/rules/other/s71003/brt061303.htm.

478 Castellani & Goodman, *The Case Against the SEC Director Election Proposal in* Bebchuk, Shareholder Access to the Corporate Ballot 20 (2004); Grundfest, *Advice and Consent* 7 et seq., www.ssnr.com/abstract=481021 (2003); Lipton & Rosenblum, 59 Bus. Law. 67, 86 (2003).

479 Bebchuk, 93 VA. L. Rev. 102, 149 (2007).

480 *Id.* at 148.

481 Until December 2007, Rule 14a-8(i)(8) SEA red as follows: "If the proposal relates to an election for membership on the company's board of directors or analogous governing body."

a director candidate whose name would be included in the company's proxy statement,[482] but not a specific election, could not be excluded by the company. For example, the SEC held in *Union Oil Co. NAL*[483] that shareholders were allowed to include proposals for director nominees in the proxy statement of the corporation if the shareholder owned, controlled, or was represented by 125,000 shares. As in many other NALs at this time, the staff reasoned that shareholder "access to the ballot" proposals did not relate to an election[484] but rather to the procedure relevant to nominate candidates in general.[485]

Later, after the increasingly successful elections of shareholder nominees, the SEC changed its policy and allowed the exclusion of proposals concerning bylaw amendments, implementing a proxy access rule. The SEC reasoned that the implementation of a proxy access rule would establish a procedure resulting in contested elections and creating a loophole in Rule 14a-12 SEA, which established disclosure requirements for contested solicitations.[486] Activists argued that such SEC practice contradicted the traditional interpretation of Rule 14a-8(i)(8) SEA and that its implementation was possible without violating the disclosure requirements of Rule 14a-12 SEA, but their arguments fell on deaf ears.[487] In *Unocal Co. NAL*,[488] the SEC allowed the exclusion of a shareholder proposal to amend the company's bylaws by allowing any shareholder owning at least 125,000 shares to present a nominee for the director elections under Rule 14a-8(i)(8) SEA. The Commission argued that "rather than establishing procedures for nomination or qualification generally, they would establish a procedure that may result in contested elections of directors."[489] The historic change of attitude of the 1990 *Unocal NAL*[490] was confirmed a week later, when the SEC issued the *Amoco NAL*[491]. The proponent argued that democratic governance in American corporations required free elections. To ensure confidentiality of votes alone would not be enough; instead, a free election also required providing shareholders with a choice of candidates.[492] In practice, management allowed only its own candidates to appear on its proxy statements, whereas shareholders had to pay significant costs in order to nominate a candidate, including separate ballots, mailings, and tabulation. Therefore, only the wealthiest shareholders could nominate their own candidates. If companies opened their proxy statements to the nominees of qualified shareholders, it would efficiently solve this problem.[493] Unimpressed by such argu-

482 Citigroup, Inc., SEC No-Action Letter, 2003 WL 1900802 (Apr. 14, 2003).

483 Union Oil Co. of Calif., SEC No-Action Letter, 1983 WL 30873 (Feb. 24, 1983).

484 Id.; Union Oil Co. of Calif., SEC No-Action Letter, 1981 WL 24701 (Jan. 29, 1981), Mobil Corp., SEC No-Action Letter, 1981 WL 26205 (Mar. 3, 1981), Unicare Servs., Inc., SEC No-Action Letter, 980 WL 15475 (May 13, 1980).

485 Citigroup, Inc., SEC No-Action Letter, 2003 WL 1900802 (Apr. 14, 2003).

486 Romanek & Krus, Mergers & Acquisitions § 21-11 (2002).

487 *Id.*

488 Unocal Corp., SEC No-Action Letter, 1990 WL 285946 (Feb. 6, 1990).

489 United Road Services, Inc., SEC No-Action Letter, 2000 WL 565126 (May 5, 2000).

490 Letter from James McRitchie, CorpGov.Net, to Jonathan G. Katz, Secretary, SEC (May 26, 2003) http://www.sec.gov/rules/other/s71003/corpgov052603.htm#P148_24999.

491 Amoco, SEC No-Action Letter, 1994 WL 43831 (Feb. 14, 1990).

492 Supporting statement by legal counsel of proponent Wulff, 1990 WL 286092 (Nov. 13, 1989).

493 *Id.*

ments, the SEC, following its new policy, upheld the exclusion of a proposal that allowed shareholders with over $100,000 market value in shares to nominate a director candidate. The SEC, citing its decision in the *Union Oil, Co. NAL*, reasoned that rather than establishing procedures for nomination or qualification of directors, the proposal would instead establish a procedure that could result in contested board elections, a problem that would be better addressed under different rules, such as Rule 14a-12 SEA. Several following NALs[494] held proxy access proposals excludable for the same reason.[495]

(3) Potential Rule 14a-11 SEA (2003)

In 2003, Citigroup obtained a no-action letter[496] when it excluded a bylaw amendment proposal allowing the holder of 3 percent of the outstanding shares to nominate a director candidate whose name would have had to be included on the corporation's proxy card. The proponent's arguments that related to the wording of Rule 14a-8(i)(8) SEA, the traditional understanding that the exclusion only concerned specific elections, and the inconsistency of the SEC's holding that a company may be required to nominate two candidates for every open board position leading to contested elections failed to sway the SEC.[497] Or did it? Surprisingly, just a few months after this last no-action letter, the SEC proposed Rule 14a-11 SEA, which, in contrast to its Citigroup decision, would allow shareholders under certain circumstances to propose director nominees. Despite its precatory character, it would put pressure on boards.

The proposal's prerequisites were that the proponent had to have held a minimum of 5 percent of the outstanding shares for a minimum of 2 years. A triggering event needed to have occurred, such as 35 percent withheld votes for one nominee[498] or a 50 percent vote in favor of the shareholder nominee[499]. The nominee had to be an independent candidate.[500] If proposed Rule 14a-11 SEA applied, the proposal was not excludable under Rule 14a-8(i)(8) SEA.[501] Up to three shareholder nominees[502] were includable on the corporate proxy card.

Reactions to this proposed rule were mixed. Main points of critique included the Commission's lack of authority to regulate matters of state law concerning corporate

494 *For many*: Bank of Boston, SEC No-Action Letter, 1990 WL 285947 (Jan. 26, 1990); Thermo Electron, SEC No-Action Letter, 1990 WL 286329 (Mar. 22, 1990).

495 http://www.corpmon.com//CitiMgt20000222.htm (last visited on Mar. 8, 2006).

496 Citigroup, Inc., SEC No-Action Letter, 2003 WL 328268 (Jan. 31, 2003).

497 Appeal of AFSCME Employees Pension Plan from no-action determination of SEC concerning shareholder proposal submitted to Citigroup, 2003 WL 1900802.

498 Alston + Bird LLP, *Shareholder Access to Proxies,* http://www.alston.com/articles/Shareholder%20Access%20to%20Proxies.pdf (last visited Feb. 6, 2006).

499 *Id.*

500 Bainbridge, *A Comment on the SEC Shareholder Access Proposal* 3, www.sec.gov/rules/proposed/s71903/bainbridge121903 (last visited Feb. 6, 2006).

501 http://www.corplawblog.com/archives/000255.html (last visited Feb. 6, 2006).

502 SEC, Briefing Paper For Roundtable Discussion on the Proposed Security Holder Director Nominations Rules (Feb. 25, 2004) http://www.sec.gov/spotlight/dir-nominations/dir-nom-briefing.htm.

affairs[503], as the Commission ignored the distinction between permissible federal regulation of voting procedure and impermissible federal regulation of the substance of elections.[504] In 2005, the SEC reversed itself due to the passage of time and announced that the proposal was no longer necessary or appropriate.[505]

(4) AFCSME v. AIG

The Second Circuit confronted this issue on appeal in *AFSCME v. AIG.*[506] This decision was highly anticipated because this legal question had not yet been the subject of regulation or a Delaware court decision. The district court's decision concerned a shareholder proposal to implement a proxy access rule concerning the election of directors and officers. The proponent's leading argument related to the lack of meaningful shareholder control over the process by which director candidates were nominated in a public corporation. Stockholders whose suggested nominees were rejected by the nominating committee had no recourse other than sponsoring a dissident election campaign. This route was so expensive that it had been rarely used outside the takeover context. The access to the company's proxy to present a shareholder nominee for a director position would be a more efficient mechanism to ensure board accountability, since it would allow competition among the nominees. The exclusion of a proposal to implement such mechanisms would therefore be dramatic.[507] AIG, on the other hand, argued primarily that the proposal failed to meet the requirements of proposed Rule 14a-11 SEA. It only required that the proponent hold 3 percent of the outstanding shares for more than one year and thus did not fulfill the conditions for an exception to the otherwise applicable Rule 14a-8(i)(8) SEA exclusion.[508] The district court argued that it was not the task of courts to create law by granting a verdict that future shareholders with similar concerns could use. Since 1999, the SEC had started to issue no-action letters in favor of the excluding companies if the proposing shareholders were unable to prove that the proposal met legal requirements. Delaware had not yet regulated direct shareholder access, nor had a Delaware court decided the issue. Furthermore, current federal regulations would not require AIG to include the proposal in its proxy statement.[509] The court underscored that it had certainly considered the Citigroup NAL, but it felt itself not bound by this SEC decision. Consequently, it did not grant the injunction in favor of the AFSCME proposal.

The Second Circuit, in contrast, ruled in favor of AFSCME and the ability to implement a proxy access rule through bylaw amendment. The court noted that the language of the rule was not particularly helpful to its interpretation. Furthermore, the Commission

503 *Id.*

504 Bainbridge, *A Comment on the SEC Shareholder Access Proposal* 6, www.sec.gov/rules/proposed/s71903/bainbridge121903 (last visited Feb. 6, 2006).

505 Verizon Commc's, Inc., SEC No-Action Letter, 2005 WL 283289 (Feb. 7, 2005); Qwest Commc's Int'l, SEC No-Action Letter, 2005 WL 283288 (Feb. 7, 2005); Halliburton Co., SEC No-Action Letter, 2005 WL 283290 (Feb. 7, 2005).

506 Am. Fed'n of County and Mun. Empls. v. Am. Int'l Group, 361 F. Supp 2d 344 (S.D.N.Y. 2005).

507 AIG, SEC No-Action Letter, 2006 WL 721899, at *5 et seq (Mar. 20, 2006).

508 *Id.* at 8 – 10.

509 *Id.* at 3.

had changed its mind in interpreting the meaning of the rule without explanation. In 2006, when it filed an amicus brief in the case, it opposed not only AFSCME's position but also its own 1976 statement after the last substantial amendment of the rule. The court deemed it appropriate to defer to that 1976 SEC statement, which was the rule's interpretation at the time of its last substantial amendment. It followed AFSCME's interpretation that *election* means a particular election, not simply the procedural rules governing elections.

(5) SEC's reaction to the Second Circuit decision

The Commission did not wait long to respond to the Second Circuit. It aimed to eliminate any uncertainty regarding the interpretation of former Rule 14a-8(i)(8) SEA. At this time, the majority of the commissioners were Republicans.[510] After elaborate reflection on the numerous arguments of both sides, in July 2007 the SEC issued two opposing proposals relating to Rule 14a-8(i)(8) SEA's interpretation of the proxy access rule.

The *first proposal* allowed the inclusion of bylaw proposals in the company's proxy materials if the proposing shareholder held 5 percent and had been entitled to vote for at least one year by the date of submission. Many legal scholars raised arguments in favor of this first proposal.[511] First, it was reasonable to interpret the wording of the exclusion of former Rule 14a-8(i)(8) SEA, "relate to an election," to mean that the rule encompassed proposals concerning the election of a specific individual, but not proposals only relating to general election procedures. The election of a specific individual requires detailed disclosure concerning that individual. This information would have to be placed in a separate proxy statement. Procedural regulations on director elections, in contrast, would not. An amendment of Schedule 14A and 13G could provide shareholders with additional information about the proponents of the nominees as well as the nominee himself.[512] The right of a corporation to exclude shareholder proposals that concern the director nomination would further undermine one of the basic rights of shareholders— the right to communicate with each other on important matters such as director elections. It would have the added effect of making rules on the federal level meant to concern only election procedures preferable to governance arrangements permitted under state law, such as shareholder proposals concerning the director election. A different interpretation would be inconsistent with the SEC's 1976 statement following the last major amendment of the rule. It would also contradict its longstanding practice of allowing shareholders to include in the company's proxy statement various proposals that may lead to contested elections, such as de-staggering the board or introducing cumulative voting.[513] Furthermore, it would lead to a proxy rule policy

510 BLOOMENTHAL, SECURITIES LAW HANDBOOK, Vol. 1, § 18.26 (2005-2006).

511 Letter of Cox, Atkins, Campos, Glassman, Nazareth, Harvard professors, to SEC (Jan. 2006) (on file with author): asking the SEC to support their opinion in the amicus curiae letter to the Second Circuit.

512 Shareholder Proposals, Exchange Act Release No. 56,160, Investment Company Act Release No. 27,913 (proposed July 27, 2007), http://www.sec.gov/rules/proposed/2007/34-56160.pdf.

513 Letter of Cox, Atkins, Campos, Glassman, Nazareth, Harvard professors, to SEC (Jan. 2006) at 2 (on file with author): asking the SEC to support their opinion in the amicus curiae letter to the Second Circuit.

that proxy rules were not intended to advance. While it would not allow shareholders to include proposed bylaw amendments to provide proxy access, it would allow the inclusion of proposed bylaw amendments to eliminate the proxy access of shareholders if the company already had a bylaw permitting proxy access. However, proxy rules are not intended to impede contested elections.[514] Finally, disclosure is not an argument against but in favor of proxy access. If proxy access proposals would be excludable according to Rule 14a-8(i)(8) SEA, it would be necessary for proponents to initiate their own proxy contests at high cost. Additionally, the SEC was said to require all relevant information about the procedure to be disclosed in a separate proxy statement prior to any solicitation according to Rule 14a-3 and 14a-12 SEA. Such consequences tend to show the importance of proxy access under the Second Circuit decision. Furthermore, concerns that shareholders would be faced with complicated and confusing documents[515] from shareholder disclosure about their own nominees according to the Rules 14a-4(d), 14a-12(c) and 14a-4(a) SEA[516] is unconvincing. There would be several ways to meet these disclosure requirements.[517] These include providing only a limited description of each nominee in the proxy statement and posting the description separately from the proxy statement, perhaps on designated websites.[518]

The *second proposal* of the Commission was an amendment to Rule 14a-8(i)(8) SEA that would allow issuers to exclude proposals relating to the nomination and election procedure of directors, including proxy access proposals. The less convincing arguments in favor of this interpretation include the rule's intention to prevent contested elections by allowing concerned companies to exclude shareholder proposals. Such a view would also be consistent with the 1976 statement. Furthermore, it would prevent possible loopholes in the disclosure requirements of Rule 14a-12 SEA by not allowing shareholders to include their nominees in the company's proxy statement. Otherwise, it would be possible for a shareholder to wage an election contest without conducting a separate proxy solicitation, thus without the required disclosures and liability applying to misrepresentations under Rule 14a-9 SEA.[519] A final argument is that Rule 14a-12 SEA would not include disclosures for nominees who are not supported by the board in the company's proxy statement.[520]

In December 2007, the SEC published its release No: 34-56914 (Dec. 6, 2007). With regard to the disclosure requirements on contested elections laid down in Rule 14a-12 SEA and Schedule A14, Rule 14a-8(i)(8) was revised according to its second proposal. Proposals could be excluded "[i]f the proposal relates to a nomination or an election for membership on the company's board of directors or analogous governing body or a procedure for such nomination or election." In consequence, shareholders were practically hindered

514 *Id.* at 3.

515 Letter from Sullivan & Cromwell, to the SEC (June 13, 2003) www.sec.gov/rules/other/s71003/sullivan061303.htm.

516 *Id.*

517 SEC Staff Report, Review of the proxy process regarding the nomination and election of directors (July 15, 2003) at 7, http://www.sec.gov/news/studies/proxyreport.pdf.

518 *Id.*

519 Shareholder Proposals, Exchange Act Release No. 56,160, Investment Company Act Release No. 27,913 (proposed July 27, 2007), http://www.sec.gov/rules/proposed/2007/34-56161.pdf.

520 Romanek & Krus, Mergers & Acquisitions § 21-11 (2002).

from impacting the selection of board members, a strong setback for all (active) shareholders. SEC Chairman Cox's hopeful pronouncement on November 28, 2007, noted that the upcoming release might not have been the SEC's last word on shareholder proxy access.[521]

(6) Excursion: the internet age

Parallel to the development of the proxy access rule, the Internet has also impacted the issue of director nominations. In 2007, the SEC enacted rules that allowed shareholders to save costs on printing and mailing proxy materials even when participating in a proxy contest in opposition to the corporation. The newly introduced e-proxy rules allow corporations and opposing solicitors to mail shareholders a short notice regarding the issue to be voted on during the next shareholder meeting that refers them to a website with the necessary solicitation materials,[522] Rule 14a-16 SEA. Shareholders can then choose whether they are satisfied with the electronic materials or whether they prefer to have those documents mailed to them at the expense of the soliciting party. Despite an exemption introduced in 1992 relative to the requirement to prepare and file proxy statements according to Rule 14a-2(b)(1) SEA, this innovation was relevant to proxy access, since pursuant to Rule 14a-2(b)(1)(iv) and (x) SEA the exception had not applied to nominees for the board or persons acting on their behalf. Even though this new enactment represented an alternative to the existing proxy distribution system, it did not guarantee sufficient cost reduction such that each motivated shareholder could lead a counter campaign. A substantial part of the shareholders usually choose to obtain a paper version at the expense of the solicitor, adding to preparation costs. Furthermore, the corporation may decide for a high-level contest, which requires response at the same level from the opposing side.

The success of the e-proxy rules has generally been limited. Issuers who informed their investors through a notice that solicitation material would be available at the company's website experienced a very low viewing rate. This was not offset by the opportunity to request free hard copies.[523] Accordingly, issuers who decided against sending out a full complement of hard copies experienced significantly lower voting participation than they did before.[524] Amendments of the Notice and Access rules responding to this situation

---

521 Hunton & Williams LLP, http://www.hunton.com/files/tbl_s10News%5CFileUpload44%5C14829%5CCorpSecGovUpdatet_SH_Rules_11.07.pdf (last visited Jan. 8, 2009).

522 Kahan & Rock, *Embattled CEOs* 34, http://ssrn.com/abstract=1281516 (2008).

523 Letter from Broadridge Financial Solutions, Inc., to Elizabeth M. Murphy, Secretary, SEC (May 5, 2009) http://www.sec.gov/comments/sr-msrb-2009-02/msrb200902-2.pdf: on the introduction of an "access equals delivery" standard in the context of municipal securities.

524 Alston + Bird LLP, Securities Law Advisory (Apr. 1, 2010) at 2, http://www.alston.com/files/Publication/20fa6af5-b847-4b56-81ee-a0bfb7d64b49/Presentation/PublicationAttachment/46626fa7-c58f-4567-a3d9-a49ba918ddb6/10-199%20SEC%20Update%20Advisory.pdf; Broadbent, Memorandum on Enhanced Disclosure and New Prospectus Delivery Option for Registered Open-End Management Investement Companies (Nov. 19, 2008), http://www.sec.gov/comments/s7-28-07/s72807-169.pdf; *see* Hogan, *Are the new e-proxy rules in the United States really more effective?*, Apr. 27, 2010, http://www.lexology.com/library/detail.aspx?g=eac43ab3-a9d4-434c-a572-9cf99f24543c: according to him a Broadridge Financial Solutions, Inc. study from 2008 published that the percent-

became effective on March 29, 2010. Whether they will fulfill their aim will be proven in the following proxy seasons.

(7) Recent developments

(a) On Delaware state level

In April 2009, a bill was signed amending the Delaware General Corporation Law by providing shareholders with the opportunity to access a company's proxy statement.[525] Among these changes were the new sections 112 and 113 concerning access to proxy solicitation materials and proxy expense reimbursement. Both became effective on August 1, 2009. According to section 112, Delaware corporations may adopt bylaws granting shareholders the right to include in the corporation's proxy solicitation materials information about one or more nominees in addition to the board's nominees. The bylaws may lay down ownership requirements, information submissions required by the shareholder and the shareholder's nominee, eligibility provisions on the number of directors to be nominated, as well as others. Section 113 allows the adoption of bylaws granting shareholders the right to demand reimbursement of the solicitation expenses made in connection with the election of directors. It also provides a non-exclusive list of permissible procedures or conditions.

(b) On federal administrative level

Shortly thereafter, in May 2009, the SEC with its new majority of democratic commissioners proposed an amended Rule 14a-8(i)(8) SEA and a new Rule 14a-11 SEA.[526] Proposed Rule 14a-8(i)(8) SEA commenced with five substantive exclusions of shareholder proposals, among them, "(iv) [n]ominates a specific individual for election to the board of directors." Nevertheless, three exceptions applied again to the exclusion according to proposed Rule 14a-8(i)(8)(iv) SEA: "[O]ther than pursuant to § 240.14a-11, an applicable state law provision, or the company's governing documents." The relevant exception represented proposed *Rule 14a-11 SEA* in contrast to a possible legal route provided by the company. The latter required ordinarily a two-step process involving at least two subsequent annual meetings, one amending the bylaw and one using the route during the following year(s).[527] Proposed Rule 14a-11 SEA, in contrast, provided (active) shareholders with the opportunity to nominate one candidate (or up to ¼ of the vacant positions) in only one shareholder meeting. The shareholder friendly ownership

age of total retail shares that voted dropped to 16,57 percent in 2008 from 34,28 percent in 2007, for companies that used the notice-only option for the first time in 2008.

525 H.R. 19, 145th Gen. Assem. (Del. 2009): to be codified at DEL. CODE ANN. tit. 8.

526 Facilitating Shareholder Director Nominations, Securities Act Release No. 9046, Exchange Act Release No. 60,089, Investment Act Release 28,765, 2009 WL 1953653 (proposed June 10, 2009); Press Release, SEC, SEC Votes to Propose Rule Amendments to Facilitate Rights of Shareholders to Nominate Directors (May 20, 2009) http://www.sec.gov/news/press/2009/2009-116.htm.

527 Bloomenthal, Securities Law Handbook, Vol. 1, § 18.27 (2009-2010).

requirements comprised a holding period of only one year and a minimum stake of 1, 3 or 5 percent[528] of the corporation's outstanding shares, as long as they did not intend to bring about a change of control. Shareholders were then able to give notice about their intent to nominate to the corporation via Schedule 14N up to 120 days before the day the registrant had mailed the proxy materials of the prior annual meeting.

With regard to the above-mentioned state regulation, the proposed rule would have effectively eliminated the potential for public companies to use the recent amendments to eliminate or restrict shareholder proxy access provided at the federal level. Delaware corporations would have remained free to expand shareholder proxy access with Rule 14a-11 SEA representing a bright line below which a corporation could no longer go.[529]

The proposed rule has, however, been strongly criticized, not only for its content.[530] Counterarguments referred also to the SEC's lack of jurisdictional authority on the matter,[531] the effectiveness of the approach, as it would have prematurely ended the search for the right provision at the state level,[532] and finally the design of the rule.[533] Such concerns were countered by reference to the SEC's regulation of the solicitation process of public corporations, which also requires that certain information be provided through the proxy materials. The latter also concerns certain shareholder proposals, such as proxy access

528 Depending on whether the nominating shareholder is a large accelerated, accelerated or non-accelerated filer under Rule 12b-2 SEA.

529 Jane K. Storero & Jeffrey M. Taylor, *Shareholder Access: The SEC, Delaware & Congress Advance the Ball,* WALL STREET LAWYER, July 2009, *available* at http://www.blankrome.com/index.cfm?contentID=37&itemID=2034.

530 Grundfest, *The SEC's Proposed Proxy Access Rules: Politics, Economics, and the Law,* http://ssrn.com/abstract=1538630 (2010).

531 For the denial of the statutory authority of the Commission could be brought forth the outcome in a similar case regarding a SEC rule barring national security exchanges and associations from listing stock of corporations which nullify, restrict or disparately reduce per share voting rights of common shareholders, *see* BRT v. SEC, 905 F.2d 406, 409 – 412 (D.C. Cir. 1990). The court denied the Commission's authority to correspondingly amend the rules of self-regulatory organizatons under § 19 (c) SEA as otherwise furthering the purpose of the Exchange Act since Congress' central concern especially with § 14(a) SEA was disclosure (J.I.Case Co. v. Borak, 377 U.S. 426, 431 (1964): "The purpose of § 14(a) is to prevent management or others from obtaining authorization for corporate action by means of deceptive or inadequate disclosure in proxy solicitation.") as belonging to the area of voting process in contrast to substance. The Commission's rule went beyond the control of voting procedure and also concerned the distribution of voting power, an authority the proponents of the Exchange Act had not intended to grant. Rather, it is the corporate state law that regulates the distribution of powers among various players in the process of corporate governance, and the Commission's leap beyond disclosure is just that kind of regulation.

532 BRT, Media Statement (May 20, 2009) http://www.businessroundtable.org/sites/default/files/2009.05.20%20SEC%20Proxy%20Access%20Statement.pdf; *see* Jane K. Storero & Jeffrey M. Taylor, *Shareholder Access: The SEC, Delaware & Congress Advance the Ball,* WALL STREET LAWYER, July 2009, *available* at http://www.blankrome.com/index.cfm?contentID=37&itemID=2034.

533 Grundfest, *The SEC's Proposed Proxy Access Rules: Politics, Economics, and the Law,* http://ssrn.com/abstract=1538630 (2010); Young/The Corporate Library for the CII, *The Limits of Private Ordering: Restrictions on Shareholders' Ability to Initiate Governance Change and Distortion of the Shareholder Voting Process*, http://www.cii.org/UserFiles/file/The%20Limits%20of%20Private%20Ordering%20UPDATED%2011-17-09.pdf (2009).

proposals. As far as the prematurely ending state-level efforts were concerned, it was argued that the Commission only provided for a minimum level of proxy access, which the states would have remained free to increase.

During the reopened comment period in December 2009,[534] the SEC asked in particular for comments on the idea of private ordering.[535] Opinions broadly diverged.

Grundfest opposed the mandatory minimum access regime proposed by the SEC and suggested adopting an *opt in* regime.[536] According to Grundfest, only a fully enabling approach to proxy access made sense since a mandatory rule would hardly be able to address the individual circumstances of the almost 12,000 publicly traded U.S. corporations.[537] Further, the SEC did not have the necessary information or the means necessary to determine the preferences of the majority of shareholders[538] and therefore lacked the prerequisites to issue a mandatory rule.[539] The opt in regime would prevent externalities resulting from interest groups using the proxy access less to advance a successful candidate than to announce their interests, as often done by labor unions and public pension funds.[540] It would further prevent shareholder disenfranchisement, as they would be able to prevent proxy access if they chose.[541] Finally, the opt in regime allegedly would prevent the otherwise arbitrary and capricious rulemaking of the SEC under the Administrative Procedure Act[542]. In addition, it would conform to the aim of making the corporate proxy process as close to the actual in-person meeting of shareholders as possible.[543] It would dissolve the contradiction that shareholders would be allowed to nominate director candidates, but not to decide the proper proxy access regime. Moreover, it would avoid a mandatory minimum access regime that precludes amendments to loosen its prerequisites[544].[545]

Bebchuk and *Hirst* raised strong arguments against an opt in regime as far as the choice between different default rules was concerned. Despite *Grundfest's* convincing argument regarding the SEC's insufficient means to assess the majority will, they underscored that the denial of a mandatory proxy access rule does not automatically point

534 Facilitation Shareholder Director Nominations, Securities Act Release No. 9086, Exchange Act Release No. 61,161, Investment Company Act Release No. 29,069, 74 Fed. Reg. 67144 (Jan. 19, 2010).

535 CII, *Governance Issues – Proxy Access*, http://www.cii.org/resourcesKeyGovernanceIssuesProxyAccess (last visited June 8, 2010).

536 Grundfest, *The SEC's Proposed Proxy Access Rule: Politics, Economics, and the Law* 7 – 8, 2, http://ssrn.com/abstract=1491670 (2010).

537 *Id.* at 1, 4.

538 *Id.* at 5, 15.

539 *Id.* at 2.

540 *Id.* at 4.

541 *Id.* at 2.

542 Administrative Procedure Act, 5 U.S.C. § 706 (2)(A) (2009).

543 Facilitating Shareholder Director Nominations, Securities Act Release No. 9046, Exchange Act Release No. 60,089, Investment Act Release 28,765, 74 Fed. Reg. 29,024, 29,025 (proposed June 10, 2009).

544 *See* § 112 DGCL, which establishes no minimum standard for proxy access permitting therefore the imposition of any lawful condition on access, while the proposed mandated minimum access prohibits that an indefinite number of lawful conditions are imposed.

545 Grundfest, *The SEC's Proposed Proxy Access Rule: Politics, Economics, and the Law* 2-3, 9-11, http://ssrn.com/abstract=1491670 (2010).

to a specific default rule.[546] The proxy access rule is most likely to represent the most efficient rule for most corporations.[547] Costs saved by shareholders who would otherwise have to spend money on distributing proxy materials[548] lead to invigorated elections[549] and therefore to reduced insulation from removal.[550] All contribute to benefits like increased director accountability[551] and shareholder value. Based on the benefits of proxy access, the choice clearly should be in favor of an *opt out* rule. This is also the case for theoretical rule-design-reasons stated *supra* in the theoretical part of the introduction to Part 1. Shareholders face substantial difficulties to initiate rule amendments under private ordering, taking into account the necessity of initiating the appropriate amendment, which is often restricted to the board of directors. Accordingly, it needs to account for the interests of shareholders and the board in designing the rule. As a corollary, it is generally advisable to design a rule in a way where the opt in or opt out favors the administration and not the shareholders. In the case of proxy access, the administration will be inclined to remove the proxy access rule. Moreover, it has the right to initiate this change and will therefore be likely to initiate an opt out while shareholders would be equipped with a veto right.[552] As a consequence, they argued, the shareholder-friendly proxy access rule needs to be designed as an opt out regime.[553]

According to the convincing approach of *Young*, the discussion about the proper default rule needs to consider the entire corporate decision-making process and the practical limits it imposes on private ordering in the interests of shareholders.[554] Shareholders face not only limitations in initiating amendments to governance arrangements, but they also need to obtain the necessary quorum for approval. For governance arrangements on the bylaw level, the shareholder initiation right seems in general to stem from the proxy rules, as held by the Delaware Supreme Court. The lack of an initiation right may be considered when designing default rules according to the recommendations of *Bebchuk/Hamdani*. However, supermajority voting requirements,[555] use of the denominator of outstanding shares instead of votes cast,[556] and multiple class stock structures

546 Bebchuk & Hirst, *Private Ordering and the Proxy Access Debate* 6, http://ssrn.com/abstract=1513408 (2010).

547 *Id.* at 5.

548 *Id.* at 7-8.

549 *Id.* at 8.

550 *Id.* at 9 n.30 – 36.

551 *Id.* at 8.

552 Bebchuk & Hamdani, 96 Nw. U. L. Rev. 489 *passim* (2002).

553 Bebchuk & Hirst, *Private Ordering and the Proxy Access Dabate passim,* http://ssrn.com/abstract=1513408 (2010).

554 Young/The Corporate Library for the CII, *The Limits of Private Ordering: Restrictions on Shareholders' Ability to Initiate Governance Change and Distortion of the Shareholder Voting Process*, http://www.cii.org/UserFiles/file/The%20Limits%20of%20Private%20Ordering%20UPDATED%2011-17-09.pdf (2009).

555 *Id.* at 7: according to which between 35,4 and 39,1 percent (separate number for each market indice) of the Russel 3000, Russel 1000 and S&P 500 companies have installed supermajority voting requirements to amend bylaws.

556 *Id.* at 6.

with unequal voting right[557] frequently impede the approval requirement. The choice of a proper default rule that considers only the limits of shareholder initiation would not overcome these measures. Rather, they show the limits of private ordering as such. They result in the consideration of other alternatives, such as the limitation of the supermajority requirements to approve the amendment of election procedures, the implementation of a one-share one-vote policy, or, more specifically, a *mandatory approach* to the proxy access rule.

(c) On federal legislative level

Shareholder proxy access also became a focal point of discussion on the federal legislative level when in 2009 Senator Charles E. Schumer, Representative Gary C. Peters, and others introduced legislation to permit shareholders to access the corporate ballot to place their nominees for board.[558] The Wall Street Reform and Consumer Protection Act of 2009, a comprehensive financial regulatory reform bill that the House of Representatives approved in December 2009, included a provision that reaffirmed the SEC's authority to issue rules granting shareholders proxy access. Senator Dodd (D. -Conn.) argued that the bill should grant proxy access if only *a single* shareholder held at least 5 percent of the corporation's outstanding shares for two years or more.[559] The later as *Dodd–Frank Wall Street Reform and Consumer Protection Act (**"Dodd-Frank Act"**)*[560] renamed and into law signed *Restoring American Financial Stability Act of 2010*[561] tossed the key issue of corporate governance back to the SEC without imposing particular ownership requirements. It therefore removed uncertainty regarding the Commission's statutory authority to adopt a proxy access rule.[562]

557 *Id.* at 8: according to which between 7,1 and 8,8 percent (separate percentage for each market indices) of the Russel 3000, Russel 1000 and S&P 500 companies have a multiple capital structure with disparate voting rights.

558 Shareholder Bill of Rights Act 2009, S. 1074, 111th Cong. § 4 (2009) sponsored by U.S. Senator Charles Schumer, introduced on May 19, 2009: providing proxy access if ownership requirements of one percent over two years are met; Shareholder Empowerment Act of 2009, H.R. 2861, 111th Cong. § 16A (b) (2009) sponsored by U.S. Representative Gary Peters, introduced on June 12, 2009: requiring that public companies provide shareholders with access to the company's proxy statement when holding in aggregate at least one percent of the outstanding shares for at least two years, and Wall Street Reform and Consumer Protection Act of 2009, H.R. 4173, 111th Congress § 7222 (2009) introduced by Representative Frank Barney on December 2, 2009: providing the SEC with the authority to issue a proxy access rule regarding shareholder nominee(s).

559 Hyatt, *Senate Negotiators Move to Limit Proxy Access in Finance Bill*, June 17, 2010, www.business-ethics.com (title into search).

560 Pub.L. 111-203, 124 Stat. 1376-2223 (2011).

561 H.R. 4173, 111th Cong. § 972 (2010), www.congress.gov (put H.R. 4173 into bill number search, chose text of legislation, choose last version).

562 Grundfest, *The SEC's Proposed Proxy Access Rules: Politics, Economics, and the Law* 16, http://ssrn.com/abstract=1491670 (2010).

(d) The final SEC move

Only one month later, on August 25, 2010, the SEC approved a proxy access rule.[563] The SEC pursued a dual approach in favor of the effectiveness of shareholder nomination and election rights. Correspondingly, amended Rule 14a-11 SEA mandated a nomination right for shareholders who have held for 3 years alone *or as a group* 3 percent of the outstanding shares entitled to vote. The Schedule 14N that needed to be filed in this case had to contain information regarding the nominating party as well as the nominee. Shareholders were able to nominate a number of candidates, between one and one-fourth of the director positions.[564] The advantage of this approach was its *mandatory* character. It provided shareholders with a mandatory right to determine a nominee independent of their initiation rights, approval quorums, and delay related to the implementation of a corresponding rule. Further, directors were unable to decide to opt out. A group was able to accumulate the ownership percentage of 3 percent. Even though the quorum was high, it balanced well the interest of those afraid that (potential) shareholder nominations would be disruptive with those afraid that the nomination right would have little practical relevance. However, the ownership duration requirement of three years prevented short-term and mid-term investors from making use of the mandatory initiation right. Despite the intention to prevent short-term investors from impacting board composition, the three-year ownership requirement went beyond that goal. Rather, it would have been sufficient to set up a twenty-four month[565] or even an eighteen month quorum.

This criticism was relative, however, because state law and shareholder-initiated provisions were able to lower the ownership criteria provided by Rule 14a-11 SEA. After the December 2007 amendment, Rule 14a-8(i)(8) SEA has been amended again, simultaneous with Rule 14a-11 SEA. The amendment clarified that a proposal relating to elections may only be excluded if the proposal "(i) Would disqualify a nominee who is standing for election; (ii) Would remove a director from office before his or her term expired; (iii) Questions the competence, business judgment, or character of one or more nominees or directors; (iv) Seeks to include a specific individual in the company's proxy materials for election to the board of directors; or (v) Otherwise could affect the outcome of the upcoming election of directors."[566] Accordingly, the SEC has decided in favor of the traditional interpretation of Rule 14a-8(i)(8) SEA after its 1976 amendment and in favor of the company bearing the costs related to potential contested elections. It aims to increase the practical relevance of the shareholder nomination right as an important accountability mechanism. The only drawback is that small companies with a public float of $75

563 Facilitating Shareholder Director Nominations, Securities Act Release No. 9136, Exchange Act Release No. 62,764, Investment Company Act Release No. 29,384 (Aug. 25, 2010).

564 Bebchuk & Hamdani, 96 Nw. U. L. Rev. 489, 409 et seq. (2002).

565 CII, Full Council Corporate Governance Policies, 3.2 Access to the Proxy, www.cii.org/policies (updated Sept. 2010): proposing at least two years of ownership duration and three percent of joint ownership.

566 Facilitating Shareholder Director Nominations, Securities Act Release No. 9046, Exchange Act Release No. 60,089, Investment Act Release 28,765, 2009 WL 1953653, at 218 et seq. (proposed June 10, 2009).

million or less will not have to comply with the regulation for the next three years. While the SEC alleges that these companies will automatically fall under the regime at that time, others doubt that this will happen.[567]

(e) The very final move on the issue

On September 29, 2010, the U.S. Chamber of Commerce and the Business Roundtable challenged the proxy access rule of the SEC in the D.C. Court of Appeals. In July 2011, the D.C. Circuit Court vacated the proxy access rule.[568] Unfortunately, the court's reasoning was mainly based on formal arguments instead of concentrating on the purpose and effect of the SEC's rule.

ii) The majority-voting rule

When the SEC shelved its 2003 proposed Rule 14a-11 SEA granting proxy access in 2005, attention shifted toward a different debate in the field of shareholder rights, the implementation of the majority-voting rule via shareholder bylaw amendment.[569] The implementation of a majority-voting rule via bylaw amendment replaces the prevailing default rule of plurality voting.[570]

(1) The prevailing default rule of plurality voting

Plurality voting pursuant to § 216(3), the traditionally applied default rule, requires that candidates in contested elections receive more votes than their competitors independent of the total number of votes cast. It allows nominees to win the election with fewer supporting votes so long as they exceed the number of votes in support of any competitor. In uncontested elections, this means a director may even be elected with only one supporting vote.

Plurality voting has been in place for decades and is, according to Delaware law, the default standard absent a provision in the articles of incorporation specifying a different standard. Plurality voting was originally implemented because of the concern that contested elections would result in failed elections.[571] Plurality voting ensured that enough

567 CII, Corporate Governance Issues, Proxy Access, www.cii.org/resourcesKeyGovernanceIssuesProxyAccess (last visited Sept. 2010).

568 Bus. Roundtable v. SEC, No. 10-1305, 2011 WL 2936808 (D.C. Cir. July 22, 2011).

569 ABA/Committee on Corporate Laws, *Discussion paper on Voting by Shareholders for the Election of Directors* 9, http://www.law.yale.edu/documents/pdf/CBL_Symposium10_05/S1-1%20aba_discuss_paper.pdf (2005).

570 CII, Majority Voting for Directors, http://www.cii.org/resourcesKeyGovernanceIssuesMajorityVotingForDirectors (last visited Jan. 7, 2011): In most U.S. public companies directors are elected by a plurality of the votes cast.

571 *For many:* Maryland legislature: Explanation of Senate Bill 659 Vote Required to Elect Directors, quoted in Ideal Fed. Sav. Bank v. Murphy, 663 A.2d 1272, 1277-78 (Md. 1995).

nominees were elected.[572] This led to valid elections in public corporations with widely dispersed shareholdings and/or a substantial number of withheld votes, since the votes of even a small number of approving shareholders were sufficient. This latter circumstance proved simultaneously to be the main argument against the plurality-voting standard. A majority of elections remain uncontested, so that the risk of failed elections is comparably low. More importantly, the plurality-voting standard allows directors to be elected even by a very limited number of shareholder votes "in favor"; even one vote suffices.[573] This appears to contradict the basic premise of the corporate structure: that shareholders delegate most of their authority to the board of directors, which makes decisions and controls the decision-making of the officers in the interests of all shareholders to increase shareholder value. The ability of shareholders to elect directors represents their main tool to ensure that directors remain accountable to the shareholders. The few shareholder votes that may suffice for a director to be elected under the plurality-voting rule raise justifiable doubts about the level of directorial accountability toward shareholders.

(2) Voting options under the plurality-voting rule

Most proxy cards distributed under the plurality-voting rule provide shareholders only with the opportunity to vote "for" a nominee or to "withhold" authority to vote for a nominee, but not to vote "against" a nominee.[574] However, in the prevailing kind of uncontested elections, only the possibility to vote "against" a nominee would make directors accountable to shareholders, as they would face the risk of losing their board seat during the next election.[575] Together with a system of plurality voting, this leads to the sentiment that "shareholders have no voice in election of directors."[576]

Opponents of majority-voting rules underscore the symbolic meaning of withholding votes as a means for shareholders to express their dissatisfaction without removing the director in question. However, the inability to vote "against" a candidate reduces his accountability even further. The reason lies in the different consequences of "withheld" votes as compared to "against" votes. The latter leads automatically to the result that a candidate with more "against" than "in favor" votes is not elected as a director. Under the prevailing system, however, candidates who receive more "withheld" votes than votes "in favor" are not automatically denied the position of a director. Shareholders rather depend on the board, which has to deny the candidate the position, before he

572 ABA/Committee on Corporate Laws, *Discussion paper on Voting by Shareholders for the Election of Directors* 5, http://www.law.yale.edu/documents/pdf/CBL_Symposium10_05/S1-1%20aba_discuss_paper.pdf (2005).

573 ISS, *White Paper on Majority Voting in Director Elections* 5 (2005) (on hold with author).

574 Rule 14a-4(b) SEA; ABA/Committee on Corporate Laws, *Discussion paper on Voting by Shareholders for the Election of Directors* 11, http://www.law.yale.edu/documents/pdf/CBL_Symposium10_05/S1-1%20aba_discuss_paper.pdf (2005).

575 ABA/Committee on Corporate Laws, *Discussion paper on Voting by Shareholders for the Election of Directors* 9 et seq., http://www.law.yale.edu/documents/pdf/CBL_Symposium10_05/S1-1%20aba_discuss_paper.pdf (2005).

576 Unofficial transcript of the SEC's Security Holder Director Nominations Roundtable on March 10, 2004, www.sec.gov/spotlight/dir-nominations/transcript03102004.pdf.

is removed. The implementation of a possible "against" vote besides the "in favor" and "withhold" votes would provide shareholders a broader range of voting opportunities, including the expression of dissatisfaction on the lower end. Automatic removal independent of a board decision would increase the ability of shareholders to hold directors accountable and would therefore increase the effectiveness of the shareholder franchise.

(3) Arguments in favor of the majority-voting rule

The majority-voting rule requires that candidates nominated for a director position have the majority of votes cast in their favor.[577] Even if no competitor exists for a vacant position, the sole nominee must still obtain the majority of the votes cast. This requirement assures the responsiveness of members of the board of directors to shareholder interests if they seek to be re-elected by the shareholders. Each director to be re-elected after his annual term of office will be held accountable for his past decisions and actions and their conformity to the shareholder interests through the number of supporting votes. Therefore, the majority-voting rule complements the functions of the proxy access rule by increasing the accountability and responsiveness of directors. As a consequence, agency costs resulting from the separation of ownership and control are further reduced.

(4) Counterarguments

Even though the replacement of plurality voting with majority voting has broad scholarly support,[578] a few voices[579] argue against majority voting.[580] Besides the *risk of failed elections*[581] and the symbolic character of its introduction due to state law *holdover rules*,[582][583] opponents argue that majority voting has the potential to *destabilize the board* due to a possible sudden removal of directors.[584] The possible removal may also have an adverse

577 CII, *Majority voting Primer – Making Shareowner's Votes Count: Majority Voting in Director Elections* (Feb. 27, 2006) http://www.cii.org/UserFiles/file/resource%20center/publications/MajorityVotingPrimer.pdf; CII, *Majority Voting for Directors*, http://www.cii.org/resourcesKey-GovernanceIssuesMajorityVotingForDirectors (last visited June 5, 2010); ISS, *White paper on Majority Voting in Director Elections* 16 (2005) (on hold with author).

578 *For many*: Bebchuk, 93 Va. L. Rev. 102 (2007).

579 ABA/Section of Business Law, 61 Bus. Law. 399 (2005); Letter from BRT, to ABA (May 26, 2005); Fairfax, 69 Ohio St. L.J. 53 (2008); Joseph Hinsey, *Corporate Governance Activists are Headed in the Wrong Direction*, http://hbswk.hbs.edu/item/5442.html (July 5, 2006).

580 Olson, A practical guide to SEC proxy and compensation rules 8-19 (2001).

581 Joseph Hinsey, *Corporate Governance Activists are Headed in the Wrong Direction*, http://hbswk.hbs.edu/item/5442.html (July 5, 2006).

582 The holdover rule in § 141 (b) DGCL provides that an incumbent director remains in office notwithstanding the failure to receive the required vote until the successor is elected unless the director resigns or the stockholders remove the director, Thacher, *Majority Voting in Director Elections: A Look Back and A Look Ahead* 2, www.stblaw.com/content/ppublications/pub560.pdf (2006).

583 ABA/Section of Business Law, 61 Bus. Law. 399, 410 (2005); Letter from BRT, to ABA (May 26, 2005) at 1; Fairfax, 69 Ohio St. L.J. 53, 63 et seq. (2008).

584 ISS, White Paper on Majority Voting in Director Elections, 15 (2005) (on hold with author).

impact on the company's ability to comply with certain *standards or requirements* such as retaining independent directors or directors with specific expertise.[585] Further, opponents argue that the possible rejection of candidates by shareholders may lead to a negative impact regarding the *mix of skills and expertise* of the members on the board.[586] In addition, majority voting may give increased power to *special interests,* which may be narrowly focused on single-issue viewpoints that may not reflect long-term shareholder value.[587] Moreover, majority voting may also *reduce the pool of qualified candidates*,[588] as some have argued in opposition to the proxy access rule. Finally, majority voting is said to be *superfluous* because of the signaling effect of withheld votes.[589]

There is truth to the claim that majority voting is one of several means to effectively install *accountability,* since it enables shareholders to express their dissatisfaction not only symbolically but also effectively by denying a candidate the necessary support for reelection.[590] The resulting increase in pressure on a single candidate occurs not only in contested elections but also in uncontested elections.[591] Plurality voting, in contrast, provides at best only a minimal monitoring device, since under the most common scenario of uncontested elections only one vote is sufficient to confirm the nominee.[592] Even a majority of withheld votes under the plurality-voting regime does not affect the removal of the concerned nominee as long as one supporting vote has been given. Therefore, even though withheld votes allow shareholders to make a statement, this impact is not comparable to the consequences of the majority voting-rule, under which a candidate without majority support will be removed from the position.[593]

As already mentioned, the *risk of failed elections* represents the main argument against majority voting. However, the number of contested elections has remained low, keeping the risk of failed elections correspondingly low. Accordingly, many so-called failed elections concern uncontested elections. Thus, a candidate's failure to win a majority vote is not related to the voting standard. Rather, it expresses the *lack of support* among the shareholders for a specific candidate in order to hold that candidate accountable for his

585 ABA/Section of Business Law, 61 Bus. Law. 399, 410 (2005); Letter from BRT, to ABA (May 26, 2005) at 2; Fairfax, 69 Ohio St. L.J. 53, 64 (2008); ISS, *White paper on Majority Voting in Director Elections* 15 (2005) (on hold with author).

586 ISS, *White Paper on Majority Voting in Director Elections*, 15, (2005) (on hold with author).

587 Letter from BRT, to ABA (May 26, 2005) at 2.

588 Katz & McIntosh, *Majority Election of Directors*, New York Law Journal, Mar. 24, 2005, at 5 (col. 1); ISS, *White Paper on Majority Voting in Director Elections* 13 (2005) (on hold with author); Verret, 62 Bus. Law. 1, 28 (2007).

589 ISS, *White Paper on Majority Voting in Director Elections* 13 et seq., (2005) (on hold with author).

590 Bebchuk, 93 Va. L. Rev. 102, 127–129 (2007).

591 Kahan & Rock, 96 Geo. L.J. 1227, 1280 (2008).

592 Sjostrom & Kim, 40 Conn. L. Rev. 459, 468 (2007).

593 IRRC/GMIRATINGS, The Election of Corporate Directors: What Happens When Shareowners Withhold a Majority of Votes from Director Nominees? 2 et seq., http://www.irrcinstitute.org/pdf/Final%20Election%20of%20Directors%20GMI%20Aug%202012.pdf (2012): only 5 % of the directors that received majority withhold votes at companies with simple plurality voting standard led directly to director removal as compared to fifty percent in companies with majority standards.

prior decisions. Therefore, the risk of failed elections does not seem to be a major risk under the majority-voting rule. For the few cases of contested elections, under which the risk of failed elections becomes relevant, *several modifications* of the majority-voting rule would reduce it. One modification represents the simple majority-voting rule, under which the majority requirement becomes reduced to one-third of the votes cast. Another one would allow the incumbent to remain in place for a very limited time until another election is held to remove the vacancy. Finally, majority voting could only be applied to uncontested elections. Proponents further argue that the board should be authorized to resolve failed election and that it should be provided with an incentive to cooperate with the shareholders to a find a mutually acceptable solution.[594] The advantage of this solution is that responsibility is placed on the board with no additional regulatory action required,[595] while at the same time the board is forced to cooperate with the shareholders.[596]

Concerns that there will be a significant *decrease in the number of willing candidates* to serve because of the damage to their reputation if their candidacy fails are unconvincing. Directors, once elected, hold comparably secure positions as long as they exhibit the necessary expertise and properly exercise their tasks. Potential directors should be conscious of increasing liability and the demands they face. If candidates are concerned that they might not be elected, they may not be the proper candidates and their concerns should not determine voting procedure.

The concern that directors might pursue *specific, narrow interests* contrary to long-term shareholder value is not convincing either due to the *supra* mentioned required majority of voted shares, which special interest groups would have to capture in order to win an election.[597]

As far as the *proper mix* of listing and other requirements of the board members is concerned, absent a proxy access rule, the board will propose the candidates and take into account these prerequisites. But even under the scenario of a proxy access rule, it seems unlikely that a majority of shareholders would elect candidates that do not qualify considering the resulting disadvantages for the corporation.

Moreover, the concern about the *destabilization* of the board due to majority voting and the potential changes in director positions may be addressed by longer terms of office than the usual annual term under U.S.-American practice.[598] This would allow a newly constituted board (rather likely with only few newly occupied positions) to grow together as a team and have more continuity in achieving certain goals without having to be concerned with being unseated from the board.

---

594 ISS, *White Paper on Majority voting in Director Elections* 10 (2005) (on hold with author).

595 Ira M. Millstein, *Unofficial copy of Roundtable Transcript of the SEC's Security Holder Director Nominations Roundtable* 10, http://www.sec.gov/spotlight/dir-nominations/transcript03102004.txt (2004).

596 Grundfest, *The SEC's Proposed Proxy Access Rules: Politics, Economics, and the Law* 10, http://ssrn.com/abstract=1491670 (2010).

597 Katz & McIntosh, *Majority election of directors*, New York Law Journal, Mar. 24, 2005, at 5 (col. 1).

598 Kraakman et al., The Anatomy of Corporate Law 61 (2009).

Finally, majority voting would neither destroy the symbolic meaning of withheld votes, nor would its implementation be *superfluous*. Rather, the implementation of a majority-voting rule would complement the means available to shareholders to express their discontent if given the chance to chose between votes in favor, against, or withheld. The latter combination would allow them to express their discontent. It may be true that some corporations react from time to time to the overwhelming number of withheld votes by replacing a candidate. However, the unreliable reaction of boards under the current system does not render the voting procedure superfluous, nor is it in accordance with an effective accountability mechanism that leaves the decision to the remaining incumbents and not the shareholders. In applying a majority-rule, the decision would lie in the hands of the shareholders.

(5) Recent moves in favor of majority voting

Accordingly, the *SEC*, in several no-action letters addressing the question whether proposals to implement a majority-voting rule could be excluded under Rule 14a-8(i)(8) SEA, did not concur in their exclusion.[599] The SEC agreed in general with the proponents' argument that such proposals concern general procedures of director election and are, therefore, not excludable under Rule 14a-8(i)(8) SEA.

As a result, law firms advised their clients seeking to avoid the implementation of a majority-voting rule, besides ignoring, challenging, or accepting it, to adopt a *modified plurality vote*.[600] This meant implementing a corporate policy under which nominees were required to step down from their elected position if they had not received a majority of all the votes cast. This approach allowed the board to affirm a candidate, who had not received the required majority in order to fill a vacant position. The director had then to obtain the required majority vote within the next 90 days or he would be removed. This approach avoided failed elections and their consequences. However, it still did not allow shareholders to cast votes against the nominees. The board still had the final choice on whether to remove a colleague or not, and it appeared likely that the board would be tempted to decide in favor of a colleague to avoid undermining collegiality. Further, this approach was not very useful in the context of takeovers, since the board was able to appoint directors to vacancies. Additionally, the final decision of the board about the removal of a colleague did not conform to the prevailing corporate governance system. Finally, such an approach was usually contrary to the articles of incorporations and provoked the disappointment of shareholders who had voted against the nominee, which again involved a problem of accountability. The expectation that a proposal to implement a majority-voting rule could be omitted according to Rule 14a-8(i)(10) SEA for reason of substantial implementation was disappointed when the SEC in January 2006 issued the *Hewlett Packard NAL*.[601] The SEC stated that a modified plurality vote would not allow

599 Lockheed Martin Corporation, SEC No-Action Letter, 2001 WL 121997 (Feb. 5, 2001).

600 David A. Katz & Laura A. McIntosh, *Director Elections and Majority Voting*, New York Law Journal, Dec. 29, 2005, at 5.

601 Hewlett Packard, SEC No-Action Letter, 2006 WL 39271 (Jan. 5, 2006).

a company to exclude a shareholder majority-voting proposal under Rule 14a-8(i)(10) SEA, since the majority rule had not yet been substantially implemented. Consequently, corporations facing shareholder majority-voting proposals were not able to continue to circumvent their implementation.

Despite the growing acceptance of majority voting among shareholders[602] and corporations,[603] the problem concerning the effectiveness of the different forms of majority voting remained, especially the consequences related to the failure of a director to obtain a majority vote. Accordingly, the *Hewlett Packard NAL* represented only one example of a number of shareholder proposals aiming to implement a variety of different majority voting standards during the 2006 and 2007 proxy seasons. They differed in regard to demand, precatory or mandatory, extent, comprising contested elections or not, and consequences of a failed majority vote. The latter focused on whether the board was allowed to second-guess shareholders, given that shareholder votes against a director candidate would assume an advisory character. Corporations continued to try to exclude them on the grounds of substantial implementation, sometimes successfully[604] and sometimes not.[605] In the 2008 proxy season, proposals were increasingly withdrawn, an expression of discussions between proponents and companies on the issue.[606]

---

602 Bloomenthal, Securities Law Handbook, Vol. 1, § 18.70: (2009-2010): The 43 tracked majority voting proposals voted on during the 2007 proxy season received an average support of 50,4 percent in 2007, as compared to 48,8 percent of the 95 proposals in 2006.

603 *Id.* at § 18.71: To an increasing extent companies are including shareholder proposals on majority voting without objection or they are adopting the Intel model. Intel's Form 8-K for January 19, 2006 includes the following bylaw provision in art. III, sec. 1: To an increasing extent corporations are including shareholder proposals on majority voting or they include the Intel model, which restricts majority voting to uncontested elections and which demands that directors not elected tender their resignation to the board, the Corporate Governance and Nomination Committee will make recommendations to the Board on whether to accept or reject the resignation. The board will act on the Committee's recommendation and publicly disclose its decision as well as the rational behind it 90 days from the date of the certification of the election results. The tendering director will not participate in the board's decision; CII states that currently (June 2010) half of all companies in the Standard & Poor 500 have a majority vote standard in director election, http://www.cii.org/resourcesKeyGovernanceIssuesMajorityVotingForDirectors; Kahan & Rock, *Embattled CEOs* 73, http://ssrn.com/abstract=1281516 (2008): the number of S&P 100 firms that have adopted the majority-voting rule since the decision have meanwhile increased from 9 percent in the 2005 proxy season before the SEC decision to 84 percent in the 2008 proxy season.

604 Citigroup, SEC No-Action Letter, 2007 WL 754965 (Mar. 8, 2007): The company bylaw, which determined that 60 days after an unsuccessful election of a director the resignation becomes effective if the board does not decide different, was held to substantially comprise the shareholder proposal to install a rule that to the fullest extent possible not make any provision to override a shareholder vote and to keep a director on the board who failed to obtain a majority vote.

605 Int'l Paper Co., SEC No-Action Letter, 2007 WL 754970 (Mar. 7, 2007): the proposal was not held to be excludable for reason of substantial implementation, as it resulted in directors being deemed not to be elected if they did not obtain a majority of the votes cast, while under the current bylaw they would be elected even if they did not obtain the necessary majority vote and would have to tender their resignation.

606 Bloomenthal, Securities Law Handbook, Vol. 1, § 18:70 (2009-2010): In the proxy season 2008, of 92 tracked proposals aiming to introduce majority voting 54 were withdrawn.

Legislation, both on the state and federal level, also moved toward majority voting. Even though the *Delaware legislator* did not amend the required vote necessary to elect a director, § 216(3), the legislator aimed to accommodate the desire to do something about plurality voting with two amendments that became effective on August 1, 2006.[607] It added to § 216 a provision that "[a] bylaw amendment adopted by stockholders, which specified the votes that shall be necessary for the election of directors shall not be further amended or repealed by the board of directors."[608] This is significant in the context of § 109(a). The success is relative, however, as the articles of incorporation may provide that any bylaw amendment must be approved by two-thirds of the outstanding shares.[609] Furthermore, an amendment to § 141(b)[610] intended to deal at least to some extent with the holdover issue of directors not elected by the required majority vote.[611] Amended § 141(b) sent. 7, 8[612] provides the corporation with the opportunity to have directors irrevocably agree to resign if they do not obtain the necessary majority vote, amending the default plurality voting standard.[613] This gives corporations the opportunity to subsequently enforce the resignation conditioned upon the director failing to achieve a specified vote for reelection.[614] Even though the amendments did not impose a majority-voting standard, as many activists would have liked it, or make it a default standard, the amendments facilitated the adoption of majority-voting standards by boards and shareholders.[615]

On the level of the federal legislation, the *supra* mentioned *Restoring American Financial Stability Act of 2010*,[616] as passed by the Senate in May 2010, also targeted majority voting. Section 971 intended to implement a new section 14B in the Securities Exchange Act of 1934. It obliged the Commission to pass not later than a year after its enactment a rule directing the national securities exchanges and associations to prohibit the listing of any security of an issuer that is not in compliance with the requirements of the subsection, section 14B(a)(1)(A) SEA. Section 14B(a)(2)(A) intended to lay down

607 *Id.* at § 18.69.

608 S. 322, 143rd Gen. Assem., Reg. Sess. § 5 (Del. 2006), www.legis.delaware.gov (search session, bill type and bill number) 75 Laws 2006, ch. 306 § 5, effective Aug. 1, 2006.

609 Bloomenthal, Securities Law Handbook, Vol. 1, § 18.69 (2009-2010).

610 S. 322, 143rd Gen. Assem., Reg. Sess. § 3 (Del. 2006), w<ww.legis.delaware.gov (search session, bill type and bill number) 75 Laws 2006, ch. 306 § 5, effective Aug. 1, 2006.

611 Bloomenthal, Securities Law Handbook, Vol. 1, § 18.69 (2009-2010).

612 „A resignation is effective when the resignation is delivered unless the resignation specifies a later effective date or an effective date determined upon the happening of an event or events. A resignation which is conditioned upon the director failing to receive a specified vote of reelection as a director may provide that it is irrevocable."

613 O'Toole & Symonds, Delaware, Laws governing Business Entities: Annotated Statutes and Rules, Vol. 1, 21 (2007 spring ed.) *available at* http://www.lexisnexis.com/csc/pdf/58559.pdf.

614 S. 322, 143rd Gen. Assem., Reg. Sess. (Del. 2006) Synopsis on amendment of § 141(b), http://legis.delaware.gov/LIS/lis143.nsf/48224c9dab6a374a852568f70050ed2c/6973d91cd3b751c-8852571630056c104?OpenDocument.

615 Milbank, Tweed, Hadley & McCloy LLP, *Delaware Legislature adopts amendments to facilitate majority voting for director elections*, Client Alert, July 17, 2006, http://www.milbank.com/NR/rdonlyres/FB16A0C1-EE30-4072-8A45-FBC1E0470F76/0/060717.pdf.

616 H.R. 4173, 111th Cong. S. 972 (as passed by the Senate, May 20, 2010).

a majority-voting standard for uncontested elections of directors. Subsection (C) determined the consequences if a director did not obtain the majority of the votes cast. Under this scenario, directors were obliged to tender their resignation to the board. The board would have been obliged to determine the date on which the resignation takeswould take effect, which has to be made public. The board would have been able to unanimously decline to accept the resignation. It would have been obliged to make public the specific reasons for that decision and that the decision was in the best interest of the issuer and its shareholders within 30 days after the vote. Even though the provision would have effectively been limited to listed corporations, it would nevertheless have been a signal for the entire corporate governance discussion on majority voting. The Act seemed to well balance the interests by leaving the final authority to decide on the resignation with the board, but at the same time demanding that the board informs the public about its decision. If tendered resignation is accepted, the board would have been obliged to publish the date of its effectiveness. If the resignation is declined, the board would have needed to unanimously support this decision and to publish its reasons as well as its benefits to the corporation and the shareholders. The obligation to publish its decision within a small timeframe aimed to enable monitoring of the board's decision. However, the restriction of the majority-voting rule to uncontested elections, aiming to prevent failed elections, would have given boards the potential to circumvent the majority-voting requirement by proposing an additional pseudo-candidate. Further, it would have prevented the simultaneous application of the proxy access rule and majority voting to contested elections with shareholder-proposed candidates. However, the Dodd-Frank Act, signed into law on July 22, 2010, dropped the Senate's proposal for a majority-voting rule.

iii) The cumulative-voting rule

Another very relevant procedural rule for active shareholders to effectively impact board composition is the cumulative-voting rule, the most popular kind of proportional voting[617] and the most effective technique to secure the representation of minority interests.[618] Cumulative voting allows a shareholder to accumulate the number of votes in a board election and to cast all of them for a single nominee when the board has multiple openings.[619] In contrast, shareholders under a straight voting rule may not give more than one vote per share to a single nominee.[620] However, alarmed by the role of cumulative voting in several proxy contests in the 1950s and the wave of hostile takeovers in the 1980s, many states eliminated cumulative voting. Mandatory cumulative voting only

617 Hopt/Roth, in: Großkomm AktG, 2006, § 101 mn.66.

618 Paul L. Davies, *The Board of Directors: Composition, Structure, Duties and Powers – Company Law Reform in OECD Countries A Comparative Outlook of Current Trends* 12, http://www.oecd.org/dataoecd/21/30/1857291.pdf (2000).

619 Balotti & Finkelstein, The Delaware Law of Corporations and Business Organizations, Vol. 1, § 7.27 (2010); Ruffner, Die ökonomischen Grundlagen des Rechts einer Publikumsgesellschaft, 2000, 189.

620 SEC, *Cumulative Voting* (Oct. 13, 2004) http://www.sec.gov/answers/cumulativevote.htm.

existed in seven states as of 2008,[621] compared to 22 states in 1950[622].[623] Delaware corporations may include the cumulative-voting rule in their articles of incorporation, § 214.

(1) Arguments for and against cumulative voting

Opinions on the desirability of cumulative voting are sharply divided.[624] Cumulative voting is designed to protect minorities by providing a method of voting which *ensures a minority*, if it is large enough or sufficiently purposeful and cohesive, *representation* on the board of directors to an extent roughly proportionate to the minority's size.[625] That is exactly the reason why it is so desirable for active shareholders aiming to overcome the separation of ownership and control and usually represented by a strong minority. While active shareholders under a plurality-voting rule or a majority-voting rule need to make comprehensive efforts to obtain board representation, this is comparably easier under cumulative voting. In the last few years of growing institutional stock ownership,[626] cumulative voting became one of the more important means for shareholders to exercise control if dissatisfied with management.[627] The effectiveness of cumulative voting is further increased when combined with the proxy access rule. A closely related advantage of cumulative voting is the *reduced costs* of obtaining board representation. In contrast to straight voting, it is sufficient to have the support of a large enough minority instead of a majority, which reduces organizational and campaign costs significantly.[628] Once the nominee has been elected, (at least) part of their control costs may be passed on to the corporation itself, which has to compensate the members of the board.[629] Cumulative voting is therefore a significant control mechanism for active shareholders of publicly owned companies.[630] The reduced efforts and costs for them to influence the composition of the board mitigate the problems of rational apathy and free-riding.[631]

At the same time cumulative voting represents a procedure under which *elected directors are independent in a genealogical sense*.[632] By adding an independent board member, critical scrutiny of management action could be factored in, thereby improving corporate decision-making and managerial accountability.[633] Accordingly, cumula-

621 ABA, Model Business Corporation Act Annotated (MBCAA), Vol. 1, 7-214 (2008).
622 Gordon, 94 Colum. L. Rev. 124, 165 (1994).
623 Gordon, 59 Stan. L. Rev. 1465, 1498 n.132 (2007).
624 ABA, Model Business Corporation Act Annotated (MBCAA), Vol. 1, 7-210 (2008).
625 *Id.* at 7-210; Gordon, 59 Stan. L. Rev. 1465, 1498 n.132 (2007); Klein & Coffee, Business Organization and Finance 117 (2008); Merkt/Göthel, US-amerikanisches Gesellschaftsrecht, 2006, 315; Rehm, in: Eidenmülller, Ausländische Kapitalgesellschaften, 2004, § 11, mn.37.
626 Gordon, 94 Colum. L. Rev. 124, 173 (1994).
627 Berrar, NZG 2001, 1113 (1115).
628 Gordon, 94 Colum. L. Rev. 124, 172 et seq. (1994).
629 Ruffner Die ökonomischen Grundlagen eines Rechts der Publikumsgesellschaft, 2000, 190.
630 *Id.* at 189 et seq.
631 Gordon, 94 Colum. L. Rev. 124, 172 et seq. (1994).
632 Gordon, 59 Stan. L. Rev. 1465, 1498 n.132 (2007).
633 Gordon, 94 Colum. L. Rev. 124, 170, 171 (1994).

tive voting is useful for securing a higher possible return from corporate activity.[634] It is therefore beneficial for all shareholders of the concerned corporation to get (active) minority shareholders represented on the board.

Just like the other electoral procedures discussed, cumulative voting has been confronted with several *counterarguments*. These include the fear that minority representation on the board will be used to extract *private benefits*[635] via threats of hold-up scenarios for greenmail[636637] or of obtaining confidential information[638]. In addition, opponents argue that the *functioning of the board could be disrupted* by minority representation, such as by subliminal disharmony, extensive debates,[639] or cycling and inconsistent decision results.[640] Furthermore, opponents are concerned about additional agency costs caused by the *interruption of proportionality between voting and participation* in gains and losses.[641] Finally, another argument relates to the concern that cumulative voting may *hinder takeovers* and therefore simultaneously *management control via the market for corporate control*.[642]

Shareholders aiming to exercise impact on the board will exercise their influence after evaluating the different opportunities under the applicable regime. Hence, the opportunity for active shareholders to choose to influence the board composition via the less costly cumulative-voting rule has many advantages. Since active shareholders will exercise their influence regardless, it seems preferable to have them do it in a canalized way that is transparent and gives fewer opportunities for strategic actions leading to *threats and disruption*.[643] Acting as a member of the board also implies that the proceedings are "more susceptible to legal scrutiny,"[644] since active shareholders in this position become subject to the duties of care and loyalty as well as to the duty of discretion, just as all other board members.[645] *Gordon* mentioned that the *concerns of disharmony and disruption* of the board's work apply only under certain ownership structures. General developments in ownership structure lead to more freefloat and fewer blockholders. Due to collective action issues leading to rational apathy, the consequence of this was

634 *Id.* at 168.

635 *See* Ruffner, Die ökonomischen Grundlagen eines Rechts der Publikumsgesellschaft, 2000, 191: who points out that it is rather a question of "how" and not "whether" shareholders with larg stakes exercise their impact upon the corporation; Williams, 33 Harv. Bus. Rev. 108, 112 (1955).

636 Greenmail being composed from Green Back (Dollar) and Black Mail. Greenmailing means repurchasing shares from a hostile acquirer by paying a substantial premium over the market price, Mäntysaari, The Law of Corporate Finance: General Principles and EU Law, Vol. III, 512 (2010).

637 Gordon, 94 Colum. L. Rev. 124, 169 (1994).

638 *Id.* at 167; Williams, 33 Harv. Bus. Rev. 108, 112 (1955).

639 Gordon, 94 Colum. L. Rev. 124, 167, 170 (1994); Williams, 33 Harv. Bus. Rev. 108, 112 (1955).

640 Easterbrook & Fischel, 26 J.L. & Econ. 395, 409, 410 (1983).

641 *Id.* at 409; Easterbrook & Fischel, The Economic Structure of Corporate Law 73 (1991).

642 Easterbrook & Fischel, The Economic Structure of Corporate Law 73 (1991); Easterbrook & Fischel, 26 J.L & Econ, 395, 409 (1983).

643 Gordon, 94 Colum. L. Rev. 124, 174 (1994); Ruffner, Die ökonomischen Grundlagen eines Rechts der Publikumsgesellschaft, 2000, 191 et seq.

644 Gordon, 94 Colum. L. Rev. 124, 171 (1994).

645 Ruffner, Die ökonomischen Grundlagen eines Rechts der Publikumsgesellschaft, 2000, 191.

a change from majority-governed to management-governed corporations. This implies that a coercive minority facing a disorganized majority may start to dictate to the corporation. Considering that institutional investors on average account for far more than fifty percent of corporate ownership, concerns about a diffuse majority confronted by a coercive minority are unjustified. Even though some of the institutional investors may remain passive, a minority of the institutional investors will nevertheless be able to coordinate their actions with many of the other shareholders. It will give the majority a voice in the corporation via an active minority and be a counterweight to management. Giving an active minority the tool of cumulative voting, which allows reducing coordination costs, represents an effective means to reduce the issue of collective action and rational apathy.[646]

The required coordination among several shareholders as well as the restrictions on directorial compensation will prevent institutional investors from aiming for *private benefits*. They will prefer to enhance corporate performance by installing an independent and sophisticated director exercising his task of controlling and consulting corporate management and reinstalling managerial accountability. As a consequence, stock prices will rise and all shareholders will profit on a shared basis.[647]

Even though the opportunity for a minority to be represented on the corporate board may lead to *discussions on the board as well as a certain delay*, this effect is outweighed by the advantages of cumulative voting. Minority shareholders get an adequate voice when they are represented on the corporate board.[648] The assertion of shareholder interests and points of view allows shareholders to potentially check the influence of managers on directors.[649] Moreover, the mere presence of an independent director enables him to bring up issues that otherwise would not have been discussed while preventing management from implementing poorly designed proposals.[650]

The *cycling concern*[651] is less a problem of smaller committees such as the board of directors.[652] Furthermore, as the highest decision committee, the board is directly responsible for the consequences of its decisions. For reputational reasons, it has low incentives to engage in changing coalitions that lead to disadvantages for the corporation.[653]

Neither is the *proportionality* of voting rights and participation in losses and return influenced by the cumulative-voting rule. Once the rule is implemented and all parties are aware of it, the number of seats occupied by each shareholder group will vary according to its ownership proportion.[654] The accessibility of all shareholders to the cumulative voting process assures the necessary proportionality.

---

646 Gordon, 94 COLUM. L. REV. 124, 170–173 (1994).
647 *Id.* at 171.
648 Williams, 33 HARV. BUS. REV. 108, 111 (1955).
649 *Id.*
650 *Id.* at 112.
651 Easterbrook & Fischel, 26 J. L. & ECON. 395, 409, 410 (1983).
652 Ruffner, Die ökonomischen Grundlagen eines Rechts der Publikumsgesellschaft, 2000, 192.
653 *Id.*
654 Williams, 33 HARV. BUS. REV. 108, 111 (1955).

Finally, administrative accountability may be furthered by means of corporate law and the market for corporate control. Reinforcing the legal means by *impeding the market means* to a certain extent does not automatically result in less total accountability. Rather, it is a question of the right balance to ensure sufficient accountability, which requires taking into account the concrete corporate circumstances.

However, a weakness of cumulative voting authorized by the certificate of incorporation lies in the opportunity for the board of directors or the shareholder majority to substantially reduce or even eliminate its *effectiveness*.[655] Thus, *staggering* the board of directors in up to three classes, § 141(d), a measure enacted to prevent takeovers, can impair cumulative voting due to the limited number of vacant positions up for election at one time.[656] The possible accumulation of votes to be cast by the minority in favor of one director is then significantly reduced.[657] The customary means of providing directors willing to leave the board with generous compensation during takeover situations may call into question the effectiveness of staggered board in any case.[658] Beyond this, staggered boards are associated with lower firm value.[659] Furthermore, the court of chancery has upheld action taken by a board of directors to *reduce the number of board seats* to preclude minority shareholders from cumulatively electing directors.[660] The number of directors can be readily reduced as their number "shall be fixed by, or in the manner provided in, the bylaws", or the certificate of incorporation, § 141(b) sent. 2.[661] Majority shareholders may even *remove director(s) elected through cumulative voting* for cause.[662] Finally, even when the certificate of incorporation guarantees cumulative voting, this provision may be removed by *amending the certificate* for the purpose of eliminating unwanted minority board representation.[663] Here, it is necessary to think again about the permissibility of board action to get rid of minority representation in general as compared to the elimination of destructive minority representation in very limited scenarios. This is particularly necessary since workable alternatives to cumulative voting that function against the will of the management do not exist.[664] Negotiated settlements may be very complex and lack transparency. The leeway they give sets incentives to act strategically.[665] Voting caps may hinder management removal in takeover situations. They

655 Welch et al., Folk on Delaware General Corporation Law, Vol. 1, § 214.2 (2010).
656 Leyens, 67 RabensZ 57, 71 n.57 (2003).
657 Balotti & Finkelstein, The Delaware Law of Corporations and Business Organizations, Vol. 1, § 7.27 (2010).
658 Merkt/Göthel, US-amerikanisches Gesellschaftsrecht, 2006, mn.1384.
659 Bates et al., 87 J. Fin. Econ. 656, 675 – 76 (2008).
660 AAR Corp. v. Brooks & Perkins, Inc., C.A. No. 6287, 1980 WL 6435 (Del. Ch. 1980).
661 Welch et al., Folk on Delaware General Corporation Law, Vol. 1, § 214.2 (2010).
662 Campell v. Loews's, Inc., 134 A.2d 852, 858 (Del. Ch. 1957); Balotti & Finkelstein, The Delaware Law of Corporations & Business Organizations, Statutory Deskbook Corp – 189 (2010); Wolcott & Rogers, Corporations and Business Organizations, Delaware Code Annotated 8 § 214 (2008).
663 Maddock v. Vorclone Corp., 147 A. 255, 256 – 257 (Del. Ch. 1929).
664 *See* Ruffner, Die ökonomischen Grundlagen eines Rechts der Publikumsgesellschaft, 2000, 191 et seq.
665 *Id.* at 192.

may therefore chill takeovers, which would render one of the primary tools for securing management responsiveness to shareholders as a class less effective.[666]

Consequently, cumulative voting has to be considered as an effective method for reducing costs and therefore collective action issues for strong shareholder minorities seeking to impact board composition to increase administrative accountability. Naturally, influencing a corporate governance process may also lead to increased agency costs. However, before rendering judgment, it is important to consider the resulting benefits, which for cumulative voting seem to outweigh the costs.

(2) Rule-of-the-game level and rule design

Today only few states allow the implementation of cumulative voting in the *bylaws*. Corresponding shareholder proposals were not excludable under Rule 14a-8(i)(8) SEA, nor according to the SEC statement after its major amendment in 1976[667] or after its amendments in 2007[668] and 2010.

The majority of states, including Delaware[669] have, however, expressly provided that directors are elected by plurality vote, while corporations may through their *articles of incorporation* opt in to the cumulative-voting rule, § 214.[670] However, there is no constitutional or statutory requirement that a Delaware corporation provide for cumulative voting.[671] Neither are shareholders able to mandate the initiation of rules-of-the game amendments laid down on the articles of incorporation level as compared to the proxy-access rule or the majority-voting rule, both laid down on the bylaw level. It lies solely in the hands of the administration. Active shareholders aiming to opt in to cumulative voting are therefore restricted to using precatory proposals recommending that the administration initiate a corresponding amendment. However, the function of cumulative voting to provide a coherent minority the opportunity to elect a candidate during director elections in a management-dominated firm[672] correlates with a restriction of the administration's authority. Hence, the success of corresponding precatory proposals is limited and the choice of the rule-maker for an opt in on the level of the articles of incorporation barely makes sense. According to the *reversible default approach* of Bebchuk/Hamdani,[673] the rule design would have needed to take into account that only the administration is able to initiate an articles of incorporation amendment. As a consequence, a better approach would have been to make cumulative voting a default

---

666 Easterbrook & Fischel, The Economic Structure of Corporate Law 73 (1991).

667 http://iblsjournal.typepad.com/illinois_business_law_soc/2008/02/securities-and.html (last visited Jan. 8, 2009).

668 Hunton & Williams LLP, http://www.hunton.com/files/tbl_s10News%5CFileUpload44%5C14829%5CCorpSecGovUpdatet_SH_Rules_11.07.pdf (last visited Jan. 8, 2009).

669 §§ 214, 216 DGCL.

670 ABA, Model Business Corporation Act Annotated (MBCAA), Vol. 1, 7-214, 7-208 (2008); Leyens, 67 RabelsZ 57 (70).

671 Maddock v. Vorclone Corp., 17 Del. Ch. 39, 147 A. 255 (Del. Ch. 1929).

672 Gordon, 94 Colum. L. Rev. 124, 169 (1994).

673 Bebchuk & Hamdani, 96 Nw. U. L. Rev. 489, 489 (2002).

rule from which corporations could *opt out* at the board's initiative. This appears more appropriate, as the administration would want to opt out and would be able to initiate rule-of-the-game amendments on the articles of incorporation level. Furthermore, the administration would need to assure the approval quorum instead of the minority. Under the current regime, the majority accumulation necessary to approve the implementation of the minority-friendly cumulative-voting rule represents the second challenge for the shareholders. Another alternative is the *amendment of the relevant rule-of-the game level* for setting up a cumulative-voting rule, from the articles of incorporation to the bylaw level. Minority shareholders would be able to initiate the necessary amendment of the rules-of-the-game on the bylaw level to opt in to the cumulative-voting rule. However, as the approval requirement would remain a practical challenge for minority shareholders, the opt out regime remains the only practical form of private ordering. Finally, the comparably more restrictive *mandatory* approach appears to be the most appropriate approach with regard to the minority character of the cumulative-voting rule.

III) Preliminary results regarding shareholder impact on nomination and election procedures

Returning to the initial thesis that in a system with a long history of shareholder primacy like the United States, active shareholders are more likely to find nominating and electoral mechanisms ensuring director's accountability, the reality is as follows.

The importance of the *shareholder right to propose bylaw amendments* results from the mandatory character of these initiation rights. Director nomination and election procedures are substantially responsible for the responsiveness of the agents to the interests of their principals. Bylaws represent the rule-of-the-game level on which most of the nomination and election procedures are laid down. The mandatory shareholder initiation right is therefore key to potential amendments of corresponding procedures aiming to restore accountability. However, only a recent amendment to the Delaware Constitution allowed the Delaware Supreme Court to decide the long-discussed issue of whether shareholders may mandate the initiation of an amendment to the director nomination and election procedures. The challenge was to balance administrative and shareholder interests. The Delaware Supreme Court underscored limitations on board authority and the interpretation of the determinative exclusionary rule and confirmed that *procedural* mandatory shareholder proposals are compatible with board authority. As a consequence, only since 2008 may active shareholders, if necessary, mandate the initiation of amendments of director nomination and election procedures to restore accountability.

A very relevant nomination and election procedure for active shareholders is the *proxy access rule.* It is the sole practical opportunity for shareholders to influence the candidates they may elect as board members. In practice, the proxy access rule allows potentially contested elections as opposed to the prevailing system of de-facto cooptation. The possibility of being replaced by a shareholder nominee increases directors' responsiveness to shareholder interests. Opportunistic behavior of board members and agency costs based on the separation of ownership and control are reduced and shareholder value increases. After decades of fighting for the proxy access rule, since 2009, Delaware corporate law provides that a bylaw may oblige the corporation to include in its proxy solicitation materials one or more shareholder-nominated individuals. It approved the shareholder right to mandate the implementation of the proxy access rule via bylaw amendment; however, the enactment requires a two-step proceeding and shareholders still face the challenge of accumulating the quorum necessary to approve this measure. In 2010, the SEC made use of its new legislative authority and issued a mandatory proxy access rule whose strict preconditions state law or corporate bylaws could reduce. However, in 2011, a court decision has vacated this proxy access rule.

The *majority-voting rule* is another important election procedure that contributes to the accountability of directors. However, under the plurality-voting rule, absent a voting option *against* the candidate, only one vote *in favor* is sufficient for a candidate in an uncontested election to be elected to the board. The limited means of expressing discontent with board members via *withheld* votes is always dependent on additional board action for the removal of a board member. The board's responsiveness to shareholder interests under this regime is therefore low. The requirement that a candidate wins a majority of the votes cast to be elected necessitates broad shareholder support and may even provide shareholders with effective means to express their discontent and to initiate the consequences. Increased responsiveness to shareholder interests, enhanced if the proxy access rule is also implemented, reduces agency costs. Currently, however, *Delaware* law's default standard is plurality voting. A corporation may opt out of the prevailing election rule via bylaw or certificate of incorporation provision. Since 2006, the board may not amend shareholder-adopted bylaw amendments that specify the votes necessary for the election of directors. Active shareholders may therefore increase directorial accountability by mandating the initiation of a bylaw provision for majority voting. Even though such a provision could not be removed by the administration, its implementation, as with the proxy access rule, still depends on the accumulation of the necessary quorum. The efforts of the American Financial Stability Act 2010 towards recommendable mandatory majority voting for listed corporations were erased when the majority-voting rule was dropped before the Dodd-Frank Act was signed. As a consequence, majority voting will need to be implemented by each corporation individually.

Finally, the *cumulative-voting rule* represents an election procedure to empower active shareholders aiming to control the administration while only holding minority stakes. It reduces the effort required to organize sufficient support to have a specific candidate elected and therefore the costs to obtain (potential) board representation. In combination with the proxy access rule, it significantly assists active shareholders in threatening or facilitating proxy contests to control the administration. Despite its importance to active minority shareholders in enabling them to effectively impact the election process, statutory state law provides only an opt in mechanism on the rule-of-the-game level of the certificate of incorporation. In contrast to the bylaw level, shareholders are restricted to approving amendments initiated by the administration. As cumulative voting increases the voice of minority shareholders during director elections and therefore the accountability of directors, it seems unlikely that directors will initiate a corresponding opt in. In regard of its function as minority right, the current rule design of cumulative voting is surprising. It underscores the significance of rule design as a key to the effective functioning of accountability-enhancing statutory nomination and election procedures.

Having an underlying theory of shareholder primacy, the U.S. system of corporate governance faces severe agency issues based on the separation of ownership and control, even though it was expected to have historically provided efficient accountability mechanisms in the form of director nomination and election procedures to increase shareholder value. This expectation could not be confirmed by the results of the analysis of the state of three nomination and election procedures essential to assuring the responsiveness of directors to shareholders interests. Under the current default regime of nomination and election rules, shareholders lack the statutory right to nominate candidates during director elections. They vote according to the plurality-voting rule while cumulative voting does not apply.

A similar evaluation applies to shareholder *means* to bring about accountability-enhancing amendments. The development of U.S. securities and corporate law finally allows (active) shareholders to amend some nomination and election procedures laid down on the bylaw level to increase director accountability, which was long overdue. In 2008, the shareholder right to mandate the initiation of rule-of-the-game amendments has been approved. It is limited to the bylaw level and does not apply to the certificate of incorporation level. Proxy-access and majority-voting rule, but not cumulative voting, may now be theoretically implemented via private ordering. In practice, however, shareholder impact remains limited. As long as the proxy-access rule and majority-voting rule are not the mandatory or at least the default standard, shareholders will face collective action issues in winning approval of the implementation of accountability-enhancing amendments.

IV) Shareholder impact on nomination and election procedures under German law

Under the German two-tier system of corporate governance, authority is allocated between a management board, supervisory board, and shareholder meeting. Supervisory board representation is most sought by active shareholders.[674]

1) Context of supervisory board nomination and election

Several factors impact the significance of nomination and election of supervisory board members under German law.

674 DAI/McKinsey, Investorendialog im Umbruch, 2009, 28.

a) Removal strategy regarding members of the supervisory board

The removal strategy of the shareholder meeting is influenced by the term length as well as by the strength of early removal rights. The removal strategy regarding the supervisory board is significantly distinct from the removal strategy applicable to the board of directors. German corporate law determines a default maximum office term for supervisory members of about 5 years, § 102 (1)[675], which prevails in practice.[676] Under U.S. law, the default of one year in most cases and three to four years for staggered or classified boards[677] is comparably shorter. In addition, German law grants the shareholder meeting a weak removal power. Even though without cause, it requires a supermajority vote of three-fourths of the votes cast, § 103 (1) sent. 2.[678] The articles of incorporation may amend this quorum and in practice corporations have often lowered it to a simple majority.[679] Formal removal procedures are in practice rather rare, as for negative publicity reasons the concerned supervisory board members usually decide to resign.[680] The long default office terms increase the importance of mid-term removals, but the weak formal removal power of the shareholder meeting does not offset the long default term. The nomination and election rules under German law therefore apply in practice less often.

b) Composition of the management board

Under U.S.-American corporate law, the board of directors formally manages the corporation and the (executive) officers are only in a contractual relationship with the corporation. The latter may be appointed and removed quite flexibly.[681] German corporate law provides that the second tier, the management board, directs and manages the corporation. As it represents one of the two administrative organs, appointment and removal procedures are more complex.

i) Appointment strategy

Once a management board position has become vacant, the supervisory board *appoints a new member*, § 84 (1) sent. 1. The supervisory board has discretion to choose whom to appoint as a director. § 107 (3) sent. 2 determines explicitly that the supervisory board may not delegate the decision about the appointment to its committees. It may, however, have the decision prepared by one of them.[682] It is controversial whether the articles of incorporation may provide a precatory proposal right to another organ of the corpora-

675 Each section in this Subpart four of Part two without further determination refers to the AktG.
676 Vetter, in: Marsch-Barner/Schäfer, Hdb börsennotierte AG, 2005, § 25 mn.45.
677 Kraakman et al., The Anatomy of Corporate Law 61 n.28 (2009).
678 Kraakman et al., The Anatomy of Corporate Law 62 et seq. (2009).
679 Obermüller et al., Die Hauptversammlung der Aktiengesellschaft, 2001, J mn.82.
680 Vetter, in: Marsch-Barner/Schäfer, Die börsennotierte AG, 2005, § 25 mn.56.
681 Merkt/Göthel, US-amerikanisches Gesellschaftsrecht, 2006, mn.607.
682 Geßler/Käppler, AktG, § 84 mn.6 (2010).

tion or a third person due to the resulting pressure exercised on the supervisory board.[683] Accordingly, not even the articles of incorporation can provide that a shareholder without supervisory board representation is able to propose a candidate.[684] Theoretically, each member of the supervisory board is allowed to propose a candidate for the vacant position(s), but the supervisory board in its entirety must later decide on one of the candidates. Without a specific statutory provision, the resolution of the supervisory board requires a simple majority of the votes cast, except for the 2/3 support of the supervisory board required pursuant to § 31 (2) sent. 3 BGB, 29 (1) MitbestG.[685] A shareholder may therefore only directly influence the composition of the management board by having the necessary majority representation on the supervisory board. It may be achieved by election through the shareholder meeting or by delegation rights pursuant to § 101 (2).[686]

In practice, however, vacant director positions for which several candidates have been suggested are filled according to the suggestion of so-called *finding committees*. These finding committees suggest only one candidate after an elaborate selection process. followed by the formulation of the corresponding employment contract. However, the delegation ban laid down in § 107 (3) sent. 2 prohibits the finding committee from concluding a binding contract prior to the supervisory board's approval.[687] Therefore, active shareholders wanting to impact management board composition via supervisory board representation have to be represented on the finding committee to impact the choice of the final candidate.

ii) Removal strategy

The removal strategy determines the actual strength of a management board position. It depends on the maximum length of an office term and the early removal requirements.[688] Under German law, the supervisory board appoints the members of the management board for a comparably long *maximum term of office* of five years, § 84 (1) sent. 1.[689] No. 5.1.2 (2) sent. 1 DCGK encourages not to generally apply the five-year maximum length to first appointments. In practice, the first term of office has, meanwhile, usually a length between two and three years, while the maximum length of five years generally applies to re-appointed management board members.[690]

Besides the relatively long term of office, the supervisory board has only a weak mandatory *early-removal* power over management board members.[691] The early removal

683 Hefermehl/Spindler, in: MüKo, 2004, § 84 mn.11.
684 *Id.* at mn.12.
685 Habersack, in: MüKo AktG, 2008, § 108 mn.20.
686 Hefermehl/Spindler, in: MüKo AktG, 2008, § 84 mn.12.
687 BGH, Urt. v. 14.11.1983, Az.: 13.11.1983, BGHZ 89, 48 (56); Hopt/Roth, in: Grosskomm AktG, § 107 mn.381.
688 Fleischer, AG 2006, 429 (429).
689 Engert, ZIP 2006, 2105 (2106).
690 Weber, in: Hölters, AktG, 2011, § 84 mn.20; Wiesner, in: Münch. Hdb. AG, Vol. 4, 2007, § 20 mn. 30.
691 Kraakman et al., The Anatomy of Corporate Law 62 (2009).

of a member always requires an important cause, § 84 (3). This rule has often been evaluated as too protective of the market position of good and solid managers and too diffuse about the requirement of an *important* cause.[692] This evaluation is mitigated by rule § 84 (3) sent. 4, however. It establishes an assumption in favor of a valid revocation, even if an important cause does not exist, as long as no contrary legally binding decision exists.[693] An important reason to oust a member of the management board is either a gross breach of duty, the inability to lead the business of the corporation, or the shareholder meeting's loss of confidence in the member of the management board, § 84 (3) sent. 2.

According to common legal opinion, the explicit or implicit pressure from shareholders does not represent an important reason allowing the supervisory board to oust a management board member. However, shareholders remain free to work toward the withdrawal of confidence through the shareholder meeting.[694] A decision by a sole majority holder outside the shareholder meeting, in contrast, does not represent the shareholder meeting's decision and is therefore not sufficient.[695] § 122 (2) allows shareholders with a stake of at least 5 percent of the outstanding shares or Euro 500,000 of the share capital for three months to request the publication of an additional agenda topic, which can be the withdrawal of confidence in a management board member.[696] However, the final decision whether to oust the director or not remains with the supervisory board, which underscores the German legislator‘s preference for stability on the management board[697].

iii) Impact on management composition in practice

The five-year office term and the early removal right for cause represent hurdles that prevent even active shareholders with supervisory board representation from impacting the management board's composition. The practical need for quicker replacements of management board members is therefore often a result of unanimous agreements between the corporation, represented by the new supervisory board, and the management board,[698] followed by an amicable termination of the office.[699] Usually, shareholders with increasing impact, who threaten to or actually block, among others, urgent corporate capital measures requiring a supermajority of shareholders are a counterpart of such agreements. Often, corresponding agreements are triggered by significant payments to the departing incumbent(s), which No. 4.2.3. DCGK recommends restricting. Obtain-

692 Fleischer, AG 2006, 429 (437).

693 *Id.* at 438.

694 Fleischer, DStR 2006, 1507 (1513).

695 BGH, Urt. v. 07.06.1962, Az.: II ZR 131/61, WM 1962, 811 (811); Hefermehl, in: Geßler et al., AktG, § 84 mn.72; Hefermehl/Spindler, in: MüKo AktG, § 84 mn.105; Mertens, in: KöKo AktG, 1996, § 84 mn.106.

696 Cornelius Goetze/Gleis Lutz-AmCham, *Shareholder Activism – (k)ein rechtliches Thema?, Presentation Evening Briefing*, May 8, 2008, 13, http://www.amcham.de/fileadmin/templates/main/pdf/Praesentation_Goetze.pdf.

697 Kraakman et al., The Anatomy of Corporate Law, 2009, 62.

698 Schäfer, NZG 2007, 900 (902 et seq.).

699 Götze, in: Von Rosen, Die Hauptversammlung vor neuen Herausforderungen, DAI studies issue 41, 2008, 119 (130); Schäfer, NZG 2007, 900 (903).

ing supervisory board representation apart from the formal regime usually requires the coordination of a blocking minority of 25 percent of the votes present during a shareholder meeting.

2) The legal analysis of the four issues

a) Mandatory shareholder initiation of rule-of-the-game amendments

i) Relevant rule-of-the-game levels

Under the German statute for corporations, corporations may apart from the articles of incorporation install up to three separate *Geschäftsordnungen*, one for each of the three corporate organs, to lay down nomination and election related rules-of-the-game. Procedural rules concerning the nomination and election of supervisory board members by the shareholder meeting, not mandated by corporate statute, may be imposed by the articles of incorporation or the *Geschäftsordnung* of the shareholder meeting. The shareholder meeting has to decide whether or not to set up its own *Geschäftsordnung*. If approved, it may contain rules regarding the preparation and arrangement of a shareholder meeting, § 129 (1), including nomination and election provisions regarding the supervisory board. Only without a mandatory statutory provision determining a deviating rule-of-the-game level for a specific nomination or election rule may the *Geschäftsordnung* of the shareholder meeting impose nomination and election procedure provisions. Matters to be laid down in a *Geschäftsordnung* of shareholder meetings are therefore rather restricted.[700]

ii) Mandatory shareholder initiation rights

Amendments on rule-of-the-game levels, articles of incorporation,[701] and *Geschäftsordnung* of the shareholder meeting may be *initiated* by a request of the shareholder meeting for the management board to prepare a corresponding amendment. The quorum necessary for such a request equals the quorum necessary to approve the requested measure, § 83 (1) sent. 1. More relevant for active shareholders, an amendment may also be initiated by minority request of shareholders pursuant to § 122 (2). The ownership requirements for such a minority request are a minimum stake of 5 percent or €500,000 of the total share capital. Shareholders need to have held these shares for a minimum of three months before the shareholder meeting has taken place and will need to continue holding them until their motion has been decided, §§ 122 (1) sent. 3, (2), 142 (2) sent. 2. The minority request aims to publish an additional topic for the agenda of an upcoming shareholder meeting to pass the necessary resolution approving the intended amendment, §§ 122 (2), 142 (2) sent. 2 or, if necessary, to have the management board

700 Ziemons, in: Schmidt/Lutter, AktG, 2010, § 129 mn.4.

701 Semler, in: Münch. Hdb. AG, Vol. 4, 1999, § 35 mn.41; Obermüller et al., Die Hauptversammlung der Aktiengesellschaft, 2001, B mn.117.

prepare the measure, § 83 (1).[702] The purpose of the minority request must relate to the competency of the shareholder meeting, for instance, by relating to matters about which the shareholder meeting has to decide on via shareholder resolution according to statute.[703] The shareholder meeting may initiate corresponding amendments per an existing *Geschäftsordnung* of the shareholder meeting or the articles of incorporation. According to amendments by the ARUG,[704] a minority demand for publication directed at and reviewed by the managing board[705] has to be *received* by the corporation thirty days prior to the shareholder meeting, § 122 (2) sent. 3. For the initiation of the amendment of the articles of incorporation, the publication request has to contain the exact wording of the amended articles of incorporation, § 124 (2) sent. 2. Once the form and content related prerequisites have been fulfilled, the management board is obliged to immediately publish the appropriate minority request, § 124 (1) sent. 1.[706] According to the purpose of § 122 to protect the minority, the provision has a mandatory character. The articles of incorporation may lower these requirements, 122 (2), (1) sent. 2.[707]

The *approval* of an amendment of a *Geschäftsordnung* for and through the shareholder meeting requires a simple absolute majority of the votes cast, § 133 (1) and three-quarters of the share capital present during the shareholder meeting, § 129 (1). Due to the restricted content and the high approval quorum, only few *Geschäftsordnungen* for shareholder meetings have been set up so far.[708] In 1998, the KonTraG raised the capital requirement to today's level, which has made the implementation of further *Geschäftsordnungen* even harder.[709] The approval of an amendment of the articles of incorporation also requires a simple absolute majority of the votes cast, § 133 (1), as well as three-fourths of the capital present during the shareholder meeting, § 179 (2).

Therefore, shareholders under German law have comparably broad initiation rights at the in practice less relevant bylaw and the certificate of incorporation level. However, amendments on both rule levels require a supermajority approval, reducing the practical relevance of private ordering.

iii) Counterarguments on mandatory shareholder initiation rights

However, minority demands pursuant to § 122 (2) are increasing under the German corporate regime because of the growing transparency of ownership structures, easing the accumulation of 5% through different shareholders.[710] The counterarguments brought forth by opponents of mandatory shareholder initiation rights under German corporate

702 Obermüller et al., Die Hauptversammlung der Aktiengesellschaft, 2001, B mn.107.
703 Kubis in: MüKo AktG, 2004, § 122 mn.31; Ziemons, in: Schmidt/Lutter, AktG, 2010, § 122 mn.17.
704 Mertens, AG 1997, 481 (485): prior to the ARUG, the request needed to reach the corporation 10 days past having published to convene the shareholder meeting, § 124 (1) sent. 2 AktG a.F.
705 Kühn, BB 1965, 1170 (1171).
706 Hüffer, AktG, § 122 mn.7.
707 *Id.* at mn.1.
708 *Id.* at § 129 mn.1a; Ziemons, in: Schmidt/Lutter, AktG, 2010, § 129 mn.4.
709 Kubis, in: MüKo AktG, 2004, § 129 mn.9.
710 Halberkamp/Gierke, NZG 2004, 494 (494); Kubis, in: MüKo AktG, 2004, § 122 mn.2.

law are comparable to those brought forth against them under U.S. corporate law as the relevant parameters are comparable.

An example is the argument that shareholders have *less information* than the administration. As under U.S. law, it may be countered with the argument that the administration may have more information than shareholders do, but it may not always have the proper incentives to use the information. Furthermore, the administration is neither obliged to nor barred from making its own statement,[711] especially when intending to spread unknown relevant information.

Another comparable concern relates to the *opportunistic use* of mandatory initiation rights. Even though the eligibility parameters under § 122 (2) differ from those under Rule 14a-8 SEA, the resulting accessibility of shareholders to initiation rights under both regimes can still be assumed comparable. While the German regime requires an ownership of only 3 months before submitting a proposal, U.S.-American law requires one year of ownership. In contrast, § 122 (2) requires five percent ownership for a minority request, whereas Rule 14a-8 SEA requires only 1 percent ownership. The two different combinations of ownership requirements produce comparable results as far as relating to concerns of nuisance proposals and the related costs. The ownership requirements assure that shareholders have a relevant economic interest in corporate well-being. Furthermore, they assure identification with the corporation while preventing a too quick involvement of new shareholders. As far as the demanded ownership percentage under the ownership requirement is concerned, the economic interest of eligible shareholders has to be even more intense under the German regime than under the U.S.- American regime. Regarding the time component of the ownership requirement, the three months requirement still assures identification and prevents a too spontaneous, possibly issue-related involvement, including share lending for a few days as a basis to exercise the minority right.[712] The latter is prevented by the three-month requirement because the publication convening a shareholder meeting is usually announced less time in advance, §§ 123, 124 (1). Therefore, even though a proponent's identification with the corporation may be weaker under the German three-month minimum ownership requirement, the proponent's economic interest in the corporation under the 5 percent minimum ownership quorum is comparably higher than under the U.S. rule and allows the assumption that the deviations under both ownership requirements compensate for each other. An additional aspect under German law concerns management board's obligation to execute the measures the shareholder meeting has resolved on, § 83 (2), which has not equivalent under U.S. law.. This obligation completes the already wider-reaching mandatory initiation right of shareholders under German law by also obliging management board to execute shareholder initiated resolutions of the shareholder meeting as long as they correspond to the responsibility of the shareholder meeting. Possible opportunism concerns based upon this aspect may, however, be appeased. In addition to the majority approval

711 Kubis in: MüKo AktG, 2004, § 124 mn.44.
712 *Id.* at § 122 mn.2.

requirement management board is not obliged to execute resolutions violating statute or articles that are contrary to the corporate interests[713].

Accordingly, the concerns about shareholder initiation rights are also unconvincing under German corporate law.

b) Shareholder nomination right

Due to the different decision-making process in German corporations, the *proxy access rule* needs to be redefined as the *shareholder nomination right* in the German context.

i) Status quo under German corporate law

It is generally the supervisory board that proposes candidates for vacant positions on the supervisory board, § 124 (3) sent. 1, who are then elected by the shareholders during the next shareholder meeting, § 101 (1) sent. 1. German corporate law provides, however, different opportunities for shareholders to propose their own nominees for a vacant supervisory board position in addition to the nominees proposed by the supervisory board.

Pursuant to §§ 127, 126, each shareholder may propose a nominee for a vacant position in advance of a shareholder meeting. These shareholder proposals must include the name of the proposing shareholder, §§ 127 sent. 1, 126 (1) sent. 1, the name, profession, and residence of the candidate, § 124 (3) sent. 3, as well as the candidate's membership in other supervisory boards or memberships in comparable foreign or German supervisory bodies of commercial enterprises, if the concerned company is listed, § 125 (1) sent. 5. The proposal for appointment may include reasoning with up to 5000 characters, §§ 127, 126 (2) sent. 2. If such a proposal is posed up to two weeks before the shareholder meeting takes place, the board of directors has to include the proposal in its complex announcements, §§ 126 (1) sent. 1, 125 (1) to (3).[714] For listed corporations, § 126 (1) sent. 3 requires publication via the corporate website. When choosing to propose a candidate prior to the shareholder meeting, shareholders representing a minimum of 10 percent of the present share capital may demand to have a vote on their candidate before one on the administrative nominee, § 137.

Another opportunity for shareholders to propose a nominee for a vacant supervisory board position is to launch the proposal during the shareholder meeting. It represents a part of the shareholders participation rights and is even granted to shareholders not entitled to vote, as long as an according agenda point exists.[715] An opportunity according to

713 Habersack, in: Großkomm AktG, 2008, § 83 mn.13.

714 Bollweg, Die Wahl des Aufsichtsrates in der Hauptversammlung der Aktiengesellschaft, 1997, 133.

715 Habersack, in: MüKo AktG, 2008, § 101 mn.16; Hopt/Roth, in: Großkomm AktG, 2006, § 101 mn.70.

§ 137 does not exist in this case; it is rather the leader of the shareholder meeting who has to decide in which order to vote on the different nominees.[716]

Both approaches need to be distinguished from the opportunity of shareholders to propose, via minority request, § 122 (2), to have the nomination of supervisory board members announced as an additional agenda topic of an ordinary or even special (§ 122 (1)) shareholder meeting.[717] This may particularly be the case in a shareholder meeting for which shareholders propose to announce the removal of supervisory board members as an additional agenda topic, § 122 (2).

Due to the lack of a comprehensive proxy process, these formal opportunities for shareholders to determine supervisory board nominees appear to be of higher practical relevance than those initially provided under U.S. law. Hence, the need to initiate an amendment of the underlying rules to enhance the shareholder nomination right seems secondary. However, practice has proven that only a few shareholders use their right to propose supervisory board nominees in public corporations and only few of them are elected.[718] An exception may apply to crucial votes involving massive efforts of the opponents to catch the attention of a substantial number of shareholders. They usually have the potential for shareholder-proposed nominees to become elected. Therefore, even though the supervisory board does not have the competency of cooptation,[719] shareholders tend to elect the administrational nominees resulting in de-facto cooptation[720] as under U.S. law. Both circumstances may result from collective action issues. They are based on the lack of information regarding potential candidates as well as the efforts necessary to convince the masses of shareholders of an opposing candidate in a corporate governance system with growing freefloat. Historic blockholders, in contrast, were able to directly impact the administrative proposals and did not have to make use of those minority means. Without the reduction of collective action issues or shareholder activism, shareholders tend to follow the administrative suggestions in specific corporate matters like elections of the supervisory board.[721] In particular, provisions intended to reduce collective action issues, for instance, the increase of the presence rate during shareholder meetings via online participation, § 118 (1), may be helpful. Shareholders may initiate such an amendment of the articles of incorporation, § 118 (1). However, to achieve the necessary approval quorum represents another challenge. Furthermore, active shareholders are able to overcome them. Under the German corporate regime, they are confronted with smaller legal barriers, for instance, to wait for a general or to

716 Habersack, in: MüKo AktG, 2008, § 101 mn.16; Hopt/Roth, in: Großkomm AktG, 2006, § 101 mn.70.

717 Habersack, in: MüKo AktG, 2008, § 101 mn.15.

718 Bernhardt, ZHR 159 (1995), 310 (314); Leyens, 67 RabelsZ 57 (81); Lutter, ZHR 159 (1995), 287 (301); Meder, DStR 2008, 1242 (1242); Roth/Wörle, ZGR 2004, 565 (577); Semler, The Practice of the German Aufsichtsrat, in: Comparative Corporate Governance, 1998, 267 (269); Semler, Rechtsvorgabe und Realität der Organzusammenarbeit in der Aktiengesellschaft, in: Schneider et al., FS Lutter, 2000, 721 (725).

719 Habersack, in: MüKo AktG, 2008, § 101 mn.18.

720 Lutter, EuZW 2009, 799 (809).

721 Baums/Fraune, AG 1995, 97 (109 et seq.).

convene a special shareholder meeting to have their nominee successfully elected. An informal alternative preferably used by active shareholders to get around them requires sufficient impact in the shareholder meeting to pressure management to cooperate. Active shareholders together with supportive shareholders may accumulate a sufficiently large stake to hinder the facilitation of capital measures or other important measures requiring shareholder approval. They may use this position to induce members of the supervisory board to resign from their office.[722] Subsequently, the shareholders will convince the management board to make the necessary application with the commercial register, § 104 (1), to restore the necessary resolution quorum of the supervisory board, § 108 (2).[723] Without the will of confrontation, it will usually consider the active shareholders' recommendation for new supervisory board members and inform the commercial register, which will in general respect those proposals. As a consequence, active shareholders with substantial personal stakes or corresponding support amongst the shareholders may obtain one or more supervisory board seats without necessarily having to wait for the next shareholder meeting.[724]

Despite the practical limitations, the design of the shareholder nomination right requires no amendment.

ii) Counterarguments on shareholder nomination right

To the arguments against shareholder nomination rights, only a few additions need to be made to those arguments raised under U.S. law. As a consequence of the shareholder nomination right, members of the administration may begin to focus even more closely on the *short-term interests* of shareholders. However, it may be countered that under the German corporate regime the office periods for members of the supervisory and management board are five years, significantly longer than the one-year period under the U.S. regime, §§ 103 (1), 84 (1). Coupled with weak removal rights they assure a comparably long term of office. This and the rather long-term compensation regime, § 87 (1), Nos. 4.2.3., 5.4.6 DCGK, allow and oblige the administration to focus on the long-term development of the corporation. Therefore, they do not need to focus on the likely short-term demands of shareholders in order to assure their re-election against competing, shareholder-proposed candidates. The issue of shortsightedness of members of the administration as a result of the shareholder nomination right is therefore not truly an issue under the German corporate regime.

As far as concerns relate to the higher costs and disruptive potential of *election contests*, the different ownership requirements under the German and U.S.-American corporate regime are relevant. According to § 127 each shareholder may propose a nominee, in contrast to the SEC's vacated mandatory proxy access rule requiring a three percent stake held for at least three years. Constant election contests seem to be the obligatory consequence of this provision. However, in German practice, shareholders

722 Schaefer, NZG 2007, 900 (902).
723 *Id.*
724 *Id.*

propose supervisory nominees only from time to time; contested elections therefore do not represent the rule.[725] In addition, the office terms of supervisory members under German law are with up to five years much longer than the one year lasting terms under U.S. law. Accordingly, concerns about higher costs and constant board disruption appear exaggerated.

c) Absolute majority-voting rule

i) Status quo under German corporate law

As in many other European countries, the standard voting rule for corporate elections in Germany is majority voting, not plurality voting.[726]

§ 133 (1) sets forth a general default rule that resolutions of the shareholder meeting require the majority of the votes cast, as long as neither statute nor the articles of incorporation deviate from this principle. For elections like those of the supervisory board, the articles of incorporation may determine different requirements, § 133 (2). Therefore, the default rule for uncontested and contested elections of members of the supervisory board requires that candidates receive a simple and a(n) (absolute) majority of the votes cast.[727] The absolute majority relates the votes obtained by a candidate to the total number of votes cast,[728] as opposed to the relative majority, except if the election is uncontested.[729] The latter measures the votes obtained by a candidate in comparison to the votes competing candidates have obtained. Shareholders may withhold their votes, vote *against*, or vote *in favor* of a candidate.[730] The withheld votes are not considered while counting the votes.[731] In contrast to the prevailing plurality voting system in the United States, the votes cast in *favor* and *against* a candidate are relevant to the election result. Withheld votes express a mild form of discontent as they have only a symbolic character.

§ 133 (2) grants the ability to introduce a relative majority-voting standard regarding the election of the supervisory board members[732] by amending the articles of incorpora-

---

725 Lutter, ZHR 159 (1995), 287 (301); Meder, DStR 2008, 1242 (1242); Roth/Wörle, ZGR 2004, 565 (577); Semler, Rechtsvorgabe und Realität der Organzusammenarbeit in der Aktiengesellschaft, in: Schneider, FS Lutter 2000, 721 (725).

726 ISS, *White Paper on Majority voting in Director Elections* 4 (2005) (on hold with author).

727 Bollweg, Die Wahl des Aufsichtsrates in der Hauptversammlung der Aktiengesellschaft, 1997, 456; Habersack, in: MüKo AktG, 2008, § 101 mn.27; Hopt/Roth, in: Großkomm AktG, 2006, § 101 mn.78.

728 Volhard, in: MüKo AktG, 2004, § 133 mn.64.

729 *Id.*

730 Hüffer, AktG, 2010, § 133 mn.18.

731 BGH, Urt. v. 20.03.1995, Az.: II ZR 205/94, NJW 1995, 1739 (1743) – Girmes; Volhard, in: MüKo AktG, 2004, § 133 mn.27.

732 Bollweg, Die Wahl des Aufsichtsrates in der Hauptversammlung der Aktiengesellschaft, 1997, 462; Breuer/Fraune, in: Heidel, Aktienrecht und Kapitalmarktrecht, 1997, § 101 mn.6; Habersack, in: MüKo AktG, 2008, § 101 mn.27; Hoffmann-Becking, in: Münch. Hdb. AG, 2007, Vol. 4, § 30 mn.15; Hüffer, AktG, § 101 mn.4, § 133 mn.32, Mertens, in: KöKo AktG, 1996, § 101 mn.14, Obermüller et al., Die Hauptversammlung der Aktiengesellschaft, 2001, J mn.50, Vetter, in: Marsch-Barner/Schäfer, Hdb börsennotierte AG, 2005, § 25 mn.23.

tion accordingly. A provision amending the simple absolute majority requirement on the rule-of-the-game level of the *Geschäftsordnung* of the shareholder meeting would therefore not be sufficient.[733] However, the legal standard of absolute majority is widespread in German corporations. The introduction of a less shareholder friendly relative majority voting standard via amendment of the articles of incorporation requires the approval of three-fourths of the voting capital, § 179 (2) sent. 1. In light of the rule design of § 133, the majority-voting standard is comparably strongly protected from hasty amendments toward a plurality-voting standard.

Regarding the accountability of members of the administration, the default regime of the absolute majority-voting rule complements well the mandatory shareholder nomination right for supervisory board members. As for the shareholder nomination right, the use of shareholder initiated rule-of-the-game amendments to amend the election procedure is unnecessary. The status quo of the rule design of the election process of the supervisory board members strongly supports their accountability.

ii) Counterarguments on majority-voting rule

For the arguments against *majority voting,* there are again only a few issues to add to the discussion under U.S. law. One addition concerns the argument that a true election process would make it difficult for corporations to assure the proper *qualification of directors* as required under different regulations. Here, the increasingly relevant criterion of independent board members is quasi-superfluous under the German two-tier regime, which implies the independence of members of the supervisory board. Another addition relates to the *concern of destabilization* of the board and fears that directors will *focus on short-term interests* of shareholders. It is also argued that this is a consequence of the potential to effectively remove directors due to majority voting. As mentioned previously, the administrative terms of office last generally five years for both tiers, §§ 103 (1), 84 (1). The compensation schemes for both boards, § 87 (1), Nos. 4.2.3., 5.4.6 DCGK, are rather long-term orientated. In addition, the majority-voting rule has been the voting standard in German corporations for decades. Only in a few cases has it been the subject of discussions. These related more to the permissibility of proportional voting in order to grant minority shareholders the opportunity to be represented on the supervisory board[734] than to the introduction of a plurality-voting rule.

d) Cumulative-voting rule

Looking back at the shareholder friendly nomination and election rules providing a comparably high level of accountability, they allow reduced agency costs arising from the separation of ownership and control in corporations with increasing freefloat. Despite these comparably low legal barriers, collective action issues seem to keep shareholders

733 Kubis, in: MüKo AktG, 2004, § 129 mn.4.

734 Hüffer, AktG, § 133, mn.33; Volhard, in: MüKo AktG, 2004, § 133 mn.78.

from comprehensively making use of their rights. Active shareholders may be able to overcome these issues. As they usually hold minority stakes and frequently threaten or actually attempt to remove supervisory board members, their costs to actively control the administration are high. They may, however, be significantly reduced by an election procedure supporting minorities during the election process, the cumulative-voting rule.

i) Permissibility of cumulative voting

The German legislator has not regulated cumulative voting. German courts have not yet decided whether the cumulative-voting procedure regarding the election of supervisory board members is admissiable.[735] They have so far only confirmed the permissibility of attenuating deviations from the general simple absolute majority quorum for elections on the level of the articles of incorporation.[736]

The discussion amongst legal scholars on election procedures deviating from the majority-voting rule concentrates on proportional voting, of which cumulative voting is the best-known form of execution. Accordingly, many of the proponents of proportional voting also support the permissibility of cumulative voting,[737] while arguments against its implementation are similar to those against proportional voting. Only few proponents of proportional voting do not support cumulative voting. However, they do not bring forward any arguments explaining the different evaluation of both voting rules.[738]

Widespread opinion rejects the implementation of the proportional-voting rule via amendment of the articles of incorporation.[739] It argues that the German legislator did decide against an obligatory minority representative in 1965[740] and that the legal systematics concerning the supervisory board expresses the legislator's will that there not be a proportional-voting rule.[741] Consequently, the argument goes, the legislator did not intend to allow implementation of a proportional-voting rule via amendment of the articles of incorporation.[742] In addition, opponents argue, §§ 101 (1), 137 requires a personal election. This would not be realized if shareholders are bound to proposed lists and therefore to certain compositions of candidates limiting the free election[743] in a way that influences the result of the election. Therefore, proportional voting rules requiring list

735 Bollweg, Die Wahl des Aufsichtsrates in der Hauptversammlung der Aktiengesellschaft, 1997, 468; Hopt/Roth, Großkomm AktG, 2006, § 101 mn.62.

736 BGH, Urt. v. 13. 3. 1980, Az.: II ZR 54/78, NJW 1980, 1465 (1466).

737 Berrar, NZG 2001, 1113 (1115); Grundmann, in: Großkomm AktG, 2008, § 133 mn.126; Roth/Hopt, in: Großkomm AktG, 2006, § 101 mn.66; Timm, NJW 1987, 977 (986).

738 Habersack, in: MüKo AktG, 2008, § 101mn.27.

739 Bollweg, Die Wahl des Aufsichtsrates in der Hauptversammlung der Aktiengesellschaft, 1997, 468 et seq.; Mertens, in: KöKo AktG, 1996, § 101 mn.14; Hoffmann-Becking, in: Münch. Hdb. AG, Vol. 4, 2007, § 30 mn.15; Obermüller et al., Die Hauptversammlung der Aktiengesellschaft, 2001, J mn.51; Vetter, in: Marsch-Barner/Schäfer, Hdb börsennotierte AG, 2005, § 25 mn.23.

740 *See,* Hopt/Roth, in: Großkomm AktG, 2006, § 101 mn.63.

741 Bollweg, Die Wahl des Aufsichtsrates in der Hauptversammlung der Aktiengesellschaft, 1997, 471.

742 Vetter, in: Marsch-Barner/Schäfer, Hdb börsennotierte AG, 2005, J mn.51.

743 *See,* Semler, in: MüKo AktG, 2004, § 101 mn.55.

elections should also be invalid for this reason. Furthermore, the limitation of delegation rights would be circumvented. According to § 101 (2), shareholders or third persons may determine up to one-third of the (shareholder) representatives of the supervisory board. Proportional voting, however, would allow the circumvention of such a limitation, since it in fact grants additional delegation rights to minority shareholders.[744] Moreover, the introduction of cumulative voting via amendment of the articles of incorporation would result in the introduction of maximum votes and plural votes contrary to § 12 (2)[745].[746] An additional argument concerns the use of the minority friendly proportional-voting rule in regard of § 103, allowing the shareholder meeting to oust members of the supervisory board with a supermajority vote as long as elected free from delegation rights.[747] Finally, they argue that in situations of codetermination, each of the shareholder representatives on the supervisory board has a key position in decision-making. This requires a high quality of homogeneity amongst the shareholder representatives.[748] Such key positions have the danger of solidarity with the employee representatives. It would therefore likely disturb the balance of interests on the supervisory board and possibly result in an over-proportional representation of minority interests on the supervisory board.[749] Therefore, proportional voting would have consequences that go far beyond the goal of ensuring minority representation.[750]

However, the predominant majority agrees on the permissibility of the introduction of a proportional-voting rule via amendment of the articles of incorporation.[751] The assumed intent of the German legislator in favor of a pure majority-voting rule would result in an over-proportional influence of majority shareholders on the composition of the members of the supervisory board. Minority shareholders, in contrast, have generally no opportunity to determine their own representative for the supervisory board except pursuant to a corresponding agreement with the majority shareholder. This circumstance leads to a significant reduction in the influence of minority and small shareholders.[752]

Furthermore, the legislator's 1965 decision against an obligatory minority representative on the supervisory board does not allow the conclusion that the legislator intended to prohibit the introduction of proportional voting through amendment of the articles of

744 Bollweg, Die Wahl des Aufsichtsrates in der Hauptversammlung der Aktiengesellschaft, 1997, 472.

745 *See,* Hopt/Roth, in: Großkomm AktG, 2006, § 101 mn.63.

746 Bollweg, Die Wahl des Aufsichtsrates in der Hauptversammlung der Aktiengesellschaft, 1997, 472 et seq.

747 Obermüller et al., Die Hauptversammlung der Aktiengesellschaft, 2001, J mn.51.

748 Bollweg, Die Wahl des Aufsichtsrates in der Hauptversammlung der Aktiengesellschaft, 1997, 471 et seq.

749 *See,* Hopt/Roth, in: Großkomm AktG, 2006, § 101 mn.63.

750 Bollweg, Die Wahl des Aufsichtsrates in der Hauptversammlung der Aktiengesellschaft, 1997, 472.

751 Grundmann, in: Großkomm AktG, 2008, § 133 mn.97; Habersack, in: MüKo AktG, 2008, § 101 mn.27; Hopt/Roth, in: Großkomm AktG, 2006, § 101 mn.64; Hüffer, AktG, 2010, § 133 mn.33; Raiser, Recht der Kapitalgeselschaften, 2001, § 16 mn.75; Spindler in: Schmidt/Lutter AktG, 2010, § 133 mn.54; Semler, in: Münch. Hdb. AG, Vol. 4, 1999, § 39 mn.86.

752 Raiser, Recht der Kapitalgesellschaften, 2001, § 16 mn.75.

incorporation.[753] Rather, § 133 (2) explicitly allows stronger and weaker requirements amending the simple absolute majority requirement of § 133 (1) for elections, including the election of the supervisory board.[754]

A further argument in favor of the permissibility of proportional voting is the fact that the democratic will of shareholders is already impacted during elections by non-voting stock, majority-voting rule, and delegation rights.[755] Furthermore, delegation rights are already a special form of minority representation.[756] The legislator restricts delegation rights to one-third of the members of the supervisory board, § 101 (2) sent. 2, assuring that the majority of shareholders may determine the majority of seats of shareholder representatives on the supervisory board. However, it does not assure that the majority of shareholders may determine the majority of the members of the supervisory board. This may be concluded from the fact that delegation rights are even granted in cases of codetermination concerning half of the representatives on the supervisory board.[757]

Moreover, the introduction of proportional voting does not violate the ban on multiple voting rights, § 12 (2), which assures that the influence of shareholders in the corporation is linked to their financial participation. The underlying principle of *one share one vote* is formally adhered to as long as minority shareholders are granted the same number of votes per share as all the other shareholders.[758] Therefore, shareholders are not treated unequally when allowed to bundle their votes in favor of one of several candidates.[759]

In addition, other related regimes provide for proportional voting. Under the codetermination regime of the MitbestG (§§ 15, 16, 18 MitbestG), proportional voting for employee representatives goes without saying. For the regime of the cooperative, the BGH[760] strongly recommends the implementation of the proportional-voting rule for the representative assembly under § 43a GenG. Regarding the corporate supervisory board, the BGH determined that implementing a proportional voting rule is a worthy aim.[761]

Finally, the basic consideration is that shareholders with a qualified minority may best control the administration, as their stake allows compensation for their efforts. Cumulative voting represents a mechanism to improve corporate governance, as it raises the incentives of qualified minorities to control the administration. It lowers their efforts and costs to be represented on the board. Once on the board, they will have access to relevant information and a corporate payment for holding the position.[762]

753 Habersack, in: MüKo AktG, 2008, § 101 mn.27; Hopt/Roth, in: Großkomm AktG, 2006, § 101 mn.65.

754 Hopt/Roth, in: Großkomm AktG, 2006, § 101 mn.65, Hüffer, AktG, 2010, § 133 mn.33, Timm, NJW 1987, 977 (986).

755 Hopt/Roth, in: Großkomm AktG, 2006, § 101 mn.65.

756 Bollweg, Die Wahl des Aufsichtsrates in der Hauptversammlung der Aktiengesellschaft, 1997, 472; Semler, in: Münch. Hdb. AG, Vol. 4, 1999, § 40 mn.86.

757 Hopt/Roth, in: Großkomm AktG, 2006, § 101 mn.65.

758 Berrar, NZG 2001, 1113 (1115).

759 *Id.*

760 BGH, Urt. v. 22.03.1982, Az.: II ZR 219/81, BGHZ 83, 228 (233 et seq).

761 BGH, Urt. v. 07.06.1962, Az.: II ZR 131/61, WM 1962, 811 (811).

762 Grundmann, in: Großkomm AktG, 2008, § 133 mn.98.

ii) Rule design proposal

The implementation of a deviating proportional election standard such as the cumulative voting standard is generally seen as a simplification of the simple absolute majority representing a "different requirement" in the sense of § 133 (2).[763] As under U.S. law, its implementation requires the amendment of the facultative part of the articles of incorporation, within the permissible borders of § 23 (5).[764]

At first glance, initiating an opt in to the cumulative-voting rule, despite the need to do so on the articles of incorporation level, requires only a five percent shareholder minority. However, as a rule-of-the-game amendment on the level of the articles of incorporation, its approval requires three-fourths of the present share capital to approve. Taking into account that the purpose of cumulative voting is to strengthen the rights of minority shareholders while limiting the impact of majority of shareholders, achieving the necessary supermajority quorum appears rather unlikely. This may explain why neither a significant number of proportional nor cumulative-voting rules have been implemented in German corporations.[765]

A system of formerly coherent majorities makes it desirable in particular to protect shareholder minorities. A system of increasing freefloat and stronger management profits from control through coherent minorities. However, the minority initiation right is not very helpful as long as the approval to opt in requires a qualified majority. A better designed rule would therefore either involve a mandatory cumulative-voting rule[766] or the default standard of cumulative voting with a qualified minority able to veto opt outs. An amendment of the relevant rule-of-the-game level from the articles of incorporation to the *Geschäftsordnung* alone, in contrast, would not represent an alternative. A corresponding amendment on the altered level would still require supermajority approval by three- fourths of the present capital, § 129 (1) sent. 1.

V) Final thesis regarding the shareholder impact on nomination and election procedures

1) Conclusion regarding German corporate law

The influence of shareholders in German corporations regarding the nomination and election of the administration is limited to their impact on the composition of the supervisory board as first tier. Only once majority representation on the supervisory board has been obtained may shareholders decide to oust a member on the second tier and to replace him with their own nominee.

763 Bollweg, Die Wahl des Aufsichtsrates in der Hauptversammlung der Aktiengesellschaft, 1997, 468; Grundmann, in: Großkomm AktG, 2008, § 133 mn.97.

764 Grundmann, in: Großkomm AktG, 2008, § 133 mn.98; Stein, in: MüKo AktG, 2005, § 179 mn.10.

765 Volhard, in: MüKo AktG, 2004, § 133 mn.78.

766 Beyer, Minderheitsvertreter im Aufsichtsrat, 2001, 35: proposing the implementation of a mandatory law that protects minority interests during election processes.

Shareholders under German corporate law historically had and still have comparably strong rights to mandatorily *initiate* amendments of rules-of-the-game on the bylaw as well as the articles of incorporation level. A minority stake of five percent or €500,000 of the share capital held for at least three months suffices to undertake such a mandatory initiation. However, since two of the three nomination and election procedures enhancing the accountability of the administration are already in place as mandatory or default rules under German law, the significance of the initiation right for the procedures at stake is accordingly lower. For the election rules at stake that leave room for private ordering, the relevant issue is therefore the required supermajority quorum to approve an articles of incorporation amendment. It protects shareholders from a premature opt out of a favorable default status. Simultaneously, it impedes shareholder-initiated opting in to minority friendly election rules.

Shareholders under German corporate law have a mandatory *right to propose a nominee* for a vacant position on the supervisory board. In listed corporations, the nominees need to be published on the corporation's website. This mandatory right not only produces contested elections. More importantly, it also confronts supervisory board members with the possibility of having to compete against another potential candidate. As a consequence, they are more responsive to the interests of the shareholders to assure their reelection. It needs to be underscored that each shareholder may propose a nominee for a vacant supervisory board position as long as he has held his shares for three months. Even though the nomination right is not frequently used in practice, the increasing impact of active shareholders and their formal or informal use of nomination rights strengthen this effect.

The default simple absolute *majority-voting standard* complements the direct shareholder nomination right. It supports the alignment of the interests of supervisory board members and shareholders, as reelection depends on the support of a majority of the voting shareholders who are able to vote *against* the candidate. Both rules help increase accountability and diminish opportunistic behavior of the supervisory board members. As a consequence, agency costs resulting from the separation of ownership and control decrease.

Finally, the implementation of a *cumulative-voting rule* reduces collective action issues for active shareholders with a strong minority position aiming to achieve supervisory board representation.[767] For a market with a historically blockholder structure, where agency conflicts focus on the relationship between minority and majority shareholders, as in times of increasing freefloat and increasing administrative power, cumulative voting reduces agency costs. Even though German courts have not yet decided whether cumulative voting is permissible, the better arguments are in its favor. In practice, the issue would not be solved with the decision about its permissibility; rather, the problem is one of rule design. In a market with still substantial stakes of concentrated ownership, one-fourth of the present capital may still veto an opt in to a cumulative-vot-

767 Paul L. Davies, *The Board of Directors: Composition, Structure, Duties and Powers – Company Law Reform in OECD Countries A Comparative Outlook of Current Trends* 13, http://www.oecd.org/dataoecd/21/30/1857291.pdf (2000).

ing rule and makes reaching the required three-fourths approval quorum difficult. A default or even a mandatory cumulative-voting rule is more appropriate.

2) Comparing results with initial thesis

The results of the analysis regarding the shareholder initiation rights on rules-of-the-game amendments as well as the three nomination and election rules in place contradict prediction of the initial thesis.

The analysis has proven that under German corporate law, two of the four rules at stake, the initiation right of rule-of-the-game amendments via minority demand and the shareholder nomination right, are already mandatory standards. The third of the rules in place, the majority-voting rule, is the default standard for elections to the supervisory board. Only the permissibility of the cumulative-voting rule via opting in has neither been laid down by statute nor have courts decided in its favor; however, the arguments of its proponents prevail. The latter two rules are subject to private ordering on the rule-of-the-game level of the articles of incorporation, majority voting as the default rule and cumulative voting requiring an opt in. The latter requires initiation and supermajority approval. However, only accountability-enhancing rules with a mandatory or default character are relevant in practice. Under current German rule design, this applies to the shareholder initiation right, the nomination right, and the majority-voting rule. As a consequence, the German corporate governance system, characterized as historically *stakeholder friendly*, grants shareholders unexpectedly strong participation rights. The nomination and election procedure of supervisory board members is accountability friendly and makes the given shareholder initiation rights on both rule-of-the-game levels largely unnecessary.

Furthermore, the impact of shareholders of German corporations has historically been and still is wider than the one that would be provided to them under the shareholder primacy orientated U.S. corporate law. Despite the financial reform, neither proxy access nor majority voting have become mandatory or default rules. It therefore remains the task of the shareholders to initiate a vote on their implementation, since Delaware has held that shareholders may launch mandatory proposals on the bylaw level that are procedurally-related. Shareholders may also use the two-step proceeding recently introduced under Delaware corporate law to implement shareholder proxy access. The opt in approach to the cumulative-voting rule on the articles of incorporation level, however, demonstrates the limits of this shareholder initiation right under U.S. law. Despite the demands of *Bebchuk*[768] to expand them to the articles of incorporation level, it is restricted to the bylaw level. Opting in to the minority shareholder friendly regime of cumulative voting depends therefore on the rather unlikely initiation through the administration.

The result is astonishing not only with regard to the historically different prevailing interests under both systems but also with regard to their historically *different share-*

768 *For many Bebchuk articles* Bebchuk, 118 Harv. 833, 867 (2005).

holder structures. In a system with dispersed ownership as in the *U.S.*, the primary agency conflict and therefore the major source of agency costs lies in the relationship between corporate management and dispersed shareholders. In these constellations, the administration tends to act opportunistically instead of in the shareholder interest, since dispersed shareholders are generally confronted with collective action issues and are subject to rational apathy and free-riding. For a very long time, the rule design of the nomination and election procedure of directors did not contribute to the reduction of this agency issue. It neither held members of the administration accountable nor provided shareholders with the necessary means to amend the relevant rules-of-the-game. The latter even prevented shareholders not following the pattern of rational apathy and free-riding from amending the corresponding rules to establish the necessary accountability. Only in 2008 has this legal obstacle been removed for the bylaw level, lowering the costs for active shareholders to initiate and adopt relevant rules. Under the *German* corporate governance system, conflicts between blockholding shareholders, who assured the consideration of their interests through the mere size of their stake, and minority shareholders, unable to assert their interests against majority shareholders, have historically been the major source of agency issues. Accordingly, it was assumed that German corporate law has implemented strong minority rights instead of strong accountability mechanisms applying to the administration. However, the results of the analysis have not proven to be consistent. The minority friendly cumulative-voting rule represents neither a mandatory nor a default voting rule under German corporate law. Rather, its implementation would require opting in. However, shareholders have a mandatory nomination right. Furthermore, the majority-voting rule represents the default rule. Therefore, the (minority) shareholder right to mandate the initiation of rule-of-the-game amendments is secondary. The nomination right and the majority-voting rule assure administrative accountability and strengthen the position of shareholders towards the administration. Recalling the current trend towards increasing freefloat and administrative power in German listed corporations as well as the growing acceptance of the shareholder primacy approach, however, this approach is appropriate. The nomination and election procedures assure administrative accountability toward shareholder interests. Surprisingly, the approach of German corporate law is in this new context a pioneer for corporate governance that has been in place in the United States for decades.

3) Transfer of experiences with nomination and election procedures

The results of the analysis not only contradict the expectations that the historically stakeholder friendly *German corporate law* is more restrictive toward shareholders and their interests than shareholder primacy based U.S. corporate law. They even go beyond that. Controversial nomination and election rules aiming to increase the administration's accountability, which have been the subject of discussion for decades under U.S. corporate law, have been in place for decades under German corporate law. As far as transferability to the U.S. system characterized by shareholder structures of substantial freefloat, the *experiences* of three of the four rules in place as mandatory or default rules under German law may also be taken into account. Two of them have still not been implemented or become effective under U.S. law.

In general, the German corporate statute provides shareholders with unlimited opportunities to make *proposals* for an upcoming shareholder meeting. Under certain conditions they will even be published on the corporate website prior to the meeting. Despite the relatively new phenomenon of shareholder activism under the German corporate governance system and the stronger publication of ownership, the use of shareholder proposals significantly increased in the last years. Concerns of rational apathy appear to be secondary. In addition, the number of nuisance proposals has been reduced significantly. The higher ownership standard of 5 percent under German law compared to 1 percent under U.S. corporate law has to be seen in the context of the different ownership structures in both countries. Accordingly, the lower U.S. quorum may satisfy the same needs as the higher German quorum. In addition, the difference is relative because of the second, alternative ownership quorum of €500,000 of the share capital under the German system. Especially in large, listed German corporations, it is in practice a simplification of the ownership participation quorum. The experiences under the German system are not without drawbacks; however, the obligation of the management board to follow minority demands is not unlimited.[769] The implementation of the minimum holding period of three months via the KonTraG in 1998 has poured oil on troubled water. It keeps outsiders from holding shares only for few days for the purpose of launching a proposal[770] and has reduced issue-related involvement. The comparably longer holding requirement of one year under U.S. corporate law aims to fulfill the same function while compensating the comparably lower stake required. The additional restriction of mandatory shareholder proposals to procedural election rules-of-the-game on the bylaw level under U.S. law further limits the potential of nuisance proposals as well as opportunistic shareholder behavior.

In larger German corporations, *nomination proposals* according to § 127 have been disproportionately often applied even though the total number of nomination proposals has remained rather low.[771] Collective action issues apply not to the nomination process as such, since each shareholder may propose a nominee for an upcoming election of the supervisory board. Rather, the challenge is achieving a sufficient number of shareholder votes for the shareholder nominee. This does not apply to nominees intended to replace a publicly controversial administrative candidate. The potential for shareholders, who usually follow the recommendation of the administration in specific corporate decisions, to deviate from this pattern is higher under these circumstances. Therefore, the campaign efforts necessary to convince the shareholders to vote for a shareholder candidate are lower. This represents significant support even for active shareholders, while in the

769 Mertens, AG 1997, 481 (481 et seq., 491): noting that even though the management board should aim to support the use of minority rights to the extent possible, as long as it is used legitimately, it may not be used for propaganda reasons disturbing the remaining agenda topics and resulting in elevated costs for the corporation.

770 Kubis, in: MüKo AktG, 2004, § 122 mn.2.

771 *Id.* at §§ 127 mn.2, 126 mn.2.

remainder of cases the efforts necessary to challenge an administrative nominee remain significant. The low number of proposed candidates and the tiny number of successfully elected shareholder candidates is an additional argument against the various concerns the vacated rule of the SEC had been confronted with. Its ownership requirements as compared to the lack of ownership requirements under the German regime would even have contributed to a reduced number of proposals. Finally, the elevated freefloat would have further impeded the accumulation of the shareholder quorum necessary to have the candidate elected. As a consequence, the very few successful cases in which shareholder nominees would have been elected under the vacated SEC proxy access rule put in perspective the concerns about communication breakdowns on divisive U.S. boards as well as costly election contests. Concerns about the shortsightedness of incumbents due to the relevant replacement risk have not been proven as relevant under the German system. The usual office period of five years as well as a compensation scheme oriented toward the sustainable development of the corporation largely insulate administrative members from the pressure of short-term focused shareholder demands. In contrast, the annual replacement risk coupled with a compensation scheme focusing mainly on quarterly reports under the U.S. system of corporate governance generally raises the director's responsiveness to short-term focused shareholder demands. The proxy access rule debate may therefore reflect an issue inherent in the U.S. corporate governance system that needs to be dealt with apart from the discussion about the implementation of a proxy access rule. Furthermore, the limited number of actual replacements by shareholder nominated candidates under German law puts in perspective the concern that replacement will incline incumbent directors to give way to corresponding shareholder demands. Consequently, the German experience adds another argument in favor of the implementation of a mandatory shareholder access rule under U.S. law.

Finally, under the German corporate governance system, the *majority-voting rule* applying to contested and uncontested elections has been in place for decades. Even though the articles of incorporation may provide for different election rules, § 133 (2) AktG, German corporations have rarely made the corresponding amendments.[772] This may be evaluated as an indicator that the risk of failed elections, usually raised against the implementation of a mandatory majority-voting rule under U.S. corporate law, has not proven as relevant in practice. Rather, it is reduced by the efforts of the administration and shareholders aiming for a strong support of their candidates. In addition, in case of a failed election, the articles of incorporation may provide for a casting vote, for instance during a third ballot.[773] Also in this context, the five-year office term and the sustainable compensation scheme applying to supervisory board members render the blackmail and destabilization potential insignificant. The positive German experience with the majority-voting rule during contested and uncontested supervisory board elec-

772 Volhard, in: MüKo AktG, 2004, § 133 mn.77.

773 Controversial, *for* the permissability of a casting vote, Grundmann, in: Großkomm AktG, 2008, § 133 mn.126; Semler, in: Münch. Hdb. AG, Vol. 4, 1999, § 39 mn.73; Semler, in: Schmidt/Lutter, AktG, 2010, § 133 mn.51: requiring that the leader of the shareholder meeting is a shareholder and was elected as having a casting vote.

tions is an additional argument in favor of its implementation as a mandatory or default rule under U.S. law.

German experiences have therefore proven that the mandatory shareholder initiation right, the shareholder nomination right, and the majority-voting rule are beneficial and seem to overcome possible drawbacks. For this reason, all three rules have been in place for a long time under German law. Despite the underlying systemic differences of the U.S. and German corporate governance systems, the mainly positive experience of their application under German law is another argument in favor of their (less restricted) implementation under U.S. law.

Conversely, *U.S. experience* with active shareholders demonstrates that active shareholders may overcome concerns related to collective action issues that restrict the application of shareholder proposals and proxy access. Despite the historically existing legal barriers under U.S. law, they have made use of both, either directly to reach their goal or indirectly to further their strategy. Active shareholders, like hedge funds, often aim to exercise impact beyond the amendment of rules-of-the-game. Very frequently, they have used their formal impact on the nomination and election of the board of directors, especially by pursuing proxy contests to pressure management,[774] to reach a specific goal apart from a board position. Their impact is expected to increase with the recently implemented and expected amendments. The collective action concerns applicable to the historically accountability friendly German rules may therefore be expected to be reduced by the increasing presence of active shareholders. In particular, the nomination right's aim to overcome de facto cooptation and to increase accountability, whose realization is impeded by collective action issues, will be enhanced by their activities.

774 Gillan & Starks, *The Evolution of Shareholder Activism in the United States* 31, www.ssrn.com/abstract=959670 (2007).

D) Part II: Transaction activism

I) Introduction

Shareholders do not only become active with the aim to enhance abstract rules-of-the-game of a corporation to increase the accountability of the administration. Some of them go beyond this abstract impact level and aim to influence specific important corporate decisions of the corporate management. Shareholders have demonstrated an elevated interest in corporate transaction decisions. Especially more active investors, like hedge funds, are not satisfied by low cost, small, systemic corporate governance amendments, as less active shareholders like mutual and public pension funds are.[775] Rather, they direct their activism towards specific aspects of a company's business or management leading often to significant changes in the concerned corporations.[776] Most hedge fund activism relates to specific transactions or, more generally, to changes in corporate strategy.[777] Less active shareholders, like mutual funds and public pension funds, tend to join the more active shareholders in impacting these specific corporate decisions.[778]

1) Definition of transaction activism

Transaction activism relates to the impact active shareholders exercise on specific corporate decisions concerning a transaction in the sense of business combinations between two constituent corporations. Their influence (officially) intends to prevent a corporate transaction decision led by opportunistic administrative interests. The most relevant types of corporate transactions are mergers, acquisitions, and divestitures, which will be the subjects of the following analysis. Mergers as fundamental corporate decisions often involve a direct shareholder vote as part of the corporate decision-making process. In practice, a tendency toward more acquisitions and two-step transactions consisting of share acquisition followed by a merger has evolved. While the number of true mergers has significantly decreased in Germany,[779] their relevance in the United States has remained comparably high.

---

775 Kahan & Rock, 155 U. Pa. L. Rev. 1021, 1043 (2007).

776 *Id.*

777 Bratton, 95 Geo. L.J. 1375, 1422 et seq. (2007); Thompson, *The limits of hedge fund activism* 13 http://escholarship.org/uc/item/5jq9d71m (2006).

778 Kahan & Rock, 155 U. Pa. L. Rev. 1021, 1045 (2007).

779 Kraakman et al., The Anatomy of Corporate Law 202 n.88 (2009): referring to the opportunity of shareholders to amend the terms of the merger once the merger has come into effect, § 15 UmwG, as one of the purposes for the reduced number of mergers in Germany.

An alternative control mechanism in the transaction context that needs to be distinguished from transaction activism is the *market for corporate control.* Investors choose corporations with a comparably low market to book value. They aim to obtain control over the shareholder meeting to replace the administration, which is assumed to have insufficiently considered shareholder interests, in order to raise its stock price. Transaction activism, in contrast, represents the impact of a shareholder minority on the administration of the targeted corporation to control a significant corporate transaction decision alone or in combination with other aspects of corporate strategy. It does not depend on, but may well involve, the (partial) removal of administrative members. Transaction activism applying to corporations to be acquired via a merger or acquisition may simultaneously involve a change of control, with the consequence that takeover provisions and case law apply. To avoid a commingling of the effects of both mechanisms, it is useful to limit the analysis of transaction activism involving both transaction types to acquiring corporations. This does not, however, concern transaction activism targeting a divesting transaction, which suggests analyzing its particularities in a selling corporation.

2) Corporate decision-making authority in the transaction context

Usually, transaction decisions represent a part of corporate strategy and therefore a management task, and they are decided by the administration alone and not by the shareholders. However, some types of transactions are of fundamental character for a corporation. They are not management decisions to be made by the administration alone. Instead, statute or precedent require that shareholders must at least approve the transaction. In practice, active shareholders target both management and fundamental transaction decisions.

3) Goals, strategies, and directions of transaction activism

The incentive of shareholders pursuing transaction activism is to win a significant *personal increase of funds* or to prevent a loss that offsets the costs required to bring about the intended transaction decision. Since corporate transactions have the potential to impact the constituent corporations significantly, the potential personal benefits of active shareholders based on the impact of the transaction on the targeted corporation are accordingly high. Active shareholders may personally benefit from the increase of the stock price of the targeted corporation, aligning corporate and shareholders interests. Alternatively, they may profit from the distribution of the corporate war chest or a sum obtained as compensation for the sale of a part of the corporation. They may also benefit from the increased share price of a third corporation or the decrease of the targeted corporation's[780] stock price.

780 Please consider especially during the second Part regarding transaction activism that the term **„targeted corporation“** relates to the corporation targeted by shareholders pursuing transaction

Active shareholders apply different *strategies* while pursuing personal goals via transaction activism. One approach to prevent a potential decrease of the share price, to increase the share price again or even to achieve distributions from the targeted corporation is to *prevent* the purchase of an overpriced third corporation. Preventing the transaction avoids the potential plunge of the stock price of the acquiring corporation or ensures its return to its initial level. Alternatively, transaction activism may aim to amend the corporate strategy to improve the efficiency of the targeted corporation and bolster its profit and stock price. This may be realized by dissolving a conglomerate through the *divestiture* of non-core business units, which results in a more profitable remaining unit. Such a procedure reduces the conglomerate discount reflected in the share price. It is based on the assumption that conglomerates comprise more and less profitable units resulting in a lower average profit than if they had fewer more profitable units.

More generally spoken, transaction activism may aim to *prevent* a transaction entirely or with regard to its specific terms. Vice versa, active shareholders may intend to *facilitate* a transaction against the will of the administration.

4) Means to pursue transaction activism

Active shareholders engaging in transaction activism make use of a variety of shareholder means during their campaigns. These means are provided to them by statute, the articles of incorporation, the bylaws, or the *Geschäftsordnung*, respectively, or case law. However, their efforts may also comprise *informal means* that go beyond these *formal means*. This distinction is less a technically compulsory distinction because of the different legal consequences related to them. Rather, it provides a clear distinction between means provided to shareholders and additional means used by active shareholders that have evolved in practice. The distinction is relevant to the legal limits applying to transaction activism as well as the conformity of their application with the underlying corporate governance theory.

5) Potential and risks of transaction activism

The transaction activism strategy aiming to compensate the personal efforts of shareholders through the resulting increase of the stock price of the target corporation especially involves beneficial transaction activism. Here the aim is to control and correct a management decision as a result of personal interests, not the interests the administration is obliged to pursue. While the administration may aim to secure or enlarge the authority and compensation related to its position, this opportunism may come at high cost to the corporation. The personal benefits related to the transaction may tempt corporate man-

activism as opposed to corporations to be acquired during a transaction. The latter are referred to as „corporation to disappear“ in the merger context or „corporation to be acquired“ in the tender offer context.

agement to overpay in a transaction, which may negatively impact the stock price and therefore shareholder interests. Alternatively, management may have abandoned focus on corporate profitability in order to secure or to enlarge its own position. As a consequence, the stock price will fall as compared to its development when focusing on a few efficient business units and leaving the diversification to shareholders. The control of such opportunistic administrative transaction decisions not only results in personal benefits to active shareholders. Rather, all shareholders are able to profit from reduced agency issues, resulting in a rising stock price.[781]

Other strategies of transaction activism bear stronger risks for the targeted corporation and its shareholders. The stock price usually aligns the interests between the corporation and shareholders. However, this alignment may not always apply. Active shareholders may be tempted to pursue interests that allow them to profit more from a certain transaction decision than the rise of the targeted corporation's stock price. They may be based on pricier stakes in the other constituent or a competing corporation or on the use of financial instruments. Their pursuit may be neutral or even detrimental to the targeted corporation and its shareholders.

6) Introducing hypothesis with regard to transaction activism

Based on their efforts to overcome collective action issues, active shareholders pursuing transaction activism use formally provided *shareholder means* to directly or indirectly impact a corporate transaction decision. In addition, active shareholders use means not set forth in the articles of incorporations, bylaws, corporate statutes, or jurisdictions to increase their limited impact, especially in the context of management transaction decisions. For *U.S. corporations*, one can predict that the characteristic freefloat provides sufficient grounds for active shareholders to pursue efforts to overcome issues of collective action. Despite the historical shareholder primacy approach in the United States, the results of the prior analysis let assume a rather limited number of fundamental transactions providing shareholders with direct impact on the corporate decision-making process. The same applies to their impact on corporate transaction decisions in general.

781 Sometimes, the expectations in well-know successful active shareholders generally focusing on transaction activism, like Wyser Pratte, are so high that the announcement of his investment in a targeted corporation results already in a stock price increase representing the entire potential of transaction activism without any amendments having been initiated yet (like Wyser Pratte, whose investment in Rheinmetall alone resulted in more than a doubled stock price (FazFinance.net, Maschinenbau Rheinmetall ohne Kursfantasie, Nov. 28, 2001, http://www.fazfinance.net/Aktuell/Boerse-und-Anlage/Rheinmetall-ohne-Kursfantasie-3188.html). The downside to this positive reaction is that the concerned investor is likely to exit the corporation without to realize the beneficial amendments if the risen share price reflects already most of the beneficial effects of shareholder activism on the target's stock price (like Wyser Pratte, who left Rheinmetall in November 2001 after only one year of investment, *Id.*). As a consequence, the share price will drop back to its initial level and the corporate strategy will often remain unchanged. However, besides the unrealized hopes of the corporate stakeholders, the short investment will generally not result in damages for the targeted corporation.

Regarding the means of providing active shareholders with indirect impact on management's transaction decisions via the use of their franchise, the results of the prior analysis again allow the prediction that they are weak. As a consequence, a wide use of informal means by active shareholders in U.S. corporations may be assumed. Despite the historical shareholder approach, the results of the prior analysis allow the assumption that active shareholders in *German corporations* apply informal means less often to compensate for a lack of effective formal means to prevent or facilitate a transaction decision. The prior analysis has demonstrated that shareholders of German corporations have stronger initiation rights and a more effective franchise. This permits the assumption that they have generally stronger participation rights in corporate transaction decisions. In addition, their formal means to indirectly influence a corporate transaction decision are more effective.

At first glance, transaction activism has great potential to significantly reduce the agency costs of targeted corporations due to the amount of financial means involved in such transactions. Active shareholders that have recognized opportunistic administrative transaction decisions control them with the help of otherwise rationally passive shareholders. They use formal and informal means to directly or indirectly impact the corporate decision-making process in the interests of the shareholders. However, the large sums involved may tempt active shareholders to increase their potential personal benefit. They may decide to pursue a deviating interest instead of benefiting from the stock price development of the targeted corporation aligning corporate and shareholder interests.[782] The question that arises is therefore whether the potential opportunism of active shareholders is effectively restrained through the existing *legal limitations* under corporate and securities law or capital markets law. This does not relate as intensively to the use of formal means in overcoming issues of collective action. Their official character allows the expectation that the necessary legal limits to restrict their potential abuse have been anticipated. Rather, it relates to the use of informal means. The expected low relevance of informal means under German law as compared to U.S. law allows the assumption that the relevant legal limits to restrain opportunistic behavior of active shareholders are more efficient. Vice versa, the longer experience with shareholder activism in the U.S. implies that legislators, administrations, and courts have compensated for possible deficits.

Closely related to the efficacy of legal limitations in restricting opportunistic transaction activism is the search for a more general *distinction between desirable and opportunistic transaction activism*. Beneficial transaction activism prevents the realization of opportunistic administrative interests via a corporate transaction decision and has positive effects for the shareholder value. These prerequisites of beneficial transaction activism are impacted by the transaction type, the direction of the activism, and the position of the targeted corporation as acquirer or seller in the transaction. The available formal and informal means in the specific transaction activism constellation decide about the frequency with which shareholders will impact the corporate decision-making process in the intended way. Based on these parameters of transaction activism con-

782 *See* Briggs, 32 J. Corp. L. 681, 701 (2007).

stellations, the question is whether some of them are more likely to involve beneficial transaction activism than others. It is assumed that some of these constellations tend to unite an underlying general personal interest of responsible administrative members contradicting the shareholder value interest and shareholder means to effectively impact the administrative transaction decision. If the assumption were affirmed by the analysis of the subsequent six constellations of transaction activism, the question to be raised would be whether this knowledge could be used to make the limitations applying to opportunistic shareholder activism more effective.

The reduction of collective action issues and the use of informal means by active shareholders pursuing transaction activism raises the final question of whether their approach conforms to the *underlying theory* of the purpose of the corporation and the authority distribution between shareholders and administration. The reduction of collective action issues seems, particularly for U.S. corporations with high ratios of freefloat, to be a way to reduce the gap between theory and practice, which appears to be less wide for German corporations. However, the conformity of the use of informal means besides formal means to impact pure management decisions appears less evident.

II) Transaction activism under U.S.-American law

1) Decision-making authority with regard to transactions

Management tasks are increasingly delegated to the executive officers in larger listed corporations. However, the board of directors remains generally responsible for important corporate strategic and policy decisions,[783] including most of the transaction decisions analyzed in this subsection. As an independent organ, the board of directors has wide discretion when deciding important management tasks and is not bound by shareholder instructions.[784] Related to this wide discretion is the risk of opportunistic behavior; the corporation and its shareholders have to bear the resulting agency costs. An exception to the board's exclusive authority over the corporate decision-making process on transactions applies if the transaction represents not a management task, as is generally the case, but a fundamental corporate decision.

2) General formal shareholder means

Shareholders have only a limited impact on the agenda of an upcoming shareholder meeting via their right to make shareholder proposals according to Rule 14a-8 SEA. Even precatory shareholder proposals are subject to substantive exclusions according to Rule 14a-8(i) SEA, which prevents the proposals from being integrated into the corporation's proxy materials. Correspondingly, shareholders are not allowed to submit countermotions regarding

783 Göthel/Merkt, US-Amerikanisches Gesellschaftsrecht, 2006, mn.567.
784 *Id.* at mn.573.

management proposals for the same shareholder meeting, Rule 14a-8(i)(9) SEA. Another relevant exemption concerns proposals relating to management's ordinary business operations pursuant to Rule 14a-8(i)(7) SEA, which would simultaneously be an improper subject for shareholder action according to Rule 14a-8(i)(1) SEA. However, state law leaves room for shareholder proposals, which have been conceived as recommendations for the administration to decide on a certain management matter, including recommendations on specific transaction decisions.[785] The administration is not allowed to exclude a corresponding shareholder proposal before the shareholders have voted. The board of directors is not bound to approve precatory shareholder proposals and to implement them, even if they have been approved by the necessary shareholder quorum. An exception applies to the already analyzed bylaw proposals as provided by state law, § 109 (a).[786] Accordingly, active shareholders may use precatory shareholder proposals solely to give a signal to the administration. Their impact on the administration depends on shareholder support.

Rule 14a-7 SEA provides shareholders with the right to demand a list of stockholders or the circulation of the requesting shareholder's materials from the corporation. In general this right is restricted to times when the corporation engages or intends to engage in a proxy contest. The corporation confronted with such a demand may, however, decide between the two alternatives. The requesting shareholder has to provide postage and sufficient copies of the materials to be forwarded to his fellow shareholders if the corporation decides for the second alternative.[787] Corporations may therefore easily restrict this type of contact between active shareholders with limited financial resources and a broad shareholder audience. Under state law, the issuer confronted with such a demand has no corresponding choice, § 219. However, the request may only be made 10 days prior to the shareholder meeting. Its practical relevance is therefore also restricted.

In the context of transaction activism, it may therefore be helpful to use the beneficial ownership reporting requirements under § 13(d)(1) SEA/Rule 13d-1(a) SEA/Schedule 13D. They apply to all beneficial owners holding more than 5 percent of the outstanding shares of the registrant with the purpose or effect of changing or influencing the control of the issuer. In contrast to the regime applying to passive investors according to § 13 (g) SEA/Rule 13d-1(b) SEA/Schedule 13G, it is likely to apply to and to prove to be helpful for shareholders pursuing transaction activism. The comprehensive data to be provided to the SEC includes the exact number of the acquired shares, the origin and value of the financial means used, and the purpose of the acquisition. The latter comprises the intent to acquire control of the issuer, to merge it with another corporation, or any other major change in its business. Active shareholders may use the disclosure to obtain information about fellow shareholders holding qualified stakes as well as their intent and (qualified) stakes in other corporations, as both Schedules are publicly available.[788] The former information, especially in regard of the difficulties shareholders face in obtaining share-

785 Clark, Corporate Law, 373 (1986); Merkt/Göthel, US-Amerikanisches Gesellschaftsrecht, 2006, mn.806.
786 Sections without a further specification in this Subpart two of Part two refer to the DGCL.
787 Eisenberg, Corporations and other Business Organizations ch. 5, sec. 3 (2005).
788 Hu & Black, 61 Bus. Law. 1011, 1040 (2006).

holder lists, may be helpful in contacting major fellow shareholders to prepare a campaign. The information on the intent of qualified shareholders, however, is usually kept rather general instead of providing useful information.

A more serious means for shareholders to exercise pressure on management based on or independent of litigation against administrative members is the threat or actual *removal of members of the board of directors*. Unlike in common law times, when the removal of a director was only possible under exceptional circumstances, today directors may generally be removed without cause, § 141(k). However, many articles of incorporation include a provision explicitly precluding removals without cause as part of the widespread takeover prophylaxis.[789] A further restriction of the early removal right results from the installation of a staggered board, § 141 (k)(1). It prevents shareholders holding a majority stake or having the corresponding support from fellow shareholders from removing directors early or limiting them to a part of the board. However, considering the average office period of one year,[790] early removals of directors are of low practical relevance compared to the election procedures analyzed *supra*. Accordingly, shareholders dissatisfied with a director's performance will instead use the annual election, whose procedure is dominated by the federal proxy rules. However, the prior analysis has demonstrated the significance of the nomination and election procedures to assure accountability as well as the practical limitations shareholders face.

The concentration on the annual election process is also a result of another circumstance. Shareholders under U.S. corporate law have no statutory right to *convene a special shareholder meeting*. According to § 211(d), the right is restricted to the board of directors. But it is not unusual for the certificate of incorporation as well as the bylaws to grant the CEO or shareholders the same right. One of the key corporate governance issues during the 2008 and 2009 proxy seasons was the introduction or the reduction of the threshold necessary for shareholders to call a special shareholder meeting. During the former season, shareholders had pushed for the ability of 25 percent of shareholders to convene a special meeting. During the 2009 season, shareholders demanded that threshold be reduced to a mere 10 percent stake. Proposals concerned Kraft, Time Warner and Pfizer.[791] Many of the corporations that had already amended their bylaws to impose a 25 percent threshold and still became subject to a 10 percent threshold proposal argued that they were excludable under Rule 14a-8(c)(10) SEA. The SEC, however, rejected the arguments put forward by the companies that they had "substantially complied" with the proposal. Even though the companies were dissatisfied with this outcome, little is expected to change in the coming proxy seasons.[792] However, the 10 percent standard still represents a relevant obstacle for active shareholders, who usually hold minority stakes around 5 percent.

789 Merkt/Göthel, US-amerikanisches Gesellschaftsrecht, 2006, mn.572.

790 *Id.* at mn.571.

791 WestlawBuiness.com, *Special Shareholder Meetings: The Epic Tug of War Between Boards and Investors* (Apr. 16, 2009), http://currents.westlawbusiness.com/Articles/2009/07/20090730_0007.aspx?cid=&src=WBSignon.

792 King & Spalding, *Key Takeaways from the 2009 Proxy Season and Preparing for 2010 A Primer for Public Company Directors*, Client Alert Corporate Practice Group (July 2, 2009), http://www.kslaw.com/Library/publication/ca070209.pdf.

Furthermore, shareholders pursuing transaction activism may choose to threaten or actually sue members of the administration responsible for the transaction decision at stake, especially for violating their fiduciary duties. The standard of review that directors or officers have violated their *duty of care* applying to business decisions amongst parties dealing at arm's length is the business judgment rule. This rule assumes that members of the administration, when making a business decision, acted on an informed basis, in good faith, and in the honest belief that the action taken was in the best interest of the company.[793]

However, the business judgment rule presupposes that directors have no conflict of interest.[794] The *duty of loyalty*, in contrast, is the principal practical constraint on directors and officers[795] and is designed to avoid the possibility of fraud or the temptation of self-interest. It ensures that the interests of stockholders are not subordinated to the personal interests of an official.[796] The duty of loyalty concerns specifically the dealings between a director or officer and the corporation for which he is a fiduciary and which therefore tend to involve a conflict between self-interest and fiduciary obligation. Dealings with the corporation are therefore subject to rigorous scrutiny.[797] A director or officer can be found liable for breach if he uses his position to promote a transaction that provides the official with material personal benefits and if the transaction is unfair.[798] He has the burden of proving to have acted in good faith and that the transaction is inherently fair.[799] Initially, it is the plaintiff who has to show the possibility of self-interest, but then the burden shifts to the defendant to demonstrate the intrinsic fairness of the transaction.[800] The burden shifts back if, based on the knowledge of the material facts, a majority of disinterested directors or a majority of disinterested shareholders approved the transaction, § 144 (a)(1) and (2).[801] The latter so-called "shareholder ratification doctrine" requires a fully informed shareholder vote approving a director action that does not legally require shareholder approval in order to become legally effective. "[T]he only director action or conduct that can be ratified is the one which the shareholders are specifically asked to approve."[802] Only justified threats seem here potentially helpful to dissuade the responsible officials from adhering to their transaction decision.

Shareholders are able to threaten to or use their *right to inspect* the corporate books and records in regards to a specific administrative decision, like a transaction decision. § 220 (b) grants every shareholder the right to make a written demand in which he

793 Aronson v. Lewis, 473 A.2d 805, 812 (Del. 1984).
794 Lewis v. S.L. & E., Inc., 629 F.2d 764, 769 (2d Cir. 1980).
795 Anabtawi & Stout, 60 Stan. L. Rev. 1255, 1263 (2008).
796 Balotti & Finkelstein, The Delaware Law of Corporations & Business Organizations, § 4.35, at 4-233 (2010).
797 Bayer v. Beran, 49 N.Y.S.2d 2, 6 et seq. (1944).
798 Anabtawi & Stout, 60 Stan. L. Rev. 1255, 1264 (2008).
799 Bayer v. Beran, 49 N.Y.S.2d 2, 7 (1944).
800 Weinberger v. UOP, Inc., 457 A.2d 701, 703 (Del. 1983).
801 *See* Weinberger v. UOP, Inc., 457 A.2d 701, 703 (1983); In re Wheelabrator Techs. Inc. S'holders Litig., 663 A.2d 1194, 1203 (Del. Ch. 1995).
802 Gantler v. Stephens, 965 A.2d 695, 713 (Del. 2009).

explains the "proper reason" for his request. The matter needs to be "reasonably related to such person's interest as a stockholder" including possible administrative wrongdoing. Even though the inspection right should "not open the door to the wide ranging discovery that would be available in support of litigation," "[f]or this statutory tool to be meaningful, ... it cannot be read narrowly to deprive a stockholder of necessary documents solely because the documents were prepared by third parties." A stockholder who bases his claim "on alleged corporate wrongdoing, and assuming that the allegation is meritorious, ... should be given enough information to effectively address the problem."[803] Mainly used to prepare proxy fights, the right of inspection may also serve to control the administration ex post,[804] for instance as a basis for litigation.

Finally, shareholders may threaten to take control of the targeted corporation, for instance via take-over bids, in order to replace the administration. If the threat appears credible, it may increase pressure on the administration to make the proper transaction decision.[805]

3) Need of active shareholders to use informal means

Shareholders of U.S. corporations pursuing transaction activism are confronted with the plenary power of the board of directors over corporate decisions, including transaction decisions, § 141 (a). Theoretically, they are limited to the general right to elect directors, to vote on fundamental corporate decisions and to sue directors and officers violating their fiduciary duty as opposed to selling their shares.[806] In practice, many articles of incorporation have implemented classified boards and staggered voting. They require that shareholders have success in more than one annual shareholder meeting to obtain control of the board. Additionally, the significant costs related to the formally provided proxy contest procedures during director elections and shareholder votes on fundamental transactions restrict their availability to shareholders with large financial resources. The right to sue is overshadowed by the deference provided to the directors by the broadly applicable business judgment rule.[807] Finally, poison pills often prevent the sale of shares to an active group aiming to acquire the majority of shares. Vice versa, their redemption depends on securing sufficient shares to elect the majority of the directors.[808] As a consequence, the efficiency of the limited number of shareholder means is in practice further impeded. These circumstances make it insufficient for active shareholders to focus on

803 Saito v. McKesson HBOC, Inc. 806 A.2d 113, 114-115 (Del. 2002).

804 Jänig, Die aktienrechtliche Sonderprüfung, 2005, 32.

805 Brav et al., *Hedge Fund Activism, Corporate Governance, and Firm Performance* 43 http://ssrn.com/abstract=948907 (2008): noting that the intention to take control of the company is the most aggressive tactic pursued by *hedge funds*, as active shareholders with the widest spectrum of tactics used.

806 Thompson, *The Limits of Hedge Fund Activism* 19, http://escholarship.org/uc/item/5jq9d71m (2006).

807 *Id.*

808 *Id.* at 19, 20.

the use of formally provided shareholder means. Rather, they apply means not explicitly provided to them to overcome these legal and factual barriers.

4) Constellations of transaction activism

The following six constellations of transaction activism differ in the targeted type of transaction, the direction of the transaction activism, and/or the position of the corporation targeted by transaction activism in the transaction.

a) Transaction activism targeting corporate ***merger*** decisions

The analysis will focus on the most relevant traditional statutory merger.[809]

i) Special formal means for shareholders of ***surviving*** *corporations*

Special formal means helpful for active shareholders intending to impact corporate merger decisions may be used in addition to the just analyzed general formal means.

(1) Under corporate law

The corporate decision to merge with another corporation represents in general a fundamental corporate decision. As the mandatory initiation right of shareholders is limited to procedural decisions on the bylaw level, the authority to initiate a specific merger is limited to the board of directors.[810] Shareholders of the constituent corporations still participate directly in the corporate decision-making process of fundamental merger decisions by approving the merger with their vote.[811] In the surviving corporation, the realization of a merger requires besides the approval of the board of directors, § 251 (b), the *shareholder approval through a majority of the outstanding shares* entitled to vote thereon. The articles of incorporation may lay down a higher quorum, § 251 (c). The rationale behind the approval requirement even for shareholders of the surviving corporations suggests the concern about the sheer size and the potential of these transactions to radically alter the power and composition of the acquiring corporation's management.[812] Still, the impact granted to shareholders remains restricted to a veto position.[813] In addition, acquiring corporations are able to avoid shareholder approval.[814] Delaware state law provides several exceptions from the shareholder approval requirement. The most relevant

809 Merkt/Göthel, US-amerikanisches Gesellschaftsrecht, 2006, mn.1158.
810 Bebchuk, 118 HARV. L. REV. 833, 846 et seq. (2005).
811 *Id.* at 846.
812 KRAAKMAN ET AL., THE ANATOMY OF CORPORATE LAW 198 (2009).
813 Bebchuk, 118 HARV. L. REV. 833, 846 et seq. (2005).
814 Kamar, *Does Shareholder Voting on Acquisitions Matter,* American Law & Economics Association Annual Meetings, Paper 64, 9, http://law.bepress.com/cgi/viewcontent.cgi?article=1799&context=alea (2006).

one is the *short form merger* if the surviving corporation holds at least 90 percent of the corporation that is to disappear during the merger, § 253. An exception to the exception applies if the dissenting shareholders have to accept any consideration other than stock, § 262 (b)(2). Another relevant exception is the *small-scale merger* involving a maximum share increase of twenty percent in the surviving corporation, § 251 (f). The implication is that a shareholder vote is unnecessary as the board of the surviving corporation is merely making a modest purchase conveniently structured as merger.[815] The prerequisite for a valid approval in listed corporations is the full and adequate disclosure of all material facts to the voting shareholders.[816] Vice versa, opposing shareholders need to lead a *proxy contest* involving separate proxy materials and proxy cards to be filed with the SEC involving substantial costs, as analyzed more closely *infra.* Active shareholders will particularly use this veto right, where applicable, to prevent unwanted mergers.

Active shareholders aiming to prevent a merger from taking place may further consider *litigation.* The *appraisal remedy* is the dominant remedy for shareholders opposing a merger transaction. According to § 262, shareholders of the "constituent corporations," who may participate in the vote on the transaction, may disinvest at an adequate price. The term constituent corporation is not defined by statute. But sections 262(b)(1)(ii) and 251 permit the conclusion that disappearing and surviving corporations are meant.[817] For appraisal purposes, the shareholder has to notify the corporation in a notice of intent to demand an appraisal prior to the shareholder meeting. During the merger vote he must either abstain or vote against the proposed merger. Within a short period of time following the shareholder meeting, the shareholder must notify the company in writing of his intent to demand payment in cash for his shares. Furthermore, he has to continue holding his shares through the effective date of the merger.[818] In addition, a comprehensive number of exclusions apply to the appraisal right.[819] They include the market out exception applying to shares listed on a national securities exchange.[820] However, the sole issue raised in an action seeking appraisal is the provision to dissenting shareholders on grounds of inadequacy of the offering price of a judicial determination of the intrinsic value of their shareholdings.[821] The court will only determine the price at which the shareholder who made use of the appraisal right may turn in his shares.[822] It will grant him damages according to the difference between the stock's actual value and the price paid to him.[823] Even if a successful appraisal right provides an exit opportunity to shareholders whose investment is involuntarily altered by a fundamental corporate change,[824]

815 KRAAKMAN ET AL., THE ANATOMY OF CORPORATE LAW 198 (2009).

816 MAYNARD, MERGERS & ACQUISITIONS 38 (2005).

817 *Id.* at 44; WELCH & TUREZYN, FOLK ON THE DELAWARE GENERAL CORPORATION LAW 722 (2009).

818 MAYNARD, MERGERS & ACQUISITIONS 46 (2005).

819 COX & HAZEN, CORPORATIONS § 22.20, 625 (2003).

820 § 262(b)(1) DGCL.

821 Cede & Co. v. Technicolor, Inc., 542 A.2d 1182, 1186 (Del. 1988); Kaye v. Pantone, Inc., 395 A.2d 369, 375 (Del. Ch. 1978).

822 Merkt/Göthel, US-amerikanisches Gesellschaftsrecht, 2006, mn.1210.

823 Poole v. N.V. Deli Maatschappij, 224 A.2d 260, 262 et seq. (Del. Ch. 1966).

824 MAYNARD, MERGERS AND ACQUISITIONS 132 (2005).

the implementation of the merger will continue unaltered. Hence, for shareholders pursuing transaction activism it is not very useful.

The appraisal right has been subject to some isolated erosion, especially in cases of fraud, misrepresentation, self-dealing, deliberate waste of corporate assets, gross and palpable overreaching, or illegality.[825] Even if applicable, the appraisal remedy does not completely exclude *equitable jurisdiction* in regards to the fairness of a merger.[826] The general standard of care for directors and officers in negotiated transactions not involving self-dealing or any other form of conflict of interest and absent fraud and bad faith was established in the *TransUnion case*[827] involving a cash-out merger.[828] It applies the general assumption under the *business judgment rule* that "in making a business decision, the directors of a corporation acted on an informed basis, in good faith and in the honest belief that the action taken was in the best interest of the company."[829] "In the context of a merger … a director has the duty … along with his fellow directors, to act in an informed and deliberate manner in determining whether to approve an agreement of merger before submitting the proposal to the stockholders."[830] To rebut, for instance, the presumption of informed business judgment, the plaintiff has to prove that a director and his fellow directors were *grossly negligent* in violating their duty to act in an informed and deliberate manner in determining whether to approve a transaction and to submit the proposal to the stockholders.[831] Under these circumstances plaintiffs are rarely successful.[832]

Once the plaintiff has proven the *material self-interest* of at least one member of the board in the transaction, the application of the business judgment rule may be rebutted. If less than the majority of the directors voting are interested in the transaction, the interested director has to control or dominate the board as a whole. Alternatively, he must have failed to disclose his interest in the transaction to the board and a reasonable board member would have regarded the existence of the material interest as a significant fact in the evaluation of the proposed transaction.[833] Such constellations invoke the concern that the transaction terms are the result of self-interested negotiations.[834] The burden then shifts to the defendant to demonstrate the intrinsic fairness of the transaction to the company. It depends on the fairness of the price paid to the shareholders as well as

825 Weinberger v. UOP, Inc., 457 A.2d 701, 714 (Del. 1983); Cole v. Nat'l Cash Credit Ass'n, 156 A. 183, 187 (Del. Ch. 1931); Umstead v. Durham Hosiery Mils, Inc., 578 F. Supp. 342 (M.D.N.C. 1984).

826 Welch & Turezyn, Folk on the Delaware Corporation Law: Fundamentals 655 (2009).

827 Smith v. Van Gorkom, 488 A.2d 858 (Del. 1985).

828 Maynard, Mergers and Acquisitions, 433, 442 et seq. (2005).

829 Aronson v. Lewis, 473 A.2d 805, 812 (Del. 1984).

830 Smith v. Van Gorkom, 488 A.2d 858, 873 (Del. 1985).

831 *Id.*: A director's duty to exercise an informed business judgment is in the nature of the duty of care, as distinguished from the duty of loyalty.

832 Cox & Hazen, Corporations § 23.01 (2010).

833 Cinamera, Inc., v. Technicolor, Inc., 663 A.2d 1134, 1153 (Del. Ch. 1994), aff'd 663 A.2d 1156, 1168 (Del. 1995).

834 Cox & Hazen, Corporations § 23.02 (2010).

the fairness of the initiation, structure, negotiation, and disclosure of the transaction.[835] Regarding the latter, once the administration has negotiated and approved the transaction, its fiduciary duty obliges it to provide shareholders with full and fair disclosure on the basis of which the shareholders are allowed to vote on the transaction.[836] Even shareholders who have accepted the merger are not barred from challenging the fairness of the consideration if they were not informed of all material facts regarding the transaction at the time the consideration was accepted.[837]

An additional concern relates to *cash outs*, especially short-form mergers according to § 253 and the lack of opportunity for minority shareholders to share in the profits of the surviving corporation.[838] Equitable remedies have concentrated on the purpose of the transaction and the fairness to the minority shareholders.[839] The Delaware Supreme Court has abandoned the former criteria.[840] Rather, courts in Delaware have concentrated on the *entire fairness test*. As far as the fairness of the price is concerned, minority interests were strengthened by an appraisal proceeding decision of Delaware's highest court. It granted shareholders frozen out in the second step of an acquisition a proportionate share of the gains resulting from the business plan agreed upon once the minority is eliminated through the second step.[841] In regards to the available appraisal remedy, courts have been rather restrained in granting equitable remedies sought in procedural settings. So far they have granted relief only in cases of purposeful manipulation of disclosure practices or operations to artificially depress the share price.[842] Other scenarios

835 Weinberger v. UOP, Inc., 457 A.2d 701, 711 (Del. 1983).

836 Delaware law imposes upon the board the fiduciary duty to disclose fully and fairly all material facts within its control that would have significant impact upon the shareholder vote, Stroud v. Grace, 606 A.2d 75, 85 (Del. 1992); Rosenblatt v. Getty Oil Co., 493 A.2d 929, 944 et seq. (Del. 1985); In re Wheelabrator Techs., 663 A.2d 1194, 1198 (Del. Ch. 1995); Cox & Hazen, Corporations § 23.01 (2010).

837 Bershad v. Curtiss-Wright Corp., 535 A.2d 840, 848 (Del. 1987): stating that a shareholder has no standing to challenge the fairness of the merger consideration once he has tendered his shares and accepted the benefits of the merger being fully informed; Clements v. Rogers, 790 A.2d 1222, 1235 et seq. (Del. Ch. 2001): explicitly following *Bershad,* turning on the fact whether the plaintiff was an *informed* shareholder at the time she tendered her shares for the merger consideration, and that the fact that she complains that there have been material omissions and misrepresentations does not mean that the plaintiffs had learned about *all* information; Trounstine v. Remington Rand, 194 A. 95, 99 (Del. Ch. 1937): referring to the general principle that "who participates in or acquiesces in an action has no standing in a court of equity to complain against it, even though the act be against the permission of the law."

838 Cox & Hazen, Corporations § 23.03 (2010).

839 Roland Int'l Corp. v. Najjar, 407 A.2d 1032, 1034, 1036 (Del. 1979); Singer v. Magnavox Co., 380 A.2d 969, 982 (Del. 1977); Tanzer v. Int'l General Indus., Inc., 379 A.2d 1121, 1124 et seq. (Del. 1977).

840 Weinberger v. UOP, Inc., 457 A.2d 701, 715 (1983); Cox & Hazen, Corporations § 23.02 (2010): proposes a more useful stricter business purpose test relating to the purpose not of the transaction in general, but instead to the reasons for cashing out the minority shareholders of the corporation.

841 Cede & Co. v. Technicolor, Inc., 684 A.2d 289, 298 et seq. (Del. 1996).

842 Berkowitz v. Power/Mate Corp., 342 A.2d 566, 573 et seq. (N.J. Ch. 1975).

concerned purposeful timing to depress the price[843] or lack of independent determination of the fairness of the price.[844] The applicability of the entire fairness test has been qualified for short-form mergers by the legislative intent. It would be frustrated if the parent corporation would be subject to the entire fairness test.[845] The exclusive remedy to the minority shareholders absent fraud or misleading or inadequate disclosure is the appraisal remedy.[846] As far as freeze-outs involve a tender offer followed by a short-form merger, Delaware courts followed *Glassman* and demanded for the merger part that the price equals the one offered during the tender offer.[847]

However, courts are unlikely to undo a completed transaction based on a fiduciary duty claim. Rather, they prefer to award money to dissenting minority shareholders, to offer them shares in the consolidated or purchasing corporation, or to obtain the fair market price of their shares at conditions of the time of sale.[848] To allow rescission, in contrast, would represent undue hardship to all other participating investors, creditors, and the constituent corporations as compared to the rights of a few shareholders.[849] It accepts that the injured parties will not always end up where they would have been without the fraud.[850] To even have a chance to enjoin the completion of a transaction on the grounds of violation of fiduciary duties, a dissenting shareholder must therefore sue prior to the consummation of the transaction.[851] Accordingly, equity-based litigation has a comparably small potential for active shareholders to directly prevent a merger from taking place. Rather, a well-founded and early made threat to launch legal proceedings may indirectly keep the board from initiating a merger. More likely is, however, the constellation that a successful fiduciary claim is led ex post against a responsible director.

843 Rabkin v. Philip A. Hunt Chem. Corp., 498 A.2d 1099, 1099, 1106 et seq. (Del. 1985): explicitely stating that restricting the evaluation to the fairness of the price where the appraisal remedy applies while otherwise the fairness of the procedure is also evaluated cannot convince.

844 Kahn v. Lynch Commc'n Sys., Inc., 638 A.2d 1110, 1120 et seq. (Del. 1994): denies a shift of burden regarding the entire fairness to the plaintiff based on the mere existence of an independent negotiation committee, since it is necessary that the committee has true bargaining power. This is not the case if it is coerced by threats to proceed with the hostile tender offer and the price has not been confirmed.

845 Glasman v. Unocal Exploration Corp., 777 A. 2d 242, 247 et seq. (Del. 2001).

846 *Id.*, Cox & Hazen, Corporations § 23.02 (2010).

847 In re Pure Res. S'holders' Litig., 808 A.2d 421, 445 (Del. Ch. 2002): In order to address the potential for coercion and unfairness posed by controlling shareholders who seek to acquire the balance of the company's shares by acquisition through some equitable reinforcement, an acquisition tender offer by a controlling stockholder is only non-coercive, when: "1) it is subject to a non-waivable majority of the minority tender condition; 2) the controlling stockholder promises to consummate a prompt § 253 merger at the same price if it obtains more than 90 percent of the shares; and 3) the controlling stockholder has made no retribute threats."

848 Cox & Hazen, Corporations § 23.02 (2010).

849 Alabama Fidelity Mortgage & Bond Co. v. Dubberly, 73 So. 911, 915 (Ala. 1916); Strassburger v. Earley, 752 A.2d 557, 579 (Del. Ch. 2000).

850 Cox & Hazen, Corporations § 23.02 (2010).

851 The same applies to claims based on grounds of illegality, fraud or abuse of power, including the violation of securities laws' disclosure provisions, especially Rule 10b-5 SEA and Rule 14a-9 SEA (Cox & Hazen, Corporations § 22.18 (2003)) as well as § 16(b) SEA (Maynard, Mergers & Acquisitions, 226 (2005)).

As a consequence, the only relevant special formal means under corporate law for active shareholders is the approval requirement. Where applicable, it grants active shareholders the right to prevent an announced merger if they have accumulated sufficient votes to hinder the necessary shareholder approval. However, the relaxation of the statutory approval requirement allows management to circumvent this potentially disruptive prerequisite.[852] For transaction activism targeting a merger without a useful approval requirement, including the aim to facilitate a merger, only the general formal shareholder means, mainly accountability measures applying to the board of directors, remain.

(2) Under securities law

In addition to the numerous state law relaxations, acquirers listed on one of the three national stock exchanges issuing less than twenty percent of their outstanding common stock for compensation purposes avoid the shareholder approval requirement.[853] However, paying the balance with substitutes is costly.[854]

As far as shareholder approval applies, federal proxy rules demand that publicly traded corporations disclose all material information necessary for shareholders to meet an informed decision regarding the transaction. Information requested under *Schedule 14A* must be included in the proxy statement pursuant to which proxies are solicited and represents the minimum level of disclosure. To prevent liability under *Rule 14a-9 SEA,* disclosure has to be full and adequate in regard to all material facts.[855] This may require disclosure beyond the line items required to be disclosed according to Schedule 14A.[856] The information to be disclosed by the administration soliciting votes approving a merger may be useful for active shareholders, as material facts may contain relevant

---

852 Thompson, *The Limits of Hedge Fund Activism* 20 et seq., http://escholarship.org/uc/item/5jq9d71m (2006).

853 Kamar, *Does Shareholder Voting on Acquisitions Matter*, American Law & Economics Association Annual Meetings, Paper 64, 9, http://law.bepress.com/cgi/viewcontent.cgi?article=1799&context=alea (2006); Thompson, *The Limits of Hedge Fund Activism* 21, http://escholarship.org/uc/item/5jq9d71m (2006); *see* NYSE Rule 312 (c) (1) and (2) and NASDAQ Stock Market Rule 5635 (a) (1) (A) and (B) both relating first to the voting power and then to the number of shares related to the outstanding shares before the increase.

854 *See* Kamar, *Does Shareholder Voting on Acquisitions Matter*, American Law & Economics Association Annual Meetings, Paper 64, 11, http://law.bepress.com/cgi/viewcontent.cgi?article=1799&context=alea (2006): referring to the strained borrowing power of the acquirer, the resulting taxability for the remainder of the consideration once the substitute exceeds 40 percent, and the general uncertainty regarding the price at which preferred stock will trade if not traded before the acquisition.

855 Basic, Inc. v. Levinson, 485 U.S. 224, 231, 232, 250 (1988): "An omitted fact is material if there is a substantial likelihood that a reasonable shareholder would consider it important in deciding how to vote" as it "would have significantly altered the total mix of information available." … "Materiality in the merger context depends on the probability that the transaction will be consummated, and its significance to the issuer of the securities. It depends on the facts of the case and this is to be determined on a case-by-case basis."

856 Maynard, Mergers & Acquisitions 236 (2005).

disadvantages of the merger. Vice versa, shareholders soliciting proxies to disapprove a merger are also subject to the complex and costly proxy regime.

Similarly, if the acquiring corporation issues stock as consideration and no exemption according to §§ 3 and 4 of the Securities Act of 1933 applies, it has to register those shares pursuant to § 5 of the 1933 Securities Act. The purpose of the registration is to inform prospective investors adequately about the issuer and the terms of the proposed offering so the investor can make an informed decision.[857] Once the distribution is registered, the acquiring corporation must file a short registration statement, in an acquisition transaction usually Form S-4, with the SEC. It comprises in Part I the prospectus to be distributed to the shareholders of the acquired corporation before the SEC declares the registration effective.[858] Regulation S-K lays down the disclosure procedure including the comprehensive disclosure requirements. The filed registration statement is then to be used in lieu of Schedule 14A. The information to be disclosed under both regimes in regard of the proposed transaction is very similar.[859] Only when the SEC review process is complete and the SEC declares the registration statement effective may the bidder issue its securities to complete the transaction.[860] Any untrue statement or omission of a material fact in this context may violate section 10(b) SEA and Rule 10b-5 SEA and result in liability.

Material information to be provided by the administration in the merger context under securities regulation can provide active shareholders useful information about the transaction for their campaign. Vice versa, active shareholders aiming to solicit proxies to veto a planned merger are confronted with the comprehensive proxy regulation they need to conform to when soliciting proxies voting against a merger.

*ii) Transaction activism aiming **to prevent** a merger*

(1) Underlying interests

Administrations in the surviving corporation tend to pursue the opportunistic aim of increasing and securing their own authority and compensation by purchasing third corporations via mergers, possibly subordinating shareholder interest. The incentives of the responsible officials encourage agreement to overpay. Informed shareholders, however, know that merger premiums are likely to be so substantial that often the entire merger gain is transferred to the shareholders of the disappearing corporation.[861] As a consequence, the stock price of surviving corporations tends to develop negatively with the announcement of the transaction, while the effect on the stock price of the disappearing corporation is positive.[862] Until the 1990s, the portfolio theory was able to put this result into perspective.

857 *Id.* at 228.

858 Merkt/Göthel, US-amerikanisches Gesellschaftsrecht, 2006, mn.1202.

859 Maynard, Mergers & Acquisitions 235 (2005).

860 *Id.* at 227.

861 Bratton, 95 Geo. L.J. 1375, 1424 (2007).

862 Andrade et al., 15 J. Econ. Persp. 103, 109 – 11 (2001); Bratton, 95 Geo. L.J. 1375, 1425 (2007); Thompson, *The Limits of Hedge Fund Activism* 14, http://escholarship.org/uc/item/5jq9d71m (2006).

It held that the combined result for the constituent corporations, relevant for diversified investors, was positive, but it was not thereafter.[863] Involved shareholders of surviving corporations therefore have the tendency to react carefully to acquiring transactions, as they assume overpayment. Moreover, the financial incentives of active shareholders are strong enough to prevail over collective action issues and the legal barriers necessary to block a planned merger. Their efforts to prevent an overpaid merger are likely to be overcompensated by preventing or offsetting a significant decrease of the stock price of the surviving corporation. Simultaneously, all shareholders of the targeted corporation are able to profit from the efforts of the active shareholders to increase the corporate shareholder value.[864] As a consequence, desirable shareholder activism is likely to occur under this constellation.

(2) Relevant shareholder means

Active shareholders of the surviving corporation have different means at hand to prevent a merger. They will try to bring forward their arguments against the specific merger decision to the responsible administrative members via telephone calls, e-mails, or personal talks. If applicable, they will try to directly impact the corporate decision-making process on the announced merger by threatening to or preventing the necessary approving quorum, § 251 (c). In practice, this represents the opportunity with the least effort for active shareholders of the surviving corporation to prevent an announced merger.[865] To realize their threat, active shareholders may decide on a costly proxy fight requiring soliciting proxy authority from fellow shareholders via general advertisements and proxy materials to be sent to fellow shareholders. Alternatively, shareholders may, to reduce their financial efforts, work around the proxy rules by encouraging fellow shareholders to vote against the merger without seeking proxy authority. This route makes it, however, more difficult to convince a sufficient number of shareholders and requires carefully considering the scope of the proxy rules.

Absent a necessary shareholder vote, active shareholders will have to apply general accountability measures and threaten with a proxy fight to replace responsible directors to keep them from approving the planned merger.[866] Shareholders have developed a wide range of means between threatening to and actually undertaking a full-scale proxy contest to remove part or the entire slate of incumbents to impact transaction decisions. The success of a threat depends on its credibility. It is impacted by the reputation of the active shareholders, the type and number of supportive fellow shareholders, and the closeness of the next general shareholder meeting or the right to convene a special meeting. They may still apply the removal strategy after the transaction has been confirmed to have a new board investigate the implemented transaction. Alternatively, shareholders may

863 Moeller et al., 60 J. Fin. 757, 769 et seq. (2005).

864 Bratton, 95 Geo. L.J. 1375, 1425 et seq. (2007).

865 Thompson, *The Limits of Hedge Fund Activism* 21, http://escholarship.org/uc/item/5jq9d71m (2006).

866 *Id.*

threaten to or sue the responsible directors or executive officers[867] for the violation of their fiduciary duties by affirming the detrimental transaction.

As the ultimate action, financially credible active investors will threaten to *take control* of the surviving corporation to replace its administration and prevent the transaction or to hold the responsible individuals accountable. The threat to apply external control is intended to support their means of internal control. However, corresponding threats have only occurred in a few cases[868] due to the complexity of defense tactics usually in place, the necessary financial commitments, and the risk this capital is subordinated[869].

With regard to the generally efficient means for shareholders to prevent a merger, (beneficial) shareholder activism is likely to frequently apply under this constellation.

(3) Examples

(a) Mylan/King

A very well known example of transaction activism is the example of Carl Icahn's ("***Icahn***") activism as a shareholder of Mylan Laboratories Inc. ("***Mylan***") against the merger between Mylan and King Pharmaceuticals Inc. ("***King***"). When Mylan announced in July 2004 it sought to acquire King in a reverse triangular merger for 0,9 Mylan shares per King share, representing a 61 percent premium for King shareholders,[870] Icahn started to purchase Mylan shares. In August 2004, he filed a 13D Schedule disclosing a stake of 6.8 percent in Mylan and his opposition to the Mylan-King merger as too dilutive and too expensive for Mylan shareholders. In early September 2004, a proxy statement[871] by Icahn followed announcing a proxy contest on the merger decision for December 2004.[872] Later in September, Icahn amended the 13D Schedule disclosing that he was holding 8.9 percent of Mylan's stock.

Parallel, hedge fund Perry Corp. ("***Perry***") who held King shares had entered into an investment strategy known as merger arbitrage, which would allow it to profit from the consummation of a merger between Mylan and King. As its profit would be higher the less likely the market evaluated chances for consummation, it initially neither filed

867 Merkt/Göthel, US-amerikanisches Gesellschaftsrecht, 2006, mn.1073, 823.

868 Brav et al., *Hedge Fund Activism, Corporate Governance, and Firm Performance* 15, 43, http://ssrn.com/abstract=948907 (2008): referring to the threat of a takeover as the last of seven possible tactics of hedge funds pursuing shareholder activism, which has only been pursued in 4,2 percent of the cases.

869 Thompson, *The Limits of Hedge Fund Activism* 22, http://escholarship.org/uc/item/5jq9d71m (2006).

870 Robert Steyer, *More Opposition to Mylan-King Deal*, Oct. 13, 2004, TheStreet.com, http://www.thestreet.com/story/10187651/more-opposition-to-mylan-king-deal.html.

871 Carl C. Icahn, Proxy statement pursuant to Schedule 14A, soliciting material pursuant to section 240.14a-12, Sept. 7, 2004, http://www.sec.gov/Archives/edgar/data/69499/000092847504000059/proxysept7.txt.

872 Charles M. Nathan, *Merger Arbitrage, Beneficial Ownership Reporting and Proxy Contests: The SEC's Perry Order*, Oct. 25, 2009, HLS Forum on Corporate Governance and Financial Regulation, http://www.lw.com/upload/pubContent/_pdf/pub2854_1.pdf.

a Schedule 13D nor Schedule 13G. In order to increase the likelihood of the consummation of the merger, it acquired voting rights of nearly ten percent of Mylan's outstanding shares allowing it to support the approving vote. Through swap transactions it had avoided any economic exposure from owning Mylan shares, whose price would decline through the approved merger.[873]

In October 2004, the second largest known shareholder of Mylan, UBS Global Asset Management (***"UBS"***), holding 3.9 percent, joined Icahn in opposition to the Mylan-King deal. After having expressed its concerns in two meetings with CEO and Vice-Chairman Coury, UBS, in a letter to Mylan's Chairman Puskar filed with the SEC on the consecutive day, expressed its discontent with the intended transaction. It would be "dilutive of long term economic value for Mylan shareholders" as King faced "rapidly approaching exclusivity losses" on some products without "any meaningful ... new product-pipeline" to compensate for the losses.[874]

Icahn intensified his opposition after King had financial problems involving the restatement of earnings as well as government and SEC investigations.[875] In November 2004, Icahn offered to purchase the rest of Mylan shares leading Perry to disclose its Mylan position in a 13D Schedule, since it no longer met the passive investor requirement.[876] In late November, Icahn sued Mylan and Perry alleging Perry's purchase had violated the principle of "one person/one vote,"[877] which he later dropped. In a letter to Mylan's board comprising a letter to Mylan's shareholders Icahn underlined his interest in shareholder democracy. He warned Mylan to restructure the deal to prevent a shareholder vote on the merger. Otherwise he would seek to replace Mylan's board as soon as possible while the new board would investigate the transaction decisions of the old board. In the letter to the Mylan shareholders he outlined his opposition as well as his reasons for his opposition to the King acquisition.[878]

In February 2005, Mylan and King agreed to terminate the merger agreement because of King's restatement of several years of earnings.[879] As a reaction, Icahn informed Mylan of his intent to nominate candidates for the election of directors.[880] Mylan responded to

873 Moeller et al., 60 J. FIN. 757, 758 (2005).

874 Robert Steyer, *More Opposition to Mylan-King Deal*, Oct. 13, 2004, TheStreet.com, http://www.thestreet.com/story/10187651/more-opposition-to-mylan-king-deal.html.

875 Robert Steyer, *Mylan and Icahn turn up the Volume*, part 3, Dec. 22, 2004, TheStreet.com, http://www.thestreet.com/story/10200481/3/mylan-and-icahn-turn-up-the-volume.html.

876 Robert Steyer, *Mylan and Icahn turn up the Volume*, part 2, Dec. 22, 2004, TheStreet.com, http://www.thestreet.com/story/10200481/2/mylan-and-icahn-turn-up-the-volume.html.

877 Robert Steyer, *Mylan and Icahn turn up the Volume*, part 3, Dec. 22, 2004, TheStreet.com, http://www.thestreet.com/story/10200481/3/mylan-and-icahn-turn-up-the-volume.html.

878 Robert Steyer, *Mylan and Icahn turn up the volume*, part 2, Dec. 22, 2004, TheStreet.com, 2, http://www.thestreet.com/story/10200481/2/mylan-and-icahn-turn-up-the-volume.html.

879 Kamar, *Does Shareholder Voting on Acquisitions Matter*, American Law & Economics Association Annual Meetings, Paper 64, 9, http://law.bepress.com/cgi/viewcontent.cgi?article=1799&context=alea (2006); *Icahn stops Mylan bid for King*, Mar. 1, 2005, http://www.independent.co.uk/news/business/news/icahn-stops-mylan-bid-for-king-485308.html.

880 Schedule 13D of Icahn Associates Corp. & affiliated companies, Exhibit 3, Febr. 27, 2005, http://www.sec.gov/Archives/edgar/data/69499/000092847505000048/mylanlab13d.txt.

Icahn's bid for Mylan stock in June 2005 with a share repurchase program for 25 percent of Mylan's outstanding shares.[881]

During his successful campaign, Icahn used a wide spectrum of special and general formal as well as informal shareholder means to oppose Mylan management's transactions plans. Immediately after the announcement of the intended merger, Icahn had started accumulating a stake of more than 5 percent, which obliged him to disclosure, but less then 10 percent, which would have qualified him as an insider and controlling shareholder under the SEA. From the beginning, he expressed his opposition to the merger and his intent to solicit proxies against the merger in well-founded public letters to the CEO, board, and shareholders of Mylan, as well as in phone calls and one-on-ones with CEO and board. Only six weeks after the merger announcement, Icahn filed a proxy statement with the SEC and credibly threatened to pursue a proxy fight regarding the shareholders' vote on the merger. His opposition was supported by the second largest shareholder, UBS, which joined in criticizing the planned transaction in a letter to Mylan's Chairman filed with the SEC. A helpful circumstance was the announcement of the potentially necessary financial restatements by King coupled with the lack of an announcement of a special shareholder meeting to vote on the merger. Icahn, an investor with the necessary financial background, intensified his credible pressure on Mylan's board by offering to tender the remaining Mylan shares. Furthermore, he sued Perry as well as Mylan for breaching the principle of "one person/one vote."[882] Moreover, in a letter to Mylan's board, he demanded that they maintain the shareholder vote on the merger instead of restructuring the deal. Otherwise, he credibly threatened[883] to nominate his own slate of directors for the next election followed by investigations into the decisions of the incumbent board and possible legal proceedings. When King confirmed that it had to restate its financials for several years, an explicit reason for termination according to the merger agreement and one of the many suspicions of Icahn, the Mylan board had no choice but to terminate the merger agreement.

Concerning the voting power necessary for the threatened proxy contests on the merger vote or the director election, Icahn held less than ten percent to avoid regulatory consequences related to insider and controlling shareholder status. A credible chance to obtain the necessary majorities for both instruments was underscored by the letter of UBS, which in June 2004 held a 3.9 percent stake, to Mylan's Chairman. UBS joined Icahn in publicly criticizing the merger with King.[884] Both appeared to act in parallel instead of jointly, therefore avoiding the insider and controlling shareholder regula-

881 Press Release, Mylan Labatories, Mylan Labatories announces § 1.25 Billion Share Buyback, expected to represent nearly 25 percent of the company's stock, June 14, 2005, http://www.sec.gov/Archives/edgar/data/69499/000095015205005135/j14467exv99w2.htm.

882 Robert Steyer, *Mylan and Icahn turn up the Volume*, part 3, Dec. 22, 2004, TheStreet.com, http://www.thestreet.com/story/10200481/3/mylan-and-icahn-turn-up-the-volume.html.

883 Having the necessary financial means, demonstrated by threat to takeover, not only for a proxy contest regarding the shareholder vote on the merger, but also for one regarding the director election.

884 Robert Steyer, *More opposition to Mylan King deal,* Oct. 13, 2004, TheStreet.com, http://www.thestreet.com/story/10187651/more-opposition-to-mylan-king-deal.html.

tions[885]. In addition, Icahn initiated legal proceedings against Mylan and Perry to prevent Perry's vote on the merger without bearing the corresponding economic risk.

The full commitment of Icahn, who did not hesitate to threaten to or to use special and general formal and informal shareholder means to prevent a truly disadvantageous corporate transaction, proved to be worth the effort. Nevertheless, it must be considered that Icahn's critique of the merger was well founded and well demonstrated to the shareholders and that shareholder means are comparably strong under this constellation. He had the experience, reputation, and the necessary financial means to back up his threats, allowing him to overcome collective action issues as well as the legal limits.

(b) Pharmacopeia/Eos Biotechnology

The transaction activism pursued by OrbiMed Advisors against the merger of Pharmacopeia Inc. (***"Pharmacopeia"***) and Eos Biotechnology Inc. (***"Eos Biotechnology"***), in contrast, is characterized by a different strategy.

On August 22, 2001, privately held Eos Biotechnology agreed to be acquired by Pharmacopeia via a stock swap initially worth $197 million; Pharmacopeia scheduled the shareholder vote on the merger for January 18, 2002.[886] Pharmacopeia's stock plunged about 26 percent in the four months following the announcement as compared to a 17 percent rise in the broader American Stock Exchange Biotech Index.[887] OrbiMed Advisors, Pharmacopeia's largest shareholder, holding approximately 10 percent, hired a proxy advisory firm and objected publicly to the transaction. In a well-reasoned letter directed to Pharmacopeia's CEO and board, OrbiMed determined the deal to be too expensive as well as dilutive, making no strategic sense. Furthermore, it determined Pharmacopeia's shares were too undervalued for merger consideration and announced it would vote against the merger and urged fellow shareholders to do the same.[888] Although OrbiMed Advisors commended other shareholders to vote against the proposed acquisition of Eos Biotechnology, it did not seek proxy authority with respect to the proposed transaction.[889] Besides its public opposition, OrbiMed concentrated its communication on a few of the larger shareholders.

In January 2002, Pharmacopeia's board, which had also hired a proxy advisory firm, obtained support from the recommendation of ISS, at that time an influential independent proxy advisory firm. In a letter to Pharmacopeia's shareholders, CEO Mollica begged them to vote in favor of the merger, as ISS had recommended voting *for* the merger.[890]

885 Pursuant to sections. 12(b)(1)(D), 16(a), (b), 20(a) SEA.

886 Adam Feuerstein, *Pharmacopeias biggest investor trying to block Eos deal*, Jan. 4, 2002, TheStreet.com, http://www.thestreet.com/story/10006204/1/pharmacopeias-biggest-investor-trying-to-block-eos-deal.html.

887 *Id.*

888 Notice of exempt proxy solicitation by OrbiMed Advisors, Dec. 19, 2001, http://www.secinfo.com/dsTKg.4F9ew.d.htm.

889 13D Schedule filed by OrbiMed, Dec. 19, 2001, 7, http://www.secinfo.com/dsTKg.4F9Ex.htm#78q.

890 Rule 425 Business communication of the Pharmacopeia board, Jan. 10, 2002, http://www.secinfo.com/dRqWm.3sd.htm.

Still, on January 17, 2002, 12 hours before Pharmacopeia's shareholders would have been asked to vote on the merger, Pharmacopeia and Eos Biotechnology terminated the merger agreement without stating any reasons.[891]

OrbiMed's success was based on a clear campaign focusing on preventing the planned merger and its disadvantages to the Pharmacopeia shareholders. It aimed to convince the administration, the fellow shareholders, and the public that abandoning the merger would be in Pharmacopeia's best interest. The low-profile communication solicited proxies only from very few large shareholders, falling therefore under the exemption of the ten-or-fewer rule according to Rule 14a-2(b)(2) SEA. The public campaign informing others about the disadvantages of the transaction without soliciting proxies did not represent a solicitation under the regime of the proxy rules, Rule 14a-1(l)(2)(iv)(A) SEA. This *just vote no campaign* could make use of relaxed proxy regulations,[892] exempting OrbiMed from a large part of the filing requirements applicable to a proxy fight. As a result, OrbiMed had to invest significantly less compared to a campaign seeking proxies, as Icahn had done, to prevent the merger.

iii) Transaction activism aiming ***to facilitate*** *a merger*

In general, shareholders in the surviving corporation of a potential merger, free of any deviating interests, tend to oppose an acquisition because of the potential decrease in the stock price of the acquiring corporation. Furthermore, administrations tend to prefer strategies allowing it to secure or increase its authority and compensation. It has therefore generally stronger (opportunistic) incentives to support an acquisition via a potential merger, instead of opposing it. As a consequence, it seems unlikely that both interest groups would simultaneously follow a pattern opposite their general interests, prerequisite for the corresponding (beneficial) constellation of transaction activism.

Additionally, the shareholder means to facilitate a merger against the will of the administration are more limited than under the opposite constellation, making the required efforts correspondingly higher. Active shareholders in the potentially acquiring corporation are often able to use their veto right to prevent a merger. It suffices if they are able to ensure that shareholders representing the majority of the outstanding shares entitled to vote on the merger vote against it. Active shareholders pursuing the opposite strategy need to initiate and approve the merger against the will of the administration. However, shareholders under U.S. law have no formal means to mandate the initiation of a fundamental corporate transaction like a merger. Only the use of general formal and informal means, most effectively the threat to remove administrative members, and favorable circumstances like outstanding transaction conditions and a majority of supportive institutional shareholders could turn the tide.

---

891 Adam Feuerstein, *Pharmacopeia and Eos call the whole thing off*, Jan. 18, 2002, TheStreet.com, http://www.thestreet.com/story/10007015/1/pharmacopeia-and-eos-call-the-whole-thing-off.html.

892 *Annual Corporate Governance Review 2002 – Shareholder Proposals and Proxy Contest* ii f, 2002, Georgeson Inc., http://www.georgeson.com/usa/download/acgr/acgr2002.pdf.

Moreover, taking into account the general effect of an acquisition on the surviving corporation's stock price and the efforts necessary to successfully pursue this strategy, it seems unlikely that the expected benefits will sufficiently compensate for those efforts. Active shareholders therefore lack the necessary financial incentives to become active. Also from this perspective, desirable transaction activism in the potentially surviving corporation aiming to facilitate a merger against the administration' will is unlikely.

Perry's efforts in favor of the board-favored Mylan-King merger, which unsuccessfully aimed to prevent Icahn's efforts to block it, in contrast, did not represent (beneficial) transaction activism. It neither opposed a transaction decision supported by the administration nor aimed to control the responsible members. Rather, it concerned the active engagement of a person with voting rights aiming to ensure that the controlling activities of Icahn would fail and the opportunistic administrative transaction decision would prevail. Perry's engagement in the potentially surviving corporation was based on opportunistic incentives. The reason Perry supported the merger of Mylan was not an exceptional constellation of beneficial transaction activism. Rather, its opportunistic efforts prevented it from economic exposure if Mylan's share price had declined after it had voted in favor of the transaction. Perry knew that Mylan would be harmed by overpaying for the acquisition of King, which in return would have resulted in Mylan's share price sinking. Perry intended to vote in favor of the merger and to counter opposition from other Mylan shareholders. It held almost ten percent of Mylan's shares. However, Perry had hedged its exposure through swaps. As a result, it could vote alongside other Mylan shareholders yet had no economic interest in the consequences of the merger for Mylan.[893] As a King shareholder, the realization of the merger would have allowed it to profit from the increased stock price of King as a disappearing corporation.

b) Transaction activism targeting corporate ***acquisition*** decisions

Another relevant transaction type is the acquisition of another corporation via tender offer. A tender offer aims at the acquisition of all of the outstanding shares of a corporation by going directly to its shareholders. The tender offer's popularity is based on the opportunity of a hostile takeover bypassing the target management altogether, in contrast to mergers or asset acquisitions.

*i) Special formal means for the **acquiring** company's shareholders*

(1) Under corporate law

Shareholders of the potentially acquiring corporation are usually not provided with special formal means to ensure the appropriate consideration of their interests. That is exactly the reason why boards expecting opposition from shareholders decide for acquisitions via tender offers, at least for the first step, to get around otherwise applicable

893 *Perry hedge fund settles with SEC over Mylan stake*, July 21, 2009, reuters.com, http://www.reuters.com/article/idUSN2126137920090721.

shareholder approval requirements.[894] Simultaneously, principal-agent issues tend to surface on the acquiring side under tender offer constellations.

The *cash* consideration is the most relevant type of consideration for the tendered shares. Again, it generally requires no shareholder approval, as compared to the *share* consideration that usually depends on an increase of authorized shares according to § 242 (b)(1). The necessary cash consideration is usually assured via a bridge loan, which will be paid back after the issuance of junk bonds.[895]

Shareholders pursuing transaction activism in acquiring corporations will therefore generally have to fall back on the use of their general formal means. Most likely, they will threaten to remove the responsible members of the administration after the transaction decision has been made or to acquire control of the corporation via tender offer. Legal proceedings against the administrative members of the acquiring corporation, however, are unlikely to be successful because of the business judgment rule. Enhanced entire fairness scrutiny for self-interested transactions will unlikely apply to tender offers depending on the decision of the individual shareholders.[896]

(2) Under securities law

Beneficial ownership reporting requirements for shareholders intending to impact a control-changing transaction of the issuer are laid down in § 13 (d)(1)/Rule 13d-1 SEA/ Schedule 13D. In practice, they provide only limited information on the intent of such shareholders. Furthermore, they oblige active shareholders to disclose information instead of providing them with useful information. Only general ownership information provides them with information about potentially interested transactions of administrative members as shareholders of the corporation to be acquired and of qualified shareholders of the acquiring corporation, who may support a possible campaign of transaction activism. Besides, acquisitions via tender offer need to be reported to the SEC if the intent is to acquire more than five percent, § 14(d)(1)/Rule 14d-1 SEA. In addition to the information provided in Schedule 13D, the report has to include information on the source and amount of funds regarding the financing of the concerned transaction[897]. The benefits of these disclosures, however, are rather limited for active shareholders of

894 Thompson, *The Limits of Hedge Fund Activism* 17, http://escholarship.org/uc/item/5jq9d71m (2006): mentioning that the acquisition of Warner by Times and the decision of Time's board to switch from a merger to a tender offer acquisition was to circumvent the shareholder approval by Time's shareholders, Paramount Commc'ns, Inc. v. Time, Inc., 571 A.2d 1140 (Del. 1990).

895 Merkt/Göthel, US-amerikanisches Gesellschaftsrecht, 2006, mn.625, 1313, 1318.

896 In re Siliconix, Inc. Shareholder Litigation, 2001 WL 716787, 6 et seq. (Del. Ch. 2001): The entire fairness test, in contrast, may not be applied, as a tender offer involves a decision of the single shareholder, who has to decide whether to tender or not. Therefore, an involved interested party of the transaction may only exercise impact on one of the constituent corporations, the acquiring corporation in making its purchase decision, while not being able to exercise impact on the other corporation, as the target corporation is not confronted with a corporate decision because its shareholders are targeted.

897 Item 7 of the special instructions for complying with Schedule TO in relation with Regulation M-A, 17 C.F.R. 229, item 1007 (a)–(c).

the acquiring corporation aiming to facilitate or prevent an acquisition against the will of the administration.

ii) Transaction activism aiming ***to prevent*** *an acquisition*

(1) Underlying interests

Transaction activism aiming to prevent an acquisition involves similar underlying contradictory interests of the administration and shareholders as the parallel constellation involving a merger. While the administration is likely to profit from the acquisition through increased authority and compensation, the stock price of acquiring corporations usually drops, as paid premiums tend to be higher than resulting synergies. Despite possibly negative consequences for shareholder value, the administration will have strong incentives to facilitate the acquisition. Active shareholders will find a wide control field for their beneficial activities, as rising stock prices of the targets will allow them to profit from their efforts.

(2) Relevant shareholder means

In addition, principal-agent issues surface even more under these acquisition constellations, as shareholders are not able to participate in the corporate acquisition decision. In contrast to a merger constellation, active shareholders are not able to concentrate on overcoming collective action issues to ensure the necessary shareholder support to veto the merger. Rather, they need to overcome legal limits besides collective action issues to apply the general accountability measures to the relevant administrative members to prevent an acquisition. These increased efforts lower the financial incentives of active shareholders as overcompensation becomes less likely.

(3) Example

As announced on May 20, 2006, Mirant Corp. *("**Mirant**")* made a cash-and-stock[898] bid for NRG Energy Inc. ("***NRG***"), which immediately turned down the offer,[899] despite a 33 percent premium[900]. NRG reasoned that the offer undervalued NRG's shares, that Mirant's stock was poor compensation, and that in light of industry growth trends it was not the time for a sale.[901]

---

898 *Mirant Withdraws its Offer to Buy NRG*, June 13, 2006, The New York Times, *available at* http://www.nytimes.com/2006/06/13/business/13energy.html.

899 Schedule 13D of Pirate Capital LLC, Item 4, Purpose of the Transaction, June 1, 2006, http://www.sec.gov/Archives/edgar/data/1010775/000114420406023271/v044689_sc13d.txt.

900 Andrew Ross Sorkin, *Dealbook; A Strategic Decision, or Self-Preservation?*, June 4, 2006, The New York Times, *available at* http://query.nytimes.com/gst/fullpage.html?res=9D05E2DD1731F937A-35755C0A9609C8B63&sec=&spon=&pagewanted=all.

901 *Mirant Withdraws its Offer to Buy NRG*, June 13, 2006, The New York Times, *available at* http://www.nytimes.com/2006/06/13/business/13energy.html.

Four hedge funds that together held about 7 percent of Mirant called on Mirant's CEO to drop the bid for NRG.[902] On June 1, 2006, Pirate Capital LLC ("***Pirate***"), which held 1.6 percent of Mirant's outstanding shares, sent a letter to Mirant's CEO. It urged him to stay away from a hostile bidding procedure, as it would not be in the best interest of Mirant's shareholders. Rather, Mirant would allegedly do well to put itself up for sale. Further, Pirate demanded a personal meeting with the board of directors in order to discuss the matter.[903] Jana Partners LLC ("***Jana***"), which held 2.3 percent of Mirant's outstanding shares, sent a letter to Mirant's board of directors. It asked it to stop bidding for NRG and to consider selling non-strategic corporate assets, to increase corporate leverage, and to return the money to the shareholders through stock buybacks and dividends. It viewed the intended acquisition as detrimental to shareholder value.[904] In a second letter of June 12, 2006, addressed to the independent directors of Mirant's board, Pirate reiterated its unanswered request to meet with Mirant's board to discuss the proposed transaction. In addition, Pirate threatened to remove part of Mirant's board in a proxy fight if Mirant did not publicly abandon its bid by June 14, 2006, and sell the company instead. More specifically, it threatened Mirant with a formal request that the board of directors convene a special shareholder meeting. Alternatively, it would solicit the necessary agent designations to meet the forty percent threshold required by the company's certificate of incorporation for shareholders to call a special meeting. The purpose of the special meeting of shareholders would be to increase the number of board members, to remove some of the incumbents, and subsequently to gain a majority of the board members. This majority would call for the immediate abandonment of the proposed NRG acquisition.[905] On the same day, Mirant withdrew its proposal to acquire NRG. It cited NRG's unwillingness to sit down to discuss the opportunities to create value for both companies' shareholders and a long, contested pursuit not being in the best interest of Mirant and its shareholders.[906] The stock price development upon this announcement was positive.[907]

Despite Mirant's arguments and NRG's takeover defense via a staggered board, another factor for the abandonment, unacknowledged by Mirant, was the strong and steady opposition of several hedge funds holding shares in Mirant. The formal letters to

902 *Mirant Withdraws Hostile $7.9 Billion Offer For NRG*, June 13, 2006, Pulp.tc, http://www.pulp.tc/html/mirant_news_20.html.

903 Schedule 13 D of Pirate Capital LLC, Exhibit B, June 1st, 2006, http://www.secinfo.com/d12TC3.vmn8.htm#Dates.

904 Jennifer McCandless, *Mirant hit by activist hedge funds*, June 2, 2006, Financial News Online, http://www.efinancialnews.com/assetmanagement/pensionfunds/content/1045135411.

905 Schedule 13D of Pirate Capital LLC, Exhibit C, amended June 12, 2006, http://209.85.135.132/search?q=cache:ZKvqp6T8V8gJ:shareholder.api.edgar-online.com/efx_dll/edgarpro.dll%3F-FetchFilingRTF1%3Fsessionid%3DA_geWt3VVIRhQHP%26ID%3D4476200%26PageBreak-StyleID%3D2+mirant+nrg+shareholder+opposition&cd=19&hl=de&ct=clnk&gl=de&client=-firefox-a.

906 *Mirant Withdraws Its Offer to Buy NRG*, June 13, 2006, The New York Times, *available at* http://www.nytimes.com/2006/06/13/business/13energy.html; Stephen Taub, *Hostile Bids, Hostile Shareholders*, June 12, 2006, CFO.com, http://www.cfo.com/article.cfm/7053828?f=related.

907 *Mirant Up on Activist Agitation*, June 21, 2006, TheStreet.com, http://www.thestreet.com/story/10293003/1/mirant-up-on-activist-agitation.html.

Mirant's CEO and board, including the request for a meeting with the board to discuss about the transaction, remained unheeded by Mirant's administration. However, it paid deference to Pirate's threat of a proxy fight if Mirant did not abandon NRG's acquisition and put itself up for sale. The threat was accompanied by a feasible method to undertake a proxy fight: apart from the annual general meeting a special shareholder meeting could be convened by 40 percent of the shareholders according to the articles of incorporation. Additionally, Pirate was supported by three other hedge funds representing together 7 percent, as demonstrated by their joint outcry against NRG's acquisition in a letter to the CEO. The additional demand of a sale of the corporation, which usually results in the loss of key administrative positions, allowed Mirant's administration to recognize the demand to abandon the NRG acquisition as the lesser of two evils. Pirate's credible threat of a proxy fight and the recommendation to sell Mirant instead of acquiring NRG, paired with the parallel complaints of several hedge funds, were an effective tactic to prevent the acquisition in the absence of a veto right.

Instead of withdrawing after the abandonment of the acquisition, the hedge funds made further demands. Pirate reiterated its request to personally meet with Mirant's board to discuss steps to enhance shareholder value.[908] The other hedge funds joined Pirate in its demand to enhance shareholder value by using corporate cash, additional debt, and divestitures to implement share repurchases and dividends.[909]

iii) Transaction activism aiming ***to facilitate*** *an acquisition*

Comparable to the parallel constellation of transaction activism aiming to facilitate a merger, the underlying interests of administrative members cause them to act more opportunistically when supporting an acquisition than when aiming to prevent it. In addition, shareholder efforts in the acquiring corporation to prevent an acquisition are more likely to enhance shareholder value than opposite efforts. Accordingly, constellations aiming to prevent a transaction provide active shareholders more often with the necessary financial incentives based on a rising stock price than constellations aiming to facilitate an acquisition. In addition, the lack of special formal means for a direct shareholder impact on the corporate acquisition decision and the increased efforts necessary to *facilitate* a corporate acquisition transaction further reduce the likeliness of sufficient financial incentives for active shareholders to pursue this strategy. Beneficial transaction activism aiming to facilitate a corporate acquisition will therefore be rather rare.

908 Schedule 13D of Pirate Capital LLC, Exhibit D, amended June 14, 2006, http://www.sec.gov/Archives/edgar/data/1010775/000090266406001656/exhibit_d.txt.

909 Schedule 13 D of Pirate Capital LLC, Exhibit E, amended June 20, 2006, http://www.sec.gov/Archives/edgar/data/1010775/000114420406025513/v045920_ex99-e.txt.

c) Transaction activism targeting corporate ***divestiture*** decisions

*i) Special formal means for shareholders of the **divesting** company*

(1) Under corporate law

Divestitures of corporate subsidiaries or divisions are usually pure management decisions. A divestiture involving the sale of part of the corporation needs to be distinguished from the corporate decision to sell (almost) all of the corporate assets, which requires shareholder participation. According to § 271(a), the purchase of all or substantially all assets of a corporation, be it for shares or cash, requires shareholder approval by a majority of the outstanding shares of the selling corporation in a meeting proceeded by a 20 day notice period. The judiciary determined the distinguishing criteria. "All or substantially all … assets" were held in *Gimbel v. Signal Companies, Inc.* (1974)[910] to be the ones "quantitatively vital … to the existence and purpose of the corporation". Active shareholders tend, however, to engage in divestiture transactions involving non-core divisions or subsidiaries when the targeted corporations are characterized by a conglomerate structure. Transaction activism targeting divestitures does not therefore usually involve corporate transaction decisions providing shareholders with a participation right pursuant to § 271(a).

Furthermore, state law does not attach an *appraisal right* to the sale of corporate assets as opposed to mergers or consolidations, § 262.[911] Its significance for active shareholders is mainly limited to the preclusion of fiduciary duty claims.

Absent relevant special formal shareholder means to impact the administrative decision about a potential divestiture, active shareholders must use general formal as well as informal shareholder means. Besides threats of a proxy fight to replace administrative members and of taking control of the corporation, they could threaten to sue the responsible administrative members for violating their fiduciary duties in the corporate divestiture decision. Fiduciary duties may not only demand that administrations implement a divestiture, but divestitures may allow the administration to more easily enforce its fiduciary duties in the future.[912] But again, a divestiture decision lies deep in the business judgment territory of the board. Absent conflicting interests, active shareholders will be confronted with a burden of proof that is hard to satisfy.

(2) Under Securities Law

Absent special shareholder means, active shareholders have recourse to shareholder proposals according to Rule 14a-8 SEA to pressure the administration. They can mandate, for instance, the initiation of accountability friendly procedural amendments on the bylaw level or launch a precatory proposal directly concerning the divestiture decision.

---

910 316 A. 2d 599, 606 (Del. Ch. 1974).

911 Cox & Hazen, Corporations § 22.20, 624 (2003); Welch & Turezyn, Folk on the Delaware General Corporation Law 722 (2009).

912 Adams & Mukherji, 68 Fordham L. Rev. 15, 47 et seq. (1999).

The general beneficial ownership reporting requirements pursuant to §§ 13(d) and 13(g) SEA allow them to identify qualified shareholders. They can contact these with the intent to convince them to support their campaign against the administrative decision regarding a divesting transaction.

*ii) Transaction activism aiming **to facilitate** a divestiture*

This form of shareholder activism aims at prodding the administration of a targeted corporation to unbundle some of its divisions or subsidiaries to slim down its conglomerate structure. The unbundling takes place via an asset sale or a spin-off.

(1) Underlying interests

A reason for the administration's general interest in abstaining from divestitures despite inefficient corporate conglomerate structures are again to be found in the aspiration for security of their current position and compensation. Directors prefer the size of a conglomerate structure for compensation reasons. Moreover, internal diversification secures the positions by reducing bankruptcy risk, while the higher market capitalization restrains takeover attempts. Finally, the size of the business allows the camouflaging of management mistakes by the average performance of the business. Divestitures, especially when applied to conglomerates, may, however, have a very positive impact on the shareholder value of the concerned corporation. The approach of active shareholders to engage in conglomerate corporations and to facilitate a divestiture has its origin in the conglomerate discount. According to a rule of thumb, it amounts to 15 percent of the stock price. Unbundling of conglomerates has been encouraged for about 25 years and the prevailing approach to explain this discount concerns the need for other divisions to subsidize underperforming, non-core subsidiaries.[913] More generally, a corporation may become more effective through a divestiture if it disposes of poorly performing units that depress its value or a subsidiary that may only unlock its true value outside of a conglomerate structure. With the sale of the concerned divisions or subsidiaries the active shareholders aim to unlock this discount and all shareholders of the targeted corporation will profit from the rising stock price or an alternative distribution. Activism aiming to facilitate divestitures is therefore likely to be a basis for desirable transaction activism.

(2) Relevant shareholder means

Active shareholders aiming to convince the administration to initiate, approve, and implement the sale or spin off of corporate divisions or subsidiaries to realign the corporate business and to get rid of the conglomerate discount need to use general formal and informal means. They may initially contact members of the administration via e-mails, letters, and phone calls or, if granted, personal meetings to present and explain the sincerity of their demands. To underscore the sincerity of their demand they may launch

913 Bratton, 95 Geo. L.J. 1375, 1392 n.73 (2007).

a shareholder proposal to pressure the administration to make the divestiture. Such a proposal may either relate directly to the divestiture or mandate a procedural bylaw amendment to increase shareholder impact. Despite Rule 14a-8(i)(1) SEA, a proposal may even relate to management tasks as long as it contains only a recommendation.[914] In order for a proposal not to fall short of its pressuring effect, sufficient shareholders need to (be likely to) vote for it. A stronger signal is the threat to launch a full-scale proxy battle if the corporation does not pursue divestiture. It depends on an unfettered replacement plan in the near future. Besides a lack of takeover defenses like classified boards, it includes the opportunity to convene a special meeting or the credible announcement to remain involved until the subsequent shareholder meeting(s). Furthermore, the usual minority position of active shareholders requires them to convey sufficient support of fellow shareholders for the proxy fight.[915] Active shareholders are able to sue members of the administration for violating their fiduciary duties by abstaining from a value-enhancing divestiture. As an ultimate means, they can suggest selling the entire corporation or even launch their own offer to acquire the entire targeted corporation, endangering the positions of the incumbents.

(3) Examples

(a) Sears' divestitures

An example of earlier shareholder activism in the 1990s aiming at the amendment of the corporate strategy by divesting parts of the targeted corporation is Sears, Roebuck & Co (***"Sears")***.[916] As a consequence of a diversification strategy in the early 1980s, Sears had combined retail and financial services divisions.[917] While the latter developed superbly, the former deteriorated with earnings declining at an annual rate of 7.7 percent in the seven years up to 1990. Many shareholders decided to exit Sears. Others decided to become active. From 1989 on and for more than three years, active shareholders targeted Sears to improve its corporate governance by increasing accountability[918] as well as its performance by divesting parts of the corporation.[919] Amongst them were the LENS Fund ("***LENS***"), holding 100 shares, and public pension fund CalPERS, holding 0.6 percent.[920]

---

914 Göthel/Merkt, US-amerikanisches Gesellschaftsrecht, 2006, mn.806.

915 Thompson, *The Limits of Hedge Fund Activism* 22, http://escholarship.org/uc/item/5jq9d71m (2006).

916 Gillan et al., 55 J. FIN. ECON. 103, 116-118 (2000): Eight of the seventeen members of the board were insiders, further board members served a median of eleven long years and had close ties to management based on joint service on other boards, and so on; Carol AS Thompson/The History of the Conspiracy Against Tobacco, The Newton Minnow Page, http://www.smokershistory.com/Minow.htm (last visited Jan. 12, 2010).

917 Gillan et al., 55 J. FIN. ECON. 103, 103 (2000).

918 Gillian et al., 55 J. FIN. ECON. 103, 119 (2000).

919 Monks & Minow, *Sears Case Study*, http://www.lens-library.com/info/sstan.html (Draft 1994).

920 Monks & Minow, *Sears Case Study*, http://www.lens-library.com/info/sstan.html (Draft 1994).

In 1989, CalPERS voiced concerns about Sears' performance. In several letters to Sears' Board Chairman and CEO, CalPERS complained about the depressed share price, the failures of its retail strategies, and its poor governance structure.[921] It sent an open letter to Sears' CEO in which it proposed the installation of a shareholders' advisory group to give the board non-binding advice. CalPERS also hinted that it preferred a major restructuring by spinning off the successful financial divisions from the plunging retail division. After discussions with Sears' officers, CalPERS agreed to set aside its shareholder proposal for an advisory group at the upcoming May 1991 shareholder meeting on condition that it receive two meetings with Sears' executives. Sears' performance continued to decline.[922]

Robert Monks, one of two founders of LENS, pursued a different strategy of shareholder activism. Due to Sears' poor performance and major governance issues, he decided to engage in a proxy contest for one of the seats on the corporate board in May 1991. Despite a shareholder nomination and a cumulative-voting rule, Monks experienced restraints most of which active shareholders today are still likely to face when attempting to have their own candidate elected. After the board denied including Monks' candidacy in the corporate proxy materials, a longtime LENS associate and Mirant shareholder nominated him based on the bylaws' shareholder nomination right. Seeking proxy authority for his own candidacy, Monks had to produce and mail solicitation materials to his fellow shareholders at his own expense. Meanwhile, the corporate proxy materials containing the board's candidates were mailed to 450,000 shareholders and 400,000 employees at Sears' expense. Providing them all with proxy materials about Monks' candidacy would have cost about $1.2 million. He therefore had to concentrate on shareholders with more than 1000 shares. Obtaining the names of these shareholders was another challenge. Usually, shareholders could request a shareholder list long before an election, § 219. An exception applied, however, if the request is not made for a "proper cause" according to § 220 (b)(1), the burden of proof being on the administration.[923] Sears hired Martin Lipton, who sued Monks, arguing that he wanted the list for an improper cause. Monks was denied the shareholder list. Furthermore, 25 percent of Sears' shares were held as part of an employee benefit plan. Direct contact with the employees was prevented by Sears' offer to only forward Monks' solicitation material to the shareholding employees for a payment of $300,000. Consequently, the 25 percent of shareholders whom Sears employed and the 20 percent of shareholders holding less then 1000 shares did not receive Monks' solicitation materials. Moreover, the SEC had to clear Monks' solicitation materials before he was allowed to send them to the remaining shareholders.[924] Regarding election procedure, under the Employee Retirement Income Security

921 Gillan et al., 55 J. Fin. Econ. 103, 118, 119 (2000).

922 Monks & Minow, *Sears Case Study*, http://www.lens-library.com/info/sstan.html (Draft 1994).

923 Gen. Time Corp. v. Talley Indus., Inc., 43 Del. Ch. 531, 533 (1968): "[T]he desire to solicit proxies for a slate of directors in opposition to management" is a "purpose reasonable" to his "interest as a stockholder" and therefore a "proper purpose" under § 220 (b) (1) and (b) sent. 3.

924 In 1992, this regulation was amended, so that shareholders can now circulate information about shareholder resolutions without pre-approval by the SEC as long as they do not concern a proxy contest for a board position, even if only concerning a slate of one or two directors, and therefore do not aim to contest control, *see* Monks & Minow, Sears Case Study, http://www.lens-library.com/info/sstan.html (1996).

Act (***"ERISA"***)[925] the voting rights of the employee shares are exercised through trustees determined by the board. Due to non-confidential voting, the trustee's vote in favor of the board's candidates was certain. Besides, officials had not undertaken any enforcement action to demonstrate to ERISA money managers that they needed to vote the proxies for the exclusive benefit of the beneficial owners. The lack of confidential voting also prevented shareholders engaged in business with Sears to vote for Monks, as did the in 1992 amended[926] "bona fide nominee" rule.[927] Finally, Sears' management shrank the board by three inside members to increase the stake necessary to elect one director under the cumulative-voting rule from 16 to 24 percent.[928] Despite CalPERS' publicly announced support for Monks' candidacy,[929] the number of impediments, some of which do not apply currently, prevented Monks from being elected to the board.[930]

Thereafter, Monks changed his strategy and supported five shareholder proposals submitted at the next shareholder meeting in 1992. The five proposals contained requests to introduce confidential voting and to evaluate the options for the divestiture of the non-merchandising divisions. LENS expressed its support for the proposals by phone calls, newspaper ads, and SEC approved solicitation letters.[931] CalPERS expressed again its support of LENS.[932] Personal conversations with Sears' management during which LENS demanded that an investment banker evaluate a break-up in exchange for the withdrawal of the shareholder resolution remained unsuccessful. However, shareholder support for the proposals during the general shareholder meeting in 1992 turned the tide. 40 percent voted in favor of the confidential voting rule and 27 percent in favor of the evaluation of divestiture options.[933] Less than six months later, in September 1992, Sears announced a major restructuring including the sale and entire or partial spin-off of its financial services divisions.[934] The positive performance of Sears' stock reflected, amongst other reasons, the successful completion of the restructuring plan.[935]

---

925 Monks & Minnow, Sears Case Study, 1996, http://www.lens-library.com/info/sstan.html (1996).

926 Regulation of Communications Among Shareholders, Exchange Act Release, Exchange Act Release No. 31326 (Oct. 16, 1992), 57 Fed. Reg. 48276, available at http://content.lawyerlinks.com/default.htm#http://content.lawyerlinks.com/library/sec/sec_releases/34-31326.htm.

927 The former "bona fide nominee" rule, Rule 14a-4 (d) SEA until 1992, practically prohibited shareholders to vote on different proxy cards, as they required that the registrant's candidates agreed to appear on the dissident's proxy card even when seeking only a minority position on the board.

928 Gillan et al., 55 J. FIN. ECON. 103, 119, 122 (2000).

929 Crutchley et al., *Shareholder wealth effects of CalPERS' activism*, Financial Services Review, http://www.lens-library.com/info/doc_list.html (1998); Lisa Holton, *Dissident Sears shareholder gains support, stock up*, April 19, 1991, CHICAGO SUN-TIMES, http://www.encyclopedia.com/doc/1P2-4050158.html.

930 Gillan et al., 55 J. FIN. ECON. 103, 119 (2000): Monks obtained 12 percent of the vote; Monks & Minow, *Sears Case Study*, http://www.lens-library.com/info/sstan.html (1996).

931 Gillan et al., 55 J. FIN. ECON. 103, 119 (2000).

932 *Most Pension Funds Aren't on Warpath*, May 1, 1992, THE SEATTLE TIMES, http://community.seattletimes.nwsource.com/archive/?date=19920501&slug=1489401.

933 Monks & Minow, *Sears Case Study*, http://www.lens-library.com/info/sstan.html (1996).

934 *Id.*, Gillan et al., 55 J. FIN. ECON. 103, 104 (2000).

935 Gillan et al., 55 J. FIN. ECON. 103, 134 (2000).

It took LENS about three years to finally win the necessary divestitures. LENS led a very public campaign against Sears' administration. The advantage of the more successful shareholder proposals compared to the proxy contest was and remains their inclusion in the company's proxy materials, which lowers the costs of the campaign substantially. The strong shareholder votes in favor of the precatory proposals, including the evaluation of divestiture options, left Sears' administration, unable to stop the declining performance by minor governance changes, without a choice but to divest.

CalPERS' less active activism during 1989 and 1992 concentrated mainly on the use of low-cost means like personal communication with Sears' management and board. To convince Sears' CEO of the necessity of personal deliberations with the administration, CalPERS offered to withdraw its proposal to install an advisory committee. This threat sufficed for the intended deliberations to take place. However, they alone did not convince Sears to divest. Thereafter, CalPERS supported Monks' and LENS' activities with public statements and contributed noticeably to the success of their campaign.

(b) Mirant's divestitures

After having successfully prevented Mirant's acquisition of NRG, Mirant's active investors continued their shareholder value enhancing activities. To increase Mirant's stock price, they intended to implement two comprehensive share buy-back programs, which they proposed to finance by different measures. Amongst these was the sale of Mirant's businesses in the Philippines and the Caribbean to generate the largest part of the necessary cash. Upon the recall of the NRG merger, Mirant's CEO received a letter from Pirate via 13D regulatory filing, which referred to the volatile character of the assets in the emerging Philippine and Caribbean markets[936].[937] In the event of a failure to raise the stock price in 2006, Pirate recommended the sale of the entire corporation.[938]

The strong recommendations by Pirate proved to be successfully timed. Mirant had only just exited from bankruptcy. The successful threats that had just prevented NRG's acquisition comprised the convening of a special shareholder meeting to hold a proxy fight to obtain the board majority and the recommendation of the sale of the entire company. They were most likely still present in the heads of Mirant's administration. Furthermore, amongst Mirant's shareholder were six further hedge funds holding each stakes between 2 and 5.7 percent.[939] Most of them had already become active in order to prevent NRG's acquisition. Succumbing to renewed pressure, Mirant exercised two stock buy-

936 *Mirant up on activist agitation*, Part 2, June 21, 2006, TheStreet.com, http://www.thestreet.com/story/10293003/2/mirant-up-on-activist-agitation.html.

937 Schedule 13D of Pirate Capital LLC, Exhibit E, amended June 20, 2006, http://209.85.135.132/search?q=cache:RYenLFCd5EsJ:shareholder.api.edgar-online.com/efx_dll/edgarpro.dll%3FFetchFilingRTF1%3Fsessionid%3DM9NUHiDyflwR6V5%26ID%3D4492525%26PageBreakStyleID%3D2+edgar+mirant+nrg&cd=14&hl=de&ct=clnk&gl=de&client=firefox-a.

938 *Id.*

939 Heidi Moore, *Mirant picks adviser for potential sale*, Apr. 10, 2007, Financial News Online, http://www.efinancialnews.com/assetmanagement/pensionfunds/content/2347527893.

backs in the third quarter of 2006 followed by the required divestitures.[940] In December 2006, Mirant sold its Philippine assets in Mirant Philippines Corporation to Tokyo Electric Power and Marubeni. This was followed by an agreement to sell six natural gas-fired plants to LS Power Group in January 2007. In April 2007, Mirant entered into a definitive sale and purchase agreement with Marubeni regarding its Caribbean Holdings.[941]

Both examples demonstrate that despite a lack of special formal means in the divestiture context and the direction of transaction activism to facilitate a divestiture, the use of general formal and informal means allows active shareholders to prevail. Especially widely supported shareholder proposals and threats of proxy contests and the sale of the corporation have been very successful. However, their effectiveness depends on additional circumstances, like the shareholder structure, the support of fellow institutional investors and the financial means and reputation of the active shareholders.

*iii) Transaction activism aiming **to prevent** a divestiture*

Beneficial transaction activism aiming to prevent a divesting transaction depends on an opportunistic intention of the administration to facilitate a divestiture. As divestitures, if concluded with third parties and not with a subsidiary, generally restrict the authority and compensation of the incumbents rather than increasing them, such a constellation will rarely occur. Moreover, preventing a divestiture would require enhancing shareholder value to provide all shareholders of the targeted corporation with a benefit. Generally, the reduction of conglomerates has been acknowledged to increase shareholder value when getting rid of underperforming units and the conglomerate discount. A corresponding acknowledgement for the opposite constellation does not exist. Finally, the available means to prevent a divestiture are limited. The required efforts for active shareholders are therefore high and the potential to have their efforts sufficiently compensated are low. Frequent beneficial transaction activism under this constellation will therefore be unlikely.

5) Transaction activism and means, conflicts of interest, legal limitations and the underlying theory

a) General analysis of the means used for transaction activism

i) Categorization of means

Active shareholders pursuing transaction activism use *formal means* provided to them by the articles of incorporation, bylaws, statutes, and precedent, as well as *informal means* not explicitly provided to them. The general *among* the former means relate to the

940 *Id.*

941 *Mirant Corporation (MIR) to Sell Caribbean Business for $1.08 Billion*, Apr. 18, 2007, StreetInsider.com, http://www.streetinsider.com/Mergers+and+Acquisitions/Mirant+Corporation+(MIR)+to+Sell+Caribbean+Business+for+%241.08+Billion/2057330.html.

administration of the corporation, to their participation in the financial stakes of the corporation, and to the protection of shareholders. Fundamental corporate decisions provide shareholders with *special formal* means to participate in this corporate decision-making process. The latter have evolved in practice to impact decisions of the administration, when shareholders have not been provided with means to directly impact the corporate decision-making process. They allow active shareholders to wield effective control over the members of the administration instead of limiting their control of management and control through directors to the use of the legally restricted formal means meant to assure accountability.[942] The qualification as informal means depends, however, strongly on the characteristics of the legal system. Accordingly, informal means under the U.S. legal system with its comprehensive and strict disclosure regime under the proxy rules are especially those means which have been developed to reduce the efforts related to the use of the proxy regime. The use of informal means to impact corporate decisions in the transaction context, amongst others, raises the question of the efficiency of existing legal limitations to restrain potential opportunism of active shareholders and their conformity to the underlying governance theories.

Only fundamental corporate transactions provide shareholders with *special formal means* to participate directly in the corporate decision-making process. Mainly in the merger context, shareholders of the constituent corporations need to approve the transaction. This provides shareholders aiming to prevent a merger with *direct impact* on the corporate decision-making process by providing them with a veto right. Alternatively or apart from such a veto constellation, active shareholders have to use general formal as well as informal means to assure the effective use of the veto right or to *(indirectly)* influence the incumbents' transaction decision. The indirect influence targets the members responsible for the transaction decision at stake and aims to impact the decision by threatening or actually holding them accountable for the unaltered transaction decision.

Finally, active shareholders may involve *solely fellow shareholders* and *members of the administration* during their campaign or involve the *public* to reach their transaction goal. In most cases, they limit their efforts to fellow shareholders and the administration. Only in rare cases do the efforts of active shareholders evolve into full public attacks,[943] such as press campaigns applying reputational mechanisms to exercise pressure on corporate management.

ii) Means under different constellations of transaction activism

The analysis of the six different constellations of transaction activism has demonstrated that transaction activism aiming to *prevent a transaction* against the will of the administration can fall back on helpful *special* shareholder means if the transaction is a fundamental one. This is the case with mergers, which in many constellations provide shareholders with a veto right. However, especially in self-dealing transactions as opposed to

942 For shareholder control of officers through the use of informal means, see OLSON, PUBLICLY TRADED CORPORATIONS: GOVERNANCE & REGULATION § 2.5 (2001).

943 Briggs, 32 J. CORP. L. 681, 696 (2007).

arm's-length combinations, administrations tend to make use of front-loaded two-tier offers. They allow potential shareholder opposition in the acquiring corporation to be avoided, while simultaneously pressuring shareholders of the acquired corporation to offer their shares to avoid having to agree to a lower second-tier price. The first tier assures by its sale that the acquiring corporation has the necessary majority for shareholder approval of a merger and obtains higher compensation. The second tier is still compensated beyond market price, but significantly below the consideration of the first tier.[944] However, state courts have not found that the pressure put on shareholders in self-dealing constellations is a violation of the substantive fairness.[945] Federal courts held that two-tier offers do not represent a manipulative device deceiving the shareholders of the acquiring corporation according to § 10(b) or § 14(e) SEA.[946] Under these and other types of transactions, like tender offers and divestitures, active shareholders have no formal means to prevent the administrative decision by directly participating in the corporate transaction decision. They therefore must use general formal and informal means to *indirectly* impact transaction decisions.

Regarding the opposite direction of transaction activism aiming to *facilitate a transaction* against the will of the administration, formal means available to active shareholders are even more restricted. Neither corporate nor securities law provide active shareholders with effective means of direct impact on the corporate transaction decisions. The initiation rights of shareholders under U.S. law regarding specific transaction decisions as opposed to abstract rule-of-the-game decisions on the bylaw level are weak. Shareholder proposals under Rule 14a-8 SEA aiming directly at the realization of a specific transaction have to work around Rule 14a-8(i) SEA by formulating a mere recommendation to the management. Their precatory character will in the best case of substantial shareholder support pressure the corporate management. However, it still remains the board of directors that will have to initiate, approve, and implement the intended transaction. In the rest of the cases, shareholders have to apply other general formal and informal means to pressure the board to facilitate the intended transaction. For fundamental transactions like mergers, active shareholders additionally need to ensure the necessary shareholder quorum to approve the transaction.

Especially constellations of transaction activism aiming to *prevent* a transaction have often turned out to be successful[947] which is not surprising in regards to the limited initiation rights of shareholders under U.S. law. In addition, active shareholders have proven to be more successful on the buy side than on the sell side.[948] This is closely related to the first fact. Based on the generally underlying interests of (active) shareholders and administration, shareholder activism on the buy side usually intends to prevent a trans-

944 Merkt/Göthel, US-amerikanisches Gesellschaftsrecht, 2006, mn.1257.

945 Alcott v. Hyman, 184 A.2d 90, 94 (Del. Ch. 1962); *aff'd,* 208 A.2d 501 (Del. 1965); Brundage v. New Jersey Zinc Co., 226 A.2d 585, 601 (N.J. 1967); *id,* at 1258.

946 Radol v. Thomas, 534 F. Supp. 1302, 1312 (S.D. Ohio 1982); Clark, Corporate Law 471 (1986).

947 Bratton, 95 Geo. L.J. 1375, 1424 (2007); Thompson, *The Limits of Hedge Fund Activism* 13, http://escholarship.org/uc/item/5jq9d71m (2006).

948 Bratton, 95 Geo. L.J. 1375, 1424 (2007).

action planned by the administration. On the sell side, however, it often aims to facilitate a transaction, which is harder for active shareholders to realize.

iii) The proxy rules and the opportunities to escape them

Proxy rules significantly determine the campaigns of active shareholders. Even though their regime has been loosened during the last decades, undertaking a full-scale proxy contest has remained very costly. As a consequence, active shareholders pursuing transaction activism, especially when intending to directly veto a transaction or to replace an incumbent by their own candidate, have to consider the proxy rules.

Pursuant to Rule 14a-2 SEA, the SEC proxy rules apply to every solicitation of a proxy with respect to securities registered according to § 12 SEA. The definitions of *proxy,* as laid down in Rule 14a-1(f) SEA, and *solicitation* according to Rule 14a-1(l) SEA are interpreted extremely broadly. The relevant SEC rule defines a *solicitation* as any communication to shareholders "under circumstances reasonably calculated to result in the procurement, withholding or revocation of a proxy."[949] It is supposed to be interpreted "in all its literal breadth." Thereafter, a solicitation may even relate to authorizations to inspect stockholder lists, necessary to obtain the quorum for inspection rights under state law, even "where obtaining the authorizations was not a step in a planned solicitation of proxies."[950] Furthermore, letters not requesting any authorization if (1) part of "a continuous plan" intended to end in solicitation and (2) "which prepare the way for its success" were held to fall under the proxy rules (known as *Okin* test).[951] The most detailed analysis of the question of what communications constitute solicitations within the meaning of the proxy rules was provided by an amicus brief filed by the SEC in *Long Island Lighting Co. v. Barbash (**"LILCO"**)*[952]. It recommends focusing on the purpose for which the communication was published, such as whether the purpose was to influence the shareholders' decision. The relevant factors to determine the purpose are the content, audience, and timing of the communication as well as the relationship between the communicator and proxy contestant.[953] However, what type of communication falls under the term solicitation is not always clear; statements regarding this question bear therefore a general litigation risk.[954]

To comply with the proxy rules, active shareholders generally need to file a preliminary proxy statement according to Schedule 14A and a proxy card to the SEC staff for review. After all comments are cleared, the shareholder is free to mail his materials to all or as many other shareholders as he wishes. However, the other shareholders need to be identified, the necessary materials printed, and finally provided to the shareholders. This usually requires hiring a professional proxy solicitation firm and represents a very complex and costly process. Once the proxy statement has been distributed, everything

949 Rule 14a-1(l) SEA.
950 Studebaker Corp. v. Gittlin, 360 F.2d 692, 695 (2d Cir. 1966).
951 SEC v. Okin, 132 F.2d 784, 786 (2d Cir. 1943).
952 779 F.2d 793 (2d Cir. 1985).
953 Amicus Curiae Brief for the SEC at 8, LILCO, 779 F.2d at 793 (No. 85-7890).
954 Briggs, 32 J. Corp. L. 681, 686 et seq. (2007).

else to be sent out by the insurgent does not need to be pre-cleared by the SEC. It allows insurgents to reply in a timely and cost-effective manner to proponent's statements through the dissemination of additional solicitation material.[955] The remaining restraint is the general proxy antifraud rule, Rule 14a-9 SEA.[956]

However, the proxy rules provide different means for shareholders to communicate with each other. These are shareholder proposals, Rule 14a-8 SEA, requests for shareholder lists or to mail the shareholder material, Rule 14a-7 SEA, and electronic shareholder forums, Rule 14a-17 SEA[957]. The interactions between shareholders that are necessary during campaigns of active shareholders usually go beyond these three means. They therefore require extensive filings[958] with the SEC, which are extremely expensive in terms of money, time, and reputation risk[959] for the active shareholders while the administration is able to access corporate funds for their campaigns. Some active shareholders focus therefore on the use of means which either do not constitute solicitation or require not as extensive a filing with the SEC. In the last years, the use of these opportunities has increased due to legal amendments and evolved practices. They shall be shortly summarized here to demonstrate the restrictions active shareholders are confronted with.

The most notable exception to the proxy rules is *Rule 14a-1(l)(2)(iv) SEA*. It authorizes ways in which a security holder may announce his intent to vote in a certain manner as well as the reasons for it. Amongst them are the bona fide publication disseminated on a regular basis, Rule 14a-1(l)(2)(iv)(A) SEA, including speeches in press releases as well as statements and advertisements on broadcast media, newspapers, and so on. This rule is of particular interest for active shareholders, as it represents one of the few efficient and at the same time low cost means for shareholders to express dissatisfaction with deficient management strategies[960] by facilitating "just-vote-no" campaigns. It allows them to publicize their decisions to withhold their votes for a part or the entire slate of the directors standing for election. Their expectation is that the announcement will influence other shareholders in their votes and that the number of withheld votes will underscore their collective dissatisfaction.[961] In the few cases in which transactions require shareholder approval, active shareholders may apply this mechanism to announce that they intend to disapprove the transaction. OrbiMed Advisors, a shareholder of Pharmacopeia, which intended to merge with EOS, pursued the latter approach. OrbiMed Advisors success-

955 Regulation of Communication Among Securityholders, Exchange Act Release No. 31.326, [1992 Transfer Binder] Fed. Sec. L. Rep. ¶ 85051 at 83365 (Oct. 16, 1992).

956 Briggs, 32 J. Corp. L. 681, 687 (2007).

957 A communication made through such a forum, which constitutes a solicitation because of its content, must comply with the proxy filing and disclosure requirements if done within the 60 days before the shareholder meeting.

958 Rule 14a-6 SEA generally demands prefiling of preliminary proxy statement and ballot 10 days before the definitive copies of these materials are expected to be sent to the shareholders and filing of definitive proxy statement with the SEC before the ballot may circulate.

959 Briggs, 50 Bus. Law. 99, 103 (1994).

960 Del Guercio et al., *Do Boards Pay Attention when Institutional Investor Activists 'Just Vote No'* 5, http://www.ssrn.com/abstract=575242 (2008); Grundfest, 45 Stan. L. Rev. 857, 937 (1993).

961 Eisenberg, Corporations and other Business Organizations ch. 5, sec. 3 (2005).

fully used the exception to lead a "vote-no campaign" to prevent the approval of the merger. It escaped from the costly proxy rule regime and even prevented Pharmacopeia's shareholder meeting, determined to approve the merger, from taking place.

Another exemption contains *Rule 14a-2(b)(2) SEA*, which excludes from most proxy requirements, except for Rule 14a-9 SEA, a stockholder's communication directed to ten or fewer persons (ten-or-fewer rule). Despite the enactment of section 13 (d) SEA and the widespread adoption of poison pills, rendering the original purpose of the exemption, to facilitate organizational activities of shareholders, obsolete, it is still extremely useful.[962] It gives an insurgent the opportunity to gauge the level of support amongst the largest shareholders without alerting management through any public proxy filing, and without incurring any significant expenses.[963] In the case of middle-market and smaller companies, where the ownership can be fairly concentrated, the insurgent's first round of telephone calls may largely determine the outcome of the entire campaign. It may be used in addition to other exceptions, for instance the former.

The "free speech rule," introduced in 1992 and laid down in *Rule 14a-2(b)(1) SEA*, bears similar consequences. It applies to any solicitation of persons not seeking, directly or indirectly, proxy authority and not requesting a form of revocation, abstention, consent, or authorization, provided that the solicitor has no substantial interest in the matter. The latter applies to a group of shareholders exceeding five percent if they have not professed a lack of interest in control of the company, Rule 14a-2(b)(1)(vi) SEA. According to the SEC, the limitation forces insurgents to make an "irrevocable election" whether to use the Rule or to retain the option of waging a proxy contest. Any later attempt to back out will potentially turn all previously exempt communication into illegal solicitations.[964] As management would be unlikely to bargain with a paper tiger, application of this safe harbor rule for contacting an unlimited number of shareholders will be restricted to just-vote-no campaigns against management proposals.[965] Actions of institutional shareholders who oppose a corporation's proxy solicitation for a proposed merger, like the mailing of a letter opposing the merger to other shareholders, including the duplicate of the previously mailed proxy card, amounted to a "form of revocation."[966]

In addition to these exemptions, dispensations from the general filing requirements, which include the preliminary filing according to Rule 14a-6 sent. 1 SEA, are provided by the *free communication Rule 14a-12 SEA*. Introduced in 1999, it proved to be a rele-

---

962 Briggs, 50 Bus. Law. 99, 105 (1994).

963 *Id.*

964 Regulation of Communications Among Shareholders, Exchange Act Release No. 31,326, Fed. Sec. L. Rep. ¶ 85,051, at 83,360-62 & n.36 (Oct. 16, 1992).

965 Briggs, 50 Bus. Law. 99, 130–131 n.165 (1994): noting that the rule appears to have been originally intended to be used largely in connection with just-vote-no campaigns, it may also be used by an investor campaigning in favor of its own Rule 14a-8 proposal; *see* Regulation of Communications Among Shareholders, Exchange Act Release, No. 31,326, Fed. Sec. L. Rep. ¶ 85, 051, at 83, 358 (Oct. 16, 1992): according to which the free speech rule is intended to permit shareholders to discuss "management performance" and express "support for, or opposition to, management or third party proposals or director nominees".

966 Mony Group v. Highfields Capital, 368 F.3d 138, 138 (2d Cir. 2004).

vant amendment.[967] As pre-filing requirements pertain to proxy statements and ballots, oral and *other* written communications, regardless of the subject matter of the solicitation, may be furnished. *Written* solicitations have to be filed with the SEC upon their first use, participants in the proxy solicitation and their shareholdings have to be disclosed, and the communication has to bear a legend advising that the proxy statement will be sent and should be read once available.[968] *Oral* communications are allowed and "do not need to be reduced to writing and filed."[969] Also a solicitor may send all the information out to the press.[970] By the time a proxy statement was issued some fights had already been decided "as management frequently decided to reach settlements with their dissident shareholders rather than risk a full-scale battle."[971] "In order to rely on Rule 14a-12, soliciting parties must intend to furnish a proxy statement to security holders."[972] But solicitations may be abandoned and then there will not be a proxy statement.[973]

Rule 14a-6 sent. 2 SEA concerns the second preliminary filing exception. It applies if the solicitation relates to a meeting in which the only matters to be acted upon are among others the election of directors, the approval of an auditor, the voting on shareholder proposals pursuant to Rule 14a-8 SEA as included in the company's proxy statement,[974] and the ratification of certain executive compensation proposals. In such cases it suffices if the proxy statement and ballot are filed contemporaneous with their use.

iv) Proxy rules in the context of transaction activism

Active shareholders have developed different practices to deal with the comprehensive and costly proxy rule regime. Roughly, one can distinguish between pure pressure campaigns and campaigns that may result in a proxy contest. However, each campaign, even if under the same regime, proceeds differently, as demonstrated *supra* by the three constellations of transaction activism. The means applied and their order vary.

---

967 Briggs, 32 J. Corp. L. 681, 689 (2007).

968 Eisenberg, Corporations and other Business Organizations ch. 5, sec. 3 (2005).

969 Regulation of Takeovers and Security Holder Communication, Securities Act Release No. 7760, Exchange Act Release No. 42,055, Investment Act Release No. 24,107, 64 Fed. Reg. 61408, 61, 414 (Nov. 10, 1999) *available* at http://www.sec.gov/rules/final/33-7760.htm.

970 Regulation of Takeovers and Security Holder Communications, Securities Act Release No. 7607, Exchange Act Release No. 40633, Investment Act Release 23,520, 67 Fed. Reg. 67,331, 67,340, 1998 WL 767321 (proposed Dec. 4, 1998).

971 *Annual Corporate Governance Review 2005-Annual Meetings, Shareholder Initiatives, Proxy Contests* 4, 2005, Georgeson Shareholder, http://www.georgeson.com/usa/download/acgr/acgr2005.pdf.

972 SEC/Div. of Corp. Fin., Manual of Publicly Available Telephone Interpretations, at Part I.D. Question No. 3 (Supp. III 2001), http://www.sec.gov/interps/telephone/phonesupplement3.htm.

973 Briggs, 32 J. Corp. L. 681, 690 (2007).

974 Schoen v. AMERCO, 885 F. Supp. 1332, 1346 (D.Nev. 1994).

(1) Testing the waters

Prior to any kind of campaign, active shareholders will test the waters. They will want to know more about the acceptance of their position amongst the fellow shareholders. This will be easier in firms with fewer shareholders or several shareholders holding larger stakes than in firms with substantial freefloat. The *ten-or-fewer rule* allows shareholders to contact up to ten shareholders without worrying about filing requirements. It makes sense for the initiators to contact the more influential shareholders with larger stakes. Often they will be able to contact them without requiring a shareholder list from the corporation, as they already know them or can identify them via their Schedule 13D filings.

Shareholders aiming to facilitate a transaction will particularly seek early contact with the administration to ascertain its attitude regarding the intended transaction in more detail. For shareholders intending to oppose a transaction suggested by management, contact is not as urgent. Contact is usually established through e-mails or phone calls. Sooner or later, the initiators will try to have a personal meeting with the administration. Whether that meeting will be granted depends on their stake and the administration's attitude. In a few cases, active shareholders have used their proposal right under Rule 14a-8 SEA to force the administration to hold at least preparatory personal talks about the transaction decision. To obtain this result, active shareholders have made governance proposals disliked by management, such as the installation of an advisory committee proposed by CalPERS as a shareholder of Sears, and offered to drop them if a personal meeting is granted.

(2) Pure pressure campaigns and "just-vote-no" campaigns

Shareholders could decide on a pure pressure campaign against the administration after gathering information about the attitude of (some) of their fellow shareholders and the administration. They would then try to achieve the same results through a low- key lobbying campaign directed at fellow shareholders and the administration instead of engaging in a high-stakes proxy contest. To block a transaction involving a shareholder vote, a low-key means would be to engage in a *"just-vote-no" campaign.* The initiation of a transaction as well as the prevention of a transaction not involving a shareholder vote may be realized directly through a *solicitation of consent.* Another means that directly targets the intended transaction decision is a shareholder proposal recommending the shareholder-value evaluation of different transaction alternatives. Sears' shareholder LENS received substantial support for its proposal to evaluate divestiture alternatives, which contributed to the Sears' administration's decision to divest. *"Vote-yes" campaigns* involving governance proposals also have indirect impact on intended transaction decisions. LENS also applied this strategy by supporting five shareholder proposals, amongst them the introduction of confidential voting, to initiate Sears' divestitures. *"Withhold-vote" campaigns* target a specific director or the entire slate as bearing the responsibility for corporate underperformance and are another means of indirect impact.[975]

(a) Pure solicitations of consent

Pure solicitations of consent are pressure campaigns not involving an upcoming shareholder vote on the issue. Shareholders may initiate this campaign by contacting management about their intention to start a corresponding campaign related to a specific issue or decision. In some cases, the threat alone will change the minds of the responsible administrative members. Otherwise, the insurgents will have to contact the shareholders apart from those already contacted during the initial phase to inform them about the campaign and its purpose. Depending on the shareholder structure, they will concentrate their efforts only on shareholders with larger stakes in the corporation or a majority of their fellow shareholders. Means of contact may involve private communications via phone calls, letters, or e-mail. Additionally, the insurgents can launch a public campaign if their financial resources allow them to do so. The goal of the *consent campaign* is for the contacted shareholders to inform the administration of their support for the campaign. Similar to the *infra* analyzed withhold-vote or vote-no campaigns, the pure solicitation of consent campaign is a cheap and easy way to express dissatisfaction with a specific management decision in the transaction context. It is purely symbolic. However, the success of corresponding campaigns in influencing specific business issues, rather than general discontent about the corporate strategy and performance, has demonstrated their effectiveness.[976]

As pure solicitation of consent campaigns relate neither to a shareholder meeting nor to an upcoming proxy contest, proxy rules do not apply to this kind of campaign.[977] A limitation of this approach occurs, however, if active shareholders possibly plan to get involved in a proxy contest after a lobbying campaign has failed. In *Chris-Craft Industries, Inc. v. Independent Stockholders Committee*,[978] the District Court of Delaware held that the whole point of "support letters of dissatisfied substantial shareholders" in support of a merger proposal was to "force management into submission" without a proxy fight instead of " prepar[ing] the way for a proxy solicitation." This impression was underscored by a subsequent derivative action. Therefore, the court ruled that neither the second part of the *Okin* test had been met nor Rule 14a-6 SEA violated.[979] The SEC, in

975 Grundfest, 45 STAN. L. REV. 857, 906 (1993).

976 Del Guercio et al., *Do Boards Pay Attention when Institutional Investor Activists 'Just Vote No'?* 11, 14, http://ssrn.com/abstract=575242 (2008): their results are based on 112 'just vote no' campaigns between 1990 and 2003 of hedge funds and other investors, in contrast to the research results of Bratton and Brav et al. concentrating on hedge funds.

977 Champion Parts Rebuilders, Inc. V Cormier Corp., 661 F. Supp. 825, 851 (N.C. Ill. 1987): "What was sought and obtained by Cormier as evidence of shareholder support ... with no shareholders' meeting in the offing, could not be characterized as "proxies."; Briggs, 50 BUS. LAW. 99, 126 n.145 (1994).

978 354 F. Supp. 895, 907 (D. Del. 1973).

979 *Id.*

contrast, refused in a similar case to issue a no-action letter. It believed that a letter-writing campaign was designed to pave the way for a proxy solicitation.[980] Shareholders considering a subsequent proxy fight thus must consider the litigation risk when designing their campaign.

The pressure exercised on management during pure consent solicitation campaigns as well as the *infra* analyzed pre-contest solicitations will be increased by the use of formal shareholder means. As a shareholder meeting draws near, active shareholders have made *mandatory shareholder proposals, Rule 14a-8 SEA,* to induce the administration to come to the table or to make the intended transaction decision. Even though the corporation needs to include these proposals and a supportive statement in its proxy materials, preliminary filings are exempted under Rule 14a-6 sent. 2 SEA. The support for these proposals has often been realized via "vote-yes" campaigns. Only in a few cases of transaction activism have active shareholders used legal proceedings based on fiduciary duty violations or appraisal claims.[981] In these few cases, they used it mainly as a threat related to a potential prior inspection of the administrative transaction decision according to § 220 to pressure the administration.[982] External control to take control of the targeted corporation is another means of pressure. Hedge funds increasingly have sufficient money to buy a corporation outright.[983] The activities of Icahn are an example. As a large minority shareholder, he proposed the purchase of Mylan to prevent the acquisition of King. His intention was to threaten the administration with the loss of their positions if they continued to pursue the transaction. Usually active shareholders do not actually intend to complete such a transaction; an actual acquisition remains the notable exception.[984] Rather, they use such an

980 Nottingham Partners, SEC No-Action Letter, [1984-1985 Transfer Binder] Fed. Sec. L. Rep. ¶ 77, 862 (Nov. 16, 1984).

981 Brav et al., *Hedge Fund Activism, Corporate Governance, and the Firm Performance* 15, 43, http://ssrn.com/abstract=948907 (2008).

982 In contrast, takeover constellations involving cashout conflicts of interest are very likely to produce litigation by target shareholders. (Kahan & Rock, 155 U. Pa. L. Rev. 1021, 1037 et seq. (2007); Thompson & Thomas, 57 Vand. L. Rev. 133, 138 (2004)) Primarily cases involving the cashout of public minority shareholders through controlling shareholders where target shareholders cannot use their vote as the controlling shareholder possesses more than 50 percent often result in successful shareholder litigation, also in reducing transaction costs resulting from opportunistic management. (Thompson & Thomas, 57 Vand. L. Rev. 133, 138 et seq. (2004); Thompson, *The Limits of Hedge Fund Activism* 15, 21, http://escholarship.org/uc/item/5jq9d71m (2006)) The opportunities of a higher compensation give active shareholders the necessary incentives, and, despite several procedural hurdles of appraisal procedures according to § 262, active shareholders have turned out to be successful in obtaining prices significantly above the initially offered cash out compensation. (Thompson, *The Limits of Hedge Fund Activism*, 21 et seq., http://escholarship.org/uc/item/5jq9d71m (2006)).

983 Briggs, 32 J. Corp. L. 681, 699 (2007).

984 Bratton, 95 Geo. L.J. 1375, 1426 et seq. (2007); Brav et al., *Hedge Fund Activism, Corporate Governance, and the Firm Performance* 15, 43, http://ssrn.com/abstract=948907 (2008); Thompson, *The Limits of Hedge Fund Activism* 13, http://escholarship.org/uc/item/5jq9d71m (2006).

offer to shake things up.[985] They put the corporation in play to pressure the members of the administration with the loss of their positions.[986]

(b) Just-vote-no campaigns

Just-vote-no campaigns involve partially similar mechanics as campaigns purely soliciting consent. However, they take place in anticipation of an expected shareholder vote and therefore require a much closer consideration of the proxy rules. Active shareholders engaging in *just-vote-no campaigns* do not seek proxy authority. They aim to ensure that a substantial number of shareholders will vote *against* the approval of a fundamental transaction, *for* a shareholder proposal, or *withhold* their vote for the election of a director[987] on the corporate proxy card. As far as a *just-vote-no campaign* is symbolic, with the exception of sufficient votes against a fundamental transaction, publicity of the purpose and the result of the campaign is key.[988] At minimum, the insurgent shareholders should place a letter with their completed proxy card stating that the reason for the campaign is to undercut the target board's ability to profess confusion or ignorance about the source of shareholders' dissatisfaction.[989] The recently amended SEC regulation, which obliges the publication of shareholder voting results, including board elections, within 4 business days after the meeting, Item 5.07 of Form 8-K, assures the quick publication of all voting results.[990] Shareholders and the press are easily able to access this data.[991]

Active shareholders pursuing a *just-vote-no campaign* are able to use different regimes. Besides the *ten or fewer rule*, which may be especially helpful in companies with concentrated ownership, a provision that greatly facilitates *just-vote-no campaigns* is *Rule 14a-1(l)(2) SEA*.[992] It allows active shareholders to publish their decision to vote *against* a transaction, to *withhold* votes from directors, or to vote *for* a shareholder proposal and the reasons for it. They can use as many words as necessary and as often as they like. However, the exemption does not allow soliciting others to vote in a certain way; they are limited to announcing and explaining their own voting decision.

985 Briggs, 32 J. CORP. L. 681, 699 (2007).

986 Bratton, 95 GEO. L.J. 1375, 1423 et seq. (2007); Thompson, *The Limits of Hedge Fund Activism* 13, http://escholarship.org/uc/item/5jq9d71m (2006).

987 The landmark case regarding withhold-vote campaigns (or vote-of-no-confidence) regarding director election concerned the case of Michael Eisner, former CEO and Chair of the Disney board, who during the 2004 general shareholder meeting experienced a withhold-campaign with 43 percent of the shareholder votes cast being withheld. As a consequence, the board of directors decided unanimously to split the positions of the Chairman and the CEO and Eisner remained solely with the CEO position. (Goldhaber, *Eisner no longer Disney Chair*, Mar. 4, 2004, http://www.mouseplanet.com/dan/bm040304mg.htm).

988 Grundfest, 45 STAN. L. REV. 857, 907 (1993).

989 *Id.*

990 Proxy Disclosure Enhancement, Securities Act Release No. 9089, Exchange Act Release No. 61,175, Investment Act No. 29,093 (Dec., 16, 2009), 61, www.sec.gov/rules/final/2009/33-9089.pdf.

991 Grundfest, 45 STAN. L. REV. 857, 907 et seq. (1993): still referring to the former content of Forms 10-Q and 10-K, item 4, which has been transferred to Form 8-K, item 5.07.

992 EISENBERG, CORPORATIONS AND OTHER BUSINESS ORGANIZATIONS ch. 5, sec. 3 (2005).

A less frequently used[993] but still very helpful exemption is the *free speech rule 14a-2(b)(1) SEA,* which was originally intended to be used for *just-vote-no campaigns.*[994] It allows *any solicitation* as long as the person seeks neither proxy authority nor has a substantial interest in the matter subject to the vote. As the type and the content of the communication are not restricted under this rule, active shareholders are able to contact fellow shareholders personally, via mailings or press releases and media to fully develop their arguments. Each written communication or script for oral communication, except for widespread communication, of shareholders with a stake of more than $5 million in market value, have to be filed with the SEC no later than 3 days after its first use.[995] Rule 14a-2(b)(1) SEA requires further that investors with a stake of more than five percent profess that they lack an interest in control.[996] Even though it may seem that this renders the exemption unavailable for most of the initiators of *just-vote-no campaigns*, there remains ample space for them to use the exclusion. They may have had to file a Schedule 13D instead of Schedule 13G, as they aim to impact the control of the corporation. This needs, however, to be distinguished from the requirement of lacking the intent to take over the corporation or actively supporting an opposing slate of nominees in a proxy contest.[997] If the Schedule 13D has been filed in "boilerplate" language, this may require formulating it more specifically to eliminate the reservation of this exemption.[998] Another relevant issue relates to the restriction of the rule's use if it represents a *revocation.* The Second Circuit held in *MONY Group, Inc. v. Highfield Capital Management. L.P.*[999] that a communication to shareholders aiming to oppose a proposed merger that contains an unmarked duplicate of management's proxy card represents a *revocation* in the sense of Rule 14a-2(b)(1) SEA. As a result, the exception was no longer available. In 2009, the SEC proposed a new rule intended to override this ruling.[1000] Later in 2009, the SEC decided to defer these considerations pending the consideration of the proposal to facilitate shareholder director nominations in company's proxy materials.[1001] Furthermore, the SEC demands an irrevocable choice between the use of this rule and maintaining the option to wage a proxy fight. Any attempt to back out of the rule will potentially turn all previously exempt communications into illegal solicitations.[1002] Finally,

---

993 Briggs, 32 J. Corp. L. 681, 700 (2007).

994 Regulation of Communication Among Securityholders, Exchange Act Release No. 31,326, [1992 Transfer Binder] Fed. Sec. L. Rep. ¶ 85,051 at 83,358 (Oct. 16, 1992).

995 Rule 14a-6(g)(1),(2) SEA.

996 Rule 14a-2(b)(1)(vi) SEA.

997 Briggs, 50 Bus. Law. 99, 130 (1994).

998 Willkie Farr & Gallagher, *„Just Vote No" Campaigns in Uncontested Director Elections – Renewed Vitality for the 2010 Proxy Season* 4-5, Sept. 24, 2009, www.willkie.com (search "just vote no", choose 5125149_7.DOC).

999 368 F.3d 138.

1000 Proxy Disclosure and Solicitation Enhancements, Securities Act Release No. 9052, Exchange Act Release 60,280, Investment Act Release 28,817 (proposed July 10, 2009), www.sec.gov/rules/proposed/2009/33-9052.pdf, 50.

1001 Proxy Disclosure Enhancements, Securities Act Release No. 9089, Exchange Act Release 61,175, Investment Act 29,092 (Dec. 16, 2009), www.sec.gov/rules/final/2009/33-9089.pdf, 8.

1002 Regulation of Communication Among Securityholders, Exchange Act Release No. 31,326, [1992 Transfer Binder] Fed. Sec. L. Rep. ¶ 85,051, at 83,360-62, n.36 (Oct. 16, 1992).

during all their activities insurgents have to keep in mind the group provisions under section 13(d) SEA.

Just-vote-no campaigns avoid many of the difficulties of other minority shareholder means. They circumvent most of the collective action issues, amongst them freeriding usually resulting in rational apathy.[1003] This results from the fact that a majority vote is not necessary for the success of such a campaign. Furthermore, its low costs make its initiation not depend on an investor who is able to bear possible costs exceeding benefits.[1004] The costs related to *just-vote-no campaigns* are trivial. Even though activist shareholders aiming to impact a transaction decision may not be able to rely on analyst reports and extensive industry discussion, as is the case when targeting firms for low overall performance,[1005] larger institutional investors may usually rely on their in-house analysis that initially provoked them to engage in favor of the specific transaction decision. They may also engage in a public dialog about the transaction decision at stake, as long as they conform to the proxy rules and do not form a "group" under § 13(d) SEA. Information- sharing techniques developed by institutional investors help them reduce their coordination costs.[1006]

The institutional barriers will most likely be the most serious ones involved, amongst them the pressure on large institutional investors not to become agents of corporate change. Another institutional barrier concerns the apathy of individual shareholders, who hold their shares in "street names" while not providing specific voting instructions for the broker, so that they are able to vote at their discretion,[1007] invariably voting client shares pro-manager.[1008] Only in July 2010 did the SEC approve an amendment to NYSE Rule 452. It excludes the elections of directors from routine matters and therefore from brokers' ability to vote on the matter at their own discretion if shareholders fail to provide specific voting instructions on the matter.[1009] As a result, shares held in street names will not be voted in an election of directors unless the holders specifically instruct their brokers how to vote.[1010] The impact on *just-vote-no campaigns* should not be underestimated, as broker votes usually represent a significant percentage of the total vote. As a consequence, the percentage of *withheld* votes in campaigns concerning director elections and therefore the effectiveness of *withhold-vote campaigns* increases.[1011] Most of the remaining barriers are not unique to

1003 Grundfest, 45 Stan. L. Rev. 857, 914 (1993).

1004 *Id.* at 913.

1005 *Id.* at 916.

1006 *Id.* at 915.

1007 402.06(D) NYSE Listed Company Manual.

1008 Grundfest, 45 Stan. L. Rev. 857, 923 (1993); Willkie Farr & Gallagher, *„Just Vote No" Campaigns in Uncontested Director Elections – Renewed Vitality for the 2010 Proxy Season* 2, Sept. 24, 2009, www.willkie.com (search "just vote no", choose 5125149_7.DOC).

1009 Self-Regulatory Organizations, Exchange Act Release No. 60,215 (July 1, 2009), www.sec.gov/rules/sro/nyse/2009/34-60215.pdf.

1010 Laura D. Richman & Mayer Brown, *Amendment of NYSE Rule 452: Elimination of Broker Discretionary Voting in Director Elections*, July 1, 2009, www.mayerbrown.com/publications/article.asp?id=7172.

1011 Willkie Farr & Gallagher, *„Just Vote No" Campaigns in Uncontested Director Elections – Renewed Vitality for the 2010 Proxy Season* 2-3, Sept. 24, 2009, www.willkie.com (search "just vote no", choose 5125149_7.DOC)

just-vote-no campaigns and may be worked around.[1012] Accordingly, their success does not depend on majority support to express a lack of confidence, and the public may be educated about systemic deficiencies (client conflicts, internal guidelines) and their impact on the achieved campaign results.[1013]

Even though *just-vote-no campaigns,* with the *supra* mentioned exceptions, are purely symbolic, according to *Del Guercio et al. (2008),* they lead to the total or partial implementation of specific shareholder demands about 37 percent of the time. For 36 percent of the campaigns that achieve shareholder support beyond 20 percent, the implementation ratio lies near 100 percent.[1014] In addition, the average return increases.[1015] For *withhold-vote campaigns* for board elections, the 31 percent CEO turnover rate within one year is twice as high as in matched control firms. The forced CEO turnover rate of 17 percent is almost nine times as high as in control firms.[1016] The overall performance, especially in cases of forced CEO turnover, increased substantially.[1017] The pressure exercised on the board by *just-vote-no campaign*s is therefore a successful mechanism to re-align the interests of shareholders and boards; in practice the latter tend to fail to discipline management effectively and in a timely manner.[1018] The increase in operating return as a result of *withhold-vote campaigns* confirms that they are beneficial to all shareholders.[1019]

(3) Pre-proxy campaigns and proxy contests

As a next or as a first step, active shareholders are able to exercise increased pressure on the administration by overtly preparing for a proxy contest in the hope of demonstrating shareholder support in order to achieve a settlement. The *final* way is the full-scale proxy contest. Pre-proxy contests as well as final proxy contests may either concern a shareholder vote on a transaction or the election of the board. The most efficient constellation for shareholders pursuing transaction activism is the former. It applies, however, only under some merger constellations or if the acquisition consideration requires a capital increase of the acquiring corporation that requires shareholder approval. In all other cases, active shareholders have to express their dissatisfaction with the administrative transaction decision during the next election.

1012 Grundfest, 45 STAN. L. REV. 857, 919 (1993).

1013 *Id.* at 919-924.

1014 Del Guercio et al., *Do Boards Pay Attention when Institutional Investor Activists 'Just Vote No'* 11, http://www.ssrn.com/abstract=575242 (2008).

1015 *Id.* at 15.

1016 *Id.* at 22.

1017 *Id.* at 28 et seq., Table 7: pointing out in Panel C that in cases of no forced CEO turnover within one year after the campaign, the increased operating returns for campaigns not stating the *overall dissatisfaction* as reason for the campaign are indifferent, while campaigns that targeted bad overall performance that did not result in disciplinary turnover still led to positive increase in performance.

1018 Denis & Denis, 50 J. FIN. 1029 (1995).

1019 Del Guercio et al., *Do Boards Pay Attention when Institutional Investor Activists 'Just Vote No'* 28, http://www.ssrn.com/abstract=575242 (2008).

(a) Pre-proxy campaigns

Insurgents may in general prepare for a proxy contest by relying on the means provided by *state corporate law*. Even though insurgents have no statutory right to call a special meeting, some corporations have authorized them to convene it according to the certificate of incorporation or the bylaws, § 211(d). Insurgents are also able to inspect the shareholder list for a proper purpose according to §§ 219, 220. The preparation of a proxy contest or the communication with other shareholders represents such a purpose.

If the proxy contest relates to an election, the insurgents can organize a slate of opposing nominees. In compliance with bylaw pre-notification requirements, insurgents are obliged to inform management two or three months before the scheduled meeting about the names of the opposing nominees and substantial information usually required by a proxy statement. This is advantageous because it gives management an early signal about the possibility of a proxy contest, allows the challengers to profit from additional publicity, and restricts management's communication with its shareholders to plain-vanilla communication.[1020]

In the past, federal law required the filing of preliminary proxy statements with the SEC for pre-proxy campaigns before pursuing solicitation activities.[1021] An important amendment was the implementation of the *free communication* Rule 14a-12 SEA in 1999. It has been used extensively since.[1022] It allows unlimited solicitations as long as no proxy statement is filed. While oral communications are freely permitted, written materials must be filed upon first use. Even though its use requires the actual intent to furnish and disseminate a future proxy statement, in several cases the provision has been used to provide an entire book of information to shareholders without providing a proxy statement. The fight had been decided and the proxy solicitation abandoned before.[1023]

Altogether, pre-proxy campaigns allow active shareholders to demonstrate their support through other shareholders to reach a settlement even before undertaking a full-scale proxy contest. Rule 14a-12 SEA especially allows active shareholders to threaten the administration at arm's length, as its use does not depend on the decision against a proxy contest with the consequence that it remains a "toothless tiger."[1024] In addition, its use neither involves substantial costs nor time in contacting other shareholders or plac-

1020 ConAgra, Inc. v. Tyson Foods, Inc., 708 F. Supp. 257, 267 – 69 (D.Neb. 1989): The court stated that ConAgra's press release to inform the public about a significant corporate development constituted gun jumping under the proxy rules, as ConAgra participated in a takeover contest over another corporation and was in the process of assembling proxy materials to be sent to the shareholders. Under the LILCO SEC test, the announcement of a pending proxy contest while complying with a company's advance notice bylaw may turn each management shareholder statement with other than plain-vanilla language into a solicitation; Exchange Act Release No. 7208, 3 Fed. Sec. L. Rep. ¶ 24,104-11, at 24,108 (Jan. 7, 1964).

1021 Briggs, 50 Bus. Law. 99, 137 (1994).

1022 Briggs, 32 J. Corp. L. 681, 696 (2007): referring to 41 campaigns led by hedge funds, of which 30 made use oft Rule 14a-12 SEA, while the rest of the campaigns involved rather "unusual circumstances".

1023 *See* Briggs, 32 J. Corp. L. 681, 696 et seq. (2007).

1024 Briggs, 50 Bus. Law. 99, 130 (1994).

ing the communication with the press. Rather, it is sufficient to file any written communication with the SEC at the time it is sent off to other shareholders.

(b) Proxy contests

Finally, shareholders may actually have to engage in a proxy contest to reach their transaction goal. The full proxy contest requires the pre-screening of the proxy statement and ballot according to Schedule 14A, which need to be provided to the SEC 10 days prior to the date at which they will be sent to the shareholders, Rule 14a-6 SEA. Once approved by the SEC, the insurgents must pay the significant costs of printing and mailing statement and card to as many other shareholders as they know and can afford.

v) Frequency and effectiveness of analyzed means

Apart from the few constellations of transaction activism involving the use of veto rights to directly prevent a merger or a transaction requiring shareholder approval for an increase in the share capital, active shareholders have recourse to general formal and informal means to impact a specific administration decision in the transaction context. Most frequently, active shareholders decide initially to communicate directly with the administration with the goal of demanding shareholder-value enhancing measures. Other means frequently used are shareholder proposals—precatory if relating to the transaction decision directly, mandatory when demanding governance enhancing procedures—and the public critique of the company for denying the demanded change. Furthermore, frequently used means relate to the removal of directors and stretch from non-confrontational removal strategies to proxy contests to the replacement of directors with a shareholder-proposed candidate. Only in a few cases have active shareholders sued the corporation or intended to take control of the corporation,[1025] such as by launching a takeover bid to reach their goal.[1026]

The most relevant and most successful tool is to threaten or actually undertake a proxy contest to replace members of the board.[1027] The formally provided path of a proxy

1025 Thompson, *The Limits of Hedge Fund Activism*, 13, 16, http://escholarship.org/uc/item/5jq9d71m (2006).

1026 Brav et al., *Hedge Fund Activism, Corporate Governance, and the Firm Performance* 15, 43, http://ssrn.com/abstract=948907 (2008): The order of frequency with which the means have been applied relates to hedge fund activism in general as the one involving the widest range of means to pursue shareholder activism. As hedge funds pursue general tactics related to the reduction of agency costs, including transaction activism, financial activism, and so on, these numbers may be used to demonstrate the frequency with which means are used to pursue transaction activism. It is representative for all other areas of shareholder activism targeting specific administrational decisions as opposed to the less active form of shareholder activism targeting the amendment of abstract corporate governance rules.

1027 *Regarding shareholder activism in general* Bebchuk, 118 Harv. L. Rev. 833, 851 et seq. (2005); Bebchuk, 93 Va. L. Rev. 102, 110, 117, 136 et seq. (2007); Briggs, 32 J. Corp. L. 681, 716 et seq. (2007); Gantchev, *The Costs of Shareholder Activism: Evidence from a Sequential Decision Model* 19, http://fisher.osu.edu/supplements/10/9861/01222010-Nickolay%20Gantchev.pdf

contest has been used by active shareholders with the financial means to undertake a proxy fight. However, the just analyzed alternative means to effectively challenge director positions by pressuring the administration without a full-scale proxy contest involve lower financial efforts while having a similar potential to remove board members. For these reasons, active shareholders have successfully used them, especially just-vote-no campaigns.[1028]

vi) Support from Delaware's courts

Delaware courts aiming to ensure shareholders the benefit of their vote have assisted active shareholders seeking to use their voting rights during campaigns.[1029] Most importantly, the Delaware Supreme Court confirmed the strict *compelling justification* standard of *Blasius*,[1030] which applies to board actions taken with the primary purpose of intervening in the effective exercise of shareholder voting rights. As a consequence, boards may not adopt *ad hoc* measures aiming to prevent upcoming, most likely successful, shareholder votes, as they did in the past. Examples are amending the bylaws, adding board members to prevent a majority shareholder from obtaining control,[1031] and amending the bylaws to introduce a supermajority quorum.[1032] In *MM Cos v. Liquid Audio, Inc.*,[1033] the Delaware Supreme Court reaffirmed the application of the *compelling justification* standard, either independently, in the absence of a hostile contest of control, or within the *Unocal* standard of review when the board's action is taken as a defensive measure.[1034] Triggering this standard requires that "the primary purpose of the board's

(2009); *opposing opinion:* Klein & Zur, 64 J. FIN. 187, 214 et seq., 216 (2009): not finding a relationship between proxy fights and the rate of success.

1028 Del Guercio et al., *Do Boards Pay Attention when Institutional Investor Activists 'Just Vote No'* 5, http://www.ssrn.com/abstract=575242 (2008).

1029 Briggs, 32 J. Corp. L. 681, 693 (2007).

1030 Blasius Indus., Inc. v. Atlas Corp., 564 A.2d 651, 655, 659, 660, 661, 663 (Del. Ch. 1988): The decision concerns the extension of a board of 7 through incumbents by 2 more seats to prevent that majority shareholders extend the board to 15 seats and therefore determine the majority of the board seats. It was held, that the *Unocal* standard (Unocal Corp. v. Mesa Petroleum Co., 493 A.2d 946 (Del. 1985)), thereafter the reasonable exercise of good faith and due care generally validates, in equity, the exercise of legal authority even if the act has an entrenchment effect, may not be sufficient for board action designed for the primary purpose of interfering with the effectiveness of a stockholder vote. Rather, an even closer scrutiny has to be accorded to such transaction. This may be justified by the fact that the shareholder vote "is critical to the theory that legitimates the exercise of power by some (directors and officers) over vast aggregations of property that they do not own." It also involves "the question who, as between the principal and the agent, has authority with respect to a matter of internal governance." Therefore, boards acting primarily to impede the exercise of stockholder voting power bear the heavy burden of demonstrating a *compelling justification* for such action. Lacking such justification, the directors, even though acting in good faith, are held to have violated their duty of loyalty with the consequence that their action will be set aside by the court.

1031 Blasius Indus., Inc. v. Atlas Corp., 564 A.2d 651, 655 (Del. Ch. 1988).

1032 Chesapeake Corp. v. Shore, 771 A.2d 293, 297 (Del. Ch. 2000).

1033 813 A.2d 1118 (Del. 2003).

1034 *Id.* at 1130.

action is to interfere with or impede the exercise of the shareholder franchise and the shareholders are not given a full and fair opportunity to vote effectively."[1035] The board's amendment of bylaws to increase the members of the board from five to seven and the subsequent appointment of two corporate nominees was a triggering event. The board's intent was to foil the insurgent's attempt to capture a majority by electing own nominees to two vacant and four new board positions.[1036] This ruling ensures a stricter review standard for board actions thwarting the use of the shareholder franchise to hold the incumbents responsible. Active shareholders also hope that board impediments to their use of the shareholder franchise, as experienced by Monks running for Sears' board, will also decrease.

b) Potential conflicts of interest of active shareholders

Active shareholders are generally frequently confronted with concerns about pursuing interests that deviate from those of the remaining shareholders. In the transaction context such concerns relate tightly to the use of (financial) instruments.

The conflicts of interest between active shareholders and the remainder of shareholders of the targeted corporation based on the use of (financial) instruments, like derivatives, needs to be distinguished from conflicts of interest between active *institutional* shareholders and the remainder of shareholders, based on the fact that institutional investors are only intermediaries. Institutional investors do not necessarily act like principals, since they always pursue further interests than solely these of their investors, beneficiaries, and so on. Institutional shareholders are only intermediaries and investment and voting decisions are not made by their investors, beneficiaries, but by the managers. These managers pursue not only the interests of their investors, but also, among others, those of the corporation behind them.[1037]

Two underlying principles of corporate governance are called into question by the use of (financial) instruments, whose use is relevant in the context of transaction activism. The *separation of ownership and control*, conceived by Berle and Means, has been the basis for constraining the authority of management and reducing the divergence between the interests of shareholders and management.[1038] *Judge Frank Easterbrook* and *Professor Daniel Fischel's* allegation that it is *impossible to separate the voting rights from the equity interest*[1039] represents an oversimplification still applying to most cases of share ownership.[1040] Both concepts have significant impact on the attitude towards (active) shareholders exercising control to discipline management.[1041]

1035 *Id.*

1036 *Id.* at 1118.

1037 For more details, see Rock, 79 GEO. L.J. 445, 469 et seq. (1991), Winkler, Die Verantwortung institutioneller Anleger als Aktionäre in Publikumsgesellschaften in Deutschland und den USA, 2008, 319 et seq., 356 et seq.

1038 Hu & Black, 61 BUS. LAW. 1011, 1013 (2006).

1039 Easterbrook & Fischel, 26 J. L. & ECON. 395, 410 (1983).

1040 Hu & Black, 61 BUS. LAW. 1011, 1020 (2006).

1041 *Id.* at 1014.

However, the use of (financial) tools may separate instead of bridging the interests of ownership and control[1042] by decoupling voting rights from the economic interest represented by shares. This leads to the allegation that, for instance, the use of (financial) instruments is a reason why shareholders should not be able to directly impact management decisions. Doing so may result in smaller, neutral, or even negative economic positions compared to the shareholder's voting rights, and therefore be in economic terms contrary to the best interests of the corporation.[1043] Three different applications of these (financial) instruments have repeatedly been discussed in the context of conflicts of interest impacting transaction activism.

i) Empty voting

Empty voting is a controversial means, which has been repeatedly applied by active investors, that unties shareholder votes from their economic interest. Empty voting can be achieved through share borrowing or an equity swap and has the consequence that shareholders exercise voting rights without having an (equivalent) economic interest in the corporation. The former alternative is often performed by borrowing shares for a short time, including the record date. It enables the borrower to exercise the voting rights during the upcoming shareholder meeting (so-called Record Date Capture). The borrower obtains shares and agrees to return the shares upon election of either side, to pay the lender the value of any dividends or other distributions on the shares during the borrowing period, and to secure the loan with cash or securities. As a consequence, the lender bears the economic risk, but has no votes, while the borrower is allowed to vote without economic ownership.[1044]

The second alternative involves the use of over the counter (“***OTC***”)—for disclosure purposes “privately traded”[1045]—derivatives.[1046] It is implemented through the purchase of shares (first step), which allow the shareholder to participate in a possible vote, for instance, a transaction vote or director election. The economic exposure is hedged by

1042 Thompson, *The Limits of Hedge Fund Activism* 35, http://escholarship.org/uc/item/5jq9d71m (2006).

1043 Alexander & Honaker, 33 Del. J. Corp. L. 749, 756 et seq. (2008): They mention few of a myriad of reasons why corporations are not run directly through shareholder vote, amongst them their missing information to make a fully informed decision, which may not be possible based on publicly available information, as the public dissemination of confidential information has to be prevented. Furthermore, some investors have different investment horizons inconsistent with the maximization of a corporation's potential value on risk adjusted basis and managers of investors may not necessarily be incentivized to act in the best interest of the investor as shareholder or the remaining shareholders of the corporation.

1044 Hu & Black, 61 Bus. Law. 1011, 1027 (2006).

1045 *Id.* at 1014.

1046 The OTC market is used for the sale of stocks, bonds, commodities and derivatives that may or may not be listed on major exchanges. The OTC market does not have a central meeting place like an exchange. Rather, it uses people called market makers who are collecting points for stocks who then deal with one another, usually over the computer or phone, to trade the stock, bond or other commodity. Not all OTC stocks are required to report to the SEC. http://www.ehow.com/about_5038098_definition-otc-stock-market.html#ixzz1CbymNaLQ.

entering into an equity swap with the short "interest" leg remaining with the shareholder while a derivative dealer takes the long "equity" leg (second step). The latter often hedge their economic exposure by selling the shares short.[1047] Again, shareholders engaging in this type of empty voting are able to participate in a transaction vote without experiencing the financial consequences of the corporation related to the vote.

A beneficial use of empty voting involves the increase of the voting power of an existing ownership position. It can help shareholders to overcome collective action issues by increasing the voting power of economically involved shareholders without requiring them to invest a proportionally increased amount of financial means. Accordingly, empty voting can provide shareholders with an increased number of votes, which lowers the coordination efforts and costs necessary to convince a sufficient number of fellow shareholders to vote alike on a specific matter. Shareholders with additional empty votes could therefore control the administration more efficiently.[1048]

At the same time, empty voting bears the often-alleged risk that shareholder votes on influential corporate decisions like transactions could not be led by an economic interest in the corporation and for the transaction decision enhancing the corporate shareholder value most. That shareholders may simultaneously hold shares in the other constituent corporation in the transaction makes this concern realistic. As already ascertained, consolidation benefits tend to be transferred entirely to the corporation to be acquired or its shareholders, which often leads to negative financial consequences for the acquiring corporation. An empty voter, who has simultaneously invested in the corporation to be acquired, could therefore vote empty in favor of the transaction in the acquiring corporation, as demonstrated by Perry's merger arbitrage strategy as a King shareholder and potential Mylan empty voter based on a swap.

ii) Hidden ownership

Hidden ownership, the counterpart of empty voting, is used to conceal ownership from disclosure obligations under the Securities Exchange Act, which mostly turn on voting rights rather than on economic ownership.[1049] It is implemented through equity derivatives, which are "cash-settled, and thus" do "not convey the right to acquire shares."[1050] The hiding shareholder remains with the long *equity* leg of a swap. The counterpart, in contrast, holds the short leg of the swap, which he is most likely to hedge with the ownership of matched shares. The *hiding* shareholder can therefore expect, even though it is not guaranteed, to re-purchase these shares including their voting rights once the swap is unwound. In this regard, he may expect that the party holding the *short swap* leg will meanwhile vote in his interest.

Hidden ownership can be used to secretly amass a larger number of shares and thereby prevent the disclosure of the stake as well as the purpose of its acquisition. Rec-

1047 Hu & Black, 61 Bus. Law. 1011, 1024 et seq. (2006).
1048 *Id.* at 1015.
1049 *Id.* at 1014.
1050 *Id.* at 1041.

ognized active shareholders are able to circumvent the payment of inflated share prices, which can be the effect of the disclosure of their intentions or augmenting stakes alone. Furthermore, it can preclude administrative actions foiling the preparation of internal shareholder protests or the use of external control means against a transaction decision. Opportunistic shareholders are, however, equally able to accumulate a substantial stake to suddenly pursue their strategies without prior disclosure.

iii) Related non-host assets

A third controversial constellation involving the pursuit of deviating interests through active shareholders in the transaction context concerns *related non-host assets* and their impact on a shareholder's overall economic interest.[1051] Related non-host assets describe the realization of an additional economic interest in a third corporation whose development is related to that of the targeted corporation. In the transaction context, such an asset usually concerns the other constituent corporation of a transaction. Otherwise, it may involve investments in competing corporations. These intentional investments in related non-host assets need to be distinguished from random participations in both constituent corporations resulting from external diversification strategies that are not expected to impose a systematic bias on transaction decisions.[1052]

Considering that the benefits of transactions can be unequally shared amongst the constituent corporations, the intention to increase the economic interest through economic stakes in both constituent corporations in such constellations requires the use of financial instruments. Accordingly, investors would need to hold shares in the acquiring corporation and to short shares in the corporation to be acquired, or vice versa. In contrast to the empty voting constellation, which involves voting rights in addition to a neutral economic position, the constellation at stake is based on an additional negative economic stake in the other constituent corporation. The increased economic interest can reduce collective action issues by increasing the benefits of a successful campaign for shareholders pursuing transaction activism in the constituent corporation with their positive economic interest, such as an overpaying acquiring corporation. However, only as long as the positive economic interest mediating the voting rights is more or equally as costly as the negative interest in the other corporation will the realization of the conflicting interest be largely excluded. Besides, other shareholders can pursue the opposite strategy, such as traditional merger arbitrage with the consequence that a battle for votes regardless of the value of the transaction evolves.[1053] Similarly, an investment in related non-host targets may also serve to increase voting impact and therefore to reduce collective action issues if used in addition to empty voting. Depending on the specific transaction, however, the empty votes have the potential to be used to the detriment of the targeted corporation if the other stake mediates a negative interest in the targeted corpo-

1051 *Id.* at 1033.

1052 Thompson, *The Limits of Hedge Fund Activism* 34, http://escholarship.org/uc/item/5jq9d71m (2006).

1053 Hu & Black, 61 Bus. Law. 1011, 1033 et seq. (2006).

ration. Finally, another relevant constellation involves positive stakes with different sizes of economic interest in two related corporations, whether competitors or constituent corporations of a transaction. Here, the risk lies in the use of the voting rights mediated through the smaller economic stake to the detriment of this corporation and the benefit of the related corporation.

iv) Lacking special regime

The application of these three strategies by active shareholders does not necessarily result in conflicts of interest between them and their fellow shareholders of the targeted corporation. Rather, it can also overcome issues of collective action through increased voting power or economic interests without the need to increase the investment proportionately. This will either reduce the campaign costs or increase the benefits of a successful campaign and, therefore, increase the financial incentives for active shareholders to become active in the interests of all shareholders. However, these potential beneficial effects cannot detract from the potential of this strategy to produce a conflict of interest between active shareholders impacting the administration and their fellow shareholders of the targeted corporation. However, there has been little evidence that hedge funds, who with their limited diversification requirements and high-profit pressure are the ones most likely to apply these means to enhance their personal profit independent of their fellow shareholders' interests, have applied corresponding "games."[1054]

Apart from Regulation SHO[1055] on naked short sales, relating to short sales without prior borrowing of the sold shares or a corresponding arrangement, which has the danger of failure and the exacerbation of market declines, a specific regime does not apply to the three constellations. In particular does empty voting via the two-step process involving OTC equity swaps not fall under the classic vote-buying precedent of *Schreiber v. Carney*[1056].[1057] This ruling recognized the positive and negative potential related to vote buying,[1058] declined its general ban, and demanded a case-by-case analysis.[1059] However, one can assume that apart from the *infra* analyzed applicable general legal regime market mechanisms, like supply and demand and competition, reduce the number of opportunistic transaction activism constellations. The use of (financial) instruments, as practiced by Perry, also depends on a counterparty willing to take the opposite position and risk. In addition, other investors can pursue the opposite strategy and therefore foil an opportunistic strategy.[1060]

1054 Briggs, 32 J. Corp. L. 681, 701 (2007).
1055 Rule 200 – 204 under 17 C.F.R. § 242.
1056 447 A.2d 17 (Del. Ch. 1982).
1057 Schreiber v. Carney, 447 A.2d 17, 23 (Del. Ch. 1982).
1058 *Id.* at 24 et seq.
1059 *Id.* at 25.
1060 Thompson, *The Limits of Hedge Fund Activism* 35, http://escholarship.org/uc/item/5jq9d71m (2006).

c) Constellations involving desirable transaction activism

A close analysis of six different transaction activism constellations has demonstrated that some of the constellations are more likely to involve conflicting interests between opportunistic members of the administration and shareholders aiming to increase shareholder value. Each of them also provides active shareholders with different means to pursue transaction activism depending on the direction of the transaction activism. They impact the strength of their financial incentives. Finally, it has also been proven that certain constellations of transaction activism are in practice more relevant than others. Regarding the three demonstrated corporate strategies that may misalign shareholder and corporate interests, the question is whether it is possible to determine transaction activism constellations that are more likely to involve desirable transaction activism than others. Furthermore, the question is also whether knowledge about such constellations could be helpful in dealing with transaction activism, especially in applying legal limitations to opportunistic transaction activism.

Desirable transaction activism occurs when active shareholders influence the administration and its opportunistic decision to engage in a transaction to advance its own interests instead of maximizing shareholder value. Active shareholders pursuing desirable transaction activism endeavor to control such a decision ex ante by preventing the opportunistic transaction decision. Alternatively, they will hold members of the administration ex ante accountable for their opportunistic decision, such as by removing them from their position. The incentives of active shareholders pursuing beneficial transaction activism are aligned with these of their fellow shareholders. They all aim to maximize the targeted corporation's stock price, which results when the opportunistic transaction decision is prevented or the opportunistic directors are removed.

Other factors, generally determined by or dependent on the specific situation, are less decisive. The available means for active shareholders under the specific constellation, the costs necessary to finance the efforts to control the opportunistic transaction decision, the shareholder structure, the expected rise in the stock price, and the size of the stake of the active shareholders are less significant in evaluating the desirability of transaction activism. Rather, such circumstances determine the likelihood of transaction activism. They influence whether the efforts necessary to amend an opportunistic transaction decision will be sufficiently compensated by its benefits and therefore their financial incentives. However, only a few of these circumstances, like the direction and the available means, can be generalized sufficiently to roughly predict the likelihood of transaction activism under certain constellations. Accordingly, the efforts to prevent an intended transaction are comparably lower, in contrast to the facilitation of a transaction denied by the administration. Moreover, the prevention of a fundamental transaction requires fewer efforts than that of another transaction.

Returning to the desirability of transaction activism under certain constellations, the general impact of each of the six analyzed transaction decisions on the shareholders and members of the administration is decisive. Based on generalizable knowledge specific to the analyzed transaction decisions, some of them tend to have a rather positive effect on the shareholders' interests. On the basis of generally applicable assumptions, some of them have a positive impact on the interests of the members of the administration. These general transaction consequences relating to the underlying interests of the shareholders and the administration make it possible to identify constellations of transaction activism that are more likely to involve desirable transaction activism. They involve contrary underlying interests of shareholders on the one hand, which need to prevail according to the underlying theory, and the interests of the administration, which need to be subordinated, on the other hand.

The prevailing *general shareholder* interests are aligned with the shareholder value expressed by the stock price development. Based on empirics, some transaction decisions tend to involve the unequal distribution of the potential benefits of a transaction. Therefore, the stock price of only one of the constituent corporations is generally likely to increase, while the other one is likely to decrease. Shareholders confronted with the latter consequences are therefore likely to reject the transaction decision, at least its initial terms. Shareholders in the opposite situation tend to support a corresponding transaction. In more detail, the acquisition of an entire corporation via merger or tender offer is usually correlated with a decrease in the bidding corporation's stock price. The premium over the market price offered to the shareholders of the targeted corporation is likely to swallow or even exceed the entire benefits of the consolidation. As a consequence the stock price of the acquiring corporation plunges and the one of the corporation to be acquired rises.[1061] Similarly, the divestiture by corporations with conglomerate structures can help to decrease a conglomerate discount and increase the selling corporation's stock price, not necessarily to the detriment of the acquiring corporation. Exceptions to the alignment of the interests of active shareholders and general shareholders and the stock price can apply, however, based on the use of the mentioned (financial) instruments leading to a pursuit of economically neutral or negative interests or based on related non-target economic interests.

Administrative interests impacted by corporate transactions in general concern the security of the administrative position as well as the related authority, compensation, and reputation. The prevention of a (partial) sale or even the acquisition of another corporation via a merger or acquisition generally impacts these interests positively. The sale (of a subsidiary or division) or an unrealized merger or acquisition, however, will be seen as negative in the eyes of the administrative members. Exceptions to this general rule apply if these disadvantages are outweighed, for instance, by exceptional financial consequences of the transaction that outweigh the interests of the administrative members.

Only where the interests of the shareholders and those of the responsible administrative members in regards to a certain transaction decision differ and the administration lets its own interests prevail will transaction activism be beneficial. Transferred to the six analyzed decisions, it can be summarized that based on the opposing general interests of shareholders and administration, three of them have the general potential for beneficial transaction activism. These are the decision to acquire another corporation

1061 Bratton, 95 Geo. L.J. 1375, 1424 et seq. (2007); Thompson, *The Limits of Hedge Fund Activism* 14, http://escholarship.org/uc/item/5jq9d71m (2006).

via merger or tender offer as well as the decision to abstain from a possible divestiture. Transferred to the constellations of potentially desirable transaction activism, they are the prevention of an acquisition of another corporation via merger or tender offer, at least in its initial terms, as well as the facilitation of a divestiture for corporations with conglomerate structure.

In contrast, the remaining three of the analyzed transaction activism constellations seem more likely to involve opportunistic shareholder activism. The generally underlying interests of shareholders and members of the administration are the same. The administration, whether aiming to enhance shareholder value or opportunistically prioritizing its own interests, will therefore make the identical transaction decision, making beneficial shareholder activism superfluous. Therefore, active shareholders of the acquiring corporation, who engage in the facilitation of an acquisition via merger by pursuing traditional merger arbitrage or a tender offer, and shareholders of a corporation with conglomerate structure, who engage in blocking a planned divestiture, are likely to act opportunistically themselves. All three strategies have the tendency to reduce instead of increasing the shareholder value of the targeted corporations. They are therefore potentially pursued by shareholders with interests decoupled from the general shareholder interests.

This approach, based on the general consequences of a transaction for the interests of shareholders and members of the administration of the targeted corporation, is not restricted to the six analyzed transaction decisions or constellations of transaction activism. It may also be *carefully* transferred to other constellations of transaction activism. Accordingly, an administrative decision *against* the *sale* of the targeted corporation via a merger or tender offer has the potential to be an opportunistic one aiming to secure the status quo of the members of the administration. Its facilitation through active shareholders has the potential of significantly increasing shareholder value, but the means of active shareholders aiming for the facilitation of such a transaction are limited. Transaction activism aiming to improve the purchase conditions for the corporation to be acquired by temporarily blocking the acquisition[1062] has better means at hand. However, purchase prices barely represent a general issue in times of premiums exceeding the entire benefits of transactions.[1063] In addition, takeover law places stricter duties upon the administration, reducing the number of cases in which opportunistic behavior of members of the administration prevents a sale. Opposite efforts of shareholders to prevent the sale of the targeted corporation via merger or tender offer may be opportunistic, since its sale usually provides significant advantages to its shareholders.

d) Legal restrictions applicable to opportunistic transaction activism

Active shareholders face a number of relevant restrictions. The concern is whether these suffice to prevent opportunistic transaction activism and, closely related, whether the prior developed distinction could be helpful to tackle it more efficiently.

1062 Bratton, 95 Geo. L.J. 1375, 1423 (2007).
1063 *Id.* at 1424.

i) Under securities law

(1) Proxy statement, § 14(a) SEA, Rule 14(a)-3(a) SEA

Disclosure obligations for shareholders involved in proxy fights according to Schedule 14A or Rule 14-12 SEA, battles to veto a transaction decision, or to vote on their own nominee during director elections are extensive. Generally, every proxy solicitation must be accompanied or preceded by a proxy statement, Rule 14(a)-3(a) SEA, containing the information specified in Schedule 14A. Only under the regime of Rule 14(a)-12 SEA, may a solicitation precede it. As part of the original promulgation of the proxy rules, the wording stems from 1956 and therefore from a time where derivatives were still unknown. Accordingly, line item 5 (b)(1)(iv) of Schedule 14A requires only that the solicitor notify "the amount of each class of security which the participant owns beneficially." Even fewer disclosure obligations will apply to communications using exemptions or limitations under the applicable proxy rules. As a consequence, this regulation dating from 1956 seems insufficient to reflect today's (financial) instruments[1064] as well as the frequent formal and informal use of exceptions and exemptions.

However, the outdated legislative wording is compensated by the *infra* analyzed *materiality* standard of facts to be disclosed under the proxy antifraud rule.

(2) Proxy antifraud rule 14a-9 SEA

The proxy antifraud rule has been specifically tailored for proxy solicitations[1065] and applies to proxy solicitations by the corporation and shareholders. It prohibits false or misleading declarations in proxy statements, form of proxy, notice of meeting, or other written or oral communication resulting from any falsely stated or omitted material fact. A fact has been interpreted as *material* in the proxy solicitation context "if there is a substantial likelihood that a reasonable shareholder would consider it important in deciding how to vote."[1066] It may be assumed that a shareholder would like to know about possible adverse interests of fellow shareholders, especially when they lead or oppose a campaign. Therefore, "material" facts include short or hedged positions, participation in the other constituent corporation, or possible bond positions. The Second Circuit has even stopped a proxy solicitation that took place under the "free speech rule" and therefore did not even involve a proxy statement[1067].[1068] As a consequence, the proxy antifraud

1064 Partnoy, 34 Ga. L. Rev. 599, 599 (2000): pointing out the difference derivatives, like swaps, make and how "corporate law has been left in the dust".

1065 Bloomenthal, Securities Law Handbook, Vol. 1, § 17:15 (2009-2010).

1066 TSC Indus., Inc. v. Northway, Inc., 426 U.S. 438, 449 (1976).

1067 Mony Group, Inc., v. Highfields Capital Mgmt., L.P., 368 F.3d 138, 148 (2d Cir. 2004): holding that "[i]n terms of adequate disclosure," the court observes that "at least one of the Appellees, Highfield, has a "short" derivative position in bonds issued by AXA that has only recently been partially disclosed and that may or may not be in sync with the interests of other MONY shareholders".

1068 Briggs, 32 J. Corp. L. 681, 704 (2007).

provision effectively complements the line item disclosure obligations under the proxy rules.

The impact of the SEC's policing of solicitations significantly increased once the U.S. Supreme Court recognized implied remedies for violations of Rule 14a-9 SEA.[1069] For active shareholders, this means that they must diligently provide the required proxy documentation, as they must expect to be confronted by an adversary in a transaction- or election-related proxy contest. However, as active shareholders' adversaries are usually the administration, this risk is relative. The last decades have shown little of such in-campaign time litigation. Management usually depends on their votes to remain in office.[1070] Additionally, today's institutional shareholders are relatively illiquid and an attack against them could have uncomfortable consequences for the management.[1071] Finally, it could alienate other shareholders.[1072]

(3) Beneficial ownership report, § 13(d) SEA

Implemented through the Williams Act, beneficial ownership reporting under section 13(d) SEA intends to alert the marketplace to every large, rapid aggregation or accumulation of securities, regardless of the techniques employed, that might result in a potential shift in corporate control.[1073]

(a) Legal standard

Under section 13(d), Rule 13d-1(a) SEA, shareholders with a stake of more than five percent of an issuer's outstanding shares have to file a statement containing the information under Schedule 13D with the issuer, the SEC, and the exchange(s).

The quorum is *triggered* through five percent of "beneficial ownership" of equity shares and refers to sole or shared voting and/*or* investment power, Rule 13d-3(a) SEA. It can be held "directly or indirectly, through any contract, arrangement, understanding, relationship, or otherwise." According to Rule 13d-3(d)(1) SEA, it includes "the right to acquire beneficial ownership … within sixty days, including … through the exercise of any option [or] warrant." Treated equally are persons who make use of arrangements with the intent to prevent the otherwise necessary disclosure, Rule 13d-3(b) SEA. All participations held by a person without regard to the reason of attribution are accumulated for reasons of notification, Rule 13d-3(c) SEA.

The extensive data to be *disclosed* comprises information on the holder and the funds used to acquire the shares, their number and percentage, and any purchase or sale within the past 60 days, Schedule 13D. *Item 4* demands the disclosure of the transaction's purpose. Furthermore, *item 6* requires disclosing "any contracts, arrangements, understand-

---

1069 J.I. Case Co. v. Borak, 377 U.S. 426 (1964).

1070 Briggs, 50 Bus. Law. 99, 136 (1994).

1071 *Id.*

1072 Briggs, 32 J. Corp. L. 681, 700 (2007).

1073 GAF Corp. v. Milstein, 453 F.2d 709, 717 (2d Cir. 1971); Morales v. Quintel Entm't, Inc., 72 F. Supp 2d 344, 347 (S.D.N.Y. 1999).

ings or relationships (legal or otherwise)" concerning a security of the issuer and the filing of related "written agreements" as exhibits. The filing has to be done truthfully and completely.[1074] Section 13(d) SEA is violated to the extent that a misstatement or omission is *material*.[1075] The applicable materiality standard is also the one set forth in *TSC Industries, Inc. v. Northway*[1076].[1077] It requires that there is a substantial likelihood that a reasonable shareholder would consider it important in making an investment decision. Any acquisition or material amendment has to be filed within ten days, section 13(d)(1) SEA.

(b) Group disclosure, Rule 13d-5(b) SEA

Several individual shareholders may be deemed a *group* with the consequence that they are treated as one person for the purpose of acquiring, holding, or disposing of securities. Under section 13(d) SEA, these shareholders would be obliged to file a Schedule 13D if their aggregate holdings exceeded five percent. They need to have agreed to act together for the purpose of acquiring, holding, voting, or disposing of equity securities of an issuer, Rule 13d-5 SEA. Parallel actions alone are insufficient.[1078] The legislative history[1079] and case law[1080] indicate that such an agreement does not need to be in writing and can be informal or inferred from circumstantial evidence.[1081] A group has therefore been affirmed in cases of information exchange amongst shareholders, patterns of coordinated share purchases, similar voting patterns, and the communication of joint aims.[1082] The number of *acting in concert* cases has, however, been reduced by stricter jurisprudence[1083]

1074 SEC v. Savoy Indus., 587 F.2d 1149, 1165 (D.C. Cir. 1978), cert. denied, 440 U.S. 913 (1979); GAF Corp., v. Milstein, 453 F.2d 709, 720 et seq. (2d Cir. 1971).

1075 CSX Corp., Inc. v. The Children's Inv. Fund Mgmt. (UK) LLP, 562 F. Supp 2d 511, 555 (S.D.N.Y. 2008): relating to the question whether the long party in a cash-settled total return equity swap, the defendant, was obliged to notify under § 13 (d) SEA.

1076 426 U.S. 438, 449 (1976).

1077 CSX Corp., Inc. v. The Children's Inv. Fund Mgmt. (UK) LLP, 562 F. Supp 2d 511, 555 (S.D.N.Y. 2008): holding that the materiality standard according to TSC Indus., Inc. v. Northway applies also in the context of § 13(d) SEA.

1078 Kahan & Rock, 155 U. Pa. L. Rev. 1021, 1079 (2007); Spindler, WM 2007, 2357 (2363).

1079 House and Senate Reports: „This provision is designed to obtain full disclosure of the identity of any person or group obtaining the benefits of ownership of securities by reasons of any contract, understanding, relationship, agreement or other arrangement." S. Rep. No. 550, 90th Cong., 1st Sess. 8 (1967); H.R. Rep. No. 1711, 90th Cong., 2d Sess. 8-9 (1968).

1080 Wellman v. Dickinson, 682 F.2d 355, 364 (2d Cir. 1982); SEC v. Savoy Indus. Inc., 587 F.2d 1149, 1163 (D.C. Cir. 1978).

1081 Bainbridge, *Constraints on Shareholder Activism in The Untited States and Slovenia* 12, http://ssrn.com/abstract=228780 (2000); Briggs, 50 Bus. Law. 99, 111-112 (1994); Clark, Corporate Law 556 (1986).

1082 Spindler, WM 2007, 2357 (2363).

1083 Spindler, WM 2007, 2357 (2363): as expressed by the amendment of the proxy rules that introduced passive investors, and precedent, see Hallwood v. Gotham, 286 F.3d 613, 616, 618 (2d Cir. 2002): which noted that the evidence of meetings of several investors of Hallwood, which comprised conversations about Hallwood, over several years as well as bursts of purchases of these investors in the same week were not sufficient to prove an *acting in concert;* VC Draper v. Millenium Partners, 260 F. Supp 2d 616, 631 -33 (S.D.N.Y. 2003): Court found sporadic e-mail

and legislative amendments.[1084] The formation of a *group* can also trigger poison pills, state antitakeover laws, and short-swing profit liability, section 16(b) SEA. Insurgents have therefore a considerable incentive to avoid becoming members of a group.[1085]

(c) Purpose disclosure, Schedule 13D item 4

Another relevant issue for active shareholders concerns the accurate disclosure of the *purpose of a transaction* to be disclosed under Schedule 13D item 4. It calls for the disclosure of any "plans or proposals" concerning many different corporate occasions, including mergers, extraordinary corporate transactions, changes on the board of directors or management, and asset sales. Any material change in the investor's plans requires the "prompt" filing of an amendment to the Schedule, Rule 13d-2(a) SEA. The intent is to alert investors to potential changes in corporate control and to give them a chance to evaluate the effects of such changes.[1086] The temptation to mislead on this obligation is extremely high, as shareholders may try to prevent the disclosure of plans that may still be frustrated by the administration or other shareholders. There have been many legal proceedings on the issue.[1087] The critical question has repeatedly been at what point preliminary ideas and thoughts have ripened into *plans and proposals*. Aiming to prevent premature disclosure and to ensure full and fair disclosure, courts have held that an investor must disclose the ultimate purpose "regardless of the definiteness or even the existence of any plans to implement this purpose."[1088] But he is only obliged to disclose his plans if they are not merely "preliminary,"[1089] "tentative,"[1090] "contingent,"[1091] or not yet "firm"[1092] or "fixed."[1093] The sometimes-applied *shotgun* approach to item 4, filling in an unlimited number of possible actions to prevent plans from leaking through disclosure, appears inappropriate. The filing requires constant updates to prevent it from becoming misleading.[1094] Therefore, active shareholders are obliged to disclose only definitively formed intentions[1095] or plans, such as the intent to conduct a proxy fight, to remain a passive investor, or to liquidate a position, under Schedule 13D.

---

contact between the investors as well as the proposal of the same slate of directors as insufficient to be convinced that the defendants acted as a group.

1084 Amendments to Beneficial Ownership Reporting Requirements, Exchange Act Release No. 39,538 (Jan. 12, 1998), http://www.sec.gov/rules/final/34-39538.txt.

1085 Briggs, 50 Law. Bus. 99, 112 (1994).

1086 Clark, Corporate Law 555 (1986); Loss & Seligmann, Fundamentals of Securities Regulation 578 (2001); Spindler, WM 2007, 2357 (2363).

1087 Briggs, 50 Bus. Law. 99, 122, 121 (1994).

1088 Chromalloy Am. Corp. v. Sun Chem. Corp., 611 F.2d 240, 247 (8th Cir. 1979).

1089 SEC v. Amster & Co., 762 F. Supp. 604, 610 – 614 (S.D.N.Y. 1991).

1090 Todd Shipyards Corp. v. Madison Fund, Inc., 547 F. Supp. 1383, 1387 (D.C.N.Y. 1982).

1091 CNW Corp. v. Japonica Partners, L.P, 874 F.2d 193, 197 (3rd Cir. 1989).

1092 Trans World Airlines, Inc. v. Icahn, 609 F. Supp. 825, 832 (D.C.N.Y. 1985).

1093 Todd Shipyards Corp. v. Madison Fund, Inc., 547 F. Supp. 1383, 1388 (D.C.N.Y. 1982): relating to not *firm fixed* plans.

1094 Spencer Cos., Inc. v. Agency Rent-A-Car, Inc., 542 F. Supp. 237, 238 (D.C. Mass. 1982).

1095 SEC v. Amster & Co., 762 F. Supp. 604, 614 (S.D.N.Y. 1991).

(d) Deviating interests of active shareholders

If interests of active investors deviate from the interest of their fellow investors, such as by the use of (financial) instruments, the question arises whether Schedule 13D sufficiently requires the disclosure of these conflicting interests. As mentioned *supra,* the *triggering* ownership quorum of five percent is required for sole or shared voting and/ or investment power, Rule 13d-3 SEA.[1096] Relevant *disclosures* comprise the *purpose of acquisition* as well as *contracts, arrangements, understandings, or relationships with respect to securities of the issuer*, items 4 and 6 of Schedule 13D.

Empty voting via *borrowing* shares, which provides the borrower with voting rights regarding a transaction decision or a director election, is likely to trigger disclosure under Schedule 13D and needs to be disclosed. Share lending seems to fall under item 6 of Schedule 13D.[1097] Therefore, most investors prefer to realize empty voting via the use of *equity swaps.* They purchase stock, sell it short, and hedge the economic risk by keeping hold of the shares. Their treatment under Schedule 13D is less clear. Short sales will not change a reporting individual's Rule 13d-3 SEA beneficial ownership since they do not amend the amount of shares in which the person has "voting or investment power." Short sales may, however, trigger a necessary amendment under Rule 13d-2 SEA if they represent a *material* amendment of the facts set forth in a filed Schedule 13D. This could require disclosure of the *source of funds*, a shift in the *purpose of transaction* as well as a *contract, agreement, understanding, or relationship with respect to securities of the issuer*, or require that an exhibit be filed, items 3, 4 and 6.[1098] *Item 4* represents a very general disclosure requirement, which does not explicitly cover derivatives. However, active shareholders involved in high-profile activism like transaction activism need to consider the materiality requirement of the general antifraud rule. It requires disclosing possible conflicts of interest resulting from derivatives, bonds, or stakes in other companies that impact their interest in the transaction.[1099] Different SEC releases underscore this by determining that *short* or future transactions could represent "a possible shift in purpose" relevant under Schedule 13D.[1100] *Item 6* does not require the disclosure of short positions, enabling investors to vote empty. However, if a large long position triggers disclosure, it

1096 Despite the amendment of the SEA's beneficial ownership provisions and the authority granted to the SEC to determine when security-based swaps grant beneficial ownership, both via the Dodd-Frank Act, the "old" beneficial ownership regime is still valid. On December 15, 2011, the SEC announced that it is (still) preparing a broad review of the beneficial ownership reporting rules.

1097 Hu & Black, 61 Bus. Law. 1011, 1041 (2006).

1098 SEC Compliance and Disclosure Interpretations, Exchange Act secs. 13(d) and 13(g) and Regulation 13D-G Beneficial Ownership Reporting, last update Nov. 16, 2009, Question 104.01, http://www.sec.gov/divisions/corpfin/guidance/reg13d-interp.htm.

1099 Briggs, 32 J. Corp. L. 681, 704 (2007).

1100 Commission Guidance on the Application of Certain Provisions of the Securities Act of 1933, the Securities Exchange Act of 1934, and Rules thereunder to Trading in Security Futures Products, Securities Act Release No. 8107, 67 Fed. Reg. 43, 234, at 43, 240 (June 27, 2002): discussing security futures; Public Disclosure of Material Short Security Positions, Exchange Act Release No. 29,278, [1991 Transfer Binder] Fed. Sec. L. Rep. (CCH) ¶ 84,806, at 88,799 n.29 (June 7,

requires the disclosure to have partially offset the economic interest by short positions.[1101] A well-known example is Perry, which had acquired 9.9 percent of Mylan's shares from banks. In addition, Perry had been involved in swap transactions offsetting the entire financial exposure of its Mylan participation. Under item 6 of its delayed Schedule 13D, it disclosed that it had engaged in security–based swap agreements and other hedging transactions involving stock loans, leaving the number of the involved shares and the terms of the hedges open.[1102] However, Wall Street observers understood immediately that Perry was effectively buying votes to support the merger Icahn opposed.[1103]

Hidden ownership via OTC cash-settled swaps does not convey the right to acquire the corresponding shares. Whether they are covered through Rule 13d-3 SEA's *arrangement, understanding, or relationship* depends on the firmness of the shareholder's expectation to be able to terminate the swaps at any time and to be able to obtain the underlying shares at any time. At this point, the SEC provides unsatisfying guidance through SEC rules and no-action letters.[1104] The position of the SEC's Division of Corporate Finance, expressed in an unofficial amicus curiae letter in 2008, gave little reason to believe that the SEC would soon clarify the issue.[1105] It stated "that a standard cash-settled equity swap agreement ... does not confer on a party ... any voting power or investment power over the shares a counterparty purchases to hedge its position." Absent any unusual circumstances, the counterparty's hedge would create "uncertainties for investors who have used equity swaps in accordance with accepted market practices."[1106] The mere "presences of economic or business incentives that the counterparty may have to vote the shares as the other party wishes or to dispose of the shares to the other party" does not amend this evaluation.[1107] However, in the context of business combinations or other change of control transactions, the Division pointed out that the existing regulatory scheme requires the disclosure of equity swaps under item 4 of a Schedule 13D if planning to acquire additional shares.

Courts have not yet decided the precise issue either. In the recent case of *CSX Corp. v. Children's Investment Fund Management (UK) LLP*,[1108] involving the accumulation of 14 percent hidden ownership, Judge Kaplan left open the qualification of the long

1991): discussing short positions, acknowledging that Schedule 13D requires to publicly report certain material long, but no short positions.

1101 Hu & Black, 61 Bus. Law. 1011, 1041 (2006).

1102 Hu & Black, 61 Bus. Law. 1011, 1042 et seq. (2006).

1103 Briggs, 32 J. Corp. L. 681, 705 (2007).

1104 Hu & Black, 61 Bus. Law. 1011, 1041 (2006); Public Disclosure of Material Short Security Positions, Exchange Act Release No. 29,278, 1991 WL 294380, *at 3 (June 7, 1991): pointing out that the Exchange Act requires the public reporting of "certain long security positions" ... "relevant to corporate control and its transfer", but not whether these comprise what is today known as "hidden ownership".

1105 Bertuccini, 31 Cardozo L. Rev. 267, 291 (2009).

1106 Exhibit to Defendant's Response to the SEC Amicus Letter: Fax from Brian V. Breheny to Lewis Kaplan, as Amici Curiae Supporting Respondent, CSX Corp. v. Children's Inv. Fund Mgmt. (UK) LLP, 562 F. Supp 2d 511 (2008) (No. 1:08CV02764), 2008 WL 7055479.

1107 *Id.*

1108 556 F. Supp 2d 511 (S.D.N.Y. 2008), aff'd in part, 292 F. App'x 133 (2d Cir. 2008).

"equity" leg of a swap under Rule 13d-3(a) SEA defining beneficial ownership. Instead, he decided in favor of the fact intensive Rule 13d-3(b) SEA and held that the defendant had acted to evade the reporting requirements under section 13(d) SEA and was therefore deemed a beneficial owner.[1109] Even though Judge Kaplan decided against qualifying a cash-settled equity swap under the idea of beneficial ownership, he still indicated that swap holders may be treated like corresponding owners.

According to some practitioners, the disclosure of long positions under cash-settled swaps is not required.[1110] Legal scholars, in contrast, offer convincing arguments that they should be disclosed, despite the fact that they do not allow voting or disposing of the underlying shares. They at least grant *investment power* under Rule 13d-3(a)(2) SEA when taking into account that investment banks usually hedge their short exposure by keeping the underlying shares and that the long party is often able to unwind the swaps prior to maturity.[1111] A corresponding interpretation also conforms to the congressional intent of the Williams Act to provide transparency for the ordinary shareholder. Furthermore, it promotes judicial efficiency by avoiding the rather fact intensive finding under Rule 13d-3(b) SEA as done by Judge Kaplan.[1112] Taking into account that derivatives developed about a decade after the SEA Rules were issued, the legislative intent in enacting the diclosure regime could not cover them.[1113] Therefore, the current regime provides the necessary means to demand the disclosure of long positions, since these permit the hiding of conflicts of interest.

Finally, for an investor holding *(opposite) economic stakes in both acquirer and target, item 6* requires the disclosure of "contracts, arrangements, understandings or relationships with respect to securities of the issuer." However, it does not include stakes in a third issuer.[1114] Only if the stake in the third corporation independently reaches the five percent threshold would an independent second filing be necessary.[1115] However, short positions are not directly called for under Schedule 13D.[1116] Item 4 covers just about the

1109 *Id.* at 548 et seq.

1110 Chin-chong Liew, *Disclosure Requirements for Purely Cash-Settled Derivatives*, Hong Kong Lawyer, June 2000, www.hk-lawyer.com (search title).

1111 Bertuccini, 31 Cardozo L. Rev. 267, 286 et seq. (2009); Hu & Black, 61 Bus. Law. 1011, 1042 (2006): Questioning the non-disclosure if focusing solely on the economic dynamics surrounding the swap, with the derivative dealer usually aiming to hedge its exposure by holding matched shares, to whom the swap party may return at any time and exchange its swap positions for the matched shares once the swap is terminated.

1112 Bertuccini, 31 Cardozo L. Rev. 267, 287 et seq. (2009).

1113 *Id.* at 285 et seq.

1114 Briggs, 32 J. Corp. L. 681, 705 (2007); Hu & Black, 61 Bus. Law. 1011, 1043 (2006).

1115 Briggs, 32 J. Corp. L. 681, 705 n.164 (2007).

1116 *See* H. Comm. on Gov't Operations, Short-Selling Activity in the Stock Market: Market Effects and The Neen for Regutlation, H.R. Rep. No. 102-414, pt. I, at 23 (1991), *reprinted in* Fed. Sec. L. Rep. (CCH) No. 1483, at 23 (Jan. 22, 1992): "short sellers who acquire a short position of this [5 percent] magnitude in a company's stock are not subject to any similar [to Schedule 13D] reporting requirement"; Public Disclosure of Material Short Security Positions, Exchange Act Release No. 29,278, [1991 Transfer Binder] Fed. Sec. L. Rep. (CCH) ¶ 84,806, at 81,796 (June 7, 1991): acknowledging that Schedule 13D "require[s] public reporting of material long (but not short) positions".

same scope of disclosure as demanded by the proxy rules. They do not require the disclosure of purely negative economic stakes without voting rights, but only derivative positions held in addition to a qualified number of shares. The latter concern only reduced or neutralized financial interests in the targeted corporation and therefore empty voting constellations, like that pursued by Perry in Mylan, represent a change in purpose.[1117]

Despite the outworn terminology, the disclosure regime represents a surprisingly efficient means to disclose circumstances indicating a potential conflict of interest if active investors hold more than five percent of the outstanding shares. Especially the materiality qualifier prevents excessive filings, burdening investors and addressees. It has the advantage of being case specific and requiring disclosure only if the specific case has relevant circumstances. However, the actions of Perry have also indicated the limits of the current system. They pointed out the doubts about the interpretation of the triggering beneficial ownership components of voting rights and economic interests, the accuracy needed to judge whether items 4 and 6 of Schedule 13D are met, and the potential risks of related non-host targets.

(e) Remedies against violations of the section 13(d) SEA regime

Remedies stretch from orders to file an amended or delinquent Schedule 13D to cease and desist orders, actions seeking civil penalties,[1118] and criminal sanctions.[1119] In its order against Perry, the SEC only charged Perry with failing to timely file a Schedule 13D when it acquired more than five percent of Mylan's outstanding shares to support the proposed merger with King. According to the SEC, Perry had not purchased the shares "in the ordinary course of business" under Rule 13d-1(b) SEA, which would have allowed it to file a Schedule 13G instead and to defer its reporting up to forty-five days after the end of the calendar year. Rather, as an institutional investor, it had effected the acquisition for the primary purpose of influencing the outcome of the transaction by voting the acquired shares accordingly. The settlement agreement with the SEC for violating section 13(d) obliged Perry to pay a $150,000 fine without admitting wrongdoing.[1120] Usually, courts order corrective disclosure. However, in some cases they enjoin the voting of the tainted stock,[1121] demand rescission of the stock acquired post violation,[1122] prohibit further stock acquisitions,[1123] or even require the disgorgement of profits.[1124] Any of these remedies would represent a danger to the success of an activist campaign if

1117 Briggs, 32 J. Corp. L. 681, 705 et seq. n.162-165 (2007).

1118 Secs. 21C and 21 (d) (3) Securities Exchange Act.

1119 U.S. v. Paul A. Bilzerian, 926 F.2d 1285,1298 (2d Cir. 1991) "[C]riminal penalties are available against one who knowingly makes a false and misleading statement of material fact on a document required to be filed by the securities laws."

1120 Stephen M. Haas, *SEC Resolves Empty Voting Action Involving King-Mylan Merger*, Aug. 19, 2009, HLS Forum on Corporate Governance and Financial Regulation, http://blogs.law.harvard.edu/corpgov/2009/08/19/sec-resolves-empty-voting-action-involving-king-mylan-merger/.

1121 Campion Parts Rebuilders, Inc. v. Cormier Corp., 661 F. Supp. 825, 825, 851 (N.D. Ill. 1987).

1122 Gen. Steel Indus., Inc. v. Walco Natl. Corp. et al., 1981 WL 17552 at 6 (E.D.Mo. 1981)

1123 Campion Parts Rebuilders, Inc. v. Cormier Corp., 661 F. Supp. 825, 851 (N.D. Ill. 1987).

1124 SEC v. Bilzerian, 29 F.3d 689, 689 (D.C. Cir. 1994).

not make it completely impossible. Moreover, a federal court injunction confirming the violation of federal securities laws would presumably cause fellow shareholders and the administration to lose respect for the activist shareholders, dooming the campaign.[1125]

(f) Practical relevance of section 13(d) SEA regime for active investors

An often-heard critique involves the allegation that active shareholders often fail to comply with their disclosure duties.[1126] In fact, active shareholders' noncompliance with disclosure obligations would be of limited practical relevance. Even though disclosure under section 13(d) SEA has the potential to disclose their conflicts of interest,[1127] hedge funds pursuing transaction activism generally hold smaller stakes. In addition, they tend to publicly announce their investments after or concurrently with their announcement to corporate management, usually long before getting close to the threshold of section 13(d) SEA.[1128] Furthermore, hedge funds need to disclose their equity holdings quarterly pursuant to section 13(f) SEA. The fact is that the disclosure regime according to section 13(d) SEA impinges substantially on investor privacy. It discourages many shareholders to hold a stake of more than 4.9 percent of the targeted corporation,[1129] as well as communication and coordination.[1130] From a policy perspective, informing the market earlier would produce an earlier price increase. The outcome would be diminished gains for active shareholders aiming to acquire additional shares and financial incentives to become active. This is confirmed by the circumstance that institutional U.S. investors frequently cite section 13(d)'s application to groups and the related liability risk as the reason for a general lack of shareholder activism.[1131] As a consequence, it seems worthwhile to eliminate the legal uncertainty related to the term *group* as specified in Rule 13d-5 SEA by excluding parallel actions instead of expanding notification obligations and increasing the SEC's enforcement actions.[1132]

(4) Short form beneficial ownership report, section 13(g) SEA

In 1998, the SEC added a new category of *passive* investors who are able to file an abbreviated disclosure statement on a short-form Schedule 13G. It calls for only basic information on the investor, the number and percentage of shares, including borrowed shares, the purchases or sales within the last 60 days, and the nature of the interest in the shares. However, it imposes no disclosure of purpose.[1133] In addition, it requires only an annual dis-

1125 Briggs, 50 Bus. Law. 99, 118 (1994).
1126 Kahan & Rock, 155 U. Pa. L. Rev. 1021, 1077 (2007).
1127 *Id.* at 1078.
1128 *Id.*; Kumpan, AG 2007, 461 (467).
1129 Bainbridge, *Constraints on Shareholder Activism in The Untited States and Slovenia* 12, http://ssrn.com/abstract=228780 (2000).
1130 *Id.* at 11.
1131 *Id.* at 13; Black, *Shareholder Activism and Corporate Governance in the United States* 8, http://ssrn.com/abstract=45100 (1997).
1132 Kahan & Rock, 155 U. Pa. L. Rev. 1021, 1079 (2007); Spindler, WM 2007, 2357 (2363).
1133 Briggs, 32 J. Corp. L. 681, 691 (2007).

closure within 45 days of the end of the calendar year, except for holdings crossing the ten percent mark, Rule 13d-1(b)(2) SEA. Record date capture without control intent is barely disclosed.[1134]

It is *triggered* when one has between 5 and 20 percent of beneficial ownership in the sense of Rule 13d-3 SEA. Under the *passive investor* regime, the person must have acquired the "securities in the ordinary course of ... business and not with the purpose nor with the effect of changing or influencing the *control* of the issuer, nor with or as a participant in any transaction having such purpose or effect", Rule 13d-1(b)(1)(i) SEA. Furthermore, one needs to fulfill additional prerequisites laid down in Rule 13d-1(b)(1)(ii) and (iii) SEA. Whether the passive investor regime applies is decided by specific facts and circumstances accompanying the solicitation and the vote.[1135] It is difficult and fact intensive.[1136] The *control* concept under this regime is not limited to cases in which a person has or seeks ownership of a majority of the outstanding shares. Rather, the realities of commerce are determinative and actual working control is key.[1137] Therefore, activist solicitations going beyond mere suggestions to management will be disqualified from further use of this regime. These include the aim to facilitate transaction decisions, such as through the sale of the targeted corporation or contested director elections to force the administration to amend its transaction decision.[1138] Rather, shareholders pursuing activities affecting corporate policy by making direct or indirect threats to management by getting fellow shareholders involved to support their proposal have to file a Schedule 13D.[1139] This includes even activities of shareholders opposed to a proposal put forth by management for shareholder approval.[1140] Accordingly, shareholders pursuing transaction activism via direct or indirect impact on the transaction decision have to file a Schedule 13D.

The recent SEC proceeding against Perry, which found it failed to timely disclose its ownership under section 13(d) SEA, confirms the limited relevance of the section 13(g)

1134 Hu & Black, 61 Bus. Law. 1011, 1041 (2006).

1135 Amendments to Beneficial Ownership Reporting Requirements, Exchange Act Release No. 39,538 (Feb. 17, 1998) http://www.sec.gov/rules/final/34-39538.txt, 23.

1136 *Id.* at 25.

1137 Graphic Scis., Inc. v. Int'l Mogul Mines Ltd., 397 F. Supp. 112, 125 (D.D.C. 1974).

1138 Amendments to Beneficial Ownership Reporting Requirements, Exchange Act Release No. 39,538 (Feb. 17, 1998), http://www.sec.gov/rules/final/34-39538.txt, 23; *compare* Egghead.com, Inc. v. Brookhaven Capital Mgmt., Inc., 194 F. Supp. 232 (S.D.N.Y. 2002): denying summary judgment on passivity issue because of intense strategic debates and seeking of possible board representation; Transcon Lines v. A.G. Becker Inc., 470 F. Supp. 356 (S.D.N.Y. 1979): ruling that mere suggestions and discussions with management about corporate policies do not constitute non-passive control purpose; Briggs, 32 J. Corp. L. 691 n.66 (2007).

1139 Transcon Lines v. A.G. Becker Inc., 470 F. Supp. 356, 379 (S.D.N.Y. 1979): ruling that mere suggestions and discussions with management about corporate policies do not constitute non-passive control purpose; Groskaufmanis & Gamer, *Monitoring the Dance: An Assessment of the SEC's Regulation 13D-G Amendments*, 6 Corp. Governance Advisor 16, 18 (1998): distinguish between demands with implicit or explicit threat to rally other substantial shareholders on the same issue (13D), and mere suggestions (13G) in regard to policy questions (here a divisional spin-off) for the analysis.

1140 Amendments to Beneficial Ownership Reporting Requirements, Exchange Act Release No. 39,538 (Feb. 17, 1998), http://www.sec.gov/rules/final/34-39538.txt, 24.

SEA regime for active shareholders. Perry, pursuing merger arbitrage, had intended to profit from the postponed disclosure of its voting rights in Mylan by initially relying on Schedule 13G. However, the SEC determined that Perry had not been entitled to defer filing pursuant to Rule 13d-1(b) SEA. The acquisition had not been effected in the *ordinary course* of its business. Rather, qualified institutional investors need to "acquire securities as part of their ordinary market making or passive investment activities." When acquiring "ownership of securities for the purpose of influencing the direction or management of an issuer or affecting the outcome of a transaction … the acquisition is not made and the shares are not held in the 'ordinary course' of business for purposes of relying on Rule 13d-1(b) SEA."[1141]

The line between a Schedule 13D and 13G filing should be clarified by explicitly requiring a Schedule 13D filing for stakes held to affect a transaction-related shareholder vote that will not affect control.[1142]

(5) Disclosure by institutional money managers, section 13(f) SEA

Section 13(f) SEA requires status-based quarterly disclosure from institutional money managers holding securities of a value of at least $100 million. Money managers are non-natural persons who invest in or buy or sell for their own account, as well as persons, natural or other, who exercise investment discretion with respect to the account of any other person, section 13(f)(5)(A) SEA. This provision also includes hedge funds.[1143] Securities in the sense of section 13(f) SEA are interpreted narrowly and comprise publicly traded U.S. common shares and exchange-traded options,[1144] but not OTC securities. Therefore, section 13(f) SEA requires neither the disclosure of hidden (morphable) ownership positions, relying usually on OTC derivatives, nor of empty voting via share borrowing or hedging of economic ownership. Under the latter scenario, only direct ownership needs to be disclosed, not its empty character.[1145]

(6) General antifraud provision

Shareholders can also be liable under the general antifraud provision, section 10(b) and Rule 10b-5 SEA. It prohibits the use of any "device, scheme, or artifice to defraud" creating liability for any misstatements or omissions of a material fact and therefore a wide range of behavior. However, absent (i) a line item disclosure requirement, (ii) insider trading, or (iii) a duty to correct, a *duty to disclose* does not apply to shareholders. Furthermore, the misstatements or omissions in company filings must be *in connection with* a security's purchase or sale. The misstated or omitted fact has to be *material.* In 1988, the

1141 Order Instituting Administrative And Cease-And-Desist Proceedings, Exchange Act Release No. 60,351, Investment Advisors Act of 1940 Release No. 2907 (July 21, 2009), www.sec.gov/litigation/admin/2009/34-60351.pdf.

1142 Hu & Black, 61 Bus. Law. 1011, 1052 (2006).

1143 *Id.* at 1043.

1144 *Id.* at 1044.

1145 *Id.*

Supreme Court held in *Basic v. Levinson*[1146] that the materiality standard of the proxy antifraud rule also applies to the general antifraud provision.[1147] It requires a substantial likelihood that a reasonable (potential) shareholder would consider it important in deciding whether to purchase or sell and that (actual/truthful) disclosure would alter the "total mix" of information available.[1148] False and misleading statements regarding material facts made in a Schedule 13D can therefore be actionable by a buyer or seller under the general antifraud provision.[1149] Conflicts of interest of active shareholders, resulting from (financial) instruments, stakes in third corporations, or loans, fall either under item 4 or item 6 of Schedule 13D.[1150] The intent to impact a major transaction decision and, if necessary, to replace the current board, which is likely to have a significant impact on the stock price, while having a neutral or even negative economic interest in the corporation, is material. As a consequence, reports of active shareholders will only under specific circumstances become subject to a filing of a buyer or seller under the general antifraud provision.

(7) Regulation of fair disclosure

The Fair Disclosure Regulation (***"Regulation FD"***) that came into force in 2000 represents another limitation that could be relevant for shareholders conducting transaction activism. It obliges the administration to simultaneously furnish the public with the same material non-public information provided to institutional investors, Rule 100 (a)(1), (b)(1)(iv) SEA. This may be satisfied by either filing a Form 8-K or by publishing it in a comparable manner, such as via a press release or a conference call, Rule 101(e) SEA. The underlying intent of Regulation FD is to strengthen the investor's belief in the capital market's integrity. Therefore, it aims to prevent selective disclosure of material non-public information to selected investors, which allows them to profit or at least to avoid loss at the cost of the uninformed. In addition, it restrains the administration from treating material information as a commodity to gain or retain the favor of its institutional investors.[1151] The violation of Rule 100(a) SEA can result in an SEC enforcement action alleging the violation of sec-

1146 485 U.S. 224 (1988).

1147 Basic, Inc. v. Levinson, 485 U.S. 224, 231 (1988).

1148 *Id.* at 231 et seq.

1149 U.S. v. Bilzerian, 926 F.2d 1285, 1298 (2d Cir. 1991); Kammerman v. Steinberg, 891 F.2d 424, 431 (2d Cir. 1989); GAF Corp. v. Milstein, 453 F.2d 709, 720 (n.22) et seq. (2d Cir. 1971): pointing out the missing parallel antifraud provision for beneficial ownership reports as compared to disclosures to be provided by tender offerees under § 14(d) and the corresponding antifraud rule § 14(e) SEA, but without a clearer indication from Congress, the fact that tender offer transactions entail methods clearly distinguishable from § 13(d) dealings, which involves extensive communications to the shareholders, which § 10(b) does not provide a remedy to shareholders while the beneficial ownership report does not entail such communication, there is a clear need for an antifraud provision; COX ET AL., SECURITIES REGULATION § 16 B, 944 (2004).

1150 Here, the approaches in regard to derivatives, loan positions and stakes in third corporations are either argued under the *purpose* item four, so done by the SEC in its releases, or under item six, so, for instance, done by Judge Kaplan in: CSX Corp. v. Children's Inv. Fund Mgmt. (UK) LLP, 562 F. Supp 2d 511, 556 (S.D.N.Y. 2008).

1151 Selective Disclosure and Insider Trading, Securities Act No. 7881, Exchange Act No. 43,154 (Aug. 15, 2000), http://www.sec.gov/rules/final/33-7881.htm.

tion 13(a) or 15(d) SEA. They can bring cease-and-desist orders or civil actions seeking an injunction and/or civil monetary penalties,[1152] but not antifraud liability under Rule 10b-5 SEA or a private cause of action,[1153] Rule 102 SEA. Despite the restricted number of remedies, this regulation has chilled the relationship between active shareholders and the administration. The latter is usually not willing to share certain information with all shareholders. However, without access to nonpublic information, the ability of shareholders to become active and enhance corporate governance is reduced.[1154] This effect on the low-cost means of private negotiation requires a reassessment in order for them to fulfill their potential as efficient governance devices.[1155]

(8) Insider trading under section 10(b), Rule 10b-5 SEA

Insider trading provisions may also be triggered in the context of transaction activism. Relevant constellations could represent share acquisition by active shareholders intending to amend corporate policy independent of or to the detriment of the targeted corporation or the request to fellow shareholders to support their strategy and to purchase additional shares. A third constellation represents communication with the administration about a specific transaction decision and the threat to sell all shares if the administration does not follow their initiative.

State insider trading law appears less relevant in the transaction activism constellation, as it requires an active misrepresentation to other investors or the corporation.[1156] Federal securities law, in contrast, also covers *silent insider trading*,[1157] also known as the "disclose or abstain-rule."[1158] Under Rule 10b-5 SEA,[1159] a finding of fraud on the unfairness of allowing insiders to profit from their special access to sensitive information frustrates the justifiable expectation of the securities marketplace that all investors have relatively equal access to material information.[1160] Thereafter, shareholders subject to a fiduciary duty towards the corporation and its shareholders have to disclose any *material* non-public information available to them as insiders when trading on the issuer's shares or to

1152 *Id.*

1153 Yockey, 61 S.C. L. Rev. 171, 210 (2009).

1154 Bainbridge, *Shareholder Activism in The United States and Slovenia* 16, http://ssrn.com/abstract=228780 (2000).

1155 Yockey, 61 S.C. L. Rev. 171, 173, 218 (2009).

1156 Merkt/Göthel, US-amerikanisches Gesellschaftsrecht, 2006, mn.975.

1157 SEC v. Texas Sulphur Co., 401 F.2d 833, 848 (2d Cir. 1968): "Thus, anyone in possession of material inside information must either disclose it to the investing public, or, if he is disabled from disclosing it in order to protect a corporate confidence, or he chooses not to do so, must abstain from trading in or recommending the securities concerned while such inside information remains undisclosed."; Merkt/Göthel, US-amerikanisches Gesellschaftsrecht, 2006, 983.

1158 Cady, Roberts & Co., 40 S.E.C. 907 (1961), 1961 WL 60638, 3.

1159 Adopted pursuant to the Commission's statutory authority under § 10(b) of the Securities Exchange Act to adopt rules to proscribe "any manipulative or deceptive device or contrivance" in connection with the purchase or sale of any security, see Cox et al., Securities Regulation 653 (2004).

1160 Cady, Roberts & Co., 40 S.E.C. 907 (1961), 1961 WL 60638, 4; SEC v. Texas Gulf Sulphur Co., 401 F.2d 833, 848 (2d Cir. 1968); Cox et al., Securities Regulation 880 (2004).

abstain from trading. The information is material if a reasonable investor would qualify it as important.[1161] With regard to an omission, a reasonable person has to attach importance to the fact omitted in determining a choice of action in the transaction in question.[1162] There has to be a substantial likelihood that the omitted fact would have assumed actual significance in the deliberations of a reasonable investor or that he would have viewed disclosure of the omitted fact as having significantly altered the total mix of information available.[1163] The duty to disclose relates only to situations that are of a special nature and that are likely to have a significant impact on the share price if the special situation is disclosed.[1164] For shareholders to fall under the obligation to *disclose or abstain,* it is not sufficient to be in the mere possession of material non-public information. It is necessary for them to be subject to a fiduciary duty toward the corporation.[1165] Finally, they need to have traded on the basis of the undisclosed material information.[1166]

Active minority shareholders intend to impact significant corporate transaction decisions with the help of fellow shareholders, which is likely to significantly impact the stock price either positively or negatively. Such information could be qualified as relevant information for the deliberations of a reasonable investor, which is able to alter the total mix of available information and therefore is material. However, taking into account the wording and the general purpose of Rule 10b-5 SEA, the share purchase by active shareholders intending to impact the corporate strategy cannot be insider trading. It does not involve insider *information*, which has been *provided* on the basis of their relationship and impact on the corporation. Furthermore, only the trading of controlling shareholders, subject to the requisite fiduciary duties, has been recognized as insider trading.[1167] Minority shareholders with initially smaller shareholdings, in contrast, are not subject to fiduciary obligations, even when intending to purchase a qualified minority stake. Equally, active shareholders sharing their plans to exercise impact on a corporate transaction decision with fellow shareholders may share *material non-public information* with fellow shareholders. However, neither one of them has been provided with the information due to an influential position in the corporation that has made them subject to fiduciary duties. Finally, the administration, knowing about the plans of active shareholders and their threat to sell all of their shares through private communication, is generally prohibited from trading on the basis of this information. Consequently, insider provisions play a minor role for active shareholders and do not constitute a helpful means to disclose possibly deviating interests.

1161 Basic, Inc. v. Levinson, 108 S. Ct. 978, 980 (1988).

1162 Branham v. Material Sys. Corp., 354 F. Supp. 1048, 1055 (S.D. Fla. 1973).

1163 TSC Indus., Inc. v. Northway, Inc., 426 U.S. 438, 449 (1976); SEC v. Champion Sports Mgmt., Inc., 599 F. Supp. 527, 534 (S.D.N.Y. 1984).

1164 Fleischer, 51 VA. L. REV. 1271, 1289 (1965).

1165 CLARK, CORPORATE LAW 322 (1986).

1166 Merkt/Göthel, US-amerikanisches Gesellschaftsrecht, 2006, mn.987.

1167 Bainbridge, *Constraints on Shareholder Activism in The Untited States and Slovenia* 15, http://ssrn.com/abstract=228780 (2000).

(9) Insider provisions, section 16 SEA

The insider reporting provision of section 16(a) SEA has "the purpose of preventing speculation based upon inside information or other abuses of their position by … large shareholders of registered corporations."[1168] Shareholders holding more than 10 percent of the outstanding shares of a corporation must report all their trades in equity securities on a monthly basis, section 16(a) SEA. Neither OTC derivatives nor share lending trigger the regime.[1169] Once *disclosure* is triggered, section 16 SEA's definition of beneficial ownership focuses on economic ownership. It requires the disclosure of most economic interests, including equity derivatives, Rule 16a-4 SEA, whether exchange traded or OTC.[1170] Even some related non-host assets are covered.[1171] A disclosure of short sales is not required, as section 16(c) SEA bans them outright.[1172] Focusing on economic ownership, section 16(a) SEA does not cover share borrowing or lending. Accordingly, section 16 SEA demands disclosure of hidden (morphable) ownership, while empty voters on the basis of borrowed shares would not need to disclose.[1173] Active shareholders try not to exceed the 10 percent threshold. However, considering further the comprehensive disclosure obligations under Schedule 13D and the proxy rules, the insider reporting rules play a minor role for active shareholders and their possibly deviating interests.[1174]

The short-swing profit rule determines that insiders must forfeit to the corporation any profit made by a purchase and sale occurring within six months if they own each time more than 10 percent, section 16(b) SEA. Especially for diversified institutional investors like mutual funds, the short-swing profit rule represents a substantial deterrent to holding large share blocks as liquidity becomes substantially reduced equating to increased risk and costs.[1175] But even for the remainder of large shareholders, it proves to be detrimental, as it keeps them from liquidating their stake when they receive negative information.[1176] The short-swing profit rule represents one of the major reasons why only a small number of larger shareholdings exist in U.S. corporations.[1177] The incentives of active investors to hold stakes above 10 percent are significantly reduced.[1178] They avoid

1168 Whiting v. Dow Chem. Co., 386 F. Supp.1130, 1133 (D.C.N.Y. 1974).

1169 Hu & Black, 61 Bus. Law. 1011, 1039, 1045 (2006).

1170 *Id.* at 1045 et seq.

1171 Opposing opinion: Briggs, 32 J. Corp. L. 681, 705 (2007).

1172 Padilla, *The Regulation of Insider Trading as an Agency Problem*, bepress Legal Series 2005 – Working Paper 641, 6.

1173 Hu & Black, 61 Bus. Law. 1011, 1045 et seq. (2006).

1174 Briggs, 32 J. Corp. L. 681, 705 et seq. (2007).

1175 *Id.* at 17; Briggs, 32 J. Corp. L. 681, 697 n.107: making short term trading impossible, active investors prefer therefore to remain below 10 percent; Padilla, *The Regulation of Insider Trading as an Agency Problem*, bepress Legal Series 2005 – Working Paper 641, 8; Roe, 27 J. Fin. Econ. 7, 17 (1990).

1176 Padilla, *The Regulation of Insider Trading as an Agency Problem*, bepress Legal Series 2005 – Working Paper 641, 8.

1177 Roe, Strong Managers, Weak Owners, 119 et seq., 270 et seq. (1996); Skrzipek, Shareholder Value versus Stakeholder Value: Ein Vergleich des des US-amerikanischen Raums mit Österreich, 2005, 93.

1178 Bhide, 34 J. Fin. Econ. 31, 37 (1993).

triggering the insider status.[1179] This is not without consequences for corporate governance. The incentives to undertake substantial efforts to exercise inside control decrease with the stake's size and the potential for overcompensation.[1180]

(10) Control person liability, section 20(a) SEA

Finally, shareholders holding more than 10 percent of the outstanding shares of the issuer are deemed controlling shareholders, section 12(b)(1)(D) SEA. They are jointly and severally liable if the controlled person is responsible under SEA provisions and they have exerted actual power or influence over the controlled person.[1181] Liability based on section 20(a) SEA can exceed the investment and remove the limited liability of the shareholder.[1182] As active shareholders, especially because of the short-swing profit rule and the beneficial ownership requirement, keep their shareholding below 5 or 10 percent, avoidance of section 20 (a) SEA is of little practical relevance for active shareholders.

(11) Reform intentions of the SEC

In July 2010, the SEC addressed the issue of empty voting and other forms of decoupling of voting rights and economic interests and launched a *concept proposal*.[1183] As a concept proposal, it formulated a variety of rather general regulatory responses. To address decoupling, it proposed to modify the current disclosure system (including section 13(d), 13(f), and 13(g)) or to develop a new disclosure regime helpful to all participants in a proxy contest by allowing them to draw the necessary conclusions. Other options comprised the obligation to certify on the proxy form that one has the full economic interest in the shares being voted or the earlier disclosure of the meeting's agenda prior to the record date, enabling shareholders having loaned their shares to timely recall them. Finally, they included the restriction of proxy voting to persons who hold pure long positions in the underlying shares and the prohibition of empty voting involving negative economic interests.

Another proposed rule stems from the SEC's authorization to regulate security- based swaps under the Dodd-Frank Act.[1184] It aims to increase transparency of the "security-based swap" ("***SBS***") market. The Dodd-Frank Act requires that certain SBS transactions must be cleared through an agency and be traded on a registered trading platform. SBS transactions (cleared or uncleared) must be reported to a registered security-based

1179 *Id.* at 37; Seyhun, Investment Intelligence from Insider Trading 31 (1998).

1180 Padilla, *The Regulation of Insider Trading as an Agency Problem*, bepress Legal Series 2005 – Working Paper 641, 7–9; Roe, 27 J. Fin. Econ. 7, 38 (1990).

1181 Durham v. Kelly, 810 F.2d 1500, 1503 et seq. (9th Cir. 1987); Kersh v. Gen. Coucil, 804 F.2d 546, 548 (9th Cir. 1986).

1182 Skrzipek, Shareholder Value versus Stakeholder Value: Ein Vergleich des des US-amerikanischen Raums mit Österreich, 2005, 93.

1183 Concept Release on the U.S. Proxy System, Exchange Act Release No. 62,495, Investment Advisors Act of 1940 Release No. 3052; Investment Company Act Release 29,340, 75 Fed. Reg. 43019 (proposed July 14, 2010), *available at* www.sec.gov/rules/concept/2010/34-62495.pdf.

1184 Sec. 712(d) of The Dodd-Frank Wall Street Reform and Consumer Protection Act (Pub. L. No. 111-203, H.R. 4173).

swap data repository ("***SDR***") or the Commission. A separate release[1185] proposed rules governing the SDR registration process, duties, and core principles. Proposed Regulation SBSR[1186] (Security Based Swap Reporting) lays out who must report what information where and which information needs to be publicly disseminated.[1187] One swap party would have to report information on the transaction to a SDR, while in turn the SDR would have to publicly disseminate part of this information.[1188]

Both approaches aim for disclosure of decoupled voting rights and economic interests and therefore for more transparency in dealing with (financial) instruments. However, the concepts are still too general to discuss their specific approaches. Rather, it has to be underscored that the goal needs to be to keep benefits and burden resulting from additional disclosure obligations in perspective. Even though the terminology of the current regime is largely outdated, the materiality qualifier of the related antifraud rules suppresses the abuse of decoupling while keeping the disclosure burden within limits. Therefore, a proposed regulation should concentrate on updating the language, especially of the underlying regime, while maintaining flexible language regarding future (financial) instruments and the resulting disclosure burden. The approach contained in Rule 13d-3 SEA linking voting and/*or* economic power appears to be a promising approach. Finally, the assimilation of instruments triggering disclosure and those that need to be disclosed would result in clearly elevated transparency.[1189]

ii) Fiduciary duties under corporate law

(1) Status quo of shareholder fiduciary duties

Potential fiduciary duties represent the most relevant restriction for shareholders pursuing transaction activism under corporate law. Absent any *statutory* fiduciary duty,[1190] courts have determined shareholders are not subject to fiduciary duty obligations.[1191] Exceptions apply only to certain shareholders under specific circumstances.[1192]

1185 Security-Based Swap Data Repository Registration, Duties, and Core Principles, Exchange Act Release No. 63,347, 75 Fed. Reg. 77,306 (proposed Dec. 10, 2010), *available at* www.sec.gov/rules/proposed/2010/34-63347.pdf.

1186 Regulation SBSR-Reporting and Dissemination of Security-Based Swap Information, Exchange Act Release No. 63,346, 75 Fed. Reg. 75,208 (proposed Dec. 2, 2010), *available at* www.sec.gov/rules/proposed/2010/34-63446.pdf.

1187 Mary L. Schapiro, Chairman of the SEC, Opening Statement of the SEC Open Meeting Item 4 – Proposed Regulation SBSR (Nov. 19, 2010) www.sec.gov/news/speech/2010/spch111910mls-item4.htm.

1188 Press Release, SEC, SEC proposes rules on Security-Based Swap Reporting (Nov. 19, 2010) www.sec.gov/news/press/2010/2010-230.htm.

1189 Hu & Black, 156 U. Pa. L. Rev. 625, 683 (2008).

1190 Anabtawi & Stout, 60 Stan. L. Rev. 1255, 1267 (2008).

1191 Ostlind v. Ostlind Valve Co., 165 P.2d 779, 788 (Or. 1946); Merkt/Göthel, US-amerikanisches Gesellschaftsrecht, 2006, mn.952; Voigt, Haftung aus Einfluß auf die Aktiengesellschaft, 2003, 152 n.994.

1192 *See* Anabtawi & Stout, 60 Stan. L. Rev. 1255, 1268 (2008).

Only *controlling shareholders* may have fiduciary duties toward the corporation and its minority shareholders.[1193] In general, shareholders directly or indirectly holding more than half of the corporation's voting power are controlling shareholders.[1194] Alternatively, a shareholder has to exercise actual control over corporate conduct due to specific business or professional relationships or otherwise to be in a position[1195] that allows him to determine who sits on the board of directors.[1196] The second test is not an easy one to satisfy. It requires that shareholders, although lacking a clear majority, have such formidable voting and managerial power as if they had majority voting control.[1197] Furthermore, it has been recognized that a number of shareholders "can *collectively* form a control group where those shareholders are connected in some legally significant way – e.g., by contract, common ownership, agreement, or other arrangement—to work together toward a shared goal." The group is then accorded "a controlling shareholder status, and therefore its members owe fiduciary duties to their fellow shareholders."[1198]

1193 Cox & Hazen, Corporations § 11.11 (2003); Hazen, 125 U. Pa. L. Rev. 1023, 1027 et seq. (1977); other approach: Guntz, Treubindungen von Minderheitsaktionären, 1997, 61 et seq.: underscoring that the duty of loyalty depends upon a specific impact on the corporation and its shareholders, pointing out several constellations under which *minority* shareholders have specific means to exercise relevant impact, 251 et seq.: mentions the example of derivative suits and the application of fiduciary duties due to sueing shareholder's representation, and, pursuant to Guntz, impact of the sueing shareholders of/upon corporation and the remaining shareholders.

1194 Wheeler v. Abilene Nat. Bank, 159 F. 391, 391, 393 et seq. (8th Cir. 1908): "The power of a single holder of a majority of the stock of a corporation devolves upon him the correlative duty on the holders of the minority of the stock to exercise good faith, care, and diligence to make the corporate property produce the largest possible amount, to protect the interests of the minority stockholders, and to secure and deliver to them their just proportion of the income and the proceeds of the property."

1195 Mayer v. Adams, 167 A.2d 729, 732 (Del. Ch. 1961).

1196 Weinstein Enters., Inc. v. Orloff, 870 A.2d 499, 506 et seq. (Del. 2005); Citron v. Fairchild Camera and Instrument Corp., 569 A.2d 53, 70 (Del. 1989): stating an exception for minority shareholders with an ownership of less than 50 percent of a corporation's outstanding stock to become a controlling shareholder if dominating a corporation through actual control of corporate conduct; Traub v. Barber, 452 N.Y.S.2d 575 (App. Div. 1982): It is not necessary to own a majority of the voting shares to be a controlling shareholder. Rather the defendant owning 20,6 percent of the outstanding shares and no other person owning more than 5 percent was enough to support a claim that the defendant was bound by fiduciary duty as a controlling shareholder.; In re PNB Holding Co. S'holders Litig., No. Civ. A. 28-N, 2006 WL 2403999, at *9 (Del. Ch. 2006): pointing out that "a controlling shareholder exists when a stockholder: 1) owns more than 50 percent of the voting power of a corporation; or 2) exercises power over the business and affairs of the corporation."; Kaplan v. Centex Corp., 284 A.2d 119, 122-123 (Del. Ch. 1971): Stock ownership alone, at least when it amounts to less than a majority, is not sufficient proof of domination and control. Control and domination may be exercised directly or through nominees. In *actual* exercise they imply at minimum a direction of corporate conduct in such a way as to comport with wishes or interests of corporation or persons doing the controlling.; Anabtawi & Stout, 60 Stan. L. Rev. 1255 (1270); Berle, 58 Colum. L. Rev. 1212, 1212 (1958): referring to the definition of "control" as the capability to chose the directors; Cox & Hazen, Corporations 252 (2003); Immenga, Die personalistische Kapitalgesellschaft, 1970, 181.

1197 In re PNB Holding Co. S'holders Litig., 2006 WL 2403999, at *10 (Del. Ch. 2006).

1198 Dubroff v. Wren Holdings, LLC, C.A. No. 3940-VCN, 2009 WL 1478697, at *3 (Del. Ch. 2009).

Such an approach has, however, to be clearly distinguished from a group of shareholders whose members have solely parallel interests.[1199] Finally, even controlling shareholders are entitled to vote to further their financial interests.[1200]

Courts have only in a limited number of cases applied fiduciary duties to shareholders, mainly when the control exercised over the firm was equivalent to that of the directors. This has primarily occurred in closed corporations or self-interested transactions, especially freeze-outs, of public corporations.[1201] The latter concerned mainly the *duty of loyalty*, such as the majority shareholder involved in a parent-subsidiary relationship or the individual shareholder standing on both sides of the transaction,[1202] invoking a potential conflict of interest. The allocation of the purchase price amongst different shareholder groups to the benefit of the strongest voting group despite a transaction between two unrelated groups can also indicate overreaching.[1203] They all invoke the concern that the transaction terms are the result of self-interested negotiations and require application of closer scrutiny.[1204] The duty of loyalty precludes controlling shareholders from using their position to extract material economic benefits at the minority's expense.[1205] *Weinberger*'s *entire fairness* inquiry applies, however, only if the controlling shareholder stands on both sides of the challenged transaction.[1206] Like directors, such controlling shareholders ordinarily bear the burden of proving the entire fairness of the transaction once the plaintiff has shown control and a potential conflict of interest.[1207] The fairness of the *consideration* demands that minority shareholders should receive the substantial equivalent in value of what they had before[1208] and participate proportionally in any non-speculative gains generated by the acquisition.[1209] The fairness of the *procedure* includes the fairness of the bargaining procedure, like timing, initiation, structure, and negotiation, as well as the approvals of the board and the shareholders.[1210] Defendants can, however, avoid the implications of a conflict of interest on the transaction terms with a ratifying vote of a fully informed and un-coerced majority of the minority, which

1199 Williamson v. Cox Commc'ns, Inc., No. Civ. A. 1663-N, 2006 WL 1586375, at *6 (Del. Ch. 2006).

1200 Thorpe by Castleman v. Cerbco, Inc., 676 A.3d 436, 444 (Del. 1996); Bershad v. Curtiss-Wrigth Corp., 535 A.2d 840, 845 (Del. 1987); Emerson Radio Corp. v. Int'l Jensen Inc., Civ. A. Nos. 15130, 14992, 1996 WL 483086, at *17 (Del. Ch. 1996).

1201 Anabtawi & Stout, 60 Stan. L. Rev. 1255, 1261, 1269, 1271-1272, 1295 (2008).

1202 Emerald Partners v. Berlin, 787 A.2d 85, 90 (Del. 2001).

1203 In re Tele-Comm. Inc. Shareholder Litig., 2005 WL 3642727, 6 et seq. (Del. Ch. 2005): entire fairness inquiry applied since the premium of a class of shares held almost exclusively by the directors experienced a substantially larger premium than the other class of shares.

1204 Cox & Hazen, Corporations, § 23.02 (2010).

1205 Jones v. H.F. Ahmanson & Co., 460 P.2d 464, 471-472 (Cal. 1969); Central Trust Co. v. Bridges, 57 Fed. 753, 766 (6th Cir. 1893).

1206 Cox & Hazen, Corporations § 23.02 (2010).

1207 Kahn v. Lynch Commc'n Sys., Inc., 638 A.2d 1110, 1115 (Del. 1994); Weinberger v. UOP, Inc., 457 A.2d 701, 710 (Del. 1983); Official Comm. of Unsecured Creditors of Color Tile, Inc. v. Investcorp S.A., 137 F. Supp 2d 502, 508, (S.D.N.Y. 2001).

1208 Sterlin v. Mayflower Hotel Corp., 93 A.2d 107, 114 (Del. 1952).

1209 Weinberger v. UOP, Inc., 457 A.2d 701, 703-704, 714 (Del. 1983).

1210 *Id.* at 711.

concerns a specific action or conduct they have been specifically asked to ratify.[1211] The burden to prove a lack of entire fairness will shift back to the plaintiff.[1212] Courts have, however, put in doubt the independence of directors once a controlling shareholder is involved. Only the interjection of an independent and diligent negotiating committee between constituent corporations with actual bargaining power to reject the transaction would put the burden of proof on the plaintiff.[1213] The legislative intent is that qualifications to the entire fairness test apply only to short-form mergers[1214] and to tender offers of majority shareholders directed at the subsidiary's shareholders.[1215]

Only in exceptional cases have shareholders become subject to the fiduciary *duty of care*, such as when the controlling shareholder knowingly sold control to a "looter" who planned to expropriate the corporate assets for himself.[1216] Again, the plaintiff needs to plead the relevant facts, including the seller's knowledge about the buyer's intentions.[1217]

Courts have underscored that even shareholders subject to fiduciary duties can vote in their own interest. They are limited by the fiduciary duty owed to other shareholders, but it is not objectionable that their motives may be for personal profit.[1218] The overall objective of the controlling shareholder's fiduciary obligation is not to bar the controlling shareholder from acting in his own self-interest, but to assure that the interests of the corporation and fellow shareholders are also served.[1219] Therefore, even controlling shareholders have the right to exercise wide liberality of judgment. They can admit per-

1211 Gantler v. Stephens, 965 A.2d 695, 713 (Del. 2009).

1212 Kahn v. Lynch Commc'n Sys., Inc., 638 A.2d 1110, 1115, 1117 (Del. 1994); Emerald Partners v. Berlin, 726 A.2d 1215, 1222 et seq. (1999); Anabtawi & Stout, 60 Stan. L. Rev. 1255, 1266 (2008).

1213 Kahn v. Lynch Commc'n Sys., Inc., 638 A.2d 1110, 1115, 1117 (Del. 1994); In re Cysive, Inc. S'holders Litig., 836 A.2d 531, 547 et seq. (Del. Ch. 2003).

1214 Glasman v. Unocal Exploration Corp., 777 A.2d 242, 247 et seq. (Del. 2001): holding that the parent company that exercises its right under the short-form merger provision to rid itself of the minority shareholders in the subsidiary does not have to establish the entire fairness for its actions, the exclusive remedy for the minority shareholders remaining the appraisal remedy, the reason being the legislative intent in providing a short-form merger procedure being frustrated if the parent corporation were subject to the entire fairness review standard.

1215 In re Siliconix, Inc. S'holder Litig., 2001 WL 716787, 6 et seq. (Del. Ch. 2001): The applicable standard to tender offers is the standard of a fair price, which requires that shareholders confronted by a tender offer are free of coercion to accept the offer or not and the information provided to them has to be free of any violation of disclosure obligations. The entire fairness test, in contrast, may not be applied, as a tender offer involves a decision of the single shareholder, who has to decide whether to tender or not. Therefore an involved interested party of the transaction may only exercise impact on one of the constituent corporations, the acquiring corporation in making its purchase decision, while not being able to exercise impact on the other corporation, as the target corporation is not confronted with a corporate decision because targeted are its shareholders.

1216 Abraham v. Emerson Radio Corp., 901 A.2d 751, 762 (Del. Ch. 2006).

1217 *Id.*

1218 Bershad v. Curtiss-Wright Corp., 535 A.2d 840 (Del. 1987).

1219 Cox & Hazen, Corporations § 11.11, 253 (2003).

sonal profit into the motives determining their decision, as long as their advantage is not obtained at the expense of fellow shareholders.[1220]

Courts have remained reserved in making minority shareholders with shareholdings below 10 percent subject to fiduciary obligations.[1221] Courts have set a high bar for finding that a minority shareholder has exercised *actual* control. A minority shareholder needs to control such a large block that it represents the majority of the shares likely to be voted, taking into account the rational apathy of the remaining shareholders.[1222] The same applies to the *collective* exercise of control. For reasons involving § 13(d) SEA, it will be hard to prove that several investors are jointly active in the same corporation. In addition, the potential conflicts of interest of active shareholders appear rather modest in contrast to the constellations involving determinative votes of controlling shareholders, which have been recognized as raising enhanced scrutiny.[1223] Active shareholders, who usually hold stakes below 10 percent and officially act only in parallel with fellow investors, will neither fall under the notion of control, nor fulfill the means of any of the accredited factional constellations. Liability of active shareholders under the current fiduciary duty doctrine is therefore in practice of limited relevance.

(2) Proposed extension of fiduciary duties

Based on the increased impact of active shareholders on management's (transaction) decisions, which often involves fellow shareholders and the use of informal means, different approaches have been proposed to extend fiduciary duties to minority shareholders.

In 1958, *Berle* mentioned the lack of a well-developed notion of control responding to the then present conditions. He considered its extension to comprise *working control*, referring to minority shareholders, and the quasi-political process to mobilize and induce sufficient other shareholders to commonly elect directors. Working control required a close relationship to the board that allowed the controlling shareholders to

1220 Heil v. Standard Gas & Elec. Co., 151 A. 303, 304 (1930); Tanzer v. Int'l General Indus., Inc., 379 A.2d 1121, 1123 (Del. 1977).

1221 An exception are the fiduciary duties applied to shareholders pursuing a derivative suit representing the corporation and its remaining shareholders: Whitten v. Dabney, 154 P. 312 (1915); Shelton v. Pargo 582 F.2d 1298 (Ct. App. 4th Circ. 1978); Clarke v. Greenberg, 296 N.Y. 146, 71 N.E.2d 443 (1947); Young v. Higbee Co., 324 U.S. 204 (1945); Wied v. Valhi, Inc. 466 A.2d 9 (1983).

1222 Smith v. Alantic Props., Inc., 422 N.E.2d 798, 801 et seq. (Mass. App. Ct. 1981): pointing away from the broad language in Donahue v. Rodd Electrotype Co., 367 Mass. 578, 593 (1975) and taking account of the moderations in Wilkes v. Springside Nursing Home, Inc., 370 Mass. 842, 848 et seq. (1976): demanding the weighing of the business interests for both sides of shareholders. It did not confirm violation of fiduciary duties, but rather adhered to standard of fair dealing applicable to nonfiduciary business situations and majority shareholders, which should also apply to minority shareholders controlling on a particular issue. The minority shareholder should therefore be able to follow the course he or she thinks is best without intending to or in fact being inimical to the corporate interests. *See* Hetherington, 1972 DUKE L.J. 921, 944, Anabtawi & Stout, 60 STAN. L. REV. 1255, 1297 (2008).

1223 Kahan & Rock, 155 U. PA. L. REV. 1021, 1074 (2007).

approve or even choose the slate of candidates for the next director election. Considering that shareholders follow administrative proposals in specific corporate matters, the ability to impact the proxy machinery accordingly coupled with a substantial minority stake allowed them to elect directors.[1224]

In 2008, Anabtawi and Stout presented a similar call for adaption to today's realities involving active shareholders, based on their growing impact and their potentially deviating interests.[1225] They proposed to extend fiduciary duties to active shareholders to prevent them from acting opportunistically when controlling specific management decisions as opposed to ad hoc solutions.[1226] The current approach, they allege, is based on two assumptions that have been eclipsed: minority shareholders lack power due to proxy voting procedures and rational apathy,[1227] which makes concerns about possibly oppressive propensities superfluous,[1228] and shareholders pursue the concomitant interest to improve corporate performance to raise the stock price.[1229] Today, however, many minority shareholders become active and are anything but powerless. They exercise immense impact on the administration. Their increasing power allows active minority shareholders not only to maximize the targeted corporation's stock price, but also to pursue deviating interests based, amongst others, on (financial) instruments or pricier investment in the other constituent corporation of a transaction.[1230] Fiduciary duties, especially the duty of loyalty, would allow for the restriction of such opportunistic behavior.[1231] Therefore, so their allegation goes, a latent duty of loyalty should apply as soon as shareholders manage to successfully influence a company's actions with regard to a particular issue.[1232] In addition, the transaction or strategy would need to bear a material, personal economic interest for the shareholder(s). The latter prophylactic notion is fact intensive and already applies when a shareholder does not share the benefits with the rest of the shareholders.[1233] As a consequence, this approach expands both the notion of *control* and the *circumstances* under which a threat to the corporation and shareholders is assumed.[1234]

This approach properly reflects the increasing impact of active shareholders based on the overcoming of collective action problems and the use of informal means, even though the necessary efforts regarding the legal barriers applying to many shareholder means are still substantial. However, the extension of the *control* notion to circumstances apart from the shareholders right to vote[1235] seems unnecessary. The practice of share-

---

1224 Berle, 58 Colum. L. Rev. 1212, 1213 (1958).
1225 Anabtawi & Stout, 60 Stan. L. Rev. 1293 (2008).
1226 Anabtawi & Stout, 60 Stan. L. Rev. 1255 (2008).
1227 *Id.* at 1267 et seq., 1275.
1228 Hetherington, DUKE L.J. 921, 933 (1972).
1229 Anabtawi & Stout, 60 Stan. L. Rev. 1255, 1268 (2008).
1230 *Id.* at 1261, 1284-92.
1231 *Id.* at 1294 et seq.
1232 *Id.* at 1297 et seq.
1233 *Id.* at 1299.
1234 *Id.* at 1295.
1235 *Id.* at 1297 et seq.

holder activism has demonstrated that the most effective means of active shareholders is the credible threat of or an actual proxy fight to impact the composition of the board. Once this impact exists, active shareholders can even impact specific transaction decisions mainly by referring to the possible impact on the board composition. As far as both argue that their approach will not promote excessive litigation,[1236] this may be true. Nevertheless, the decisive argument is not the limited number of shareholders making use of the relevant means of litigation or threatening campaigns.[1237] This contradicts their argument of a significant increase in the number of shareholders impacting management decisions in such a way that revision of fiduciary duties is necessary. Rather, the number of control cases under the expanded *control* notion is expected to remain the same for the *supra* mentioned reason.

As far as the expansion of the relevant factual circumstances is concerned, the approach stands in strong contrast to decades-applicable doctrine. Corporate investors, whether holding a majority or minority stake, may generally vote merely to further their own interest by maximizing the value of their shares.[1238] It is therefore not the impact resulting from control as such, but only the realization of selfish decisions *to the detriment of the rest of the shareholders*, which fiduciary duties aim to prevent. Anabtawi and Stout's approach, however, restricts this notion. It only allows shareholders to pursue material self-interest in the transaction if all benefits are shared with the other shareholders.[1239] This prophylactic standard might seem appealing at first glance. At second glance, however, it represents an overly broad approach. It implies a standard of protection that all shareholders have to share in the benefits of a transaction. This does not conform to the corporate approach to self-interested transactions. It aims to protect the corporation and its shareholders from the harm resulting from such transactions instead of completely prohibiting them, as in agency and trust law.[1240] This has been the corporate law approach applicable to directors and officers. It is not convincing that the standard should be even stricter for minority shareholders, especially when taking into account the efforts confronting shareholders who seek to actually impact a management decision.

Finally, mechanisms developed over time impose relevant limitations likely to restrict even opportunistic behavior of minority shareholders. These are in particular the disclosure obligations under the federal securities laws, which are efficiently complemented by the proxy and general antifraud provision. They ensure case-specific disclosure of all material information, including possible conflicts of interest based on (financial) instruments. These have to be set in the context of the majority-voting requirement mentioned by Anabtawi/Stout, as well as the issue of collective action not applicable to the administration. They make a corresponding extension of the fiduciary duties and the possibly resulting litigation unnecessary. It seems therefore reasonable to restrict share-

1236 *Id.* at 1303 et seq.

1237 *Id.* at 1300 et seq.

1238 Fletcher, Cyclopedia of the Law of Corporations 12B § 5713 (2010).

1239 Anabtawi & Stout, 60 Stan. L. Rev. 1255, 1299 et seq. (2008).

1240 *Id.* at 1264.

holder fiduciary duties to transactions involving potential self-interest of controlling shareholders coupled with the remaining shareholders' inability to express their will on the transaction.

iii) (More) Legal restraints and transaction activism constellations

The disclosure regime including its antifraud rules and the range of remedies under securities law has, despite contrary discussions amongst legal scholars,[1241] efficiently hindered shareholders from pursuing deviating interests to become active to the detriment of the remaining shareholders. The deficits in sufficiently addressing current (financial) instruments have, however, already been recognized by the SEC, among others, in its amicus curiae letter in *CSX v. TCI* of June 4, 2008. They are subject to reforms proposed by then SEC Chairman Schapiro. The hope is that the planned reform will efficiently tackle the challenge to provide increased transparency and therefore legal certainty in dealing with (financial) instruments. Under corporate law, the current fiduciary duty regime restricts potentially disloyal behavior of corporate actors. For active minority shareholders pursuing deviating interests it will only be of limited relevance.

Both consequences are also relevant to the use of knowledge about distinct transaction activism constellations based on the generally underlying interests of shareholders and the administration to distinguish opportunistic from beneficial transaction activism. The disclosure regime applies independently of whether an actual conflict of interest becomes relevant, for instance during a specific transaction activism engagement. It only requires the disclosure of all material information to allow shareholders to be able to draw relevant conclusions for their investment decisions. In this context, the mentioned distinction may be helpful for the remaining shareholders of the targeted corporation. However, it will not be able to help increase the efficiency of the disclosure regime by uncovering active shareholders with diverging interests. The narrowly interpreted impact prerequisite of the fiduciary duty regime will exclude most of the activities of active minority shareholders from becoming subject to the conflicts of interest notion. A general distinction between constellations of desirable and opportunistic transaction activism for conflicts of interest as a trigger of the fiduciary regime remains irrelevant, therefore. The same applies to the determination of potential fiduciary duty violations to the detriment of the corporation and fellow investors or a sole impact on the burden of proof.

e) Transaction activism and underlying corporate governance theories

The question remaining is whether by overcoming issues of collective action and by using informal and formal means to impact fundamental or management's transaction

1241 Briggs, 32 J. Corp. L. 681, 707 (2007): proposes to amend the proxy rules on the disclosure side to comprise derivatives, short positions, debt and other obligations ... and their practical effects and to consider derivatives under Schedule 13D for the ownership quorum triggering the disclosure regime as well as items to be disclosed.

decisions, active shareholders are usurping management tasks and therefore not acting according to underlying corporate governance theories.

Despite the prevailing theory of shareholder primacy, shareholders in U.S. corporations are faced by a reality of director primacy based on *insufficient incentives* and *collective action issues* as well as *legal obstacles*. These keep shareholders from effectively exercising their franchise. As a consequence, shareholders, in practice, do not exercise the impact that is theoretically attributed to them by underlying corporate governance theory. The question in regards to active shareholders impacting *specific* corporate decisions is whether they close the gap between practice and theory or cross this line and usurp management tasks?

Active shareholders successfully engage in transaction activism. Hedge funds in particular usually hold a sufficiently large number of shares since they invest mainly in an undiversified manner and therefore take larger stakes in one corporation, allowing them to profit significantly from a rising stock price of the targeted corporation. Furthermore, institutional active shareholders usually have a sufficient number of like-minded colleagues, who are willing to take their side when it is necessary and worth the effort. Finally, the concentrated and undiversified investment of hedge funds allows them to bear the costs necessary to hire lawyers to circumvent possibly relevant legal barriers or proper proxy fights. As a consequence, active shareholders have the necessary *incentives* to become active; they are able to overcome *collective action issues* as well as *legal and practical restrictions*.[1242]

While overcoming the issue of collective action inherent in a shareholder structure characterized by freefloat is broadly welcomed and contributes to closing the gap between theory and practice, it alone does not characterize transaction activism. Rather, the overcoming of legal and practical restrictions, including the ineffective nomination and election process, the comprehensive and costly proxy rules regime, the limited number of direct votes on corporate (transaction) decisions, and the limited shareholder impact on the corporate decision-making process in general, have been traced with skepticism.

The initial question concentrates therefore on the use of informal means by active shareholders. The answer to the initial discussion about the ultimate authority in a corporation referred to the shareholders. Active shareholders applying formal and informal means to overcome legal and factual obstacles to impact transaction decisions are, under the principal-agent doctrine, not usurping management's authority. Rather, the surprise about the impact shareholders can actually exercise is a result of the decades long practice of director-primacy. Based on legal and factual obstacles, the impact of dispersed shareholders was very much limited and prevented the success of several attempts by shareholders to overcome these limitations, the last of which represented the market for corporate control. While takeover attempts have been successfully defeated by the anti-takeover devices of the administrations, shareholder activism can hardly be restricted from the administrative side. This is the reason for the allegations of inconsistency between shareholder activism and underlying theories of corporate governance.

1242 *Id.* at 711 et seq.

Most importantly, by overcoming legal and practical obstacles, also with the help of informal means, active shareholders can effectively use their franchise, especially in the many constellations not providing shareholders with direct means to participate in the corporate decision-making process. The threat to or the actual use of the shareholder franchise represents the most frequently used and efficient means for active shareholders to control specific decisions of the administration. It allows shareholders to exercise control over board members, who either make the decision themselves or have to control the responsible management. Its effective use therefore allows the more active among the active shareholders to reduce the agency issues resulting from the separation of ownership and control.[1243] The use of informal means remains either below the impact of the formally provided means (amongst others personal contact) or it supports the formally provided channels of shareholder power. The latter involves the few cases in which a shareholder vote is provided on a specific corporate (transaction) decision, and, more often, the use of the shareholder franchise to hold members of the administration accountable. As a consequence, active shareholders do not usurp management tasks.

A separate question is, however, whether the increasing separation of economic ownership and (retained) control rights based on the use of (financial) instruments and the increasing impact of institutional investors as intermediaries amends *Berle & Means'* fundamental assumption that owners should be in control.

III) Preliminary results regarding transaction activism

1) Means of active shareholders

The analysis of U.S.-American law in the context of transaction activism has proven the following: apart from collective action issues, the impact of shareholders on corporate transaction decisions through formal means is very limited. Shareholders have the right to participate in corporate decision-making by approving the decision only in a very limited number of fundamental transactions, mainly some merger constellations. The shareholders' initiation rights in fundamental and indeed in all transaction decisions are limited. They are restricted to precatory shareholder proposals. Even if the shareholder meeting approves the proposal by a significant percentage, the administration decides whether to implement the proposal. The result is similar for shareholder means granting them the opportunity to *indirectly* impact these decisions through the use of effective accountability means applicable to the responsible administration. Corporate statutes and securities laws do not provide shareholders with the means necessary to effectively remove members of the administration who are responsible for opportunistic transaction decisions. The nomination and election rules and their recent and expected amendments have for a long time effectively kept and will continue to keep shareholders from effectively exercising their franchise. The minimum mandatory proxy access rule, recently adopted on the federal level (and currently not in force), granting shareholders access

1243 Dent, 1989 Wis. L. Rev. 881, 882 (1989).

who have held a three-percent stake for more than three years, has limited the expectations that effectiveness will be significantly increased. In addition, the proxy rules relevant for direct and indirect impact have been opened by granting exceptions or even restricting their applicability through the 1992 and the millennium amendments. However, the successful use of a proxy contest is still very costly and time consuming. The communication amongst shareholders is still limited by them, which reinforces existing issues of collective action.

Active shareholders engage in transaction activism based on a qualified minority position and often using less costly informal means. Both combined reduce the costs of the efforts while allowing them to benefit from their efforts. This provides them with the necessary incentives. Besides overcoming their own lack of incentives, they often convince the remainder of shareholders to join them in their use of informal means. Due to the shareholder structure of U.S. corporations, the involvement of a sufficient number of other shareholders requires a correspondingly strong involvement of the active shareholders. Active shareholders have often had the opportunity to convince fellow institutional shareholders to join them in a promising campaign. Very often, they start their campaigns with the low-cost means of private conversations with the relevant members of the administration. Only if these are unsuccessful will active shareholders under U.S. law focus on means involving shareholder votes, which either directly or indirectly impact the transaction decisions and/or involve the public. Especially in transaction constellations granting shareholders useful *direct* impact, they use informal means like *just-vote-no* campaigns or other exceptions from the proxy rules to get around the still pricey and time-consuming proxy contest. Such a proceeding allows them to communicate in a less expensive and less time consuming way with management as well as with other shareholders in order to engage them in the campaign. The hiring of expensive lawyers may be necessary in many cases, however. Regarding the exercise of *indirect* impact in the majority of the remaining transaction activism constellations via the shareholder franchise, active shareholders of U.S. corporations pursue a similar approach as far as their means are concerned. Accordingly, active shareholders until recently used a withhold-vote campaign absent a proxy access rule and will most likely continue to do so even if the new minimum mandatory proxy access rule again comes into force. Shareholders need to have held their stakes for at least three years, which is usually not the case for active shareholders. However, instead of aiming for the removal of administrative members in order to impact a transaction decision, they prefer to only make credible threats. It prevents them from becoming an insider subject to fiduciary duties. The (threat to use the) shareholder franchise, despite its obstacles, is therefore the most relevant of the shareholder tools for active shareholders.

2) Efficiency of existing legal limitations

The legal regime relies on disclosure to restrict the opportunistic behavior of (active) shareholders under U.S. law and less on the fiduciary duty regime and other constraining provisions. It focuses on qualified minority investors' general obligation to disclose extended circumstances, which could be the basis of a conflict of interest. Similarly, shareholders engaging formally in an upcoming shareholder vote have to meet comprehensive notification requirements. Surprisingly, neither triggers nor line items seem to cover the (financial) instruments possibly responsible for the conflicts of interest of active shareholders. However, especially the *interest* and *purpose* items under the proxy statement and the beneficial ownership report and the *material* qualifiers of the anti-fraud rules assure the efficient disclosure of the circumstances responsible for conflicts of interest. Contrary to the initial assumption, the traditional disclosure regime largely prevents active shareholders from pursuing special interests.

In addition, the amendments of the proxy rules in 1992 and 2000 have effectively mitigated the prohibitive character of the proxy regime and simultaneously increased control over shareholders aiming to circumvent the above-mentioned disclosure regimes. They have reduced the time- and cost-related burdens of shareholders' activities in relation to an upcoming shareholder vote or an election. Active shareholders especially use the (additional) exceptions from the proxy rules and have developed efficient ways to use them to impact shareholder votes or elections while preventing the costs and loss of time still related to a proxy contest. However, even by providing exceptions, the proxy rules ensure that abusive techniques used to pursue special interests barely have a chance because of the way the exempted actions or solicitations have to be exercised. Accordingly, the potential to abuse the very effective and frequently used low-cost means of *just-vote-no campaigns* to pursue special interest purposes is restricted by the proxy rule regime. It assures that soliciting materials directly provided to selected shareholders address only a very limited number of shareholders. For most campaigns of active shareholders, this alone is not sufficient. Another relevant exception allows shareholders to publicly state how and why they will vote on an upcoming issue without soliciting proxy authority. This will also inform the administration pursuing a shareholder-enhancing transaction of possibly deviating interests of shareholders. The absence of proxy authority solicitation will simultaneously reduce the impact of active shareholders. The third exemption similarly allows solicitations as long as shareholders neither solicit proxy authority nor have the intent to get involved in a proxy contest. Shareholders choosing this exception significantly reduce their bargaining power with the administration. The pre-filing exceptions of pure solicitation materials preceding the proxy statement and ballot require that the solicitation material be simultaneously filed with the SEC. All these exceptions have the effect of channeling the activities that aim to circumvent the proxy rules and therefore to keep them under control.

3) Separation of transaction activism constellations

Based on the general underlying interests of shareholders and the administration, it is possible to distinguish transaction activism constellations, which more often involve desirable transaction activism from constellations involving opportunistic activism. However, this distinction is, contrary to the initial thesis, only of limited relevance for the efficiency of the legal regime that prevents opportunistic shareholder behavior. Potential liability for opportunistic behavior of active shareholders based on the violation of fiduciary duties fails due to the control notion. The effective disclosure regime, however, links to the actual interests or purpose of transactions of the concerned shareholder. It leaves it therefore to the fellow shareholders to draw the necessary conclusions from their actions. Only they may fall back on the distinction in deciding whether to support their campaign.

4) Transaction activism and underlying governance theories

Finally, active shareholders have strong enough incentives to counter opportunistic administrative transaction decisions. They can overcome collective action issues and other factual and legal barriers restricting the impact of shareholders. Making use of their shareholder franchise to indirectly impact a transaction decision by overcoming collective action issues and numerous legal and factual barriers related to the nomination and election process and a proxy contest allows active shareholders to hold the responsible individuals accountable. Similarly, active shareholders with sufficient incentives to overcome collective action issues and to get around obstacles inherent in the proxy regime may be able to exercise direct impact on fundamental transaction decisions.

The exercise of direct impact on fundamental transaction decisions closes the gap between the theory that shareholders as owners have an actual say on a fundamental issue and their practice of primarily following administrative recommendations, whether shareholder-enhancing or not. The exercise of (indirect) impact on management transaction decisions, mainly via the threat to or the actual use of the shareholder franchise, conforms to the prevailing theory of shareholder primacy. According to it, the shareholders may call the shots not only in regards to the interests to be pursued by a corporation, but also in regards to who has the final say in the relationship between the shareholders and administration. As (economic) owners, shareholders have delegated their decision rights to the board of directors while maintaining the control right restricted to the members of the board. Accordingly, they should use their control right to prevent opportunistic administrational transaction decisions. The use of means like the threat of or the actual use of the shareholder franchise to correct opportunistic administrational decisions therefore seems foreign to the long-term practice of director primacy. It conforms, however, to the underlying corporate governance theories. The necessary financial means would be reduced and its availability extended by adopting the proposed amendments to the nomination and election rules.

IV) Transaction activism under German law

1) Authority distribution in the transaction context

The corporate statute provides that the *management board* generally manages the affairs of the corporation, § 77 (1) AktG.[1244] The management comprises all legal and factual activities that aim for the realization of the corporate purpose.[1245] However, the management board not only must tend to the daily operations of the corporation,[1246] particularly corporate earnings.[1247] It is also responsible for the direction § 76 (1) and therefore the strategic leadership of the corporation,[1248] including corporate planning and coordination.[1249] This involves transaction decisions, like the purchase of other corporations or the sale of corporate branches. In contrast to daily management questions, the entire management board must deal with fundamental management tasks.[1250] The management board is generally free to act as it see fit; the instructions of the supervisory board or the shareholder meeting are generally non-binding.[1251] This is reflected in the business judgment rule, § 93 (1) sent. 2, which under German law also establishes the presumption that management board members have acted in accordance with their fiduciary duties.[1252]

The *supervisory board*, as the administrative control organ, is generally excluded from management tasks like strategic decisions. It controls the directorial management tasks in the sense of § 76 (1)[1253], § 111 (1), (4) sent. 1. The supervisory board controls their legality as well as their usefulness and efficiency.[1254] The separation between management and control is, however, lessened through the general consultation task of the supervisory board regarding planning future corporate policy. According to the Federal Civil Court of Justice, the supervisory board can shape the entrepreneurial activity of the management board by exercising preventive control.[1255] Since the management board needs to convince the supervisory board of its entrepreneurial plans, the supervisory board has the right and the duty to

1244 Sections without further specifications in this Subpart four of Part two relate to the AktG.
1245 Mülbert, in: Großkomm AktG, 2008, § 119 mn.40.
1246 Kropff, AktG 1965, 95 et seq.
1247 Kort, in: Großkomm AktG, 2006, Vor § 76 mn.10; Raisch, Unternehmensrecht Vol. 2, 1974, 43.
1248 Spindler, in: MüKo AktG, 2008, § 76 mn.16.
1249 Kort, in: Großkomm AktG, 2006, § 76 mn.38; Mertens, in: KöKo AktG, 1996, § 76 mn.5.
1250 Kort, in: Großkomm AktG, 2006, § 77 mn.42; Mertens/Cahn, in: KöKo AktG, 2010, § 77 mn.16; Spindler, in: MüKo AktG, 2008, § 77 mn.62.
1251 Kort, in: Großkomm AktG, 2006, Vor § 76 mnn.8, 13.
1252 Von Hein, Die Rezeption US-amerikanischen Gesellschaftsrechts in Deutschland, 2008, 919 et seq.
1253 Drygalla, in: Schmidt/Lutter, AktG, 2010, § 111 mn.11.
1254 BGH, Urt. v. 25.03.1991, Az.: II ZR 188/89; NJW 1991, 1830 (1831); Drygalla, in: Schmidt/Lutter, AktG, 2010, § 111 mnn.20–21: referring primarily to legality and regularity; Hopt/Roth, in: Großkomm AktG, 2006, § 111 mnn.301 et seq.: demonstrating convincingly that the regularity of a management task has besides the criteria of legality and usefullness and efficiency no additional content.
1255 BGH, Urt. v. 21.04.1997, Az.: II ZR 175/95, NJW 1997, 1926 (1928)-ARAG/Garmenbeck.

advise the management board on the issue.[1256] More specifically, the veto right under § 111 (4) sent. 2 provides the supervisory board with an important means of preventive control. The articles of incorporation or the supervisory board can determine "certain kinds of corporate actions" which require the approval of the supervisory board. These transactions have to be specific and of a fundamental character for the corporation, as opposed to general management tasks. They need to have a significant impact on the corporate assets as well as the financial and profit situation of the corporation.[1257] The most important veto rights of the supervisory board concern corporate consolidations and the acquisition or sale of companies.[1258] These transactions either generally require supervisory board approval, as they exceed customary business operations, or the need to approve depends on the financial volume of the transaction.[1259] In practice, the purchase or sale of corporate divisions or subsidiaries is contained in all veto catalogues.[1260] Neither the consultation right nor approval requirements grant the supervisory board a right to initiate management tasks or to issue instructions on them.[1261] A denial of the approval does not even impact the authority of the management board to represent the company in such a transaction. The management board can only be held liable under § 93 (2) for ignoring a denied, but required, supervisory board approval[1262] if sued by the supervisory board, § 112.

Shareholders, as economic owners, are generally excluded from the corporate decision-making process on management matters, § 119 (2). However, the shareholder meeting has to approve recurring, structural, and fundamental measures, as laid down in § 119 (1) or by statute. For a shareholder meeting's vote suitable and *repetitive* topics concern the exoneration of the management or supervisory board, § 120, or the use of the net profit, § 174.[1263] Individual cases with regard to administrative accountability relate to the dismissal of supervisory board members, § 103 (1), the withdrawal of confidence in management board members, § 84 (3), the enforcement of indemnification claims, § 147 (1), or the appointment of a special auditor, § 142 (1).[1264] Moreover, the shareholder meeting has to approve transactions of *fundamental* character. Only in a limited number of scenarios does the shareholder meeting have subsidiary management authority. Either the management board asks for its binding decision, § 119 (2),[1265] or the supervisory board denies its approval according to § 111 (4) sent. 2 and the management board demands that the share-

1256 Drygalla, in: Schmidt/Lutter, AktG, 2010, § 111, mnn.4, 18 et seq.; Habersack, in: MüKo AktG, 2008, § 111 mn.100.

1257 Drygalla, in: Schmidt/Lutter, AktG, § 111 mn.56; Habersack, in: MüKo AktG, 2008, § 111 mnn.106-109.

1258 Hopt/Roth, in: Großkomm AktG, 2006, § 111 mn.654.

1259 Habersack, in: MüKo AktG, 2008, § 111 mn.110.

1260 Hopt/Roth, in: Großkomm AktG, 2006, § 111 mn.654.

1261 Bork, ZGR 1989, 1 (21): notes that the supervisory board has no right to direct or veto the management tasks of the management board, the supervisory board may only disapprove management tasks, decide ad-hoc on approval requirements or take personnel consequences; Habersack, in: MüKo AktG, 2008, § 111 mn.97.

1262 Drygalla, in: Schmidt/Lutter, AktG, 2010, § 111 mn.61.

1263 Hüffer, AktG, § 119 mn.11.

1264 Mülbert, in: Großkomm AktG, 2008, § 119 mn.39.

1265 *Id.* at mnn.38, 54.

holder meeting approves it, § 111 (4) sent. 3.[1266] Both can apply to management's transaction decisions. In addition, shareholders have to approve a small number of management decisions in the transaction context. They mark the dividing line between the management competency and fundamental corporate decisions[1267] and need to have a structurally significant impact on the corporation, as determined by *Holzmüller/Gelatine*[1268].[1269] It lies in the management board's hands to submit them to the shareholder meeting for approval.[1270] Finally, § 119 (2) concerns only the management board's *decision* authority.[1271] It leaves room for shareholders to discuss management issues relating to a topic of the shareholder meeting's agenda. With a recommending resolution, shareholders can indirectly comment on the work or a specific decision of the management board.[1272] Such an unrequested resolution is not, however, binding on the management board.[1273]

2) General formal shareholder means

a) Initiation rights

Shareholders have several ways to initiate a corporate decision or measure. Regarding an upcoming shareholder meeting, *each* shareholder may launch a *countermotion* regarding an administrative proposal. A countermotion relates to a specific agenda topic and has content that is contrary to or deviates from that of the targeted administrative proposal.[1274] The countermotion has to reach the corporation at least 14 days before the shareholder meeting to oblige the management board to make it, its reasoning, and a possible administrative statement accessible, § 126 (1), to credit institutes, shareholder associations, shareholders, and members of the supervisory board, § 125 (1) – (3). Only illegal or abusive countermotions do not have to be made accessible, § 126 (2). Countermotions can also be launched as late as during the shareholder meeting, since they do not need to be announced prior to the shareholder meeting, § 124 (4) sent. 2.

Furthermore, shareholders can also initiate shareholder resolutions or discussions that do not represent countermotions without their prior publication, § 124 (4) sent. 2. A shareholder may propose a shareholder resolution even right before the shareholder meeting. The motion needs to be launched during the shareholder meeting and to relate

1266 Mülbert, in: Großkomm AktG, 2008, § 119 mn.43: however not being of practical significance; Drygalla, in: Schmidt/Lutter, AktG, 2010, § 111 mn.60.
1267 Mertens, in: KöKo AktG, 1996, § 76 mn.3.
1268 BGH, Urt. v. 25.02.1982, Az.: II ZR 174/80, NJW 1982, 1703-Holzmüller; BGH, Urt. v. 26.04.2004, Az.: II ZT 155/02, NZG 2004, 571-Gelatine.
1269 Hüffer, AktG, § 119 mnn.5, 16 et seq.
1270 Spindler, in: MüKo AktG, 2008, § 77 mn.7.
1271 Mülbert, in: Großkomm AktG, 2008, § 119 mn.39.
1272 Eckardt, in: Geßler et al., AktG, 1973, § 119 mn.13; Hüffer, § 119 mn.11; Mülbert, in: Großkomm AktG, 2008, § 119 mn.39; Spindler, in: Schmidt/Lutter, AktG, 2010, § 119 mn.14; Zöllner, in: KöKo AktG, 1985, § 119 mn.26.
1273 Eckardt, in: Geßler et al., AktG, 1973, § 119 mn.31; Habersack, Großkomm AktG, 2008, § 82 mn.27; Mülbert, in: Großkomm AktG, 2008, § 119 mn.60.
1274 Hüffer, AktG, § 126 mn.2.

to an agenda topic, § 124 (4) sent. 2, 2nd alt.[1275] Apart from countermotions, these motions usually complement or amend administrative motions.[1276] An example represents the demand to directly appoint a special auditor, § 142 (1). Without a prior announcement, it can be requested during the topic that administrative members be discharged if the concerned periods are identical.[1277] Reconsidering that § 119 (2) grants the management board only a *decision* competence, the shareholders can also discuss agenda-related management matters and comment on them via a recommending resolution.[1278]

In this context, it is controversial whether shareholders can initiate the removal of or withdrawal of confidence in a member of the supervisory or management board in relation to the topic of discharging administrative members, § 120. Some[1279] support such an opportunity, as long as the reason lies in the time period subject to the discharge. They argue that shareholders have no specific need to be protected, which would make specific publication necessary.[1280] The similar situation of initiating the removal of an administrative member in relation to the topic presenting the report of a special auditor has also been recognized to not requiring separate publication.[1281] Furthermore, they assert that the withdrawal of confidence in a management board member does not yet represent the final decision. Rather, the supervisory board takes it.[1282] The more convincing approach,[1283] however, declines the opportunity to have either motion initiated according to § 124 (4) sent. 2. Its proponents defend it by arguing that the withdrawal of confidence constitutes more than the refusal to discharge a member of the management board. It allows the supervisory board to remove the concerned member. Furthermore, those authorized to vote for others would often not know how to vote in such a situation. As a consequence, the number of votes cast would be significantly reduced and would likely result in accidental majorities.[1284] Removal tactics therefore require prior publication under § 124.

Finally, shareholders can initiate the addition and publication of an agenda topic for an upcoming shareholder meeting, § 122 (2). This right is subsidiary. It only applies if an intended shareholder motion may not be dealt with under the topics announced by the

1275 Eckardt, in: Geßler et al., AktG, 1973, Vor § 118 mn.53 et seq., § 122 mn.11, § 126 mnn.1 et seq.

1276 Marsch-Barner, in: Marsch-Barner/Schäfer, Hdb börsennotierte AG, 2005, § 34 mn.89.

1277 Hüffer, AktG, § 142 mnn.9, 10; Marsch-Barner, in: Marsch-Barner/Schäfer, in: Hdb börsennotierte AG, 2005, § 34 mn.89; Werner, in: Großkomm AktG, 2008, § 124 mn.87.

1278 Mülbert, in: Großkomm AktG, 2008, § 119 mn.39.

1279 Hüffer, in: AktG, 2012, § 124 mn. 19; Willamowski, in: Spindler/Stilz, AktG, 2007, § 124 mn.18; Zöllner, in: KöKo AktG, 1985, § 124 mn.15; Kubis, in: MüKo AktG, 2004, § 124 mn.73: only when a special audit report has been announced to be submitted.

1280 Ziemons, in: Schmidt/Lutter, AktG, 2010, § 124 mn.60.

1281 Kubis, in: MüKo AktG, 2004, § 124 mn.73; Rieckers, in; Spindler/Stilz, AktG, 2010, § 124 mn.56; Werner, in: Großkomm AktG, 2008, § 124 mn.89,.

1282 In the context of § 84 (3) AktG: Ziemons, in: Schmidt/Lutter, AktG, 2010, § 124 mn.60.

1283 LG München I, Urt. v. 28.07.2005, Az.: 5 HKO 10485/04, ZIP 2005, 1598; Drinhausen, in: Hölters, AktG, 2011, § 124 mn. 24; Hopt/Roth, MüKo AktG, 2006, § 103 mn.12; Kubis, in: MüKo, 2004, § 124 mn.73; Werner, in Großkomm AktG, 2008, § 124 mn.89.

1284 Regarding § 103 (1) AktG: Hopt/Roth, in; Großkomm AktG, 2006, § 103 mn.12 n.49; Notthoff, WiB 1997, 848 (850); with regard to § 84 (3) AktG: Werner, in: Großkomm AktG, 2008, § 124 mn.89.

administration according to § 124 (4) sent. 2, 2nd alt. or § 126.[1285] For at least three months and throughout the decision on the request, the shareholder(s) need to have held and continue to hold a stake of at least five percent of the shares or of Euro 500,000 of the share capital. Since the ARUG, the initiation of an additional topic and its publication must be requested up to 31 days prior to the shareholder meeting, § 122 (2) sent. 3. The topic needs to relate to a matter authorized for the shareholder meeting.[1286] Most importantly for transaction activism-pursuing shareholders, a minority request can concern the removal of a supervisory board member, § 103 (1), or the withdrawal of confidence in a management board member, § 84 (3) sent. 2.[1287] Management topics[1288] like corporate strategy or policy are, in contrast, generally excluded.[1289] It is controversial, however, whether shareholders are allowed to initiate a measure that is subject to Holzmüller/Gelatine jurisprudence. Some endorse the initiation right for these management tasks.[1290] Others deny an initiation right to the shareholder meeting in management matters, even if these need to be approved under the Holzmüller/Gelatine jurisprudence.[1291] They limit the shareholder meeting's initiation right to the exceptional scenario that such a measure has already been initiated by the management board and it is likely that the management board will ignore the approval requirement. Solely the management board has the authority to initiate management matters. The shareholder meeting does not have it.[1292] A third approach argues that even though the exception makes sense, the general refusal to initiate a management measure that *always* requires the shareholder meeting's approval represents an overly strict approach.[1293] Rather, the admission of an initiation of a *recommending* shareholder resolution preceded by a possible discussion on the issue sufficiently considers both the management character and the approval requirement. Therefore, the final initiation authority rests with the management board. Due to the structural consequences of the potential transaction, the shareholders can

1285 Eckardt in: Geßler et al., AktG, 1973, § 122 mnn.11 et seq.; Semler, in: Münch. Hdb. AG, Vol. 4, 1999, § 35 mn.39.

1286 Hüffer, AktG, § 122 mn.15; Kubis, in: MüKo AktG, 2004, § 122 mnn.31, 15 et seq.; Kühn, BB 1965, 1170 (1171); Obermüller et al, Die Hauptversammlung der Aktiengesellschaft, 2001, B mn.107; Werner, Großkomm AktG, 2008, § 122 mnn.26 et seq.

1287 Eckardt in: Geßler et al., AktG, 1973, § 122mn.12; Werner, in: Großkomm AktG, 2008, § 122 mn.17.

1288 Eckardt in: Geßler et al., AktG, 1973, § 122 mn.10, 11.

1289 Ziemons, in: Schmidt/Lutter, AktG, 2010, § 122 mn.40.

1290 OLG Frankfurt a.M., Beschl. v. 15.02.2005, Az.: 20 W 1/05, AG 2005, 442 (442): an intended resolution about management measures will only allow to convene a shareholder meeting if the shareholder meeting's responsibility is based on Holzmüller/Gelatine; Ziemons, in: Schmidt/Lutter, AktG, 2010, § 122, mnn.40, 17: supports the minority initiation right with regard to contracts subject to Holzmüller/Gelatine.

1291 LG Duisburg, Beschl. v. 29.05.2002, Az.: 21 O 106/02, NZG 2002, 643 (644)–Babcock Borsig: confirming this approach, however, not limiting it expressly to these circumstances; Kubis in: MüKo AktG, 2004, § 122 mn.15; Schaaf, Die Praxis der HV, 1999, mn.89; Semler, in: Münch. Hdb. AG, Vol. 4, 1999, § 35 mn.16; Werner, in: Großkomm AktG, 2008, § 122 mn.27.

1292 Kubis, in: MüKo, AktG, 2004, § 122 mn.15; Semler, in: Münch. Hdb. AG, Vol. 4, 1999, § 35 mn.16; Werner, in: Großkomm AktG, 2008, § 122 mn.28: an initiation right is only given once the management board has decided about whether the transaction will take place.

1293 Halberkamp/Gierke, NZG 2004, 494 (497).

request the publication of an additional agenda topic covering a recommending shareholder vote on the issue.[1294] Successful requests are added to the convocation notifications, § 125, or published, § 124 (1). The management board can ignore § 122 (2) proposals that are contrary to the law or the articles of incorporation.

If the § 122 (2) request targets a measure or contract that requires *preparation* through the management board, the shareholder resolution is limited to demanding the preparation (and conclusion) of the measure or the contract, § 83 (1) sent. 1, 2.[1295] As under § 122 (2), the initiation right does not concern measures or contracts representing management tasks for which the management board is solely responsible.[1296] *Measures* under § 83 (1) sent. 1 include the election of members of the supervisory board, the discharge of the management and supervisory board, amendments of the articles of incorporation, the increase and decrease of the share capital, or the removal of members of the supervisory board.[1297] Parallel to the controversy whether shareholders can initiate transactions subject to the Holzmüller/Gelatine precedent under § 122 (2) is the debate whether the management board needs to prepare such an initiating shareholder vote. For similar reasons, the management board can be asked to prepare a recommending shareholder resolution on the issue.[1298] This does, however, not amend the principle that based on the provision's purpose to allow the shareholder meeting a proper decision on measures for which it is solely responsible, the shareholder meeting cannot require the preparation of management measures that only require an internally relevant shareholder approval[1299]. Furthermore, the shareholder meeting can initiate the preparation and signing of *contracts*, which require shareholder approval, § 83 (1) sent. 2. Merger contracts, §§ 13, 65, 73 UmwG, represent one example.[1300] The initiation right is justified, as the management board has limited authority to conclude consolidating and similar contracts.[1301] For that cause, it applies even

1294 Halberkamp/Gierke, NZG 2004, 494 (497).

1295 Eckardt, in: Geßler et al., AktG, 1973, § 122 mn.15; Obermüller et al., Die Hauptversammlung der Aktiengesellschaft, 2001, B mn.107; Werner, in: Großkomm AktG, 2008, § 122 mn.31; For an even more practical approach and against a too formal approach, demanding a § 83 resolution if it appears for sure that the minority request will obtain the necessary shareholder support for a structural measure, whose quick realization is in the corporate interest, resulting in the duty of the management board to cooperate and provide the necessary documentation, based on which shareholders will be able to decide on the measure during the current shareholder meeting, Ziemons, in: Schmidt/Lutter, AktG, 2010, § 122 mn.26.

1296 Spindler, in: MüKo, AktG, 2008, § 83 mn.2.

1297 Eckardt, in: Geßler et al., AktG, 1973, § 122 mn.15; Spindler, in: MüKo, AktG, 2008, § 83 mnn.2, 6; Weber, in: Hölters, Aktiengesetz, 2011, § 83 mn.3.

1298 Other view in favor of the preparation of a *mandatory* shareholder vote: Habersack, in: Großkomm AktG, 2008, § 83 mn.6; Hüffer, AktG, 2010, § 83 mn.2; Seibt, in: Schmidt/Lutter, AktG, 2010, § 83 mn.4; Spindler, in: MüKo AktG, 2008, § 83 mn.6; Weber, in: Hölters, AktG, 2011, § 83 mn.3; Other opinion denying the applicability of § 83: Werner, in: Großkomm AktG, 2008, § 122 mn.29: without a corresponding necessity he declines to restrict the responsibility of the management board in management matters and to transfer the initiation right in such matters to the shareholder meeting, as it is limited to *statutory* shareholder responsibilities.

1299

1300 Habersack, in: Großkomm AktG, 2008, § 83 mn.7; Spindler, in: MüKo AktG, 2008, § 83 mn.10.

1301 Spindler, in: MüKo AktG, 2008, § 83 mn.2.

if the administration opposes its conclusion.[1302] Finally, the request needs to be approved by the quorum needed to approve the measure or contract, § 83 (1) sent. 3.

Complementary to § 122 (2), a shareholder minority has the mandatory right[1303] to convene a *special shareholder meeting*. It needs to hold at least a stake of five percent for a minimum of three months and throughout the decision on the request, §§ 122 (1), 142 (2) sent. 2. The demand has to be submitted in writing to the management board. It needs to state the reasons and the purpose. Parallel to § 122 (2), the latter needs to consider the limitations of the shareholder meeting's responsibility.[1304] The request cannot be abusive, as when its aim is unattainable or is not as urgent and may therefore wait for the next general meeting.[1305] The corporation bears the costs of the meeting, § 122 (4).

Few shareholder rights, especially the minority rights to appoint special auditors, §§ 142 (2), (4), 258 (2) sent. 3, or to assert corporate claims of damage, §§ 147, 148, can be applied without shareholder approval and therefore apart from a shareholder meeting. Consequently, their use does not depend on the §§ 122, 83[1306], 124 (4), 126 regimes.

b) Shareholder approval rights

The mentioned initiation rights are tightly coupled with the shareholder meeting's responsibility. Most importantly, shareholders are able to initiate a shareholder resolution *ousting members of the supervisory board*. Shareholders can remove supervisory board members early and even without cause, § 103 (1), if approved by at least three-fourths of the votes cast. Regarding the early removal of management board members for cause, § 84 (3), an exception to the principle that pressure of shareholders alone, whether exercised by majority[1307] or minority shareholders,[1308] to remove a member is generally not *a relevant cause* only applies if the corporation would suffer a significant danger, which can only be prevented by removal of the member.[1309] Courts have yet to approve a corresponding constellation, however. Shareholders can nevertheless initiate the *removal of management board members for cause* through the supervisory board. Besides the initiation of such a shareholder resolution, the shareholder resolution needs to withdraw confidence in a

1302 Habersack, in: Großkomm AktG, 2008, § 83 mn.8; Hüffer, AktG, 2010, § 83 mn.3; Mertens, in: KöKo AktG, 1996, § 83 mn.3: for contracts requiring a qualified majority, since they go far beyond management tasks; Spindler, in: MüKo AktG, 2008, § 83 mn.9.

1303 Ziemons, in: Schmidt/Lutter, AktG, 2010, § 122 mn.4.

1304 Obermüller et al., Die Hauptversammlung der Aktiengesellschaft, 2001, B mn.107.

1305 Hüffer, AktG, § 122 mn.6.

1306 Habersack, in: Großkomm AktG, 2008, § 83 mn.10; Hüffer, AktG, 2010, § 83 mn.4; Mertens, in: KöKo AktG, 1996, § 83 mn.5: denying an analoguous application since the management board would then be obliged to follow the demand of the minority contrary to the will of the minority and at the same time would send itself to his doom; different opinion: Spindler, in: MüKo AktG, 2008, § 83 mn.12: argueing that the minority with its initiation right replaces the shareholder meeting, therefore justifying the extension of the requirement to minority demands.

1307 *See* BGH, Urt. v. 7. 6. 1962, Az.: II ZR 131/61, WM 1962, 811 (811 et seq.).

1308 Fleischer, DStR 2006, 1507 (1513): uses *a fortiori* approach with regard to majority shareholders; Hoffmann et al., Mitbestimmungsgesetz, 1987, § 31 mn.55.

1309 Mertens/Cahn, in: KöKo AktG, 2010, § 84 mn.131.

member of the management board, § 84 (3) sent. 2. Initiated through such resolution, it is at the supervisory board's discretion[1310] to remove the member, § 84 (3) sent. 1.

Contested is whether a shareholder resolution not discharging a member of the management board, § 120, simultaneously withdraws confidence, § 84 (3). One approach declines the need for a formal procedure and supports the possibility that declining to discharge may simultaneously express the withdrawal of confidence in a member of the management board.[1311] The proponents argue that the discharge of the members of the management board expresses confidence in the members and their work, while declining to discharge them expresses a withdrawal of confidence. Even if the discharge concerns past behavior, it may hardly be concluded that the shareholder meeting remains uninfluenced in regard of its confidence in current or future actions of the concerned member.[1312] The more convincing opinion, however, opposes this approach. It underscores that not every declining of discharge needs to represent a withdrawal of confidence. Rather, this intent needs to be clearly expressed. The discharge relates not only to a past time period, but its decline may also be based on disapproval of a single measure. The withdrawal of confidence, however, expresses that confidence in the concerned member has been lost. Accordingly stricter are the consequences of a potential removal.[1313] For the supervisory board, this is reflected by the qualified default quorum to remove a supervisory board member.[1314] The denied discharge alone is insufficient.[1315]

1310 BGH, Urt. v. 21. 4. 1997, Az.: II ZR 175/95, DStR 1997, 880 (882)-Arag/Garmbeck; Hopt/Roth, in: Großkomm AktG, 2006, § 116 mn.153.

1311 Kort, in: Großkomm AktG, 2008, § 84 mn.165: the discharge expresses usually an element of confidence, while the opposite constellations expresses a withdrawal of confidence, even though discharging concerns a behavior in the past, it may not be concluded that the shareholder meeting has currently or for the future confidence in the actions of the concerned management board member; Mertens, in: KöKo AktG, 1996, § 84 mn.105; Mertens/Cahn, in: KöKo AktG, 2010, § 84 mn.127; *see* Obermüller et al., Die Hauptversammlung der Aktiengesellschaft, 2001, C IV 3 a, especially n.552: which evaluates each denial of discharge simultaneously as withdrawl of confidence; Wiesner, in: Münch. Hdb. AG, Vol. 4, 1999, § 20 mn.49.

1312 Kort, in: Großkomm AktG, 2008, § 84 mn.165.

1313 Spindler, in: MüKo AktG, 2008, § 84 mn.127.

1314 KG, Urt. v. 3.5.2007, Az.: 23 U 102/06, AG 2007, 745 (746); LG München I AG 2005, 701 (702); Fleischer, in: Spindler/Stilz, AktG, 2010, 441; Hopt/Roth, in: Großkomm AktG, 2006, § 103 mn.12: notes that it may not be concluded from the denial to discharge that a member of the supervisory board may be removed, rather, the resolution must explicitely state that the member will be removed from its position; Hüffer, AktG, § 84 mn.30: notes that it may be a withdrawal of confidence, but does not have to, as disapproval for the past does not necessarily mean that the shareholder meeting intends to break with this member for the future; Kubis, in: MüKo AktG, 2004, § 120 mn.35; Seibt, in: Schmidt/Lutter, AktG, 2010, § 84 mn.51: arguing that the withdrawal of confidences relates to the future; Spindler, in: MüKo AktG, 2008, § 84 mn.127; Thüsing, in: Fleischer, Hdb Vorstandsrecht, 2006, § 5 mn.27; Vetter, Marsch-Barner/Schäfer: Hdb börsennotierte AG, 2005, § 25 mn.58: The denial to discharge is not a removal in the sense of § 103 (1) AktG, the removal of a member of the supervisory board needs to be explicit subject of a separate shareholder resolution; Zimmermann, in: FS Rowedder, 1994, 593 (594 et seq.); Zöllner, in: KöKo AktG, 1985, § 119 mnn.41 et seq.

1315 Eckardt, in: Geßler et al., AktG, 1973, § 120 mn.46; Hüffer, AktG, § 103 mn.3; Mülbert, in: Großkomm AktG, 2008, § 120 mn.47; Obermüller et al., Die Hauptversammlung der Aktiengesellschaft, 2001, I mn.42.

Furthermore, the surviving or acquiring corporation of a merger or acquisition will need to finance the purchase. Depending on the amount of free cash, the purchase price, and the kind of contribution offered, an increase of the share capital, combined with an exclusion of preemptive rights, will need to be implemented. *Contingent share capital increases* according to § 192 (2) No. 2 automatically exclude preemptive rights. In practice, however, they are barely used for consolidations.[1316] *Authorized capital* can enable the management board to increase the share capital by a maximum of fifty percent for up to five years, §§ 202 et seq. It may even enable the board to decide on the exclusion of preemptive rights, § 203 (2). Otherwise, an *ordinary share capital increase* will generally require a shareholder approval by three-fourths of the present capital, § 182 (1) sent. 1. Based on the restricted approach of Community law regarding preemptive rights exclusions, Art. 29 Second European Company Directive, preemptive rights can only be waived by a qualified majority vote of three-fourths of the voting capital, § 186 (3) sent. 2.[1317] A less relevant alternative to accumulate the necessary shares is finally the accumulation of the corporation's own shares. Independent of the purpose of the repurchase, the management board can for up to five years be authorized by the vote of a simple majority of the present capital to implement a repurchase of no more than 10 percent of the outstanding shares, § 71 (1) No. 8. In most of the cases, however, the necessary financial means will exceed 10 percent of the share capital. Furthermore, repurchases bind a significant amount of corporate assets.[1318]

Finally, the transaction could impact the type of business or the purpose of the acquiring corporation and therefore require amending the *articles of incorporation*. According to § 179 (1), (2), three-fourths of the voting capital need to approve an amendment.

c) Other shareholder rights

The *shareholder right to information*, § 131 (1), intends to provide shareholders with the necessary information to use their membership rights. For shareholders in listed corporations it is of significant meaning.[1319] Generally, a shareholder can request information relating to the affairs of the corporation during the shareholder meeting. If the demand is particularly comprehensive, it may be raised prior to the shareholder meeting, though this is an exception.[1320] Affairs of the corporation also relate to corporate policy and must be necessary for an evaluation of a topic on the shareholder meeting's agenda.[1321]

Another relevant shareholder right is the general *motion for a special auditor* regarding specific completed or at least initiated management measures, including the control

1316 Fuchs, in: MüKo AktG, 2005, § 192 mnn.60. 6: noting the limited practical relevance in the context of consolidations, as the contingent capital results in unwanted publicity of entrepreneurial projects, as the shareholder meeting has to determine its purpose and distribution price.
1317 Kraakman et al., The Anatomy of Corporate Law 148 (2004).
1318 Fuchs, in: MüKo AktG, 2005, § 192 mn.7; Hüffer, AktG, 2010, § 192 mn.2.
1319 Spindler, in: Schmidt/Lutter, AktG, 2010, § 131 mnn.1, 11.
1320 *Id.* at mn.26.
1321 *Id.* at 28, 30.

and approval responsibility of the supervisory board.[1322] It is used to prepare the discharge of, § 120, or possible litigation against, members of the administration,[1323] § 142 (1). The appointment of a special auditor needs to be announced on the agenda, § 124 (1), except if relating to a discharge that concerns the same time period,[1324] § 124 (4) sent. 2, 2nd alt. To initiate a motion, a shareholder requires a stake of 1 percent or one representing Euro 100,000 of the share capital. The shareholder meeting needs to appoint a specific auditor through a simple majority vote. Once the shareholder meeting has denied the appointment, shareholders who have held such a stake for three months and will continue holding it until the motion has been decided can use the minority right, i.e. obtain a court order, § 142 (2). Their motion needs to be justified by facts that indicate irregularities or gross violations of law or the articles of incorporation through the concerned measure.

Shareholders may *assert claims of the corporation* against members of the management or supervisory board according to §§ 93, 116 or §§ 823 et seq. BGB[1325], § 147 (1) sent. 1, 2nd alt. The shareholder meeting needs to approve it by a simple majority. In general, claims for damages need to be announced as separate agenda topics, § 124 (1). An exception pursuant to § 124 (4) sent.2, 2nd alt. applies, for instance, if a special audit report that analyzes potential claims for damages is one of the topics on the agenda.[1326] Subsidiary to the enforcement by the corporation, § 148 (3), a shareholder minority holding a stake of 1 percent or Euro 100,000 of the share capital may assert the corporate claim according to § 147 (1) in its own name, § 148.

d) Capital markets law

Finally, shareholders can fall back on the publicly available information about their fellow investors, especially when aiming to launch a campaign against a transaction decision that depends on the support of fellow shareholders. Corresponding information is publicly accessible via the website of the Bundesanstalt für Finanzdienstleistungsaufsicht (***"BaFin"***)[1327] and the issuer as well as the business register (*Unternehmensregister*), § 8b HGB. Shareholders are obliged to immediately inform the BaFin and the issuer when they have reached, exceeded, or fallen below stakes representing voting rights of 3, 5, 10, 15, 20, 25, 30, 50 and 75 percent of an issuer, 21 (1) WpHG. Once it has received the information, the issuer must immediately publish it and forward it to the business register and the BaFin, § 26 WpHG.

The shareholder forum allows shareholders to be contacted independent of the size of their stake, § 127a. As part of the Electronic Federal Gazette (*Elektronischer Bunde-*

1322 Bezzenberger, in: Großkomm AktG, 2008, § 142 mnn.12, 13, 19.

1323 Hüffer, AktG, 2010, § 142 mnn.4 et seq., 16; Spindler, in: Schmidt/Lutter, AktG, 2010, § 142 mnn.14, 16.

1324 Hüffer, AktG, 2010, § 142 mn.9.

1325 Spindler, in: Schmidt/Lutter, AktG, 2010, § 147 mn.3.

1326 Hüffer, AktG, 2010, § 147 mn.3.

1327 The Bundesanstalt für Finanzdienstleistungsaufsicht [BaFin] [Federal Financial Supervisory Authority] is the German banking regulatory authority.

*sanzeiger "**eBAnz**")*, shareholders are allowed to communicate with each other without having to worry about acting in concert. So far, shareholders have barely used it.[1328]

3) Constellations of transaction activism

a) Transaction activism targeting corporate ***merger*** decisions

*i) Special formal means for shareholders of **surviving** corporation*

With the *Umwandlungsgesetz*[1329] ("***UmwG***"), the German legislator has laid down detailed merger procedures to safeguard shareholder decision rights during a merger.[1330] It distinguishes the in practice more relevant[1331] mergers into an existing corporation (§§ 2 No. 1, 4 et seq., 60 et seq. UmwG) or into a newly founded corporation. For the surviving company, the former and here analyzed form does not result in a control change.

(1) Report based shareholder approval

German law requires each of the constituent corporation's administrations to generate a *merger report, § 8 UmwG,* to provide shareholders with the fundamentals of the transaction.[1332] Its purpose is to provide shareholders with a reliable basis to evaluate whether the merger makes economic sense and whether it conforms to the relevant rules.[1333] It needs to explain and to justify the merger process and the details of the merger contract. For reasons of shareholder protection, § 5 (1) UmwG has laid down the minimal content of such a contract.[1334] In addition, it has to explain the determined exchange ratio legally as well as economically.[1335]

Furthermore, independent and knowledgeable auditors have to evaluate the legal and economic considerations that have induced the responsible individuals to undertake a merger[1336] and summarize them in an audit report. Art. 10 Third Company Law Directive (***"Merger Directive"***) requires audit reports regarding the fairness of the merger terms.[1337] Correspondingly, the German UmwG requires that merging companies commission *audit reports by independent experts* on the substantive terms of the merger prior to the decisive shareholder meeting, §§ 11 UmwG, 319 HGB. These terms relate

---

1328 Ziemons, in: Schmidt/Lutter, AktG, 2010, § 127a, mn.2.
1329 Umwandlungsgesetz [Reorganization Act], Oct. 28, 1994, BGBl. I at 3210 (F.R.G.).
1330 Kraakman et al., The Anatomy of Corporate Law 135 (2004).
1331 Stengel, in: Semler/Stengel, Umwandlungsgesetz, 2012, § 2 mn.23.
1332 Gehling, in: Semler/Stengel, Umwandlungsgesetz, 2012, § 8 mn.2.
1333 Lutter/Drygalla, in: Lutter/Winter, UmwG, Vol. 1, 2004, § 8 mn.14.
1334 Pfeifer, Schutzmechanismen bei der Umwandlung von Kaptitalgesellschaften, 2001, mn.500; Schumacher, Das Informationssystem der Verschmelzung unter Beteiligung von Aktiengesellschaften, 2004, 14.
1335 Gehling, in: Semler/Stengel, Umwandlungsgesetz, 2012, § 8 mn.22.
1336 Pfeifer, Schutzmechanismen bei der Umwandlung von Kaptitalgesellschaften, 2001, mn.508.
1337 Kraakman et al., The Anatomy of Corporate Law 135 (2004).

to the accuracy of the details of the merger contract, its completeness and in particular the adequacy of the exchange ratio.[1338] The latter aspect assures that shareholders know the true value of the involved corporations when deciding whether to support the merger or to veto unjustified exchange ratios.[1339] Its function is the same as the fairness opinion of an investment banker obtained by public U.S. corporations prior to a merger seeking protection from shareholder suits.[1340] Based on an administrative proposal, the responsible court determines the auditor, § 10 UmwG.

An *exception* to both *merger and audit report* requirements applies only to upstream mergers of wholly owned subsidiaries, §§ 8 (2), 12, 60 and §§ 9 (2), 60 UmwG, Art. 24 of the Merger Directive[1341], or if all shareholders waive them, §§ 8 (3), 9 (3), 60 UmwG.

The requirement under German law that the shareholder meetings of the constituent corporations *approve the merger*[1342] also underscores the fundamental nature of the merger decision, which cannot be made by the agents alone.[1343] In preparation for the shareholder meeting, shareholders have to be able to access relevant documents, like the merger contract as well as the merger and audit reports, § 63 (1), (3) UmwG. In addition, they have the right to inquire into all important matters regarding the merger during the shareholder meeting, § 64 UmwG. The quorum for approval is *three-fourths* of the present share capital; the articles of incorporation can impose a higher threshold, §§ 13 (1) sent. 1 and 2, 65 (1) sent. 1 and 2 UmwG. Therefore, German law imposes a higher threshold than the two-thirds of the cast votes required by Art. 7 of the Merger Directive.[1344] An exception applies to *group mergers*. The surviving corporation needs to already own 90 percent of the share capital of the corporation to be acquired, § 62 (1) UmwG.[1345] A shareholder minority with a stake of 5 percent of the share capital in the surviving corporation may still demand the convening of a shareholder meeting to vote on the merger, § 62 (2) UmwG.

(2) Legal proceeding with regard to a merger

A powerful means for shareholders of the disappearing corporation who are dissatisfied with the adequacy of the compensation is the *appraisal proceeding* (*Spruchverfahren*), § 15 UmwG. These shareholders have the right to challenge the fairness of the merger price by suing the surviving company for the difference between the value of the shares previously owned and the value of the shares obtained.[1346] Despite its *inter omnes* effect, it only leads to cash adjustments without impacting the merger as such, § 14 (2)

1338 Zeidler, in: Semler/Stengel, Umwandlungsgesetz, 2012, § 12 mn.1.
1339 Lutter/Drygalla, in: Lutter/Winter, UmwG, Vol. 1, 2004, § 9 mn.4.
1340 Kraakman et al., The Anatomy of Corporate Law 200 (2009).
1341 Diekmann, in: Semler/Stengel, Umwandlungsgesetz, 2012, § 60 mn.4.
1342 Stratz, in: Schmitt et al., UmwG, UmwStG, 2009, § 65 mn.2.
1343 Lutter/Drygalla, in: Lutter/Winter, UmwG, Vol. 1, 2004, § 13 mn.4.
1344 Kraakman et al., The Anatomy of Corporate Law 197 et seq (2009).
1345 Kraakman et al., The Anatomy of Corporate Law 135 (2004).
1346 *Id.*

UmwG[1347], comparable to class actions under U.S. law.[1348] As the appraisal proceeding impacts the merger terms after the effective date, it has deterred mergers in Germany.[1349]

Similarly, shareholders of the corporation to disappear have under a limited set of circumstances, including the merger of a private corporation into a public corporation, a *right to exit* by selling their shares to the surviving corporation, as provided in the (draft of) the merger contract, § 29 UmwG. Despite the side effect of making merger decisions expensive, this exit opportunity does not help active shareholders.[1350]

Shareholders supporting a merger are further protected against the consequences of potential *rescission claims* by opposing shareholders via the merger's registration with the commercial register.[1351] The registration may even take place when a rescission claim has been brought against the approval of one of the constituent corporations. It requires a court order, which upon application of the concerned constituent corporation confirms that the rescission claim does not oppose the registration, §§ 16 (3) sent. 1, (2) UmwG. For the court to issue such an order, the claim needs to be impermissible or evidently ill-founded, the plaintiff needs to be unable to prove that he has been holding a stake worth Euro 1000 when the convention was announced, or the disadvantages to the constituent entities outweigh the disadvantages to the respondent if the violation is not especially serious, § 16 (3) UmwG.

A broad discussion has developed regarding whether the purpose of the merger resolution requires a *material reason to justify the merger*, similar to the justification requirement applying to the exclusion of a preemptive right[1352]. This is relevant to shareholders aiming to prevent a merger, since legal proceedings against the effectiveness of the merger resolution cannot be based on the exchange ratio, § 14 (2) UmwG. The Higher Regional Courts of Frankfurt and Jena as well as a majority of legal scholars thinks such a measure is unnecessary.[1353] Some legal scholars[1354] and the Higher Regional Court in

1347 Pfeiffer, Schutzmechanismen bei der Umwandlung von Kaptitalgesellschaften, 2001, mnn.536, 542.

1348 Kraakman et al., The Anatomy of Corporate Law 202 n.90 (2009).

1349 *Id.* at 202 n.88.

1350 Kraakman et al., The Anatomy of Corporate Law 200 et seq. (2009).

1351 Pfeiffer, Schutzmechanismen bei der Umwandlung von Kaptitalgesellschaften, 2001, mnn.517, 522.

1352 BGH, Urt. v. 13.03.1978, Az.: II ZR 142/76, BGHZ 71, 40 (40)–Kali & Salz: Regarding the exclusion of preemptive rights, the decision of the Federal Court of Justice requires a justification, which needs to comprise the suitability, necessity and commensurability of the exclusion of the preemptive rights.

1353 OLG Jena, Urt. v. 5. 11. 2008, Az.: 6 W 288/08, NJW-RR 2009, 182 (183); OLG Frankfurt, Beschl. v. 8.2.2006, Az.: 12 W 185/05, NJOZ 2006, 870 (879); Gehling, in: Semler/Stengel, Umwandlungsgesetz, 2012, § 13 mn.23; Heckschen, in: Widman/Mayer, Umwandlungsrecht, Vol. 1, 2009, mn.163.27; Hügel, Verschmelzung und Einbringung, 1993, 136: providing an excpetion for circumventing scenarios; Lutter, ZGR 1981, 171 (180); Lutter/Drygalla, in: Lutter/Winter, UmwG, Vol. 1, 2004, § 13 mn.35; Zimmermann, in: Kallmeyer, Umwandlungsgesetz, 2010, § 13 mn.12.

1354 Limmer, Hdb der Unternehmensumwandlung, 2007, mn.645: considers the auditing at least in certain cases as permissible after considering the different applicable minority protection devices, but with a reduced standard of auditing focused on the abuse of discretion as well as

Stuttgart[1355] demand a material justification. The demand for a material justification has been brought up in the context of preventing a dilution of the voting rights of the involved shareholders.[1356] It must be distinguished from capital dilution, which the appraisal procedure and the right to appeal against the merger resolution are supposed to prevent[1357]. Proponents of the material control requirement interpret the legislator's reasoning[1358] as having left this issue expressly open,[1359] while systematic and teleological interpretations claim its necessity. § 8 (1) UmwG demands an administrative merger report that demonstrates the usefulness and profitability of the transaction. Further merger rules aim to protect minority shareholders against decisions that harm their interests. Accordingly, it is argued that a substantive justification requirement is permissible.[1360] As far as the *telos* of the applicable rules is concerned, the alleged control requirement is justified with necessary qualification for the protection of minority shareholders in a majority system.[1361] It would assure that material reasons in the interest of the corporation justify the transaction. However, it would be necessary to counterbalance the interests of the involved shareholders instead of assuming the absolute prevalence of majority decisions and protecting minority shareholders only against arbitrary decisions and providing them with claims compensating financial losses.[1362]

The prevailing and convincing opinion, in contrast, is that a material merger control to prevent the dilution of voting rights is unnecessary. It declares the risk of dilution to be approved by the legislator, since no preemptive right has been granted in the context of a capital increase before a merger, § 192 (2) No. 2, which could be interpreted as a legislative waiver of the justification requirement. Furthermore, the UmwG comprises a struc-

heavily incorrect decisions; Martens, ZGR 1979, 493 (496 et seq.); Timm, ZGR 1987, 403 (421 et seq.): focusing on group scenarios which require to control decisions of stable majorities; Wiedemann, ZGR 1980, 147 (156 et seq.).

1355 OLG Stuttgart, Urt. v. 23.11.1994, Az.: 3 U 77/94, WM 1995, 1355 (1355 et seq.): considering whether shifting of the merger costs towards the remaining corporation constitutes a violation of a fiduciary duty which justifies appealing the merger resolution, it is rather a general question of designing a contract than a core issue of a merger resolution (Heckschen, Widmann/Mayer, Umwandlungsrecht, Vol. 1, 2009, mn.163.19 n.2.).

1356 Wiedemann, ZGR 1980, 147 (156).

1357 Lutter/Drygalla, in: Lutter/Winter, UmwG, 2004, § 13 mn.34.

1358 RegE eines Gesetzes zur Bereinigung des Umwandlungsrechts [Draft Law of the Federal gGvernment of an Act about the Adjustment of Reorganization Act], Apr. 2, 1994, BR-Drucks 75/94, Reasoning UmwG 95, in: Widman/Mayer, Vol. I, Gesetzesbegründungen, 2009, § 13 UmwG: according to which "The legislator does not agree to the opinion, which has been developed by the courts and scholars according to which for a material control of important shareholder resolutions it has to be laid down the interest of the legal person as well as the necessary and commensurable means. It appears already doubtful, whether these fundamentals developed so far for the capital increase under exclusion of preemptive rights may be transferred just like that to merger resolutions. Accordingly, it appears to be impossible to regulate this basic issue of corporate law only for the special case of a merger, but not generally for important shareholder resolutions."

1359 Limmer, Hdb der Unternehmensumwandlung, 2007, mn.645.

1360 *Id.*

1361 Timm, ZGR 1987, 403 (421 et seq.).

1362 Martens, ZGR 1979, 493 (496 et seq.); Wiedemann, ZGR 1980, 147 (156 et seq).

turally arranged protection of minority shareholders, which ensures sufficient protection of their interests.[1363] Sufficient means already exist through the administrative merger report, §§ 8, 60 UmwG, control through independent auditors, §§ 9, 12, 60 UmwG, comprehensive shareholders' information rights,[1364] qualified shareholder approval requirements in the constituent corporations, §§ 13, 65 UmwG, and the right to exit for cash, § 29 UmwG[1365].[1366] General corporate fiduciary duties complete the minority protection measures.[1367] Moreover, it is hard to apply the criteria of suitability, necessity,[1368] and adequacy to a merger. For instance, the transaction with another entity represents an *aliud* and therefore not a potentially more suitable or alternative transaction.[1369] The justification requirement would therefore result in unintended legal uncertainty.[1370] Finally, the counterargument that it is unjustified to treat a capital increase for contribution in kind under the exclusion of preemptive rights differently than a merger into a surviving corporation[1371] can be rebutted by the comprehensive merger procedure. It prevents a circumventing use of a merger to avoid the justification criteria that generally applies to such share capital increases.[1372] Consequently, a substantive justification requirement comparable to the one developed for the exclusion of preemptive rights does not apply to mergers. It can therefore not serve as a ground for rescission claims.

(3) Shareholder participation in necessary financial measures

Finally, shareholders of surviving corporations may have to approve the necessary capital measures for the surviving corporation to be able to compensate the shareholders of the acquired corporation. The implementation of the capital increase needs to be registered with the commercial register of the surviving corporation before the merger can be registered, § 66 UmwG. An exception applies only to rarely used contingent capital; the registration of the shareholder resolution approving the capital increase is then suf-

1363 Gehling, in: Semler/Stengel, Umwandlungsgesetz, 2012, § 13 mn.23; Heckschen, in: Widman/Mayer, Umwandlungsrecht, Vol. 1, 2009, mn.163.27; Lutter, ZGR 1981, 171 (180); Schumacher, Das Informationssystem der Verschmelzung unter Beteiligung von Aktiengesellschaften, 2004, 90; Zimmermann, in: Kallmeyer, Umwandlungsgesetz, 2010, § 13 mn.12.

1364 Gehling, in: Semler/Stengel, Umwandlungsgesetz, 2012, § 13 mn.23; Heckschen, in: Widman/Mayer, Umwandlungsrecht, Vol. 1, 2009, mn.163.27; Lutter, ZGR 1981, 171 (180); Zimmermann, in: Kallmeyer, Umwandlungsgesetz, 2010, § 13 mn.12.

1365 Gehling, in: Semler/Stengel, Umwandlungsgesetz, 2012, § 13 mn.23; Heckschen, in: Widman/Mayer, Umwandlungsrecht, Vol. 1, 2009, mn.163.27; Lutter, ZGR 1981, 171 (180); Zimmermann, in: Kallmeyer, Umwandlungsgesetz, 2010, § 13 mn.12.

1366 Gehling, in: Semler/Stengel, Umwandlungsgesetz, 2012, § 13 mn.23; Hügel, Verschmelzung und Einbringung, 1993, 135.

1367 *Id.* at mn.24; Zimmermann, in: Kallmeyer, Umwandlungsgesetz, 2010, § 13 mn.12.

1368 Heckschen, in: Widman/Mayer, Umwandlungsrecht, Vol. 1, 2009, mn.163.27; Lutter, ZGR 1981, 171 (180).

1369 Hügel, Verschmelzung und Einbringung, 1993, 134 et seq.; Lutter/Drygalla, in: Lutter/Winter, UmwG, 2004, § 13 mn.36.

1370 Heckschen, in: Widman/Mayer, Umwandlungsrecht, 2009, Vol. 1, mn.163.27.

1371 Hirte, Bezugsrechtsausschluss und Konzernbildung, 1986, 70 et seq.

1372 Heckschen, Widman/Mayer, Umwandlungsrecht, Vol. 1, 2004, mn.163.27.

ficient.[1373] Therefore, mergers for share contributions usually require the preceding registration of the implementation of the capital increase under the exclusion of preemptive rights in the surviving corporation before registering the merger.

*ii) Transaction activism aiming **to prevent** a merger*

(1) Underlying interests

Their underlying interests make it likely that the members of the administration will support a potential merger. It allows them to secure their positions while increasing their responsibilities and compensation. Shareholders, in contrast, will fear that a potential merger will cause the stock price to plunge while preventing it will cause the price to rise again. It thus provides financial incentives for proceeding against potentially opportunistic administrative behavior.

(2) Relevant shareholder means

The UmwG provides shareholders with special formal means to prevent a merger by blocking the required shareholder vote of three-fourths of the present capital to approve a merger, §§ 13, 65 UmwG. Despite this high quorum, transaction activism under this constellation is relevant, as shareholders tend to follow management's recommendations in specific business matters. Accordingly, active shareholders can use this veto right by accruing votes of more than one-fourth of the present capital to vote against the merger. Blockholders or coalitions of minority shareholders are able to use the veto right to block a potential merger.[1374] To accumulate the necessary threshold, active shareholders can turn *privately* to other blockholders or qualified minority shareholders to convince them to oppose the merger. Information on the names of shareholders with a stake of more than 3 percent can be found on the website of the BaFin or the publicly accessible business register (*Unternehmensregister*). This strategy saves money since shareholders need only contact a few blockholders or qualified minority shareholders to accumulate the necessary threshold. Considering the shareholder structure in German corporations, characterized by comparably low freefloat despite the dissolution of *Deutschland AG*, this strategy appears to be promising. Absent a sufficient number of privately contactable shareholders, active shareholders have to contact a larger number of undisclosed shareholders. A theoretically helpful means in this context is the *shareholder forum,* § 127a. However, its acceptance has been limited. Therefore, active shareholders must contact and convince other shareholders by informing the *public* of the true administrative incentives of the transaction and the consequences of the merger for the surviving corporation's shareholders. The latter method involves comparably greater efforts and therefore significant costs.

1373 Diekmann, in: Semler/Stengel, Umwandlungsgesetz, 2007, § 66 mn.13.
1374 Kraakman et al., The Anatomy of Corporate Law 200 (2009).

An alternative or parallel strategy to prevent the merger is the *impact on the positions of the members of the administration*. The management board initiates the merger. The supervisory board will most likely have to approve the *initiation* of a fundamental decision like a merger according to § 111 (4) sent. 2, except if the shareholder meeting has initiated the transaction.[1375] Proponents of another approach object that such a veto right would grant the supervisory board the right to block the shareholder meeting's decision-making process even if it has not been explicitly provided with a corresponding opportunity.[1376] This argument is exaggerated, however, as one must distinguish between the initiation through the management board and the approval of fundamental transactions through the shareholder meeting. Only the former represents a management task that may be subject to a veto of the supervisory board according to § 111 (4) sent 2. To deny the supervisory board's veto right would not sufficiently distinguish the steps and responsibilities in the corporate decision-making process. Only if the shareholder meeting initiates a fundamental transaction, which the management board has to prepare and implement pursuant to § 83, will the supervisory board not have to approve the initiation of the transaction.[1377] Accordingly, active shareholders aiming to prevent a merger initiated by the management board can also target the members of the supervisory board and convince them to veto the initiation. This impact can be exercised via informal means. These include personal communication with the members of the administration via e-mails, phone calls, formal letters, or even personal talks. In addition, the public can be given specific information about the administration's incentives and the consequences of the merger for the surviving corporation and its stockholders and/or a general critique of the responsible members of the administration. The pressure to convince members of the administration can also be generated by threatening to use general formal means. These include the initiation and approval of the early removal of the responsible supervisory board members or the initiation of the early removal of management board members. Shareholders of German corporations have different ways of implementing such accountability measures. They can be initiated spontaneously by a motion on an announced topic of a *shareholder meeting*, § 124 (4) sent. 2. If publication according to § 124 (1) is necessary, a shareholder minority can request the addition and publication of the topic to the general meeting agenda up to 31 days prior to the shareholder meeting, §§ 122 (2), (83 (1)). The motion can even be combined with the demand to convene a *special shareholder meeting*, § 122 (1). These initiation rights underscore the credibility of the threats of active shareholders to use formal general shareholder means. The ultimate threat remains to acquire the corporation.

1375 Habersack, in: MüKo AktG, 2008, § 111 mn.114; Hopt/Roth, in: Großkomm AktG, 2006, § 111 mn.640 n.2461; Martens, ZHR 147 (1983), 377 (386 n.23); other opinion: Mertens, in: KöKo AktG, 1996, § 111 mn.71; Timm, DB 1980, 1201, 1203 et seq.

1376 Mertens, in: KöKo AktG, 1996, § 111 mn.71; Timm, DB 1980, 1201, 1203 et seq.

1377 Hopt/Roth, Großkomm AktG, 2006, § 111 mn.640; Martens, ZHR 147 (1983), 377 (386 n.23).

(3) Example

An example of shareholder activism involving a potential merger concerned Volkswagen AG's (*"Volkswagen"*) preparation to acquire Porsche SE (*"Porsche"*), which was implemented in 2012. In 2009, Porsche held 51 percent of Volkswagen's voting rights and Volkswagen agreed to hold 42 percent of Porsche.[1378] The transaction concerned the trading corporation Porsche Holding Salzburg and Porsche's car production, including debt of Euro 15,9 billion, mainly from Porsche's initial attempt to take over Volkswagen as part of a family rivalry. The transaction was financed through the distribution of additional preferred stock with a value of Euro 4 billion by Volkswagen in 2010.[1379] Volkswagen's minority shareholders Norwegian Government Pension Fund NBIM, with a 0.15 percent stake of common shares and 4 percent of preferred shares, and DWS, with a stake of less than 3 percent[1380], opposed the merger.[1381] Due to Volkswagen's shareholder structure, three major shareholders jointly representing 77 percent of the share capital (Porsche 50 percent, State of Niedersachsen 20 percent; Qatar 7 percent) supported the transaction, so their efforts to prevent the merger focused on delaying the process and increasing the transaction costs.[1382]

Their critique targeted conflicts of interest that they alleged had determined the transaction decision in breach of good management principles.[1383] They were based on the fact that the head of the supervisory board of Volkswagen, F. Piech, is also the member of one of the families that owns all of Porsche's common shares, while only Porsche's preferred shares are traded. Therefore, he has a personal interest in a maximum purchase price, while as head of the supervisory board of Volkswagen he has to assure that the purchase price is at arms' length. It is alleged that Porsche was using the transaction to get rid of its debt by using Volkswagen's available cash, which totals about Euro 10 billion. This sum had not been accessible to Porsche when it initially tried to take over Volkswagen, due to Niedersachsen's veto position under the Volkswagen Act. The price to be paid for Porsche, including a part of its debt, was considered too high in light of Porsche's

1378 *Stolpersteine für die VW-Porsche-Fusion*, Oct. 19, 2010, boerse.ARD.de, http://www.boerse.ard.de/content.jsp?key=dokument_478308.

1379 *Investoren formieren sich gegen Porsche-Deal*, Oct. 9, 2009, HANDELSBLATT, http://www.handelsblatt.com/unternehmen/industrie/investoren-formieren-sich-gegen-porsche-deal;2466219.

1380 Capital market publication for Volkswagen AG, Oct. 2, 2007, referring to the status on Sept. 26, 2007, Business register, www.unternehmensregister.de.

1381 *Nordischer Gegenwind*, Oct. 8, 2009, FINANCIAL TIMES DEUTSCHLAND, http://www.ftd.de/unternehmen/industrie/autoindustrie/:nordischer-gegenwind-grossaktionaer-droht-vw-mit-klage-gegen-porsche-kauf/50020523.html?page=2.

1382 *Id.*

1383 *Großaktionär greift VW wegen Porsche-Übernahme an*, Oct. 8, 2009, DiePresse.com, http://diepresse.com/home/wirtschaft/international/513571/print.do; *Nordischer Gegenwind*, Oct. 8, 2009, FINANCIAL TIMES DEUTSCHLAND, http://www.ftd.de/unternehmen/industrie/autoindustrie/:nordischer-gegenwind-grossaktionaer-droht-vw-mit-klage-gegen-porsche-kauf/50020523.html?page=2; *Investoren formieren sich gegen Porsche-Deal*, Oct. 9, 2009, HANDELSBLATT, http://www.handelsblatt.com/unternehmen/industrie/investoren-formieren-sich-gegen-porsche-deal;2466219, Handelsblatt.com.

problematic financial position. Furthermore, they alleged that the purchase price was not transparent, as additional requested information regarding the price calculation had not been provided.[1384] The financing of the transaction via the distribution of additional preferred stock would likely dilute the value of the existing preferred stock,[1385] while the voting authority related to the common shares of the Porsche and Piech families would remain untouched.[1386] In addition, they were unable to access the strategy behind the acquisition of Porsche Holding Salzburg.[1387] To win the support of Niedersachsen in favor of the merger, Volkswagen had amended its articles of incorporation to secure Niedersachsen's right to delegate 2 of the 20 supervisory board members. Under the old version of the Volkswagen Act, Niedersachsen had held a blocking minority, despite its stake of 20.1 percent, and a right to determine 2 of Volkswagen's 20 supervisory board members. However, the European Court of Justice had held in October 2007 that the Volkswagen Act violated Community law. A 2008 amendment to the Volkswagen Act had only maintained Niedersachsen's veto position.[1388]

Due to the particular shareholder structure of Volkswagen, the critique expressed by the minority shareholders opposing the intended merger concentrated on the use of informal means and general formal means not depending on majority approval. Information about personal conversations between active shareholders and the administration of Volkswagen has not been reported. Six months after the public announcement of the merger in April 2009,[1389] the NBIM Fund criticized the transaction in a public letter addressed to the head of the supervisory board, F. Piech. Furthermore, it predicted that the information policy pursued would lead to a significant increase in capital costs.[1390]

1384 *Großaktionär greift VW wegen Porsche-Übernahme an*, Oct. 8, 2009, DiePresse.com, http://diepresse.com/home/wirtschaft/international/513571/print.do; *Nordischer Gegenwind*, Oct. 8, 2009, Financial Times Deutschland, http://www.ftd.de/unternehmen/industrie/autoindustrie/:nordischer-gegenwind-grossaktionaer-droht-vw-mit-klage-gegen-porsche-kauf/50020523.html?page=2; *Widerstand gegen VWs Porsche-Deal* , Oct. 9, 2009, Finanznachrichten, http://www.finanznachrichten.de/ausdruck/2009-10/15159916-widerstand-gegen-vws-porsche-deal-022.htm.

1385 *Widerstand gegen VWs Porsche-Deal*, Oct. 9, 2009, Finanznachrichten, http://www.finanznachrichten.de/ausdruck/2009-10/15159916-widerstand-gegen-vws-porsche-deal-022.htm.

1386 *VW-Aktionäre ebnen Weg für Porsche-Übernahme*, Dec. 4, 2009, Boerse.ARD.de, http://boerse.ard.de/content.jsp?key=dokument_399258; *Kleinanleger greifen VW-Führung an*, Dec. 3, 2009, Hannoversche Allgemeine, http://www.haz.de/Nachrichten/Wirtschaft/Deutschland-Welt/Kleinanleger-greifen-VW-Fuehrung-an.

1387 *Investoren formieren sich gegen Porsche-Deal*, Oct. 9, 2009, Handelsblatt, http://www.handelsblatt.com/unternehmen/industrie/investoren-formieren-sich-gegen-porsche-deal;2466219.

1388 Girndt/Boeckler foundation, *Das VW Gesetz schreibt Geschichte*, 2010, http://www.boeckler.de/pdf/magmb_2010_07_girndt.pdf; *VW drückt bei bei Porsche-Übernahme auf die Tube*, Dec. 3, 2009, Wirtschaftsblatt http://www.wirtschaftsblatt.at/home/boerse/binternational/400224/index.do?from=rss; *Autobauer Volkswagen hält Kurs bei Porsche-Übernahme*, Dec. 3, 2009, Wirtschaftswoche, http://www.wiwo.de/unternehmen-maerkte/volkswagen-haelt-kurs-bei-porsche-uebernahme-415852/print/.

1389 *Volkswagen spielt Porsche-Übernahme durch*, Apr. 23, 2009, T-online.de, http://wirtschaft.t-online.de/automobilindustrie-vw-spielt-porsche-uebernahme-durch/id_18539130/index.

1390 *Großaktionär greift VW wegen Porsche-Übernahme an*, Oct. 8, 2009, DiePresse.com, http://diepresse.com/home/wirtschaft/international/513571/print.do; *Nordischer Gegenwind*, Oct. 8, 2009,

The NBIM Fund also announced its intention to sue members of the supervisory board for damages and to report a criminal offence in the form of a breach of trust, § 266 StGB,[1391] recommending that other shareholders follow its example.[1392] Two days later, DWS publicly supported the NBIM Fund's allegations in an interview with the daily *Handelsblatt.*[1393] Only a few weeks later, the Hermes Fund joined the critique in a published letter. It demanded more transparency, the installation of special committees, and the use of independent auditors for evaluation purposes.[1394]

During a special Volkswagen shareholder meeting in December 2009, the shareholder meeting authorized a contingent capital increase via the distribution of additional preferred stock and approved amendments to the articles of incorporation via a supermajority of the three major shareholders.[1395] Several minority shareholders made use of their right to speak during the meeting[1396] and questioned the management board on the transaction as well as the other constituent corporation, § 64 UmwG. They used their right to significantly criticize and extensively question the administration on the circumstances of the transaction, accusing them of implementing it to pay off Porsche's debt to the detriment of Volkswagen' minority shareholders.[1397] Four days later, Volkswagen increased its Porsche stake to 49.9 percent.[1398]

The accessible information on the intended merger of Volkswagen and Porsche shows the desirability of the shareholder activism and the opportunism of a Volkswagen administration riddled with conflicts of interest. These conflicts of interest result from

---

ftd.de, http://www.ftd.de/unternehmen/industrie/autoindustrie/:nordischer-gegenwind-grossaktionaer-droht-vw-mit-klage-gegen-porsche-kauf/50020523.html?page=2.

1391 *Ferdinand Piech-Verdacht auf Untreue?*, Nov. 26, 2009, Boerse-go.de, http://www.boerse-go.de/nachricht/Ferdinand-Pich-Verdacht-auf-Untreue-VW-Volkswagen,a2018936.html.

1392 *Nordischer Gegenwind*, Oct. 8, 2009, Financial Times Deutschland, http://www.ftd.de/unternehmen/industrie/autoindustrie/:nordischer-gegenwind-grossaktionaer-droht-vw-mit-klage-gegen-porsche-kauf/50020523.html?page=2.

1393 *Investoren formieren sich gegen Porsche-Deal*, Oct. 9, 2009, Handelsblatt, http://www.handelsblatt.com/unternehmen/industrie/investoren-formieren-sich-gegen-porsche-deal;2466219.

1394 Daniel Schäfer, *Großaktionäre heizen VW ein*, Nov. 16, 2009, Financial Times Deutschland http://www.ftd.de/unternehmen/industrie/autoindustrie/:porsche-uebernahme-grossaktionaere-heizen-vw-ein/50037928.html.

1395 *VW übernimmt knapp die Hälfte von Porsche*, Dec. 7, 2009, Hannoversche Allgemeine, http://www.haz.de/Nachrichten/Wirtschaft/Deutschland-Welt/VW-uebernimmt-knapp-die-Haelfte-von-Porsche.

1396 Kremer, in: Ringleb et al., Deutscher Corporate Governance Kodex, 2008, mn.255: according to whom the right to speak is derived from § 118 AktG, as it is not expressely laid down in the Stock Corporation Act, but in No. 2.2.3 DCGK.

1397 Gregor Haake/Margret Hucko, *Porsche-Übernahme: Aktionäre drehen VW-Führung durch die Mangel*, Dec. 3, 2009, Financial Times Deutschland, http://www.ftd.de/unternehmen/industrie/autoindustrie/:porsche-uebernahme-aktionaere-drehen-vw-fuehrung-durch-die-mangel/50045682.html; *Kleinanleger greifen VW-Führung an*, Dec. 3, 2009, Hannoversche Allgemeine, http://www.haz.de/Nachrichten/Wirtschaft/Deutschland-Welt/Kleinanleger-greifen-VW-Fuehrung-an.

1398 *VW übernimmt knapp die Hälfte von Porsche*, Dec.7, 2009, Hannoversche Allgemeine, http://www.haz.de/Nachrichten/Wirtschaft/Deutschland-Welt/VW-uebernimmt-knapp-die-Haelfte-von-Porsche.

the majority positions of the Porsche and Piech families in both corporations as well as the position of F. Piech as head of Volkswagen's supervisory board. The transaction is designed to circumvent Niedersachsen's veto and grants Porsche access to Volkswagen's war chest.

With a qualified majority of shareholders in favor of the merger, the active shareholders could not use special formal means to veto the fundamental transaction by a vote of more than twenty-five percent of the present capital (§§ 13, 65 UmwG, § 202). The same applied to the effective general formal means depending on (qualified) majority approval (§§ 103 (1), 84 (3)). Volkswagen's active minority shareholders used informal shareholder means involving the public by targeting the reputations of the administrative members, especially the supervisory board members. They used letters released to the public and interviews with journals to publicly express their discontent with the merger and to support each other. During Volkswagen's special shareholder meeting, the minority shareholders extensively used their general right to speak and their special right to question management about the transaction and the other constituent corporation. Their opposition gained more public attention. Furthermore, they threatened legal proceedings and reported a breach of trust and simultaneously referred to several like-minded shareholders likely to support them. Finally, they predicted increased capital costs as a capital market reaction to the lack of transparency about the strategy and price of the Porsche acquisition.

Claims for damages by several investment funds and Porsche shareholders of more than several billion U.S. dollars based on wrong information and manipulation of the market price were the most severe obstacle facing the merger.[1399] In Germany, Piech is now under attack for having violated his duties as a member of Porsche's supervisory board. In Febrary 2012, the Higher Regional Court of Stutgart held that he had violated his main duties as supervisory board member with regard to Porsche's attempt to take over Volkswagen.[1400] The court set aside the exoneration of the entire supervisory board for the year 2008/09.

*iii) Transaction activism aiming **to facilitate** mergers*

Considering the generally underlying interests, an opportunistic administration aims to facilitate a merger. Shareholder-value orientated shareholders in the surviving corporation aim, in contrast, to prevent an acquisition, which is likely to transfer the entire benefits of the merger to the shareholders of the acquired corporation. In parallel, the facilitation of a merger will hardly provide shareholders of the surviving corporation with the necessary incentives to become active, as the stock price is unlikely to rise upon

---

1399 *Volkswagen/Porsche Milliardenklagen gefährden Fusion*, Feb. 17, 2010, MANAGER MAGAZIN, http://www.manager-magazin.de/unternehmen/artikel/0,2828,678473,00.html; *Klageflut könnte VW-Porsche-Fusion verzögern*, Oct. 19, 2010, DIE ZEIT, http://www.zeit.de/wirtschaft/unternehmen/2010-10/porsche-vw-verschmelzung.

1400 OLG Stuttgart, Urt. v. 29.02.2012, Az.: 20 U 3/11.

the announcement of a merger. As a consequence, the constellation is unlikely to involve beneficial transaction activism.

Shareholders of German corporations can initiate the shareholder meeting's decision to have the management board prepare and later implement a merger contract via minority motion, §§ 122 (1), 83 for the next general or a requested special shareholder meeting, § 122 (2). The initial motion needs to be brought by shareholders holding (jointly) a stake of 5 percent or a stake of Euro 500,000 of the share capital if it takes place during a general shareholder meeting. Moreover, the shareholder meeting is responsible for mergers, as the relevant statute requires the shareholder meeting to approve the merger contracts.[1401] Since a merger contract needs to be prepared prior to the required shareholder vote, the minority motion is restricted to a request that a shareholder vote be held on the demand that the management board prepare it, § 83 (1) sent. 2. This applies also if the administration opposes a merger. The intention is to provide shareholders with initiation rights on fundamental matters.[1402] However, the specific approval quorum, §§ 13, 65 (1) UmwG, § 83 (1) sent. 3, represents a substantial practical hurdle for active shareholders to facilitate a merger. Taking into account that shareholders are likely to follow management's recommendations[1403] in specific business matters,[1404] management's support of the merger seems to be key. Therefore, active shareholders would need to change the management board's mind via the use of the entire spectrum of general formal and informal means, including those involving the public. Accordingly, even if the facilitation of a merger would be subject to potential transaction activism, the lack of helpful special means to reduce active shareholders' campaign costs makes the necessary financial incentives less likely.

b) Targeting ***tender offer*** decisions

*i) Special formal means of shareholders of the **acquiring** company*

(1) Regarding general acquisitions

The corporate decision whether to acquire another corporation is generally considered to be a management task falling under the management board's authority, § 76 (1).[1405] The control of such management tasks falls under the responsibility of the supervisory board. A shareholder vote on the corporate decision to acquire another corporation is therefore generally not required.

1401 Hüffer, AktG, 2010, § 83 mn.3; Spindler, in: MüKo AktG, 2008, § 83 mn.6, 10.

1402 Hüffer, AktG, 2010, § 83 mn.3; Mertens, in: KöKo AktG, 1996, § 83 mn.3; Spindler, in: MüKo AktG, 2008, § 83 mnn.9 et seq.

1403 Choi & Guzman, 87 Va. L. Rev., 961, 985 (2001), Clark, Corporate Law 94 (1986).

1404 Bebchuk, 118 Harv. L. Rev. 833, 875 et seq. (2006): while denying this circumstance for well known corporate governance issues, which shareholders are able to inform themselves about without too large efforts, they may be most likely to follow management recommendations on specific business decisions, usually requiring sophisticated information on the matter for evaluation reasons.

1405 Fleischer, in: Hdb Vorstandsrecht, 2006, § 22 mn.42; Wagner DStR 2004, 141 (141).

Shareholder approval is necessary, however, if an amendment to the articles of incorporation is required for the transaction, § 179. This is the case when the line of business specified in the articles of incorporation does not cover the business of the acquiring corporations or does not comprise the *acquisition of participations* as part of the line of business,[1406] § 23 (3) No 2.

(2) Regarding significant participation acquisitions

It is controversial whether the shareholder approval requirement under the *Holzmüller/Gelatine*[1407] *cases* also applies to the *acquisition* of participations. The initial *Holzmüller* case decided by the Federal Court of Justice concerned the spin-off of the only valuable part of a corporation. The court decided that the management board was reasonably required to ask the shareholder meeting for approval pursuant to (only internally relevant) § 119 (2).[1408] In its later *Gelatine* decision relating to the corporate restructuring of a subsidiary into a lower-tier subsidiary, the court changed its underlying dogmatic reasoning to one of judicial amendment of the law (*offene Rechtsfortbildung*). Since the measure so closely impacts the membership rights of shareholders and their financial interest that it is almost tantamount to an amendment of the articles of incorporation, the mediatization of the shareholder rights necessitates a vote of the shareholder meeting.[1409]

The question is, however, whether and when *Holzmüller/Gelatine* applies to corporate acquisitions of participations. The "*if*" is much debated amongst scholars.[1410] One opinion interprets the verdict's text literally,[1411] with the consequence that even major share acquisitions fall solely under management's responsibility. Shareholder approval is only required once management requires that the shareholder meeting approve the decision according to § 119 (2).[1412] Proponents argue that the acquisition of participations only constitutes an asset

1406 Kubis, in: MüKo AktG, 2004, § 119 mn.66.

1407 BGH, Urt. v. 25.02.1982, Az.: II ZR 174/80, NJW 1982, 1703-Holzmüller; BGH, Urt. v. 26.04.2004, Az.: II ZT 155/02, NZG 2004, 571-Gelatine.

1408 BGH, Urt. v. 25.02.1982, Az.: II ZR 174/80, NJW 1982, 1703-Holzmüller.

1409 BGH, Urt. v. 26.04.2004, Az.: II ZT 155/02, NZG 2004, 571 (573)-Gelatine; Beisel, in: Beisel/Klumpp, Der Unternehmenskauf, 2009, ch. 8, mn.81.

1410 BGH, Urt. v. 25.02.1982, Az.: II ZR 174/80, NJW 1982, 1703 (1705)-Holzmüller: Discussed passage distinguishes sharply between measures which fall under the *Holzmüller* doctrine, since they concern the core area of the corporation's business and they are capable of impacting the legal position of the shareholders significantly, in contrast to the usual management of the corporation to which belongs in general the setting-up, acquisition and equipment of a subsidiary with the necessary capital.

1411 Renner, NZG 2002, 1091 (1093); Sünner, AG 1983, 169 (170); other opinion: BGH has left this question open: BGH, Urt. v. 25.02.1982, Az.: II ZR 174/80, NJW 1982, 1703 (1705); *see* Henze, in: FS Ulmer, 211 (229); Wagner, DStR 2004, 141 (142).

1412 *Busch*, AG 2002, 145 (148): a takeover offer through a corporation requires regularly no shareholder resolution; *Ebenroth/Daum*, DB 1991, 1105 (1109); *Groß*, AG 1994, 266 (273 et seq.): based on the understanding that the *Holzmüller* doctrine applies only if the transaction interferes with the membership position of shareholders, not even a major participation acquisition demanding the transfer of a major part of the corporate assets requires an approval by the shareholder meeting, since the acquisition of a participation constitutes the use of assets which is part

exchange by which shareholder interests are not impacted. The application of the *Holzmüller* doctrine is therefore unnecessary.[1413] Neither the shareholders' administrative nor financial rights are impacted significantly by major share acquisitions:[1414] the right to participate in shareholder meetings and to vote on issues according to the articles of incorporation and statute are neither formally nor substantially violated. Shareholders, so goes the argument, do not have the right to impact the composition of the assets, nor does an explicit statutory provision (as is the case for transfers of assets, capital measures, corporate contracts, mergers, but not for acquisitions of shares[1415]) apply to share acquisitions.[1416] Accordingly, proponents argue, solely the management board determines the use of corporate assets, as is the case with the acquisition of shares and other investments. Shareholders, in contrast, are only allowed to determine the use of net profit stated in annual financial statements.[1417] In addition, the financial shareholder rights are not fundamentally impacted by a significant share acquisition. The liquidation value of a stake usually equals its fair value. The claim to profit as such is not influenced by a share acquisition, since it comprises only the right to participate in the shareholder decision about the use of the annual net profit. The law also protects against the abuse of retained profits in subsidiaries.[1418] Furthermore, the risk of loss exists under each of the investments made by management and is therefore not particular to the acquisition of participations in a third corporation.[1419] Finally, the approach of the proponents of shareholder approval has the potential to cause legal uncertainty.[1420]

Other legal scholars[1421] argue that major share acquisitions should be approved by a shareholder vote. However, their approaches diverge. Besides the approach pursued by

---

of the management. The shareholder meeting may therefore get only involved in participation acquisition transactions if the management board requires that the shareholder meeting approves it according to § 119 (2) AktG; *Joost*, ZHR 163 (1999), 164 (183); *Mertens*, in: KöKo AktG, 1996, § 76 mn.51; *Renner*, NZG 2002, 1091 (1093 et seq.); *Sünner*, AG 1983, 169 (170): unwritten competence of shareholder meeting under the scenario of setting up, acquisition and equipment as little as under sale of subsidiaries or shares; *Wagner*, DStR 2004, 141 (146); *Werner*, ZHR 147 (1983), 429 (447 et seq.).

1413 Ebenroth/Daum, DB 1991, 1105 (1109).

1414 Groß, AG 1994, 266 (273); Renner, NZG 2002, 1091 (1092); Sünner, AG 1983, 169 (170); Wagner, DStR 2004, 141 (142).

1415 Renner, NZG 2002, 1091 (1093).

1416 Groß, AG 1994, 266 (273).

1417 *Id.*; Renner, NZG 2002, 1091 (1093); Wagner, DStR 2004, 141 (143).

1418 Groß, AG 1994, 266 (274 et seq.); Renner, NZG 2002, 1091 (1093); Wagner, DStR 2004, 141 (143 et seq.).

1419 Renner, NZG 2002 1091 (1092).

1420 Geßler, Einberufung und ungeschriebene Hauptversammlungszuständigkeiten, in: Lutter et al., FS Stimpel, 1985, 771 (786); Sünner, AG 1983, 169 (170).

1421 *Fleischer,* Hdb Vorstandsrecht, 2006, § 22 mn.42; *Geßler*, Einberufung und ungeschriebene Hauptversammlungszuständigkeiten, in: Lutter et al., FS Stimpel, 1985, 771 (786 et seq.); *Habersack*, in: Emmerich/Habersack, Aktien- und GmbH-Konzernrecht, 2010, Vor § 311 AktG, mnn.42, 46: applicable *Holzmüller* doctrine in case of acquisition of share participation concerning 80 percent of the acquiring corportaion's value; *Lutter*, in: FS Stimpel, 1985, 825 (850 et seq.): distinguishes between management decisions and structural decisions, the latter require a shareholder approval if they are very similar to a merger, conversion, obligation to transfer entire assets or exclusion of subscription rights. By now, Lutter supports a rather restricted appli-

Holzmüller/Gelatine based on the mediatization of the shareholder rights, some scholars demand approval of extraordinary transactions, which include the acquisition of major participations. Finally, others view *Holzmüller/Gelatine* as part of the group building control.

Most of the proponents of shareholder approval agree that shareholders in the acquisition of a major participation suffer from the same *mediatization effect* as under the spin-off scenario underlying the *Holzmüller* decision.[1422] According to the reasoning of the BGH in the *Holzmüller* and *Gelatine* decisions, shareholder interests are at risk due to the mediatization resulting from the transfer of competency in favor of the management board, which exercises the shareholder rights in a subsidiary. Shareholders of the parent corporation have only indirect influence on the newly acquired operational assets as compared to direct impact on the (exchanged) financial assets.[1423] The diluting effect depends on the participation rate of the parent corporation.[1424] Furthermore, there is the financial risk that shareholders will pay more for the acquired participation than was initially paid for it, transferring wealth to outside shareholders of the subsidiary.[1425] Even if a 100 percent stake is acquired, the same

---

cation of the *Holzmüller* doctrine. Therefore, he points out that in the normal case of forming a group by acquiring a participation or by setting up a subsidiary the shareholder meeting should not get involved as long as the articles of incorporation admit an acquisition of a participation,*Lutter*, 25 Jahre AktG, 53 et seq. (71 n.50); *Lutter/Leinekugel*, ZIP 1998, 225 (230); *Mecke*, Konzernstruktur und Aktionärsentscheid, 50 et seq., 161 et seq.; *Mülbert*, Aktiengesellschaft, Unternehmensgruppe und Kapitalmarkt, 371: supports the equal treatment of spin-off and acquisition of a share participation; Süßmann, in: Geibel/Süßmann, WpÜG, 2008, § 25 mn.2: declares *Holzmüller/Gelatine* doctrine as applicable under § 25 WpÜG; *Timm*, Die Aktiengesellschaft als Konzernspitze, 1980, 71 et seq. (76); *Timm*, ZIP 1993, 114 (116 et seq.): no shareholder approval necessary as long as the group building measures relate to a subsidiary which does not constitute the essential asset of the parent corporation, the question is therefore whether the measure has a corresponding weight in order to be qualified as an amendment of the material aim of the firm; *Wollburg/Gehling*, Umgestaltung des Konzerns – Wer entscheidet über die Veräußerung von Beteiligungen einer Aktiengesellschaft?, in: Niederleithinger et al., FS Lieberknecht, 1997, 133 (133 et seq., 152): Authors point out the requirement of shareholder approval under the *Holzmüller* doctrine for the scenario of the purchase and sale of essential participations but also the necessary reservation of its use in the corporate practice and the application of the *Holzmüller* doctrine regarding world wide operating groups. For the context of a sale of a participation: Even though the acquisition of a participation is generally covered by the general authority of the management board to manage the corporation this may not be transferred to the (acquisition or) sale of essential participations.

1422 *Fleischer*, Hdb Vorstandsrecht, 2006, § 22 mn.42; *Habersack*, in: Emmerich/Habersack, Aktien- und GmbH-Konzernrecht, Vor § 311, mnn.20, 15, 14; *Hirte*, Bezugsrechtsausschluss und Konzernbildung, 1986, 162 et seq.: underscores the equal necessity for protection whether the withdrawal concerns substance or liquidity, in balance sheet terms spin-off and acquisition both involve the exchange of assets, spin-off and acquisition result therefore both in a mediatisation of shareholder rights; *Mülbert*, Aktiengesellschaft, Unternehmensgruppe und Kapitalmarkt, 1996, 371; *Wollburg/Gehling*, Umgestaltung des Konzerns – Wer entscheidet über die Veräußerung von Beteiligungen einer Aktiengesellschaft?, in: Niederleithinger et al., FS Lieberknecht, 1997, 133 (155).

1423 *Habersack*, in: Emmerich/Habersack, Aktien- und GmbH-Konzernrecht, 2010, Vor § 311, mnn.42, 34; *Lutter/Leinekugel*, ZIP 1998, 225 (230).

1424 Timm, ZIP 1993, 114 (116).

1425 Habersack, in: Emmerich/Habersack, Aktien- und GmbH-Konzernrecht, 2010, Vor § 311, mn.34.

risk exists indirectly as outside shareholders could be integrated later, while the risk of dilution of shareholder impact remains.[1426] Both risks could be compensated by unwritten approval competencies of the shareholder meeting applying to essential share acquisitions that involve about 80 percent of the assets of the acquiring corporation.[1427]

Some scholars, including *Lutter*, require an unwritten approval competency of the shareholder meeting (also) for decisions that concern the underlying principles of the corporation[1428] or the core area of the corporate concept.[1429] They are *one-time decisions.*[1430] These measures are not governed by statute requiring shareholder approval and are therefore formally covered by the authority of the management board.[1431] However, they are so close to the fundamental measures, which, according to statute, need to be approved by a shareholder vote that they clearly do not fall under the general management competence of the management board.[1432] A corresponding evaluation is found in § 119 (1).[1433] The consequences of these unwritten measures requiring shareholder approval have to be economically or legally, partially or entirely, comparable to the ones governed by statute that require shareholder approval.[1434]

A third approach interprets *Holzmüller/Gelatine* as requiring shareholder approval for group building scenarios.[1435] Accordingly, it applies to newly formed groups as well as to enlargements of groups,[1436] as long as the relevant measure has a certain weight for the acquiring corporation.[1437] Besides the mediatization concerns related to the administrative and financial shareholder rights mentioned by the BGH,[1438] additional aspects need to be considered to justify the necessity of shareholder approval for a major share acquisition. These include the impact of group building on the corporate structure and

1426 *Id.*; oposing opinion: Renner, NZG 2002, 1091(1092).

1427 Habersack, in: Emmerich/Habersack, Aktien- und GmbH-Konzernrecht, 2010, Vor § 311, mn.46.

1428 Lutter, Organzuständigkeiten im Konzern, in: Lutter et al., FS Stimpel, 1985, 850 et seq.

1429 Lutter/Leinekugel, ZIP 1998, 225 (230).

1430 *Id.*

1431 *Id.*

1432 Lutter, Organzuständigkeiten im Konzern, in: Lutter et al., FS Stimpel, 1985, 825 (850).

1433 Lutter/Leinekugel, ZIP 1998, 225 (230).

1434 Geßler, Einberufung und ungeschriebene Hauptversammlungszuständigkeiten, in: Lutter et al., FS Stimpel, 1985, 771 (786).

1435 *Id.*; Habersack, in: Emmerich/Habersack, Aktien- und GmbH-Konzernrecht, Vor § 311 mnn.20, 15, 14 (2001), 34 (2010): now pointing out that determining is not the group building scenario, but the limitation of the shareholder rights through the mediatisation of the shareholder rights resulting, for instance, from the acquisition of a participation, even if in practice most of those cases will be group building scenarios; Liebscher, Konzernbildungskontrolle, 1995, 86-91; Mecke, Konzernstruktur und Aktionärsentscheid, 1992, 50 et seq., 161 et seq.; Mülbert, Aktiengesellschaft, Unternehmensgruppe und Kapitalmarkt, 1996, 370 et seq.: who focuses on group building processes as far as they involve a shifting of financial means to subsidiaries, which involve the factual reduction of shareholder rights, 371; Timm, ZIP 1993, 114 (116 et seq.); Wagner, DStR 2004, 141 (144).

1436 Mülbert, Aktiengesellschaft, Unternehmensgruppe und Kapitalmarkt, 1996, 370 et seq.

1437 Timm, ZIP 1993, 114 (117).

1438 *Id.* at 116; Habersack, in: Emmerich/Habersack, Aktien- und GmbH-Konzernrecht, 2010, Vor § 311, mn.14; Mecke, Konzernstruktur und Aktionärsentscheid, 1992, 80–182; Mülbert, Aktiengesellschaft, Unternehmensgruppe und Kapitalmarkt, 1996, 371, 372 et seq.

the tasks and responsibilities of the parent corporation's organs.[1439] They are also relevant to the evaluation of whether the transaction comes close to an amendment of the corporate objective, which would require amendment of the articles of incorporation.[1440]

The arguments of opponents of a shareholder approval for participation acquisitions are not convincing. They are only of a formal nature. Negating the impact of the acquisition of a major participation on any of the administrative or financial shareholder rights by taking a rather descriptive look on each of the relevant rights, this approach is unappealing. Rather than formally distinguishing the *Holzmüller* spin-off scenario from the participation acquisition scenario by the means involved,[1441] a functional approach that not only concentrates on the impact on the separate legal categories of shareholder rights but also on the factual consequences should prevail.[1442]

The three remaining approaches all support the necessity of shareholder approval for the acquisition of significant participations. The remaining question is therefore whether a specific acquisition justifies the shareholder approval requirement in the acquiring corporation. Decisive is its impact on the distribution of authority amongst shareholders as principals and the management and supervisory board members as agents. The necessity of shareholder approval for the acquisition of share participation must be answered by considering the *functional* background of the distribution of power between principals and agents. Under corporate law, economic ownership and the authority to dispose of corporate assets are split up. Shareholders as economic owners of the corporation have the authority to determine the articles of incorporation's content, including the nature of the corporation's business. Due to the costs of a complete contract, the necessarily incomplete contract is supplemented by shareholder competencies concerning repetitive and fundamental decisions laid down in §§ 119 (1) No 1, 2, 3, 4 and 5, 6, 8 as well as throughout the corporate statute. On the other hand, shareholders are generally excluded from managing the corporation, § 119 (2). The management board members, in contrast, have to direct and to manage the daily affairs of the corporation within the line of business specified in the articles of incorporation, §§ 76 (1), 77. Such distribution of authority assures efficient leadership of the corporation, which prevents strategic or daily decisions from having to be met by unsophisticated shareholders acting rationally apathetically on management decisions. With regard to fundamental decisions, such as the acquisition of major participations, sufficient information is usually publicly available to the shareholders nor does the rational apathy scenario apply to such decisions. Furthermore, a major acquisition significantly impacts the distribution of competencies between shareholders and the management board. While the shareholders remain formally responsible for the fundamental decisions in the (future parent) corporation, their factual impact is significantly reduced. Management exercises the shareholder rights in the subsidiary comprising the decisions on significant structural matters, while the participation represents the major assets of the

1439 Timm, ZIP 1993, 114 (116); Mecke, Konzernstruktur und Aktionärsentscheid, 1992, 183.

1440 Busch, AG 2002, 145 (148); Mecke, Konzernstruktur und Aktionärsentscheid, 1992, 183 et seq.; Timm, ZIP 1993, 114 (117).

1441 Renner, NZG 2002, 1091 (1092).

1442 Mülbert, Aktiengesellschaft, Unternehmensgruppe und Kapitalmarkt, 1996, 371.

corporation. Here, the distribution of authority as laid down in §§ 76 (1) and 119 (1), (2) has shifted significantly in favor of management, leading to the mentioned mediatization of shareholder rights as well as to the risk of diluting the financial value of the membership right. Funds available to realize the operational part of the business may be significantly reduced. As a result, the realization of the corporate objective can be difficult, making an amendment to the line of business and therefore an amendment of the articles of incorporation necessary. Finally, the focus on the violation of shareholder rights instead of on the *structural character* of the measure would have the consequence that other major transactions would not need to be approved, even though their impact may be significant.[1443] As a consequence, allegations that *group provisions* in the articles of incorporation of acquiring corporations make shareholder approval of the acquisition of participation unnecessary, as shareholders are aware of them and their effects making additional protection superfluous,[1444] are not convincing. The exceptional character of transactions subject to *Holzmüller/Gelatine* and their closeness to a required amendment to the articles of incorporation underscores that general group provisions have no impact.[1445]

The relevant border that determines whether a specific participation acquisition requires shareholder approval should be determined on this basis. Accordingly, the valuation of corporate law in general and of structural decisions specifically should be the starting point. As raised by the BGH in *Gelatine*, the legislative intent is clearly to provide the management board with the necessary discretion to efficiently manage the corporation. Only a very limited number of structural decisions require shareholder approval.[1446] Statutory shareholder approval concerns only extreme situations. § 179a requires the obligation to transfer the entire corporate assets. However, it applies as soon as the obligation leads to a lack of sufficient assets to further pursue the corporate objective.[1447] The wording of the norm underscores that only extreme situations are covered, while it is not applied word-for-word, but rather according to its functional purpose. Requiring a structural impact of the measure and considering the statutory reservation to requiring shareholder approval, unwritten shareholder competencies need to be handled in a restrictive manner. The determination of the border should therefore be oriented toward the purpose of the approval requirement rather than on straight numbers. Even though the absence of a bright line approach triggering shareholder approval for participation acquisitions leads to a certain extent of legal uncertainty,[1448] a *qualitative approach* does justice in each case.[1449] It needs to be dealt with similarly to vague legal terms (*unbestimmte Rechtsbegriffe*).[1450] Finally, the restriction that in cases requiring a shareholder resolution the approval can only be

1443 Lutter/Leinekugel, ZIP 1998, 225 (230).

1444 Krieger, in: Münch. Hdb. AG, Vol. 4, 1999, § 69 mn.7; Joost ZHR 163 (1999), 164, 183.

1445 Habersack, in: Emmerich/Habersack, Aktien- und GmbH-Konzernrecht, 2010, Vor § 311 mn.42.

1446 BGH, Urt. v. 26.04.2004, Az.: II ZT 155/02, NJW 2004, 1860 (1864)-Gelatine.

1447 Hüffer, AktG, § 179a mn.5.

1448 Geßler, Einberufung und ungeschriebene Hauptversammlungszuständigkeiten, in: Lutter et al., FS Stimpel, 1985, 771 (786); Sünner, AG 1983, 169 (170).

1449 Fleischer, NJW 2004, 2335 (2339).

1450 Geßler, Einberufung und ungeschriebene Hauptversammlungszuständigkeiten, in: Lutter et al., FS Stimpel, 1985, 771 (786).

denied for *appropriate reasons*[1451] suffers from a lack of practicability, which results from the difficulties of proving the appropriateness of each denial.[1452]

As a consequence, in the rare cases when *Holzmüller/Gelatine* applies to qualitative relevant acquisitions of participations, an approval by three-fourths of the present share capital is required. The BGH has justified the qualified majority requirement with the closeness of the concerned measure to an amendment of the articles of incorporation. According to § 179 (1), (2), it requires an equal approval through the shareholder meeting. Even though the decision does not require an amendment of the articles of incorporation, its influence on the shareholders comes very close to a decision requiring their amendment.[1453]

In practice, the validity of a public offer to acquire a participation, which does not represent a mandatory offer, §§ 39, 35 (2) WpÜG,[1454] depends on the required approval of the shareholder meeting. § 25 WpÜG provides that the public offer to acquire a corporation may be conditioned by the approval of the shareholder meeting of the bidding corporation. It is an exception to the general principle that conditions which depend on the bidder are bannd from public offers, § 18 WpÜG, which in turn represents an exception to the general permissibility of conditions on public offers, § 11 (2) Nr. 5 WpÜG.[1455] The shareholder meeting's approval has to take place at the latest 5 days before the offer expires.[1456] It is controversial, however, whether an approval under § 25 WpÜG needs to be based on an explicit provision or whether it may be based on *Holzmüller/Gelatine*. Cases in favor exist only in the form of *obiter dictum*.[1457] It must be supported to keep the procedure free of competency issues.[1458]

1451 Schneider, in: Assmann et al., WpÜG, 2005, § 25 mn.2.

1452 Süßmann, in: Geibel/Süßmann, WpÜG, 2008, § 25 mn.4.

1453 BGH, Urt. v. 26.4.2004, Az.: II ZR 154/02, NZG 2004, 575 (579)-Gelatine; Hübner, Die Ausgliederung von Unternehmensteilen in aktien- und aufsichtsrechtlicher Sicht, in: Lutter et al., FS Stimpel, 1985, 791 (795 et seq.); Raiser, Recht der Kapitalgesellschaften, 2001, § 16 mn.15; Habersack, in: Emmerich/Habersack, Aktien- und GmbH-Konzernrecht, 2010, Vor § 311 mn.50; other opinion in favor of a simple majority: Hüffer, Zur Holzmüller-Problematik: Reduktion des Vorstandsermessens oder Grundlagenkompetenz der Hauptversammlung, in: Habersack et al., FS Ulmer, 2003, 279 (297 et seq.); Semler in: Münch. Hdb. AG, Vol. 4, 1999, § 34 mn.42.

1454 Wertpapiererwerbs- und Übernahmegesetz [WpÜG] [Acquistition and Takeover Act], Dec. 20, 2001, BGBl. I at 3822 (F.R.G.).

1455 Busch, AG 2002, 145 (145); Noack/Holzborn, in: Schwark/Zimmer, Kapitalmarktrechts-Kommentar, 2010, § 25 mn.1; Süßmann, in: Geibel/Süßmann, WpÜG, § 25 mn.2.

1456 Süßmann, in: Geibel/Süßmann, WpÜG, 2008, § 25 mnn.2, 3.

1457 LG Stuttgart, Urt. v. 8.11.1991, Az.: 2 KfH O 135/91, AG 1992, 236 (237 et seq.)–not legally binding: questions concerning the core area of the corporation, as it is the case with spin-offs but also with the administration of participations including the acquisition and their sale, have to be put at shareholder approval in order to prevent that membership rights and the function of the shareholder meeting become gauged; LG Duisburg, Urt. v. 27.6.2002 Az.: 21 O 106/02, AG 2003, 390 (390, 391)–Babcock Borsig AG/HDW–not legally binding: the acquisition or sale of a participation requires the approval of the shareholder meeting as far as the measure concerns the core area of the business of the firm and the corporate structure undergoes a radical change.

1458 Fleischer, Hdb Vorstandsrecht, 2006, § 22 mn.43; Noack/Holzborn, in: Schwark/Zimmer, Kapitalmarktrechts-Kommentar, 2010, § 18 WpÜG mn.12; § 25 WpÜG, mn.2; Steinmeyer, in: Häger/Steinmeyer, WpÜG, 2007, § 18 mn.12.

*ii) Transaction activism aiming **to prevent** an acquisition*

(1) Underlying interests

Opposing underlying interests between an opportunistic-acting administration aiming to realize the acquisition of another corporation and shareholders aiming to enhance shareholder value by avoiding overpaying for an acquisition are the basis of beneficial shareholder activism. Simultaneously, the constellation bears the potential to provide active shareholders with the necessary financial incentives to become active and to oppose to an opportunistic administrative decision. They are based on potentially rising stock prices and distributable war chests. So far, the constellation is comparable to that targeting a merger decision.

(2) Relevant shareholder means

The corporate decision to acquire another corporation is usually a management decision requiring no shareholder approval due to the high standards of *Holzmüller/Gelatine*, except for scenarios requiring shareholder approval of certain financial measures. Only the supervisory board has to approve a corresponding direct management decision, § 111 (4) sent. 2.

Therefore, active shareholders aiming to prevent a proposed acquisition are limited to the use of general formal and informal means because of a lack of special formal means like a veto right. Active shareholders are therefore limited to convincing either the management or the supervisory board to change its opinion and reject the transaction. After contacting a sufficient number of fellow investors to assure their support, they will communicate their critique of the transaction, especially possible overpayment, and their support from like-minded shareholders. They will contact the administration, especially the management board or the head of the supervisory board, via e-mails, phone calls, or private conversations. In addition, active shareholders may underscore their demand with the threat to use general formal means including the removal of supervisory board members and the (precatory) initiation of the removal of a management board member. Furthermore, they may threaten to introduce a motion for a special auditor or to recommend a shareholder resolution relating to an administrative agenda topic[1459] during the next general meeting or a special shareholder meeting upon minority request.[1460] Absent success through these threats alone, they must implement them by using their initiation rights and proving that they have the necessary support from fellow shareholders. Finally, active shareholders may in parallel or independently *publish* their criticism of the transaction or the performance of certain administrative members via public letters or directly by informing the media. Apart from a shareholder vote, such a campaign aims to trigger the reputational mechanism and move the concerned members of the

1459 Mülbert, in: Großkomm AktG, 2008, § 119 mn.39.

1460 Semler, in: Münch. Hdb. AG, Vol. 4, 1999, § 35 mn.16.

administration to abandon the transaction. However, if the active shareholders have initiated a shareholder vote, such a campaign aims to ensure its success.

In the rare case that the corporate decision to acquire another corporation falls under *Holzmüller/Gelatine*, the shareholder meeting will use the qualified approval requirement of three-fourths of the present share capital to veto the acquisition. If management ignores the necessity of such shareholder approval, common opinion[1461] allows a minority of shareholders to initiate a shareholder vote on the acquisition according to § 122 (1), (2), (3).

(3) Example

The combined use of general formal and informal means by active shareholders of the acquiring corporation is well demonstrated by the attempt of Deutsche Börse AG ("***Deutsche Börse***") to acquire the London Stock Exchange ("***LSE***") via a cash tender offer. Deutsche Börse went public in 2001. Traditional German investment funds and international institutional shareholders, amongst them Merrill Lynch, Fidelity, and Capital, held its name shares. In October 2004, the hedge fund The Children Investment Fund ("***TCI***"), holding a 1 percent stake, met with Deutsche Börse's management to talk about the corporation and the industry in general.[1462] Later, an employee of TCI warned Deutsche Börse to have the shareholders decide on any deal with LSE. On December 13, 2004,[1463] Deutsche Börse launched an offer of 530 pence per LSE share[1464] without prior shareholder consultation. Due to sufficient cash reserves, Deutsche Börse did not need to convene a special meeting to have the shareholders approve financial measures and preferred to avoid a request according to § 119 (2). The latter not only would have required Deutsche Börse to provide shareholders with the necessary information on the issue,[1465] leading to insight into the company's deliberations about valuation, but it would have also bound management to the approved price.[1466] TCI, holding 1.8 percent at this time, initially confirmed its support for the offer.[1467] But about a month later, after TCI

1461 LG Düsseldorf, Beschl. v. 29.05.2002, Az.: 21 O 106/02, NZG 2002, 643 (643 et seq.): granting an injunction with regard to the ad hoc announcement of Babcock Borsig to sell the significant participation in the Howaldtswerke Deutsche Werft AG ("***HDW***") in favor of Wyser Pratte Management & Co. Inc., which as shareholder of Babcock Borsig aimed to prevent this sale by demanding the court to authorize a special shareholder meeting, § 122 (3), intended to realize the shareholder vote necessary according to *Holzmüller/Gelatine*; Halberkamp/Gierke, NZG 2004, 494 (497); Kubis, in: MüKo AktG, 2004, § 122 mn.15; Semler, in: Münch. Hdb. AG, Vol. 4, 1999, § 35 mn.16.

1462 Seifert, Invasion der Heuschrecken, 2006, 26.

1463 Von Heusinger/Storn, Die Zeit, 30.6.2006, 29.

1464 Seifert, Invasion der Heuschrecken, 2006, 102.

1465 BGH, Urt. v. 15.1.2001, Az.: II ZR 124/99, NJW 2001, 1277 (1277, 1278); Hüffer, AktG, § 119 mn.13.

1466 Seifert, Invasion der Heuschrecken, 2006, 107.

1467 *Id.* at 26 et seq.; other opinion: Kamp/Krieger-Boeckler foundation, *Die Aktivitäten von Finanzinvestoren in Deutschland,* working paper 103, 2005, 50, http://www.boeckler.de/pdf/p_arbp_103.pdf: noting that TCI opposed the transaction from the beginning.

acquired a 5 percent stake, it contacted Deutsche Börse, informing it that the offer was overpriced[1468] and demanding a special meeting to dismiss Rolf Breuer, head of the supervisory board of Deutsche Börse, § 103 (1), in order to stop the offer for LSE. Simultaneously, TCI informed the press[1469] of its request. The management board declined the request, since TCI did not fulfill the ownership requirement to have held its 5 percent stake for at least *three months* before the meeting, §§ 122 (1) sent. 3, 142 (2) sent. 2. Critical investors did not hesitate to express their discontent about the overpriced offer for LSE via the press. Deutsche Börse's management, in contrast, was restricted by the rules of the British Panel on Takeovers and Mergers,[1470] which made it difficult for them to provide their shareholders with well-founded data demonstrating that the price was justified. It would have required them to *publish* this sensitive information.[1471] Fidelity and Merrill Lynch, who had increased their holdings by this time to 8 percent, as well as several hedge funds, as confirmed by separate faxes or e-mails, together had a stake of about 30 percent of Deutsche Börse. They all argued for the cancellation of the LSE deal.[1472] Some of them, amongst them TCI as a leading opponent, wanted a shareholder vote on the offer and complained about the corporate governance in general and the communication policy of the head of the management board, Werner Seifert, and Rolf Breuer.[1473] In addition, they demonstrated their power by pointing out that they would have the opportunity to dismiss part of the supervisory board at the next general shareholder meeting, which was only eleven weeks away. TCI's e-mails followed corresponding press articles. They justified their lack of confidence in the administration by arguing it had failed to consider shareholder interests.[1474] The generally low attendance rates at German shareholder meetings, the provision of the articles letting suffice a simple majority for the removal of supervisory board members, the opponents' stake of 30 percent, and the press support constituted sufficient pressure for Deutsche Börse's man-

1468 Kamp/Krieger-Boeckler foundation, *Die Aktivitäten von Finanzinvestoren in Deutschland,* working paper 103, 2005, 50 et seq., http://www.boeckler.de/pdf/p_arbp_103.pdf.

1469 Seifert, Invasion der Heuschrecken, 2006, 106.

1470 „The Panel on Takeovers and Mergers (the "Panel") is an independent body, established in 1968, whose main functions are to issue and administer the City Code on Takeovers and Mergers (the "Code") and to supervise and regulate takeovers and other matters to which the Code applies in accordance with the rules set out in the Code. It has been designated as the supervisory authority to carry out certain regulatory functions in relation to takeovers pursuant to the Directive on Takeover Bids (2004/25/EC) (the "Directive"). Its statutory functions are set out in and under Chapter 1 of Part 28 of the Companies Act 2006. The Panel regulates takeover bids and other merger transactions (however effected) for companies which have their registered offices in the United Kingdom, the Channel Islands or the Isle of Man, if any of their securities are admitted to trading on a regulated market in the United Kingdom or on any stock exchange in the Channel Islands or the Isle of Man." http://www.thetakeoverpanel.org.uk/structure/about-the-panel.

1471 Seifert, Invasion der Heuschrecken, 2006, 109.

1472 *Id.* at 27.

1473 Kamp/Krieger-Boeckler foundation, *Die Aktivitäten von Finanzinvestoren in Deutschland,* working paper 103, 2005, 51, http://www.boeckler.de/pdf/p_arbp_103.pdf: so done by DSW

1474 Seifert, Invasion der Heuschrecken, 2006, 30 et seq.

agement to give in. In March 2005, it terminated the transaction[1475] and initiated share buyback programs. The stock price rose, which was not only welcomed by investors but also by the administration, which hoped to keep investors from continuing to impact corporate strategy and the supervisory board positions. However, instead of exiting, the active shareholders continued raising their voice. They increased their stakes to 35 percent (TCI 7.9 percent, Atticus 5.1 percent, Capital Group Companies 5.0 percent, Capital Group International 4.7 percent, others 12.3 percent). Furthermore, they pressured the administration to remove a substantial number of supervisory board members as well as Werner Seifert to ensure that the LSE acquisition would not happen and to extract additional money. On May 9, 2005, after a special meeting of the supervisory board and before the general meeting on May 25, 2005, Werner Seifert resigned his position as head of the management board. Rolf Breuer, whose resignation had also been sought initially by TCI's motions for the upcoming general meeting and who, based on the investors' pressure, had already announced his resignation, remained in office at the request of some investors until the end of 2005.[1476]

For the German corporate landscape, the shareholder activism that successfully prevented Deutsche Börse's acquisition of LSE kicked off a new form of shareholder activism.[1477] It had significant consequences for the planned acquisition and the targeted corporation and its administration.[1478] Regarding LSE's acquisition, the activism involved primarily informal means, such as personal e-mails, letters, and "one-on-ones" between TCI's head (or other investors) and the head of Deutsche Börse's management board, paired with their simultaneous publication. Pressure was also exercised by threatening the removal of the heads of management and supervisory board at a special meeting. Only the ownership requirement of §§ 122 (1) sent. 3, 142 (2) sent. 2 prevented the meeting from taking place and served its purpose of keeping short-term shareholders from convening special meetings to threaten the administration with removal. However, it did not hinder them from transferring their threat to the next general meeting. Its credibility depended most importantly, however, on significant stock purchases and parallel support for their position by 30 percent of the shareholders. Due to low shareholder attendance, it sufficed to pressure management to amend its decision without necessitating the use of removal rights.

Similar to the *group* regime for disclosure purposes under U.S. securities law, shareholders of German corporations *acting in concert* may be subject to the notification regime, § 22 (2) WpHG, or may trigger the obligation to launch a mandatory offer once they have jointly reached a 30 percent stake, §§ 30 (2), 35 (2) WpÜG. On October 19,

---

1475 *Deutsche Börse verzichtet auf LSE*, Mar. 6, 2005, DER SPIEGEL, http://www.spiegel.de/wirtschaft/0,1518,345083,00.html.

1476 Kamp/Krieger-Boeckler foundation, *Die Aktivitäten von Finanzinvestoren in Deutschland,* working paper 103, 2005, 51, http://www.boeckler.de/pdf/p_arbp_103.pdf.

1477 Engert, ZIP 2006, 2105 (2105); Fiesler et al., *Von der "Wall Street Rule" zu den "Media Rules" Bedeutung, Anliegen und Instrumente aktiver Aktionäre*, in: Meckel et al., Verkauft und nichts verraten, 2008, 16 (17), *available at* http://www.faz.net/m/%7BE5065EB2-29A7-4977-8117-6B3641E1FCBD%7DPicture.PDF.

1478 Engelhardt, *Activist Investing aus Unternehmenssicht*, M&A Review 4/2008, 194 (195).

2005, the BaFin published its decision that it was unable to prove that Deutsche Börse's investors had acted in concert.[1479] The BaFin perceived as determative that many shareholders had been dissatisfied with the lack of discussion of management's offer, which had resulted in criticism from different shareholders and in different ways. Based on this evidence, the BaFin was unable to prove with sufficient certainty that the investors had coordinated their behavior to strongly and consistently impact Deutsche Börse's administration while following a joint entrepreneurial interest or an overall plan[1480] through votes during the shareholder meeting.[1481] The parallel share acquisition and the communication amongst the several investors to hinder the acquisition of a competitor via factual impact on the management board were insufficient.[1482]

iii) Transaction activism aiming ***to facilitate*** *an acquisition*

Opportunistic behavior of the administration in the acquisition context is more likely to take place in the facilitation of (overpriced) acquisitions of other corporations, as they allow directors to secure or improve their position and compensation. Often, the prevention of an acquisition is for the shareholders of the surviving corporation more advantageous than the facilitation of an acquisition. In parallel, the facilitation of an acquisition generally does not provide incentives for active shareholders to become active compared, for instance, to the prevention of an overpriced acquisition. The share price should only be expected to rise upon its announcement if the corporation would profit from the synergies of the acquisition.

In addition, the financial benefits to the active shareholders need to sufficiently compensate their efforts in order to have them convince the administration to undertake the acquisition. The acquisition of another corporation is usually a pure management decision as opposed to a fundamental corporate decision or a decision subject to *Holzmüller/ Gelatine*. Therefore, active shareholders need to make use of general formal and informal means. Moreover, the direction of activism aims at facilitating a transaction against the will of the administration. Despite the comparably wide range of initiation rights under German corporate law, shareholders have no mandatory initiation right under § 122 to initiate a management decision.[1483] Even in the exceptional case that the shareholder meeting would need to approve the acquisition under *Holzmüller/Gelatine*, the decision remains a management task. Shareholders aiming to facilitate such an acquisition could therefore only initiate a shareholder meeting's discussion as well as a recommending

1479 Press release, BaFin, BaFin stellt bei der Deutschen Börse kein Acting in Concert fest (Oct. 19, 2005) http://www.bafin.de/cln_161/nn_721290/SharedDocs/Mitteilungen/DE/Service/PM__2005/pm__051019__actinconcb_C3_B6rse.html?__nnn=true.

1480 *Id.*; Ralf Thaeter, *Acting in Concert – Alle Fragen bleiben offen*, Börsenzeitung, Oct. 25, 2005, 6.

1481 BGH, Urt. v. 28.09.2006, Az: II ZR 137/05, NZG 2006, 945 (945).

1482 Spindler, WM 2007, 2357 (2358).

1483 Henn et al., Hdb des Aktienrechts, 2009, ch. 9, mn.65; Werner, in: Großkomm AktG, 2008, § 122 mn.27.

resolution.[1484] Both circumstances increase the required efforts for successful activism and make overcompensation of active shareholders less likely. Under this constellation, desirable transaction activism will therefore be comparably rare.

c) Targeting ***divestiture*** decisions

i) Special formal means of shareholders of the ***divesting*** *corporation*

Corporate divestiture decisions are usually a management decision.[1485] The question is, however, whether the *sale* of participations, parallel to the opposite constellation of the acquisition of participations, could become subject to *Holzmüller/Gelatine.* The answer is almost as controversial as the *supra* analyzed question regarding the *acquisition* of participations. Former rulings[1486] and some legal scholars[1487] endorse the applicability of the *Holzmüller/Gelatine* doctrine to the sale of participations. Recent rulings, especially of the second senate of the BGH, in charge of corporate law,[1488] and legal scholars[1489] reject its applicability to the sale of participations.

The opponents argue with the similarities to the sale of other corporate assets, that there is no legislative basis for an approval requirement for the shareholder meeting and the articles of incorporation's usual authorization of the acquisition or sale of participations.[1490] The sale of a subsidiary is just the opposite act of setting up, acquiring, or equipping a subsidiary, falling under the authority of the management board.[1491] In addition, it does not pose the same danger to shareholder rights, since it does not lead to the mediatization of shareholder rights,[1492] as does the group-building scenario of the *Holzmüller* decision, but rather unwinds it[1493]. The sale of a subsidiary amends therefore

1484 *For many* Halberkamp/Gierke, NZG 2004, 494 (497).

1485 OLG Stuttgart, Urt. v. 13.07.2005, Az.: 20 U 1/05, BeckRS 2005, 08092.

1486 OLG München, Urt. v. 10.11.1994, Az.: 24 U 1036/93, AG 1995, 232 (233)–„EKATIT Riedinger Verwaltungs-AG"; LG Duisburg, Urt. v. 27.6.2002, Az. 21 O 106/02, AG 2003, 390 (390)–Babcock Borsig AG/HDW; LG Frankfurt, Urt. v. 29.7.1997, Az.: 3/5 O 162/95, AG 1998, 45 (46).

1487 Beisel, in: Beisel/Klumpp, Der Unternehmenskauf, 2009, ch. 8, mn.82; Lutter/Leinekugel, ZIP 1998, 225 (230); Wollburg/Gehling, Umgestaltung des Konzerns – Wer entscheidet über die Veräußerung von Beteiligungen einer Aktiengesellschaft?, in: Niederleithinger et al., FS Lieberknecht, 1997, 133 (161).

1488 BGH, Urt. v. 20 November 2006, Az.: II ZR 226/05, NZG 2007, 234 (234); OLG Köln, Urt. v. 15.01.2009, Az.: 18 U 205/07, BeckRS 2009, 04001; OLG Hamm, Urt. v. 19.11.2007, Az.: 8 U 216/07, NZG 2008, 155, 157; OLG Stuttgart, Urt. v. 13.07.2005, Az.: 20 U 1/05, BeckRS 2005, 08092.

1489 Götz, AG 1984, 85 (89); Groß, AG 1994, 266 (275 et seq.); Habersack, in: Emmerich/Habersack, Aktien- und GmbH-Konzernrecht, 2010, Vor 311, mn.43; Joost, ZHR 163 (1999) 164 (185 et seq.); Koppensteiner, in: KöKo AktG, 2004, Vor § 291 mn.41; Sünner, AG 1983, 169 (170); Werner, ZHR 147 (1983) 429 (447 mn.48).

1490 Koppensteiner, in: KöKo AktG, 2004, Vor § 291 mn.41.

1491 Sünner, AG 1983, 169 (170).

1492 BGH, Urt. v. 20 November 2006, Az.: II ZR 226/05, NZG 2007, 234 (234).

1493 Habersack, in: Emmerich/Habersack, Aktien- und GmbH-Konzernrecht, 2010, Vor 311, mn.43 n.212.

only the composition of the corporate assets[1494] without violating shareholder rights[1495]. Moreover, preemptive rights protect only the maintenance of the proportional participation of each shareholder related to the share capital of the corporation, but not against the amendment of the corporate assets or their value.[1496] The relevant requirement in this context is instead § 179a AktG,[1497] which would be useless if the approach of the proponents of shareholder approval was followed.[1498] As a consequence, shareholder approval becomes necessary only if the line of business specified in the articles of incorporation would not be filled out past the sale of the subsidiary anymore and requires the amendment of the articles of incorporation.[1499]

Proponents of the approval requirements under *Holzmüller/Gelatine* argue that the violation of shareholder rights is determinative. They may not only be violated through their mediatization in group-building constellations. Fundamental corporate decisions, including the sale of important participations, may formally be covered by the administrative authority, since they do not violate the line of business specified by the articles of incorporation but may still require shareholder approval. The authority of the administration ends if a measure amends the corporate appearance and structure so fundamentally that it amends the core of the corporation.[1500] Therefore, these one-time-decisions require shareholder approval.[1501]

As far as § 179a is concerned, it aims to protect shareholders from the loss of the means necessary to realize the corporate purpose against unfavorable contractual terms.[1502] Considering its wording and its location in the section about the amendment of the articles of incorporation, leading often, but not always, to actual amendment of the articles of incorporation,[1503] there is no evident reason why § 179a should be exclusive.[1504] Absent the exclusive character of § 179a, however, it does not prevent other shareholder rights violation scenarios that require shareholder approval.[1505]

The counterargument of neutralizing an existing mediatization via the sale of a subsidiary cannot be convincing either, since according to the BGH it is not solely the mediatization of the shareholder impact that demands shareholder approval. Rather, all shareholder rights violations resulting from fundamental structural changes amend the

---

1494 Koppensteiner, in: KöKo AktG, 2004, Vor § 291, mn.41.

1495 Groß, AG 1994, 266 (275).

1496 *Id.* at 275 et seq.

1497 BGH, Urt. v. 20 November 2006, Az.: II ZR 226/05, NZG 2007, 234 (234).

1498 Joost, ZHR 163 (1999) 164 (185 et seq.).

1499 Groß, AG 1994, 266 (276); Habersack, in: Emmerich/Habersack, Aktien- und GmbH-Konzernrecht, 2010, Vor 311, mn.20; Koppensteiner, in: KöKo AktG, 2004, Vor § 291, mn.40.

1500 Beisel, in: Beisel/Klumpp, Der Unternehmenskauf, 2009, ch. 8, mn.82.

1501 Lutter/Leinekugel, ZIP 1998, 225 (230).

1502 Stein, in: MüKo AktG, 2005, § 179a AktG mnn.7, 8.

1503 *Id.* at mn.11.

1504 Wollburg/Gehling, Umgestaltung des Konzerns – Wer entscheidet über die Veräußerung von Beteiligungen einer Aktiengesellschaft?, in: Niederleithinger et al., FS Lieberknecht, 1997, 133 (155).

1505 *Id.*

corporation at its core.[1506] The sale of a subsidiary does not concern the question whether decisions made in the subsidiary should instead be decided by involvement of the shareholders of the parent corporation. It is not about preventing the dilution of shareholder rights or an additional investment to maintain the participation rate either. Consequently, group dimensional thinking or remarks on preemptive rights do not cover the issue.[1507]

Rather, the issue must be approached by considering the distribution of authority between the shareholder meeting and the management board of a corporation, based on the determinations of the articles of incorporation and corporate law. In order to require shareholder approval, the sale has to be of such significance as to put the determined distribution seriously in doubt. It has to be close to the corporation's core area of business and to an amendment of the articles of incorporation. In the *Holzmüller* decision, it was the gap between the articles of incorporation and the actual corporate line of business that led the court to require shareholder approval, but not an amendment of the articles of incorporation, for the spin-off of the major Seehafen.[1508] In the *LG Duisburg* decision, the management's intended sale of Babcock Borsig AG's (***"Babcock"***) participation in the Howaldtswerke Deutsche Werft AG (***"HDW")*** was determined to be close to the core of the entrepreneurial activity of the corporation and to fundamentally amend the corporate structure.[1509]

For these reasons, the latter approach is more convincing. Active shareholders aiming to impact the management decision regarding a sale of a subsidiary can therefore only expect an approval requirement applying to the decision under exceptional circumstances. Either the *Holzmüller/Gelatine* fundamentals apply or the line of business has been so severely impacted by the transaction that it requires amendment of the articles of incorporation.[1510]

ii) Transaction activism aiming ***to prevent*** *a divestiture*

The underlying interests of administrative members suggest that an opportunistically acting management will aim to prevent the sale of a division or subsidiary rather than undertaking divestitures. Internal diversification may help to reduce insolvency risk and increase market capitalization to reduce takeover attempts, which secure management's position. In addition, shareholders profit from increased corporate efficiency and profit by reducing internal diversification and a potential conglomerate discount resulting from facilitated divestitures rather than their prevention. In parallel, active shareholders

1506 *See* Beisel, in: Beisel/Klumpp, Der Unternehmenskauf, 2009, ch. 8, mn.82; Wollburg/Gehling, Umgestaltung des Konzerns – Wer entscheidet über die Veräußerung von Beteiligungen einer Aktiengesellschaft?, in: Niederleithinger et al., FS Lieberknecht, 1997, 1331 (152).

1507 Wollburg/Gehling, Umgestaltung des Konzerns – Wer entscheidet über die Veräußerung von Beteiligungen einer Aktiengesellschaft?, in: Niederleithinger et al., FS Lieberknecht, 1997, 133 (153 et seq.).

1508 *Id.* at 156.

1509 LG Duisburg, Urt. v. 27.06.2002, Az.: 21 O 106/02, AG 2003, 390 (390 et seq.).

1510 Habersack, in: Emmerich/Habersack, Aktien- und GmbH-Konzernrecht, 2010, Vor 311 mn.20; Koppensteiner, in: KöKo AktG, 2004, Vor § 291 mn.40.

with aligned interests are more likely to profit from facilitated divestitures resulting in a rising stock price and a potentially distributable purchase price. In addition, the decision to forgo a divestiture is usually a management decision requiring the supervisory board's approval, § 111 (4) sent. 2. Absent a veto right, which applies only under exceptional circumstances, active shareholders have to undertake substantial efforts to amend the management or supervisory board's decision to facilitate the divestiture. The likelihood of beneficial activism is therefore limited under this constellation.

iii) Transaction activism aiming ***to facilitate*** *a divestiture*

(1) Underlying interests

An opportunistically acting management aims to secure its own position from insolvency and takeovers by diversifying internally.[1511] The administration's incentives for internal diversification result from its own concentrated investment in the corporation in the form of human capital.[1512] Management's risk aversion is furthered by the fact that the shareholders and not the administration are the ones to profit from successful risky decisions, while management is the one held responsible for resulting losses.[1513]

Shareholders, in contrast, pursue their interest in increasing the corporate return through divesting strategies. The strategy to dissolve corporate conglomerates, which still appear frequently on the German market, has the goal of obtaining overall more profitable corporations. The sale of marginally profitable or non-core divisions lacking synergies with the remaining corporation or very volatile business parts increases the remaining corporation's overall profitability. As a result, the stock market will evaluate the remaining corporation's shares without a discount.[1514] Similarly, the purpose could be to unlock the suppressed value of a subsidiary, whose profits are set off by the deficits of the remainder of the group or whose integration into another group would produce significant synergies. The concentration on the profitability of the targeted corporation rather than on internal diversification caused by shareholders' diversified investment strategies sufficiently protects them from the insolvency risk of single investments.[1515] It also makes economic sense that corporations incur risk, which is more easily and cheaply diversified on the level of the equity provider than through the corporations.[1516]

In parallel, the financial incentives of active shareholders are based on the expected increase in the stock price. In addition, the expectation is that their proceeds will be distributed to the shareholders if an investment opportunity with returns beyond capi-

1511 Kuhner, ZGR 2004, 244 (264).

1512 *Id.*

1513 Ruffner, Die ökonomischen Grundlagen eines Rechts der Publikumsgesellschaft, 2000, 218.

1514 Drill, Jahrbuch 2009, 60.

1515 Arnold, ZCG 2008, 221 (223); Ruffner, Die ökonomischen Grundlagen eines Rechts der Publikumsgesellschaft, 2000, 218.

1516 Brealey & Myers, The Principles of Corporate Governance 148, 824 (1991); Ruffner, Die ökonomischen Grundlagen eines Rechts der Publikumsgesellschaft, 2000, 218.

tal costs is lacking. As a consequence, beneficial activism of this kind will be likely to occur frequently.

(2) Relevant shareholder means

Divestitures are pure management decisions. Shareholders cannot fall back on special formal means that would ease the realization of their strategy to facilitate a divestiture. The general mandatory *initiation rights* of the shareholder meeting cannot be directly applied to measures for which the management is responsible,[1517] such as the sale of a subsidiary. Rather, they must use informal and general formal measures, granting them only indirect impact on facilitating a divestiture decision. The shareholders may try to convince the administration through personal communications on the intended sale. In most cases, shareholders must go beyond convincing the management board to initiate at least a shareholder resolution according to § 119 (2) to have the shareholder meeting express its position toward the potential divestiture. They will need to employ pressure by applying the threat to initiate a vote on the removal of members of the supervisory board, §§ 103 (1) and/or on the withdrawal of confidence in members of the management board, § 84 (3) sent. 2, §§ 83 (1) sent. 1, 122 (2). A credible threat depends on substantial support amongst fellow investors, however. This must be demonstrated by votes on the request to prepare these measures, § 122 (2), 83 (1) sent. 1[1518], either during the next general meeting, § 124 (4) sent. 2 or § 122 (2), or a special meeting, §§ 122 (1), (2). Additional or pure public criticism about a denied divestiture in particular or the quality of the job done by the responsible administrative members in general can contribute to the active shareholders reaching their goal.

(3) Example

The activities of John Fredriksen ("***Fredriksen***") and other active shareholders of TUI AG ("***TUI***") are an example of transaction activism aiming to facilitate the divestiture of a subsidiary which represented the most valuable part of the targeted corporation.[1519] Their aim was to have TUI sell Hapag-Lloyd. TUI anchor shareholder West-LB's December 2004 sale of its 31.3 percent stake to RIU and Caja de Ahorros del Mediterráneo, who each received about 5 percent, and to other investors had led to a free float of 90 percent, which was mainly held by institutional investors.[1520] The acquisition of CP Ships in 2005 led, as intended, to TUI's higher market capitalization. Hapag-Lloyd became the fifth largest container-shipping corporation. Active shareholders such as DWS and Union Invest complained about TUI's unsuccessful performance under

1517 Werner, in: Großkomm AktG, 2008, § 122 mn.25.
1518 Seibt, in: Schmidt/Lutter, AktG, 2010, § 83 mn.4.
1519 Letter from Fredriksen, Monteray Enterprises Ltd., to the shareholders of TUI AG, Apr. 17, 2008, 1, Die Welt, http://www.welt.de/multimedia/archive/00549/aktionaersbrief_549482a.pdf.
1520 Annual reports of TUI Group of 2005 and 2006, 125 et seq. and 125, www.tui-group.com.

the "two pillar strategy" combining a shipping and a travel line,[1521] which they viewed as responsible for Hapag-Lloyd's undervaluation.[1522] During the 2006 general meeting, Union Invest threatened management with the refusal of its exculpation, § 120. Later, it demanded in a thesis paper the disentanglement of the two pillars. In October 2006, Hermes Funds personally handed over a list of demands with the premise that the company should split the shipping and travel businesses within six to eighteen months.[1523] Management announced the merger of TUI's tourist line with First Choice, with 51 percent of the common corporation remaining with the TUI group.[1524] In fall 2007,[1525] Fredriksen purchased a stake of about 5 percent.[1526] During several personal meetings[1527] with Michael Frenzel, TUI's head of the management board, he demanded concentration on the container shipping business and complete withdrawal from the travel business.[1528] TUI's freefloat declined to about 75 percent during this time.[1529] The publication of the merger of Hapag-Lloyd into the TUI parent corporation to prevent a divestiture in January 2008 resulted in the stock price plunging to a three-year low. Fredriksen sent the supervisory and management board a public letter demanding a seat on the supervisory board and the separation of Hapag-Lloyd from the TUI group.[1530] His demand resulted in a public discussion about the issue and the abandonment of the plan[1531] due to sufficient support for Fredriksen's demand on the supervisory board.[1532] On March 4, 2008, Fredriksen, who in the meantime had become the largest shareholder with 11.75 percent,[1533] and his team turned again to TUI's management and supervisory board and encouraged them to consider a spin-off of Hapag-Lloyd to unlock its true value in favor of TUI's shareholders. Due to a very positive market reaction[1534] and support from lead-

1521 Letter from Fredriksen, Monteray Enterprises Ltd., to the shareholders of TUI AG, Apr. 17, 2008, 2, Die Welt, http://www.welt.de/multimedia/archive/00549/aktionaersbrief_549482a.pdf.

1522 Krieger/Boeckler foundation, *TUI AG – ein Konzern unter dem Druck des Kapitalmarktes*, 2009, 11, http://www.boeckler.de/pdf/mbf_finanzinvestoren_tui.pdf.

1523 *Id.*

1524 *Id.*

1525 *Id.* at 16.

1526 *Id.*

1527 Letter from Fredriksen, Monteray Enterprises Ltd., to the shareholders of TUI AG, Apr. 17, 2008, 2, Die Welt, http://www.welt.de/multimedia/archive/00549/aktionaersbrief_549482a.pdf.

1528 Jörg Eigendorf, *Auf die Führung der TUI ist kein Verlaß*, Apr. 27, 2008, Die Welt, http://www.welt.de/wams_print/article1941960/Auf_die_Fuehrung_der_TUI_ist_kein_Verlass.html.

1529 TUI group annual report 2007, 125, www.tui-group.com: Fredriksen and the Russian investor Mordaschow had accumulated around 5% each while management besides RIU and Caja de Ahorros del Mediterano, both with 5%, had further found the support of CDG, a Moroccan investor.

1530 Krieger/Boeckler foundation, *TUI AG – ein Konzern unter dem Druck des Kapitalmarktes*, 2009, 17, http://www.boeckler.de/pdf/mbf_finanzinvestoren_tui.pdf.

1531 Letter from Fredriksen, Monteray Enterprises Ltd., to the shareholders of TUI AG, Apr. 17, 2008, 2, Die Welt, http://www.welt.de/multimedia/archive/00549/aktionaersbrief_549482a.pdf.

1532 Jörg Eigendorf, *Auf die Führung der TUI ist kein Verlaß, Apr. 27, 2008, welt.de,* http://www.welt.de/wams_print/article1941960/Auf_die_Fuehrung_der_TUI_ist_kein_Verlass.html.

1533 *Id.*

1534 *Investoren lassen Aktien links liegen*, Mar. 7, 2008, Die Welt, http://www.welt.de/welt_print/article1768846/Investoren_lassen_Aktien_links_liegen.html; *Deutsche Aktien leiden unter*

ing shareholders, TUI agreed to the separation from Hapag-Lloyd. This represented a success for the four-year shareholder campaign against the "two pillar strategy."[1535] However, TUI left open the specific transaction type.[1536] Based on the negative development of the container shipping market and the correspondingly lower price expected for Hapag-Lloyd, Fredriksen later opposed the sale of Hapag-Lloyd. Instead, he demanded that its shares be spun off to TUI's shareholders.[1537] In several letters to the management and supervisory board, Fredriksen, who held a stake of 15 percent at that time, demanded a shareholder vote on the divestiture transaction. Furthermore, he demanded the removal of Jürgen Krumnow, head of the supervisory board, who he believed was incapable of controlling management, and Michael Frenzel, who had pursued the "two pillar strategy" despite four years of continuous shareholder resistance. Having aligned tourist-orientated blockholders close to the RIU family and Russian cooperation partner Alexey Mordaschow (***"Mordaschow"***), who together held a stake of about 30 percent, the supervisory board countered that a spin-off would require a buyback of bonds over €2 billion.[1538] Before the general meeting in 2008, Fredriksen informed the shareholders in a public letter about his intention to replace Jürgen Krumnow and Franz Vranitzky, a supervisory board member. This would allow him to be adequately represented both as a major shareholder and as a representative of the interests and know-how relating to the container-shipping branch.[1539] The replacement would re-establish the efficiency and independence of the supervisory board to properly exercise its control and support function toward the management board, especially regarding the expected spin-off of Hapag-Lloyd.[1540] Franz Vranitzky resigned and was replaced by a Mordaschow representative after the delay for motions regarding the general meeting had elapsed. Fredriksen declined the offer to also determine a representative.[1541] During the general meeting, Fredriksen's representative Troim spoke strongly about the major shareholder's frustrations. They focused on management's "two pillar strategy," which had produced a weak stock price, and the insufficiency of Krumnow's exercise of his control responsibilities. Fredriksen had 42 percent of the 76 percent present shareholders behind him. He was unable to reach the necessary 50 percent +1 vote quorum to oust Krumnow. 69.2

Euro und Ölpreis, Mar. 6, 2008, Die Welt, http://www.welt.de/finanzen/article1764471/Deutsche_Aktien_leiden_unter_Euro_und_Oelpreis.html.

1535 Krieger/Boeckler foundation, *TUI AG – ein Konzern unter dem Druck des Kapitalmarktes*, 2009, 17, http://www.boeckler.de/pdf/mbf_finanzinvestoren_tui.pdf.

1536 Letter from Fredriksen, Monteray Enterprises Ltd., to the shareholders of TUI AG, Apr. 17, 2008, 2, Die Welt, http://www.welt.de/multimedia/archive/00549/aktionaersbrief_549482a.pdf.

1537 Krieger/Boeckler foundation, *TUI AG – ein Konzern unter dem Druck des Kapitalmarktes*, 2009, 17, http://www.boeckler.de/pdf/mbf_finanzinvestoren_tui.pdf.

1538 Letter from Fredriksen, Monteray Enterprises Ltd., to the shareholders of TUI AG, Apr. 17, 2008, 1, Die Welt, http://www.welt.de/multimedia/archive/00549/aktionaersbrief_549482a.pdf.

1539 *Id.* at 4.

1540 *Id.* at 4 et seq.

1541 *TUI booted Großaktionär Fredriksen aus*, Apr. 28, 2008, Die Welt, http://www.welt.de/wirtschaft/article1946458/TUI_bootet_Grossaktionaer_Fredriksen_aus.html.

percent of the present shareholders voted to exonerate Frenzel.[1542] The following year, Mordaschow and Fredriksen increased their holdings to 15.03 percent[1543] and 18 percent plus debt instruments,[1544] with a remaining 55 percent freefloat.[1545] TUI's management decided to form a joint corporation with the consortium of Albert Ballin KG, formed to prevent that a non German investor would purchase Hapag-Lloyd. It retained a 43 percent share[1546] and had to exit the DAX.[1547] During TUI's general meeting in 2009, Troim criticized management for missing the best opportunity to sell Hapag-Lloyd. Furthermore, he pointed to the risks of the high debt and commitments of TUI, its poor overall performance, the unjustifiably high salary of Michael Frenzel, and the lack of control through the supervisory board.[1548] While management, supported by Mordaschow, was able to align 35 percent of the capital behind it, Fredriksen had the support of only 25 percent of the capital.[1549] He was unsuccessful in ousting Krumnow and another supervisory board member, in initiating a special audit of Frenzel's earnings, and in preventing a shareholder resolution authorizing a share buyback[1550].[1551]

Fredriksen's activism aimed to have TUI abandon its unprofitable "two-pillar strategy" by separating its two unrelated business lines and allowing Hapag-Lloyd to

1542 *Tui-Vorstand gewinnt Machtkampf*, May 7, 2008, Die Welt, http://www.welt.de/jahresrueckblick-2008/mai/article2726710/TUI-Vorstand-gewinnt-Machtkampf.html.

1543 *TUI: Russe zieht langsam gleich im Kampf der Milliardäre*, July 22, 2008, Die Welt, http://www.welt.de/welt_print/article2237174/TUI_Russe_zieht_gleich_im_Kampf_der_Milliardaere.html.

1544 *Fredriksen scheitert auf der Tui-Hauptversammlung,* Sept. 13, 2009, fazfinance.net, http://www.fazfinance.net/Aktuell/Fredriksen-scheitert-auf-der-Tui-Hauptversammlung-0238.faz.

1545 TUI group annual report 2008, 58, www.tui-group.de: 15 percent held be Fredriksen, 15 percent by Mordaschow, 15,1 percent by RIU, Caja de Ahorros and CDG Group, and 55 percent freefloat remaining.

1546 Jens Koenen/Eberhard Krummheuer, *TUI stutzt Pläne mit Air Berlin*, Sept. 9, 2009, Handelsblatt, at 9; Hans Seidenstücker, *Hapag Lloyd Gesellschafter einigen sich auf Finanzpaket Kreise,* Aug. 13, 2009, Finanzforum, http://www.finanzinform.de/wirtschaftsnews/11381/UPDATE:-HapagLloydGesellschafter-einigen-sich-auf-Finanzpaket-Kreise.html.

1547 *Düngemittelhersteller K+S verdrängt TUI im DAX*, Sept. 3, 2009, Die Welt, http://www.welt.de/finanzen/article2392860/Duengemittelhersteller-K-S-verdraengt-TUI-im-Dax.html.

1548 E. A. Ginten/G. Nikolai, *TUI-Großaktionär Fredriksen verliert Machtkampf*, May 13, 2009, Die Welt, http://www.welt.de/wirtschaft/article3735219/TUI-Grossaktionaer-Fredriksen-verliert-Machtkampf.html.

1549 *Großaktionär Fredriksen erhöht vor der Hauptversammlung den Druck*, May 12, 2009, Wirtschaftswoche, http://www.wiwo.de/unternehmer-maerkte/grossaktionaer-fredriksen-erhoeht-vor-der-hauptversammlung-den-druck-396843/.

1550 Arno Schütze/Kerstin Dörr, *Großaktionär scheitert mit Sturz von TUI-Aufsichtsratschef*, May 13, 2009, de.reuters, http://de.reuters.nsatc.net/article/deEuroRpt/idDEWEA220720090513: even though Fredriksen's anticipated blockade, which would have been successful due to a necessary support of 25 percent +1 vote of the present capital and a given support of 25 percent of the total capital of TUI, led to an amendment of the resolution preventing management from redistributing the bought back shares.

1551 *Fredriksen auf TUI-Hauptversammlung unterlegen*, May 13, 2009, Finanznachrichten, http://www.finanznachrichten.de/nachrichten-2009-05/13902574-fredriksen-auf-tui-hauptversammlung-unterlegen-016.htm; *Fredriksen scheitert auf der Tui-Hauptversammlung*, Sept. 13, 2009, fazfinance.de, http://www.fazfinance.net/Aktuell/Fredriksen-scheitert-auf-der-Tui-Hauptversammlung-0238.faz.

develop its true value. As a consequence, TUI's suppressed shareholder value would have increased and TUI's shareholders would have profited. Fredriksen pursued an additional goal through the intended spin-off of Hapag-Lloyd, however. As the owner of a shipping company, he had a personal strategic interest in acquiring Hapag-Lloyd. With the public spin-off, he would have come closer to realizing it.[1552] The alignment of both interests, increasing TUI's shareholder value and Fredriksen's opportunistic interest, allowed him to concentrate publicly on the former goal. This assured him the necessary shareholder support to pressure management while his other goal increased his incentives to become active. This transaction demonstrates the potential for transaction activism to be abused and the limits of opportunistic transaction activism because of the need to have supportive fellow investors, which usually requires an increase in shareholder value.

Absent special formal means, Fredriksen's efforts comprised the entire spectrum of general formal as well as private and public informal means. He began his campaign with non-public informal means. Informal means involving the publication of criticism followed before he threatened to apply general formal accountability measures to the responsible administrative members. As far as is known, he initially tried to convince the head of the management board during "one-on ones" to abandon the corporate "two-pillar strategy." These measures did not produce the desired results, however, as TUI's management subsequently published its intention to merge Hapag-Lloyd into the TUI group. Fredriksen responded by sending opposition letters to the members of the supervisory and the management board. His demands were backed up by a years-low stock price resulting from management's announcement and the subsequent public discussion, which convinced the supervisory board. Fredriksen's subsequent efforts to convince the supervisory and management boards to separate from Hapag-Lloyd again led to a significant positive stock price reaction. It compelled TUI's management to abandon the "two pillar strategy" and to separate from Hapag-Lloyd. However, as far as the transaction type was concerned, Fredriksen's strategy was less successful. After sending fruitless letters to try to convince the management to spin-off and not sell Hapag-Lloyd, he employed accountability measures against the responsible officials. He threatened Krumnow with ouster, alleging Krumnow was responsible for failure to control the unsuccessful "two pillar strategy." However, two ambitious campaigns during two general meetings were unsuccessful in holding Krumnow accountable or in preventing the sale of a major part of Hapag-Lloyd. Fredriksen lacked the necessary majorities.

Fredriksen's activism in TUI demonstrated clearly the *effectiveness of informal shareholder means*. The publication of criticism regarding listed corporations has the advantage of producing a positive stock price reaction that benefits active shareholders, who aim to enhance the targeted corporation's shareholder value. Especially if prior, contrary management plans have been made public and have produced a negative stock price reaction, this development will pressure management to correspondingly amend the corporate strategy. Fredriksen experienced very positive stock price development

1552 Krieger/Boeckler foundation, *TUI AG–ein Konzern unter dem Druck des Kapitalmarktes*, 2009, 16, http://www.boeckler.de/pdf/mbf_finanzinvestoren_tui.pdf.

upon demanding Hapag-Lloyd's spin-off after management's merger plans had had the opposite effect.

The administration's maneuvers, in contrast, were successful in maintaining its position. It amended its corporate strategy just enough to smooth significant stock price variations resulting from public critique. Management's stability resulted from the successful involvement of anchor shareholders who supported management's strategy in times of up to 90 percent freefloat. After West-LB sold more than half[1553] of its 31.3 percent stake to RIU and partners, the management increased TUI's market capitalization by €2 billion through the purchase of CP Ships. Michael Frenzel continued to secure his position. Besides the support of RIU, Caja de Ahorros del Mediterráneo, and CDG, holding together around 15 percent, he convinced Mordaschow to back TUI's management by measures such as forming a joint venture in the Russian tourist market. Consequently, a reliable 30–35 percent stake assured management's majority.

Despite major criticism by influential shareholders and several removal attempts, the administration and its only partially amended strategy stayed, due to anchor shareholders and low shareholder attendance. They prevented Fredriksen from making successful use of general formal accountability measures. He was unable to appoint a special auditor, § 142 (1), to prevent the discharge of the head of the management board, § 120 (1), or to remove (inefficient) supervisory board members, § 103 (1). Corporate management continued to pursue its amended "two pillar strategy." The undervaluation of one of the branches and the miserable total stock development persisted and resulted finally in TUI's DAX exit.

Consequently, published shareholder criticism coupled with the threat to apply accountability measures against the responsible administrative members represents an effective means to successfully pursue activism under this constellation. However, in times of low shareholder presence, their success turns on the number of supporting shareholders.

4) Transaction activism and targets, means, conflicts of interest, legal limitations and the underlying theory

a) Transaction activism targets under German shareholder structure

The investigation of sixteen cases of transaction activism in German corporations has demonstrated that it does not just target corporations with a shareholder structure dominated by freefloat (for instance KuKa with 100 percent freefloat in 2003), which are similar to corporations on the U.S. market. Even corporations with several blockholders apart from the DAX are targeted by transaction activism (Volkswagen: three blockholders holding 77 percent in 2005; Babcock: three blockholders holding 37 percent in 2002). Consequently, active shareholders do not shrink from blockholding structures

1553 *Id.* at 10.

and activism will not be limited to the slowly increasing number of corporations with higher freefloat, which are currently mainly DAX-listed.

b) General analysis of means used for transaction activism

i) Categorization of means

The preceding analysis of transaction activism in German corporations has demonstrated that active shareholders use a variety of means to impact corporate transaction decisions. The categorization of these means is almost the same as under U.S. law. Active shareholders use *formal means*, explicitly provided to shareholders by statute, articles of incorporation, *Geschäftsordnung,* and precedent, as well as *informal means* not explicitly laid down therein.[1554] The formal shareholder rights comprise voting rights as well as other rights.[1555] The voting rights are primarily used by active shareholders in the transaction context. The use of informal means usually takes place outside the shareholder meeting and prior to the decision-making process through personal contact with the administration or public campaigns.[1556] While the development of informal means under U.S. law is dominated by the presence of the filing regime of the proxy rules, the informal means applied under the German legal system aiming to increase the shareholder impact are not. The few campaigns that actually involved the public[1557] targeted the transaction decision as such and/or used the reputation mechanism to prod the responsible administrative members to pursue their transaction goal. Finally, the *impact* exercised by shareholders pursuing transaction activism on the concerned decisions may be *direct*, if they aim to prevent or facilitate a fundamental transaction decision or to prevent a transaction requiring a shareholder approval for the necessary capital increase or an exceptional shareholder approval. In general, however, the impact of active shareholders will be *indirect.* They will apply accountability measures to the administrative members responsible for transaction decisions, either by threatening or actually using the general formal means according to §§ 103 (1), 84 (3) AktG.[1558] Finally, the means in the above-mentioned categories may be combined differently during transaction activism. The active shareholders may only use formal means, they may combine them with private or public informal means, or they may only apply informal means. Equally, they may combine means granting them direct impact on a transaction decision, if available, with those of indirect impact.

1554 Strenger, Corporate Governance und Anteilseigner, insbesondere institutionelle Anleger, in: Hommelhoff et al., Hdb Corporate Governance, 2003, 697 (708 et seq.).

1555 Thaeter/Guski, AG 2007, 301 (302).

1556 Arnold, ZCG 2008, 221 (224).

1557 DAI/McKinsey, Investorendialog im Umbruch, 2009, 31 et seq.

1558 Thaeter/Guski, AG 2007, 301 (302).

ii) Relevance of formal and informal means

(1) Formal means

Formal means grant shareholders under a few scenarios useful direct impact on a targeted transaction. However, most transaction activism constellations involve the use of formal means providing shareholders with only indirect influence by impacting the responsible deciding or controlling administrative members. Many of the formal means require that active shareholders overcome increasingly important collective action problems to fulfill the necessary (qualified) shareholder quorum.

(a) Initiation rights

In contrast to shareholders of U.S. corporations, shareholders of German corporations have mandatory initiation rights to impact *specific* corporate decisions or measures. They may not only launch motions relating, § 124 (4) sent. 2, 126, or not, § 122 (2), to agenda topics of the next general meeting. Rather, they may also request the convening of a special meeting, § 122 (1), and determine its topic(s), § 122 (2) upon minority motion. Finally, they can demand that the management board prepare measures or contracts, § 83 (1). Active shareholders use them to initiate *direct* or *indirect* impact on a transaction decision.

To initiate a *fundamental transaction* against administrative will, §§ 122 (2), 83 (1) provides minority shareholders with the right to request a shareholder resolution approving the management board's preparation and conclusion of the underlying contract. However, the requirements to initiate such a merger against the will of the administration are high, as the initiation, § 83 (1) sent. 3, requires the same quorum as its approval, § 13, 65 UmwG. The few transaction decisions that are subject to the *Holzmüller/Gelatine* doctrine can only be initiated by shareholders on a precatory basis via a recommending shareholder vote on the transaction, §§ 122 (2), 83 (1). The final initiation authority remains, however, with the management board, controlled by the supervisory board. Finally, shareholders can use their initiation rights to apply *means with indirect impact* on corporate transaction decisions, either to prevent or to facilitate a transaction. While this represents the only way to use formal means to impact management's transaction decisions, this way may also be chosen as a means of direct impact on corporate transaction decisions. While the initiation of some shareholder means requires preparation through the management board, § 83, for others, for instance §§ 142 (2, 4), 147, this is unnecessary[1559]

(b) Direct impact

(i) Fundamental transactions

Fundamental corporate decisions enable shareholders not only to mandate their initiation, but also to veto their implementation. Theoretically, active shareholders are there-

1559 Habersack, in: Großkomm AktG, 2008, § 83 mn.10; Hüffer, AktG, 2010, § 83 mn.4; Mertens, in: KöKo AktG, 1996, § 83 mn.5; different opinion: Spindler, in: MüKo AktG, 2008, § 83 mn.12.

fore able to prevent an announced merger and to facilitate an unwanted merger against the will of the administration. In practice, however, the qualified approval quorum eases the way for active shareholders aiming to *prevent* a merger, as they only need to accumulate a supportive minority of more than 25 percent of the present share capital to prevent it. The contrary situation, that active shareholders aim to *facilitate* a merger against the will of the corporate management, requires stronger efforts from active shareholders. Both the initiation of preparation by the management board, § 83 (1) sent. 2, and the approval of the merger require equally that active shareholders accumulate 75 percent of the present capital to vote in favor of the merger, §§ 13, 65 (1) UmwG, 83 (1) sent. 3.[1560]

Active shareholders aiming to impact a corresponding transaction decision need to concentrate on *overcoming collective action issues* to ensure that a sufficient number of otherwise rationally passive fellow shareholders will support the necessary vote for the merger. Even though active shareholders may still use generally applicable shareholder means provided to ensure the administration's accountability in order to indirectly impact the decision, they are likely to focus on the more effective special formal means providing direct impact. The different demands applying to the two directions of transaction activism targeting a merger decision and the related potential of overcompensation qualify the *prevention* of a merger as a practically relevant constellation.

(ii) Transactions subject to Holzmüller/Gelatine

Another rare opportunity for shareholders to directly impact corporate transaction decisions without having to apply general formal accountability measures relates to transactions subject to *Holzmüller/Gelatine*. Besides the precatory initiation right, shareholders also have in this case the right to approve such a measure with a qualified threshold of three-fourths of the present share capital.[1561] Parallel to the merger constellation and intensified by precatory character of the initiation right, the only practical direction of transaction activism is the prevention of such a transaction.

(iii) Approval of capital measures

Finally, active shareholders in *acquiring* corporations that depend on the approval of capital measures to afford the purchase consideration can prevent a transaction for which the management board is responsible. Relevant capital measures in the transaction context are the unlimited ordinary increase of the share capital, §§ 182 et seq., combined

1560 Kropff, AktG 1965, 104; Hefermehl/Spindler, in: MüKo AktG, 2004, § 83 mn.8; Weber, in: Hölters, AktG, 2011, § 83 mn.6.

1561 BGH, Urt. v. 26.04.2004, Az.: II ZR 154/02, NZG 2004, 575 (579); Altmeppen, DB 1998, 49 (51); Fleischer, Hdb Vorstandsrecht, 2006, § 17 mn.153: requiring a simple majority of votes besides a qualified majority of the present share capital; Habersack, in: Emmerich/Habersack, Aktien- und GmbH Konzernrecht, Vor § 311 mn.50; Hübner, Die Ausgliederung von Unternehmensteilen in aktien- und aufsichtsrechtlicher Sicht, in: Lutter et al., FS Stimpel, 1985, 791 (795 et seq.); Joost, ZHR 163 (1999), 164 (171 et seq.); Priester, ZHR 163 (1999), 187 (199 et seq.); Raiser, Recht der Kapitalgesellschaften, 2001, § 16 mn.15, d).

with the exclusion of preemptive rights, § 186 (3), both requiring the approval of three-fourths of the represented share capital. Alternatively, the management board can use an existing authorization valid for up to five years to increase the share capital by half. It may comprise the management board's authorization to exclude preemptive rights, §§ 202 et seq., 203 (2). Consequently, in cases requiring approval of a capital-related measure, a minority of 25 percent + 1 vote of the present capital could in practice veto the necessary capital measure and therefore the facilitation of the transaction.

(c) Indirect impact

In all other cases, statutory corporate law provides active shareholders the general right to indirectly impact management's (transaction) decisions via the use of shareholder means aiming to ensure the administration's accountability. The in-practice most often used means to indirectly impact a transaction decision is challenging the position of one or several members of the administration responsible for the concerned transaction decision.[1562] The exercise of indirect impact on management's transaction decisions through active shareholders, especially via pressure on members of the administration, represents the most typical kind of shareholder activism in practice. It aims to enhance the shareholder meeting's control regarding the supervisory board and therefore the control by the latter of the management board to reduce its opportunistic actions and therefore part of the agency costs that reduce shareholder value in the targeted corporation.

(i) Removal of supervisory board members, section 103 (1)

Active shareholders apply or threaten to apply the removal mechanism in § 103 (1), intended to assure shareholder confidence in supervisory board members, *to pressure the administration* to enforce a transaction decision in their interest. § 103 (1) generally requires a qualified shareholder vote of three-fourths of the votes cast. Despite active shareholders' minority stakes and generally low *attendance rates,* the strong initiation rights, §§ 124 (4) sent. 2[1563], 122 (1), (2), and reduced thresholds of 50 percent in some articles of incorporation allow active shareholders to repeatedly convince sufficient shareholders to participate in a credible threat. Instead of being confronted with legal or practical limitations, active shareholders need to focus solely on overcoming collective action problems. In the hands of active shareholders, it is therefore a practically relevant means of exercising indirect impact on the administration. Especially in the context of the five-year office term, the early removal is a more important and effective accountability mechanism than in the U.S. regime with its annual elections.

1562 Besides confirmation through the different examples provided, careful transfer of U.S. data and experience mentioned by Bebchuk, 118 Harv. L. Rev. 833 (2005) and 93 Va. L. Rev. 102 (2007), Briggs, 32 J. Corp. L. 681 (2007), and Kahan & Rock, 155 U. Pa. L. Rev. 1021 (2007), as opposed to Klein & Zur, 14 J. Fin. 187 (2009) regarding the effectiveness of proxy fights/threats.

1563 Only if the report of a special auditor is on the agenda (Werner, in: Großkomm AktG, 2008, § 124 mn.89, Kubis, in: MüKo AktG, 2004, 124 mn.73), but not if the discharge of the adminstrative members, § 120 AktG, is concerned, see discussion *supra*.

(ii) Removal of management board members, section 84 (3)

The shareholder right to initiate a early removal of management board members complements this accountability mechanism. Through a corresponding vote, shareholders are able to withdraw their confidence in a management board member and therefore provide an important reason for his removal, § 84 (3) sent. 2. The supervisory board retains discretion to remove the member, § 84 (3) sent. 1. In practice, the supervisory board's discretion is reduced by the shareholder right to remove supervisory board members, § 103 (1), and the supervisory board's need for discharge, § 120. The same initiation rights applying to § 103 (1), §§ 124 (4)[1564] and 122 (1), (2), increase the credibility of a threat with this precatory initiation right.

(iii) Special auditor, section 142

Another means to pressure the administration is the motion (or threat to ask for the motion) to appoint a special auditor according to § 142 (1), including the minority right to have a court appoint a special auditor pursuant to subsection 2.[1565] For shareholders pursuing transaction activism, the reduced quorum of 1 percent under the UMAG[1566] is a lower hurdle to use the right pursuant to § 142 (2) if appointment through approval by the shareholder meeting failed.[1567] A negative audit report could not only pressure the concerned administrative member(s) for reputational reasons. The agenda topic for the submission of a special audit report also allows shareholders to integrate their motion to vote on the removal of an administrative member, § 124 (4) sent. 2, 2nd alt.[1568] However, practical experiences are very limited and so far, the effect of the provision is of preventive nature.[1569]

(iv) Litigation, sections 147 et seq.

Rarely do active shareholders threaten or actually pursue corporate claims for damages against members of the administration.[1570] These can be based on alleged violations of fiduciary duties that have resulted in corporate damage, §§ 93, 116. Corresponding litigation impacts neither the transaction decision nor the administrative position directly. It is rather a means based on reputational concerns. Shareholders use it to complement the impact of other measures or as a means of last resort, demonstrated by the NBIM Fund's attempt to prevent the Volkswagen-Porsche merger.

1564 Only if a report of a special auditor is on the agenda (Werner, in: Großkomm AktG, 2008, § 124 mn.89, Kubis, in: MüKo AktG, 2004, 124 mn.73), but not as far as the discharge of the adminstrative members, § 120 AktG, is concerned, see discussion *supra*.

1565 Wilsing/Ogorek, GWR 2009, 281217 (=GWR 2009, 75).

1566 DAV-Handelsrechtsausschluss, NZG 2004, 555 (559): critizing the introduction of the low quorum, which leads practically to the introductions of a popular proceeding.

1567 Duve/Basak, BB 2006, 1345 (1347); Wilsing/Ogorek, GWR 281217 (= GWR 2007, 75).

1568 Werner, in: Großkomm AktG, 2008, § 124 mn.89, Kubis, in: MüKo AktG, 2004, 124 mn.73.

1569 Hüffer, AktG, 2008, § 142 mn.1.

1570 DAI/Mc Kinsey, Investorendialog im Umbruch, 2009, 31: In about 4 of the 29 analyzed cases of shareholder activism, active shareholders referred to the opportunity of legal proceedings.

(2) Informal means

The use of informal means allows active shareholders to exercise additional impact on the administration and its transaction decision. They are often directed solely toward influencing the administration, but they may simultaneously target fellow shareholders and their supports with the use or threat of use of formal shareholder means that depend on a shareholder vote.

The most successful[1571] and most frequently used means of impacting the administration is private communication via telephone calls, personal conversations, e-mails, and letters. Personal conversations take place during bilateral rounds of talks, road shows, and shareholder meetings.[1572] Members of the administration are most often targeted, especially the heads of the management and supervisory boards, as well as the investor relation department.[1573] This impact through the contact may be increased by referring to like-minded fellow shareholders, through hints at future voting behavior and the possibility of convening a special shareholder meeting.[1574]

Significantly less often applied are the use of or threat of use of public relations ("*PR*") measures, which usually reflect a significant escalation.[1575] PR measures aiming to impact a corporate transaction decision can target the concerned transaction decision directly or the general work of specific members of the administration. As in the case of Fredriksen, the publication of a proposed approach to a transaction-related issue has the potential to produce significant positive stock price reactions. They are a powerful means to underline the demands of active shareholders. PR campaigns involving the qualification and performance of administrative members are especially useful during transaction decisions not providing for direct shareholder participation. They can prepare a threat or the use of the general accountability measures, like §§ 103 (1), 84 (3). PR measures represent an effective way to inform, contact, and activate fellow investors in corporations with high freefloat and a limited amount of public ownership disclosures. They, in turn, can demonstrate their support by independently contacting the administration and/or by voting for the formal accountability means. This strategy was successfully pursued by TCI, which prevented LSE's acquisition by Deutsche Börse. The parallel unanimous expression of a shareholder position can have the same impact on the responsible administration as a strong stock price reaction.

iii) Transaction activism constellations and shareholder means

Transaction activism applies to fundamental transaction decisions and to management's transaction decisions. Unlike under U.S. law, transaction decisions representing a management task may exceptionally require shareholder approval if they are subject

1571 Bassen, Einflußnahme institutioneller Investoren auf Corporate Governance und Unternehmensführung, 2001, 8.

1572 DAI/McKinsey, Investorendialog im Umbruch, 2009, 31, 32, 34.

1573 *Id.* at 31, 32.

1574 *Id.* at 31.

1575 *Id.* at 31 et seq.

to *Holzmüller/Gelatine*. Similar principles apply to transactions depending on qualified shareholder approval for an increase of the share capital and the exclusion of preemptive rights to finance the purchase price.

The accumulation of a vetoing minority of more than twenty-five percent of the present capital is sufficient for the *prevention* of transactions depending on mandatory shareholder approval, as is the case for fundamental transactions, those falling under the *Holzmüller/Gelatine* doctrine, and those requiring a share capital increase. Transaction decisions made by the management alone, can, in contrast, only be prevented indirectly through the use of general formal and informal means targeting the responsible administration.

The means to *facilitate* transactions under each of the three constellations differ in theory. The facilitation of a fundamental transaction decision provides active shareholders with the opportunity to mandate the initiation of a corresponding decision process with a minority position. However, the administration is only obliged to implement the decision once the shareholder quorum in favor equals the qualified quorum necessary to approve a merger. The facilitation of exceptional transaction decisions that require shareholder approval under *Holzmüller/Gelatine* still depends on initiation through the administration. Shareholders are restricted to debating the issue and formulating a precatory shareholder resolution. Approval also requires the approval of a qualified majority of the present capital. Finally, shareholders have no formal initiation or approval rights for the facilitation of transactions representing pure management tasks, even if dependent on a capital measure requiring a shareholder approval. The initiation and approval of such transaction decisions can only be achieved through the use of general formal and informal means, which represent the practical strategy for all three constellations.

Practical relevant means to pursue transaction activism under German law

Transaction Type / **Direction transaction activism**	**Fundamental transactions**	**Management's transaction decisions with approval requirement**	**Management's transaction decision**
Prevent transaction	*Veto*	*Veto*	*General formal/informal means*
Facilitate transaction	*General formal/ informal means*	*General formal/ informal means*	*General formal/informal means*

c) Constellations of desirable transaction activism

The analysis of six exemplary transaction activism constellations based on the generally underlying interests of administrations and shareholders as well as the available means has demonstrated that certain constellations are a better basis for (beneficial) transaction activism than others.

Transaction activism is *desirable* if it aims to prevent management's opportunistic transaction decisions. It requires that the interests of the active shareholders and the remainder of shareholders to enhance shareholder value through influence on the specific transaction decision, even under the modified shareholder approach, are aligned and contradict the interests of the opportunistically acting administration. It needs to be distinguished from transaction activism pursuing aims that deviate from the interests of the corporation and fellow shareholders. In practice, certain transaction decisions, based on the underlying general interests of the members of the administration and the assumed impact of certain transactions on shareholders' interests, have a greater potential to deviate from the determinative shareholder interests. As transaction decisions opposing opportunistic transaction decisions are likely to enhance shareholder value, they simultaneously provide active shareholders with certain financial incentives through the expected rise of the stock price. The means available under each of the constellations of transaction activism impact whether the likely benefits of an engagement will sufficiently compensate the efforts necessary to amend the opportunistic transaction decisions.

As far as the six analyzed transaction constellations are concerned, three of them are likely to involve desirable transaction activism: the prevention of the acquisition of a third corporation via merger, the prevention of the acquisition via tender offer both through active shareholders in the surviving or acquiring corporation, and the facilitation of a divestiture through shareholders of the selling corporation. The three constellations are the same as under U.S. law. The general underlying interests of the administration and shareholders under these three constellations of transaction activism are opposite. While the administration is obliged to follow the interests of the shareholders (to primarily increase shareholder value if there are conflicts with the interests of other stakeholders), it may still decide differently when making a transaction decision and pursue its personal interests instead. As in the United States, the underlying interests of the administrative members responsible for opportunistic transaction decisions are to secure their position and to maintain or increase their authority and compensation. In general, they demand deviating transaction decisions in three of the six constellations as compared to the assumption regarding which of the six transaction decisions were generally expected to enhance shareholder value. In general, decisions enhancing shareholder value are decisions against acquisitions via merger or tender offer and in favor of divestitures. Shareholders opposed to opportunistic transaction decisions to maintain or increase shareholder value pursue interests aligned with the interests of their fellow investors. This *may* even be the case in constellations where shareholders pursue mainly interests apart from those of the fellow shareholders (see *supra* Deutsche Börse/LSE or TUI/Hapag-Lloyd), providing them with additional financial incentives to become active. Determinative are that they oppose opportunistic administrative decisions and that the amended transaction decision is beneficial to the shareholder value of the targeted corporation. The determination of the three constellations is, however, only based on *assumptions* regarding the impact of certain transactions on the shareholder value of the targeted corporation and the interests of the deciding administrative interests. Upon corresponding deviations, they may also involve opportunistic transaction activism. However, the *general* distinction between constellations usually involving beneficial transaction activism and others might be helpful when analyzing the relevant limitations of (opportunistic) shareholder activism.

d) Potential conflicts of interest

Also under German law, the use of (financial) instruments is responsible for many of the cases in which investors pursuing transaction activism engage in deviating interests. They vote empty, hide from disclosure, or engage in related non-host assets.

The latter was the case when TCI became involved in Deutsche Börse. The interests of the hedge fund that led the campaign, TCI, were particularly complex as TCI held shares in Deutsche Börse but also sold shares of the other constituent corporation in the merger, LSE, short.[1576] It also held a substantial stake of shares in a major competitor Euronext.[1577] Focusing on TCI's long position in Deutsche Börse and its short position in LSE, TCI's efforts to prevent the acquisition were compensated by the rising stock price of Deutsche Börse, by preventing overpayment for LSE, and by the falling stock price of LSE once the most promising bidder left the scene. The general interests of TCI and its fellow investors in Deutsche Börse were not aligned. TCI would have aimed to prevent the acquisition even if it would not have resulted in a rising Deutsche Börse stock price, as long as the termination of the transaction resulted in a sufficient decrease in LSE's share price to sufficiently compensate it for potential losses from its long stake in Deutsche Börse.[1578] TCI's additional stake in Deutsche Börse competitor Euronext underscored the deviating interests of TCI and its fellow investors in Deutsche Börse.[1579]

As under U.S. law, the use of (financial) instruments by active shareholders under German law has the potential of overcoming collective action issues by increasing the incentives of active shareholders to engage in and therefore to strengthen management's control. They also have the potential, however, to be used by active shareholders to pursue interests not aligned with those of their fellow shareholders in a way that is detrimental to the latter. Those cases have remained rare so far, however.[1580] The following will also analyze whether the current legal regime efficiently prevents the abuse of the mentioned (financial) instruments through opportunistic active shareholders.

1576 Schmolke, ZGR 2007, 701 (711).

1577 According to the Dutch authority „Autoriteit Financiele Markten" 8,54 percent on 9.5.2006, www.afm.nl/registers/.

1578 Engert, ZIP 2006, 2105 (2107 et seq.); Schmolke, ZGR 2007, 701 (711n.57).

1579 Engert, ZIP 2006, 2105 (2107 et seq.).

1580 *See* Briggs, 32 J. Corp. L. 681 (2007): his empirical results relating to shareholder activism in U.S. corporations may be carefully transferred to shareholder activism in German corporations.

e) Legal limitations for active shareholders

The use of informal means and (financial) instruments by active shareholders raises the question whether there are sufficiently effective limitations on active shareholders to prevent them from opportunistically exercising impact to the detriment of the corporation and its shareholders.

i) Under corporate law

(1) Impact on decision-making process

(a) Abuse of rights, section 242 BGB[1581]

The use of formal shareholder rights by active shareholders to pursue deviating interests could be an abuse of rights pursuant to § 242 BGB, general provision for good faith.[1582] The applicability of § 242 BGB requires that the concerned provision not already contain exclusive limitations, as is the case for countermotions according to subsection two of § 126.[1583] Under § 242 BGB, active shareholders are restricted in their use of formal shareholder rights if they pursue neither justified interests as corporate partners nor general shareholder interests, but instead use the right contrary to its purpose to pursue special interests.[1584] The corporate management has to prove the incongruence between the measure and purpose as well as the improper motive.[1585] The latter can be derived from several factors based on a comprehensive view.[1586] In practice, it has remained a challenge for administrations to prove abuse of means by active shareholders seeking to impact corporate decisions.[1587]

The threat of initiating the removal of administrative members via the § 122 (1), (2), (3) – minority rights is a way for active shareholders to convince management to abandon or to pursue transaction decisions if prior communication was unsuccessful. Despite its purpose of protecting the minority, the right to convene a special meeting or to add an agenda topic can be abused if it lacks a justifying purpose.[1588] This is the case if, under a comprehensive evaluation of all relevant circumstances, the purpose of the special meeting or the additional topic is evidently illegal or violates the fiduciary duty

1581 Bürgerliches Gesetzbuch [BGB] [German Civil Code].

1582 Demonstrated with an example of an abusive rescission action: OLG Stuttgart, Urt. v. 13.3.2002, Az.: 20 W 32/01, AG 2003, 456 (457).

1583 Hüffer, AktG, § 126 mn.1; Werner, in: Großkomm AktG, 2008, § 126 mn.36.

1584 OLG Stuttgart, Urt. v. 13.3.2002, Az.: 20 W 32/01, AG 2003, 456 (457).

1585 *Id.* at 456 et seq.; Thaeter/Guski, AG 2007, 301 (303).

1586 OLG Stuttgart, Urt. v. 13.3.2002, Az.: 20 W 32/01, AG 2003, 456 (456 et seq.)

1587 Thaeter/Guski, AG 2007, 301 (303).

1588 OLG Köln, Urt. v. 15.06.1959, Az.: 8 W 61/59, WM 1959, 1402 (1404); KG, Beschl. v. 03.12. 2002, Az.: 1 W 363/02, AG 2003, 500 (505), NZG 2003, 441; Mertens, AG 1997, 481 (489); Semler, in: Münch. Hdb. AG, Vol. 4, 1999, § 35 mn.17.

of the shareholder initiating it.[1589] This would be the case when the shareholder intends to damage the corporation.[1590] The purpose of § 122 is to provide minority shareholders with the right to convene a special meeting[1591] to determine a matter to be discussed and decided on by the shareholders, including the opportunity to persuade other shareholders of a certain position. If the request is denied, the shareholders are able to initiate a judicial investigation, § 122 (3) sent. 1. Therefore, restrictions of these minority rights should be interpreted narrowly.[1592] Nevertheless, corporate efforts required by a special meeting are substantial, including possible negative publicity.[1593] The efforts related to § 122 (2) are comparably lower.[1594] The general costs caused by a special meeting and its reputational consequences alone are insufficient for a corporation to suffer damages, however.[1595] Rather, its consequences must go beyond these. This has been recognized for shareholders intending to withdraw their confidence in a management board member regardless of the lack of an objective reason to expose the corporation to such reputation damage.[1596] Despite lower costs and less sensation, similar restrictions apply to added topics.[1597]

Active shareholders usually convene a special meeting and/or request an additional agenda topic to oust supervisory board members, § 103 (1), and/or to express no confidence in members of the management board, § 84 (3) sent. 2. The purpose is to pressure the responsible administrative members into changing their transaction decision. This strategy is pursued because of the lack of means to directly impact the decision.

The shareholder meeting is generally authorized to initiate the removal of a management board member if it has lost its confidence in him, § 84 (3) sent. 2. An attempt to remove a member of the administration must, however, relate to the work done by the concerned member. Shareholders cannot use it solely to demonstrate their authority or to shatter an established authority structure.[1598] Accordingly, abuse results from the intent to damage the corporation by removing a management board member without substan-

---

1589 BayObLG, Urt. v. 02.08.1968, Az.: 2 Z 54/68, AG 1968, 330 (330, 331); KG, Beschl. v. 03.12. 2002, Az.: 1 W 363/02, NZG 2003, 441 (443); KG, Urt. v. 06.04.1979, Az.: 1 W 4076/78, WM 1979, 954 (955).

1590 KG, Beschl. v. 03.12. 2002, Az.: 1 W 363/02, AG 2003, 500 (505), NZG 2003, 441 (444); *see* Halberkamp/Gierke, NZG 2004, 494 (498); Kubis, in: MüKo AktG, § 122 mn.22; Werner, in: Großkomm AktG, 2008, § 122 mn.37; other opinion: Eckardt, in: Geßler et al., AktG, 1973, § 122 mn.29: who denies the right of the management board to decline the request with the reasoning that it may damage the corporation.

1591 KG, Beschl. v. 03.12. 2002, Az.: 1 W 363/02, AG 2003, 500 (503).

1592 *Id.* at 502; Semler, in: Münch. Hdb. AG, Vol. 4, 1999, § 35 mnn.(39) 17.

1593 Kubis, in: MüKo AktG, 2004, § 122 mn.18.

1594 KG, Urt. v. 06.04.1979, Az.: 1 W 4076/78, WM 1979, 954 (956); LG Frankfurt, Beschl. v. 10.12.2003, Az.: 3/16 T 17/03, AG 2004, 218 (218); Hüffer, AktG, § 122 mn.9; Kubis, in: MüKo AktG, 2004, § 122 mn.31; Werner, in: Großkomm AktG, 2008, § 122 mn.51; Zöllner, in: KöKo AktG, 1985, § 122 mn.9.

1595 Kubis, in: MüKo AktG, 2004, § 122 mn.22.

1596 Werner, in: Großkomm AktG, 2008, § 122 mn.37.

1597 KG, Beschl. v. 03.12. 2002, Az.: 1 W 363/02, NZG 2003, 441 (443); Semler, in: Münch. Hdb. AG, Vol. 4, 1999, § 35 mnn.39, 17.

1598 Thaeter/Guski, AG 2007, 301 (303).

tive reasons for the removal in order to harm the corporation's reputation.[1599] The same applies when using the measure for a purpose that is illegal or violates the shareholder's fiduciary duty.[1600] The usefulness of past management decisions may not be subject to evaluation; rather, it must be evaluated by the management board.[1601] Case law regarding the withdrawal of confidence for unreasonable reasons (*unsachliche Gründe*) according to § 84 (3) sent. 2 is a guideline. This provision intends to prevent the management board from being concerned about removal without cause.[1602] The concern is justified when the removal is only pretextual, arbitrary, or if the pursued purpose is illegal and violates good faith,[1603] especially if it represents a reaction to management's refusal to follow an illegal shareholder instruction.[1604] As the management board has to resolve a matter of its own interest in deciding about a request according to §§ 122, 84 (3), an abuse must be handled very strictly.[1605] Usually, it is necessary that the minority expressly states its intent to damage the corporation[1606] or that the purpose is evidently harassing.[1607] Finally, it must be taken into account that even the successful withdrawal of confidence in a management board member does not automatically lead to removal. Rather, the supervisory board decides about the removal of the management board member.[1608]

Opportunistically acting shareholders' purpose is to threaten the management board with removal to have it change its proper transaction decision in their interest, independent of the consequences for or to the detriment to the corporation. These requests are generally illegal. Since the concerned management board member has acted according to its duties in regards to the transaction decision, they usually do not have the necessary reason to initiate his removal and therefore to pursue such a procedure, which harms the corporation's reputation.[1609] The evaluation of such a minority request needs, however, to consider the totality of the circumstances, including the shareholder structure and the demand's likelihood of success § 84 (3).[1610] Especially if the minority request is likely to be successful, it needs to be taken into account that fellow shareholders opposing a corresponding shareholder resolution would be confronted with the risks and costs of a long

1599 Werner, Großkomm AktG, 2008, § 122 mn.37.

1600 KG, Beschl. v. 03.12. 2002, Az.: 1 W 363/02, NZG 2003, 441 (444).

1601 OLG Köln, Urt. v. 15.06.1959, Az.: 8 W 61/59, WM 1959, 1402 (1404).

1602 Messer, Die Abberufung des Vorstandes der AG wegen Vertrauensentzugs durch die Hauptversammlung, Bruchhausen et al., FS Nirk, 1992, 681 (683).

1603 BGH, Urt. v. 28.04.1954, Az.: II ZR 211/53, NJW 1954, 998 (998)-Gerling.

1604 Kort, in: Großkomm AktG, 2006, § 84 mn.166; Mertens, in: KöKo AktG, 1996, § 84 mn.105, Mertens/Cahn, in: KöKo AktG, 2010, § 84 mn.127; Messer, Die Abberufung des Vorstandes der AG wegen Vertrauensentzugs durch die Hauptversammlung, in: Bruchhausen et al., FS Nirk, 1992, 681 (692).

1605 KG, Beschl. v. 03.12. 2002, Az.: 1 W 363/02, NZG 2003, 441 (444), Werner, in: Großkomm AktG, 2008, § 122 mn.37.

1606 Kubis, in: MüKo AktG, 2004, § 122 mn.22.

1607 Halberkamp/Gierke, NZG 2004, 494 (498).

1608 Kort, in: Großkomm AktG, 2006, § 84 mn.167; Mertens/Cahn, in: KöKo AktG, 2010, § 84 mnn.105, 122; Messer, Die Abberufung des Vorstandes der AG wegen Vertrauensentzugs durch die Hauptversammlung, in: Bruchhausen et al., FS Nirk, 1992, 681 (683).

1609 KG, Beschl. v. 03.12. 2002, Az.: 1 W 363/02, NZG 2003, 441 (444).

1610 *Id.* at 443 et seq.

rescission process. Additionally, they would generally not have interim legal protection against illegal shareholder resolutions, but only against their execution.[1611] Therefore, the initiation of such a removal is pursued for unobjective reasons according to the case law developed around § 84 (3) sent. 2.[1612] It is likely to damage the reputation of the corporation. If the requested management measure has detrimental consequences apart from the consequences related to the removal procedure, the active shareholder simultaneously violates his fiduciary duties,[1613] even if he is only a minority shareholder.[1614] The purpose behind the initiation of the removal procedure and the use of the minority rights of § 122 to damage the corporation is therefore inappropriate and illegal and results in an abuse of these rights. Whether the high demands for an abuse through the intended withdrawal of confidence in the management board members have evidently been met depends on the specific circumstances of a case. It would make a request for a special shareholder meeting and/or for an (additional) agenda topic abusive as well.

A similar evaluation applies to the abuse of minority rights under § 122 when shareholders opportunistically intend to use them to (threaten to) remove supervisory board members, § 103 (1). The shareholder meeting is authorized to remove them at any time without any objective reason guaranteeing the confidence of the shareholder meeting in the supervisory board.[1615] However, under certain circumstances it is abusive to use these rights according to § 122 to initiate a removal under § 103 (1). In contrast to the initiation right pursuant to § 84 (3), the initiated and approved removal by the shareholder meeting directly removes the member from his position on the supervisory board. Taking into account the purpose of the use of the minority right to initiate the removal of a member of the supervisory board, it is, in parallel to the valuations applicable to § 84 (3), an abuse if the supervisory board has successfully opposed the opportunistic demand by active shareholders to prevent a specific transaction decision.[1616] Rather, it is at the supervisory board's discretion whether to approve management decisions or measures or to intervene, for instance, by exercising the veto right, § 111 (4) sent. 2. The removal is not related to the performance of this specific member, but aims to amend a specific transaction decision. It is also an abuse if the initiation of a removal aims to ease the displacement of incumbents on the management board with the goal of overcoming the administrative opposition to unsuccessfully impacted management measures.[1617]

As a consequence of an abuse of the rights according to §§ 84 (3) sent. 2, 103 (1), 122, the management board is allowed to deny the shareholder request.[1618] A controversy

1611 *Id.* at 444; Schmidt, in: Großkomm AktG, 1996, § 246 mnn.128-130; Hüffer, in: MüKo AktG, 2001, § 243 mnn.143 et seq.

1612 KG, Beschl. v. 03.12. 2002, Az.: 1 W 363/02, NZG 2003, 441 (446); Mertens/Cahn, in: KöKo AktG, 2010, § 84 mn.127.

1613 KG, Beschl. v. 03.12. 2002, Az.: 1 W 363/02, NZG 2003, 441 (445).

1614 BGH, Urt. v. 20.03. 1995, Az.: II ZR 205/94, AG 1995, 368 (377)–Girmes.

1615 Hopt/Roth, in: Großkomm AktG, 2006, § 103 mn.4; Hüffer, AktG, § 103 mn.3.

1616 KG, Beschl. v. 03.12. 2002, Az.: 1 W 363/02, NZG 2003, 441 (446 et seq.).

1617 *Id.* at 447.

1618 Hüffer, AktG, § 122 mn.7.

evolved regarding § 84 (3), which requires a decision on the supervisory board's own account.[1619]

Finally, the denial of an information request pursuant to § *131 (1)* for reasons of abuse is not excluded by the exclusive catalog in § 131 (3), which in sentence two expresses the exclusivity of these reasons. Rather, the abuse of the request for information not aiming at the clarification of facts,[1620] but at other purposes, eliminates the right to demand information preventing the applicability of the catalogue in subsection 3.[1621]

Consequently, active shareholders are at least in theory prohibited from using the entire spectrum of formal shareholder rights for the sole purpose of pressuring members of the administration to amend a transaction decision in their own interest. Rather, especially §§ 84 (3), 103 (1), 122 require performance-related reasons to initiate or approve the ouster of a member of the administration. Therefore, impact on transaction decisions to prevent opportunistic administrative decisions can be based on reference to these rights as far as the responsible members or other given performance issues are concerned. Impact led by opportunistic shareholder interests alone, in contrast, can at least theoretically not refer to these shareholder rights. In practice, however, the administration needs to prove the abuse.

(b) Fiduciary duty

(i) General applicability to active shareholders

Fiduciary duties protect the interests of the corporation and fellow investors of active shareholders.[1622] In contrast to U.S.-American corporate law, as interpreted by jurisprudence and the majority of legal scholars, it is recognized today that not only majority shareholders have the fiduciary duty to facilitate the corporation, to act loyally towards fellow shareholders, and to abstain from damaging the corporation.[1623] In general, minority shareholders may also be subject to fiduciary duties,[1624] especially the ban on

1619 Mertens/Cahn, in: KöKo AktG, 2010, § 84 mn.127.

1620 Thaeter/Guski, AG 2007, 301 (303).

1621 BayObLG, Beschl. v. 08.05.1974, Az.: 2 Z 73/73, NJW 1974, 2094 (2094); Decher, in: Großkomm AktG, 2001, § 131 mnn.295, 176; Ebenroth, Das Auskunftsrecht des Aktionärs und seine Durchsetzung im Prozeß, 1970, § 35 et seq., 38; Eckardt, in: Geßler et al., AktG, 1973, § 131 mn.132; Hüffer, AktG, § 131 mn.33; opposing opinion: Mayer-Landrut, Der "Mißbrauch" aktienrechtlicher Minderheits- oder Individualrechte, insbesondere des Auskunftsrechts, in: Fischer et al., FS Schilling, 1973, 235 (242 et seq.): determining the motives of the questioning shareholder as irrelevant since the requirements laid down in subsection one of § 131 AktG, requiring that the question concerns *matters of the corporation,* which are *necessary to judge the concerned topic of the agenda,* are sufficiently protecting the corporation and the participants of the shareholder meeting; Meilicke/Heidel, DStR 1992, 113 (115).

1622 Kumpan, ZHR 170 (2006), 39 (70).

1623 BGH, Urt. v. 1.02.1988, Az.: II ZR 75/87, DNotZ 1989, 14 (19)–Linotype; Henze, ZHR 162 (1998) 186 (187); Lutter, JZ 1976, 225 (230 et seq.); Lutter, ZHR 162 (1998), 164 (177).

1624 BGH, Urt. v. 20.03.1995, Az.: II ZR 205/94, NJW 1995, 1739 (1739)–Girmes; Henze, ZHR 162 (1998), 186 (187); Lutter, JZ 1995, 1053 (1054); Thaeter/Guski, AG 2007, 301 (303).

damaging the corporation or fellow investors when making use of shareholder rights.[1625] As the judiciary has developed the fiduciary duty, it is only applicable as long as statutory restrictions of shareholder rights are not exclusive, as is the case for §§ 126 et seq.[1626], but not for § 131.[1627] In order to determine that a violation has taken place, it is necessary to consider the circumstances of the specific case, especially the structure of the corporation. Egoistic shareholder behavior alone is not sufficient.[1628] Rather, the balancing of the involved interests of the corporation and the shareholder's interests has to demonstrate that the concerned shareholder(s) have exceeded the limit.[1629] If this is the case, the corporation or shareholders may demand restriction of the concerned shareholder's rights,[1630] as may be done under the principle of the abuse of rights, both overlapping in this context.[1631] They can challenge a resulting shareholder resolution or pursue a claim for damages against the shareholders who acted with the necessary intent[1632].[1633]

The question in the context of transaction activism is whether the procedure of active shareholders to impact corporate transaction decisions is limited by their fiduciary duties. As active shareholders are usually minority shareholders with stakes below ten percent, they are in most of the cases not subject to fiduciary duties according to the second senate of the BGH.[1634] A different evaluation may, however, result from the fact that active shareholders tend to pursue their own strategic goals with the support of fellow shareholders. In this context, consideration of the dogmatic approach to the fiduciary duty may prove helpful; the BGH has not yet decided the issue.[1635]

According to the prevailing *content-related opinion*,[1636] it is the duty of consideration (*Pflicht zur Rücksichtnahme*), § 705 BGB, which obliges shareholders to take into

1625 Schmidt, Gesellschaftsrecht, § 28 I, 801; Werner, Zur Treupflicht des Kleinaktionärs, in: Bierich et al., FS Semler, 1993, 419 (424).

1626 Hüffer, AktG, § 126 mn.1; Werner, Zur Treupflicht des Kleinaktionärs, in: Bierich et al., FS Semler, 1993, 419 (425).

1627 *See* mn.1648 for the possible abuse of the information right, similar evaluations applying to the fiduciary duty, Decher, in: Großkomm AktG, 2001, § 131 mn.295.

1628 Schmidt, Gesellschaftsrecht, § 28 I, 802; Thaeter/Guski, AG 2007, 301 (303).

1629 Thaeter/Guski, AG 2007, 301 (303).

1630 Marsch-Barner, ZHR 157 (1993), 172 (179).

1631 Hueck/Windbichler, Gesellschaftsrecht, § 26 mn.26.

1632 BGH, Urt. v. 20.03.1995, Az.: II ZR 205/94, NJW 1995, 1739 (1746)-Girmes; OLG Düsseldorf, Teilurt. v. 14.6.1996, Az.: 7 U 110/93, ZIP 1996, 1211 (1212 et seq.); Bungeroth, in: MüKo AktG, Vor § 53a mn.43: argueing with the *ratio legis* of former § 117 (7) No. 1 as well as with the consideration that uncertainty about the liability risk may keep shareholders from exercising their voting rights; Grunewald, Rechtswidrigkeit und Verschulden bei der Haftung von Aktionären und Personengesellschaften, Forster et al., FS Kropff, 1997, 89, 98: argueing with the intent to reduce the liability risk for minority shareholders, as they need to be encouraged to vote; Lutter, JZ 1995, 1053 (1055).

1633 Bungeroth, in: MüKo AktG, Vor § 53a AktG, mnn.32 et seq.; Hüffer, AktG, § 53a mn.21; Marsch-Barner, ZHR (157 (1993), 172 (188, 191).

1634 BGH – Urt. v. 20.03.1995, Az.: II ZR 205/94, NJW 1995, 1739 (1741).

1635 *Id.*

1636 Bungeroth, in: MüKo AktG, Vor § 53a mn.25; Hueck/Windbichler, Gesellschaftsrecht, § 26 mn.26; Lutter, JZ 1995, 1053 (1054); Marsch-Barner, ZHR 157 (1993), 172 (173).

account the purpose of the corporation, to consider the interests of fellow shareholders, and to prevent damage to them when exercising corporate influence.[1637] The fiduciary duty is, however, of particular significance for shareholders with a significant stake. Due to their position, they can exercise relevant (causal) influence on the corporate destiny and fellow shareholders' interests.[1638]

Proponents of an *impact-related approach*[1639] see the fiduciary duty as linked to the influence of shareholders in the corporation. Individual minority shareholders are therefore generally not subject to fiduciary duties,[1640] while collectively acting minority shareholders may be.[1641] According to the impact-related approach, a fiduciary duty would only apply to shareholders bundling their votes via agreement on a specific vote or voting right authorization to ensure conformity and effective votes of all participating shareholders, even in the case of short-term amendments.[1642] Parallel voting of shareholders, for instance in regard to a countermotion, § 126, in contrast cannot respond to short-term amendments and is a minor impact not triggering the fiduciary duties of the involved shareholders.[1643] As active shareholders usually pursue the latter approach, they would under this approach not be subject to fiduciary duties independent of the content of their votes. Proponents of this approach argue that the relationship of influence and responsibility equals the principle of the corporate statute as expressed in many rules, among them §§ 117, 243 (2), 254 (1), 255 (2), as well as group law.[1644] Thereafter, balancing the involved interests and considering the structure of the corporation for each singular case determines the border.[1645] The stronger their impact is the stronger are their fiduciary duties.[1646]

Under the prevailing *content-related approach*, however, shareholders not bundling their votes with those of fellow shareholders may still be subject to a fiduciary duty.[1647] Proponents of the content-related approach argue convincingly that whether to apply the

1637 Heider, in: MüKo AktG, § 2 mn.49; Henze, ZHR 162 (1998), 186 (186 et seq.).

1638 Bungeroth, in: MüKo AktG, Vor § 53a mn.26; Lutter, JZ 1995, 1053 (1054).

1639 RGZ 132, 149 (163): From the authority also to decide via majority resolution for the minority and therefore to indirectly dispose of their property rights results the duty of the majority to consider the justified interests of the minority sufficiently and not to restrict their rights unnecessarily when considering the overall interest; Dreher, ZHR 157 (1993), 150 (154-156); Zöllner, Die Schranken mitgliedschaftlicher Stimmrechtsmacht bei den privatrechtlichen Verbänden, 1963, 342 n.18; Zöllner, in: KöKo AktG, 1984, Introduction, mn.169.

1640 BGH, Urt. v. 1.02.1988, Az.: II ZR 75/87, ZIP 1988, 301 (305)–Linotype.

1641 Dreher, ZHR 157 (1993), 150 (156 et seq.).

1642 BGH, Urt. v. 20.03.1995, Az.: II ZR 205/94, BGHZ 129, 136 (151)-Girmes; Dreher, ZHR 157 (1993), 150 (158 et seq.); Thaeter/Guski, AG 2007, 301 (303).

1643 Dreher, ZHR 157 (1993), 158 et seq.

1644 *Id.* at 155.

1645 Thaeter/Guski, AG 2007, 301 (303).

1646 BGH, Urt. v. 01.02.1988, Az.: II ZR 75/87, NJW 1988, 1579 (1583); Schmidt, Gesellschaftsrecht, § 28 I, 800; Zöllner, in: KK, 1984, Introduction mn.169: applying fiduciary duties also to coincidental majorities obliging them to consider corporate interests as well as those of minority shareholders.

1647 Bungeroth, in: MüKo, AktG, Vor § 53a mn.26; Lutter, JZ 1995, 1053 (1054); Henze, BB 1996, 489 (496).

duty to respect the interests of the corporation depends primarily on the subject matter of the resolution, which is determining for pursuing the corporate purpose. Accordingly, the existence, intensity, and continuity of the fiduciary duty toward the corporation depends on the content of shareholder votes and the purpose for which shareholder means, amongst them §§ 122 (1), (2), 131, are used. If the subject matter of the resolution impacts the interests of other shareholders, the voting shareholder needs to consider the necessity and adequacy of the mildest available means. If it also impacts the interests of the corporation, it is also necessary to determine whether corporate interests justify the measure. Accordingly, based on the administrative proposal, the single shareholder voting on a shareholder resolution needs to balance the interests involved prior to voting. Otherwise, he acts contrary to his fiduciary duty. Whether a vote or action violating the fiduciary duty will actually become legally relevant depends on whether the corresponding position reaches the necessary quorum. However, this represents only a question of causality.[1648] Furthermore, the proponents of this approach point out that the fiduciary duty applies equally to all shareholders, independent of the coordination of the concerned shareholder rights. Rather, a violation depends on the content. This allows evaluating the votes of all shareholders equally, independent of whether they voted bundled or not. Moreover, it conforms to the rescission practice of shareholder resolutions due to fiduciary duty violations, which have to be evaluated equally for all shareholders. Similarly to shareholders holding a stake necessary to launch a motion or a blocking minority, shareholders bundling their rights have no more responsibility than those related to their participation in the share capital.[1649] The bundling of votes becomes therefore solely relevant in regard to the causality of resulting damage[1650].[1651] As a consequence, active shareholders using shareholder rights to realize interests to the detriment of the corporation, which will certainly lead to corporate damage or to the irrelevance of corporate interests, violate their fiduciary duty toward the corporation and their fellow shareholders.[1652] In contrast, active investors aiming to increase shareholder value of the targeted corporations often act according to the interests of the corporation and its shareholders.

If shareholders pursuing transaction activism apply the informal means to *publicly* advertise new corporate strategies and to criticize management's strategy or performance, in contrast, the substantiated criticism not involving false facts or the disparagement or defamation[1653] of the administration must, in regard to the shareholder's freedom of opinion, conform with the shareholder's fiduciary duty.[1654]

1648 Henze, BB 1996, 489 (496).
1649 *See* BGH, Urt. v. 20.03.1995, Az.: II ZR 205/94, NJW 1995, 1739 (1741 et seq.).
1650 Lutter, JZ 1995, 1053 (1054).
1651 *See* Schäfer, ZHR (1993), 192 (192).
1652 Thaeter/Guski, AG 2007, 301 (304).
1653 Werner, Zur Treupflicht des Kleinaktionärs, in: Bierich et al., FS Semler, 1993, 419 (425).
1654 *Id.* at 424 et seq.; Arnold, ZCG 2008, 221 (224).

Finally, the corporation or the shareholder(s) invoking a violation of the fiduciary duty have the *burden of proving* the violation. In practice, this is a significant burden that limits the relevance of fiduciary duty violations.[1655]

(ii) Fiduciary duties and empty voting

The use of empty voting to pursue deviating interests could be a violation of fiduciary duty. Capital markets law has not specifically regulated the phenomenon of empty voting (yet). Limitations under corporate law aimed at restricting the egoistic exercise of voting rights in constellations in which a shareholder usually does not contribute in a desirable way to the voting decision are laid down in §§ 71b, 136, 142 (1) sent. 2.[1656] Empty voters are, however, not barred by them. Empty voting is not an explicitly regulated case of suspension from voting rights, § 136. Its analogous application has been generally rejected[1657].[1658] Empty voting does not fall under the general doctrine of the *Abspaltungsverbot*, which, based on § 717 BGB and laid down for corporations in § 8 (5), bans the separate transfer of assets or administrative rights, such as the right to vote,[1659] based on the corporate membership of a shareholder. Empty voting is not, however, based on the transfer of a right related to the membership of a shareholder as required by the *Abspaltungsverbot.*[1660] It does not represent a forbidden purchase of a voting right, §§ 405 (3) No. 6, 7, as the voter does not obtain any compensation for his vote.[1661] It can, however, be observed that empty voting similar to the purchase of votes collides with the *purpose* of these comparably old-fashioned provisions aiming to ensure genuine decision-making of the shareholder meeting.[1662]

Therefore, the general limitations under corporate law, especially the fiduciary duty aiming to prevent the abuse of exercised shareholder rights, represents an appropriate principle to deal with so far unknown constellations of conflicting interests, such as empty voting. A violation of fiduciary duty would grant the right to file a rescission claim regarding a shareholder resolution involving empty votes according to § 243 (1).[1663] Pertinent case law regarding *borrowed shares* concerned only the special constellation of a squeeze out.[1664] The consequences of the votes involving borrowed shares were restricted to the exclusion of the concerned minority shareholders. Therefore, they did not concern any (potentially negative) future development for the corporation and its shareholders. Based on legislative value judgment and its intentions, an application of

1655 Thaeter/Guski, AG 2007, 301 (303).

1656 Bachmann, ZHR 173 (1999), 596 (611 et seq.).

1657 Hüffer, AktG, § 136 mn.18.

1658 Fleischer, ZGR 2008, 185 (216); Theusinger/Möritz, NZG 2010, 607 (609).

1659 Hüffer, AktG, § 133 mn.17; K. Schmidt, Gesellschaftsrecht, § 19 III, 560 et seq.; Schöne, in: Bamberger/Roth, Beck'scher Online-Kommentar BGB, 2010, § 717 mn.6.

1660 Fleischer, ZGR 2008, 185 (216); Kumpan/Mittermeier, ZIP 2009, 404 (405); Seibt, ZGR 2010, 795 (798).

1661 Theusinger/Möritz, NZG 2010, 607 (609).

1662 Bachmann, ZHR 173 (2009), 596 (614 et seq.).

1663 Kumpan/Mittermeier, ZIP 2009, 404 (410).

1664 BGH, Urt. v. 16.03.2009, Az.: II ZR 302/06, NJW-Spezial 2009, 335.

borrowed shares during a squeeze out decision rarely is an abuse.[1665] For the remainder of the constellations involving share lending, this potential is significantly larger, however. They therefore require a different legal qualification.

Legal scholars pursue two approaches to restrict the potentially abusive use of empty voting. *One approach* applies equal control of all kinds of empty voting on a case-by-case basis. It is based on the shareholder's fiduciary duty whose duty of consideration may be violated when voting empty in contrast to the interests of the corporation and its shareholders.[1666] Another, *broader approach* applies different standards to empty voting: the doctrine of institutional abuse of rights for empty voting based on share lending and fiduciary duties on a case-by-case basis for the remaining empty voting constellations.[1667] Thereafter, share lending represents a generally acknowledged legal principle. However, its use to construe empty votes does not represent a legally acknowledged function, as opposed to the generally recognized purposes of overcoming supply shortages or admitted price management.[1668] Accordingly, temporary share borrowing with the purpose of voting empty represents a voting authorization, which is a source for the falsification of the corporate decision-making process.[1669] For dogmatic reasons, it is therefore not appropriate to apply a content-related fiduciary duty approach filtering shareholder behavior disregarding the duty of consideration toward the corporation and fellow shareholders to empty voting based on lended shares. Rather, the fiduciary duty with its flexible prerequisites and legal consequences represents the ideal limitation for the remainder of the different types of empty voting.

The proponents of the former content-based fiduciary duty approach argue that empty voting can also be realized through mechanisms other than share lending to which the valuations of the general approach based on the abuse of rights may not apply.[1670] Furthermore, they allege that the broad approach to empty voting based on share lending leaves its potentially positive ability to reduce principal-agent conflicts unconsidered by declaring empty voting based on share lending as generally unlawful.[1671] These positive functions are, however, of particular relevance in reducing agency issues usually aimed at when pursuing shareholder activism. Therefore, it seems inappropriate to evaluate empty voting, even if only based on share lending, as contradicting the values of corporate law. On the other hand, the separation of legitimate from illegitimate empty votes on a case-by-case basis under the fiduciary duty approach could result in more

1665 Kumpan/Mittermeier, ZIP 2009, 404 (411).

1666 Eidenmüller, DStR 2007, 2116 (2118, 2120); Fleischer, ZGR 2008, 185 (216 et seq.); Kumpan/Mittermeier, ZIP 2009, 404 (410 et seq.); Theusinger/Möritz, NZG 2010, 607 (610).

1667 Bachmann, ZHR 173 (2009), 596 (617).

1668 Gsell, Wertpapierleihe und Repurchase Agreement im deutschen Recht, 1995, 128 et seq.: distinguishes between permissible forms of share lending, in order to realize short sales or to fulfill contractual obligations, and impermissible forms of lending shares, such as to accumulate for a short time a large amount of voting rights in order to impact important corporate decisions.

1669 Bachmann, ZHR 173 (2009), 596 (617 et seq.).

1670 Theusinger/Möritz, NZG 2010, 607 (609).

1671 Fleischer, ZGR 2008, 185 (217); Hu & Black, 79 S. Cal. L. Rev. 811, 820 et seq., 889, 907 (2006); Theusinger/Möritz, NZG 2010, 607 (609).

legal uncertainty due to the absence of a bright line. This could lead to an increased number of (potentially abusive) rescission actions with increased costs for the remainder of shareholders.[1672] Vice versa, a general prohibition of empty voting based on share lending has the potential to increase litigation even more.[1673] This may be the case as the illegality of empty voting according to the broader approach depends solely on the (improper) purpose of share lending,[1674] and such a purpose may be (too) easily assumed once share-lending periods comprise a record date.

Taking into account the potentially positive purposes of empty voting discussed *supra*, whether based on share lending or the use of financial instruments, it seems appropriate to apply the same legal regime to all types of empty voting. Therefore, the application of the fiduciary duty on a case-by-case basis seems to be the appropriate way to limit potential abuse while considering its potentially positive impact on corporate governance. It is violated whenever empty voting coincides with a conflict of interest between the voting shareholders and the interests of the corporation and its shareholders,[1675] which has to be evaluated by taking into account the specific circumstances. These include the interests pursued by the empty voting shareholder and the effect of the votes on the corporation and its shareholders.[1676] To increase the effectiveness of fiduciary duty-based limitations of empty voting, it seems preferable that courts ease the burden of proof as soon as the plaintiff provides indications of a conflict of interest on the part of the empty voting shareholder.[1677] In the transaction activism context, this could be an area in which the distinction between constellations likely to involve desirable transaction activism or not could become useful.

(c) Ban on damages under group law, sections 17, 311 AktG

Considering the still prevailing shareholder structure of German corporations with at least one large shareholder, the German legislator established limitations for the impact of entrepreneurial shareholders.[1678] Impact under German group law, § 17 (1), requires

---

1672 Bachmann, ZHR 173 (2009), 596 (618): argues in favor of the general invalidity of votes based on borrowed shares with the legal certainty and therefore the prevention of another opportunity for abusive rescission claims.

1673 Kumpan/Mittermeier, ZIP 2009, 404 (410); Theusinger/Möritz, NZG 2010, 607 (609 et seq.).

1674 Bachmann, ZHR 173 (2009), 596 (617): His third approach of the institutional rights abuse regarding empty voting based on share borrowing distinguishes between institutional abusive and permissible empty voting based on the *purpose* of share borrowing alone. While share borrowing to overcome shortages or to impact the stock price are permissible purposes, share borrowing for strategic puposes is impermissible, as share borrowing in general may not be used to pursue strategic purposes through empty voting.

1675 Zetsche, NZG 2009, 692 (697).

1676 Kumpan/Mittermeier, ZIP 2009, 404 (410).

1677 Theusinger/Möritz, NZG 2010, 607 (610).

1678 Koppensteiner, in: KöKo AktG, 2004, Vor § 311 mn.1 et seq.; Kropff, in: MüKo AktG, 2000, Vor § 311 mn. 2.

consistent, structurally-based influence.[1679] Even a minority stake may be sufficient if correlated with legal or factual circumstances ensuring sufficient impact on the corporate personnel policy or important corporate decisions. Voluntary, non-binding cooperation ensures not such impact.[1680] Active shareholders usually hold only single digit stakes. Despite low attendance rates during shareholder meetings, they alone do not ensure a voting majority. The necessary support through further (active) shareholders or the administration to impact strategic decisions does not represent a sufficiently reliable form of support assuring the consistency of the influence required by § 17.[1681] Consequently, active shareholders are generally not subject to German group law.

(d) Claim for damages, section 117 (1) AktG

Another important provision is § 117 (1). Fiduciary duties and § 117 may be violated simultaneously.[1682] § 117 (1) provides the corporation or the shareholders who have suffered damages with a claim for damages against someone who has intentionally used his impact on, amongst others, members of the administration to damage the corporation or its shareholders.

Share ownership suffices to provide the *impact* necessary under § 117.[1683] It requires any kind of influence onthe corporation, which enables corporate or factual impact[1684] on the corporation. Even minority shareholders[1685] holding a blocking or only a motion minority[1686] under German corporate law have the necessary influence.

The offender needs to *apply his influence* to order (*zu bestimmen*) specific members of the administration. Every type of influence is sufficient, as long as it causes the intended action by the administrative member.[1687] It does not have to be obnoxious.[1688] The behavior of active shareholders aiming to convince the management board to amend its strategy, by implicitly or explicitly referring to potential impact based on the parallel actions of several shareholders in applying general formal means, meets this requirement. Furthermore, active shareholders usually target members of the management or the supervisory board, § 117 (1) sent. 1, to address their request.

1679 BGH, Urt. v. 4.03.1974, Az.: II ZR 89/72, NJW 1978, 855 (857); BGH, Urt. v. 26.03.1984, Az.: II ZR 171/83, NJW 1984, 1893 (1893); Raiser/Veil, Recht der Kapitalgesellschaften, § 51 mnn.15 et seq.

1680 BGH, Urt. v. 13.10.1977, Az.: II ZR 123/76; NJW 1978, 104 (104); OLG Frankfurt a.M., Urt. v. 30.04. 1997, Az.: 23 U 89/95, NZG 1998, 229 (229); Emmerich, in: Emmerich/Habersack, Aktien- und GmbH-Konzernrecht, § 17 mn.18.

1681 Arnold, ZCG 2008, 221 (224).

1682 Spindler, in: MüKo AktG, 2008, § 117 mn.6.

1683 Brüggemeier, AG 1988, 93 (95); Kropff, in: Geßler et al., AktG, 1973, § 117 mn.14; Thaeter/Guski, AG 2007, 301 (304).

1684 Brüggemeier, AG 1988, 91 (95); Hüffer, AktG, § 117 mn.4; Schall, in: Spindler/Stilz, AktG, 2010, 117 mn.15.

1685 Thaeter/Guski, AG 2007, 301 (304).

1686 Kort, in: Großkomm AktG, 2006, § 117 mn.118; Spindler, in: MüKo AktG, 2008, § 117 mn.3.

1687 Hüffer, AktG, § 117 mn.4.

1688 Kropff, in: Geßler et al., 1973, AktG, § 117 mn.18.

Moreover, the impact applied needs to have ordered the targeted administrative members to act to the detriment of the corporation. Due to the discretion of administrative members, the question arising in this context is under what circumstances have their actions been ordered by the impact of active shareholders' demands?

Considering the *wording* of § 117, *manipulate into* implies a certain pressure behind the impact exercised. Therefore, personal talks between active shareholders and corporate management involving pure recommendations of active shareholders regarding a specific corporate strategy do not fulfill this requirement. Threats of active shareholders to remove supervisory board members or to initiate a removal of management board members if the corporate strategy is not amended according to their demands must be evaluated differently. They exceed the impact level that allows management board members to block them solely by reference to § 76 (1)[1689] and its discretion in strategic matters. Consequently, it may represent a determination in the sense of § 117 (1).

Another argument could be derived from the *purposes* of § 117 (1). Its purpose to protect the corporate assets and the corporate- and membership-related financial shareholder interests is undisputed.[1690] A lively discussion has evolved, however, about the content of an *additional purpose* of § 117 (1).

Some determine the *integrity of administrative actions* as an additional purpose. Integrity is violated when administrative members act objectively contrary to their duty; the focus lies on exceeding the administrative discretion.[1691] One objectively acts against his duty when he exceeds the boundaries of entrepreneurial actions, which focus solely on the well-being of the corporation and are pursued with responsibility and based on carefully investigated evidence.[1692] In favor of this approach, it may be argued that the administration is granted relatively wide discretion to meet its entrepreneurial decisions. It is in the shareholders' interests for management to incur risks that correlate to the potential to increase the stock price. Risky administrative decisions alone, which result in damage to the corporation and its shareholders, should not fall under § 117, as it is not the purpose of this norm to transfer general market risk away from the corporation to the influencing person.[1693] According to § 317 (2), not even a controlled company would be able to demand compensation under this scenario.[1694] Derived from the damage requirement, only an inducement to administrative members to act objectively against their duty is an order pursuant to § 117.[1695] However, this approach would result in lia-

1689 Thaeter/Guski, AG 2007, 301 (304): excluding pressure on the management board from determinations in the sense of § 117 AktG as long as management is able to resist the ambitions of active shareholders by referring to § 76 AktG.

1690 BGH, Urt. v. 22.6.1992, Az.: II ZR 178/90, NJW 1992, 3167 (3172); Hommelhoff/Witt, in: Schmidt/Lutter, AktG, 2010, § 117 mn.1; Voigt, Haftung aus Einfluss auf die Aktiengesellschaft, 2003, 37.

1691 Hüffer, AktG, § 117 mn.1; Kort, in: Großkomm AktG, 2006, § 117 mnn.6, 7; Kropff, in: Geßler et al., AktG, 1973, § 117 mnn.6, 23.

1692 BGH, Urt. v. 21.04.1997, Az.: II ZR 175/95, BGHZ 135, 244 (253 et seq.); Kort, in: Großkomm AktG, 2006, § 117 mn.7.

1693 Voigt, Haftung aus Einfluss auf die Aktiengesellschaft, 2003, 41–43.

1694 *Id.* 44.

1695 *Id.* at 40.

bility gaps to the extent that the impacting person uses the discretion of administrative members. This is especially relevant when the impacting person cheats the administrative member.[1696] Thereafter, a member can act within his business judgement, but the risk resulting from the impact exercised on the administrative member can still damage the corporation and/or its shareholders.[1697] Another systematic counterargument can be derived from subsection 2. Administrative members can also be held liable if they act contrary to their duty. Considering this additional liability of administrative members if they act contrary to their duties while being influenced to do so by another person makes it unlikely that subsection one implicitly protects the integrity of the administration. Finally, recent statutory amendments have deprived the approach of one of its main arguments. Former § 117 (7) No. 1 specified that shareholder votes do not represent influence in the sense of § 117 (1).[1698] Its proponents argued that the formally provided way for shareholders to influence the corporate decision-making process could not constitute impact in the sense of § 117 (1). In 2005, the UMAG repealed former § 117 (7) No. 1 to delete the resulting privilege of majority shareholders.[1699]

Another approach supports the idea that § 117 (1) protects the *autonomy of the decision-making process* of the independent corporation from the *competence adverse impact* of third persons or corporate members.[1700] A corresponding interpretation of § 117 's purpose would be particularly relevant for shareholders pursuing opportunistic transaction activism. Active shareholders threatening the administration in order to achieve specific transaction decisions to the detriment of the corporation and its shareholders would be liable for resulting damages. The protection of the autonomy of the corporate decision-making process is drawn from the wording *to order someone to do something,* which is necessary in addition to financial damage to the corporation or shareholders.[1701] However, impact used with the purpose of damaging the corporation or its shareholders would never have been institutionally guaranteed. Therefore, the additional requirement of violation of the corporate competency is not convincing.[1702] Furthermore, a decision-making procedure below the management or supervisory board level, also covered

1696 Mertens, in: KöKo AktG, 1996, § 117 mn.17.

1697 Voigt, Haftung aus Einfluss auf die Aktiengesellschaft, 2003, 46.

1698 *Id.* at 47.

1699 RegE eines Gesetzes zur Unternehmensintegrität und Modernisierung des Anfechtsungsrechts [UMAG] [Draft Law of the Federal Government of an Act on the Corporate Integrity and Modernization of the Rescission Right], Mar. 14, 2005, BT-Drucks 15/5092, 12: The elimination of § 117 (7) No. 1 AktG equals the elimination of a privilege of majority shareholders, who, despite the use of their voting power, were able to order the administration to act in a way resulting in a damage for the corporation and could not be held liable for it.; Hommelhoff/Witt, in: Schmidt/Lutter, AktG, 2010, § 117 mn.29.

1700 Brüggemeier, AG 1988, 91 (96); Hommelhoff/Witt, in: Schmidt/Lutter, AktG, 2010, § 117 mn.1; Kropff, in: MüKo AktG, 2004, § 117mn.2; Spindler, in: MüKo AktG, 2008, § 117 mn.2; *similar* Kort, AG 2005, 453 (453); Windbichler/Hueck, Gesellschaftsrecht, § 23 mn.28: protection of the independence and the corporate decision-making structure.

1701 Brüggemeier, AG 1988, 91 (95 et seq.).

1702 Mertens, in: KöKo AktG, 1996, § 117 mn.13; Voigt, Haftung aus Einfluss auf die Aktiengesellschaft, 2003, 47.

by § 117 (1), has not been statutorily provided for and is therefore hard to protect. As a consequence, impact on authorized representatives as influenced persons could not be enforceable.[1703] The protection of autonomy apart from competency leaves unanswered what is understood as the *autonomy of the corporate decision-making process*.[1704] Furthermore, the systematic argument relating to § 117 (2) again becomes relevant. It also requires that the concerned administrative members acted against their duty for liability. If the fact that the administration opened its decision to the impact of others to the detriment of the corporation already constituted a breach of duty, § 117 (2) requiring a breach of duty by the administrative members would consequently be superfluous. Therefore, the impact on management and supervisory board members alone cannot be forbidden.[1705] Finally, the protection of the autonomy of the corporate decision-making process does not correspond to the risk resulting from heteronomy.[1706] Rather, it would burden the influencing person with general market risk, as the impact on administrative members could make them consider the proposed action and follow the proposal while normal market risk eventually harms the corporation.[1707] It would be unfair and economically unwarranted to burden with augmented market risk influential persons like majority shareholders in difficult corporate situations with possibly incapable management.[1708] Therefore, the protection of the autonomy of the corporate decision-making process cannot be a purpose of § 117 (1).[1709]

The third and final approach suggests the protection of the corporation from *impact contrary to its interest*.[1710] This approach prevents the impact's specific risk and the general market risk from being commingled, and the influencer from being held liable even if market risk causes the harm. The focus on the general corporate interest allows partial liability for corporate damage based on the purpose of the regulation.[1711] This interpretation considers that despite the impact exercised on the administration, the decision remains an entrepreneurial decision.[1712] As far as the systematics of § 117 is concerned, the impact demanded according to § 117 (1) is qualified in comparison to the sole impact on management, but distinct from the separately regulated § 117 (2) sent. 1. It therefore conforms to the distinction between the liability provisions in subsections one and two. Finally, this interpretation considers that even though the administration has wide

1703 Voigt, Haftung aus Einfluss auf die Aktiengesellschaft, 2003, 48 et seq.

1704 *Id.* at 50, Kort, in: Großkomm AktG, 2006, § 117 mn.13.

1705 Voigt, Haftung aus Einfluss auf die Aktiengesellschaft, 2003, 50.

1706 Kort, in: Großkomm AktG, 2006, § 117 mn.50.

1707 Voigt, Haftung aus Einfluss auf die Aktiengesellschaft, 2003, 52.

1708 *Id.* 52.

1709 *Id.*

1710 *Id.* at 61: who sees the reason for the liability in the quasi affiliation of the person that makes use of alien management authority; Schall, in: Spindler/Stilz, Aktiengesetz, 2010, § 117 mn.6: pointing out that § 117 AktG does not establish a corporate duty for the impacting person, but just the justification of the everybody-duty to not damage the corporation via illegal influence.

1711 Schall, in: Spindler/Stilz, AktG, 2010, § 117 mn.6; Voigt, Haftung aus Einfluss auf die Aktiengesellschaft, 2003, 56, 60.

1712 LG Mainz, Urt. v. 3.3.1988, Az.: 1 O 104/87, AG 1988, 171 (177).

discretion to consider all relevant interests in each particular situation, it is capable of pointing out the determinative interests for its decision-making process.[1713]

In light of the arguments for the *enlightened shareholder value approach*, this approach needs to be adapted. It demands respect for the interests of all stakeholders with shareholder interests taking precedence. The adaptation takes account of the coercive economic arguments in favor of the enlightened shareholder value approach while considering all of Voigt's arguments in favor of the final approach. Consequently, § 117 (1) protects not only the corporate assets and the shareholders' assets, but it also intends to protect from influence that is contrary to the interests relevant to the corporate decision-making process under the enlightened shareholder value approach. It holds the influencer responsible if the influence results in damages while respecting the administration and its discretion. In the context of transaction activism, the approach properly distinguishes between shareholders pursuing deviating interests, potentially subject to liability according to § 117 (1), and those advocating enhanced corporate governance.

Consequently, wording, purpose, and systematics suggest that § 117 (1) covers the impact exercised by active shareholders pursuing opportunistic goals and applying intensive pressure to administrative members, rendering their reference to § 76 (1) ineffective.[1714]

Furthermore, the corporation needs to suffer from *damage* based on the impact, which has to be kept strictly separate from damage resulting from entrepreneurial risk. The looting of a corporation would be relevant damage. Another example is a decreased stock price caused by the impact of active shareholders pursuing deviating interests based on empty voting or costlier participations in constituent or competing corporations. The same applies to a financially negative corporate disposition.[1715] More generally, it comprises the results of the shareholder impact following a corporate strategy opposed to that of management, which has proven to be detrimental to the corporation.[1716]

Finally, the concerned impact has to be *illegal* and the offender needs to have *acted intentionally*. The illegality exists if the impacted member of the administration objectively breaches his duty. The intent requires the knowledge about the breach of duty and the general suitability of the action or omission to damage the corporation. *Dolus eventualis* suffices.[1717] As a consequence, even active shareholders who coerce administrative members to act according to their deviating interests no matter what the consequences for the targeted corporation may be are liable under § 117 (1) if the targeted corporation suffers a damage.

The plaintiff, the corporation or the shareholders, need to demonstrate that the preconditions of § 117 (1) have been met. A shift in the *burden of proof* or simplifications regarding the intent required are generally not provided. A factual assumption that a cor-

1713 Voigt, Haftung aus Einfluss auf die Aktiengesellschaft, 2003, 54.

1714 Thaeter/Guski, AG 2007, 301 (304).

1715 OLG Düsseldorf, Urt. v. 16.10.1990, Az.: 19 W 9/88, AG 1991, 106 (109): noting the sale under value or the share package purchase over value; Thaeter/Guski, AG 2007, 301 (304).

1716 Thaeter/Guski, AG 2007, 301 (304).

1717 BGH, Urt. v. 20.03.1995, Az.: II ZR 205/94, BGHZ 129, 136 (162)–Girmes; Schall in: Spindler/Stilz, AktG, 2010, § 117 mn.25; Spindler, in: MüKo, AktG, 2008, § 117 mnn.40-42.

responding impact has been exercised applies, however, once damage to the corporation and a corresponding shareholder advantage have been proven.[1718] The requirement to prove that the influenced member of the administration acted based upon the influence to the detriment of the corporation is a practical hurdle. The concerned members usually fear to be held liable themselves under § 117 (2)[1719] and therefore decide not to testify regarding § 117 (1). These concerns are very relevant in the context of transaction activism and significantly limit the effect of § 117 (1) to prevent opportunism among active shareholders.[1720]

This contradicts the purpose of § 117 (1) to also screen active shareholders who do not pursue transaction activism to improve corporate performance, but who instead opportunistically act independent of or to the detriment of the corporation to satisfy their own interests. To satisfy the legislative intent and the practical need for limitations allowing the screening of opportunistic behavior of active shareholders, either courts or the legislator could adapt the applicable fundamentals concerning the burden of proof. The practical difficulties, similar to the ones applying to the fiduciary duty, relate not only to proving the intent of the coercive shareholders, but also to the impact applied and the resulting action of the member of the administration. A careful shift of the burden of proof for a limited number of constellations likely to involve the opportunistic behavior of active shareholders would be a possible solution. In the context of transaction activism, this could be based on the generally underlying interests and incentives of administrative members and shareholders based on the assumptions about the impact of certain transaction decisions on shareholder value. For the six analyzed constellations this would concern three of them. Consequently, an existing statutory mechanism could have relevance in limiting opportunistic shareholder behavior.

(e) Liability as shadow director

Another relevant limitation could be the liability as a so-called shadow director. It is controversial whether liability may result solely from pursuing actions for which management is responsible.[1721] Even when following the argument that liability should be based solely on the actions of the concerned person, an active minority shareholder influencing management's transaction decision will not fulfill the necessarily strict requirements. Shareholders pursuing transaction activism neither administer specific functions of the

1718 Spindler, in: MüKo AktG, 2008, § 117 mn.43.

1719 Kropff, in: MüKo AktG, 2004, § 117 mn.19.

1720 Thaeter/Guski, AG 2007, 301 (304 et seq.).

1721 *For such liability* Fleischer, AG 2004, 517 (523 et seq.); Hefermehl, in: Geßler et al., AktG, § 93 mn.8; Spindler, in: MüKo AktG, 2008, § 93 mn.17; Zöllner/Noack, in: Baumbach/Hueck, GmbHG, 2010, § 43 mn.3: demanding that the actions appear to the outside and that they originally belong to management's tasks; Mertens, in: Hachenburg, GmbHG, 1997, § 43 mn.7: against a liability for reasons of factual management, with reference to sufficient liability opportunities resulting from contract, tort and membership related law, legal certainty and the criminal analogy ban; Hüffer, AktG, § 93 mn.12: requiring a formal appointment act; Mertens, KöKo AktG, 1996, § 93 mn.12: requiring either an appointing act or the displacement of the legitimate organ as responsible.

concerned organ such a way that the organ would undertake that function,[1722] nor do they take over a material part of the management function[1723].[1724] Rather, the indirect impact exercised by active shareholders with minority stakes in transaction decisions aims to amend the behavior of the responsible management board members, with or without pressure, in a limited number of matters. This stands in clear contrast to the prerequisite that one must create the impression of acting as a management board member to the outside.[1725] The impact is not intense enough to even get close to a significant part of management's function in the corporation. Consequently, the actions of active shareholders are not likely to fall under this liability regime.

(f) Immoral damage, section 826 BGB

Shareholders assuming transaction activism while adhering to deviating interests may intentionally and immorally act to harm others, § 826 BGB. § 826 BGB applies independent of § 117 (1).[1726] The measure(s) utilized by the active shareholders must harm the corporation or its shareholders. Furthermore, the damage of the measure must be disproportionate to its benefits for it to violate the sense of decency of all fair and just thinking people under [corporate] law.[1727] The shareholder must act with intent, which must include the damage.[1728] As the shareholder's intent can be inferred from the circumstances, the most important indicium to prove intent is whether the facts that are responsible for the destructive effect of the measure are cognizable.[1729] It does not suffice, therefore, that the impact harms the corporation or the shareholders. Rather, the measure needs to contradict the corporate interests so significantly that there is no doubt that it is detrimental to the targeted corporation. These latter circumstances will rarely occur. The ability of § 826 BGB to restrict the opportunistic behavior of active shareholders is comparably low.[1730]

(2) Impact prior to decision-making process

These provisions, especially §§ 242, 826 BGB, and the fiduciary duty[1731] can equally restrain impact exercised prior to the corporate decision-making process.

1722 BGH, Urt. v. 21.3.1988, Az.: II ZR 194/87, NJW 1988, 1789 (1790); Fleischer, AG 2004, 517 (524).
1723 *Id*; the stricter approach demands the complete replacement of the corporate management by the shareholder in question so that the usually responsible person is completely detracted from liability: Mertens, KöKo AktG, 1996, § 93 mn.12; Stein, Das faktische Organ, 1984, 184 et seq.
1724 Thaeter/Guski, AG 2007, 301 (305).
1725 BGH, Urt. v. 25.2.2002, Az.: II ZR 196/00, NJW 2002, 1803 (1803).
1726 Wagner, in: MüKo BGB, 2009, § 826 mm.44, 125.
1727 BGH, Urt. v. 20.03.1995, Az.: II ZR 205/94, AG 1995, 368 (377)-Girmes.
1728 Palandt, BGB, 2010, § 826 mn.10 et seq.
1729 Wagner, in: MüKo BGB, 2009, § 826 mn.47.
1730 Arnold, ZCG 2008, 221 (224); Fleischer, ZGR 2008, 185 (210).
1731 Thaeter/Guski, AG 2007, 301 (303).

(a) Extra-institutional activities

Neither the corporate statute nor case law (explicitly) provide shareholders with the opportunity to impact the corporate decision-making process that falls under the sole responsibility of the management board, apart from the shareholder meeting and the scenarios laid down in §§ 119 (2), 111 (4) sent. 3 and determined by *Holzmüller/Gelatine*.[1732] Therefore, individual shareholders have no right to request additional administrative rights, such as that a certain management measure will be omitted or facilitated.[1733] However, the question remaining is whether shareholders are forbidden from influencing administrative members in their decision on management matters apart from the shareholder meeting. Such could be extra-institutional activities that allow the administration to demand omission.[1734]

The compelling character of the corporate statutory rules expressed in § 23 (5), for reasons of legal certainty protecting investors of public corporations, allows additions as long as the concerned rules have not been explicitly determined as exclusive.[1735] Therefore, the (indirect) impact of (individual) shareholders on the management board and its transaction decisions outside the shareholder meeting is as such not prohibited. The management board, with its wide discretion and final responsibility,[1736] may consider whether to talk to an investor or not. Furthermore, management's discretion allows it to decide whether to take their arguments into account while making its decision aiming for the general benefit of the corporation and its shareholders. The compelling character of the corporate statute implementing the management board's responsibility for management matters, § 76 (1), requires that the management board remains the one to make the final transaction decisions that represent pure management decisions. Once this border has been crossed, corporate law provides the opportunity to take action either against the resulting measure or against the impacting shareholder. Absent the opportunity to directly impact a transaction decision, active shareholders will, with or without means of pressure, impact the responsible administrative members. However, it will always remain the administration's decision to make. As a consequence, the active shareholder's impact exercised outside the shareholder meeting regarding transaction decisions will generally not represent such extra-institutional action.

(b) Information and equal treatment

Another closely related question is whether the administration is allowed to consider the demands of minority shareholders. Private conversations between administrative members and individual active shareholders involving information about future corporate decisions, such as transactions, could constitute the unequal treatment of shareholders

1732 BGH, Urt. v. 25.02.1982, Az.: II ZR 174/80, NJW 1982, 1703–Holzmüller; BGH, Urt. v. 26.04.2004, Az.: II ZT 155/02, NZG 2004, 571–Gelatine.
1733 Mülbert, in: Großkomm AktG, 2008, Vor §§ 118–147 mn.222.
1734 *See* Thaeter/Guski, AG 2007, 301 (305 et seq.).
1735 Röhricht, in: Großkomm AktG, 2004, § 23 mn.167.
1736 Schaefer, NZG 2007, 900 (901).

who are in the same position[1737], § 53a. The administration would be obliged to decline the demand for such conversations.

A first objection could be based on the requirement of § 53a of shareholder *treatment*. This provision addresses the corporation and applies to the measures of its organs,[1738] including the supervisory and management board. Sole personal conversations between representatives of the administration and active shareholders concerning the corporate decision-making process have in general no immediate legal consequences for the shareholder going beyond the conversation.[1739] Regarding the provision's wording, they could therefore be denied the quality of *treatment*.

Furthermore, differentiation based on capital participation does not apply to auxiliary rights like the information right exercised outside the shareholder meeting.[1740] The informational equal treatment, as expressed in No. 6.3 DCGK, therefore requires that every shareholder, independent of the size of his stake or other reasons related to his person, obtains or is able to obtain the same information from the corporation.[1741] On the other hand, it does not negate that certain shareholders, like active shareholders actually using the information in contrast to most of their passive fellow shareholders, have a legitimate reason to request more information.[1742] This thought is supported by the special provision § 131 (4).[1743] Thereafter, shareholders have the right to request information other shareholders have already obtained earlier at the next shareholder meeting, as long as it does not need to be published ad hoc, § 15 WpHG.[1744] The right is not only restricted by the need to know about the information provided to a specific shareholder, but also by its delay up to the subsequent shareholder meeting.[1745] The provision restricts the equal treatment to a restoration of equal information during the next shareholder meeting. Furthermore, it does not prohibit the exchange of information. Rather, it is the prerequisite to a corresponding request. Applied to conversations with active shareholders, the information usually exceeds the necessary capital market information.[1746] The information presented to active shareholders on the occasion of road shows[1747] or during private conversations is subject to § 131 (4). Therefore, it cannot generally be forbidden. To fulfill their information demand must serve the general corporate interest, however, §§ 93 (1) sent. 3, 404. That might well be so, not only for general reputational reasons,[1748] but also by preventing active shareholders interested in certain transaction decisions from becoming more aggressive or voting with their feet.[1749]

1737 Art. 42, Second Council Directive, 1977 O.J. (L 26) 12.
1738 Hüffer, AktG, § 53a, mn.4.
1739 Thaeter/Guski, AG 2007, 301 (306).
1740 Henze/Notz, in: Großkomm AktG, 2004, § 53a mn.58.
1741 V. Werder, in: Ringleb et al., Deutscher Corporate Governance Kodex, 2008, mn.1225.
1742 *Id.*
1743 Hüffer, AktG, § 131 mn.42.
1744 *Id.*; Wilde, ZGR 1998, 423 (461).
1745 Grüner, NZG 2000, 770 (778); Wilde, ZGR 1998, 423 (462).
1746 Schiessl, VGR Vol. 2 (2000), 57 (68).
1747 Decher, in: Großkomm AktG, 2001, § 131 mn.357.
1748 Wilde, in: ZGR 1998, 423 (460).
1749 Grüner, NZG 2000, 770 (777).

ii) Capital markets law

(1) Notification obligations, sections 21, 22 (1), (2), 25, 25a, 27a WpHG

(a) Legal status quo

Active shareholders not intending to take over the targeted corporation are generally subject to the notification requirements under §§ 21, 25, 25a, 27a WpHG. Shareholders holding more than 3 percent of the voting rights have to provide notification in this circumstance, as well as when they cross the thresholds of 3, 5, 10, 15, 20, 30, 50 and 75 percent, § 21 (1) WpHG. In contrast to the U.S.-American approach under § 13 SEA, the initial idea of the EU notification regime was to generally base the notification obligations solely on voting rights while generally not considering economic ownership. However, under certain other conditions, §§ 22 (1), (2) WpHG attributes (additional) voting rights, such as when a person owns shares for the account of a third person and has an, *infra* discussed, impact on the vote, § 22 (1) No. 2 WpHG, or a person able to acquire shares which is solely dependent on its own declaration of intent, § 21 (1) No. 5 WpHG. Voting rights are also attributed to a person who exercises voting rights as a representative, but at his own discretion, § 22 (1) No. 6 WpHG, or who acts in concert with other shareholders, § 22 (2) WpHG. The issuer and the BaFin must be notified within 4 working days.

In 2007, the *Transparenzrichtlinie-Umsetzungsgesetz*[1750] introduced § 25 WpHG, which complements the notification obligations of § 21 WpHG. It requires considering positions that involve the use of financial instruments to build up stakes and can therefore be understood as run-up protection.[1751] These financial instruments must grant their holder a legally binding right to acquire shares with voting rights. Notification obligation triggering thresholds equal those laid down in § 21 WpHG, except for three percent. In 2008, the *Risikobegrenzungsgesetz*[1752] implemented § 25 (1) 3 WpHG. For notification purposes, it generally requires the addition of actual voting rights and those mediated by financial instruments. Since the *Anlegerschutz- und Funktionsverbesserungsgesetz* (***"AnsFuG"***)[1753], the notification obligations under § 25 WpHG are even triggered if *other instruments* grant their holder a legally binding right to acquire shares with voting rights, § 25 (1) 1. The AnsFuG also introduced § 25a WpHG, which demands the notification of financial or other instruments which grant the opportunity to acquire voting rights.

Finally, all shareholders with share-based voting rights of 10 percent and over need, amongst others, to disclose within 20 working days their aims with regard to the acquired voting rights, § 27a WpHG. In contrast to the U.S.-American approach, the obligation is not limited to the control context. The specifications have to address possible strate-

1750 Transparenzrichtlinie-Umsetzungsgesetz [Transparency Directive Implementation Act], Jan. 10, 2007, BGBl. I at 10 (F.R.G.).

1751 Weber/Meckbach, BB 2008, 2022 (2029).

1752 Risikobegrenzungsgesetz [Risk Limitation Act], Aug. 12, 2008, BGBl. I at 1666 (F.R.G.).

1753 Anlegerschutzes und Verbesserung der Funktionsfähigkeit des Kapitalmarkts [Investor Protection and the Functionality Improvement Act], Apr. 5, 2011, BGBl. I at 538 (F.R.G.).

gic aims and the intent to increase the voting rights within the next year to impact the administration's composition or the corporate capital structure, § 27a (1) WpHG.

Notification obligations are the key mechanism to prevent the abuse of derivatives that decouple voting rights and economic interests to the detriment of the corporation and its shareholders. As under U.S. law, derivatives such as swaps not only have the potential to overcome issues of collective action. They also carry the risk that they could be used to circumvent notification obligations or to vote independently of or even in opposition to the interests of the corporation and its shareholders because of a negative or a lack of economic interests coupled with the voting right.

(b) Hidden ownership

Hidden ownership can be practiced in several ways, most importantly through share lending or derivatives such as cash-settled equity swaps. The *share lender* remains theoretically with only an obligatory restitution claim. However, German model contracts often comprise an anticipated agreement about a factual claim (*Realanspruch*) for retransfer that allows the lender to terminate the loan through unilateral declaration.[1754] The holder of the *long "equity" leg of a cash-settled swap* has an economic stake in the development of the underlying share's price and dividend payments, but has no formal rights regarding the reference assets.[1755] In particular the latter constellation has been used to prevent early disclosure and a mandatory bid when accumulating stakes in a takeover. It raised the question whether economic stakes should trigger notification obligations. Since the adoption of the AnsFuG in 2011, §§ 25 and 25a WpHG provide an answer for both constellations of hidden ownership, but the solution provided by the AnsFug has come a long way.

The initial example of hidden ownership in the takeover context is Schaeffler KG's (***"Schaeffler"***) acquisition of Continental AG (***"Continental")***. In July 2008, Schaeffler surprisingly announced that it had accumulated about 36 percent of Continental's shares without prior notice. Schaeffler held 2.97 percent of Continental's shares and financial instruments, granting it the right to acquire a further stake of 4.95 percent. In addition, it had entered into cash-settled equity swaps of more than 28 percent with nine different banks. Each hedged its short position by physically holding the reference shares (each of the banks also remaining under 3 percent according to § 21 (1) WpHG). The BaFin was unable to determine that Schaeffler had been obliged to notify under the then relevant regime.[1756]

For active shareholders, hidden ownership via cash-settled swaps was a mechanism to circumvent the transparency of stakes in order to leave the administration and fellow shareholders uncertain about the size of their stake as well as the stakes of supporting shareholders. It allowed them either to exaggerate the size of their stake when pressuring management or to surprise and impress them with the size of their precise stakes once it

1754 Bachmann, ZHR 173 (2009), 596 (633).
1755 Von Bülow, in: KöKo WpHG, 2007, § 22 mn.87.
1756

became necessary. For active shareholders this had the equal advantage of permitting the accumulation of stakes at an unchanged price. Furthermore, it prevented management from opposing their stake building, for instance by looking for an anchor shareholder. Hidden ownership provided active shareholders with an opportunity to reduce costs and collective action issues to exercise effective internal supervision of the administration in the interest of shareholders and apart from the imperfect external control mechanism. Hidden stake building through active shareholders had the potential, however, to allow these shareholders to secretly amass stakes to prepare opportunistic actions. Furthermore, management may have been intimidated by alleged majorities and have given in prematurely to the demands of the active shareholders to avoid a public campaign or a removal, even before the information became available to the market.[1757]

In the equally concerned takeover context active shareholders were sometimes confronted with, objections related to hidden ownership were that acquirers could pay too low consideration as they saved the premium for all hidden acquired shares. The achieved *toehold*[1758] prevented some alternative bidders from getting involved.[1759] Another concern related to the equal distribution of the control premium amongst the remaining shareholders. Finally, the targeted administration was and is, apart from investor relation purposes, interested in knowing about a new blockholder.[1760] For potential acquirers, however, surprise attacks had the advantage of not necessitating the sharing of "privately produced information" with others. Therefore, they dared more often to risk a costly takeover attempt promoting the market for corporate control in general.[1761]

(i) The notification regime prior to the AnsFuG

Prior to the implementation of the AnsFuG, it was controversial whether and under which provision of the §§ 21 et seq. WpHG the notification of economic interests of (active) shareholders realized through share lending or cash-settled derivatives was required.

1. Notification obligation under former section 25 WpHG

Proponents of a notification obligation under former § 25 (1) WpHG argued that cash-settled equity swaps represent *financial instruments* under the legal definition of § 2 (2b) WpHG. § 25 (1) WpHG requires based on a binding agreement the *right* to acquire shares with voting rights. A holder of a short position under a cash-settled equity swap,

1757 Engert, ZIP 2006, 2105 (2110).

1758 Bulow et al., 107 J. Political Econ. 427 et seq. n.1 (1999).

1759 Zetsche, NZG 2009, 692 (696).

1760 Fleischer/Schmolke, NZG 2009, 401 (405 et seq.).

1761 Fleischer, ZGR 2008, 185 (206 et seq.); Fischel, 57 Tex. L. Rev. 1, 13 et seq. (1978); Grossman & Hart, 11 Bell J. Econ. 42, 60 (1980): noting that the disclosure obligations under the Williams Act of 1968 may have the unintended consequence to make raids more difficult instead of making them easier, management uses the disclosure obligations to drag some raiders to court, which increases costs of raids even more, while the 5 percent quorum paired with the intent disclosure of Schedule 13D filers does not only encourage competition from other raiders, but also encourages shareholders to freeride.

however, usually has the choice between cash and shares to perform the contract. The holder of a long position has to accept this choice and cannot insist on performance in shares.[1762] The proponents argued, however, that the provision's purpose to hinder unrecognized accumulations of stakes has to outweigh the wording in favor of a wide interpretation of the term to also cover circumventing scenarios.[1763] In practice, holders of the short position under a cash-settled swap have the choice of whether to perform in cash or shares to circumvent notification obligations, which depends on the holder of the long position's right to demand the delivery of shares.[1764] It has therefore to suffice that both parties have the understanding that shares will be delivered and the short party feels, for reasons of a businessman's decency or a gentlemen's agreement, obliged to perform by delivering shares when the long party intends to build up a block.[1765] Consequently, pursuant to the proponents, the long party's right in the legal sense was unnecessary[1766] and many of the controversial, relevant hidden ownership constellations had to be notified under former § 25 WpHG.[1767]

These arguments were unconvincing, however. The legislator had intentionally choosen the provision's narrow wording[1768] and the long party under a cash-settled equity swap does not have a restitution *right* regarding the referenced shares.[1769] Besides the *practical difficulties* regarding proof of a gentlemen's agreement,[1770] the wide interpretation ignored the *legislator's intent.* In 2007, the German legislator[1771] had decided to follow the explicitly narrow European interpretation[1772] and had laid down the requirement of a *binding agreement,* which grants the *right* to obtain shares for notification obligations regarding future share positions. These European specifications did not

1762 Baums/Sauter, ZHR 173 (2009), 454 (469); Schiessl, Der Konzern 2009, 291 (296).
1763 Schneider/Anzinger, ZIP 2009, 1 (7); Schneider/Brower, AG 2008, 557 (564).
1764 Schneider/Brouwer, AG 2008, 557 (563).
1765 *Id.* at 564; Schneider/Anzinger, ZIP 2009, 1 (7).
1766 Schneider/Anzinger, ZIP 2009, 1 (7); Schneider/Brouwer, AG 2008, 557 (564).
1767 Schneider/Anzinger, ZIP 2009, 1 (8).
1768 Eichner, ZRP 2010, 5 (6); Weber/Meckbach, BB 2008, 2022 (2024).
1769 Baums/Sauter, ZHR 173 (2009), 454 (469).
1770 Merkner/Sustmann, NZG 2010, 681 (682).
1771 Gesetzesentwurf zur Umsetzung der Richtline 2004/109/EG des Europäischen Parlaments und des Rates vom 15. Dezember 2004 zur Harmonisierung der Transparenzanforderungen in Bezug auf Information über Emittenten, deren Wertpapiere zum Handel auf einem geregelten Markt zugelassen sind, und zur Änderung der Richtlinie 2001/34/EG [Draft Law of an Act to Implement Directive 2004/109/EC], Sept. 4, 2006, BT-Drucks 16/2498, at 36 et seq.
1772 European Parliament and Council Directive 2004/109/EC, art. 13, 2004 O.J. (L 390) 49 "The notification requirement … shall also apply to a natural person or legal entity who holds, directly or indirectly, financial instruments that result in an entitlement to acquire, on such holder's own initiative alone, under a formal agreement, shares to which voting rights are attached, already issued, of an issuer whose shares are admitted to trading on a regulated market."; Commission Directive 2007/14/EC, art. 11, 2007 O.J. (L 69) 32 "[S]waps …shall be considered to be financial instruments, provided that they result in an entitlement to acquire, on the holder's own initiative alone, under a formal agreement, shares to which voting rights are attached, already issued, on an issuer whose shares are admitted to trading on a regulated market."

cover cash-settled equity swaps.[1773] Since the requirements laid down in the underlying European Directive were minimum requirements, the German legislator would have been able to impose a higher standard and to interpret the term *right* widely. The legislator's decision against such a wide version and in favor of the narrow interpretation found explicit expression in § 25 WpHG; therefore, it could not be circumvented based on teleological arguments.[1774] Even the amendment of § 25 WpHG by the *Risikobegrenzungsgesetz* in August 2008 explicitly left this formulation untouched after balancing efforts and benefits. Therefore, it did not cover cash-settled equity swaps.[1775] At that time, the transparency issue related to long positions of cash-settled equity swaps had been clearly demonstrated through Schaeffler's announcement to acquire Continental AG in July 2008 that had preceded the amendment.

As far as *share lenders* were concerned, they theoretically hold an obligatory restitution claim, which is often of *factual* nature in practice. It was therefore not the question whether the share lender holds a corresponding right, but rather whether he holds a financial instrument in the sense of § 25 WpHG. Until 2008, the BaFin affirmed the obligation of a lender to notify under § 25 WpHG[1776], as the restitution claim was qualified as a financial instrument in the sense of a derivative, § 2 (2) No. 1 WpHG. The restitution claim is bindingly agreed on by both sides, it is timely delayed, and its value depends on the underlying shares. However, strong opposition led the BaFin to change its mind in its 2009 guidelines and to explicitly exclude a notification obligation for share lenders.[1777] It had been argued that share lending is not a financial agreement in the sense of a forward transaction. The agreements listed in § 2 (2) No. 1 WpHG are all agreements with reciprocal obligations that may be performed with a timely delay. The restitution claim, in contrast, has no such reciprocal character and the transfer of the shares as well as the consideration have to be performed without delay.[1778] Even though the approach was rather formal, the amendment to the BaFin guidelines underscored the delicacy of the issue and demonstrated the need for legislative intervention in this area.[1779]

1773 Antwort der Bundesregierung auf eine kleine Anfrage–BT-Drucks 16/10094 [Response of the Federal Government regarding an Inquiry–BT-Drucks 16/10094] Aug. 26, 2008, BT-Drucks 16/10167, 4.

1774 Weber/Meckback, BB 2008, 2022 (2024).

1775 Antwort der Bundesregierung auf eine kleine Anfrage–BT-Drucks 16/10094 [Response of the Federal Government regarding an Inquiry–BT-Drucks 16/10094] Aug. 26, 2008, BT-Drucks 16/10167, 4 et seq.; Fleischer/Schmolke, NZG 2009, 401 (404); Fleischer/Schmolke, ZIP 2008, 1501 (1506 et seq.).

1776 BaFin, Draft of the Emittentenleitfaden [guidelines for issuers] 2009, 40, www.otto-schmidt.de/wirtschaftsrecht/news_8724.html (link „Entwurf Konsultation 15/2008 – Emittentenleitfaden Teil 1: Neue Kapital).

1777 BaFin, Emittentenleitfaden [guidelines for issuers] 2009, V.3.7.12, 103, VIII.2.5.2.2, 140 et seq., VIII.2.8.3.2 166, www.bafin.de (search Veröffentlichungssuche Leitfäden).

1778 Bachmann, ZHR 173 (2009), 596 (635); V. Bülow/Stephanblome, ZIP 2008, 1797 (1800): against the qualification of share lending as financial instrument; DAV-Handelsrechtsausschuss, NZG 2009, 175 (176).

1779 Bachmann, ZHR 173 (2009), 596 (635).

2. Notification obligation under section 22 (1) sent. 1 No. 2 WpHG

Another scholarly approach to hidden ownership via the use of swaps or share lending related, and due to its lower threshold of 3 % still relates, to § 22 (1) sent. 1 No. 2 WpHG. Thereafter, voting rights are attributed to the beneficiary.[1780] Its proponents made legal, economic, and comparative arguments that the shares held by the share borrower and the short party are held for the account of the lending party and the long party under a swap.

a. Shares belonging to a third person

The shares need to belong to a third person. In the context of *share lending*, the shares belong to the borrower and therefore to a third person. For derivatives like equity *swaps*, the necessary ownership of the party holding the short position is mostly affirmed when the short party hedges the economic risk by physically holding the underlying shares.[1781] The relationship between the long party and the physically held shares by the short party is insignificant, as long as the shares are held.[1782]

b. Shares held for the beneficiary

The shares have to be held for the person that bears the economic risk and the potential benefits related to the shares, the beneficiary. The *borrower* holds the shares for the lender as long as he does not transfer them to an unbound third person,[1783] which is usually not the case under hidden ownership scenarios. The lender has the economic interest in the borrowed shares. Dividends need to be transferred to him and after the termination of the lending period he has to accept the shares at the current market price. He participates in the stock price development as if he had never lent the shares.[1784] The *long swap party* bears the economic interest in the reference shares held by the short party.[1785]

c. Impact on exercise of voting right

Controversial was the beneficiary's *impact* on the voting rights.

1780 Habersack, AG 2008, 817 (818); Schanz, DB 2008, 1899 (1902); Schanz/Schalast, Frankfurt-School working paper No. 100, 2008, 19 et seq., www.frankfurt-school.de/dms/Arbeitsberichte/Arbeits100.pd; Weber/Meckback, BB 2008, 2022 (2024).

1781 Baums/Sauter, ZHR 173 (2009) 454, 465; Schanz, DB 2008, 1899 (1903).

1782 Schanz, DB 2008, 1899 (1902 et seq.): based on publicly available information, in the case of Schaeffler, it was uncertain whether the banks with which Schaeffler had entered into cash swaps were holding the reference shares or not.

1783 BaFin, Emittentenleitfaden [guidelines for issuers] 2009, VIII. 2.5.2.2., 141, www.bafin.de (Veröffentlichungssuche Leitfäden); Bachmann, ZHR 173 (2009), 596 (627); Burgard, BB 1995, 2069 (2073 et seq.): regarding the same provision which in 1995 was § 22 (1) No. 1 WpHG.

1784 Bachmann, ZHR 173 (2009), 596 (627 et seq.); Schneider, in: Assmann/Schneider, WpHG, 2006, § 22 mn.68.

1785 Habersack, AG 2008, 817 (818); Weber/Meckback, BB 2008, 2022 (2026).

i. Abstract or specific voting impact

The BaFin and some legal scholars followed a broad approach.[1786] They assumed that a person bearing the economic interest in shares has the *abstract* opportunity to impact the exercise of the voting rights.[1787] A positive confirmation of the impact was not required under this approach.[1788] Therefore, the *long party* under a cash-settled equity swap had to notify under § 22 (1) sent. 1 No. 2 WpHG, as the actual impact on the voting rights of the short party physically holding the underlying shares to hedge its risk was irrelevant.[1789] Equally, the *share lender* had to notify.[1790]

A similar approach generally assumed the necessary impact on the voting right as long as the person was bearing the economic interests in the referred shares, but *allowed rebuttal of the presumption* by proof of the opposite. For *share lenders* as well as for *long parties* under cash-settled equity swaps, a notification obligation was assumed as long as the person had not proven to lack an opportunity to impact the exercise of the voting right.[1791] Applied to share lending or equity swaps to hide ownership with the aim of

1786 BaFin, Emittentenleitfaden [guidelines for issuers] 2009, VIII.2.5.2, 140, www.bafin.de (Veröffentlichungssuche Leitfäden); Engert, ZIP 2006, 2105 (2110); Habersack, AG 2008, 817 (818 et seq.): requiring factual impact on the exercise of the voting rights, which is usually given when the parties agree that the short party hedges the risk by physically holding the underlying shares and the short party is factually obliged to offer the shares to the long party once the swap becomes terminated; Schanz, DB 2008, 1899 (1902 et seq.): refusing the requirement of an impact regarding the exercise of the voting rights, sees the prerequisites fulfilled when the short party under the swap physically holds the underlying shares; Schanz/Schalast, Frankfurt-School working paper No. 100, 2008, 19 et seq., www.frankfurt-school.de/dms/Arbeitsberichte/Arbeits100.pd; Weber/Meckback, BB 2008, 2022 (2028): with regard to cash-settled equity swaps, as long as the short party has purchased the underlying shares.

1787 BaFin, Emittentenleitfaden [guidelines for issuers] 2009, VIII.2.5.2, 140, www.bafin.de (Veröffentlichungssuche Leitfäden): determining an abstract view (on whether share lending means to hold for the account of a third person) as sufficient, making a case-by-case evalution whether impact on the voting right was exercised in the specific case superfluous; VG Frankfurt, Urt. v. 18.05.2006, Az.: 1 E 3049/05, BKR 2007, 40 (43): determines that it is sufficient for § 22 (1) sent. 1 No. 5 WpHG that the person underlying the notification obligation due to the economic risk he bears is typically able to legally or factually direct the formal holder of the shares, which does not exclude an attribution in cases were directions regarding the exercise of the voting rights are excluded.

1788 *See* Bachmann, ZHR 173 (2009), 596 (629): for share lending; Engert, ZIP 2006, 2105 (2110): for derivatives, as long as parties demand at least factual that the contracting partner holds the shares and exercises them in the interest of the contractual partner, as he has assumed the economic interest.

1789 Schanz, DB 2008, 1899 (1902).

1790 BaFin, Emittentenleitfaden [guidelines for issuers] 2009, VIII. 2., 140 et seq., www.bafin.de (Veröffentlichungssuche Leitfäden); *see* Bachmann, ZHR 173 (2009) 596, 628: noting that this approach lets suffice that one party is bearing the economic risk and potential, which grant him a certain impact on the exercise of the voting right; Bayer in: MüKo AktG, § 22 app. § 22 WpHG mn.21; Kumpan/Mittermeier, ZIP 2009, 404 (406).

1791 Bachmann, ZHR 173 (2009), 596 (629): for share lending a notification obligation is dependent on the circumstance that the borrower keeps the shares, which will be the case when pursueing strategic goals, and that the lender has reserved the right to impact the voting rights; Weber/

impacting strategic management decisions, they were not an a-typical constellation that allowed rebuttal of the presumed impact, like for investment purposes.[1792]

The BGH[1793] and the majority of legal scholars[1794] proposed a narrower approach. They required the *positive confirmation* that the economically interested person was able to impact the exercise of the voting rights. However, the type of impact they demanded differed.

Proponents of the broad approach argued with the *wording* of § 22 (1) sent. 1 No. 2 WpHG. Without a deviating legal definition,[1795] the term *for the account* does not explicitly demand an actual impact on the voting right and allows a purely economic interpretation.[1796] Proponents of a narrower interpretation, in contrast, warned against overstretching this provision. Especially the more recent phenomenon of cash-settled derivatives is not explicitly encompassed by the provision, while especially more recent foreign provisions comprise them. The wording of a provision could not for teleological reasons alone be endlessly stretched.[1797]

Proponents of the broad interpretation also cited the *purpose* of § 22 (1) sent. 1 No. 2 WpHG and the underlying European Directive.[1798] The European Transparency Directive intended to provide greater transparency on investments for reasons of investor protection as well as increased market efficiency.[1799] The German legislator added the purpose of providing the corporation with a better overview of the shareholder structure and control.[1800] Therefore, the issuer protection from investors aiming to takeover the corporation or to exercise impact on corporate strategies through this provision demanded disclosure

---

Meckbach, BB 2008, 2022 (2028): assuming a corresponding impact on the voting right as soon as the short party is physically holding the underlying shares. Thereafter, it may be distinguished whether an obedience of the short party can be assumed, which is usually the case for a-typical cases like recognizable takeover plans or other strategies pursued by the long party.

1792 Bachmann, ZHR 173 (2009), 596 (630); Weber/Meckbach, BB 2008, 2022, 2028.

1793 BGH, Urt. v. 16.03.2009, Az.: II ZR 302/06, ZIP 2009, 908 (908, 913).

1794 Baums/Sauter, ZHR 173 (2009), 454 (465 et seq.): demanding additionally that the economic owner may exercise directions with regard to the underlying shares, like the restitution or utilization for his own account; V. Bülow, in: KöKo WpHG, 2007, § 22 mn.66: requires the opportunity to impact the exercise of the voting rights, *Id.* at 84: denying an attribution of the voting rights to the lender, *Id.* at: 87 denying an attribution for swaps; Eichner, ZRP 2010, 5 (6); Merkner/Sustmann, NZG 2010, 681 (682): denying an attribution for swaps; Opitz, in: Schäfer/Hamann, Kapitalmarktgesetze, § 22 WpHG mn.30: requires a possible impact on the voting rights based on the underlying legal relation in general, *Id.* at 48: denying therefore an attribution to the share lender; Schiessl, Der Konzern 2009, 291 (295); Schwark, in: Schwark, Kapitalmarktrecht, 2010, § 25 WpHG mn. 4.

1795 Schanz, DB 2008, 1899 (1902); Schanz/Schalast, Frankfurt-School working paper No. 100, 2008, 17, www.frankfurt-school.de/dms/Arbeitsberichte/Arbeits100.pdf.

1796 Schanz, DB 2008, 1899 (1902 et seq.); Schanz/Schalast, Frankfurt-School working paper No. 100, 2008, 17, www.frankfurt-school.de/dms/Arbeitsberichte/Arbeits100.pdf.

1797 Fleischer/Schmolke, ZIP 2008, 1501 (1505); Opitz, in: Schäfer/Hamann, Kapitalmarktgesetze, § 22 mn.60.

1798 Habersack, AG 2008, 817 (819).

1799 European Parliament and Council Directive 2004/109/EC, recital 1 and 2, 2004 O.J. (L 390) 38.

1800 RegE zum Zweiten Finanzmarktförderungsgesetz [draft law of the federal government of the Second Financial Markets Promotion Act], Jan. 27, 1994, BT-Drucks 12/6679, 52.

of cash-settled equity swaps often used by silently approaching acquirers or active shareholders.[1801] The European capital markets regulation had been strongly impacted by the development of the U.S.-American and U.K. capital markets law. The already mentioned *CSX v. TCI* case was a clear signal in favor of a broad interpretation. Thereafter, notification obligations were triggered by economic positions under cash-settled equity swaps if the short party agreed on hedging by physically holding the underlying shares. The short party was then factually forced to offer them to the long party upon termination of the swap, which represented a sufficient basis for the attribution.[1802] As a consequence, an extensive interpretation of the wording of § 22 (1) sent. 1 No. 2 WpHG was required to serve the *purpose* of also covering circumventing constellations.[1803] The opponents countered that the purpose of § 22 WpHG is to consider certain significant positions granting impact on the exercise of *voting rights* of third persons for notification purposes.[1804] Even though the purpose-related arguments of the proponents weighed heavily, they were not convincing. Especially in regard to the limits resulting from the wording of the provision, they tried to achieve wishful thinking.

From a *systematic* point of view, the proponents of the broader interpretation cited the equivalence of the attribution provisions § 22 WpHG and § 16 (4). The latter attributes voting rights of shares not belonging to the person obliged to notify if the person bears the economic interests of the participation. § 16 (4) applies, for instance, to trusts. It is not relevant that the trustor is bound to the trustee, but that the trustee bears the economic consequences of the participation. Proponents of the broader approach argued that the same had to apply to the parallel norm of § 22 (1) sent. 1 No. 2 WpHG.[1805] Furthermore, § 22 (1) sent. 1 No. 3 and 6 WpHG explicitly exclude scenarios under which the potentially notifying party has no discretion to exercise the voting right or the third person will exercise the voting rights independent of his instructions. Their reverse conclusion was that in provisions without a corresponding prerequisite specific voting impact was unnecessary.[1806] The more convincing systematic arguments were, however, brought forth in favor of the narrow interpretation. The basic provision § 21 WpHG focuses expressly on voting rights for notification purposes. This approach continues in § 22 (1) WpHG.[1807] Under the parallel provision § 22 (1) No. 1 WpHG, the necessary voting impact on the shares held by the subsidiary is mediated in an institutional way without expressly requiring it.[1808] As a consequence, § 22 (1) sent. 1 No. 2 WpHG needs to be interpreted as requiring that the economically interested person has the opportunity to impact the exercise of the voting right of the lent or physically held shares. (Former) § 25 WpHG, in contrast, concerned only financial instruments and demanded explicitly a

1801 Schneider, WpHG, Vor § 21 mn.4: with regard to takeover attempts.
1802 Habersack, AG 2008, 817 (819).
1803 Hirte, in: KöKo WpHG, § 21 mn.7; Bayer, in: MüKo AktG, 2008, § 22 app., § 22 WpHG mn1.
1804 V. Bülow, in: KöKo WpHG, 2007, § 22 mn1.
1805 Schanz, DB 2008, 1899 (1902); Schanz/Schalast, Frankfurt-School working paper No. 100, 2008, 17, www.frankfurt-school.de/dms/Arbeitsberichte/Arbeits100.pdf.
1806 Bachmann, ZHR 173 (2009), 596 (629).
1807 V. Bülow, in: KöKo WpHG, 2007, § 22 mn.66.
1808 BGH, Urt. v. 11.02.2009, Az.: 23 O 44/08, ZIP 2009, 906 (913).

binding agreement, which grants the right to acquire the referenced shares. It was not a special provision in relation to § 22 WpHG. Even though its later implementation did not intend to restrict § 22 WpHG,[1809] it clearly expressed the legislative intent to require the disclosure of financial instruments only under the specific circumstances laid down in § 25 (1) WpHG.[1810] Moreover, § 22 (1) sent. 1 No. 3, 5, and 6 WpHG represent comparably specific provisions with correspondingly specific prerequisites. A very broad, boilerplate interpretation of § 22 (1) sent. 1 No. 2 WpHG to prevent circumvention scenarios would contradict the rather casuistic structure of § 22 (1) sent. 1 WpHG.[1811] Finally, the narrow interpretation was strongly emphasized by the statutory consequences of violating the notification obligations. This could not be countered by reference to the necessity of hindering the circumvention of capital market transparency by broadly interpreting the norm.[1812] § 28 WpHG explicitly determines the loss of the attributed (voting) rights if the notification obligations under consideration of § 22 (1) sent. 1 No. 1 and 2 WpHG have been violated. For a share lender, such a remedy would only make sense if he were able to impact the exercise of the voting rights through the borrower.[1813] For the holder of a long position under cash-settled equity swaps, this remedy appears inappropriate, as it denies the exercise of rights which are not mediated by a long position. Rather, it focuses on the economic interest of the underlying shares. With regard to the civil fine remedy laid down in § 39 WpHG, which may result in substantial fines, the BGH interpreted narrowly § 22 WpHG. This required sticking closely to the wording of the provision while prohibiting analogous interpretations, Art. 103 (2) GG and § 3 OWiG.[1814] Thereafter, even the approach that shifted the burden of proof regarding borrowed shares[1815] and derivatives[1816] by generally assuming that the necessary impact on the voting right existed but may be rebutted had to be declined.[1817]

ii. Legal or factual specific impact

The proponents[1818] of a *law-based impact* on the exercise of the voting rights refused a notification obligation for holders of a *long position* or *lenders* without corresponding

1809 Weber/Meckback, BB 2008, 2022 (2029).
1810 Fleischer/Schmolke, ZIP 2008, 1501 (1506).
1811 Eichner, ZRP 2010, 5 (6); Fleischer/Schmolke, ZIP 2008, 1501 (1506).
1812 Eichner, ZRP 2010, 5 (6).
1813 BGH, Urt. v. 11.02.2009, Az.: 23 O 44/08, ZIP 2009, 906 (913).
1814 BGH, Urt. v. 18.09.2006, Az.: II ZR 137/05, DStR 2006, 2042 (2044): regarding the parallel provision of § 30 WpÜG; Eichner, ZRP 2010, 5 (6); Fleischer/Schmolke, ZIP 2008, 1501 (1506).
1815 Bachmann, ZHR 173 (2009), 596 (629).
1816 Weber/Meckbach, BB 2008, 2022 (2028 et seq.).
1817 Eichner, ZRP 2010, 5 (6).
1818 Von Bülow, WpHG, 2007, § 22 mnn.84, 87; Fleischer/Schmolke, ZIP 2008, 1501, 1506: declaring swaps relevant for notification purposes if, in exceptional cases, the holder of the long position has voting right impact; Schiessl, Der Konzern 2009, 291 (295): refers not explicitely to the necessary qualifaction of the basis of the impact on the voting rights, but refers to the usually missing agreement for the long party to exercise voting rights and the allocation in the trading portfolio according to § 23 (5) WpHG when the banks decide not to use their voting rights.

contractual provisions. Their opponents[1819] required only a *factual influence* of the exercise of the voting rights; they differentiated, however, regarding notification obligations of a long party and lender. Applied to hidden ownership via cash-settled equity swaps, the necessary factual obligation to vote as required by the party holding the *long position* was primarily based on the economic set of interests.[1820] The short party allegedly regularly purchases the underlying shares to hedge the risk resulting from a short sale and will hold them until the swap is terminated. The short party physically holding the underlying shares is factually obliged to sell the shares later to the long party. To maintain this opportunity, the short, hedged party will have to support the plans of the long party, which means mainly that the short party votes according to the interests of the long party.[1821] To sell the shares to the market, either at once or over a longer period of time, is hardly an alternative. The sale of substantial positions at once and for a stable price is impossible and a sale over a longer period for hedging reasons unsatisfying. The sale of the shares to the swap partner, in contrast, assures a good sales price, and takes place at once and at the right time when the swap is terminated. A future long party may even choose its counterparty according to its potential voting behavior.[1822] Consequently, short parties hedging their risk by physically holding the underlying shares will de facto exercise their voting rights according to the interests of the long party.[1823] For share *lenders,* the economic incentives are different. The share lender has to take back the shares at the price at termination. In practice, the borrower will absent deviating contractual clauses exercise the voting right according to his will. Under both approaches, lenders did not have to notify pursuant to § 22 (1) No. 2 WpHG.

To evaluate the long party's notification obligation under § 22 (1) No. 2 WpHG, the question was therefore whether the impact on the voting rights needed to be of *legal* or *factual nature*. In favor of the former interpretation, it was argued that § 28 WpHG requires a legal right first, which may then be lost in the case of a violation.[1824] This interpretation also had the advantage of increasing legal certainty. The requirement of a factual impact on voting rights was highly uncertain, however, which could not conform to the principles of a state under the rule of law.[1825] Demonstrated for the example of cash-settled swaps, factual voting rights would depend on whether the swap partner is

1819 Baums/Sauter, ZHR 173 (2009), 454 (467): assuming even in hedging cases when the short party physically holds the underlying shares that a factual impact on the exercise of the voting rights is typically not given, since banks, for reasons of § 23 (1) WpHG, usually do not exercise their voting rights and usually lend the shares to third persons; V. Bülow, in: KöKo WpHG, 2007, § 22 mnn.87, 3: noting that a factual impact on the voting rights is sufficient for the shares to be held for the account of the long party, that, however, the long party has no impact regarding the voting rights, even if the short party has for hedging reasons decided to acquire the shares; Habersack, AG 2008, 817 (818): argueing with the economic considerations which alledgedly establish the necessary impact on the voting rights.

1820 *See* Fleischer/Schmolke, ZIP 2008, 1501 (1505).

1821 Habersack, AG 2008, 817 (818).

1822 *See* Fleischer/Schmolke, ZIP 2008, 1501 (1505).

1823 Habersack, AG 2008, 817 (818).

1824 BGH, Urt. v. 11.02.2009, Az.: 23 O 44/08, ZIP 2009, 906 (913).

1825 Schanz, DB 2008, 1899 (1902).

hedging his short position by physically holding the underlying shares or not. It appeared awkward to make the notification obligation dependent on the purely internal hedging decision of the swap partner.[1826] Avoidance of legal uncertainty would have required that the swap counterparty abstained from hedging by physically holding the reference shares.[1827] Despite the underlying purpose of increasing market transparency, it was necessary to maintain the conformity of the regime as well as legal certainty in applying it. Only the narrow interpretation was able to achieve this. In addition, the physical holding of the underlying shares is not the rule. According to studies of ISDA[1828] and SIFM,[1829] the hedging of short positions under a swap is in practice not always realized by physically holding the underlying shares,[1830] but rather through other positions in the underlying shares.[1831] In addition, banks tend to allocate their shares in the trading portfolio and are therefore not allowed to vote at all.[1832]

Finally, a comparative approach demonstrated that other countries, like France,[1833] Switzerland,[1834] the UK,[1835] and Australia[1836] had also decided that the obligation to disclose cash-settled derivatives like swaps could not be resolved by means of interpretation. Rather, they had decided to amend their legislation and explicitly include them as trigger for notification purposes.[1837]

1826 *Id.* at 1904.

1827 *Id.*

1828 International Swap and Derivatives Association, Inc. (***"ISDA"***).

1829 Securities Industry and Financial Market Association (***"SIFM"***).

1830 Brief of International Swaps and Derivatives Association, Inc. and Securities Industry and Financial Markets Association, as Amici Curiae supporting Respondents at Argument I.B., CSX Corp. v. Children's Inv. Fund Mgmt. (UK) LLP, 562 F. Supp 2d 511 (2008) (No. 08 Civ. 2764 (LAK)) 2008 WL 2397247.

1831 Schanz, DB 2008, 1899 (1903).

1832 Schiessl, Der Konzern 2009, 291 (296).

1833 Art. L223-7 Ic) Code de Commerce, targets solely the economic effect similar to the one of shares or voting rights, specified through Art. 223-14 III No. 3 Règlement Général of the *Authorité des Marchés Financiers (AFM),* refering specifically to contracts of difference, equity swaps and financial instruments that are related to an index, and so on.; *see* BDI, Eckpunkte für mehr Transparenz am Kapitalmarkt, February 15, 2010, 3, http://www.bdi.eu/download_content/KonjunkturStandortUndWettbewerb/Transparenz_am_Kapitalmarkt(1).pdf.

1834 Art. 20 (2bis) BEHG („Als indirekter Erwerb gelten namenlich auch Geschäfte mit Finanzinstrumenten, die es wirtschaftlich ermöglichen, Beteiligungspapiere im Hinblick auf ein öffentliches Kaufangebot zu erwerben.") proposes disclosure of cash-settled derivatives in takeover context only.

1835 No. 5.3.1, 5.7.1, 5.8.2 (4) of the Disclosure Rules and Transparency Rules (***"DTR"***) [part of the FSA Handbook], www.fsahandbook.info/FSA/html/handbook/DTR. Rule 5.3.1. comprises "financial instruments … which have similar economic effects to (but which are not) qualifying financial instruments."

1836 *See* BDI, Eckpunkte für mehr Transparenz am Kapitalmarkt, Feb. 15, 2010, 3, http://www.bdi.eu/download_content/KonjunkturStandortUndWettbewerb/Transparenz_am_Kapitalmarkt(1).pdf.

1837 Fleischer/Schmolke, ZIP 2008, 1501 (1506).

3. No notification under former regime, alternatives for new regime

Therefore, under the former §§ 21, 22, 25 WpHG regime, cash-settled derivatives like equity swaps did not have to be considered as counting toward the quorum triggering notification duties. Share lending only triggered notification duties if the underlying contract granted the lender the right to impact the voting right. The different foreign approaches not only underscored that the current version of § 22 (1) sent. 1 No. 2 WpHG was more than challenged by the use of share lending or new financial instruments to hide ownership. In regard to cash-settled derivatives, they simultaneously raised the question whether a potential legislative expansion of disclosure requirements should only comprise the initially demonstrated takeover context or generally require the disclosure of (long positions under) cash-settled derivatives.[1838] In favor of the smaller solution was argued that it is usually in takeover scenarios in which the issue arises, as in the case of Schaeffler/Continental. The benefits of the use of derivatives in this constellation are especially high. Early disclosure would prevent the undiscovered accumulation of a toehold, which usually prevents alternative offers and would take into account the interest of the shareholders in participating in the control premium.[1839] Disclosure under this restricted but most urgent area would allow the consequences of a corresponding provision to be experienced without having to incur as substantial costs as under a broad regime. Finally, the narrow approach would allow the collection of more data about the benefits of shareholder activism as a corporate governance mechanism re-establishing the administration's control by overcoming collective action issues. In favor of a broad legislative approach was argued that the purpose of the underlying Transparency Directive and the §§ 21 et seq. WpHG is to broadly provide transparency on investments in general. Moreover, it would prevent potential attempts to circumvent the provisions, as Perry did as Mylan's investor, referring initially to the Schedule 13G regime to delay disclosure before finally filing a Schedule 13D, and would evade problems of differentiating relevant from irrelevant constellations.[1840] However, the limited knowledge about the factual background of hidden ownership, the substantial costs of the broader approach, and the potential flood of disclosures that would deter the intended transparency suggested pursuing the narrower approach restricted to takeover constellations.[1841]

(ii) The legislative response, the AnsFuG

In 2010, the Federal Ministry of Finance (*"BMF"*), delayed by the financial crisis, decided to tackle the issue by requiring the notification of hidden ownership through the use of financial and other instruments. In May 2010, the BMF presented a discussion draft of the AnsFuG[1842] that pursued the broader approach applying not only in the take

1838 *Id.* at 1510.

1839 Schiessl, Der Konzern 2009, 291 (298).

1840 Fleischer/Schmolke, ZIP 2008, 1501 (1510 et seq.).

1841 Fleischer, ZGR 2008, 185 (217).

1842 Diskussionsentwurf des Gesetzes zur Stärkung des Anlegerschutzes und Verbesserung der Funktionsfähigkeit des Kapitalmarktes [Discussion Draft of the Federal Government of the Act

over scenario. In September 2010, a government draft, that required to add up all the different positions that need to be notified under §§ 21 et seq. WpHG, followed.[1843] On February 1, 2012, the for this context relevant part of the AnsFuG, which also doubled the relevant fine, came into effect.[1844]

The AnsFuG extended § 25 WpHG and implemented a new § 25a WpHG for further notification requirements. § 25a (1) sent. 1 WpHG introduced a notification obligation to direct and indirect holders of *financial and other instruments* not covered by § 25 WpHG which *grant the opportunity* of acquiring shares with voting rights. The BMF reasoned that factual and economic opportunities to acquire shares granting voting rights were subject to expanded notification requirements.[1845] The abstract formulation has the advantage of covering not only currently used instruments like cash-settled equity swaps, but also instruments that will be used in the future to pursue hidden ownership. The risk of such a wide provision is, however, a substantial flood of notifications that would not only significantly increase the costs. Furthermore, it would deter its purpose of increasing the capital market's transparency and protecting investors from the special advantages of some investors. The two listed examples in § 25a (1) sent. 2 WpHG appear too weak to establish the necessary definiteness.[1846] They include instruments, which allow hedging the risk of the counterparty by acquiring the underlying shares, § 25a (1) sent. 2 No. 1 WpHG, like long positions under cash-settled equity swaps. § 25a (1) sent. 2 No. 1 WpHG's wording expresses what is confirmed by the legislator's reasoning. The notification obligation depends not on the actual exercise of the hedging opportunity through acquisition of shares.[1847] For the reason of legal certainty, this fact is particularly welcome. Furthermore, § 25a (4) WpHG authorizes the BMF to adopt a regulation that specifies instruments that trigger notifications, the calculation of the number of voting rights as well as possible safe harbors. In regards to the variety and complexity of the concerned instruments and the abstract character of 25a (1) sent. 1 WpHG, this authorization is highly necessary as it may establish the necessary legal certainty.[1848]

---

to Strengthen Investor Protection and to Improve the Functioning of the Capital Market] May 3, 2010, www.bundesfinanzministerium.de (search „title").

1843 RegE des Gesetzes zur Stärkung des Anlegerschutzes und Verbesserung der Funktionsfähigkeit des Kapitalmarktes [Draft Law of the Federal Government of the Act to Strengthen Investor Protection and to Improve the Functioning of the Capital Market] Sept. 22, 2010, www.bundesfinanzministerium.de (search „title").

1844 Gesetz zur Stärkung des Anlegerschutzes und Verbesserung der Funktionsfähigkeit des Kapitalmarktes[Law of the Federal Government of the Act to Strengthen Investor Protection], Apr. 5, 2011, BGBl. I at 538.

1845 *Id.* at 26.

1846 Merkner/Sustmann, NZG 2010, 681 (684): pointing out the legislative intent to establish a more specific provision through the two examples.

1847 Diskussionsentwurf des Gesetz zur Stärkung des Anlegerschutzes und Verbesserung der Funktionsfähigkeit des Kapitalmarkts [Discussion Draft of the Act to strengthen Investor Protection and to improve the Functioning of the Capital Market], May 3, 2010, 39, www.bundesfinanzministerium.de (search "title").

1848 Merkner/Sustmann, NZG 2010, 681 (687).

Furthermore, the notification obligation arises once the instrument held grants the opportunity to acquire shares representing *five percent or more* of the voting rights, § 25a (1) sent. 1 WpHG. The number of voting rights usually results from the number of shares that may be acquired. As far as the financial instrument contains no indication about the number of voting rights mediated, it may be determined by the number of shares necessary to hedge the risk, § 25 (2) sent. 2 WpHG. Moreover, these positions need to be accumulated with positions to be disclosed under §§ 21, 22, 25 WpHG, § 25a (1) sent. 7 WpHG. Even though these newly covered instruments do not govern a right to acquire shares, they allow a much clearer picture to be drawn by adding given and potential voting rights to the potential total position of an investor.[1849]

Sanctions apply, when the holder does not notify the issuer and the BaFin within 4 trading days, § 21 (1) WpHG. Not the loss of rights according to § 28 WpHG, but a civil fine, augmented to a maximum of €1.000.000, §§ 39 (4), (2) No. 2 f) WpHG, may be the consequence of a violation. In regards to the sums involved in large takeovers or other transactions, the deterrent effect of such an amount is, however, still doubtful.[1850]

In addition, the AnsFuG amended § 25 WpHG. It established a parallel between §§ 25 and 25a WpHG by extending § 25 WpHG to *other instruments*. According to the official reasoning of the draft law, the provision now also comprises agreements which grant a right to acquire voting rights without falling under the term of financial instruments according to § 2 (2b) WpHG.[1851] As a consequence, even the restitution claim of the share lender is covered since share lending represents only an *other instrument*.[1852] The expansion of § 25 WpHG therefore represents an effective way of preventing the other frequent manner of hidden ownership, share lending. The advantage is to demand the disclosure of all current types of hidden participation.[1853]

For active shareholders, however, who usually hold minority positions below ten percent, the new and amended provisions §§ 25 and 25a WpHG brought about significant restrictions. Lent shares and long positions under cash-settled equity swaps trigger notifications under §§ 25 and 25a WpHG as soon as they accumulate to 5 percent. The accumulation of stakes under §§ 21, 22, 25 WpHG and § 25a WpHG prevents an accumulation of almost 10 percent of stakes (or even beyond) without having to notify. Rather, they need to notify as soon as they hold shares or ((further) financial/other) instruments

1849 RegE des Gesetzes zur Stärkung des Anlegerschutzes und Verbesserung der Funktionsfähigkeit des Kapitalmarktes [Draft Law of the Federal Government of the Act to Strengthen Investor Protection and to Improve the Functioning of the Capital Market] Sept. 22, 2010, 27, www.bundesfinanzministerium.de (search „title").

1850 Merkner/Sustmann, NZG 2010, 681 (687): with regard to the €500.000 suggested before.

1851 RegE des Gesetzes zur Stärkung des Anlegerschutzes und Verbesserung der Funktionsfähigkeit des Kapitalmarktes [Draft Law of the Federal Government of the Act to Strengthen Investor Protection and to Improve the Functioning of the Capital Market] Sept. 22, 2010, 26, www.bundesfinanzministerium.de (search „title").

1852 Diskussionsentwurf des Gesetzes zur Stärkung des Anlegerschutzes und Verbesserung der Funktionsfähigkeit des Kapitalmarktes [Discussion Draft of the Act to Strenghten the Protection of Investors and to Improve the Functionality of the Capital Market], May 3, 2010, 38, www.bundesfinanzministerium.de (search „title").

1853 Fleischer/Schmolke, NZG 2010, 846 (853).

granting their holders the economic or factual possibility to acquire shares with at least 5 percent of the voting rights. The increased transparency reduces surprises to the administration to (potential) voting stakes of 5 percent; it therefore increases the costs for active shareholders to accumulate substantial stakes, and eases the opposition to active shareholder campaigns. The lack of incentives and the collective action issues shareholders aiming to control the administration were confronted with under the former regime have therefore even increased under the new regime.

The approach of the discussion draft of the Federal Ministry of Finance[1854], in contrast, would have limited the notification of hidden stakes to a size relevant only in the takeover context, while allowing active shareholders to accumulate stakes below 10 percent. This would have allowed the collection of data and experience on the optimal transparency level before further increasing the notification obligations instead of implementing a maximum number of disclosure obligations right away, which may even limit the information efficiency.[1855] Especially in regards to shareholder activism, it would have provided the necessary period of time to compare restraints on beneficial shareholder activism with those on opportunistic shareholder activism. The current approach, in contrast, allows the efficient disclosure of underlying conflicts of interest of active shareholders. At the same time, however, it potentially limits the activities of active shareholders by raising the costs necessary to effectively control the administration. Further criticism of the adopted approach concerns its restricted remedies, especially in the takeover context. It is necessary to either augment the maximum fine or the loss of established voting rights.[1856] Finally, the specific wording of § 25a WpHG does not even cover the second of the two examples, which does not appear convincing with regard to the potential constructs of financial instruments to be expected in the future. Therefore, the formulation of the current provision and the approach with regard to its potential economic and corporate governance consequence are suboptimal.[1857]

(iii) European moves

The amendments of the European Transparency Directive[1858] proposed by the European Commission[1859], allow the expectation of a soon amendment of the notification regime which will concern the issue of hidden ownerhip. The proposal pursues an approach

1854 Diskussionsentwurf des Gesetzes zur Stärkung des Anlegerschutzes und Verbesserung der Funktionsfähigkeit des Kapitalmarktes [Discussion Draft of the Federal Government of the Act to Strengthen Investor Protection and to Improve the Functioning of the Capital Market] May 3, 2010, www.bundesfinanzministerium.de (search „title").

1855 *Id.* at 853, 854.

1856 Not specifically related to the adopted regime, but to the issue of separated economic interests and administrative rights (especially voting rights), Seibt, ZGR 2010, 795 (831).

1857 Merkner/Sustmann, NZG 2010, 681 (684): proposing a formulation.

1858 European Parliament and Council Directive 2004/109, 2004 O.J. (L390) 38 (EC).

1859 Commission Proposal for a Directive of the European Parliament and of the Council amending Directive 2004/109/EC on the harmonisation of transparency requirements in relation to information about issuers whose securities are admitted to trading on a regulated market and Commission Directive 2007/14/EC, COM (2011) 683 final (Oct. 25, 2011).

of maximum harmonization with regard to the financial instruments that need to be notified. The Commission proposes the notification of financial instruments that either grant the holder (the discretion as to) a right to acqire the underlying shares or financial instruments with similar economic effects, Art. 13 (1) (a) and (b). All financial instruments and held shares would need to be aggregated for notification purposes. The national legislators would only remain free in setting up lower thresholds than those suggested as well as with regard to the sanctions applied (minimum sanctions would need to be considered). Limiting the evaluation to the consequences for the new German notification regime, this would require that the just implemented notification of *instruments* granting the right to acqire shares under § 25 (1) WpHG would need to be rescinded. As a consequence, hidden ownership via share lending would, after a short period of notification requirement, become possible again. Apart from the consequences of such frequent amendments of the notification prerequisites with regards to legal certainty, this provision has been introduced based on a justified need, which had not only been confirmed on a German level. An exclusion of instruments granting the right to acquire shares from the harmonized notification regime would therefore provide only an incomplete legislative response to the underlying practical need.

(c) Empty voting

Also under German law, frequently applied means to vote empty are the short selling of shares held under cash-settled equity swaps or the borrowing of shares.

(i) Current notification regime

De lege lata, empty voting via cash-settled equity swaps or borrowed shares does not need to be disclosed. Share lenders as well as the long party under a cash settled swap need to notify pursuant to §§ 25, 25a WpHG in addition to the share borrower or a short swap party physically holding the underlying shares. However, they still do not need to notify the deviation of their economic interest from their voting rights as long as the economic interest is not negative.

(ii) Discussion on disclosure of empty voting

Despite the benefits of empty voting for active shareholders to increase their incentives and to overcome collective action issues, disclosure of empty voting represents the cornerstone in protecting against the abuse of voting rights lacking a proportional economic exposure. It allows shareholders to better evaluate the true motives of active shareholders pursuing a campaign for certain transaction decisions to make a well-informed voting decision. Where necessary, it helps to enforce fiduciary duties.[1860] To efficiently deal with empty voting, the deviation of the economic interests of shareholders from the corresponding number of voting rights needs to trigger notification

1860 Theusinger/Möritz, NZG 2010, 607 (611).

obligations.[1861] These include the partial and complete neutralization of the shareholder's economic interest. However, expanding shareholder disclosure obligations have limits as well. As for hidden ownership positions, a corresponding disclosure regime needs to serve the aim of increasing the transparency and the protection of investors in the capital market while preventing special advantages, instead to compromising these goals. The expansion of disclosure requirements to negative(ly deviating) economic positions may, however, result in substantial compliance and information processing costs, which are potentially not justified by few such cases mediating relevant shareholder impact.[1862] For the latter reason, some have argued that shareholders' fiduciary duties as well as the ban on market manipulation, § 20a WpHG, provide sufficient protection by preventing the effectiveness of abusive shareholder votes.[1863] However, it can be objected that disclosures usually represent the prerequisite to realizing fiduciary duty claims against empty voters. Another opinion proposes, parallel to the hidden ownership issues, to restrict the approach to disclosure of deviations between voting positions and the corresponding economic interest to the *takeover context*.[1864] Also under the given context, this would allow the legislator to collect more data on the relevance of the separation of voting rights and economic interest. At the same time, it would restrict the regime's application and its costs to an area with its highest benefits. Even though the experience and cost-related arguments are convincing, the improvement of investor protection and the increase in market efficiency apply beyond the takeover context. In addition, the disclosure regime would not deter the use of empty voting to increase the incentives of active shareholders and to reduce relevant collective action issues, as long as their interests remain aligned with those of their fellow shareholders. Rather, the design of the provision could consider relevant cost and experience arguments, such as through a deviation threshold between economic interests and voting rights.

(iii) Recent statutory provisions concerning short sales

On July 26, 2010, the adoption of the *Gesetz zur Vorbeugung gegen missbräuchliche Wertpapier- und Derivategeschäfte*[1865] banned the naked short sales of shares, § 30h WpHG. Since March 26, 2012, § 30i (1) WpHG demands the notification of net short positions of 0.2 percent and beyond to the BaFin and of 0.5 percent and beyond additionally to the public via eBAnz. However, the recently adopted provision will not require disclosing the neutralization of the shareholder's economic interest if short positions are hedged by physically holding the underlying shares, as usual for empty voting constellations via swaps.

1861 Seibt, ZGR 2010, 795 (829).

1862 *Id.* at 829 et seq.

1863 Zetsche, NZG 2009, 692 (696 et seq.).

1864 Fleischer, ZGR 2008, 185 (217 et seq.).

1865 Gesetz zur Vorbeugung missbräuchlicher Wertpapier- und Derivategeschäfte [Act to Prevent Abusive Business with Securities and Derivatives], July 26, 2010, BGBl. I at 945 (F.R.G.).

In regard of the substantial problems that result from the use of naked short sales for the financial market,[1866] the differentiation between naked and covered short sales is justified. However, the restriction of the disclosure obligations to *net short* positions excludes the disclosure of empty voting positions used to enhance economic stakes in third corporations independent of the effects for the corporation voted in. Perry, as an empty voter in Mylan, intended such traditional merger arbitrage. Negative deviations of economic interest from corresponding voting rights can help to reduce collective action issues and to increase the incentives of active shareholders. They bear, however, the risk that they will be applied to the detriment of fellow shareholders, especially when the economic interest drifts towards zero. To achieve more meaningful transparency about the use of short positions, it is necessary to notify significant positive and negative economic interests separately.[1867]

Only experience with amended § 25 (1) sent. 1 WpHG and § 25a (1) WpHG will prove whether the approach of having the counterparties of the empty voters disclose their positions will effect the intended transparency for empty voting based on share borrowing or equity swaps.

(iv) European moves

Regarding *empty voting*, no direct approach has been developed yet. In September 2011, the European Securities and Markets Authority (***"ESMA"***) launched a Call for Evidence on Empty Voting. Purpose of the call was to evaluate whether the provided evidence about empty voting would prove the need for regulatory action with regard to empty voting. On June 29, 2012, the ESMA issued its Feedback Statement according to which contributers were unable to support the ESMA with the necessary evidence about the empty voting practices. With regard to the responses provided and the progress of the European Commission with regard to the Transparency Directive, ESMA evaluated the responses as not sufficiently convincing. Therefore, ESMA concluded that at this stage evidence did not require any further regulatory action on the European level.[1868]

The proposed amendment of the Transparency Directive would, however, not bring about a higher transparency level than under the current German notification regime. The notification of certain economic stakes mediated through financial instruments, as demanded by both regimes, grants only limited conclusions on empty voting positions. Whether this level of transparency is sufficient and the adequate comprise will therefore

1866 Trüg, NJW 2009, 3202 (3204).

1867 Committee of the European Securities Regulators (CESR), Consultation Paper, CESR/09-1215b, Jan. 2010, note 42, www.cesr.eu/popup2.php?id=6481; European Market Expert Group (***"ESME"***), Views on the issue of transparency of holdings of cash-settled derivatives, Nov. 2009, 13. http://ec.europa.eu/internal_market/securities/docs/esme/tdcash_en.pdf; opposite opinion: Seibt, ZGR 2010, 795 (831): proposing netting of short and long positions while proposing to extend § 27a WpHG to economic positions of 10 percent or beyond.

1868 ESMA, Feedback Statement – Call for Evidence on Empty Voting, June 29, 2012, 5, 12, http://www.esma.europa.eu/system/files/2012-415.pdf .

already demonstrate the experience under the current expanded German notification system.

(d) Related non-host assets

The final constellation that is likely to involve deviating interests of active shareholders concerns related non-host assets referring to costlier (negative) stakes in the other constituent or a competing corporation. Notification requirements are triggered by (voting) rights in the targeted corporation. They do not require disclosing economic stakes in third corporations, even if their stock price may be related to the one of the targeted corporation. § 27a WpHG is only triggered once the voting rights of the targeted corporation have reached 10 percent or more, which active shareholders are unlikely to do. In addition, its formulation is too broad to demand the disclosure of stakes that result in conflicts of interest.

Currently, related stakes will only need to be notified if they independently trigger such an obligation under §§ 21 et seq. WpHG. As far as deviating interests are based on related non-host assets in the form of costlier negative economic positions, the independent disclosure obligation for net short positions under § 30i WpHG will help to disclose them. It will allow the shareholders of the targeted corporation to better evaluate the true interests of campaigning shareholders and is therefore a valuable means in the fight against conflicts of interest of active shareholders.

(2) Acting in concert

(a) Legal standard

The delimitation drawn by the acting in concert rules under capital markets law can be compared to the line drawn by § 117 and the fiduciary duty under corporate law. The latter determine how much shareholder impact to admit to overcome the principal-agent problem of lacking control of the management board while preventing detrimental impact on corporate organs. Correspondingly, the definition of acting in concert has to separate parallel shareholder actions based on coincidentally conforming interests from tactical cooperation of shareholder groups in the forefront of impacting the administration to pursue deviating interests.[1869] It does not decide about claims for damages, but whether shareholders have to sum up their individual stakes for transparency reasons under §§ 21 et seq. WpHG and the WpÜG's minority shareholder protection applies.[1870]

The acting in concert regime implemented by the *Risikobegrenzungsgesetz* in 2008 aimed to allow a constructive dialog among shareholders and with the issuer.[1871] Amongst others, it had been initiated by the circumstance that after months of investigation in 2005, the BaFin had not been able to ascertain that the hedge funds in Deutsche

1869 Diekmann, DStR 2007, 445 (446); Spindler, WM 2007, 2357 (2358 et seq.).

1870 Spindler, WM 2007, 2357 (2359).

1871 Bericht des Finanzausschusses [Report of the Financial Committee] June 26, 2008, BT-Drucks 16/9821, 11.

Börse had coordinated their activities in a way that would have obliged them to submit a mandatory offer under the WpÜG.[1872] The amended version of concerted action rules demands coordinated behavior regarding the issuer to the attribution of voting rights. The coordination may either be based on an *agreement* on the exercise of voting rights, § 22 (2) sent. 1, sent. 2, 1st alt. WpHG, or in *another manner* with the aim to significantly *and* lastingly impact the entrepreneurial direction of the issuer, § 22 (2) sent. 1, 2, 2nd alt. WpHG.[1873] Despite systematic arguments and the intent to maintain the just recently increased level of shareholder communication, the exception for single cases of coordination, § 22 (2) sent. 1, applies according to the wording and the legislative materials of the Financial Committee only to individual agreements in the sense of the first alternative.[1874] Furthermore, it is the legislator's intent to interpret the exception formally and broadly in order to maintain the just recently increased communication between shareholders and legal security.[1875] Accordingly, agreements regarding several topics during a shareholder meeting, or the identical topic during several shareholder meetings and also preliminary agreements about nominees for the supervisory board, represent only individual cases, § 22 (2) sent. 1 WpHG.[1876]

Shareholder *agreements* on the *exercise of voting rights* are only concerted actions when they are part of a long-term strategy of shareholders jointly pursuing entrepreneurial goals, as underscored by the single agreement exception.[1877] It was the legislator's intent to maintain the fundamentals which had applied under former subsection two of § 22 WpHG.[1878] Unlike under U.S. law, the prevention of specific entrepreneurial mea-

1872 Press release, BaFin, BaFin did not ascertain acting in concert of Deutsche Börse shareholders (Oct. 19, 2005) http://www.bafin.de/cln_161/nn_721140/SharedDocs/Mitteilungen/EN/2005/051019.html: in the matter of Deutsche Börse AG/London Stock Exchange plc.; Spindler, WM 2007, 2357 (2357).

1873 Schwark, in: Schwark/Zimmer, Kapitalmarktrechts-Kommentar, 2010, § 22 mn.28.

1874 Bericht des Finanzausschusses [Report of the Financial Committee] June 26, 2008, BT-Drucks 16/9821, 11 et seq.: referring to „Abstimmungen" in the sense of the first alternative as opposed to „Vereinbarungen" including also the second alternative, furthermore, all the mentioned examples for singular case exceptions concern shareholder votes; other opinion: Von Bülow/Stephanblome, ZIP 2008, 1797 (1799): even though the *wording* of the first sentence would allow concluding that the exception in singular cases applies only to the first alternative, the *purpose* of the provision requires to apply it to both alternatives of § 22 (2) sent. 2 WpHG; Schwark, in: Schwark/Zimmer, Kapitalmarktrechts-Kommentar, 2010, § 22 mn.24: applying the exception to both alternatives and applying a formal-material standard.

1875 This corresponds to the formal approach pursued in the verdict of BGH, Urt. v. 18.09.2006, Az.: II ZR 137/05, NZG 2006, 945 (947) shortly prior to the legislative amendments through the *Risikobegrenzungsgesetz*; other opinion: Schwark, in: Schwark/Zimmer, Kapitalmarktsrechts-Kommentar, 2010, § 22 mnn.24 et seq.

1876 Bericht des Finanzausschusses [Report of the Financial Committee] June 26, 2008, BT-Drucks 16/9821, 12; other opinion: Schwark, in: Schwark/Zimmer, Kapitalmarktrechts-Kommentar, 2010, § 22 mn.24.

1877 Bericht des Finanzausschusses [Report of the Financial Committee] June 26, 2008, BT-Drucks 16/9821, 12; Gätsch/Schäfer, NZG 2008, 846 (850).

1878 Bericht des Finanzausschusses [Report of the Financial Committee] June 26, 2008, BT-Drucks 16/9821, 11; Von Bülow/Stephanblome, ZIP 2008, 1797 (1798): requiring a permanent and sustainable coordination of voting rights (BGH, Urt. v. 18.09.2006, Az.: II ZR 137/05, ZIP 2006, 2077

sures with the aim of maintaining the status quo do not, in contrast, have the quality of exercising control[1879]. This is also crucial for the circumvention of § 35 (2) WpÜG,[1880] which is triggered by the similarly interpreted[1881] § 30 (2) WpÜG, according to the legislative intent.[1882]

The legislative aims and the remedies applying under WpHG and WpÜG suggest a narrow interpretation of the second alternative, relating to *another impact* other than voting intended to *permanently and significantly amend the entrepreneurial alignment* of the corporation.[1883] Therefore, it needs to be based on a joint strategy, exercised via direct or indirect referral to the voting rights provided by corporate law and aiming to amend the entrepreneurial alignment of the corporation,[1884] as defined and realized by the management board.[1885] An example is the separation from major business divisions or the amendment of the business strategy.[1886] Agreements to jointly purchase shares of the issuer alone, which are usually met outside the shareholder meeting and could therefore only fall under the second alternative, are expressly excluded by the legislative materials, as they exercise no impact on the issuer.[1887] Finally, the concerted action needs

---

(2080)) as well as a regular impact of certain weight (OLG Frankfurt/M, Beschl. v. 25.06.2004, Az: WpÜG 5/03, ZIP 2004, 1309 (1312)).

1879 Bericht des Finanzausschusses [Report of the financial committee] June 26, 2008, BT-Drucks 16/9821, 11.

1880 Schockenhoff/Wagner, NZG 2008, 361 (362).

1881 RegE eines Risikobegrenzungsgesetz [Draft Law of the Federal Government for a Risk Limitation Act], Dec. 7, 2007, BT-Drucks 16/7438, 13: with the aim to avoid irritations on the capital market; Von Bülow/Stephanblome, ZIP 2008, 1797 (1797 et seq.): underscoring the different regulatory aims of the §§ 21 et seq. WpHG, concerning the information of the capital market regarding essential voting impacts, and § 35 WpÜG, protecting the minority shareholders in the case of a missing obligatory takeover offer, as well as the different underlying European specifications, which may contradict the identical interpretation in specific cases; Gätsch/Schäfer, NZG 2008, 846 (848); Weber-Rey, DStR 2008, 1967 (1968): supporting the identical interpretation for reasons of transparency in the market and legal certainty; Drinkuth, ZIP 2008, 676 (679): proposing a wide definition of the acting in concert for § 22 (2) WpHG and a narrow interpretation for § 30 (2) WpÜG, especially with regard to the different purposes of both rules and their different consequences.

1882 Gätsch/Schäfer, NZG 2008, 846 (850).

1883 Von Bülow/Stephanblome, ZIP 2008, 1797 (1798); Süßmann, in: Geibel/Süßmann, WpÜG, § 30 mn.31.

1884 Bericht des Finanzausschusses [Report of the Financial Committee] June 26, 2008, BT-Drucks 16/9821, 12; Gätsch/Schäfer, NZG 2008, 846 (850).

1885 Von Bülow/Stephanblome, ZIP 2008, 1797 (1798); Gätsch/Schäfer, NZG 2008, 846 (850).

1886 Bericht des Finanzausschusses [Report of the Financial Committee] June 26, 2008, BT-Drucks 16/9821, 12; Gätsch/Schäfer, NZG 2008, 846 (850).

1887 Bericht des Finanzausschusses [Report of the Financial Committee] June 26, 2008, BT-Drucks 16/9821, 11; Von Bülow/Stephanblome, ZIP 2008, 1979 (1799); Gätsch/Schäfer, NZG 2008, 846 (848); other opinion: Schwark, in: Schwark/Zimmer, Kapitalmarktrechts-Kommentar, 2010, § 22 mn.29: argueing that the coordinated acquisition of shares is the first step in impacting the corporate management, if the aim is to significantly and for certain period of time to impact the corporate management, there is not reason to exclude a corresponding behavior.

to be intended to impact the entrepreneurial alignment. The general suitability alone is insufficient.[1888]

Only the coordination as such, not the success of its impact, results in the attribution of the voting rights of the involved shareholders.[1889]

(b) Acting in concert and transaction activism

The *first alternative* of the concerted action regime becomes relevant only in constellations of transaction activism involving a shareholder vote. Transactions requiring a shareholder vote are either of a fundamental nature or require shareholder approval under *Holzmüller/Gelatine* or for a related capital measure. Furthermore, the activism needs to intend the amendment of the status quo, which would only apply to the rare scenario that shareholders intend to undertake a fundamental transaction. Finally, the single coordination exception needs to be taken into account for strategies involving shareholder votes relating to the positions of administrative members, as it has been acknowledged for agreement about the nomination of supervisory board members.

More relevant in the context of transaction activism is therefore the *second alternative* of § 22 (2) sent. 2 WpHG. The intention of transaction activism needs to be to permanently *and* significantly amend the entrepreneurial alignment of the corporation. This does not apply when shareholders aim to prevent a singular transaction to maintain the status quo, but it usually does when they intend to facilitate divestiture. This constellation has been explicitly mentioned by the Financial Committee,[1890] as it is usually not limited to the transaction alone. Rather, the intent is often more generally to reduce the conglomerate discount by re-aligning the corporate focus. Active shareholders usually target the responsible management board or supervisory board members. The incentives of active shareholders are not limited to facilitating the transaction to realign corporate business. Rather, they often continue by demanding to have the free cash distributed to the shareholders and thus also impact the capital corporate structure of the corporation. The entire process is usually not only significant for the targeted corporation, but it will also take its time. Still, the question whether the impact on the entrepreneurial alignment is significant and permanent needs to be answered for each specific case, depending on its circumstances. Even though transaction activism comes comparably close to the requirements laid down in the new second alternative of acting in concert, a general evaluation of transaction activism constellations is impossible. The only valuable rule of thumb relates to the circumstance that shareholders aiming to jointly maintain as opposed to amend the corporate status quo through transaction activism are not subject to the concerted action regime. This conforms to the legislative intent of allowing a constructive dialogue amongst shareholders, especially for the discussion and jointly speaking up for the maintenance of the status quo and against the amendment of the corpo-

1888 Von Bülow/Stephanblome, ZIP 2008, 1797 (1799); Weber-Rey, DStR 2008, 1967 (1968).

1889 Spindler, WM 2007, 2357 (2359).

1890 Bericht des Finanzausschusses [Report of the Financial Committee] June 26, 2008, BT-Drucks 16/9821, 12.

ration's entrepreneurial strategy.[1891] Whether the *Risikobegrenzungsgesetz* has achieved the intended legal certainty has therefore to be considered doubtful.[1892]

Considering the concerted action legislation's function and the practically relevant constellations for active shareholders to impact the administration's strategy, the second alternative's limitation to shareholder impact via means provided by corporate law[1893] allows group and control building without requiring the submission of a mandatory offer, § 35 (2) WpÜG.[1894] The amendments made by the *Risikobegrenzungsgesetz* are therefore only the first steps into the proper direction, but to reach its mark it would need to also include coordinated shareholder impact solely based on the use of informal means. Especially regarding the consequences (§ 35 (2) WpÜG) dependent on the applicability of § 30 (2) WpÜG, the amendment will have to coincide with a separate interpretation or wording of both provisions.

Finally, and in practice most relevant, the *Risikobegrenzungsgesetz* has left the burden of proof untouched. It remains the task of the BaFin to prove that the circumstances of a certain case fulfill the conditions of a concerted action. In practice, the BaFin has often failed to prove the necessary facts absent any statutorily laid down presumptions or facts allowing *prima facie* evidence[1895] and is expected to continue doing so. This circumstance appears to be responsible for the low success rates of administrative procedures based on § 22 (2) WpHG, and the acknowledged indicators of acting in concert constellations provided under U.S. corporate law[1896] are a possibility to reduce the issue.

Returning to the kick-off case of Deutsche Börse, the in 2008 adopted *Risikobegrenzungsgesetz* requires that the impact outside the shareholder meeting is of long-lasting and significant nature, while the share acquisition is insufficient.[1897] Based on the lack of an amendment to the burden of proof,[1898] the BaFin would have still had a hard time proving that investors had *acted in concert* with the consequence that they be obliged to disclose their joint stake and, due to the parallel provision of § 30 (2) WpÜG, to launch an obligatory offer to the remainder of investors. While the disclosure of their joint stakes would have been an appropriate means, the latter consequence would have not, underscoring the need for a different understanding of *acting in concert* in both contexts. As a consequence, the parallel acquisition of a joint stake followed by coordinated actions of shareholders outside the shareholder meeting will remain an efficient way to impact management decisions without triggering a notification obligation.

1891 *Id.* at 11.

1892 Accordingly Schwark, in: Schwark/Zimmer, Kapitalmarktrechts-Kommentar, 2010, § 22 mn.24: who underscores this constatation and proposes absent legal certainty to extent the singular case exception to both alternatives of acting in concert and further to interpret the exception not only formally, but also materially.

1893 Bericht des Finanzausschusses [Report of the Financial Committee] June 26, 2008, BT-Drucks 16/9821, 12: "gesellschaftsrechtlich vermittelter Einfluss" or impact based on corporate law.

1894 Schneider, ZGR 2007, 440 (450 et seq.).

1895 Spindler, WM 2007, 2357 (2362).

1896 *See* Spindler, WM 2007, 2357 (2362 n.113–115).

1897 Gätsch/Schäfer, NZG 2008, 846 (848).

1898 Spindler, WM 2007, 2357 (2362).

(c) Acting in concert and conflicts of interest

Finally, the acting in concert rules under the WpHG have proven to be just as relevant in disclosing conflicts of interest as they are for transaction activism in general. An agreement that the swap partner purchases the underlying shares to hedge the risk alone, without further aim regarding the targeted corporation, is not subject to the concerted action regime.[1899] However, investors and banks do not in general agree about the use of voting rights or coordinate their actions in a different way with the aim of permanently and significantly amending the strategic corporate orientation. In practice, they usually do not even agree on the acquisition of shares, since banks decide on their own if and how to hedge. But under the new disclosure regime, the acquisition of shares as such is insufficient, since acting in concert according to the first alternative requires an agreement on the coordination of voting rights.[1900] The same applies to share lending, as the lender will in general remain without impact on the shares voted by the borrower. In this context, the amendments of the disclosure provisions under §§ 25 and 25a WpHG and on European level are expected to increase the relevant transparency.

(3) Insider trading

(a) Active shareholders and section 14 (1) WpHG

(i) Purchase of shares to impact corporate strategy in a beneficial way

§ 14 (1) No. 1 WpHG could ban active shareholders who are pursuing specific strategic plans for the targeted corporation from increasing their stake in the targeted corporation. This requires that their plan to impact corporate strategy in a specific way is insider information, § 13 WpHG. Insider information concerns circumstances that are able to significantly impact the stock price if published.[1901] The question is therefore whether the intent to impact the corporate strategy in a specific way represents such a circumstance. A "circumstance" in the sense of § 13 WpHG refers to the past, present, and future.[1902] Even the plans of a person as an internal matter may constitute insider information.[1903] However, there is a consensus that the purchase of shares by shareholders to implement specific corporate strategy, at least if done to benefit the corporation, is not banned under insider trading law. The rationales differ: The first criminal law senate of the BGH requires that for *internal* circumstances to be relevant insider information need to have been shared with a third person.[1904] The BGH's argument finds support

1899 Baums/Sauter, ZHR 173 (2009), 454 (468).

1900 Schiessl, Der Konzern, 2009, 291 (296).

1901 Wilde, ZGR 1998, 423 (461).

1902 Schwark/Kruse, in: Schwark/Zimmer, Kapitalmarktrechts-Kommentar, 2010, § 13 WpHG mn.8 et seq.

1903 *Id.* at mn.75.

1904 BGH, Urt. v. 6.11.2003, Az.: 1 StR 24/03, ZIP 2003, 2354 (2355 et seq.)–Sascha Opel: decision concerning former law, but referring to the new Market Abuse Directive and requiring that information had contact with a third person; Arnold, ZCG 2008, 221 (225); Fleischer, ZGR

in the Market Abuse Directive's wording, which uses insider *information* instead of *circumstances* whereas the preamble of the directive declines to find that one's own entrepreneurial decisions can have the status of insider information[1905].[1906] Finally, the German legislator's deliberations about the Second Financial Market Promotions Act[1907] based on the Directive support this approach. Another view denies that plans intended for personal use should be given the status of inside information for systematic reasons.[1908] The system of the insider trading bans laid down in § 14 (1) No. 1 – 3 WpHG comprises a ban on personal use (No. 1) and two prohibitions relating to the time prior to the external uses (transmission and recommendation, No. 2 and 3). Actions prior to the internal use, such as the purchase of shares to realize the plan to impact the corporate strategy, is not subject to the prohibition.[1909] The legislative intent to distinguish between internal and external use in § 14 WpHG must be considered when evaluating active shareholders' purchase of shares to amend the corporate strategy prior to an internal use under the insider regime.[1910] Finally, a third approach considers the plan to impact the corporate strategy while purchasing the issuer's shares to constitute *insider information*, § 13 WpHG, which has been *used* to purchase the shares of the issuer, § 14 (1) No. 1 WpHG.[1911] Due to the lack of an evaluative element related to the term *use of the information*, § 14 (1) No. 1 WpHG's applicability is denied based on a *teleological reduction* comparable to takeover scenarios during which shareholders, despite their plan to take over a corporation, are allowed to purchase a substantial part of the issuer's shares.[1912] Both scenarios are allegedly permissible, since the realization of an internal entrepreneurial decision must be allowed without being banned by insider regulations.[1913] Correspondingly, the purpose of the insider regime is to prevent the use of inside information

---

2008, 185 (219); Schäfer, in: Schäfer/Haman, Kapitalmarktgesetze, § § 13 WpHG mn.22 (Supp. 4 2009); Schmolke, ZGR 2007, 701 (731); In favor of inside information: Assmann, in: Schneider/Assmann, WpHG, 2006, § 13 mn.10; Engert, ZIP 2006, 2105 (2108 et seq.); Thaeter/Guski, AG 2007, 301 (307).

1905 Market Abuse Directive 2003/6/EG, recital 30, 2003 O.J. (L 96) 18, *available at* http://eur-lex.europa.eu/LexUriServ/LexUriServ.do?uri=OJ:L:2003:096:0016:0025:EN:PDF; Schäfer, in: Schäfer/Haman, Kapitalmarktgesetze, § 13 WpHG mn.22 (Supp. 4 2009).

1906 With the same argument, but with the result that it is insider information, but it is not being *abused/used*: C-J391/04, Ypourgos Oikonomikon u.a./Charilaos Georgakis, 2007, E.C.R. I-3741, para.39 – for the old Insider Directive 89/592/EWG; Grundmann, in: Ebenroth et al., Handelsgesetzbuch, Vol. 2, 2009, § 14 WphG mn.IV101; Schwark/Kruse, in: Schwark/Zimmer, Kapitalmarktrechts-Kommentar, 2010, § 14 mn.23.

1907 RegE des zweiten Finanzmarkförderungsgesetzes [Draft law of the Federal Government of a Second Financial Markets Promotions Act], Jan. 27, 1994, BT-Drucks 12/6679, 47.

1908 Weber, NJW 2000, 562 (563).

1909 *Id.*

1910 *Id.*

1911 Engert, ZIP 2006, 2105 (2109).

1912 *Id.*

1913 *See* Arnold, ZCG, 2008, 221, 225; Caspari, ZGR 1994, 530 (542); Engert, ZIP 2006, 2105 (2109 et seq.); *see* Schmolke, ZGR 2007, 701 (731); Schwark/Kruse, in: Schwark/Zimmer, Kapitalmarktrechts-Kommentar, 2010, § 14 WpHG mn.23; Thaeter/Guski, AG 2007, 301, 307.

to the advantage of the insiders that incurs disapproval,[1914] which is alleged to be the case when the acquirer pursues a strategy to the detriment of the corporation and its stock price[1915] or other shareholders.[1916] A restriction going beyond this and preventing entrepreneurs from harvesting the fruits of their beneficial ideas would, however, weaken the incentives of capital market participants. It would prevent them from developing ways to amend corporate strategies and to convince the administration of them to the benefit of the corporation, its shareholders, and its stock price.[1917] Therefore, active shareholders purchasing shares with a specific plan to amend corporate strategy in favor of the corporation and its stock price are not subject to § 14 (1) No. 1 WpHG.

(ii) Purchase of shares to pursue special interests

Different consequences of the insider regulation could, however, apply to shareholders purchasing shares to impact the corporate strategy independent of the consequences or even to the detriment of the corporation. The evaluation of such scenarios differs with the above-mentioned approaches. The proponents of the first approach still deny that something is insider information if the information is not communicated to a third party.[1918] For the supporters of the systematically reasoned approach,[1919] the activity prior to an internal use is not subject to § 14 (1) No. 1 WpHG. Only for the proponents of the teleological reduction does such a plan constitute insider information according to § 13 WpHG, which is used in the sense of § 14 (1) No. 1 WpHG. The insider regime's purpose is to prevent the use of inside information for the unacceptable advantage of insiders. Its teleological reduction is therefore superfluous under scenarios in which the purchasing shareholder plans to influence a transaction decision independent of the consequences for or the detriment to the corporation.[1920]

(iii) Sharing insider information with cooperating shareholders

Finally, the sharing of insider information with fellow active shareholders to convince the administration of a certain transaction decision could be subject to § 14 (1) No. 2 WpHG. Again, the outcome of the legal evaluation depends on the kind of reasoning applied: The proponents of the first or second approach affirm insider information due to a third-person-relation or a situation prior of a transfer and therefore § 14 (1) No. 2 WpHG.[1921] Advocates of the teleological reduction, in contrast, deny the applicability of § 14 (1) No. 2 WpHG. As long as the activist co-partners join the initiator by increasing

1914 RegE des zweiten Finanzmarktförderungsgesetzes [Draft Law of the Federal Government of the Second Financial Markets Promotions Act], Jan. 27, 1994, BT-Drucks 12/6679, 47.
1915 Thaeter/Guski, AG 2007, 301 (307).
1916 Arnold, ZCG, 2008, 221 (225).
1917 Engert, ZIP 2006, 2105 (2109).
1918 Schmolke, ZGR 2007, 701 (731 n.186).
1919 Weber, NJW 2000, 562 (563).
1920 Engert, ZIP 2006, 2105 (2109 et seq.).
1921 Schmolke, ZGR 2007, 701 (731 n.187).

their stakes to increase their joint impact on the administration and their potential profit to the benefit of the corporation, the coordination must be permitted.[1922]

(iv) Teleological approach and shareholder activism

Only the third approach based on teleological reduction, according to which insider law disapproves the use of insider information to the exclusive advantage of the insiders, but not that entrepreneurs harvest the benefits of their entrepreneurial and beneficial ideas, seems to lead to results in conformity with the separation of beneficial and opportunistic shareholder activism. While it allows shareholders with a plan to amend corporate strategy to benefit all other shareholders to purchase shares, it bans purchases by shareholders aiming to amend the corporate strategy to pursue deviating interests. Even the cooperation of shareholders for the corporation's benefit, necessary in practice due to minority positions of active shareholders, would not fall under the insider regime. Both other approaches, even if completed by teleological reductions, do not lead to equally appropriate results. The outcome for active shareholders aiming to amend corporate strategy to the benefit of the corporation according to this teleological approach conforms to the intent of the Market Abuse Directive as well as the Second Financial Market Promotions Act based on the Directive. Both have neither the intent to prohibit the realization of one's own entrepreneurial plans nor the acquisition of share packages while pursuing such a plan. Taking a closer look at the insider regime's purpose, however, it intends to hinder the use of a knowledge advantage to the disadvantage of other investors in the sense of preventing the violation of the equal treatment principle by preventing fellow shareholders from participating in the financial advantage.[1923] Explicitly excluded, however, are self-initiated control procedures like the acquisition of control of the targeted corporation in order to acquire the corporation.[1924] Under this premise, it can be argued that the lack of knowledge of the fellow shareholders about the deviating interests of fellow shareholders allows the active shareholders with deviating interests to profit from a shareholder vote needed to ensure the active shareholder's advantage. However, this process goes beyond the sole use of information. It is based on additional actions of the active shareholders. It appears therefore closer to stake building for an alternative control mechanism, the market for corporate control, explicitly excluded from the insider regime. It has been excluded without distinguishing whether it is intended to be beneficial for fellow shareholders or not. When the Directive was adopted in 1994, the phenomenon of shareholder activism was not as frequent. The fact that shareholder activism is not equally mentioned by the Directive does not permit the conclusion that there should be an equivalent exception to the insider regime. Consequently, considering that the provision's wording and structure represent arguments against the coverage of

1922 Engert, ZIP 2006, 2105 (2110).
1923 Schwark/Kruse, in: Schwark/Zimmer, Kapitalmarktrechts-Kommentar, 2010, § 14 mn.17.
1924 Directive on Insider Dealing and Market Manipulation, 2003/6/EC, recital 29, 2003 O.J. (L 96/16).

corresponding constellations while its purpose does not truly urge this distinct interpretation, the wish for a distinguishing means alone is insufficient.

(b) Administration and section 15 WpHG

Furthermore, insider obligations may arise for the administration if insider information has been provided during private conversations with active shareholders.[1925] The fact that management has met with active shareholders and the content of the conversation may represent insider information.[1926] Therefore, shareholders informing the administration that they wish to sell their entire package of shares if the corporation does not change the corporate strategy as demanded represent insider information if the information is able to significantly impact the share price.[1927] The administration is then obliged to make an ad hoc-announcement, § 15 (1) WpHG.[1928]

(4) Ban of market manipulation, section 20a (1) WpHG

§ 20a WpHG protects the confidence of market participants in the reliability and truth of price building in the securities exchanges.[1929] A violation may result in an administrative fine or have criminal consequences, §§ 38 (2), 39 (1) No. 1 WpHG. Covered *short sales*, as opposed to (abusive) banned naked short sales, are, without manipulative market behavior via the sale of shares intending to lower the stock price, not subject to the market manipulation provision.[1930] Hidden ownership is only in extreme cases, like a market squeeze, subject to the ban of market manipulation, §§ 20a (1) No. 3 WpHG, § 4 (3) No. 1 MaKonV.[1931] Neither is relevant for active shareholders, whether involved in conflicts of interest or not.

iii) Further legal restrictions

If administrations are confronted with strong pressure from active shareholders that prevents them from referring the shareholders to their corporate rights and/or to its own discretion, § 76 (1), criminal law provisions may be relevant. Furthermore, their violation may represent the basis for a claim of damages, § 823 (2) BGB.

Fraud under § 263 StGB is relevant to false facts presented to the administration while trying to convince it to make a specific transaction decision. It requires a disposition of corporate assets with an immediate impact on the corporate capital. Only in rare

1925 Schäfer, NZG 2007, 900 (901).
1926 *Id.*
1927 Assmann, in: Assmann/Schneider, WpHG, § 15 mnn.70 et seq.
1928 Wilde, ZGR 1998, 423 (461).
1929 Sorgenfrei, in: Park, Kapitalmarktstrafrecht, pt. 3, ch. 4, T 1 mn.10.
1930 Trüg, NJW 2009, 3202 (3205); for a general relevance with regard to empty voting through derivatives Zetsche, NZG 2009, 692 (696 et seq.).
1931 Fleischer/Schmolke, NZG 2010, 846 (852).

cases will this be the consequence of transaction activism.[1932] Furthermore, the financial loss required for *blackmail* according to § 253 StGB and *fraud* under § 263 StGB may not be based on alternative strategic decisions and related expectations. *Duress* pursuant to § 240 StGB, which requires that the goal pursued by the shareholders does not relate to the means applied to convince management of a certain decision, has proven to be more relevant in the transaction activism context.[1933] Finally, facts that have not been proven[1934] and are brought out during public campaigns of active shareholders targeting the reputation of members of the administration may represent *defamation* pursuant to § 186 StGB.[1935]

iv) Legal limitations and transaction activism constellations

(1) Disclosure of deviating interests

Since the implementation of the AnsFuG, hidden ownership based on share lending or a short position under a cash settled equity swap is, at least until the effectiveness of the European harmonization approach, belongs to the past. However, unlike under U.S. securities law, empty voting based on cash-settled equity derivatives or share lending as well as related non-host assets do not trigger notification or disclosure. Only net short positions of 0.2 percent and more require notification. It ensures that not only qualified positive interests mediating voting right but also negative (related non-host) financial interests without physical holding of the reference shares will need to be disclosed independently. Reduced or neutral economic positions often used to pursue empty voting will, however, not trigger notification.

(2) Liability and transaction activism constellations

Shareholders of German corporations pursuing deviating interests when exercising transaction activism that results in disadvantages for the targeted corporation and its shareholders may, in contrast to U.S. law, become subject to claims for damages. These may be based on fiduciary duty violations or on impact exercised to order members of the administration to act in a way that results in damage to the corporation or shareholders, §§ 117 AktG, 826 BGB. Unfortunately, the theoretical availability of such restraints on opportunistically acting active shareholders differs significantly from their practical relevance. The main obstacle to pursuing either claim is the burden of proof of the corporation or the damaged shareholders.[1936] As already recognized by the legislator of the

1932 Thaeter/Guski, AG 2007, 301 (303).
1933 Götze, in: Gleiss Lutz/AmCham, Shareholder Activism – (k)ein rechtliches Thema, 2008, 14, http://www.amcham.de/fileadmin/templates/main/pdf/Praesentation_Goetze.pdf.
1934 Kühl, in: Lackner/Kühl, StGB, 2011, § 186 mn.7.
1935 Götze, in: Gleiss Lutz/AmCham, Shareholder Activism – (k)ein rechtliches Thema, 2008, 15, http://www.amcham.de/fileadmin/templates/main/pdf/Praesentation_Goetze.pdf.
1936 Arnold, ZCG 2008, 221 (226).

Risikobegrenzungsgesetz,[1937] it is necessary to ease the burden of proof for the corporation and the shareholders to allow them to establish liability for opportunistic actions of active shareholders.[1938] This may be realized by determining the relevant indicators for the objective and the subjective elements of fact of the concerned provisions, either by the legislator or courts, under the premise that the plaintiffs usually have no access to the means necessary to prove the claim.

An *approach* aiming to meet the practical need to efficiently restrict shareholder activism driven by deviating interests should *provide effective but limited notification obligations* covering circumstances that are usually the basis for deviating. In addition, it should comprise the under German law already provided mechanisms to prevent or compensate corporate damages resulting from the impact exercised by (minority) shareholders. This raises the question whether the knowledge of the generally underlying interests of the members of the administration and the shareholder-value orientated (active) shareholders could be helpful in determining constellations of transaction activism under which the burden of proof, which is a hindrance in practice, could be shifted and therefore the efficiency of the available liability measures increased.

Desirable transaction activism aims to prevent an opportunistically acting administration from pursuing a decision that would lower shareholder value of the corporation or prevent it from increasing. Its occurrence is therefore more likely where the underlying interests of both shareholders and the administration are generally contradictory. In regard to the six analyzed transaction activism constellations, three of them would be implicated. Without contradicting underlying interests, it may be assumed that for the other three constellations of transaction activism the active shareholders act opportunistically themselves by pursuing interests that are not aligned with those of their fellow shareholders. If the latter three constellations involve an increased risk of opportunistic shareholder behavior, they could be subject to the mentioned shift in the burden of proof.

The assumption of *opportunistic transaction activism* may be reversed by the active shareholders proving, that they have acted in the corporate interests in the sense of an enlightened shareholder approach. The applied transaction activism would therefore have been aligned with the interests of the corporation and the fellow shareholders. As a consequence, the specific transaction decision may have been led by opportunistic interests of the administration and not by the corporate interests. However, due to the business judgement rule applying to the adminstration, § 93 (1) sent. 2, the reversal would not automatically lead to a liability of the administrative members. As long as they would be able to document the prerequisites of the unrevocable presumption to have acted according to their duty, they would not be held liable either. The remaining "lia-

1937 Das Risikobegrenzungsgesetz, Oct. 2007, Linklaters.com, http://www.linklaters.com/pdfs/publications/GER_Div/NL_Risikobegrenzungsgesetz.pdf: Aim of the *Risikobegrenzungsgesetz* is to complicate or hinder undesirable activities of financial investors without impacting efficient financial or corporate transactions. The intention was also to expand the applicability of acting in concert, also by reducing problems with regard to *proving* acting in concert.

1938 Fleischer, ZGR 2008, 185 (203); opposing opinion: Arnold, ZCG 2008, 221 (226): noting that the seldom applicability of the above-mentioned legal restrictions lies in the very nature of things. To prove that an active shareholder has the intent to damage the corporation is not done easily.

bility gap" would, however, be narrowed down. The reason for such a deviation between administrative and corporate interests could be the deviating impact of the transaction on the shareholder value of the targeted corporation compared to its generally assumed impact and/or deviating personal interests of the administration. The same may also apply to the opposite constellations likely to involve *beneficial transaction activism*. Opportunistic acting shareholders under a deviating constellation have the advantage of using the generally explanatory models applying to beneficial activism, like overpriced compensation, to assure the support of fellow shareholders. Despite these possible deviations from the general impact of certain transactions on the share price and the underlying administrative interests, certain constellations are more likely than others to involve opposing or equal interests of the actors. They do not prohibit use of this knowledge to prevent opportunistic transaction activism as long as the concerned shareholders have the opportunity to prove the opposite. A shift in the burden of proof in constellations more likely to involve opportunistic behavior of active shareholders could apply when transaction activism in these constellations leads to damage to the targeted corporation. It would have the advantage that the shareholders having access to the relevant information would be the ones that would need to prove an exception. Nor would the approach keep active shareholders from engaging in transaction activism, as they usually become active in constellations typically involving desirable transaction activism and they are able to prove the opposite when engaging in a deviating constellation. Finally, the approach would increase the practical relevance of existing liability provisions, which are currently diminished by the distribution of the burden of proof.

Besides the mentioned deviations from the underlying assumptions, it must be underscored that the possible generalization of the impact of a specific corporate measure on shareholder value applies only to a limited set of corporate decisions in the transaction context. Viewed from a more distant perspective of shareholder activism in general, it puts into perspective the usefulness of the approach based on the underlying interests of the actors to a generally applicable structural problem of lacking practical relevance of given provisions and regimes.

f) Transaction activism and underlying corporate governance theories

With the exception of fundamental transaction decisions, corporate transaction decisions represent management tasks. They are to be made by the administration alone, except if subject to *Holzmüller/Gelatine*.

The success of active shareholders impacting (opportunistic) transaction decisions in German corporations results, amongst other reasons, from the reduction of collective action issues of shareholders in corporations with increasing freefloat. It allows active shareholders to impact transaction decisions via the use of formal means requiring the support of a majority of shareholders to exercise direct or indirect impact on the decision process. In addition, active shareholders use informal means to increase their impact on management and its transaction decisions beyond the ones provided by statute, articles of incorporation, by-laws, or precedent.

The effect of active shareholders *overcoming collective action issues* to get a majority of shareholders engaged for their aim allows them, even in corporations with significant freefloat as opposed to the traditional blockholding shareholders, to effectively use the shareholder means provided by statute, articles of incorporation, by-laws, or precedent. So far, shareholder activism compensates factual deficits of shareholder impact resulting from collective action issues based on the rather recent phenomenon of increasing freefloat in listed corporations, which had not been sufficiently considered by the legislator. This concerns not only the exercise of shareholder initiation and approval rights of fundamental transaction decisions as well as those under *Holzmüller/Gelatine*. More importantly, it relates to the use of the general formal means ensuring accountability like the removal and election of members of the supervisory and management board to impact transaction decisions representing pure management tasks. Overcoming the increasing collective actions issues is (even more) critical under German law, as the legal obstacles concerning the initiation of fundamental transaction decisions and the accountability mechanisms are comparably insignificant. As a consequence, active shareholders overcoming collective action issues ensure that the intended competencies between shareholders and the administration are implemented in practice despite the increasing freefloat of listed corporations. Overcoming collective action issues through active shareholders usually represents an uncontroversial and welcome mechanism to (re)install the balance of authority and control between the administration and shareholders.

The expansion of shareholder means beyond those provided by statute, articles of incorporation, bylaws, and precedent frequently raises the question whether it is still compatible with underlying corporate governance theories, most notably the authority distribution in and the purpose of a corporation. The use of *informal means* can enhance the communication between more influential shareholders (larger stake or reputation as successful active shareholders) and the administration. Their use allows shareholders to directly contact the administration or even the public and confront it with a corporate issue. They either complement the use of formal means or are applied independently. The augmented impact of shareholders resulting from the use of informal means increases the chance that their interests will be considered. Even though the increased impact may be based on means not explicitly provided to shareholders, their use does not represent an extra-institutional action if the management board continues making the management decisions. Rather, it grants shareholders additional means to effectively impact opportunistic administrative decisions in violation of the *enlightened shareholder approach* covered by the "cloak" of the stakeholder approach.

As far as shareholders use informal means to impact pure management decisions by underscoring the possibility of the exercise of their franchise, such proceedings of active shareholders conform to underlying corporate governance theories. According to them, shareholders as principles have delegated most of their decision and control rights. They have only maintained control rights in regards to the supervisory board, which tend to be exercised rather rarely. As a consequence, the supervisory board tends to correspond less to the shareholder interests to more effectively control the management board.

The use of informal means to increase the effective use of the shareholder franchise, as done in transaction activism constellations targeting management transaction decisions, reduces the increasing agency costs based on the separation of ownership and control in German corporations.

Parallel to the analysis under U.S. corporate law, active shareholders are not limited to remedying the separation of ownership and control by overcoming collective action issues and using informal means. They may go beyond that by directly impacting management transaction decisions through the use of informal means alone and therefore ensure that members of the management board, as *agents*, act under the enlightened shareholder value approach in the interests of their *principals*, the shareholders. However, the use of informal means by active shareholders underscores the need for effectively functioning legal limitations that will prevent active shareholders from engaging, based on deviating interests, to detriment of the corporation and fellow shareholders.

Finally, transaction activism constellations aiming for divestitures by the targeted corporation in order to concentrate on the core business of the company and to reduce the conglomerate discount are where a conflict of the underlying theory specific to German corporations surfaces. It concerns the conflict of the traditionally prevailing stakeholder approach and the increasingly accepted enlightened shareholder approach. The former is still pursued by many administrations in Germany and is likely to be used as a justification for opportunistic administrative behavior. The latter represents more and more the reality of listed corporations, which have to correspond to the demand of a (international) capital market demanding a shareholder primacy approach. German administrations have traditionally acted in the interest of all stakeholders, including shareholders aiming for increased shareholder value, employees demanding secure employment and creditors requiring secure repayments in due time.[1939] Accordingly, they exercised their discretion in pursuing management tasks in the *common corporate interest*. This allowed the administration to compensate for potential deficits of one division by the profits of other one as long as the average profit of the conglomerate was sufficient. More recently, they have been confronted with the international capital market and its shareholder value focused (active) investors.[1940] They are willing to use the entire spectrum of shareholder means to increase the shareholder value of a corporation. Active shareholders targeting the elimination of inefficiencies resulting from internal corporate diversifications are likely to find the potential to increase shareholder value. It simultaneously allows reducing potentially opportunistic behavior of the administration. This is exactly one of the reasons for the decline of the stakeholder approach, which allows the administration to increase and secure its own authority and compensation with the justification of pursuing stakeholder interests. The applicable enhanced shareholder value approach therefore represents the theoretical basis of the activities of the active shareholders. Their aim for increased efficiency and return of the targeted corporation is key, even if they simultaneously raise the insolvency risk and therefore concerns of employees and creditors to

1939 Kuhner, ZGR 2004, 244 (264).

1940 The current emphasis on long-term goals and sustainability as opposed to the concern of short-termism of active shareholders will be dealt with in Part III.

a certain extent. Investors are able to protect themselves from insolvency at lower cost through external diversification,[1941] even if this raises concerns of other stakeholders.

V) Final thesis regarding transaction activism

1) Means

As expected, the means formally provided to shareholders pursuing transaction activism under U.S. and German law differ. Under both jurisdictions, active shareholders have developed effective ways to compensate their theoretically or practically lacking impact in order to influence fundamental and management transaction decisions.

a) Direct impact

Under both jurisdictions, shareholders have been provided with direct impact on the decision-making process of *fundamental corporate transaction decisions*, like most mergers. The *Holzmüller/Gelatine* doctrine under German law has even expanded these constellations by providing shareholders for a limited number of structurally significant management decisions with approval rights. Active shareholders are able to *prevent* such transactions by overcoming collective action issues and having a sufficient number of fellow shareholders veto the transaction. In addition, the shareholders of the acquiring corporation usually have the necessary incentives to prevent an opportunistic merger. Under U.S. law, active shareholders aim to ensure such a veto face bigger hurdles. They need to take account of the proxy regime and are confronted with stronger collective action issues based on the stronger freefloat.

Regarding the *facilitation* of fundamental transactions, shareholders under German law have mandatory (minority) initiation rights and a precatory initiation right regarding management decisions subject to the *Holzmüller/Gelatine* doctrine. In addition, they have the right to convene a special shareholder meeting, even if the administration opposes it. However, as the necessary quorum to initiate the preparation of future transaction decisions equals the one necessary to approve the transaction, fundamental transactions have been seldom realized against the will of the administration. Active shareholders of U.S. corporations, in contrast, have already in theory rather limited initiation rights with a purely precatory character while the list of circumstances under which such proposals may be excluded even before the precatory vote takes place is a long.

As already assumed on a general level, it can be affirmed that shareholders of German corporations have wider applicable and stronger means to *directly* impact transaction decisions. This simultaneously decreases the number of cases requiring falling back on the general accountability measures and/or informal means. However, in practice they are required under both jurisdictions to facilitate (even fundamental) transactions.

1941 *Id.*, Arnold, ZCG 2008, 221 (223); Ruffner, Die ökonomischen Grundlagen eines Rechts der Publikumsgesellschaft, 2000, 218.

b) Indirect impact

The most relevant means for shareholders to (indirectly) influence transaction decisions, especially when representing pure management decisions in either direction, are under both jurisdictions the threat to or the actual use of the franchise. Shareholders under German law have due to a supermajority requirement only limited removal rights, which are significant due to five-year office periods, but strong nomination and election rights regarding the supervisory board members. If they hold a majority stake or the corresponding support amongst the present shareholders they can initiate the replacement of a management board member through the supervisory board which depends on the shareholder meeting's vote withdrawing confidence in the member. The minority right to convene a special meeting and/or to initiate either measure complements these rights. *Active* minority shareholders able to overcome collective action issues find a wide array of useful means to pursue transaction activism.

Under U.S. law, shareholders have comparably weak nomination and election rights, which are paramount due to the annual re-election process. The broad and overly long discussion about nomination and election procedures to reduce the legal obstacles to which important accountability measures are subject to has only been partially successful in some but still not all issues. The long discussed about and sough for mandatory proxy access rule was vacated shortly after it had finally been adopted. Accordingly, active shareholders have to use the annual shareholder meetings to propose the adoption of bylaws granting the shareholders the right to include into the corporation's proxy materials nominees before proposing their own candidates and to ensure the necessary support to have them elected. For a shorter process, they need to resort to the costly means of a proxy fight or the use of informal means to replace a director.

As expected, the accountability measures under German law are, despite the five-years term of officials, in practice much more effective for active shareholders than under U.S. law. Shareholders of German corporations have the right to initiate the removal of an administrative member during each general meeting as well as during special meetings. Furthermore, they are able to nominate their supervisory board candidates.

c) Informal means

Under U.S. law, the comparably long experience of shareholder activism is reflected by the development of elaborate informal means. They have allowed active shareholders to complement their limited formal means and/or to get around legal obstacles. Correspondingly, they have developed means that systematically use the increasing number of limitations and exceptions from the costly and time-consuming proxy regime relevant for shareholders to communicate with each other. Furthermore, conversations with administrative members or public campaigns complement the picture.

In Germany, internationally active shareholders experienced in transaction activism have often made use of the comparably wider spectrum of formal shareholder means under German law. In addition, they have often started their campaigns with low-cost means of direct communications with members of the administration before surprising administrations with their often successful methods of influencing transaction decisions by using the wide array of formal means. Only in extreme scenarios did they use public campaigns.

As assumed, shareholders under German law need to use or develop informal means far less often to complement the wide regime of formal shareholder means. An exception is the frequently used means of communication with administrative members in advance of a campaign.

2) Limitations relevant for active shareholders

Shareholders applying transaction activism have only in a limited number of cases attempted or succeeded in pursuing interests deviating from those of the corporation and their fellow shareholders.

a) Disclosure

Under U.S. law, deviating interests of active shareholders have been effectively disclosed, despite the rather traditional wording of the line items of the disclosure rules and thanks to the effective materiality qualifier of the antifraud rules. The pursuit of conflicting interests via transaction activism usually requiring the support of a substantial number of shareholders has or would have been successfully undermined in cases where the conflict was disclosed. Especially the beneficial ownership definition of voting *and/ or* investment power, that is used infrequently, has the potential to disclose deviating shareholder interests that are based on (financial) means separating voting rights from economic interests. It is therefore an approach that could be picked up by the expected revision of the relevant provisions.

In 2010, the German legislator adopted an act demanding the disclosure of net short positions likely to be involved in some constellations involving related non-host assets. In 2011, the adoption of the AnsFuG, which covers share lenders and long swap parties, introduced disclosure obligations for the relevant *hidden ownership* constellations. Despite good arguments for a cautious introduction of new disclosure obligations, it has not been limited to takeover scenarios. However, it still leaves room for *empty voting*. The initially expected response of the European legislator in this regard cannot be expected anymore after the publication of the concluding statement on the Call for Evidence on Empty Voting of the ESMA. Rather, the proposed European approach allows the expectation that hidden ownership via share lending may soon become possible again.

Both, the German and the European legislator, might consider the U.S. approach, which *triggers* disclosure obligations by (positive or negative) economic interests and/ or voting rights (or those expected based on legal, economic or factual opportunities). Furthermore, it requires the *disclosure of* positive or negative economic interests and (legal, economic, or factual opportunities to dispose of) voting rights if these prove to be material. Such a transparency-based approach takes into account the (potential) benefits of the corresponding strategies while disclosing current and expected strategies that allow pursuit of deviating interests. In addition, the *material qualifier* prevents a flood of disclosures, which would hinder rather than encourage the increased transparency of critical circumstances.

b) Liability

Potential liability of active shareholders of U.S. corporations based on the detrimental impact exercised on administrative members is usually ruled out due to the minority positions of active shareholders. As a consequence, they tend not to fall under the *control* notion necessary to become subject to the fiduciary duty. This is, however, compensated by the efficient disclosure obligations and their effective enforcement mechanisms.

Under German law with its not as effective disclosure regime, a liability regime applies when shareholders impact administrative members to the detriment of the corporation and its shareholders. However, the targeted or harmed corporation or the shareholders have to prove the prerequisites of fiduciary duty violations and the provisions §§ 117 AktG, 826 BGB. This has limited their practical effect dramatically and requires the consideration of amendments to increase their effect.

As expected, the U.S.-American regime is effective in fighting deviating interests pursued with or without the application of informal means by means of disclosure, even though the disclosure regime has not been specifically amended to target the issue yet. This is expected to take place in the near future, however. The German regime, in contrast, is less effective in countering potential shareholder impact based on deviating interests. The disclosure regime has only recently covered hidden ownership constellations. The European legislator may, however, restrict this approach soon. The disclosure of empty voting constellations had been tackled on the European level, but has been set aside again. Here, it could fall back on U.S. experiences. Furthermore, the relevant liability provisions lack practical relevance.

3) Constellations of desirable transaction activism

To generally distinguish constellations of desirable from undesirable (transaction) activism based on the generally underlying interests of shareholders and the administration to approach practical deficits is the intent of this thesis. Such an approach would likely be of less relevance to U.S. law under which active minority shareholders are not subject to a liability regime. But it could be helpful in increasing the practical relevance of the liability provisions under the current German regime by easing or shifting the burden of proof under undesirable (transaction) activism constellations. Such an approach could discourage active shareholders from pursuing deviating interests at the cost of the targeted corporation and its shareholders until the German legislator installs an effective disclosure regime.

The practicability of such an approach is not deterred by the possible deviations applying to the assumed underlying interests of the analyzed transaction activism constellations. Rather, it is the lack of available, generalizable data on the impact of certain measures beyond the six analyzed corporate decisions on the shareholder value and therefore the underlying shareholder interests that prevents the general application of the approach to shareholder activism. However, in the area of transaction activism with its specific potential for opportunistic activism and during the time in which an efficient disclosure regime is not provided courts could allow the plaintiffs to bring a prima facie case in constellations likely to involve opportunistic transaction activism. The respondent, who has access to the relevant documents, would be able to rebut such a presumption.

4) Underlying corporate governance theories

Finally, the impact of active shareholders on corporate transaction decisions including fundamental decisions and management decisions has been shown to conform to the underlying corporate governance theories of U.S. and German law. Active shareholders do not limit themselves to overcoming the lack of incentives shareholders have and the general collective action problems that undermine shareholder control of the administration. The corresponding use of general formal means to impact management's transaction decisions also lessens the agency issues resulting from the separation of ownership and control. The use of informal means contributes further to this effect, as it allows active shareholders, especially under U.S. law, to overcome some of the still present legal obstacles in order to use special and general formal means. Finally, their use conforms to the shareholders' position as *principals* of the corporation that aim to enhance the *shareholders value*. What has been established for decades under U.S. law is based on the growing impact of the international capital market, increasingly recognized in the form of the governance theories of principal-agent and the enlightened shareholder under German law. The *supra* mentioned legal limitations bear the task of preventing or compensating potentially opportunistic shareholder behavior applying formal or informal means.

E) Part III: Financial activism

I) Introduction

The third relevant area for shareholder activism relates to the financial structure of targeted corporations. Active shareholders, especially hedge funds,[1942] pursue rather generalized strategies, like the payout of excess cash via dividends and share repurchases and/or the increase of corporate leverage to mitigate agency costs.[1943] The impact of active shareholders on the financial structure has the advantage that it often involves a direct return flow from the corporation to the shareholders.[1944] These cash-focused one-time effects allow them to realize short-term maximization of personal shareholder value.[1945] Especially in regard to the latter effect, active shareholders pursuing financial activism are frequently confronted with substantial critique. Active shareholders often apply impact on the corporate financial structure as part of a more comprehensive strategy. Particularly in relation to the successful pursuit of the sixth of the analyzed transaction activism constellations (facilitating divestitures), they tend to subsequently impact the financial structure.

1) Underlying interests of actors involved in financial activism

According to Berle and Mean's understanding of the separation of ownership and control, directors deciding how to invest corporate funds tend to act opportunistically. They tend to make investment decisions not necessarily to maximize corporate value by choosing the projects with the highest net present value according to shareholders' interest, but to further their own goals. Active shareholders may intervene against this kind of opportunism and aim to reduce the resulting agency costs by exercising impact on the financial structure of the targeted corporation. This reduces inefficiencies in the use of available corporate capital, especially excess cash, and increases shareholder value through better externally invested funds and outside control through the capital market. Concerns regarding financial activism relate, in parallel to the risks of transaction activism, to the potential for financial activists to abuse the impact exercised by acting opportunistically to further own interests, harming the corporation or fellow shareholders.

1942 *See* Klein & Zur, 64 J. Fin. 187, 226 (2009): noting that only hedge funds extract free cash flow by demanding share repurchase, dividends and increased leveraging.

1943 Clifford, 14 J. Corp. Fin. 323, 330 (2008).

1944 DAI/McKinsey, Investorendialog im Umbruch, 2009, 25.

1945 Götze, in: Gleiss Lutz/AmCham, Shareholder Activism – (k)ein rechtliches Thema, 2008, 7, http://www.amcham.de/fileadmin/templates/main/pdf/Praesentation_Goetze.pdf.

2) Corporate financial measures

Active shareholders preferably impact a number of different financial measures. Means allowing direct financial return from the corporation to the shareholders include share repurchases, augmented general dividends, and special dividends. In addition, active shareholders often, but less frequently, focus on an increase of corporate debt (leveraging) to finance the distributions.[1946] Combined mid-term strategies may include the sale or spin-off of a non-core division or subsidiary to eliminate a conglomerate discount, the prevention of an acquisition, as was the case for Mirant,[1947] and the sale of corporate assets freeing undisclosed reserves. These strategies simultaneously provide the basis for subsequent financial measures of the above-mentioned kind. The following Part on financial activism will concentrate on the most relevant financial measures initiated by active shareholders: share repurchases, dividends, and increased corporate leveraging.

3) Means to impact corporate financial decisions

Without efficient special formal means to directly impact corporate decisions on the financial structure, active shareholders have to use the general formal (accountability) means provided to them and the informal means developed by them to convince the administration to consider their interests. The general formal and informal means are those analyzed in the transaction activism Part. Therefore, the following analysis relies on the analysis of the prior Part when discussing general formal and informal means and focuses on the particularities applying to the financial activism context.

4) Firms targeted

Active shareholder aiming to initiate distributions tend to target large firms. The amounts distributed correlate positively and proportionally with the firm's size, primarily its market capitalization.[1948] As primarily large corporations provide regular dividends and periodically repurchase shares, these findings make sense.[1949] Simultaneously, large corporations are able to pay off active shareholders who are pressuring the administration

1946 Bratton, 95 Geo. L.J. 1375, 1418 (2007): only in about 19,5 percent of the payout cases; DAI/McKinsey, Investorendialog im Umbruch, 2009, 25 et seq.: in 10 of the 31 analysed cases.

1947 Emma Trincal, *Mirant up on activist agitation*, June 21, 2006, thestreet.com, http://www.thestreet.com/story/10293003/1/mirant-up-on-activist-agitation.html: One week after Mirant had withdrawn its offer to acqire NRG due to transaction activism, Pirate Capital demanded in a 13D filing a share buyback programm.

1948 Bratton, *Hedge Funds and Corporate Governance Targets; Long-Term Results*, 16, www.ssrn.com/abstract=1677517 (2010); Bratton, 95 Geo. L.J. 1375, 1415 (2007).

1949 Bratton, *Hedge Funds and* Corporate *Governance Targets: Long-Term Results* 16, www.ssrn.com/abstract=1677517 (2010); Fama & French, *Disappearing dividends: Changing Firm Characteristics or Lower Propensity to Pay?* 2, 20, http://ssrn.com/abstract=203092 (2000).

before they achieve a board position. The majority of the smaller firms targeted are cash rich ex ante.[1950]

5) Corporate modes to fund distributions

Corporations confronted with the demands of active shareholders to make distributions to shareholders have several ways to finance them. As the firms targeted by financial activism are not primarily cash-rich ex ante, except for the subset of small corporations representing a rather small part of the targets,[1951] the demands will not be primarily satisfied by the use of cash reserves. In the first place, successful demands of active shareholders are financed through the proceeds of liquidated corporate assets or liquidated or spun off corporate divisions or subsidiaries (de-conglomeration).[1952] Besides the distribution of existing cash reserves, in some cases corporations have to borrow the necessary financial means to satisfy the demands of their shareholders.[1953] Finally, some of the targeted firms rely on their future cash flows to finance the payouts.[1954] Only the majority of the ex-ante cash-rich firms had to use existing cash to finance payouts. The rest of them combined it with other sources, comparable to the remainder of the targeted firms.[1955]

6) Concerns confronting financial activism

The impact of active shareholders on the corporate financial structure of targeted corporations has been repeatedly criticized. Concerns relate particularly to the extraction of capital from the corporation to its shareholders and its opportunistic implementation to the detriment of the targeted corporation or by leaving out fellow shareholders. This may be realized through the excessive extraction of money from the corporation far beyond the excess cash as well as by realizing the distribution solely to the advantage of the active shareholders while skipping their fellow shareholders. Critique has also evolved regarding increased corporate leveraging. Excessive leveraging is alleged to

1950 Bratton, *Hedge Funds and Corporate Governance Targets: Long-Term Results* 16, www.ssrn.com/abstract=1677517 (2010); Bratton, 95 GEO. L.J. 1375, 1416 (2007).

1951 Bratton, *Hedge Funds and Goverance Targets: Long-Term Results* 16, www.ssrn.com/abstract=1677517 (2010); Bratton, 95 GEO. L.J. 1375, 1415 et seq. (2007).

1952 Bratton, *Hedge Funds and Goverance Targets: Long-Term Results* 16 et seq., www.ssrn.com/abstract=1677517 (2010): "cash sales preceded and roughtly matched … 44 percent of the subsample"; Thompson, *The Limits of Hedge Fund Activism* 17, http://escholarship.org/uc/item/5jq9d71m (2006).

1953 Bratton, *Hedge Funds and Goverance Targets: Long-Term Results*, 17 et seq., www.ssrn.com/abstract=1677517 (2010): "17 percent of the payout firms"; Bratton, 95 GEO. L.J. 1375, 1380 (2006): Borrowing was the mode of financing used only in a minority of cases (19,5 percent) analyzed by Bratton.

1954 Bratton, *Hedge Funds and Goverance Targets: Long-Term Results*, 17, www.ssrn.com/abstract=1677517 (2010): "Six payors relied entirely on cash flows from operations."

1955 Bratton, 95 GEO. L.J. 1375, 1416 et seq. (2007).

force administrations to forego promising projects[1956] and to leave targeted corporations with unsustainable capital structures.[1957] Finally, active shareholders are generally, but most specifically in the context of financial activism, confronted with the allegation that they are short-term orientated and therefore act most likely to the detriment of the corporation and its long-term orientated shareholders.[1958]

7) Introducing hypothesis

Active shareholders pursing financial activism are frequently accused of aiming to profit from short-term gains at the expense of the long-term value of the targeted corporation or financially profiting to the detriment of the remainder of shareholders. Corporate mechanisms to pursue these deviating interests via financial activism allegedly comprise distributions via share repurchases and dividend payments, whose amounts can be increased through substantial corporate leveraging. From the prior Parts of the analysis, it can be assumed that these accusations tend to ignore the benefits of financial activism and shareholder activism in general.

The results of the preceding analysis of the shareholder franchise and transaction activism permit the assumption that the number of special means provided to shareholders under U.S. law will, in the context of financial activism, be more limited than those under German law. Therefore, and in regards to the shareholder structure, active shareholders of U.S. corporations are expected to face stronger challenges in carrying out financial activism that requires the use of informal means and stronger general efforts than under German law.

The criticism shareholders pursuing financial activism are primarily confronted with differs from the one applying to shareholders who pursue corporate governance related or transaction activism. An exception is the allegation of short-term behavior, which is still most characteristic of financial activism. Transferring the results from the prior parts of the analysis, the criticism needs to be treated with caution. Besides their expected benefits, factual and legal limitations are expected to restrict shareholder opportunism. More effective legal limitations to restrict potentially opportunistic shareholder behavior can be expected under U.S. law. An exception may, however, apply in regards to the possible overreaching of fellow shareholders. Here, the traditional German blockholder structure with its primary agency conflict amongst majority and minority shareholders permits one to assume that the fellow shareholders are more effectively protected from unequal treatment.

1956 *See* Bratton, 95 GEO. L.J. 1375, 1415 (2007).

1957 *See id.* at 1410.

1958 *See* Bratton, *Hedge Funds and Goverance Targets: Long-Term Results* 1, www.ssrn.com/abstract=1677517(2010).

II) Financial activism under U.S.-American law

1) Authority distribution regarding corporate financial decisions

The impact of active shareholders on the corporate decision-making process regarding financial measures, including the distribution of corporate capital via share repurchases or (increased) dividends and increased leveraging, is a common phenomenon in the United States.[1959] Delaware corporate law provides shareholders with generally few direct decision rights, mainly those concerning mergers and the amendment of the articles of incorporation, but not regarding financial decisions involving distributions and leveraging.[1960] Even when granted, the shareholder impact is usually restricted to approval rights and does not include the ability to mandate the initiation of the matter.[1961] Especially in the financial activism context the latter would be particularly useful for active shareholders. In contrast, corporate law does not evaluate specific business decisions like "scaling-down decisions"[1962] in the form of distributions as involving the kind of fundamental decision that calls for a shareholder veto right. Despite their potentially significant economic impact on the corporation, decisions about corporate distributions are considered part of ordinary business and delegated to management's sole privilege.[1963] Under U.S. corporate law, therefore, active shareholders have no special formal means to impact financial decisions. Rather, they have to use the general formal and informal means analyzed in the preceding Part in order to impact specific business decisions.

2) Capital distributions

One of the most common goals of active shareholders, especially hedge funds, is the distribution of corporate funds through share repurchases or dividends.[1964]

1959 Brav et al., *Hedge Fund Activism: A Review* 13, www.ssrn.com/abstract=1551953 (2010): in 17,4 percent of the sample activism targeted the firm's payout policy and capital structure; Brav et al., *The returns to hedge fund activism* 5, http://ssrn.com/abstract=1111778 (2008): who have determined an average of 12,7 percent of cases of shareholder activism targeting the capital structure; Greenwood & Schor, *Investor Activism and Takeovers* 23, www.ssrn.com/abstract=1003792 (2009): activism agendas of hedge funds related to the capital structure in about 10,08 percent.

1960 KRAAKMAN ET AL., THE ANATOMY OF CORPORATE LAW 73 et seq. (2009).

1961 The separation of ratification and initiation rights is a mechanism to reduce agency costs, as emphasized by Fama & Jensen, 26 J. L. & ECON. 301 (1983), *available at* www.ssrn.com/abstract=94034.

1962 Bebchuk, 118 HARV. L. REV. 833, 837 (2005).

1963 *Id.* at 847.

1964 Gantchev, *The Costs of Shareholder Activism: Evidence from a Sequential Decision Model* 18, http://www.cob.ohio-state.edu/fin/dice/seminars/Nickolay_Gantchev.pdf (2009); Gillan & Starks, *The Evolution of Shareholder Activism in the United States* 30, www.ssrn.com/abstract=959670 (2007), Klein & Zur, 64 J. FIN. 187, 197 (2009).

a) Active shareholders and share repurchases

The empirical work of *Klein/Zur* analyzing data about hedge funds and other entrepreneurial confrontational activists' campaigns from 2003 to 2005 shows a positive success rate of hedge funds' buyback demands as compared to their general success rate of 60 percent.[1965] However, evidence based on a wider data set puts this overly positive success rate in perspective.[1966]

i) Functional background of share repurchases

The demand of active shareholders to repurchase shares is a valuable means in the context of the shareholder value approach.[1967] Repurchases paying out *free* cash reduce agency costs.[1968] They avoid administrative overinvestments, investment expenditures beyond those required to maintain assets in place and support financing new investments with a positive net present value.[1969] Therefore, *temporarily* available corporate capital that cannot be invested for competitive profits should be re-distributed to the investors via share repurchases to allow them to invest it externally for more profit.[1970] Reduced resources under administrative control reduce not only its authority, but also most likely its compensation, its incentive to grow firms beyond their optimal size. Share repurchases make it more likely that administrations will become subject to monitoring through the capital market when in need of new capital.[1971] Without distributions like repurchases, internal financing prevents such external monitoring, including the risk of unavailability or higher prices for new capital,[1972] which makes the former preferable to the administration. Consequently, it is desirable that administrations with (temporarily available) substantial free cash repurchase stock[1973] to distribute free cash otherwise invested below capital costs or even wasted.[1974] Furthermore, share repurchases may

1965 Klein & Zur, 64 J. Fin. 187, 211 (2009): 100 percent as compared to 60 percent in general.

1966 Boyson & Mooradian, *Hedge funds as shareholder activists from 1994 – 2005* 9, www.ssrn.com/abstract=992739 (2007): based on data considering a time frame from 1994 to 2005, general capital structure changes are successful in about 63 percent of the scenarios; Brav et al., *Hedge Fund Activism: A Review* 58, Table 1, www.ssrn.com/abstract=1551953 (2010): based on data from 2001 to 2007, capital structure related demands are in average (partially) successful in about 52 percent; Brav et al., *Hedge Fund Activism, Corporate Governance, and Firm Performance* 42, www.ssrn.com/abstract=948907 (2008): based on data from 2001 to 2006, hedge funds (partially) successful facilitate capital structure amendments, including share repurchases, in about 64 percent of the scenarios.

1967 Hirsch, Der Erwerb eigener Aktien nach dem KonTraG, 2004, 51.

1968 Jain, 59 J. Econ. Bus. 406, 407 (2007); Jensen, 76 Amer. Econ. Rev. 323, 323 (1986), *available at* http://ssrn.com/abstract=99580.

1969 Richardson, 11 Rev. Acc. Stud. 159, 160 (2006).

1970 Arnold, ZCG 2008, 221 (223); Merkt/Göthel, US-amerikanisches Gesellschaftsrecht, 2006, 551; Mülbert, ZGR 1997, 129 (132).

1971 Jensen, 76 Amer. Econ. Rev. 323, 323 (1986).

1972 Rozeff, 5 J. Fin. Research 249, 250 – 251 (1982).

1973 Excessive distributions result in substantial increase of costs for capital, see *id.* at 250-251.

1974 Jensen, 76 Amer. Econ. Rev. 323, 324 (1986).

serve price management purposes.[1975] By increasing the demand while the number of offered shares remains stable, the stock price rises.[1976] Share repurchases are also used for signaling purposes in order to express administration's confidence that the stock price is undervalued.[1977] From a management perspective, this opportunity is particularly significant. In the United States, the share price is an index showing whether management is sufficiently considering shareholder interests, especially the interest to maximize the share price.[1978] The latter two purposes are, however, not uncontroversial; to maintain investor's confidence demands compensation via sufficient disclosure.[1979] Moreover, share repurchases impact the shareholder structure, reducing the freefloat by repurchasing from odd-lot shareholders and therefore the communication costs.[1980]

The incentives for shareholders to control the administration by impacting the corporate financial structure via the facilitation of share repurchases are not only based on the usually positive impact on the shareholder value of the targeted corporation. Rather, shareholders participating in the repurchase will also experience an *immediate* return on their investment,[1981] as the repurchase price is usually above market level.[1982]

ii) Examples

(1) KMG

Hedge funds have pressured companies into large share repurchases on several occasions. One of the more recent cases involves the energy company *Kerr-McGee* (***"KMG"***). It underperformed its peers and had ample opportunity for financial and strategic restructuring. Icahn spearheaded a group of investors, including hedge fund Jana holding 7.6 percent of KMG's outstanding shares. They had unsuccessfully criticized KMG for destroying shareholder value with a high-risk exploration program instead of selling some of its oil and natural gas production.[1983] Icahn finally sent signs of a potential proxy battle[1984] by nominating Barry Rosenstein and himself to take the maximum number of board seats up at the shareholder vote on May 10, 2005. On April 14, 2005, KMG's

1975 Clark, Corporate Law 628 et seq. (1986).

1976 Last, Der Erwerb eigener Aktien als Rückkaufinstrument, 2006, 17.

1977 *Id.* at 18.

1978 Hirsch, Der Erwerb eigener Aktien nach dem KonTraG, 2004, 51; Oechsler, in: MüKo AktG, 2008, § 71 mn.6.

1979 Last, Der Erwerb eigener Aktien als Rückkaufinstrument, 2006, 18.

1980 Bezzenberger, Erwerb eigener Aktien durch die AG, 2002, mn.81; Posner, AG 1994, 312 (316).

1981 Thompson, *The Limits of Hedge Fund Activism* 16, http://escholarship.org/uc/item/5jq9d71m (2006).

1982 Merkt/Göthel, US-amerikanisches Gesellschaftsrecht, 2006, mn.551.

1983 *Icahn Criticizes Kerr-McGee's Exploration Programm*, March 11, 2005, The New York Times, http://query.nytimes.com/gst/fullpage.html?res=9B03E1DF143CF932A25750C0A9639C8B63; Greg Levine, *Kerr-McGee Agrees To Buy Stock, Drop Suit—If Icahn Ceases Proxy Talk*, Apr. 14, 2005, Forbes.com, http://www.forbes.com/2005/04/14/0414autofacescan06.html.

1984 Greg Levine, *Kerr-McGee Agrees To Buy Stock, Drop Suit—If Icahn Ceases Proxy Talk*, Apr. 14, 2005, Forbes.com, http://www.forbes.com/2005/04/14/0414autofacescan06.html.

management settled with Icahn, announcing a $4 billion buyback at a minimum premium of 15 percent over the current stock price.[1985] Furthermore, KMG agreed to divest oil and gas properties valued at $2 to $2.5 billion and to use the proceeds to reduce its debt.[1986] Finally, KMG reduced its dividend.[1987] In return, Icahn and Jana immediately ceased their proxy-solicitation activities by withdrawing their board nominees before the upcoming annual shareholder meeting.[1988] As a consequence, KMG was downgraded by the rating agencies.[1989] Later, it agreed to be acquired by Anadarko Petroleum for $70.50 per share, as compared to the $30 per share at which it had been traded before Icahn's engagement.[1990]

(2) Mirant

Another target of active shareholders is *Mirant*. In 2006, it was confronted with a demand for a substantial buyback program. Hedge fund Pirate Capital LLC (***"Pirate Capital"***) and three other funds had successfully convinced Mirant's management to withdraw its almost $8 billion unsolicited bid for NRG Energy Inc. They had successfully demanded the sale of the corporation and threatened a proxy contest supported by several other institutional investors. Just a week later, Jana sent a letter to the Chairman and CEO of Mirant requesting a $4.7 billion repurchase. The buyback proposal concerned about 60 percent of Mirant's outstanding shares and was expressed through a Schedule 13D filing.[1991] The founder of Pirate Capital included a detailed financial analysis in his filing as well as recommendations of how to maximize long-term stockholder value. He suggested the generation of $4.7 million by using the cash available on the balance sheet as well as the proceeds from the recapitalization plan for the company's Philippine assets.

1985 City Group, *Hedge Funds at the Gate*, Sept. 22, 2005, 12, 21, http://docs.google.com/viewer?a=v&q=cache:ZMvebuWeB5IJ:bschool.washington.edu/cfoforum/CitiGroup%27s%2520hedge-funds-at-the-gate.pdf+hedge+funds+at+the+gate&hl=en&pid=bl&srcid=ADGEESjUCurL-S4nsym_VRUp3aMGBUPQL3CyAM904quc6QSqkYUdenR2BrOYcIYgf2DsQReHMQ5LY-oYwHc0hU4qTWeboUFIRvpYqY7vduiFz2vQqCKT6zhFvQchUpd9gP9INrywVOQo38&sig=AHI-EtbSeoLOM6SaDX0f-y1WIcIxtrhbZAA.

1986 *Kerr-McGee buys back $4 billion shares*, Apr. 14, 2005, msnbc, http://www.msnbc.msn.com/id/7501342.

1987 *Id.*; Stephen Taub, *Big Buyback Ends Kerr-McGee Proxy Fight*, Apr. 15, 2005, cfo.com, http://www.cfo.com/article.cfm/3881047?f=related.

1988 Stephen Taub, *Big Buyback Ends Kerr-McGee Proxy Fight*, Apr. 15, 2005, cfo.com, http://www.cfo.com/article.cfm/3881047?f=related.

1989 *Id.*

1990 Samuel Brothwell & Angela Ho, *Back to the future: The new corporate raiders*, Sept. 2006, Public Utilities Fortnightly, 24, http://www.fortnightly.com/pubs/09012006_BusinessMoney.pdf; Greg Levine, *Kerr-McGee Agrees To Buy Stock, Drop Suit—If Icahn Ceases Proxy Talk*, Apr. 14, 2005, Forbes.com, http://www.forbes.com/2005/04/14/0414autofacescan06.html.

1991 Schedule 13D of Pirate Capital LLC, Exhibit E, June 20, 2006, http://209.85.135.132/search?q=-cache:RYenLFCd5EsJ:shareholder.api.edgar-online.com/efx_dll/edgarpro.dll%3FFetch-FilingRTF1%3Fsessionid%3DM9NUHiDyflwR6V5%26ID%3D4492525%26PageBreak-StyleID%3D2+edgar+mirant+nrg&cd=14&hl=de&ct=clnk&gl=de&client=firefox-a: regarding the improvement of shareholder value.

In addition, he proposed borrowing and the use of the proceeds of the future sale of the remaining Philippine equity and the Caribbean assets. The financial rationale of the suggested sales of the Philippine equity and the Caribbean assets was to eliminate volatile emerging market exposure and to transform the company into a pure U.S. player appealing to U.S. investors.[1992] Based on the prior pressure from the funds opposed the bid for NRG Energy, Mirant announced it planned to repurchase 43 million shares via a Dutch tender worth around $1.25 billion. It was to be funded by the sale of its Caribbean and Philippine power assets.[1993] Mirant undertook two stock buybacks for a total of $1.35 billion, one in July and one in September 2006. The buybacks followed divestitures. In December 2006, the utility sold its assets in the Philippines for $3.4 billion to Tokyo Electric Power. In January 2007, it agreed to sell six natural gas-fired plants for $1.41 billion to LS Power Group,[1994] and in August 2007 sold its Caribbean assets for $1.08 billion to Japan's Marubeni.[1995]

iii) Means and limitations

U.S.-American corporate law has a stronger tendency to protect shareholders than creditors.[1996] Accordingly, share repurchases are generally admitted under U.S. corporate law, section 160,[1997] and they have no caps. The administration determines the timing, procedure, and amount of shares to be repurchased; it is protected by the business judgment rule. Its discretion and the singular character of share repurchases allow the administration to take into account the current corporate liquidity surplus before deciding whether to retain capital or to distribute it.[1998] Shareholder participation is not granted in the corporate decision-making process about share repurchases. Due to the lack of shareholder impact, active shareholders need to apply general formal (especially the threat of or an actual proxy fight) and informal means (primarily personal conversations and means to circumvent the proxy fight regime) to impact management decisions. This can be compared to transaction activism targeting management transactions. Therefore, if financial activism is applied post-transaction activism, the continuing impact of the recently applied means or just the reference to them may be sufficient to bring about the intended change in the financial structure. The specific legal limitations in the financial context relevant to the administration are therefore simultaneously relevant limitations for the active shareholders impacting the administrative decision-making process.

1992 Emma Trincal, *Mirant Up on Activist Agitation*, June 21, 2006, TheStreet.com, http://www.thestreet.com/story/10293003/1/mirant-up-on-activist-agitation.html.

1993 Samuel Brothwell & Angela Ho, *Back to the future: The new corporate raiders*, Sept. 2006, Public Utilities Fortnightly, 24, 26, http://www.fortnightly.com/pubs/09012006_Business-Money.pdf.

1994 Heidi Moore, *Mirant picks adviser for potential sale*, Apr. 10, 2007, Financial News Online, http://www.efinancialnews.com/assetmanagement/pensionfunds/content/2347527893.

1995 *Japanese Co. buys Mirant's Caribbean assets*, June 1, 2007, Thefreelibrary, http://www.thefreelibrary.com/Japanese+Co.+buys+Mirant%27s+Caribbean+assets.(ARUBA)-a0164112068.

1996 Posner, AG 1994, 312 (312).

1997 Any section without specification in this subpart two of Part three refers to the DGCL.

1998 Leven/Helm, BHV-News & Aktienkultur, 3/1996, 5 et seq.

Share repurchases need to be financed out of the corporate *surplus*, which means repurchases are prohibited when the capital is impaired or the repurchase would cause impairment, § 160 (a) (1).[1999] Recent net profits alone are not sufficient for share repurchases.[2000] This provision is intended to prevent boards from draining corporate assets to the detriment of creditors and the long-term health of the corporation.[2001] However, the effectiveness of the surplus criteria should be kept in perspective because the board of directors determines the stated capital. The stated capital represents the basis of the surplus criteria and needs, at a minimum, to equal the sum of the face amounts of the shares issued, §§ 154, 244. Furthermore, the board has broad discretion in evaluating the corporate assets to determine the corporate surplus and is not bound to the book value or another formal procedure.[2002] Courts usually deny review.[2003] The surplus criterion has therefore lost its practical significance.[2004]

Furthermore, share repurchases may be appealed under the fraudulent transfer statute in the Delaware Uniform Fraudulent Transfer Act (***"UFTA"***) or the federal Bankruptcy Code (***"B.C."***). The latter is, however, restricted to transfers two years prior to filing the petition and is therefore less important in insolvency constellations.[2005] A fraudulent transfer requires that the repurchasing corporation transferred money or assets without obtaining a reasonable equivalent. The repurchase of one's own shares represents such a scenario.[2006] In addition, the corporation needs to be insolvent, § 5 UFTA. Alternatively, it needs to have incurred debt beyond its ability to pay as such debt matures or be engaged in a business for which the remaining assets are unreasonably small, §§ 4(a)(2)(ii),(i) UFTA. Then the intent to hinder, to delay, or to defraud any creditor will be implied (constructive fraud).[2007] Creditors and the bankruptcy trustee, § 544(b)(1) B.C., can attack the transfer within four years, § 9(b) UFTA. As a consequence, the trustee may recover the property transferred or its value for the benefit of the estate, § 550(a) B.C.

The board's statutory liability, §§ 174, 172, based on its impact on the surplus calculation is rather limited. Due to the extensive entrepreneurial discretion of the board of directors and the applicability of § 102(b)(7)[2008] in the distribution context, directors may only be held liable for the violation of their duty of loyalty.[2009] Even though it is unsettled when directors have to grant creditors' interests priority over the usually pre-

1999 Cox & Hazen, Corporations 576 (2003).

2000 Westlaw, Corporate Dividends and Stock Repurchases, § 6.8, n.2.

2001 Klang v. Smith's Food & Drug Ctrs., Inc., 702 A.2d 150, 154 (Del. 1997).

2002 Randall v. Bailey, 23 N.Y.S.2d 173, 184 (1940).

2003 Morris v. Standard Gas & Elec. Co., 63 A.2d 577, 583 (Del. Ch. 1949).

2004 Engert, in: Lutter, ZGR special issue 17, 2006, 743 (759); Kumpan, AG 2007, 461 (464).

2005 Engert, in: Lutter, ZGR special issue 17, 2006, 743 (770).

2006 In re Roco Corp., 701 F.2d 978, 982 et seq. (1st Cir. 1983): considering the economic position of the repurchasing corporation when determining whether the corporation has obtained a reasonably equivalent value; Vadnais Lumber Supply, Inc. v. Byrne, 100 BR. 127, 136 (Bankr. D. Mass. 1989); Engert, in: Lutter, ZGR special issue 17, 2006, 743 (772).

2007 Kumpan, AG 2007, 461 (464).

2008 Prod. Res. Group, L.L.C. v. NCT Group, Inc., 863 A2.772, 793 et seq. (Del. Ch. 2004)

2009 Engert, in: Lutter, ZGR special issue 17, 2006, 743 (782 et seq.).

vailing shareholder interests, such constellations are rather irrelevant with regards to the targeted repurchase constellations.

Only under limited circumstances do the administration's common law duties permit it to deal selectively with its stockholders.[2010] The details are determined by the rational business purpose test, according to which the administration has to prove that it acted to compensate an existing danger and therefore pursued a proper business purpose with the repurchase program instead of solely securing its own position.[2011] In the context of share repurchases, the administrative fiduciary obligations efficiently protect the minority shareholders.[2012] As minority shareholders, active shareholders are not likely to be held liable under the fiduciary duty regime.

In addition, repurchases of registered common shares, § 12 SEA, oblige the issuer to disclose them, which grants shareholders the opportunity to inform themselves comprehensively about them, Rule 703 Regulation S-K and S-B. The disclosure has to take place in the annual reports according to Form 10-K – pt. II Item 5 (c)[2013] as well as in the quarterly financial reports according to Form 10-Q – pt. II Item 2 (c)[2014].[2015] Furthermore, the knowledge of an initiated repurchase program is insider knowledge, which may result in liability pursuant to Rule 10b-5 SEA if abused.[2016] Rule 10b-18 SEA provides a safe harbor preventing liability for manipulation under § 9(a)(2) SEA as well as Rule 10b-5 SEA if there is voluntary compliance with certain manner, timing, price, and volume conditions.

b) Active shareholders and dividends

The initiation of additional regular or special dividend payments is another technique active shareholders use to have corporate capital distributed to the shareholders. Active hedge funds, in contrast to other entrepreneurial investors, aim to augment dividend payments and have according to *Klein & Zur (2009)* proven to be very successful in achieving this goal.[2017] According to their analysis, the dividend of targeted corporations rose by an average of 11.2 cents per share in the year following the initial 13D filing. It

2010 Frantz Mfg. Co. v. EAC Indus., 501 A.2d 401, 408 (Del. 1985).

2011 Chef v. Mathes, 199 A.2d 548, 554 (Del. 1964); Kaplan v. Goldsamt, 380 A.2d 556, 568 (Del. Ch. 1977): granting wide discretion to directors: as long as they appear to act in good faith, with honest motives, for honest ends, the exercise of discretion will not be interfered by the courts, the presumption of sound business judgement reposed in a Board of Directors will not be disturbed if any rational business purpose can be attributed to its decision.

2012 Kraakman et al., The Anatomy of Corporate Law 150 (2004).

2013 Form 10-K, 9, http://www.sec.gov/about/forms/form10-k.pdf.

2014 Form 10-Q, 6 http://www.sec.gov/about/forms/form10-q.pdf.

2015 Purchases of Certain Equity Securities by the Issuer and Others, Securities Act Release No. 8335; Exchange Act Release No. 48,766, Investment Company Act Release No. 26,252 (Nov. 10, 2003), http://www.sec.gov/rules/final/33-8335.htm#P241_86234; *see* Merkt/Göthel, US-amerikanisches Gesellschaftsrecht, 2006, mn.550.

2016 Oechsler, in: MüKo AktG, 2008, § 71 mn.295.

2017 Klein & Zur, 64 J. Fin. 187, 197 (Panel E), 212 (Table IV) (2009): suggesting a success rate of 100 percent for the demands of hedge funds to pay a dividend.

almost doubled in volume compared to the period prior to intervention and represents a change significantly higher than in the control sample. Common stock dividend initiations for the subsequent year were even higher. In contrast, the rise of dividends in corporations targeted by other entrepreneurial activists proved to be only insignificantly higher than the one in the control sample.[2018] In parallel to share repurchases, evidence based on a wider data set puts this this overly positive success rate in perspective.[2019]

i) Functional background of dividends

Dividends represent the traditional vehicle for distributing profits to shareholders.[2020] The corporation shares those profits with the shareholders it is unable to reinvest for a proper return. Shareholder value considerations justify a shareholder demand for (an increase in) the dividend payment if the corporation does not follow these considerations.[2021] The distribution via dividends, similar to share repurchases, reduces agency costs caused by the administration investing excess cash not necessarily efficiently. Dividend payments oblige administrations wishing to finance new ventures to access the capital market. This requires proof of prior corporate performance and future plans. The results affect feasibility and terms.[2022] Regular dividend payments have a more disciplining effect in contrast to share repurchases, as the latter leave the administration with discretion regarding the future payout policy.[2023] While the latter may be exercised sporadically depending on the performance of the corporations, the former oblige the administration to distribute capital continuously for signaling reasons. Investors distrusting the financial information provided by companies prefer corporations that practice (regular and gradually increasing[2024]) dividend payments. Firms that exaggerated their reported income would not be able to follow an indefinitely increasing payout policy.[2025] This behavior appears rational as long as it is based on the imperfections in the auditing process, which, even though the costly SOA regime reduced the incidence of fraud, does not always assure that insider fraud is discovered and reported.[2026] As a consequence,

2018 Klein & Zur, 64 J. FIN. 187, 224 (2009).

2019 Boyson & Mooradian, *Hedge funds as shareholder activists from 1994 – 2005* 9, www.ssrn.com/abstract=992739 (2007): based on data considering a time frame from 1994 to 2005, attempts forcing the firm to pay dividends were successful in about 33 percent of the scenarios; Brav et al., *Hedge Fund Activism: A Review* 58, Table 1, www.ssrn.com/abstract=1551953 (2010): based on data from 2001 to 2007, capital structure related demands are in average (partially) successful in about 52 percent; Brav et al., *Hedge Fund Activism, Corporate Governance, and Firm Performance* 42, www.ssrn.com/abstract=948907 (2008): based on data from 2001 to 2006, hedge funds (partially) successful(ly) facilitate capital structure amendments in about 64 percent of the scenarios.

2020 Bratton, 93 GEO. L.J. 845, 846 (2005), *available at* http://ssrn.com/abstract=535462, 3.

2021 Merkt/Göthel, US-amerikanisches Gesellschaftsrecht, 2006, mn.551.

2022 CLARK, CORPORATE LAW 599 (1986).

2023 Bratton, 93 GEO. L.J. 845, 847 (2005), *available at* http://ssrn.com/abstract=535462, 3.

2024 Lintner, 46 AM. ECON. REV. 97, 99 (1956).

2025 Pape, BB 1998, 1783 (1783).

2026 CLARK, CORPORATE LAW 598 (1986); Donna Nabel, *Upfront: Fraud after Sarbanes-Oxley*, Business Finance Magazine, Feb. 1, 2007, http://businessfinancemag.com/article/upfront-fraud-after-the lowering of the dividend would signal to the capital market a strongly negative development of the corporate profit situation.[2027] Administrations will therefore try to avoid a corresponding signal, as dividend cuts usually result in significantly decreased stock prices. This represents a consistent reaction as the optimal dividend level represents a control mechanism.[2028] Furthermore, a high dividend level helps align managers' interests. It forces the administration to continuously increase annual payments and thus to return more often to the capital markets to finance new ventures instead of being able to finance the dividends from retained earnings. Furthermore, it increases the risk of corporate failure by increasing the debt-equity ratio. Both force the administration to concentrate on profitable investments that provide the basis for these distributions.[2029] Another difference of the regular dividend payment in comparison to repurchases lies in the sharing strategy. Paid out pro rata,[2030] their discriminative potential is relatively low. Dividends are more transparent while share repurchases may escape the periodic ex post disclosure regime[2031]. Manipulations are therefore restricted to the withholding of dividends to squeeze out minority shareholders and to excessive dividends depriving the corporation of its financial basis.

Special dividends, in contrast, are closer to share repurchases. They allow the distribution of temporarily available corporate capital without raising expectations by signaling that the future dividend level will rise correspondingly. By withdrawing excessive cash, they reduce also the risk of overinvestments while increasing the likelihood that the administration will have to access the financial market and be subject to its external monitoring. Consequently, special dividends may reduce agency costs and raise shareholder value.

---

sarbanes-oxley-0201: "[T]he incidence of fraud in the nation's businesses has notably declined. Yet fraud hasn't gone away[.]"; Ribstein, 28 J. Corp. L. 1 (2002), *available at* http://ssrn.com/abstract=332681, 1 et seq., 34 et seq., abstract: "[N]ew regulation in general, and Sarbanes-Oxley in particular, is unlikely to do a better job than markets."; Sewe, *The Sarbanes Oxley Act and its Impacts on Corporate Finance and Corporate Governance Behavior*, 2012, http://com/abstract=21111505, 4: The negative effects [of the SOA] include reduction in stock value of firms, increase in audit fees; inflexible rules, coupled with managerial fear from greater opportunities for prosecution and stiffer penalties negatively affecting firms' profitability; high monitoring costs and fewer benefits from outside monitoring.

2027 Pape, BB 1998, 1783 (1783); Trost, Determinanten der Ausschüttungspolitik, 2009, 35 et seq.

2028 Jensen, 76 Am. Econ. Rev. 323, 324 (1986).

2029 Pape, BB 1998, 1783 (1783); Posner, Economic Analysis of Law 442 (2007).

2030 Gordon v. Elliman, 306 N.Y. 456, 456 (N.Y. 1954): The decision targets the equality issue rather indirectly via discussion on the procedural realization of the dividend payment to all shareholders. Accordingly, the court denies a shareholder's individual cause of action to recover dividends that have not been declared. "All he can do is to sue in equity to cause the court to perform a corporate function which the directors would have executed except for their bad faith.; Bratton, 93 Geo. L.J. 845, 847 (2005), *available at* http://ssrn.com/abstract=535462, 3.

2031 Purchases of Certain Equity Securities by the Issuer and Others, Securities Act Release No. 8335, Exchange Act Release 48,766, Investment Company Act Release No. 26,252 (Nov. 10, 2003), http://www.sec.gov/rules/final/33-8335.htm *at IV: introduced in 2004, demanding *ex post* quarterly disclosures of the repurchases shares, the average price paid, the number of the purchases, the maximum number of shares remaining under the programm, and so on.

ii) Example

An example of active shareholders initiating a distribution of corporate capital in the form of dividends to the shareholders are the activities of the hedge fund Barington Capital Group (***"Barington"***) as shareholder of the U.S. shoe retailer Steve Madden, Ltd. (***"Steve Madden"***). In July 2004, Barington, which held a 7.7 percent stake in Steve Madden, strongly suggested that it investigate opportunities to be acquired.[2032] Later that month, Barington sent a strongly worded letter to the independent directors of Steve Madden. It stated concerns about the women's retail business and demanded several amendments, amongst them the hiring of a more seasoned CEO, the removal of conflicts of interest from the board, and the distribution of excess cash in the form of dividends or share repurchases.[2033] In February 2005, Barington and Steve Madden reached an agreement. To avoid a proxy fight, Steve Madden agreed to meet with Barington on a regular basis. The CEO was not removed, but an additional independent director with knowledge of the retail sector was added to the board. Furthermore, the board of Steve Madden agreed to spend a substantial amount for the payment of dividends in 2005.[2034]

iii) Means and limitations

Under Delaware corporate law, the distribution of corporate capital, including dividends, is at the sole discretion of the board of directors. Shareholders, in contrast, are generally prohibited from forcing dividend payments.[2035] They have generally no right to initiate a decision about a dividend, even if in prior years a dividend has been distributed regularly.[2036] Even precatory shareholder proposals demanding specific dividend amounts, in stock or cash, are excludable by the administration, Rule 14a-8(i)(13) SEA.[2037] Only in very rare cases does an exception apply if the business situation does not require the retaining of capital and a dividend is denied for the board's own profit.[2038] The inadequate compensation of insiders may be evidence of such improper motives.[2039] A right to demand dividends may also result from an interpretation of the articles of incorporation.[2040] Beyond these, however, shareholders can only challenge inadequate dividends. The board of directors decides whether a dividend is going to be distributed or not,

2032 Kahan & Rock, 155 U. Pa. L. Rev. 1021, 1030 (2007).

2033 Clifford, *Are Hedge Funds Evil*, Business Lexington, http://www.bizlex.com/Articles-c-2008-11-25-82999.113117_Are_Hedge_Funds_Evil.html (2008).

2034 *Id.*; Kahan & Rock, 155 U. Pa. L. Rev. 1021, 1031 (2007).

2035 Bebchuk, 118 Harv. L. Rev. 833, 847 (2005): Corporate law sees decisions about distributions not as the kind of fundamental change that calls for shareholder power, but rather as ordinary conduct of business delegated to management.

2036 Berwald v. Mission Dev. Co., 185 N.W. 480, 482 et seq. (Del. 1962).

2037 Bloomenthal, Securities Law Handbook, Vol. 1, § 18.50 (2009-2010).

2038 Keough v. St. Paul Milk Co., 285 N.W. 809, 823 (Minn. 1939); Dodge v. Ford Motor Co., 170 N.W. 668, 682 (Mich. 1919); Clark, Corporate Law 602 (1986); Cox & Hazen, Corporations § 20.07, 552 (2003).

2039 Murphy v. Country House, Inc., 349 N.W.2d 289, 293 (Minn. Ct. App. 1984).

2040 Crocker v. Waltham Watch Co., 53 N.E.2d 230, 234 et seq. (Mass. 1944).

protected by the business judgment rule shielding it from judicial control,[2041] as long as the decision can be attributed to any rational business purpose and unless the plaintiff is able to demonstrate that the dividend payments resulted from improper motives and amounted to waste.[2042] Also in the dividend context, active shareholders are limited to the use of general formal and informal means to convince the administration to facilitate special or general dividends within applicable legal limits.

The board's discretion in determining the dividend's size is, however, almost unlimited. As Delaware follows a system of impairment of capital status, dividends may not only be paid from capital *surplus*,[2043] as defined in § 154, but also from earned surplus, paid-in surplus, revaluation surplus, and reduction surplus,[2044] § 170 (a)(1), (2). The provision's intention is to prevent boards from draining corporate assets not only to the detriment of corporate creditors, but also for the long-term health of the corporation and its shareholders.[2045] Its effectiveness is, however, also restricted by the mentioned circumstance that the board determines the share capital and the value of the corporate assets. Nimble dividends additionally liberate the surplus requirement. They are distributed from the net profits of the current and/or the preceding fiscal year if the corporation has no distributable surplus and the distribution therefore impairs the stated capital, § 170 (a)(2).[2046] This exception is justified on the grounds that the surplus limitations become at times unreasonably strict and arbitrary.[2047]

The previously mentioned effective fraudulent transfer regime under the UFTA and the B.C. also prevents excessive (special) dividend payments. Dividends especially are transferred corporate cash without reasonably equivalent value.[2048] Even bona fide shareowners need to return them upon the demand of the bankruptcy trustee.[2049]

Furthermore, dividends are granted proportionally. Once a corporate board has decided to grant a dividend, every shareholder has a claim for payment.[2050]

Holding directors and committee members liable for the unlawful payment of dividends, §§ 174, 172, could enforce dividend limitations. The board's wide discretion in determining the dividends' volume limits these provisions' practical relevance. In

2041 Clark, Corporate Law 594 (1986).

2042 Sinclair Oil Corp. v. Levien, 280 A.2d 717, 721, 722 (Del. 1971); Merkt/Göthel, US-amerikanisches Gesellschaftsrecht, 2006, mn.534.

2043 "Surplus" referring to the excess of total net worth (or "stockholders' equity") over the company's legal (or stated) capital, Clark, Corporate Law, 603 n.3 (1986); Cox & Hazen, Corporations § 20.07, 557 (2003).

2044 Cox & Hazen, Corporations § 20.07, 557 (2003); Merkt/Göthel, US-amerikanisches Gesellschaftsrecht, 2006, mn.538.

2045 Klang v. Smith's Food and Drug Ctrs., 702 A.2d 150, 154 (Del. 1997): referring to the purpose of § 160; Cox & Hazen, Corporations § 20.07, 558 (2003); Merkt/Göthel, US-amerikanisches Gesellschaftsrecht, 2006, mn.536.

2046 Merkt/Göthel, US-amerikanisches Gesellschaftsrecht, 2006, mn.540.

2047 Cox & Hazen, Corporations 563 et seq. (2003).

2048 Engert, in: Lutter, ZGR special issue 17, 2006, 743 (771 et seq.).

2049 *Id.* at 779.

2050 Gordon v. Elliman, 306 N.Y. 456 (N.Y. 1954): noting implicitely, by discussing a derivative action in favor of a dividend payment to the sueing shareholder and all other shareholders.

addition, the directors' common law duties apply to excessive dividend payments or if certain shareholders profit more from a transaction with the corporation. Instead of applying a regime distinguishing between permitted and impermissible distributions, the fiduciary duties of directors and controlling shareholders apply to such distributions.[2051] Public corporations characterized by a shareholder structure of freefloat and based on the *supra* mentioned reasons require only a judicial evaluation once conflicts of interest are involved.[2052] In this context, the corporation may not exempt directors from liability, § 102 (b)(7). The distributions at stake are, however, not subject to directorial conflicts of interest. Dividends violating statutory provisions are primarily seen as a wrong by the deciding directors. That is why the relevant statute imposes no liability on shareholders who receive dividends.[2053] Nor are active shareholders subject to fiduciary duties.

c) Active shareholders' distribution preferences

Both instruments, dividends and share repurchases, redistribute corporate capital to the shareholders. According to the *Modigliani & Miller* model of a perfect market, the dividend policy does not impact the value of the corporation.[2054] The preference of active shareholders for either one of the instruments in the actual market and their choice for corporations with the corresponding distribution policy (clientele effect[2055]) will depend on distinct factors.

One of these factors is the tax treatment of the two distributions. While dividends are treated as ordinary income, increased share value is not taxed and an increase in the share price in a subsequent sale is treated as capital gain.[2056] Legislative amendments in 2003, prolonged in 2005,[2057] have resulted in the equal taxation of dividends and capital gains income at a rate of fifteen percent[2058] for most taxpayers.[2059] However, capital losses may be deducted from capital gains without any limitation, while a deduction

---

2051 The Mann-Paller Found., Inc. v. Econometric Research, Inc., 644 F. Supp. 92, 96 (D.C. Cir. 1986); Engert, in: Lutter, ZGR special issue 17, 2006, 743 (763); Kumpan, AG 2007, 461 (463).

2052 Engert, in: Lutter, ZGR special issue 17, 2006, 743 (759, 782 et seq.).

2053 Cox & Hazen, Cox & Hazen on corporations, Vol. 3, § 20.25, 1256 (2003).

2054 Miller & Modigliani, 34 J. Bus. 411, 414 (1961).

2055 *Id.* at 431 et seq.: Investor portfolio decisions may be influenced by certain types of market imperfections, among them transaction costs and and different tax rates, as sufficiently important imperfections cause investors to tend to concentrate their portfolio holdings with securities that prove a means for reducing these costs. They termed the tendency of investors to gravitate towards certain types of dividend-paying securities, in an effort to reduce these costs, clientel effect.

2056 Clark, Coporate Law 595 et seq. (1986); Baker, Didivends and Dividend Policy 246 (2009).

2057 Jobs and Growth Tax Relief Reconciliation Act of 2003, H.R. 2, 108th Cong. (2003), prolonged by: The Tax Increase Prevention and Reconciliation Act of 2005, H.R. 4297, 109th Cong. (2006): until 2009.

2058 Jobs and Growth Tax Relief Reconcilitation Act of 2003, H.R. 2, 108th Cong., §§ 301 – 303 (2003), prolonged by: The Tax Increase Prevention and Reconciliation Act of 2005, H.R. 4297, 109th Cong. § 102 (2006): amended § 303 declaring the provisions applicable until December 31, 2010, instead until 2008.

2059 NATP, http://www.natptax.com/taxact2003.pdf (last visited Apr. 8, 2010).

from ordinary income is limited to $3000.[2060] From a tax perspective, shareholders prefer share repurchases to dividend distributions.[2061]

In practice, however, corporations prefer to share corporate profits through the payment of dividends.[2062] In regards to the described tax advantages related to share repurchases, this seems paradoxical and is described as *the dividend puzzle*[2063]. Different authors have tried to explain it. *Clark (1986)* argues several factors as responsible for a dividend policy. Amongst them are untaxed and lightly taxed investors, regulated preferences for high dividend-yielding, income-producing and other stocks, transaction cost considerations, signaling, and agency cost reduction.[2064] *Shleifer/Vishny (1986)* see it as a compensation scheme for larger shareholders, who profit from tax deductions on dividends.[2065] *Brennan/Thakor (1990)* argue that dividends are the preferable form of distribution for smaller amounts, from the perspective of the usually uninformed majority of individual investors. The non-proportional aspect of repurchases renders individual, less well-informed shareholders more vulnerable to expropriation by the better informed. The proportionality of dividend distributions ensures that all investors, independent of their level of information, profit equally. Furthermore, large shareholders are likely to use distributed capital for monitoring purposes. As large tax bracket group investors profit more from share repurchases, management prefers dividends to avoid increased control.[2066] Finally, *Allen et al. (1999)* argue that tax exemptions applying to institutions make dividend-paying corporations attractive to them. The distributed will allow them to monitor the corporation while managers take advantage of the detecting abilities of these institutions.[2067]

The determining question is whether active shareholders with minority positions and often as institutional investors have the same preference as their fellow shareholders or whether their interests conform to the practice of most administrations. For the longest time it had been in particular *tax reasons* that had been cited in favor of the dividend preference of larger institutional shareholders. They were able to profit from tax deductions on what were until 2003 heavier taxed dividends.[2068] Other non-tax related argu-

---

2060 26 U.S.C. §§ 1211, 1212 (Internal Revenue Code).

2061 Baker, Dividends and Dividend Policy 246 (2009); Merkt/Göthel, US-amerikanisches Gesellschaftsrecht, 2006, mn.564.

2062 Shleifer & Vishny, 94 J. Political Econ. 461, 465 (1986).

2063 Black, *The Dividend Puzzle*, J. Portfolio Mgmt., 8 *passim* (Special Issue 1996, originally 1976).

2064 Clark, Corporate Law 597–600 (1986).

2065 Shleifer & Vishny, 94 J. Political Econ. 461, 478 (1986): referring to the different effective tax rates applying to individual shareholders in comparison to large shareholders, which are often corporations, to which a reduction of received dividends of 70 percent applies, 26 U.S.C. § 243 (a)(1); opposing opinion: Black, *The Dividend Puzzle*, J. Portfolio Mgmt., at 9 (Special Issue 1996, originally 1976): doubting the impact of corporate investors and their different effective taxation in contrast to individual shareholders on the market.

2066 Brennan & Thakor, 45 J. Fin. 993, 1015 – 1016 (1990).

2067 Allen et al., *A Theory of Dividends Based on Tax Clienteles* 1-2, http://citeseerx.ist.psu.edu/viewdoc/download?doi=10.1.1.35.8843&rep=rep1&type=pdf (1999).

2068 *Id.* at 40; Redding, J. Fin. Intermediation 224, 225, 246 (1997); Shleifer & Vishny, 94 J. Pol. Econ. 461, 465 (1986).

ments supported this opinion. They included the prudent man rule[2069] according to the common law or ERISA, restrictions laid down in the articles of incorporations of institutional investors prohibiting investments in non-paying stock,[2070] and the obligation of some fiduciaries and non-profit organizations to spend income but not the principal.[2071] A newer, more convincing opinion[2072] alleges that institutional shareholders' prefer *share repurchases* in contrast to individual shareholders' preference for dividends. It contradicts the tax-based clientele hypothesis as well as the hypothesized preference of institutional investors for dividend payments for non-tax reasons.[2073] Supported by empirical evidence focusing on the different preferences of individual and institutional shareholders, the argument is based on the assumption that the share price is not the perfect aggregator of information on the firm's prospects and that collection of information by investors is costly.[2074] With fixed costs for the acquisition of information, only the large and institutional shareholders will have incentives to become better informed in regards to the repurchase. Small and individual shareholders will remain uninformed.[2075] Non-proportionate share repurchases, in contrast to proportionate dividends, allow large shareholders to exploit this information advantage. Therefore, larger, institutional shareholders prefer share repurchases to dividends, as they profit at the expense of the less-informed, individual shareholders vulnerable to expropriation.[2076]

Therefore, the interests of active shareholders conform to those of the majority of shareholders, as opposed to the practice of many administrations. As a consequence, the interests of shareholders and active shareholders are aligned and equally opposed to the potential administrative distribution policy. Accordingly, active shareholders are able to count on the necessary support of their fellow shareholders in, for instance, credibly threatening a proxy fight. This increases their incentives and lowers collective action issues.

2069 Hutchinson, 22 Vill. L. Rev. 15, 15 n.8 (1977): A prudent man rule requires a fiduciary – including an investment manager with discretion over the investment of fund assets – "to discharge his duties with the care, skill, prudence, and diligence under the circumstances then prevailing that a prudent man acting in a like capacity [stricter standard under ERISA: … and familiar with such matters] would use in the conduct of an enterprise of a like character and with like aims."

2070 Brav & Heaton, *Did ERISA's prudent man rule change the pricing of dividend omitting firms?* 4 -5, 16 – 17, http://ssrn.com/abstract=98568 (1998).

2071 *See* Feldstein & Green, 73 Amer. Econ. Rev. 17, 17 et seq. (1983).

2072 Brennan & Thakor, 45 J. Fin. 993, 1015–1016 (1990); Grinstein & Michaely, J. Fin. 1389, 1422 (2005); Jain, 59 J. Econ. Bus. 406, 407 (2007).

2073 Jain, 59 J. Econ. Bus. 406, 407 (2007).

2074 Brennan & Thakor, 45 J. Fin. 993, 994 (1990).

2075 *Id.* at 1015.

2076 *See* Baker, Dividends and Dividend Policy 246 (2009); Jain, 59 J. Econ. Bus. 406, 407 (2007).

3) Active shareholders and corporate leveraging

Only a small part, less than one-fifth, of the payouts achieved by active shareholders involves leveraging for the targeted corporation.[2077] Determinative for leveraging is not only the lack of alternative modes of funding, like assets that may be sold, available cash to make payouts, or sufficient future cash flows, but also the sum to be distributed to the shareholders, as the use of additional leveraging implies a larger sum. This applies, however, only to a minor extent.[2078] More relevant in regards to the distributed sums is the size of the concerned corporation.[2079]

Even though the actors of today's shareholder activism are sometimes still the same as the raiders in the 1980s, the resulting debt-equity ratios of current activism remain significantly below those of that era.[2080] Corporations targeted by shareholder activism involving leverage remain on average with a debt-equity ratio of 0.94, compared to the average ratio of non-borrowing target of 0.29.[2081] The targets of hedge funds experience the most significant increase in leverage, while the targets of other entrepreneurial activists do not experience discernible changes in debt-equity ratios.[2082] This result is consistent with the fact that hedge fund activists address free cash flow issues more frequently than other activists.[2083] The limited numbers and amounts of supportive leveraging may be explained through today's stricter lending standards. Furthermore, the bargaining activists are constrained by the fact that once they have rejected a voluntary administrative offer, they are usually in need of the support of longer-term orientated fellow shareholders. Finally, payout demands often are only a part of a broader strategy also applying the threat to purchase the firm that makes low leverage essential.[2084]

a) Functional background of leveraging

Increased leverage is another technique for active shareholders to discipline the administration to reduce the agency costs of the targeted corporation. Long-term debt reduces the cash flow available at the discretion of the administration[2085] and therefore the agency costs related to free cash flow, which management usually prefers to invest in undervalued projects or to waste before disgorging it. According to Jensen's *control hypothesis*, long-term debt restricts management's control of the future cash flow comparable to a

---

2077 Bratton, *Hedge Funds and Corporate Governance Targets: Long-Term Results* 17, www.ssrn.com/abstract=1677517 (2010); Bratton, 95 Geo. L.J. 1375, 1417 et seq. (2007).

2078 Bratton, 95 Geo. L.J. 1375, 1417 et seq. (2007).

2079 Bratton, *Hedge Funds and Corporate Governance Targets: Long-Term Results* 15 et seq., www.ssrn.com/abstract=1677517 (2010).

2080 Bratton, *Hedge Funds and Corporate Governance Targets: Long-Term Results* 17 et seq., www.ssrn.com/abstract=1677517 (2010).

2081 Bratton, 95 Geo. L.J. 1375, 1418 (2007).

2082 Klein & Zur, 64 J. Fin. 187, 224 (2009).

2083 *Id.*

2084 Bratton, *Hedge Funds and Corporate Governance Targets: Long-Term Results* 18, www.ssrn.com/abstract=1677517 (2010); Bratton, 95 Geo. L.J. 1375, 1418 (2007).

2085 Jensen, 76 Am. Econ. Rev. 323, 323 et seq. (1986); Eidenmüller, DStR 2007, 2116 (2117).

dividend payment, but it is preferable over sole distributions, as it represents a stronger promise for the future. Distributions not financed through debt may require that the administration access the capital market to have new corporate ventures financed. Even though more continuous than share repurchases, dividends can still be reduced in the future. A dividend cut will only result in a stock price decrease, a consistent reaction since the optimal dividend level represents a control mechanism.[2086] Debt, however, requires management to provide the corporate creditors regularly with the necessary payments, information, and maybe more (covenants). Otherwise, they are able to take the corporation into insolvency.[2087] The disciplining effect of debt prevents the administration from deviating too much from a profit-maximizing corporate policy,[2088] reducing inefficient or wasteful practices. However, increasing leverage implies increasing agency costs as well as bankruptcy costs.[2089] Strategies involving the increase of corporate leverage are therefore preferably applied to corporations with high cash flow[2090] and low growth prospects.[2091] Moreover, incurred debt may result in a positive leverage effect and reduce corporate capital costs. Especially during low interest rate phases, distributions financed through debt can substitute equity with cheaper debt with the consequence of increasing return on the (remaining) equity.[2092]

b) Example

The activities of Icahn, a 1980s veteran,[2093] as a shareholder of Mylan, are an example of financial activism resulting in a substantial amount of corporate debt for the target. Icahn, who held almost 10 percent of Mylan's outstanding shares,[2094] had initially prevented the acquisition of King via a stock-for-stock merger. It would have granted King a 61.8 percent premium over the pre-announcement market price. The threat of a proxy fight at the approaching shareholder meeting sufficed to prevent the transaction in February 2005.[2095]

2086 Jensen, 76 Am. Econ. Rev. 323, 324 (1986).

2087 *Id.*

2088 *Id.*

2089 *Id.*; Eidenmüller, DStR 2007, 2116 (2117).

2090 Klein & Zur, 64 J. Fin. 187, 189, 224 (2009); Zanoni, *Hedge Funds' Empty Voting in Mergers and Acquisitions: A Fiduciary Duties Perspective* 8 et seq., http://ssrn.com/abstract=1285589 (2009).

2091 Jensen, 76 Am. Econ. Rev. 323, 324 (1986).

2092 Posner, AG 1994, 312 (314).

2093 Bratton, *Hedge Funds and Corporate Governance Targets: Long-Term Results* 17, www.ssrn.com/abstract=1677517 (2010).

2094 Len Boselovic, *No Icahn and no fireworks as Mylan shareholders meet*, May 29, 2010, Pittsburgh Post-Gazette, http://www.post-gazette.com/pg/05302/597042-28.stm.

2095 Bratton, 95 Geo. L.J. 1375, 1377 (2007).

Icahn continued his activities. Dissatisfied by management missteps,[2096] including too few inside directors and excessive CEO compensation,[2097] he reiterated his offer to buy Mylan for $20 per share and announced his opposition slate of directors for Mylan's annual shareholder meeting in October 2005[2098]. The administrative response consisted of a bylaw amendment that included a preclusive advance notice requirement. Icahn responded with a second lawsuit. In June 2005, Mylan announced a $1.25 billion share repurchase in the form of a Dutch auction self-tender for up to 25 percent of the outstanding common stock,[2099] funded by a credit line of more than $1 billion[2100].[2101] In addition, Mylan doubled its dividend and revamped the board.[2102] Icahn took his pro rata share of the buyback fund, dropped the proxy fight and the offer to purchase Mylan, and sold the rest of his shares on the market. After Icahn had left Mylan, the stock was trading 32 percent higher than before his entry. But instead of having no debt, Mylan was left with an 87 percent debt-equity ratio.[2103]

c) Means and limitations

Again, shareholders under U.S. law do not have formal means to directly impact the capital structure of target firms, including the amendment of their debt-equity ratio. Active shareholders need to make use of the general (accountability) measures, including (threats of) proxy fights, litigation, or the threat to acquire the corporation, in order to impact a corresponding management decision.

The administration has almost no additional restrictions when deciding whether to incur corporate leverage to finance distributions. A limitation can result from the corporate leverage guidelines, whose violation, if not publicly amended prior to the decision, may result in liability according to Rule 10b-5 SEA.[2104] Beyond that provision, hardly any limitations apply. Only a leverage-financed distribution so critical that it may constitute constructive fraud under the UFTA or B.C. regime may be subject to a

2096 Pam Kasey, *Icahn's Stock Sale May Life Pressure on Mylan*, The State Journal, July 29, 2005, http://www.allbusiness.com/company-activities-management/company-structures/11508453-1.html.

2097 Len Boselovic, *No Icahn and no fireworks as Mylan shareholders meet*, May 29, 2005, Pittsburgh Post-Gazette, http://www.post-gazette.com/pg/05302/597042-28.stm.

2098 Bratton, 95 Geo. L.J. 1375, 1378 (2007); Pam Kasey, *Icahn's Stock Sale May Life Pressure on Mylan*, The State Journal, July 29, 2005, http://www.allbusiness.com/company-activities-management/company-structures/11508453-1.html.

2099 *Dutch Auctions*, Lawyer-Links, http://content.lawyerlinks.com/default.htm#http://content.lawyerlinks.com/sec/Deals/dutch_auctions.htm (last visited May 1, 2010).

2100 Summary Term Sheet, Mylan Laboratories Inc. Offer to Purchse for Cash, 2005, at 9, 18 et seq., http://www.sec.gov/Archives/edgar/data/69499/000095012305007416/y09827exv99wawlwa.htm#101.

2101 *Dutch Auctions,* Lawyer-Links, http://content.lawyerlinks.com/default.htm#http://content.lawyerlinks.com/sec/Deals/dutch_auctions.htm (last visited May 1, 2010).

2102 Len Boselovic, *No Icahn and no fireworks as Mylan shareholders meet*, May 29, 2005, Pittsburgh Post-Gazette, http://www.post-gazette.com/pg/05302/597042-28.stm.

2103 Bratton, 95 Geo. L.J. 1375, 1378 (2007).

2104 Weiner v. Quaker Oats Comp., 129 F.3d 310, 315 et seq. (3rd Cir. 1997).

rescission claim that may even hold the creditor liable.[2105] As a consequence, a debtor's obligation becomes invalid or subordinated.[2106] The efficiency of the relevant precedent relates to the fact that the relationship between the creditor financing these distributions and the debtor is put into the context of the entire transaction.[2107] If the transfer aims only to replace equity with debt, the transaction is evaluated as if the creditor paid the sum directly to the shareholders. Therefore, he has to direct his claims to the shareholders, even if the claim has been secured through corporate capital, but not to the corporation.[2108] Such creditor responsibility for financed distributions keeps them from financing distributions, even if secured, if the corporate creditworthiness is doubtful.[2109] Besides existing convenants, directors may therefore be confronted with additional practical limitations on incurring corporate debt to finance distributions.

4) Means to facilitate capital structure amendments

Special formal means for active shareholders to impact the corporate capital structure by repurchasing shares, increasing dividend payments, and increasing corporate debt are not provided under U.S. corporate law. All three decisions are management decisions. The success rate for share buybacks and (higher) cash dividends upon the demand of active shareholders is at least as high as the average demand of their requests.[2110] They are also very successful in increasing the leverage of targeted corporations.[2111] The success of their campaigns does not, therefore, depend on the existence of special formal means, as they exist for fundamental transaction decisions. Rather, it can be based on the use of general formal and informal means. In this context, the immediate positive financial effect coinciding with share repurchases and dividends provides not only active shareholders with strong incentives to control the administration. It also gives their fellow shareholders the necessary incentives to support them in applying general formal or informal means.

In about eighty-two percent of their successful demands to distribute corporate capital addressed to large and mid-cap firms, active shareholders applied pressure to the admin-

2105 Engert, in: Lutter, ZGR special issue 17, 2006, 743 (772); Kumpan, AG 2007, 461 (465 et seq.).

2106 Pajaro Dunes Rental Agency, Inc. v. Spitters, 174 B.R. 557, 596 et seq. (Bankr. N.D. Cal. 1994).

2107 Engert, in: Lutter, ZGR special issue 17, 2006, 743 (780).

2108 Pajaro Dunes Rental Agency, Inc. v. Spitters, 174 B.R. 557, 596 (Bankr. N.D. Cal. 1994).

2109 Engert, in: Lutter, ZGR special issue 17, 2006, 743 (772); Kumpan, AG 2007, 461 (466).

2110 Klein & Zur, 64 J. Fin. 187, 211 (2009): determining an overly positive success rate of 100 percent for buy backs and dividend demands, even though they determine that only hedge funds, but no other entrepreneurial activists expressed these demands; more reserved: Boyson & Mooradian, *Hedge funds as shareholder activists from 1994 – 2005* 9, www.ssrn.com/abstract=992739 (2007); successful in about 63 percent of the scenarios; Brav et al., *Hedge Fund Activism: A Review* 58, Table 1, www.ssrn.com/abstract=1551953 (2010): capital structure related demands are in average successful in about 52 percent; Brav et al., *Hedge Fund Activism, Corporate Governance, and Firm Performance* 42, www.ssrn.com/abstract=948907 (2008): hedge funds (partially) successful(ly) facilitate share repurchases in about 64 percent of the scenarios.

2111 Klein & Zur, 64 J. Fin. 187, 224 et seq. (2009).

istration.[2112] They used general formal as well as informal means to pressure the administration to enforce their proposals. The most successful means for active shareholders are the threat of or actual proxy contests regarding a board election,[2113] as demonstrated by the prior four examples. Active hedge funds, prevailing in the impact on the financial corporate structure, use them in about 40 percent of their campaigns. Other active entrepreneurial shareholders preferring other measures apply them in only 31 percent of their campaigns.[2114] However, only 18 percent of the distributing targets surrendered board seats,[2115] as equally demonstrated by the examples. Explanations can be found in the huge amount of money still necessary to launch a full-scale proxy contest as well as the commitment resulting from the boardroom entry even by minority funds with only one or two representatives. The fiduciary duty obligations of a representative(s) toward the corporation as a whole as well as to its shareholders would force them to pursue a cooperative value agenda.[2116] Furthermore, the mechanisms of the applicable federal securities laws would turn them into long-term investors of the targeted corporation with consequences unlikely to conform to the incentives of the engaged funds.[2117]

The relevance of threatened or actual proxy election contests also stems from the fact that board elections take place annually. Especially given the general lack of shareholder initiation rights and of the ability to convene a special meeting, the reliable rhythm of director elections supports its use to impact administrative decisions.

Often, financial activism is applied prior to or subsequent to the impact on corporate transaction decisions, which can be key to providing (part of) the capital for the demanded distributions. The successful implementation of the analyzed constellations to prevent a transaction in the form of a merger or tender offer or to facilitate the divestiture of underperforming divisions potentially makes substantial sums available. In addition, the learning curve of the administration will significantly reduce the necessary efforts to influence the administration further. The influence exercised by general formal and informal means, often based on general points of criticism is usually still present when

2112 Bratton, 95 Geo. L.J. 1375, 1405 et seq., 1416 (2007): as compared to 80 percent of the successful shareholder demands in general.

2113 Bebchuk, 118 Harv. L. Rev. 833, 851 (2005): the "key element of the corporate structure is the shareholder franchise"; Bebchuk, 93 Va. L. Rev. 102, 105 et seq., 150 et seq. (2007): shareholder franchise is key, shareholder franchise is a current means of hedge funds, which are less confronted by legal barriers, but would be supported by a further reform; Bratton, 95 Geo. L.J. 1375, 1406 (2007); Briggs 32 J. Corp. L. 681, 716, 723 (2007); Klein & Zur, *Entrepreneurial Shareholder Activism: Hedge Funds and Other Private Investors* 4 et seq., http://ssrn.com/abstract=1280672 (2006): position of frequent use of proxy solicitation process as a weapon of active shareholders; other opinion: Klein & Zur, 14 J. Fin. 187, 215 et seq. (2009): find no evidence of a relationship between proxy fight and the rate of success of campaigns of active shareholders.

2114 Klein & Zur 64 J. Fin. 187, 215 (2009).

2115 Bratton, 95 Geo. L.J. 1375, 1406, 1416 (2007): as compared to 20 percent of all the "successfully targeted" corporations.

2116 Bratton, 95 Geo. L.J. 1375, 1428 (2007); Briggs, 32 J. Corp. L. 681, 718 (2007).

2117 Briggs, 32 J. Corp. L. 681, 717-718 (2007): trading limitations resulting from the "affiliate" status, most likely applicable insider trading rules, as well as from the necessity to disgorge short-term trading profits according to § 16 SEA.

active shareholders subsequently demand distributions. The reference to them may suffice to convince the management to agree to the distribution.

5) Criticism relating to financial activism

The increasing impact of active shareholders, especially hedge funds, on the corporate financial structure has been criticized. This criticism relates especially to the development of corporate value. Accusations concern excessive distributions to shareholders, potentially financed by substantial amounts of debt, depriving managers of the targeted firms of the necessary capital to finance new projects[2118] as well as to make necessary R&D investments.[2119] The "sharpest"[2120] criticism relates, however, to the allegation that active shareholders invest short-term, focusing only on short-term gains by demanding payouts to the detriment of optimal long-term corporate growth.[2121] Another issue is whether active shareholder gains based on distributions come at the expense of other constituents. This concern relates to disproportionate distributions, especially when shares are repurchased. So may knowledgeable insiders or influential shareholders profit from a distribution, while less knowledgeable shareholders are excluded from its benefits.[2122] As share repurchases usually involve a share price above the market price, the shareholders not participating in the repurchases are likely to bear the costs.[2123] Such concerns concentrate on greenmailing-like constellations,[2124] which are relevant when active shareholders have the potential to remove the incumbents. In addition, they could prevent the installment of a new administration, despite the share price strongly indicating the need for a new management.[2125] Even if they lack the necessary support of fellow shareholders to impact board positions via the shareholder franchise, other means may provide them with the bargaining power to have the incumbents facilitate disproportional share repurchases in their favor. These means include the corporation's potential acquisition or reputation damaging fact-based campaigns.

2118 *See* Bratton, 95 Geo. L.J. 1375, 1415 (2007).

2119 *See* Bratton, *Hedge Funds and Governance Targets: Long-Term Results* 13 et seq., www.ssrn.com/abstract=1677517 (2010).

2120 Kahan & Rock, 155 U. Pa. L. Rev. 1021, 1083 (2007).

2121 Bolton et al., 30 J. Corp. L. 721, 725 (2005); *see* Bratton, *Hedge Funds and Governance Targets: Long-Term Results* 7, www.ssrn.com/abstract=1677517 (2010); Bratton, 76 Tul. L. Rev. 1276, 1284 (2002); Chandler, 67 U. Cin. L. Rev. 1083, 1092 et seq. (1999); *see* Kahan & Rock, 155 U. Pa. L. Rev. 1021, 1083 (2007); Lipton & Rosenblum, 59 Bus. Law. 67, 78 (2003); *see* Maatman & Raaijmaker, *Hedge funds in company law: virus or vaccine?* 15, http://ssrn.com/abstract=931884 (2006); Stout, *Why Carl Icahn Is Bad For Investors*, Wall Street Journal, Aug. 1, 2008, at A11; Strine, 119 Harv. L. Rev. 1759, 1764 et seq. (2006); *see* Thompson, *The Limits of Hedge Fund Activism* 2, http://escholarship.org/uc/item/5jq9d71m (2006).

2122 Kraakman et al., The Anatomy of Corporate Law 149 (2004), *id.* at 79 (2009).

2123 Merkt/Göthel, US-amerikanisches Gesellschaftsrecht, 2006, mn.551.

2124 An example is the investment of K-Kapital Partners LLC in Gyrodyne Co. of America Inc., which pursuant to a settlements sold part of its stake back to the issuer at a premium and the rest into the market, Bratton, 95 Geo. L.J. 1375, 1413 (2007).

2125 Merkt/Göthel, US-amerikanisches Gesellschaftsrecht, 2006, mn.551.

a) Foregoing interesting projects

One of the concerns is that administrations may have to forego interesting projects to finance distributions by depriving managers of ready capital to finance new projects.[2126] It can be objected that good projects will usually find the necessary financial support, if necessary by debt financing. Restrictions for management may only result if the concerned corporation is already highly leveraged, or where the payouts, as in the 1980s, were financed through substantial borrowing.[2127] The small number of payout cases involving *leverage* and the moderate amounts borrowed in relation to the corporate equity[2128] do not, however, justify this concern.

b) Reduction of R&D expenses

As far as opponents fear that allegedly short-term focused active shareholders reduce R&D expenses to the detriment of the long-term value of the corporation and its shareholders, such concerns have not been substantiated by empirical investigations. First, corporations targeted by active shareholders have generally low levels of R&D expenses.[2129] This has the advantage that the efforts pursued by active shareholders in such uncomplicated targets to enhance corporate effectiveness are rapidly reflected in the market price.[2130] In addition, financial activism does not result in a significant drop in R&D expenses that could justify the concerns of long-term orientated shareholders.[2131] Hedge funds that most successfully engage in the winning distributions have caused little or no changes in R&D expenditures. Other entrepreneurial activists have decreased R&D expenditures, but still significantly less than under the control sample. These results conform not only to the purposes stated by the active shareholders in their initial Schedule 13D filings.[2132] They make also sense when taking into account that active shareholders pursue rather generalized strategies based on publicly available information as compared to cost cutting whose consequences are unforeseeable and may

2126 *See* Bratton, 95 Geo. L.J. 1375, 1415 (2007).

2127 Bratton, 95 Geo. L.J. 1375, 1415 (2007).

2128 Bratton, *Hedge Funds and Governance Targets: Long-Term Results* 17 et seq., www.ssrn.com/abstract=1677517 (2010); Bratton, 95 Geo. L.J. 1375, 1418 (2007).

2129 Boyson & Mooradian, *Hedge funds as shareholder activists from 1994 – 2005* 10, www.ssrn.com/abstract=992739 (2007); Brav et al., *Hedge Fund Activism: A Review* 21, www.ssrn.com/abstract=1551953 (2010); Brav et al., *The returns to hedge fund activism* 7, http://ssrn.com/abstract=1111778 (2008); oposing opinion: Klein & Zur, 64 J. Fin. 187, 204 (2009): finds not difference between targets of hedge funds and other entrepreneurial investors with regard to research and development expenditures.

2130 Brav et al., *The returns to hedge fund activism* 8, http://ssrn.com/abstract=1111778 (2008).

2131 Bratton, *Hedge Funds and Governance Targets: Long-Term Results* 15 www.ssrn.com/abstract=1677517 (2010); Bratton, 95 Geo. L.J. 1375, 1415 (2007); Klein & Zur, 64 J. Fin. 187, 223, 225 et seq. (2009): there is little to no drop in mean R&D expenditures in the first year as compared to a drop for targets of other entrepreneurial activists, which may be carefully transferred as a preliminary result for the two year period.

2132 Klein & Zur, 64 J. Fin. 197, 223 et seq. (2009).

therefore easily damage the targeted corporation.[2133] Consequently, the increased returns from shareholder activism are not based on the reduction of long-term investments, such as R&D investments.

c) Short-termism

The "sharpest and most comprehensive"[2134] criticism of distributions initiated by active shareholders and of shareholder activism in general is short-termism, which when impacting management decisions may be detrimental to the long-term investments of the remainder of shareholders.[2135] The general issue for corporate managers comprises the conflict between their intent to pursue long-term investments to maximize corporate value while aiming for positive development of the stock price, which may increase through different investment decisions. The impact of allegedly short-term invested active shareholders focusing on short-term results on management's decisions permits the conclusion that management will focus more on short-term stock price highs than on the long-term maximization of corporate value.[2136] Most controversial is the shareholder impact on management decisions involving the sale of some of the corporation's lines of business, increased borrowing, and the distribution of proceeds to the shareholders via share repurchases and dividends.[2137]

Despite a comprehensive analysis of the issue, no convincing evidence has yet been established in support of this critique.[2138] In contrast, the evidence has demonstrated that the most active shareholders who primarily pursue financial activism, hedge funds, invest far longer than the average investment period of six months, namely around two years. This makes them mid-term investors.[2139] Quickly trading investors usually have

---

2133 Bratton, *Hedge Funds and Governance Targets: Long-Term Results* 15, www.ssrn.com/abstract=1677517 (2010).

2134 Kahan & Rock, 155 U. Pa. L. Rev. 1021, 1083 (2007).

2135 Lipton & Savitt, 93 Va. L. Rev. 733, 745 et seq. (2007); *see* Kahan & Rock, 155 U. Pa. L. Rev. 1021, 1083 et seq. (2007).

2136 Bratton, *Hedge fund activism and Governance Targets: Long-Term Results* 8, www.ssrn.com/abstract=1677517 (2010).

2137 *See* Brav et al., *The returns to hedge fund activism* 5-6, http://ssrn.com/abstract=1111778 (2008); *see* Dent, 35 Del. J. Corp. L. 97, 125 (2010); Partnoy & Thomas, *Gap Filling, Hedge Funds, and Financial Innovation* 35, http://ssrn.com/abstract=931254 (2006).

2138 Dent, 35 Del. J. Corp. L. 97, 100, 122 (2010): calling the charges therefore myths; Joe Nocera, *A defense of short-termism*, The New York Times, July 19, 2006, at B1, B 8, *available at* http://faculty.fuqua.duke.edu/~charvey/Media/2006/NYT_July_26_2006.pdf.

2139 Boyson & Mooradian, *Hedge funds as shareholder activists from 1994 – 2005* 2, 8, www.ssrn.com/abstract=992739 (2007): distinguishes between "communication only" categories of activism, holding shares in average 1 1/3 years as compared to "communication then aggressive" and "aggressive" activism, holding shares in average "just over two years"; Bratton, *Hedge Funds and Governance Targets: Long-Term Results* 9, 11, www.ssrn.com/abstract=1677517 (2010): hedge funds in the sample hold their stakes for around two and a half years, they tend to hold for an intermediate term; Bratton, 95 Geo. L.J. 1375, 1411, 1413 (2007); Brav et al., *Hedge Fund Activsm: A Review* 17 et seq., www.ssrn.com/abstract=1551953 (2010); Brav et al., *The returns to hedge fund activism* 2, 8, http://ssrn.com/abstract=1111778 (2008): determining an average hold-

different reasons for doing so, like mutual funds that need to ensure a certain level of liquidity to be able to redeem shares at any time.[2140] In many of these situations, investors do not try to profit particularly from the short investment term, but instead own shares briefly and treat their shares like long-term owners.[2141] Therefore, they do not make myopic demands on corporate governance.[2142] This understanding corresponds with the standard theories of market behavior, according to which even short-term investors have incentives to maximize long-term value.[2143]

Furthermore, a number of recent studies support the beneficial impact of hedge fund activism not only on the short-term stock performance of targeted corporations, but also on their long-term operating performance.[2144] This applies even after they have already left the corporation.[2145] Hedge fund activism successfully enhances operating performance, increases payouts, and reduces agency costs, improving corporate governance.[2146] Another study confirms excess stock returns and improvements in operating performance, however not in long-term returns more than one year after the intervention. Even though it does not confirm excess returns for the two-to-three-year period following the initial filing, it provides additional evidence that firms targeted by hedge

---

ing period of twenty-two months, *see* Thompson, *The Limits of Hedge Fund Activism* 30, http://escholarship.org/uc/item/5jq9d71m (2006).

2140 Duan, *The Role of Mutual Funds in Corporate Governance: Evidence from Mutual Funds' Proxy Voting and Trading Behavior* 2, http://ssrn.com/abstract=1028367 (2008).

2141 Velasco, *Shareholder Ownership and Primacy*, manuscript, 38-39, http://ssrn.com/abstract=1274244, U. ILL. L. REV. (forthcoming 2010).

2142 Dent, 35 DEL. J. CORP. L. 97, 122 (2010).

2143 *See* Dent, 35 DEL. J. CORP. L. 97, 122 et seq. n.106 (2010).

2144 Boyson & Mooradian, *Hedge funds as shareholder activists from 1994 – 2005* 8, www.ssrn.com/abstract=992739 (2007); Brav et al., *Hedge Fund Activism: A Review*, 31, www.ssrn.com/abstract=1551953 (2010); Klein & Zur, 64 J. FIN. 187, 225 (2009): transferring the positive results of one year after the event carefully to the two year period past the event; opposing, long-term return based opinion: Bratton, *Hedge Funds and Governance Targets: Long-Term Results* 2, 4, www.ssrn.com/abstract=1677517 (2010): despite a 88 percent success rate of governance-related demands of active shareholders, regarding the long-term development of returns, only a minority of the stock prices of targeted corporations beat the market indices over the period of engament, with financial underperformance being particularly notable in cases where the hedge funds entered target boardrooms, suggesting that hedge funds may only beneficially target matters to be interrogated from the outside of the target, like cash distribution, assets sales and sale of the targets as compared to others–which may be countered with the negative bias in the estimate of change in ROA due to the sample election effect, *see* Brav et al., *Hedge Fund Activism: A Review* 38 et seq., www.ssrn.com/abstract=1551953 (2010).

2145 Brav et al., *Hedge Fund Activism: A Review* 38 et seq., www.ssrn.com/abstract=1551953 (2010): noting that except for the return on assets, whose positive deviation returns to the pre-event level two years past the event, the Tobin q increases significantly past the intervention, payout policies occur sooner, the net leverage increases only insignificantly, as does the overall creditworthiness of the targeted firms and two years past the event the safety of debt claims has increased significantly. One year after the event, the CEO turnover has increased significantly, CEO compensation is lowered to a level indistinguishable to that of peers and within two years pay-for-performance increases significantly.

2146 Brav et al., *Hedge Fund Activism: A Review* 40, www.sssrn.com/abstract=1551953 (2010).

funds are not suffering from depressed long-term value.[2147] "Collectively, the evidence in these studies broadly supports the hypothesis that hedge fund activism enhances firm performance by reducing agency costs associated with free cash flow and by subjecting managers to increased discipline."[2148] It confirms the initial theoretical perception that shareholder activism reduces the agency costs based on the separation of ownership and control. It increases the control over management and reduces agency problems responsible for agency costs based on management decisions focusing on personal benefits rather than on maximizing shareholder benefits, which reduce the shareholder value.

Moreover, it is far from evident that corporate decisions favored by shareholders with high turnover strategies would generally deviate from those of long-term investors. Rather, it is likely that corporate decisions detrimental to corporate long-term profitability will also be reflected in the company's stock price.[2149] Evidence for alleged market myopia, meaning that the market price focuses rather on short-term results than on the corporate long-term potential, has so far only been vague.[2150] The sole argument in favor of market myopia is the phenomenal growth of private equity firms, which could represent a way to handle alleged short-term market perspective.[2151] This still leaves open whether private equity substitutes a problem aggravated by hedge funds or whether it only represents a good complement to shareholder activism.[2152] Rather, it appears convincing that the market takes into account the short-term as well as long-term potential of a firm, requiring that both be brought into the proper balance.[2153]

Finally, active shareholders generally hold a stake of 5 – 10 percent in the targeted corporations. They are therefore far from taking control. Even when obtaining a board seat, they do not solely represent their own interests.[2154] It remains corporate management that has to achieve compromises between the independent directors, traditional institutional investors, and active shareholders. Active shareholders aiming to pressure the corporate management to make a specific decision which it is not willing to make voluntarily depend on the support of other shareholders.[2155] Active shareholders who pursue a strategy contrary to the interests of their fellow shareholders would thus lack the necessary support for their initiatives. In the few cases in which active shareholders have obtained a board position, the affiliate status has the consequence that corporate fiduciary duties

2147 Clifford, 14 J. Corp. Fin. 323, 330 (2008).

2148 Brav et al., *Hedge Fund Activism: A Review* 40, www.sssrn.com/abstract=1551953 (2010).

2149 Bebchuk, 118 Harv. L. Rev. 833, 884 (2005); Kahan & Rock, 155 U. Pa. L. Rev. 1021, 1987 (2007); Joe Nocera, *A defense of short-termism*, The New York Times, July 19, 2006, at B1, B 8, *available at* http://faculty.fuqua.duke.edu/~charvey/Media/2006/NYT_July_26_2006.pdf.

2150 Kahan & Rock, 155 U. Pa. L. Rev. 1021, 1085 (2007).

2151 *Id.* at 1086.

2152 *Id.* at 1087.

2153 Joe Nocera, *A defense of short-termism,* New York Times, 19 July 2006, at B1, B 8, *available at* http://faculty.fuqua.duke.edu/~charvey/Media/2006/NYT_July_26_2006.pdf: pointing out that it is a question to find the right balance between long-term actions of the corporate management, as it was the case in the 1980's when corporate raiders became an issue, and the in recent times in management's focus prevailing requirements for the next quarterly report.

2154 Kahan & Rock, 155 U. Pa. L. Rev. 1021, 1088 (2007).

2155 *Id.* at 1089.

and trading restrictions, especially section 16 SEA, prevent possible short-term gains to the detriment of long-term investors.[2156] In contrast, taking into account the interest of the manager close to retirement in short-term focused earning schemes, the short-term orientated investor communication, especially quarterly earnings reports,[2157] and the annual re-election periods, one could ask whether it is the managers who primarily suffer from myopia.[2158] The dispute about short-termism appears therefore to be about the proper course of action, and maybe the actions proposed by active shareholders are more valuable.[2159]

Consequently, based on empirical evidence and the opinion of many scholars, short-termism is (at least) not (proven to be) an issue specifically related to shareholder activism.[2160] Rather, it appears as if a general short-term pressure on capital markets results from the focus on short-term based corporate publications and incentive structures that encourage corporations and investors to pursue short-term gains without regard for long-term effects. It seems therefore necessary to make rather general amendments allowing the administrations to find the proper balance between short-term and long-term corporate performance instead of accusing active shareholders of short-termism for seeking corporate governance enhancements that the administration finds inconvenient. Within this context and due to market forces, adaptive devices available to the individual corporation to reduce their *Achilles heel*,[2161] and the securities and corporate law regime, provisions targeting the short-termism of active shareholders are unnecessary and even counterproductive to their beneficial impact.

d) Opportunistic repurchases

Classic greenmailing faces two objections, inequality and agency costs.[2162] Similarly, active shareholders could face the objection that they enforce payouts at substantial premiums for their personal financial benefit while other shareholders are inequitably excluded from participating. Since under U.S. law equal treatment is only enforced for the payment of dividends, the criticism could only concern share repurchases. Targeted share repurchases, even above market price, are permissible under U.S. corporate law.[2163] Closely related is the second concern, which similar to classic greenmailing alleges that

2156 *See* Briggs, 32 J. Corp. L. 681, 717 et seq. (2007).

2157 *See* Dent, 35 Del. J. Corp. L. 97, 105 (2010); Joe Nocera, *A defense of short-termism*, New York Times, July 19, 2006, at B1, B 8, *available at* http://faculty.fuqua.duke.edu/~charvey/Media/2006/NYT_July_26_2006.pdf; The Aspen Institute, *Long-Term Value Creation: Guiding Principles For Corporations and Investors*, June 2007, 2 et seq., http://www.aspeninstitute.org/sites/default/files/content/docs/business%20and%20society%20program/FINALPRINCIPLES.pdf.

2158 Kahan & Rock, 155 U. Pa. L. Rev. 1021, 1088 (2007).

2159 *Id.*

2160 *Id.* at 1089 et seq.

2161 Martin Lipton/Wachtell, Lipton, Rosen & Katz, Key Issues for Directors, Client Memorandum, *Attacks by Activist Hedge Funds*, Mar. 7, 2006; Kahan & Rock, 155 U. Pa. L. Rev. 1021, 1089 et seq. (2007).

2162 Macey & McChesney, 95 Yale L.J. 13, 14 et seq. (1985).

2163 Kraakman et al., The Anatomy of Corporate Law 97 (2009).

active shareholders provide the administration with incentives to act opportunistically. Through their offer to sell their minority share package to the corporation at an elevated price, the administration has the chance to get rid of shareholders who exercise effective internal control, including seeking the removal of administrative members. The latter represents the parallel to external control via the market for corporate control, as under classic greenmailing.[2164]

Classic greenmailing occurred mainly between 1980 and 1984. Later, block repurchases did not usually involve greenmailing. Several reasons account for its demise, amongst them the decline of merger and repurchase activity since the 1980s and the tax law amendments[2165] making greenmailing more expensive and less attractive. Finally, the proxy process reform since 1992 has provided the shareholders with another more attractive alternative besides exit.[2166] In addition, the courts' response to greenmailing relied on the standard strategy, referring to the fiduciary duties of the administration and forbidding a selective repurchase of shares at *any* price.[2167] Despite concerns that administrations could support package repurchases to retain their individual positions, courts exceptionally allowed greenmailing when economic arguments spoke in favor of block repurchases.[2168] The *rational business purpose test* requires that the administration prove that it acted to compensate an existing danger and therefore for a proper business purpose instead of solely to secure its own position.[2169] Considering the primary purpose of the repurchase program, it may even justify a package repurchase for a control premium.[2170] As long as a proper business purpose is given, it may therefore even justify the perpetuation of control through the administration. This has been confirmed in cases of a planned liquidation of the corporation or a disadvantageous amendment of corporate policy.[2171] Accordingly, an administration satisfies its burden under the test by proving that a consideration apart from the perceived threat to control was the primary reason for the repurchase. Alternatively, the repurchase was primarily intended as a takeover maneuver and the change in control would have represented a clear threat to the future business or the existing, successful business policy of the corporation.[2172]

2164 Berle & Means, The Modern Corporation and Private Property 119 et seq. (1933); Jensen & Meckling, 3 J. Fin. Econ. 305, 308 (1976), *available at* http://ssrn.com/abstract=94043, 4 et seq.: determining the costs incurred by management opposite to the interests of the principal as residual loss, which are part of the agency costs.

2165 26 U.S.C. § 5881 (a): "Hereby, it is imposed on any person who receives greenmail a tax equal to 50 percent of gain or other income of such person by reason of such receipt."

2166 Manry & Stangeland, 6 Stan. J.L. Bus & Fin. 217, 235 et seq. (2001).

2167 Donahue v. Rodd Electrotype Company of New England, Inc., 328 N. E. 2[d] 505 (Mass. 1975).

2168 Bradley & Wakeman, 11 J. Fin. Econ. 301, 305 (1983).

2169 Chef v. Mathes, 199 A.2d 548, 554 (Del. 1964); Kaplan v. Goldsamt, 380 A.2d 556, 568 (Del. Ch. 1977): Allows wide discretion to directors. As long as they appear to act in good faith, with honest motives, for honest ends, the exercise of discretion will not be interfered by the courts. The presumption of sound business judgement will be reposed in a board of directors if any rational business purpose can be attributed to its decision.

2170 Chef v. Mathes, 199 A.2d 548, 554 (Del. 1964).

2171 *Id.*

2172 Crane Co. v. Harsco Corp., 511 F. Supp. 294, 305 (D. Del. 1981).

Evidence of the existence of side deals between active shareholders and administrations in which active shareholders used payout constellations to divert money to themselves by convincing management to pay them to exit instead of increasing control over the administration has not yet been provided.[2173]

Regarding the closeness to classic greenmail, most of the explanations possibly responsible for the decline of classic greenmail apply also to greenmailing constellations involving active shareholders. The substantial tax burden,[2174] the increasingly effective shareholder means to elevate the share price through activism as an alternative to the exit via greenmail, and the criticized[2175] precedents may have kept active shareholders from greenmailing. Another explanation could relate to the reputation mechanism and the bad name greenmail got during the 1980s, so that boards do not dare offer and active shareholders would not risk accepting greenmail offers.[2176] Closely related is the fact that active shareholders' minority stakes make them concerned about their reputation in general, since they usually depend on the support of fellow shareholders to realize their control goal. Other shareholders may refuse to support them if the active shareholders' reputation is such that they fear these shareholders may consider exiting the corporation through a greenmail-like constellation.[2177] Finally, in regards to the frequency of shareholder activism, it would most likely make little sense for administrations to get rid of some activists by paying them. As long as the problems targeted by active shareholders persist, they would soon attract new active shareholders.[2178] Without corresponding evidence and considering the arguments, greenmailing like constellations do not seem to be a problem fellow shareholders have to worry about.

III) Preliminary results on financial activism

1) Benefits

The analysis regarding the impact exercised by active shareholders on the financial structure of the targeted corporations has underscored its beneficial effect on the shareholder value of the targeted corporation. This beneficial effect is based on increasing control over administrations with the consequence of reducing agency costs resulting from retaining excess cash and administrative overinvestments. It has also demonstrated the different impact of the distinct financial means on the administrations. Despite the often large amounts involved in share repurchases and special dividends, they at least constrain the administration. Regular dividend payments, in contrast, *animate* administrations regularly to continuously increase the distributions. Incurred debt to finance either type of disgorgement binds future excess cash, *obliging* the administration to

2173 Briggs, 32 J. Corp. L. 681, 703 (2007); Kahan & Rock, 155 U. Pa. L. Rev. 1021, 1082 (2007).

2174 Hirsch, Der Erwerb eigener Aktien nach dem KonTraG, 2004, 82.

2175 Clark, Corporate Law 632 et seq. (1986); Merkt/Göthel, US-amerikanisches Gesellschaftsrecht, 2006, mn.555.

2176 Kahan & Rock, 155 U. Pa. L. Rev 1021, 1082 (2007).

2177 *Id.*

2178 *Id.*

make regular payments to creditors. As a consequence of each distribution type, excess cash is returned to the shareholders. The administration will have to act more diligently with the remaining capital and concentrate on the most profitable investments, as additional control through the capital market will apply once new investments are required. As a consequence, agency costs will be reduced and return on equity will increase. The immediate distribution to the shareholders and the increased shareholder value confirmed by the beneficial impact on the target's stock price and long-term performance provides active shareholders and their fellow shareholders with the necessary financial incentives to become active or to support such activism. The preference of sophisticated active shareholders like hedge funds is usually for share repurchases, as they are assumed to allow them to extract the greatest benefits by the use of their knowledge and to reduce free-riding. Based on tax premises, fellow shareholders are assumed to have similar preferences, ensuring their necessary support.

As initially assumed, financial activism has beneficial impact on the corporate governance of targeted corporations by reducing agency costs resulting from the separation of ownership and control.

2) Shareholder means

Corporate decisions impacting the corporate financial structure are management tasks. As assumed, active shareholders under U.S. law aiming to pursue financial activism are therefore restricted to the use of general formal and informal means. Despite the lack of special formal means granting direct impact on financial decisions, the success rate is at least as high as the average success rate of shareholder activism. This reveals that a credible threat or actual attempt to remove members of the administration from their positions via a proxy fight represents an effective means in the hands of active shareholders to enforce their demands. The effectiveness of active demands to amend the corporate financial structure may result from the aligned interests of fellow shareholders and active shareholders in increasing shareholder value. In addition, amendments of the financial structure result comparably soon in financial benefits for the shareholders of the target. Neither rule-of-the-game amendments nor transaction activism alone will cause a comparably immediate financial benefit for the shareholders. As a consequence, it may be assumed that under these scenarios even fellow shareholders have disproportionally strong incentives to support a threat or actual proxy fight aiming to facilitate the requested financial measure. Simultaneously, the relevance of the threat to or the actual use of the shareholder franchise in the transaction *and* financial activism context underscores the need to remove the legal barriers that still reduce the effectiveness of this important accountability mechanism.

3) Concerns

Active shareholders pursuing financial activism are frequently confronted with a number of charges. However, little evidence has been presented to prove that shareholders have actually pursued corresponding strategies. Regarding some of them, the evidence proves the opposite. Correspondingly, active shareholders who successfully convince administrations to incur or increase corporate debt to finance distributions do not do so to such an extent that they prevent later investments in promising projects. Nor do active shareholders chose targets with significant R&D expenditures or significantly cut the target's R&D costs. Even for those who do not believe in market efficiency,[2179] recent evidence has proven that active shareholders are mid-term investors. The benefits of their impact on the targeted corporation lead not only to short-term elevated stock prices, but evidence also shows that it even positively impacts the long-term performance of targeted firms, or at least does not fall below the long-term performance level of the control group. The impact of active shareholders on the corporate financial structure is therefore likely to increase the long-term performance of the targeted firms instead of having a detrimental impact on it. Finally, insufficient evidence has been provided that active shareholders pursuing financial activism have won any greenmailing-like package deals. This is supported by several considerations as well as the effective relevant precedent, which accepts selective repurchases only under exceptional circumstances that are not likely to apply to corresponding demands of active shareholders.

In contrast to the expectation of the initial thesis of this Part, the legal limitations to contain these potential deviating interests are only of secondary relevance. As far as concerns remain, it can be assumed that the current legal regime will largely contain potentially deviating interests.[2180] Apart from the disclosure regime analyzed in the transaction activism Part, relevant limitations are less the statutory capital requirements than the law against fraudulent transfers,[2181] the director liability arising under common law,[2182] and the greenmail doctrine. Consequently, the caution regarding the number of concerns argued against financial activism has proven to be justified.

IV) Financial activism under German corporate law

1) Authority distribution regarding corporate financial decisions

German corporations confronted with active shareholders primarily face demands regarding their financial structure.[2183] German corporate law provides active shareholders with several ways to maximize their personal shareholder value by impacting the

2179 Anabtawi & Stout, 60 Stan. L. Rev. 1255, 1291 et seq. (2008).
2180 Briggs, 32 J. Corp. L. 681, 701 (2007): referring to all conflicts of interest, including hedging.
2181 Engert, in: Lutter, Das Kapital der Aktiengesellschaft in Europa – ZGR-Sonderheft 17, 2006, 743 (769 et seq.); Kumpan, AG 2007, 461 (463); Marx, DZWIR 2006, 401 (401).
2182 Marx, DZWIR 2006, 401 (401).
2183 Böhm/Grothe, Hedgefonds-Aktivismus in Deutschland, BVAI Newsletter IV 2009, 14 (16), www.bvai.de/newsletter (choose BAI Newsletter IV/2009): about 25 percent of hedge fund activ-

financial structure of the target corporation. The most frequently used means are share repurchases, dividend payments, including special dividends, and the facilitation of supporting leverage, which lead to or increase a direct return flow to the shareholders.[2184] Corporations tend not only to underestimate the significance of financial measures for institutional investors, but also the impact shareholders may exercise in this area.[2185] This contradicts the comparably generous statutory decision rights of shareholders to participate in corporate financial decisions. Under German corporate law, shareholders have been generally granted direct decision rights in the form of approval rights if corporate decisions concern regularly repeating and structural measures or special cases.[2186] These comprise amendments of the articles of incorporation, fundamental transactions, and certain financial decisions. In the context of financial decisions, shareholders have to approve the use of net earnings, the increase or reduction of share capital, and the authorization of the management board to repurchase shares, §§ 119 (1) No. 2 and 6[2187], 174, 182 et seq. and § 71 (1) No. 8, sent. 5 and 6.[2188]

2) Distributions

In the context of financial activism, active shareholders most frequently demand distribution in the form of share repurchases and dividends. However, only 25 percent of the total cases of shareholder activism (through the in the financial context particularly present hedge funds) led to distributions to shareholders.[2189] Based on the evidence, according to which active shareholders request corresponding financial measures in about 50 percent[2190] of the shareholder activism scenarios, the success rate is around 50 percent.

a) Financial activism example facilitation repurchase and dividend

An example of financial activism that also led to distributions in the form of share repurchase programs and a substantial dividend is the impact of TCI and other funds on Deutsche Börse. After the active funds had successfully prevented Deutsche Börse's bid for LSE,[2191] based on their threat to express no confidence in the CEO, Deutsche Börse still had a war chest. The activist funds demanded its distribution to the shareholders. Their

ism events in German corporations resulted in distributions; DAI/McKinsey, Investorendialog im Umbruch, 2009, 23.

2184 DAI/McKinsey, Investorendialog im Umbruch, 2009, 25 et seq.

2185 Bassen, Einflußnahme institutioneller Investoren auf Corporate Governance und Unternehmensführung, 2001, 17.

2186 Spindler, in: Schmidt/Lutter, AktG, 2010, § 119 mn.7.

2187 Any section without further specification in this Subpart four of Part three refers to the AktG.

2188 Mülbert, in: Großkomm AktG, 2008, § 119 mnn.11 et seq.

2189 Böhm/Grothe, Hedgefonds-Aktivismus in Deutschland, BVAI Newsletter IV 2009, 14 (16), www.bvai.de/newsletter (choose BAI Newsletter IV/2009).

2190 DAI/McKinsey, Investorendialog im Umbruch, 2009, 25.

2191 Jens Masuhr, *Aktienrückkäufe Volles Programm*, Febr. 22, 2006, Focus Money, http://www.focus.de/finanzen/boerse/aktien/aktienrueckkaeufe-volles-programm_aid_256480.html.

demands were legitimized through shareholder value arguments.[2192] Despite the approval of a distribution of more than €448 million within two weeks after the termination of the bid,[2193] the funds demanded additional distributions. They also threatened to remove supervisory board members and the CEO during the upcoming May 2005 general meeting.[2194] In the beginning of May 2005, Deutsche Börse approved the distribution of the entire war chest of €1,5 billion until May 2007.[2195] Nevertheless, TCI continued attempting to remove the heads of boards and was successful.[2196] TCI's continuous demands for distributions to be financed from divestitures were underscored by the announcement that it was pooling voting rights with those of the second major shareholder, hedge fund Atticus. Both held jointly a stake of 20 percent.[2197]

Deutsche Börse ended up distributing the war chest of over €1.5 billion, which corresponded to $1.8 billion, to its shareholders via share repurchases and dividends.[2198] € 74 million were distributed as dividends, tripling the dividend. The lion's share was used to repurchase 10 percent of Deutsche Börse's outstanding shares,[2199] the maximum admissible by law.

b) Active shareholders and share repurchases

Share repurchases under German corporate law are generally prohibited. In 1998, significant liberalization was been achieved by the implementation of the shareholder meeting's right to authorize the administration to repurchase up to 10 percent of the outstanding shares without having to specify a purpose for it, § 71 (1) No. 8.[2200] The implementation of § 71 (1) No. 8 through the KonTraG was based on Art. 19 (b) of the Second Company Directive.[2201] It intended to harmonize the financial instruments of German corporations with those used internationally. Its aim was to prevent disadvan-

---

2192 *Lautstarkes Gezerre, Teil 2: Zwischenruf aus Mailand*, Mar. 3, 2005, Manager Magazin, http://www.manager-magazin.de/geld/artikel/0,2828,344550-2,00.html.

2193 *Seifert auf Schmusekurs*, Mar. 23, 2005, Manager Magazin, http://www.manager-magazin.de/geld/artikel/0,2828,347902,00.html.

2194 *Quartalszahlen läuten Countdown für die HV der Deutschen Börse ein*, Apr. 29, 2005, Die Welt, http://www.welt.de/print-welt/article667966/Quartalszahlen_laeuten_Countdown_fuer_die_HV_der_Deutschen_Boerse_ein.html.

2195 Achim Achilles, *Deutsche Börse beugt sich Aktionären*, May 3, 2005, Manager Magazin, http://www.manager-magazin.de/geld/artikel/0,2828,354441,00.html.

2196 Dietmar Palan, *TCI-Chef verliert Verbündete*, Sept. 25, 2008, Manager Magazin, http://www.manager-magazin.de/geld/artikel/0,2828,580245,00.html.

2197 *Id.*

2198 Voth, Transparenz und Fairness auf einem einheitlichen europäischen Kapitalmarkt, 2007, 62; Gerard Wynn, *Hedge funds target cash-rich corporates*, June 23, 2005, reuters.com, http://www.reuters.com/article/idUSL2338447220050623.

2199 David Ben-Ur/Corbin Capital Partners, *Shareholder Activism*, 2007, 9, www.pionline.com/assets/docs/CO19344522.PDF; Jens Masuhr, *Aktienrückkäufe Volles Programm*, Febr. 22, 2006, Focus Money, http://www.focus.de/finanzen/boerse/aktien/aktienrueckkaeufe-volles-programm_aid_256480.html.

2200 Hüffer, AktG, § 71 mnn.3, 19d; Lutter/Drygalla, in: KöKo AktG, 2010, § 71 mn.123.

2201 Council Directive 77/91/EEC, art. 19, 1976 O.J. (L 026) 0001- 0013.

tages for German corporations in comparison with corporations from other countries, amongst them the United States,[2202] and to allow them to profit from the positive effects of share repurchases.[2203] Since then, shareholder meetings have increasingly made use of this provision[2204] and about two-thirds of administrations have used the authorization[2205]. Nevertheless, in about 58 percent of the shareholder activism scenarios, active shareholders have requested the initiation of the share repurchase programs.[2206]

i) Functional background of share repurchases

Under German law, share repurchases have several purposes that are similar to those under U.S. law, yet not the same.[2207] Most relevant are the increase of the shareholder value, its signaling function, and its use as distribution alternative and acquisition currency.[2208] Most important for active shareholders, share repurchases can *enhance shareholder value* by reducing agency costs related to excess cash and overinvestment. The excess cash that cannot be invested with a return above the capital cost will be re-distributed to shareholders.[2209] This increases the return on the remaining shares and imposes additional external control upon the administration. Concerned are in particu-

2202 RegE eines Gesetzes zur Kontrolle und Transparenz im Unternehmensbereich [Draft Law of the Federal Government of an Act for Control and Transparency in Business], Jan. 28, 1998, BT-Drucks 13/9712, 13; Von Hein, Die Rezeption US-Amerikanischen Gesellschaftsrechts in Deutschland, 2008, 235.

2203 RegE eines Gesetzes zur Kontrolle und Transparenz im Unternehmensbereich [Draft Law of the Federal Government of an Act for Control and Transparency in Business], Jan. 28, 1998, BT-Drucks 13/9712, 13; Von Hein, Die Rezeption US-Amerikanischen Gesellschaftsrechts in Deutschland, 2008, 235 et seq.

2204 Hackethal & Zdantchouk, 20 Fin. Mkts. Portfolio Mgmt. 123 (2006), *available at* http://ssrn.com/abstract=920815; Wettberg, Der Rückkauf eigener Anteile im deutschen Finanzsystem, 2003, 123: about 49 percent of the listed corporations had been authorized to repurchase own shares.

2205 Wettberg, Der Rückkauf eigener Anteile im deutschen Finanzsystem, 2003, 127.

2206 DAI/McKinsey, Investorendialog im Umbruch, 2009, 25.

2207 Oechsler, in: MüKo AktG, 2008, § 71 mn.6.

2208 DAI, Der Erwerb eigener Aktien in Deutschland, 1999, 10, *available at* http://www.dai.de/internet/dai/dai-2-0.nsf/0/10CDCA1365C31F28C12574890032A37F/$FILE/7B0FFBC6B438C-495C125747C0053B113.pdf?openelement&cb_content_name_utf=aktienrueckkauf.pdf: noting that share repurchases are primarily used as acquisition currency as well as to amend the capital structure; Kellerhals/Rausch, AG 2000, 222 (225): according to their results, it is the leverage effect, which is the primary purpose of share repurchases in practice, followed by the impact on the stock price due to the signaling effect.; *see* Kitanoff, Der Erwerb eigener Aktien, 2009, 36; *see* Last, Der Erwerb eigener Aktien als Ausschüttungsinstrument, 2006, 27 et seq.: who determines the distribution of excess capital and a sustainable increase of the stock price as the two prevailing motives, which may well be combined; Oechsler, in: MüKo AktG, 2008, § 71 mn.6; Schremper, Aktienrückkauf und Kapitalmarkt, 2002, 119: stating that the elimination of undervaluation issues as well as signaling purposes as prevailing for share repurchases in German corporations.

2209 Bezzenberger, Der Erwerb eigener Aktien durch die AG, 2002, mnn.73, 75; Merkt, in: Großkomm AktG, § 71 mn.18; Mülbert, ZGR 1997, 129 (132); Oechsler, in: MüKo AktG, 2008, § 71 mn.6.

lar large firms with good returns in mature markets,[2210] whose administrations should be prevented from forming large capital reserves, which make them independent from shareholder approval and reduce shareholder value.[2211] Share repurchases serve also to *signal* that the stock is undervalued and likely to rise in the near future.[2212] Its credibility increases through reasonable administrative explanations and private administrative purchases. The better-informed agents help the principals to overcome their information deficit about positive corporate progress.[2213] The four times stronger total abnormal returns related to the open market repurchase announcements on the German market may be explained by the higher credibility of undervaluation signals attributed to the stringent repurchase process prescribed by German law.[2214] Furthermore, share repurchases represent an alternative to dividends to *distribute corporate profits* in the form of one-time distributions to avoid mistaken expectations *during times of temporary liquidity*. Dividend elevations, in contrast, require constant liquidity.[2215] Besides, repurchases give shareholders the choice between retaining their shares and selling.[2216]

ii) Means and limitations

(1) Means

Through the authorization requirement for share repurchases not falling under one of the scenarios of § 71 (1) No. 1 to 7, the management board depends on the approval of the shareholder meeting before implementing a share repurchase program. The authorization is of limited duration according to § 71 (1) No. 8,[2217] and has been extended through the ARUG from 18 months to 5 years. Based on Directive 2006/68/EC,[2218] amending the Second Company Directive 77/91/EEC, it aims to enhance the administration's flexibility to react promptly to market developments affecting the share price. Still, its remaining limitation efficiently guarantees the shareholder meeting's right to decide on corporate capital measures, comparable to authorized capital.[2219]

2210 Bezzenberger, Der Erwerb eigener Aktien durch die AG, 2002, mn.75.

2211 Oechsler, in: MüKo AktG, 2008, § 71 mn.7.

2212 Last, Der Erwerb eigener Aktien als Ausschüttungsinstrument, 2006, 28; Oechsler, in: MüKo AktG, 2008, § 71 mn.4: undersoring that signaling is the only one of the different theoretical approaches aiming to explain the stock price reactions of share repurchases, which has been supported by corresponding data.

2213 Kellerhals/Rausch, AG 2000, 222 (224); Oechsler, in: MüKo AktG, 2008, § 71mn.1.

2214 Hackethal & Zdantchouk, 20 Fin. Mkts. Portfolio Mgmt. 123 (2006), *available at* http://ssrn.com/abstract=920815.

2215 Bezzenberger, Erwerb eigener Aktien durch die AG, 2002, mn.74; Last, Der Erwerb eigener Aktien als Ausschüttungsinstrument, 2006, 11 et seq.; Oechsler, in: MüKo AktG, 2008, § 71 mn.20.

2216 Oechsler, in: MüKo AktG, 2008, § 71 mn.8.

2217 Hüffer, AktG, § 71 mn.19e.

2218 Directive of the European Parliament and the Council 2006/68/EC, 2006 O.J. (L 264) 34.

2219 RegE für ein Gesetz zur Umstzung der Aktionärsrechterichtlinie (ARUG) [Draft Law of the Federal Government of an Act Implementing the Shareholder Rights Directive (ARUG)], Jan. 21, 2009, BT-Drucks 16/11642, 25.

Despite the shareholder meeting's right to authorize a share repurchase program, its implementation still represents a typical management task.[2220] Shareholders may only impact the "how," but not the "whether," of an authorized share repurchase.[2221] The management board is, however, solely obliged to prepare and implement measures that fall into the shareholder meeting's responsibility, § 83 (1).[2222] Shareholders do not have a mandatory initiation right, therefore, that would oblige the management board to prepare or implement the authorized repurchase program, § 83.[2223] For the same reason, the minority rights pursuant to § 122 do not apply either. Shareholders must thus use the general formal as well as informal means to convince the management board to implement a (n authorized) repurchase program.

(2) Limitations

Under German corporate law, share repurchases, especially the authorization through the shareholder meeting, contain a number of specific restrictions to protect creditors and minority shareholders. The acquisition volume of the authorization is restricted to a maximum of *10 percent of the share capital*, § 71 (1) No. 8. It prevents the management board from implementing excessive share reductions to significantly impact the share price or to abusively impact the corporate shareholder structure.[2224] Furthermore, it complements the capital maintenance requirements laid down in § 71 (2)[2225] by limiting the corporation's ability to hold its own shares to 10 percent of the share capital, § 71 (2) sent. 1. These provisions require that repurchases are made *from distributable profits* without falling back on share capital or reserves required by statute or the articles of incorporation, § 71 (2) sent. 2. The former restriction limits the risks related to share repurchases. The latter aims to prevent too much capital from being used for the repurchase.[2226]

Due to the limited distribution volume, the practical possibilities of increasing the net profit or accessing other reserves to augment the distributable capital[2227] are less relevant in the repurchase than in the dividend context. It will therefore be analyzed *infra.*

Finally, the 10 percent mark complements the protection of fellow shareholders as laid down in §§ 71 (1) No. 8 sent. 3 and 4, 53a. They demand the equal treatment of shareholders during purchases and sales of one's own shares, as long as no objective reason or approval legitimizes other measures.[2228] This aims to prevent specific shareholders

2220 Oechsler, in: MüKo AktG, 2008, § 71 mn.23.

2221 Merkt, in: Großkomm AktG, 2008, § 71 mn.272.

2222 Götze, in: Gleiss Lutz/AmCham, Shareholder Activism – (k)ein rechtliches Thema, 2008, 11, http://www.amcham.de/fileadmin/templates/main/pdf/Praesentation_Goetze.pdf.

2223 Hüffer, AktG, § 83 mn.2.

2224 Hüffer, AktG, § 71 mn.19e; Last, Der Erwerb eigener Aktien als Ausschüttungsinstrument, 2006, 41.

2225 Bezzenberger, Erwerb eigener Aktien durch die AG, 2002, mn.45; Hüffer, AktG, § 71 mn.20.

2226 Merkt, in: Großkomm AktG, 2008, § 71 mn.322.

2227 Schulz, Der Einfluss von Dividenden auf Aktienrenditen, 2006, 21.

2228 BGH, Urt. v. 6.10.1960, Az.: II ZR 150/58; NJW 1961, 26 (27); Engert, in: Lutter, special issue 17, 2006, 743 (753); Last, Der Erwerb eigener Aktien als Ausschüttungsinstrument, 2006, 52; Merkt, in: Großkomm AktG, 2008, § 71 mn.66.

from being released from firm-specific risk or foregoing profitable developments or that the management board arbitrarily repurchases shares at augmented prices from certain shareholders, for instance those declining to discharge them, § 120.[2229]

To prevent insider trading, § 15 (1) sent. 1 WpHG requires generally that the corporations publish share repurchases, as long as they are not just implemented for technical reasons and with a limited impact on the share price. This has been affirmed for repurchases concerning 5 percent or more of the share capital or resulting in a stock price reaction of 5 percent or more.[2230] The safe-harbor provisions of Regulation No. 2273/2003[2231] relevant for § 14 (2) sent. 1 WpHG apply exclusively to three purposes of share repurchase plans, which are usually irrelevant for active shareholders. Controversial has remained the exact timing of the publication, as the decision-making process under § 71 (1) No. 8 comprises several stages. These are the administrative decision to ask the shareholder meeting for authorization, the shareholder meeting's authorization, and the administrative decision to implement the repurchase.[2232] Any of these steps could represent insider information pursuant to § 13 (1) WpHG.[2233] The question is which of these announces with sufficient probability, § 13 (1) sent. 3 WpHG, that the upcoming share repurchase will take place.[2234] One opinion denies the management board's obligation to publish its intentions to repurchase shares, as their announcement impacts only indirectly the value of the corporation, is non-binding, and has uncertain impact on the stock price.[2235] The prevailing opinion argues that the time at which the capital market can be certain about the share repurchase is typically the final administrative decision.[2236] The recent amendment of § 71 (3) that revoked sent. 3 with its duty to report an authorization to the BaFin has shed light on the discussion. The underlying reasoning states that the authorization by the shareholder meeting has no significant relevance for the stock price, as they have become a very common instrument. Therefore, the BaFin must be informed once the final administrative decision on the implementation of the

2229 Engert, in: Lutter, ZGR-Sonderheft, 2006, 743 (753); Merkt, in: Großkomm AktG, 2008, § 71 mn.67.

2230 Kraft/Altvater, NZG 1998, 448 (451); Last, Der Erwerb eigener Aktien als Ausschüttungsinstruement, 2006, 145; Merkt, in: Großkomm AktG, 2008, § 71 mn.45.

2231 Commission Regulation 2273/2003, art.3, 2003 O.J. (L 336) 33, 35, *available at* http://www.jura.uni-augsburg.de/fakultaet/lehrstuehle/moellers/materialien/materialdateien/020_europaeische_gesetzgebungsgeschichte_ril/ril_2003_006_eg_marktmissbrauch_geschichte/ril_2003_006_eg_pdfs/vo_eg_2003_2273_en_pdf.pdf.

2232 Last, Der Erwerb eigener Aktien als Ausschüttungsinstrument, 2006, 146.

2233 Kitanoff, Der Erwerb eigener Aktien, 2009, 213.

2234 *Id.* at 214.

2235 Martens, AG 1996, 337 (340 et seq.).

2236 BaFin, Emittentenleitfaden [guidelines for issuers] 2009, 40, http://www.bafin.de/SharedDocs/Downloads/DE/Service/Leitfaeden/emittentenleitfaden__2009,templateId=raw,property=-publicationFile.pdf/emittentenleitfaden_2009.pdf; Kitanoff, Der Erwerb eigener Aktien, 2009, 214–215; Last, Der Erwerb eigener Aktien als Ausschüttungsinstrumenet, 2006, 146; Merkt, in: Großkomm AktG, 2008, § 71 mn.47: argueing that exceptions may apply if at an earlier point the realization of a share repurchase programm becomes very probable, which may be the case when the shareholder meeting approves the repurchase programm, recommending to publish even the resolution of the administration to prevent insider trading.

share repurchase has been made.[2237] In addition, a corporation aiming to repurchase shares over the open market generally has to make a public announcement, §§ 10 (1), (3) WpÜG.[2238] As a consequence, fellow shareholders of active shareholder initiating a share repurchase on the basis of an existing shareholder authorization will be informed as soon as its implementation has been actually decided on. They will have the equal opportunity to sell (part of) their shares if the repurchase has not exceptionally been restricted to certain shareholders.

Moreover, § 71 (3) sent. 1 requires a full statement during the shareholder meeting following the transaction of the motives of the repurchase, the number of the acquired shares and their proportion to the share capital, and compensation paid.[2239] It provides shareholders who did not participate and who may fear disadvantages through the share repurchase with the opportunity to check its prerequisites and the conditions of the facilitated repurchase.

Finally, shareholders have to inform the corporation and the BaFin if they fall below a relevant ownership percentage according to § 21 (1) WpHG. The corporation is obliged to publish the information obtained from the shareholders, § 25 WpHG, as well as its own shareholdings if passing a relevant quorum, despite § 71b, as clarified in § 25 (1) sent. 3 WpHG. Active shareholders initiating a share repurchase program to exit the corporation while enjoying a premium on their share price would therefore be required to inform the BaFin and the corporation in case they had previously owned more than 3 percent. This draws the attention of the fellow shareholders to take a second look at the conditions that applied to the repurchase.

c) Active shareholders and dividends

The second most frequent demand of active shareholders on German corporations is for dividends as well as special dividends. In 42 percent or 35 percent of the contacts, the active shareholder demanded the increase of dividends or the distribution of a special dividend.[2240]

i) Functional background of dividends

Dividend payments under German law serve similar purposes as under U.S. law. They are used to *distribute corporate profits* to the shareholders.[2241] Furthermore, they serve

2237 RegE für ein Gesetz zur Umsetzung der Aktionärsrechterichtlinie (ARUG) [Draft Law of the Federal Government of an Act Implementing the Shareholder Rights Directive (ARUG)], Jan. 21, 2009, BT-Drucks 16/11642, 25 et seq.; Hüffer, AktG, § 71 mn.23a.

2238 The applicability of the WpÜG to the repurchase of shares is controversial, for a summary *see* Oechsler, in: MüKo AktG, 2008, § 71 mn.228 et seq., in favor of the applicability of § 10 WpÜG Hackethal & Zdantchouk, 20 Fin. Mkts. Portfolio Mgmt. 123, 129 (2006), *available at* http://ssrn.com/abstract=920815; Merkt, in: Großkomm AktG, 2008, § 71 mn.54; Oechsler, in: MüKo AktG, 2008, § 71 mn.232.

2239 Merkt, in: Großkomm AktG, 2008, § 71 mnn.345 – 346.

2240 DAI/McKinsey, Investorendialog im Umbruch, 2009, 25 et seq.

2241 Oechsler, in: MüKo AktG, 2008, § 71 mn.8.

as an information tool on the future cash flow for less well-informed shareholders. The difference in the prior year's dividend shows the corporation's performance during the past year.[2242] As shareholders prefer stable dividends demonstrating stable entrepreneurial corporate conditions and sanction decreased dividends indicating economic difficulties, administrations aim for dividend continuity[2243].[2244] Their goal is to cautiously elevate the dividend level in good times to avoid having to lower it in bad times.[2245] The credibility of *signaling* via dividends is based on their costs. They make mistaken signals useless.[2246] The main purpose for active shareholders to increase dividends is to *reduce agency costs* resulting from opportunistic administrative behavior based on excess cash. Administrations tend to invest it with a profit below the capital costs to further own goals, including securing and increasing their own position and compensation while reducing costs related to searching for new profitable ventures.[2247] Active shareholders aim to prevent such overinvestment of excess cash and to have it distributed to allow them to invest it externally with a higher return.[2248] The signaling effect supports the effects by keeping an achieved dividend level stable. Moreover, the administration faces the potential necessity of having to access the capital market to finance new projects and of being subject to additional external monitoring.[2249] Finally, such profit-orientated control of capital is a desired allocation of an economically rare resource.[2250]

Special dividends, legally the same, function similarly, but with the exception that their unique character does not raise expectations of the capital market that would result in falling stock prices if disappointed.[2251] Typically, they are based on extraordinary profits resulting, amongst others, from the dissolution of corporate reserves.[2252] They are a true alternative for corporations with a *temporary* high cash flow[2253] or with a high debt-equity ratio to prevent the reduced agency costs of equity from being overcompensated by the increased agency costs of debt, which could result from a continuous augmentation of debt.[2254] Special dividends may be used to *distribute* a larger amount of

---

2242 Gebhardt et al., Hdb des Finanzmanagments, 1993, 282 – 284; Prinz, in: Kessler et al., Konzernsteuerrecht, 2008, § 10 mn.310.

2243 Lintner, 46 AM. ECON. REV. 97, 99 et seq. (1956).

2244 König, Ausschüttungsverhalten von Aktiengesellschaften, 1990, 34.

2245 Prinz, in: Kessler et al., Konzernsteuerrecht, 2008, § 10 mn.310; Schulz, Der Einfluss von Dividenden auf Aktienrenditen, 2006, 19.

2246 Swoboda, Betriebswirtschaftliche Finanzierung, 1991, 207 et seq.

2247 Jensen, 76 AM. ECON. REV. 323, *available at* http://ssrn.com/abstract=99580, 1 et seq.; Jensen & Meckling, 3 J. FIN. ECON. 305 (1976), *available at* http://ssrn.com/abstract=94043, 12 et seq.; Niedernhuber, Ausschüttungsregelungen für Aktiengesellschaften, 1988, 195.

2248 Gebhardt et al., Hdb des Finanzmanagements, 1993, 270.

2249 Jensen, 76 AM. ECON. REV. 323, *available at* http://ssrn.com/abstract=99580, 1; Rozeff, 5 J. FIN. RESEARCH, 249, 250 et seq. (1982), *available at* http://ssrn.com/abstract=82031.

2250 Gebhardt, Hdb des Finanzmanagements, 1993, 272; Pütz/Willgerodt, Gleiches Recht für Beteiligungskapital, 93.

2251 Obermüller et al., Die Hauptversammlung der Aktiengesellschaft, 2001, H mn.92.

2252 Götze, in: Von Rosen, Die Hauptversammlung vor neuen Herausforderungen, DAI studies issue 41, 2008, 119 (127).

2253 Schulz, Der Einfluss von Dividenden auf Aktienrenditen, 2006, 19.

2254 Wenger/Kaserer, ZBB 2005, 1 (15).

profit to the shareholders at once. They *avoid overinvestments* in times of high liquidity often reflected by corresponding stock price discounts. If special dividends are credibly reasoned the stock price is likely to rise.[2255] Finally, like classic dividends, they may be used as a reliable *signal* of positive earnings prospects, even though investors interpret it usually as non-repetitive with correspondingly lower stock price reactions.[2256]

ii) Means and limitations

(1) Legal frame for dividends

The dividend regime under German corporate law is comparably complex.[2257] The legislator decided the underlying owner-management goal conflict in favor of the protection of creditors and capital maintenance by limiting the amount distributable via dividends.[2258] The administration may limit the distributions by retaining earnings, depriving them to this extent of their choice to invest externally for reasons of diversification or higher returns.[2259]

A specific dividend claim of a shareholder depends on an approved corporate net profit on the financial statements and a shareholder resolution approving a dividend payment, 174. The distribution policy is based on the annual financial statements, more specifically the therein-determined net profit, § 174 (1), and determined annually. The management board is generally obliged to distribute at least 50 percent of the annual net profits to the shareholders, § 58 (2) sent. 1. Once the management board has set up the annual financial statements, § 170 (1) sent. 1, and after the audit, § 316 (1) HGB, the supervisory board will usually have to approve them, § 172. Once approved and confirming a net profit, the shareholders have the right to seek a resolution on the use of the available net earnings, § 58 (3).

The shareholder meeting's authority to decide about the use of the corporate profit is limited to the bindingly determined, § 174 (1) sent. 2, and approved corporate net profit, §§ 58 (3), 174. This correlates to the restriction on distributions to the net profit prior to the corporate dissolution, § 57 (3), and the prohibition on the re-transfer of shareholders' capital contributions, § 57 (1). The former provision represents also the relevant limitation for special dividends, which may also only be derived from the corporate net profit.[2260] The shareholder resolution is based on the administrative proposal about the use of the net profit,[2261] §§ 124 (3) sent. 1, 170 (2). The administration must generally

2255 *Id.* at 14.
2256 *Id.* at 15 et seq.
2257 Von Rosen/DAI, Verhalten und Präferenzen deutscher Aktionäre, DAI studies issue 42, 2009, 38.
2258 Prinz, in: Kessler et al., Konzernsteuerrecht, 2008, § 10 mn.315.
2259 Bungeroth/Hefermehl, in: Geßler et al., AktG, § 58 mn.3; Henze, in: Großkomm AktG, 2000, § 58 mnn.11 et seq.; Lutter, in: KöKo AktG, 1988, § 58 mn.5.
2260 Götze, in: Von Rosen, Die Hauptversammlung vor neuen Herausforderungen, DAI studies issue 41, 2008, 119 (127); Kumpan, AG 2007, 461 (468 et seq.); Lenz, NZG 2006, 534 (534).
2261 Weber/Schalast, Handlungsspielräume von Staatsfonds in Deutschland, 2009, 63.

propose distribution of a minimum profit of 4 percent in relation to the shareholders' participation in the share capital. Exceptions apply when this amount is necessary to assure the viability and the ability of the corporation to resist for a reasonable period of time, § 254 (1). The proposal can also comprise the payment of a special dividend, § 170 (2) No. 1, the installment of a further amount as retained earnings or carried forward profit, or the distribution of an additional amount to the shareholders.[2262] The shareholder meeting is not bound by the proposal.[2263] Once the shareholder resolution has determined the amount to be distributed, the shareholders have a corresponding claim against the corporation, § 58 (4) in relation to the resolution.[2264] Within the mentioned limitations, it is therefore the shareholder meeting which decides about the use of the net profit and the distributed amount, §§ 119 (1) No. 2, 174.

It has remained controversial whether the dividend regime is successful in counterbalancing the underlying interests.[2265] Some evaluate the competence distribution as adequate.[2266] A few judge it as too strict on the administration.[2267] The dominating opinion amongst legal scholars, however, criticizes it as too restrictive on the shareholders.[2268] Against the latter opinion it has been argued that the administration's freedom to evaluate the corporate assets or to form undisclosed reserves has been substantially restricted under the current regime.[2269] Besides, a special auditor can be appointed to verify the evaluation process, §§ 258 et seq.[2270] The overall literature counters that the administration is provided with excess leverage. In addition to its right to determine the use of half of the corporate profit, § 58 (2), the articles of incorporation, § 58 (2) sent. 2, majority shareholder decisions, § 58 (3), and the multiple use of § 58 in groups may amend this proportion in favor of the administration. Besides, equity may also be strengthened through the increase of the share capital. Reserves, in contrast, represent an allocation brake for the capital market.[2271]

2262 *Id.* at 64.

2263 Henze, in: Großkomm AktG, 2000, § 58 mn.94; Hüffer, AktG, § 174 mn.5.

2264 Hüffer, AktG, 2010, § 58 mn.28.

2265 Bungeroth/Hefermehl, in: Geßler et al., AktG, § 58 mnn.5 et seq.

2266 Gesetzentwurf der Fraktionen CDU/CSU und FDP eines Gesetzes für kleine Aktiengesellschaften und zur Deregulierung des Aktienrechts [Draft Law of the Political Groups CDU/CSU and FDP of an Act for Small Corporations and for the Deregulation of Corporate Law], Jan. 1, 1994, BT-Drucks 12/6721, 8; Henze, in: Großkomm AktG, 2000, § 58 mn.5.

2267 Eßer, AG 1966, 24 (26): pointing out the necessary knowledge of the administration, in contrast to the shareholders, to determine how much of the corporate profit has to be retained to assure the existence of the corporation; Jagenburg, AG 1965, 156 (165-168): noting that only the management board has the knowledge about the very complex issues of the economic process, allowing a judgement about the amount of reserves necessary to secure the existence of the corporation for a longer time, pointing out the up to ten times higher reservers of U.S.-American corporations in comparison to the share capital.

2268 Bungeroth/Hefermehl, in: Geßler et al., AktG, § 58 mnn.6 – 8; Henze, in: Großkomm AktG, 2000, § 58 mn.13.

2269 Kropff, in: MüKo AktG, 2003, § 174 mn.2.

2270 Bungeroth/Hefermehl, in: Geßler et al., AktG, § 58 mn.4.

2271 *Id.* at mnn.6–8; Henze, in: Großkomm AktG, 2000, § 58 mn.13.

(2) Means

The impact of active shareholders using special formal shareholder means to increase the amount to be distributed to the shareholders is restricted through the statutory distribution authority. As shareholders have the authority to decide about the use of the annual net profit and its distribution, §§ 119 (1) No. 2, 174, they may ask the management board to prepare a corresponding shareholder resolution, § 83 (1), once the annual financial statements have been approved. They may increase the distribution volume proposed by the administration as late as during the shareholder meeting, § 124 (4) sent. 2,[2272] and up to the entire net profit determined in the financial statements, § 174 (1) sent. 2.[2273] A motion aiming to distribute a sum exceeding the corporate net profit needs not be made accessible, but often is (to expose the shareholder as incompenten and discredit other motions), as a corresponding shareholder resolution would be illegal, § 126 (2) No. 2.[2274] To have a larger part than the proposed amount distributed depends on the support of a simple majority, § 133 (1).

Key for active shareholders aiming to significantly increase the distribution volume is therefore to impact the administration prior to the determination and approval of the financial statements.[2275] The impact may either target the distribution of a larger part of the expected net profit or even the increase in the net profit. As their statutory means to impact the dividend are limited to deciding about the use of the net profit, active shareholders will need to use the known general formal and informal means to impact the administrative net profit determination.[2276] In most cases, active shareholders will need to pressure the administration to amend an overly restrictive dividend policy. Beyond personal conversations with administrative members, they will need to threaten to or actually remove them, threaten to takeover the corporation, or engage in a public campaign.

(3) Limitations on distribution volume

Before encouraging administrations to increase the net profit to facilitate a (n increased) regular or special dividend payment and due to a lack of an available war chest, active shareholders have to take into account several things. They need to consider the relevant charter and statutory provisions and the corporate financial situation, each potentially limiting an increase of the net profit.

2272 Drinhausen, in: Hölters, Aktiengesetz, 2011, § 124 mn 24, n.91.

2273 Götze, in: Gleiss Lutz/AmCham, Shareholder Activism – (k)ein rechtliches Thema, 2008, 10, http://www.amcham.de/fileadmin/templates/main/pdf/Praesentation_Goetze.pdf.; Hüffer, AktG, 2010, § 174 mn.3; Weber/Schalast, Handlungsspielräume von Staatsfonds in Deutschland, 2009, 64.

2274 Pentz, in: Fleischer, Hdb Vorstandsrecht, 2006, § 17 mn.82.

2275 Götze, in: Gleiss Lutz/AmCham, Shareholder Activism – (k)ein rechtliches Thema, 2008, 10, http://www.amcham.de/fileadmin/templates/main/pdf/Praesentation_Goetze.pdf.

2276 *Id.*

The relevant statutory provisions are complex: corporate reserves comprise capital reserves resulting from paid-in surplus, and so on, § 272 (2) HGB, as well as retained earnings, § 272 (3) HGB. Retained earnings consist of legal reserves, §§ 266 (3) A. III. No. 1 HGB, 150 (1), and other reserves, § 266 (3) A. III. No. 2-4 HGB. Legal reserves have to contain 5 percent of the annual surplus, until capital reserves according to § 272 (2) No. 1 to 3 HGB and legal reserves accumulate as a reserve fund 10 percent of the share capital, § 150 (2). The capital reserve, § 150 (3), even if it exceeds 10 percent of the share capital, § 150 (4), as tends to be the case for corporations that often accumulate a multiple of their share capital,[2277] cannot be distributed to the shareholders.[2278] Share capital, legal reserves, and the main part of the capital reserves are therefore blocked for distributions. Active shareholders aiming to convince the administration to amend their distribution policy may therefore only refer to the net profit, the profit carried forward, the other reserves, and the voluntary capital reserve according to § 272 (2) No. 4 HGB for distribution reasons.[2279] The net profit may, however, be increased through the generation of extraordinary profits by lifting hidden reserves through transaction activism (divestiture)[2280] or the reduction of the share capital, § 222 et seq.[2281] The former measure represents a pure management task allowing active shareholders to exercise impact on the administration prior the confirmation of the annual financial statements to increase the maximum amount of regular or special dividends. The latter needs to be approved by the shareholders, providing additional protection for minority shareholders from the impact of active shareholders.

(4) Limitations on distribution key

Finally, each shareholder generally has the right to participate in the dividend distribution *proportionate to the par value of his shareholding under consideration of the paid-in contributions.*[2282] Exceptions, like for preferred stock, may be based on the articles of incorporation, § 60 (3). The distribution key applies to the amount of the net profit determined to be distributed by the shareholder resolution, § 174, based on the annual financial statements as determined and approved by the administration and audited. It represents a concretization of the equal treatment doctrine laid down in § 53a[2283]. Minority shareholders holding at least 5 percent of the outstanding shares are granted additional protection from being starved by the so far unused rescission right laid down in § 254. The challenge is justified if the retained and the carried forward profits are unnecessary to securing the corporate viability and resistance in regards to its economic and financial needs over a reasonable period of time. Furthermore, shareholders must lack the 4 percent for their paid-in contributions. To prevent circumventions by hidden

2277 Falkenhausen, NZG 2009, 1096 (1097).
2278 *Id.* at 1096; Hüffer, AktG, § 150 mnn.8, 11.
2279 Prinz, in: Kessler et al., Konzernsteuerecht, 2008, § 10 mn.333.
2280 Götze, in: Gleiss Lutz/AmCham, Shareholder Activism: (k)ein rechtliches Thema, 6.
2281 Schneider, AG 2006 577 (579).
2282 Lutter, in: KöKo AktG, 1988, § 71 mn.6.
2283 *Id.* at mn.6.

distributions via transactions between the corporation and selected shareholders (*verdeckte Gewinnausschüttung*), capital maintenance requirements prohibit transactions materially disproportionate to the performance and counter-performance.[2284]

The comprehensive statutory capital requirements and the equal treatment distribution key in addition to the hidden distribution case law provide comprehensive restrictions to effectively prevent dividend payments that exploit the corporation or disadvantage fellow shareholders.

d) Distribution preferences

The corporate tax reform in 2008 has introduced equal taxation of 25 percent plus a solidarity surcharge of dividends and gains related to the sale of shares concerning up to 1 percent of the outstanding shares of a corporation. Beyond, the partial income regime considers 60 percent of the income that is taxed at the personal rate. The increasing dividend taxation has therefore almost reached the level of taxation that applies to profits resulting from the sale of shares. Empirical evidence underscores that as a consequence *private* investors are mainly indifferent in their preference between dividends and share repurchases.[2285] Over the last years, their preference for share repurchases has decreased and a well-balanced preference between dividends and share repurchases has been developed.[2286] Most *institutional* shareholders are indifferent as far as the distribution's tax treatment is concerned. A smaller, yet significant part, affirms its significance.[2287] In contrast to private investors, three-fifths of the institutional investors prefer share price increases to increased dividends.[2288] Their preference may be explained by the usually larger and more flexible character of share repurchases. In addition, share repurchases lack proportionality that could be used by knowledgeable institutional shareholders. Finally, the largely international background of institutional investors, including many U.S. investors, who usually prefer share repurchases, may be a reason. As private investors prefer balanced distributions via dividends and share repurchases, active shareholders will need to take this into account to ensure their support when aiming for distributions, as reflected in the previously mentioned numbers.

2284 KG, Urt. 15.03.1999, Az.: 8 U 4630/98, AG 2000, 183 (183); OLG Frankfurt, Urt. v. 30.01.1992, Az.: 16 U 120/90, AG 1992, 194 (196); Engert, in: Lutter, ZGR special issue 17, 2006, 743 (753); Hüffer, AktG, 2010, § 57 mnn.8-11.

2285 Von Rosen/DAI, Verhalten und Präferenzen deutscher Aktionäre, DAI studies issue 42, 2009, 37 et seq.

2286 *Id.* at 36 et seq.

2287 *Id.* at 50, 133, table A.6.7: for 56,64 percent taxation is irrelevant, for 43,36 percent it is relevant.

2288 *Id.* at 50, 132 table A.6.6: 43,31 percent prefer a higher increase in share price and a lower dividend and 17,32 percent prefer no dividend and a very high increase in share price.

3) Active shareholders and corporate leveraging

A corporation has several ways to incur corporate debt, including bank loans, bonds, convertible and participating bonds, and participating rights. Sometimes the administration will need to use them to finance capital distributions, like dividends or share repurchases.[2289] In a not insignificant number of active shareholder approaches involving distributions,[2290] they also demand increasing the corporate debt-equity ratio. Taking into account that leverage may increase the distribution volume and that active shareholders evaluate increased corporate leverage as positive,[2291] such combined demands make sense.

a) Functional background of incurring corporate debt

Under German law, an increase in the corporate debt-equity ratio allows for the *reduction of agency costs*, especially those that result from opportunistic administrative use of the available free cash flow, which the corporation is unable to invest with a return exceeding capital costs. Depending on circumstances like whether the corporation has already incurred debt, its industry, and the applicable interest rates, debt financed distributions may sustainably prevent overinvestment. Administriation will have to manage the corporate closer to profit maximization to ensure regular interest payments are made in oder to avoid insolvency. Such *disciplining character on the administration* will therefore enhance shareholder value.[2292] It has a stronger impact than e.g. sole share repurchases.[2293] In addition, incurring corporate leverage can be used to adjust the corporate capital structure by substituting part of the equity through debt, the so-called *leverage effect*. The lower amount of equity reduces the corporate capital costs if the return expectations of equity holders are higher than those of debt holders. As a consequence, the return per share will increase[2294] to the point where the risk premium compensates these benefits.[2295]

2289 These scenarios have to be distinguished from LBO's where leverage is incurred in order to finance the acquisition of the corporation as such.

2290 DAI, Investorendialog im Umbruch, 2009, 26: of 31 corporations 18 experienced a demand for share repurchases, 13 for an increase of dividend, 11 were confronted with a demand for a special dividend, and 10 with the request to increase the corporate leverage. Even though it has not been expressely stated that corporations confronted with distribution demands were also the ones that faced a demand for additional leverage, the text on page 26 indicates it, since the text equates less leverage in economically bad times with fewer demands for distributions.

2291 *Id.* at 25 et seq.

2292 Arnold, ZCG 2008, 221 (223); Baums/Institute for Law and Finance, Die Fremdkapitalfinanzierung der Aktiengesellschaft, 2006, 24, n.110; Eidenmüller, DStR 2007, 2116 (2117).

2293 Beyer, Die Beziehungen zwischen Leverag-Effekt, Verschuldensgrad, Aktienrückkauf und Shareholder Value, 2000, 3, http://www.economics.phil.uni-erlangen.de/lehre/bwl-archiv/lehrbuch/hst_kap5/shv_bezie/shv_bezie.PDF.

2294 Bezzenberger, Der Erwerb eigener Aktien durch die AG, 2002, mn.73; Last, Der Erwerb eigener Aktien als Ausschüttungsinstrument, 2006, 17; Oechsler in: Grosskomm AktG, 2008, § 71 mn.19.

2295 Kellerhals/Rausch, AG 2000, 222 (223).

b) Means and limitations

Decisions on the financial structure of corporations related to raising outside capital are generally a management task. It is the management board that decides whether to borrow from a bank or issue bonds to raise necessary capital. Neither the shareholder meeting's nor the supervisory board's participation is required, as long as the articles of incorporation or the supervisory board, § 111 (4) sent. 2, have not determined otherwise.[2296] An exception applies only if the decision to incur additional debt significantly differs from the day-to-day operations of the corporation because it fundamentally amends the financial situation of the corporation, No. 3.3 sent. 2 DCGK.[2297]

Exceptions apply for reasons of shareholder protection to special forms of obligations.[2298] *Participating bonds*, § 221 (1) 2nd alt., involve some form of participation in the corporate profit instead of a fixed interest rate. These obligations are economically so close to non-voting preference bearer shares that their issuance is, for the protection of the remaining shareholders, treated like the issuance of new shares.[2299] *Convertible bonds*, § 221 (1) 1st alt., more precisely the exchange of bonds for shares, impact the number of the issued shares, the share capital, the ownership structure, and, therefore, the participation. Finally, *participating rights*, § 221 (3), grant a right to participate in the corporate profit and liquidation proceeds. Together with *warrant bonds*, granting subscription rights, they have developed into very popular financial instruments.[2300] According to statute, the shareholder meeting has to approve or authorize for up to five years the issuance of convertible and participating bonds and participation rights by a three-fourths majority of the present capital, § 221 (1) sent. 1, 2. However, since the approval requirement is only internal, the shareholder meeting is not provided with a mandatory *initiation* right according to § 83 (1).[2301] The impact of active shareholders is, if it exists at all, limited to a formal *veto* right if any of these tools is used to incur corporate debt. The implementation of these financial tools grants only a veto right due to the closeness or convertibility to an equity stake. They will, however, not be primarily targeted by active shareholders aiming to increase the corporate debt-equity ratio. Besides, active shareholders usually aim to increase the debt-equity ratio rather than to prevent an increase. Correspondingly, the formal veto right is of little use to them.

The formal shareholder initiation rights, essential for amending the capital structure, §§ 83 (1), 122 do not, however, apply to management tasks[2302] such as the increase of the corporate debt-equity ratio through borrowing or issuing bonds. Initiating an increase

---

2296 Kübler/Assmann, Gesellschaftsrecht, 2006, 244.

2297 Götz, NZG 2002, 599 (602 et seq.); Habersack, in: MüKo AktG, 2008, § 111 mn.109; Hüffer, AktG, § 111 mn.17.

2298 Hüffer, AktG, § 221 mn.1.

2299 Kübler/Assmann, Gesellschaftsrecht, 2006, 244.

2300 Hüffer, AktG, § 221 mn.2.

2301 Hüffer, AktG, § 83 mn.2; Spindler, in: MüKo AktG, 2008, § 83 mn.8; Werner, AG 1972, 93 (98 et seq.).

2302 Halberkamp/Gierke, NZG 2004, 494 (497); Kubis, in: MüKo AktG, 2004, § 122 mn.15.

in the debt-equity ratio requires active shareholders to use the known range of general formal and informal means.

Finally, the *financial assistance provision* bans only transactions that finance the purchase of shares of a targeted corporation through a loan, security, or other transaction of the targeted corporation. The *capital maintenance provisions* prohibit the re-distribution of contributions prior to the dissolution of the corporation, §§ 71a, 57. They provide rather weak protection from potentially excessive leverage incurred upon active shareholders' distribution demand and contrary to the long-term value of the targeted corporation. In contrast, the right to attack intentional transfers by the debtor to hurt his creditors in the *ten* years prior to his insolvency grants recourse to the funds in question, to old shareholders and credit institutions, § 133 InsO. It provides comparably stronger protection against potentially excessive leverage.[2303]

c) Example[2304]

A typical example of an attempt by active shareholders to facilitate a debt-financed special dividend is the case of the CeWe Color Holding AG ("***CeWe***"). CeWe was a photo-finishing corporation, which in 2005, based on investments over €380 million, was involved in transferring from analog to digital photography technology. It had an equity ratio of 41.5 percent and a cash flow of about €15 million. Its shareholder structure included 35 percent of freefloat and several large institutional investors holding stakes below 10 percent. In 2005, the heirs of the firm's founder decided to sell their 22.5 percent stake with voting rights while retaining a non-voting stake of 27.4 percent. Soon after, K Capital Partners LLC, a U.S.-American investment company, announced that it had acquired 10.7 percent of CeWe's outstanding shares. Hedge fund MarCap Investors (***"MarCap"***) held 4.5 percent. In spring 2007, Guy Wyser-Pratte & Co. announced it had acquired a stake of 3 percent in CeWe, later increased to 5.07 percent.

Only one year after their investments, the two former investors started to complain that the transfer from analog to digital technology proceeded too slowly. They criticized the suboptimal capital structure of 100 percent equity in times of exceptionally low interest rates, which necessitated the lowering of capital costs by incurring debt and distributing the freed equity to the shareholders. Furthermore, CeWe's administration had only a 3 percent annual growth target and was therefore alleged to be incapable of reaching at least 80 percent of the 22 percent average annual growth in the photo industry. Therefore, the investors demanded a credit-financed dividend of €5 per share. After several phone calls and personal conversations between investors and administration, CeWe's administration agreed on a dividend of €1.20 per share. As a consequence, MarCap demanded a special meeting to oust four of the six supervisory board members[2305] and

2303 Eidenmüller, DStR 2007, 2116 (2121).

2304 The entire data regarding the activities of K Capital Partners and MarCap against CeWe are drawn from the following publication: Blome-Drees/Rang-Boeckler foundation, Die Aktivitäten von Finanzinvestoren in Deutschland am Beispiel der CeWe Color AG, 2009, 6-34, www.boeckler.de/pdf/mbf_finanzinvestoren_cewecolor.pdf.

2305 Regarding the other two members, the articles of incorporation determined a delegation right.

proposed to launch a vote of no confidence in the three management board members. In the beginning of 2007, the public controversies intensified. A CeWe supervisory board member and MarCap consultant alleged that an agreement between a supervisory board member and a management board member intended to manipulate CeWe's stock price to force the institutional investors to give up.

CeWe's management board reacted with a press release. It stated that CeWe's liquidity represented a strategic resource. Invested in CeWe's growth strategy, it would assure above average return. Therefore, it was the basis for sustainable shareholder value. While the current dividend amounted to €1.20 and was intended to be kept stable, the growth potential would allow investors to profit even more medium-term, once the transformation process was completed in 2007. A larger distribution, in contrast, would only serve short-term interests. Besides, CeWe's management declined distributions, as many employees had to leave CeWe due to the technology transfer. Finally, it rejected the existence of the alleged agreement and the demand that it convene a special meeting due to a general meeting in three months.

The general shareholder meeting in 2007 took place after the very positive development in the 2005-2006 corporate earnings had been announced. The CeWe administration asked for professional support and was accompanied by a sophisticated team who took the necessary steps to prepare for the showdown. It was prepared to communicate a consistent message explaining the corporate mission and strategy. This clear communication strategy, which accused the active shareholders of using incorrect statements and of lacking expertise, entailed the support of the CeWe employees. They called for the shareholders to vote for the administration and against the proposals of the active shareholders. In addition, the heirs of the founder transferred their a-typical silent partnership via the exercise of preemptive rights to shares (with voting rights). Together with the Nord/LB, a state-owned bank, they held 32.8 percent in support of the administration. The financial statements had been set up early by the management board and had been confirmed by the supervisory board. The shareholder meeting was therefore bound to the therein-determined maximum distributable amount. This was significant in regards to the active shareholder's demand for a special dividend. Finally, proxy authorities had been widely granted to react to possible countermotions and potential reasons to challenge shareholder resolutions had been precluded where possible.

The preparations proved to be worth the efforts. The shareholder presence during the meeting was successfully elevated from 37 percent during the last meeting to 87.1 percent. More than 150 questions from the active shareholders were unable to weaken the general passive shareholders and employees' support of the administration. The active shareholders' countermotions aimed to deny discharging three of the management board members. They proposed four candidates for supervisory board positions. Their intent was to replace the majority of the supervisory board members in order to appoint a distribution-friendly management board. For the same reason, they proposed voting against the administrative proposal to amend the articles of incorporation to require 75 percent support of the votes cast to elect supervisory board members. Based on the high participation rate, 59 percent of the present capital confirmed the supervisory board members and discharged the management board members. A qualified majority of the present capital confirmed the amendment of the articles of incorporation. Later filed rescission claims were dismissed or abandoned.

4) Means to pursue financial activism

Despite the comparably comprehensive number of shareholder participation rights in the context of the corporate decision-making process regarding the corporate financial structure, the special formal shareholder means to facilitate a distribution are limited. Even though shareholders may authorize the management board to repurchase shares representing up to ten percent of the share capital independent of the repurchase's purpose, they are not authorized to mandate the initiation of a share repurchase program. Regarding the distribution of dividends, active shareholders may initiate a distribution of the *entire* approved net profit, if the administration had proposed distributing less. The majority of the present share capital needs to approve the increase. To *increase* the distributable *net profit* prior to its approval by the administration, to convince the administration to use a repurchase authorization, or to facilitate supportive leveraging, active shareholders have to apply the known (accountability) means granting them indirect impact on these decisions. The immediate return for the (participating) shareholders ensures them stronger support from their fellow shareholders.

5) Concerns related to financial activism

Comparable to U.S. financial activism, the most serious concern relates to the length of the investment term of active shareholders and their corresponding impact on management's decisions to the detriment of long-term corporate value. More specifically, it relates to excessive leveraging, forcing the administration to forego promising projects or to cut R&D costs. Another concern is that active shareholders force allocation of corporate capital for their own benefit and to the detriment of their fellow shareholders.

a) Forced to forego promising projects

Detailed data about financial activism in German corporations, especially regarding the ex post debt-equity ratio of targeted firms, are lacking. Based on the limited number of supportive leverage demands[2306] and a careful transfer of U.S.-American statistics,[2307] it can only be assumed that the increase of the debt-equity ratio of German corporations targeted by financial activism is limited. As a consequence, financial activism is not expected to force target management to forego promising projects.

2306 DAI/McKinsey, Investorendialog im Umbruch, 2009, 26: 10 of 31 of the corporations that have been confronted with financial activsm have been asked to increase their debt equity ratio.

2307 Bratton, *Hedge Funds and Governance Targets: Long-Term Results* 17 et seq., www.ssrn.com/abstract=1677517 (2010); Bratton, 95 Geo. L.J. 1375, 1418 (2007).

b) Reduction of R&D costs

As in the United States, active shareholders in Germany are charged with significantly reducing R&D expenditures[2308] in order to use those funds for short-term focused distributions, decreasing corporate long-term value. Studies on the reduction of R&D expenditures through active shareholders in German firms are still not available. The careful transfer of U.S. statistics suggests, however, that active shareholders, especially the hedge funds who are most likely to initiate amendments to the financial structure, prefer corporations with initially low R&D expenditures.[2309] These uncomplicated corporations permit the efforts of active shareholders to be reflected quickly in the stock price.[2310] Furthermore, U.S. data suggest that active shareholders usually do not reduce the target corporation's investment in R&D after their investment in the company.[2311] This corresponds to their filings[2312] and to the notion that the reduction of R&D expenses, solely based on publicly available information, may result in unwanted harm to the corporate business[2313].[2314]

c) Short-termism

The most serious objection made against U.S. active shareholders, short-termism,[2315] is also raised against shareholder activism in German corporations. The concern is that active shareholders focus on short-term benefits to the detriment of long-term value-related research and innovation costs, preventing the development of new products, access to new markets, and the creation of new jobs.[2316] In addition, it is alleged that they increase the net profit relevant for distributions at the expense of substance through sales of corporate divisions, revealing hidden reserves, or decreasing the share capital.[2317]

The justified concerns of long-term investors require a *market that is myopic*[2318] and therefore inappropriately evaluates long-term strategies.[2319] This would require a rising share price in the face of short-term measures that have a detrimental effect on the long-term value of the corporation and therefore reduce the corporate net present value. The

2308 *See* Eidenmüller, DStR 2007, 2116 (2117): referring explicitely to private equity buy-out funds while later referring to these remarks with regard to hedge funds; Schneider, AG 2006, 577 (578): pointing out that they are lacking a long-term interest in R&D.

2309 Brav et al., *The returns to hedge fund activism* 7, http://ssrn.com/abstract=1111778 (2008).

2310 *Id.* at 8.

2311 Bratton, 95 Geo. L.J. 1375, 1415 (2007).

2312 Klein & Zur, 64 J. Fin. 197, 223 et seq. (2009).

2313 Bratton, *Hedge Funds and Govenance Targets: Long-Term Results* 15, www.ssrn.com/abstract=1677517 (2010).

2314 With the same result Eidenmüller: DStR 2007, 2116 (2117).

2315 Kahan & Rock, 155 U. Pa. L. Rev. 1021, 1083 (2007).

2316 Schneider, AG 2006, 577 (578).

2317 *Id.* at 579.

2318 *See* for the different myopia models: Ruffner, Die ökonomischen Grundlagen eines Rechts der Publikumsgesellschaft, 2000, 384 et seq.

2319 Arnold, ZCG 2008, 221 (223); Eidenmüller, DStR 2007, 2116 (2118); Schmolke, ZGR 2007, 701 (712).

market is not as knowledgeable as management, however, since economic property and control are separated[2320] and the market knows these asymmetries.[2321] The question is therefore whether the capital market tends to lose reliance on management and its strategies too quickly.[2322] This would justify the fear of excessive application of alternative disciplining mechanisms, like shareholder activism[2323] or takeovers, forcing myopia upon corporate management.[2324] And if restructuring through active shareholders in myopic markets increased the stock price, active shareholders could count on the support of other investors with short-term investment horizons.[2325]

As already mentioned *supra*, the opinions of financial market theorists diverge on the theme of allocation efficiency and myopia of capital markets.[2326] Besides disciplining measures, like takeovers, imposing short termism on management, some judge the short-term orientation of capital market participants to the quarterly published figures and the high profits and commissions gained by shareholders and intermediaries in restructurings as proof of the capital markets' myopia.[2327] Others counter that efficient markets do not differentiate between short- and long-term investment projects. Share prices reflect solely the present value of the discounted future cash flows while price reactions on quarterly figures are the result of announcing amended future cash flows. Therefore, management acts myopically only when not owning shares or when acting based on a short-term-based compensation system.[2328] Empirical studies on market myopia give no

2320 Engert, ZIP 2006, 2105 (2106).

2321 Bebchuk, 118 HARV. L. REV. 833, 880 et seq. (2005); Gordon, 60 U. CIN. L. REV. 347, 353 et seq. (1991).

2322 Engert, ZIP 2006, 2105 (2106): The distrust of investors in the corporate management results not only from information asymmetries, but also from the circumstance that many investors invest little to form a well founded opinion on the through management pursued corporate strategy and therefore barely exercise effective control over management. The latter circumstance is the reason for the distrust of investors in management's longer-term strategies. As far as investors do not form their own opinion, their judgment changes as soon as the market – truly or assumedly – looses trust in corporate management. For empirical support, Engert refers to a study of Gaspar et al., 76 J. FIN. ECON. 135, 146 et seq. (2005), which relies on data of U.S. corporations. The focus of the study lies on the impact of short-term investors in target corporations on the acquisition premium as well as the stock price performance around the announcement date, which is the lower the larger the number of short-term investors. Relevant data for the context confirm that according to Schedule 13F a median institutional investor holds an average stock for a period of around 15 months in his portfolio, 142-144.

2323 Engert, ZIP 2006, 2105 (2106).

2324 Ruffner, Die ökonomischen Grundlagen eines Rechts der Publikumsgesellschaft, 2000, 355 et seq., 383 et seq.

2325 *Id.* at 455.

2326 *See* Ruffner, Die ökonomischen Grundlagen eines Rechts der Publikumsgesellschaft, 2000, 383 et seq.

2327 *See* id, at 383 et seq. n.153.

2328 Jensen, *The Takeover Controversy: Analysis and Evidence* 11, www.ssrn.com/abstract=173452 (1986).

clear results as far as extent and size are concerned.[2329] Meanwhile, data confirm that markets and financial investors appreciate long-term focused corporations.[2330]

Evidence on the *lengths of investment periods* of active shareholders in German corporations mitigates concerns that active shareholders focus on short-term strategies to the detriment of long-term value. Rather, they focus on the long-term development of the targeted corporation.[2331] The majority of active shareholders of German corporations invest for two years or longer, as compared to the average turnover twice a year.[2332]

Furthermore, firms that have been impacted by active shareholders have a permanently better return on equity and assets compared to peer companies due to reduced agency costs and enhanced corporate governance.[2333] Data on *long-term effects* of shareholder activism on German corporations have not been collected and evaluated yet. However, different studies outside the United States permit the assumption that the positive empirical results may also be transferred to hedge fund activism outside the United States.[2334] *Becht et al. (2010)* examine private and publicly available information. They conclude that public interventions are associated with large positive abnormal returns in several jurisdictions, for Germany at a significant level, while private activism (in Germany stakes below 3 percent) is less profitable. Hostile interventions and interventions by specialist funds, like hedge funds, result in larger returns.[2335] *Mietzner & Schweizer (2008)* collect filings related to the acquisition of at least 5 percent of the voting rights of public firms in Germany and compare the performance of hedge funds to that of private equity funds as shareholder activists. According to them, the market perceives the announcement of the acquisition of large stakes in target firms favorably for both groups of investors.[2336] *Stokman (2008)* studied 94 hedge fund activism events from 2000 to 2007 in Europe and compares them with an equal number of similar events in North America, mostly in the United States. He concludes that hedge fund activism results not only in significant positive abnormal returns around the filing date, but also 6 months after.[2337]

2329 Eidenmüller, DStR 2007, 2116 (2118); Schmolke, ZGR 2007, 701 (713); *see* Kahan & Rock, 155 U. Pa. L. Rev. 1021, 1085 et seq. (2005).

2330 *Vorbild Familienunternehmen*, Febr. 19, 2007, Handelsblatt, www.handelsblatt.com/unternehmen/mittelstand_aktuell/vorbild-familienunternehmen;1226987.

2331 Von Rosen/Wieandt, Active Shareholders: Consensus Instead of Confrontation, Finanzplatz 3/2009, 22 et seq.

2332 DAI/McKinsey, Investorendialog im Umbruch, 2009, 16; Von Rosen/Wieandt, Active Shareholders: Consensus Instead of Confrontation, Finanzplatz 3/2009, 22 (22 et seq.).

2333 Böhm/Grothe, Hedgefonds-Aktivismus in Deutschland, BVAI Newsletter IV 2009, 14 (16), www.bvai.de/newsletter (choose BAI Newsletter IV/2009); Eidenmüller, DStR 2007, 2116 (2118 n.20, 21).

2334 Brav et al., *Hedge Fund Activism: A Review* 7, www.ssrn.com/abstract=1551953 (2010).

2335 *Id.* at 22 et seq.

2336 Mietzner & Schweizer, *Hedge Funds versus Private Equity Funds as Shareholder Activists – Differences in Value Creation* 19 et seq., www.ssrn.com/abstract=1100945 (2008).

2337 Stokman, *Influences of hedge fund activism on the medium term target firm value* 49, www.ssrn.com/abtract=1019968 (2008).

Regarding the allegation that active shareholders *exploit* their *targeted corporations*, no evidence has been provided so far. The majority of cases of shareholder activism where targeted corporations later went bankrupt involved no prior distribution requests. In the few cases in which activist shareholders had successfully facilitated distributions, the later insolvency was not causally linked to the prior distribution.[2338]

These empirical findings are supported by theoretical and practical considerations. *The shorter the time horizon* of an investor and the more important liquidity is for him, *the less he profits from active control of management.*[2339] Short-term investors preferring high liquidity aim to avoid conflicts with management, which would lock them into the company in case of friction with management and resulting sinking prices. Rather, they prefer to free-ride when there is a chance for quick profits independent of whether the positive stock price reaction results from an inflation of the profit in myopic markets or the efficient use of the firm's resources.[2340] However, active shareholders focusing on the impact on the corporate financial structure, operational and strategic aspects, sales and purchases of corporations, and corporate governance issues require a longer period of time to implement them and to benefit from them.[2341] In addition, active shareholders usually depend on the *support of* a majority of *fellow shareholders*. Even though some short-term investors may exist, the necessary support by a majority of fellow investors necessary to credibly threaten the administration requires that the demands conform to the long-term interests of the average shareholder.

Not only these considerations but also relevant *legal provisions* support the empirical findings. Since 2002, the DCGK recommends the management of listed corporations pursue a long-term orientation. Accordingly, No. 4.1.1 DCGK recommends that the management board manage the corporation with the aim of sustainable value creation, otherwise requiring a negative disclosure pursuant to § 161. Long-term orientated compensation schemes are recommended to assure the alignment of management board incentives with long-term strategies. The variable parts of management compensation are to be based on an assessment of the performance of several years, No. 4.2.3. (2) DCGK. Since the implementation of the *Gesetz zur Angemessenheit der Vorstandsvergütung* (***"VorstAG"***)[2342] in August 2009, the compensation of management board members of listed corporations must focus on the sustainable development of the firm and is binding for new contracts,[2343] § 87 (1) sent. 2. The wording is not very fitting. From a business perspective, sustainability

---

2338 Böhm/Grothe, Hedgefonds-Aktivismus in Deutschland, BVAI Newsletter IV 2009, 14 (16), www.bvai.de/newsletter (choose BAI Newsletter IV/2009).

2339 Ruffner, Die ökonomischen Grundlagen der Publikumsgesellschaft, 2000, 458.

2340 *Id.* at 460.

2341 Von Rosen & Wieandt, Active Shareholders: Consensus Instead of Confrontation, Der Finanzplatz 3/2009, 22 et seq.

2342 Gesetz zur Angemessenheit der Vorstandsvergütung, [Act on the Appropriateness of Management Board Compensation], Aug. 5, 2009, BGBl. I at 2509 (F.R.G.).

2343 Beschlussempfehlung und Bericht des Rechtsausschusses zum Entwurf des VorstAG [Recommendation and Report of the Legal Committee regarding the Draft Law of the VorstAG], June 17, 2009, BT-Drucks 16/13433, 10; Bauer/Arnold, AG 2009, 717 (724); Hoffmann-Becking/Krieger, NZG 2009, Supp. Issue 26, No. 27.

stands for a realignment of the management under ecological aspects, while the provision targets the time-horizon conflict of management members. For career reasons such as a close firm change or retirement, management members focus on corporate short-term profits instead of equally considering the long-term effects and therefore the entire net present value.[2344] However, through the VorstAG, the German legislature has clearly expressed its intent that corporations avoid short-term exaggerated success at the price of substance and a later slump in the share price by selling the corporate future. Rather, the aim is to have corporations invest in technologies that promise long-term success,[2345] which allow healthy growth and sufficient yields, the prevention of risk,[2346] and an equity provision for hard times.[2347] The seriousness of the legislative intent is underlined by liability consequences for supervisory board members not following this requirement, § 116 sent. 3.[2348] The focus on the *development* of the firm, as compared to the narrower *value* of the firm in DCGK, aims to prevent success built on shifting sands. It allows the supervisory board to decide on strategic aim(s). These could include the increase of the value of the firm, as demanded by the DCGK, but may also include the increase of earnings, sales, or innovative capability. Finally, compensation may pursue other aims.[2349] More specifically, the *variable* parts of compensation are to be founded on an assessment basis of several years, § 87 (1) sent. 3. The focus lies on the permanent, several compensation periods lasting corporate success instead of punctual success parameters.[2350] For interpretative reasons, the prolonged delay of two to four years in § 193 (2) No. 4, determined as an interpretative aid,[2351] and the in practice usual office term lengths of three to five years for management board members need to be taken into account.[2352] Consequently, in the future agreed-on[2353] variable compensation needs to take into account the performance of the last two years, § 87 (1) sent. 3[2354], or more.[2355] The assessment basis for variable compensation may be adjusted in

2344 Fleischer, NZG 2009, 801 (802).
2345 Bauer/Arnold, AG 2009, 717 (721); Thüsing, AG 2009, 517 (520).
2346 Fleischer, NZG 2009, 801 (803).
2347 Seibert, WM 2009, 1489 (1490).
2348 Fleischer, NZG 2009, 801 (802).
2349 Thüsing, AG 2009, 517 (520).
2350 Hüffer, AktG, 2010, § 87 mn.4c.
2351 Gesetzentwurf der Fraktionen der CDU/CSU und SPD eines Gesetzes zur Angemessenheit der Vorstandsvergütung (VorstAG)[Draft Law of the Political Groups CDU/CSU and FDP of an Act on the Appropriateness of Management Board Compensation (VorstAG)], Mar. 17, 2009, BT-Drucks 16/12278, 5; Hoffmann-Becking/Krieger, NZG 2009, Supp. Isse 26, No. 19: pointing out § 193 (2) No. 4 as a non-binding interpretation aid, since the legislator decided during the legislative process to set up an independent rule for other compensation means apart from stock options and determined independently that those means need an assessment basis of several years.
2352 Fleischer, NZG 2009, 801 (803).
2353 *Id.*
2354 Annuß/Theusinger, BB 2009, 2434 (2435); Bauer/Arnold, AG 2009, 717 (722 et seq.): requires a minimum of two years, and despite the increase of the minimum delay for share options from two to four years, no more than three years, for practical reasons; Hoffmann-Becking/Krieger, NZG 2009, Supp., Issue 26, No. 17; Hüffer, AktG, § 87 mn.4d.
2355 Seibert, WM 2009, 1489 (1490): proposing 3 to 4 years with regard to § 193 (2) No. 4.

cases of special effects resulting from extraordinary developments like the sale of parts of the corporation or the release of hidden reserves, § 87 (1) sent. 3.[2356] Even compensation schemes mixing short- and long-term incentives are permitted, as long as they result in long-term orientated management incentives.[2357] The provisions oblige the supervisory board to implement a compensation scheme that provides strong incentives for the long-term orientated development of the corporation while granting it sufficient discretion to decide about the specific target of sustainability. It provides the management with strong incentives as well as justifications to counter possible demands of (active) shareholders to pursue short-term strategies to the detriment of the long-term value and the net present value of the firm. A limitation on the sustainable compensation regime is the business judgment rule, § 93 (1) sent. 2. Management decisions are based on prognoses and need broad discretion, as the significance of certain measures is hard to determine ex ante while inactivity may endanger the economic development of a corporation.[2358]

Even without comprehensive data on the consequences of financial activism in German corporations, the concern that active shareholders may successfully realize short-term profits to the detriment of corporate long-term strategies is even less justified than for U.S. firms.[2359]

d) Distributions excluding fellow investors

Another concern relates especially to negotiated repurchases between the management board and active shareholders at the expense of the remaining shareholders. By threatening the administration with removal via means of internal control, active shareholders could convince the management board to repurchase their shares at a significant premium.

Already the underlying *European law* intends to protect minority shareholders through the maintenance of capital and proportional distributions to shareholders, like dividends, Art. 15 Second Company Directive[2360].[2361] Share repurchases do not represent

2356 Fleischer, NZG 2009, 801 (803).

2357 Beschlussempfehlung und Bericht des Rechtsausschusses zum Entwurf des VorstAG [Recommendation and Report of the Legal Committee regarding the Draft Law of the VorstAG], June 17, 2009, BT-Drucks 16/13433, 10; Annuß/Theusinger, BB 2009, 2434 (2436 et seq.); Bauer/Arnold, AG 2009, 717 (722); Fleischer, NZG 2009, 801 (803): short-term incentives are still permissible as long as they do not run contrary to the long-term development of the firm; Thüsing, AG 2009, 517 (520).

2358 Bauer/Arnold, AG 2009, 717 (721).

2359 Eidenmüller, DStR 2007, 2116 (2117): Noting that the allegation that hedge fund activism aims only for short-term profits is barely viable. Even though the timely investment horizon may be short, it does not mean that they have no interest in long-term strategies.

2360 Council Directive 77/91/EEC, 1976 O.J. (L 026) 0001-0013.

2361 Engert, in: Lutter, Das Kapital der Aktiengesellschaft in Europa – ZGR-Sonderheft 17, 2006, 743 (753 n.31); Fleischer, in: Lutter, Das Kapital der Aktiengesellschaft in Europa – ZGR-Sonderheft 17, 2006, 114 (119): both pointing out that the German understanding is that the general doctrine of equal treatment laid down in Art. 42 of the Second Company Law Directive prohibits also hidden distibutions to single shareholders, which influential shareholders may try to use in order to circumvent the doctrine of equal treatment.

a distribution in the sense of the Directive. They are, however, constrained by the general equal treatment principle applying to all shareholders in a comparable position, Art. 42 Second Company Directive.[2362] Furthermore, they need to meet the capital requirements applying to distributions, to be authorized by the shareholders, and are capped at ten percent of the share capital, Art. 19 (1a-c) Second Company Directive. For legal reasons, greenmail-like repurchases are rare in the E.U.[2363]

Under *German corporate law*, the principle of equal treatment correspondingly applies not only to share repurchases authorized by shareholders pursuant to § 71 (1) No. 8, sent. 3. According to § 53a, it also applies to the rest of share repurchases, § 71 (1) No. 1 – 7.[2364] The relevant question is therefore whether negotiated repurchases with active shareholders could represent exceptionally justified deviations from the equal repurchase or treatment principle. Especially for listed corporations, the permissibility of negotiated repurchases has remained controversial. Only a few view the acquisition from few shareholders as a violation of the principle of equal treatment and deny an objective justification.[2365] They argue with the government's reasoning in the KonTraG that implemented § 71 (1) No. 8. It determines that a repurchase offer needs to address all shareholders.[2366] The majority convincingly counters that repurchase offers generally have to address all shareholders, while objective reasons may justify an exceptional unequal treatment.[2367] It refers to the general equal treatment doctrine that also provides the opportunity to justify unequal treatment with objective purposes. Furthermore, the government draft's reasoning concerning the implementation of § 71 (1) No. 8 states the opportunity to justify an unequal repurchase and even mentions an example.[2368] Moreover, an exclusion from the general equal treatment principle needs to be authorized by a shareholder resolution confirming that it is objectively justified.[2369] Finally, in a few

2362 Engert, in: Lutter, Das Kapital der Aktiengesellschaft in Europa – ZGR-Sonderheft 17, 2006, 743 (753); MÄNTYSAARI, THE LAW OF CORPORATE FINANCE: GENERAL PRINCIPLES AND EU LAW, Vol. III, 512 (2010).

2363 MÄNTYSAARI, THE LAW OF CORPORATE FINANCE: GENERAL PRINCIPLES AND EU LAW, Vol. III, 512 (2010).

2364 Oechsler, in: MüKo AktG, 2008, § 71mn.96.

2365 Hüffer, AktG, 2010, § 71 mn.19k; Kitanoff, Der Erwerb eigener Aktien, 2009, 163 et seq.: arguing with the neutrality obligation of the management board and the liquidity of the secondary market for shares making an impact on the shareholder structure via share repurchases unnecessary; Peltzer, WM 1998, 322 (329); Von Rosen/Helm AG 1996, 434 (439).

2366 RegE eines Gesetzes zur Kontrolle und Transparenz im Unternehmensbereich [Draft Law of the Federal Government of an Act on Control and Transparency in Business], Jan. 28, 1998, BT-Drucks 13/9712, 13.

2367 Bezzenberger, Erwerb eigener Aktien, 2002, mn.120 et seq.; Bosse, NZG 2000, 16 (18 et seq.); Martens, AG 1996, 337 (344); Merkt in: Großkomm AktG, 2008, § 71 mn.78; Oechsler, in: MüKo AktG, 2008, § 71 mn.243 et seq.

2368 RegE eines Gesetzes zur Kontrolle und Transparenz im Unternehmensbereich [Draft Law of the Federal Government of an Act on Control and Transparency in Business], Jan. 28, 1998, BT-Drucks 13/9712, 14.

2369 RegE eines Gesetzes zur Kontrolle und Transparenz im Unternehmensbereich [Draft Law of the Federal Government of an Act on Control and Transparency in Business], Jan. 28, 1998, BT-Drucks 13/9712, ZIP 1997, 2059 (2060): A violation of the equal treatment doctrine that has

situations, such as the exclusion of a shareholder that is not intended to become public by selling the stake on the stock market or when the prevention of a takeover is in the corporate interest, they have significant advantages over the remaining opportunities.[2370]

To determine the circumstances under which an unequal repurchase in a listed corporation is objectively justified and whether these could be relevant for active shareholders is more difficult, however. The corporate interest behind the selected repurchase as well as the consequences for the rest of the shareholders need to be taken into account.[2371] Once the corporate interest has been determined, it needs to justify the restriction of the remaining shareholders' rights. The smaller the number of shareholders able to sell their shares[2372] and the higher the re-purchase price within the limits of § 57 (1) 2,[2373] the more complex are the demands upon the objective justification to balance the relevant interests.

Objective reasons justifying an unequal treatment embody circumstances that fall under § 71 (1) No. 1. The *telos* of § 71 (1) No. 1 requires that the damage is prevented by repurchasing from a specific person.[2374] Such scenarios occur only under exceptional circumstances. They concern, for instance, shareholders who pursue rescission claims that are very likely unfounded while the timely delay of the concerned measure would result in substantial disadvantages to the corporation, such as insolvency, or who have only appealed to blackmail the corporation[2375].[2376] Such claims are, however, not at stake here and the ARUG's amendments to § 246a will reduce the relevance of these scenarios. Another constellation concerns a very strong confrontation between certain shareholders that is likely to result in the corporation's contracting partners losing confidence

---

not been objectively justified may result in the defeasibility of the shareholder resolution; BHG, Urt. v. 6 October 1960, Az.: II ZR 150/58; NJW 1961, 26 (27)– inimax II: concerned the unequal distribution of new shares based on authorized capital for the by the court approved reason to prevent the realization of the intent of a large shareholder to control the corporation to destroy it; opposing opinion: Kitanoff, Der Erwerb eigener Aktien, 2009, 163 et seq.: denying the necessity and validity of this precedent under todays circumstances, including the administrative obligation of strict neutrality, which does not allow it to directly impact the composition of the shareholder structure, and the liquidity of the secondary market, making strategies pursued with the help of share repurchases to impact the shareholder structure of listed corporations superfluous, which have been set up for a continuous change in shareholders.

2370 Bosse, NZG 2000, 16 (18 et seq.).

2371 Hirsch, Der Erwerb eigener Aktien nach dem KonTraG, 2004, 105; different opinion: Bezzenberger, Erwerb eigener Aktien durch die AG, 2002, mn.144: noting that the principle of equal treatment prevails for listed corporations, meaning that an objective reason alone does not justify an unequal treatment, rather it is necessary that the remaining shareholders approve the transaction.

2372 Merkt, in: Großkomm AktG, 2008, § 71 mn.78.

2373 Oechsler, in: MüKo AktG, 2008, § 71 mn.224; Barz, in: Großkomm AktG, § 71 annot.8; Paefgen, AG 1999, 67 (70).

2374 Oechsler, in: MüKo AktG, 2008, § 71 mn.98.

2375 *Id.* at mnn.118 et seq.; Wiesner, in: Münch. Hdb. AG, Vol. 4, 1999 § 15 mn.11: for the termination of rescission actions only in exceptional cases, e.g. to terminate evidently unreasoned rescission claims delaying the increase of corporate capital or a merger; different oppinion: Hüffer, AktG, § 71 mn.10; Lutter, in: KöKo AktG, 1988, § 71 mn.26.

2376 Merkt, in: Großkomm AktG, 2008, § 71 mn.173.

in the corporation.[2377] Further scenarios involve a share package that is hard to sell on the market and whose placement would damage the corporation, as well as the repurchase to secure corporate claims.[2378] § 71 (1) No. 1's particularity is that the shareholder meeting does not need to approve an exclusion from the repurchase offer, as this might hinder the corporation from effectively averting the danger.[2379] Taking these exceptions into account, the concern that active shareholders could use their minority position to coerce the administration to repurchase their shares at a high premium seems unjustified. Even the general establishment of a control majority would not justify a selective repurchase to prevent a change of control § 71 (1) No. 1.[2380] Arguing *a majore ad minus*, the potential of some active shareholders to initiate the replacement of part of the administration to exercise internal control does not represent damage in the sense of § 71 (1) No. 1 either.

Returning to § 71 (1) No. 8, falling back on the corresponding shareholder authorization to prevent shareholder activism could be an abuse, especially as shareholder activism of hedge funds proves to be rather advantageous for fellow shareholders. The administration would therefore abuse its authorization in order to eliminate active shareholders and to save its own positions, depriving the remaining shareholders of the advantages of shareholder activism.[2381] Such an evaluation appears to conform to the limited number of cases under which an objective justification has been recognized. According to the government's reasoning, this concerns corporations with a limited number of entrepreneurial shareholders, which through a targeted repurchase intend to maintain their homogeneity.[2382] Greenmailing, even though limited to 10 percent of the outstanding shares under § 71 (1) No. 8, is recognized as a violation of § 71 (1) No. 8 sent. 3, as an unequal repurchase cannot be justified solely by the circumstance that shareholders may be able to remove the incumbents from their positions.[2383] Nothing else may therefore apply to active shareholders threatening to initiate the removal of administrative members by overcoming collective action issues and applying internal accountability measures if not repurchasing their shares above the market price. An exception applies

2377 *Id.* at 79, 172; Oechsler, in: MüKo AktG, § 71 mn.118 et seq.; different oppinion: Hüffer, AktG, § 71 mn.10; Lutter, in: KöKo AktG, 1988, § 71 mn.26.

2378 Merkt, in: Großkomm AktG, 2008, § 71 mn.79; Oechsler, in: MüKo AktG, 2008, § 71 mn.244.

2379 Merkt, in: Großkomm AktG, 2008, § 71 mn.79.

2380 Lutter, in: KöKo AktG, 1988, § 71 mn.24; Oechsler, in: MüKo AktG, 2008, § 71 mnn.104 et seq., 113; Bezzenberger, Erwerb eigener Aktien durch die AG, 2002, mn.51: noting that exceptions apply when there exists a serious concern that the acquirer will exploit the corporation, exclude it from the market, etc.

2381 Bezzenberger, Erwerb eigener Aktien durch die AG, 2002, mn.52: noting that share repurchases based on § 71 (1) No. 8 AktG to prevent a takeover, which is usually positive for the shareholder of the corporation to be acquired, are abusive; *similar* BREALAY & MYERS, PRINIPLES OF CORPORATE FINANCE ch. 16.2, 417 et seq. (2000): for the classic constellation that the target of an attempted takeover buys off the hostile bidder by repurchasing its shares at a price that satisfies the potential acquirer but not the other shareholders of the target;.

2382 RegE eines Gesetzes zur Kontrolle und Transparenz im Unternehmensbereich [Draft Law of the Federal Government of an Act on Control and Transparency in Business], Jan. 28, 1998, BT-Drucks 13/9712, 14; Oechsler, in: MüKo AktG, 2008, § 71 mn.244.

2383 Bezzenberger, Erwerb eigener Aktien durch die AG, 2002, mn.136; Oechsler, in: MüKo AktG, 2008, § 71 mn.245; Peltzer, WM 1998, 322 (327).

only if the authorizing shareholder resolution agrees to an unequal repurchase.[2384] Independent of the relevant approval quorum, it appears unlikely that a sufficient number of fellow shareholders will agree to such special treatment.[2385] The 10 percent cap restricts the blackmail potential of active shareholders substantially, as it allows only one or few of them, for reasons of pressure likely a larger stake of jointly operating investors, to exit via the repurchase program. Consequently, approval does not represent a practical alternative for active shareholders either.

Due to the otherwise ineffective contractual obligations and the liability of the responsible administrative members, §§ 93 (2), (3) No. 3, 116,[2386] the equal treatment doctrine efficiently protects fellow shareholders from the impact of (active shareholders) on the shareholder structure.[2387]

V) Final thesis regarding financial activism

1) Facts and benefits

Even though in both jurisdictions the most relevant financial measures for active shareholders are equivalent, the ratio with which they have been demanded compared to all activist events and their success ratio are different. Under U.S. law, approximately 13 to 17 percent of their demands were for the distribution of excess cash.[2388] 17 to 20 percent of the successful scenarios were financed through borrowing.[2389] In Germany, about 50 percent of corporations confronted by demands of active shareholders were subject to

2384 Bezzenberger, Erwerb eigener Aktien durch die AG, 2002, mn.121: demanding a unanimous approval for a justified unequal treatment, but declares also a majority approval of the shareholders not participating in the repurchase as sufficient, recommending to differentiate voluntarily between market purchases, for which a usual approval of the shareholder meeting suffices, and off-market purchases, which require an approval by ¾ of the remainder of shareholders; Last, Der Erwerb eigener Aktien als Ausschüttungsinstrument, 2006, 56; Merkt, in: Großkomm AktG, 2008, § 71 mn.80: requires the approval of all shareholders in order to circumvent the requirement of a justifying reason; Oechsler, in: MüKo AktG, 2008, § 71 mnn.98, 224: requires a *simple majority* according to § 133 AktG, as § 71 (1) No. 8 sent. 5 refers only to the re-distribution of the repurchased shares; *id.* at 244: refers to Bezzenberger, Erwerb eigener Aktien durch die AG, 2002, mn. 121: but demands shareholder approval of *all* shareholders.

2385 Merkt, in: Großkomm AktG, 2008, § 71 mn.80: pointing out the low attendence during shareholder meetings with regard to the approval quorum of all excluded shareholders.

2386 Bezzenberger, in: Schmidt/Lutter, AktG, 2010 § 71 mnn.71, 74.

2387 Kitanoff, Der Erwerb eigener Aktien, 2009, 148.

2388 Bratton, *The Returns to Hedge Fund Activism* 5, 21, www.ssrn.com/abstract=1111778 (2008): based on data from 2001 to 2006, in 12,7 percent of the cases hedge funds target excess cash, under-leverage, dividends and repruchases; Brav et al., *Hedge Fund Activism: A Review* 13, www.ssrn.com/abstract=1551953 (2010): based on data from 2001 to 2007, hedge funds target the firm's payout policy and capital structure in about 17,4 percent of the cases.

2389 Bratton, *Hedge Funds and Governance Targets: Long-Term Result* 16 et seq., www.ssrn.com/abstract=1677517 (2010): eight of fortyeight targets; Bratton, 95 Geo. L.J. 1375, 1418 (2007): eight of fortyone targets.

payout requests via share repurchases, dividends, and special dividends. One-third of these demands require financing through supportive leverage.[2390] In the United States, their general success rate (including partial successes) amounts to about two-thirds[2391], while 82 percent of the mid- and large-capitalization targets did so as a reaction to pressure.[2392] In Germany, 50 percent of these demands were successful.[2393]

Even though distributions have to a certain extent different functions in both jurisdictions, the functions that are relevant for active shareholders are equivalent. Accordingly, shareholders demanding the distribution of corporate capital usually aim to reduce the agency costs resulting from opportunistic administrative behavior, such as the overinvestment of excess cash. Furthermore, the potential need to access the financial market for new ventures increases the control of the administration. In addition, the leverage effect may decrease corporate capital costs. Besides elevated shareholder value, the direct financial benefits provide active shareholders with strong incentives to become active.

Under both jurisdictions, the shareholder preference for the different distribution types deviate. Private shareholders of U.S. corporations, just like institutional investors, prefer, most likely for tax reasons, share repurchases. Private investors in German corporations prefer a balance of dividends and repurchases, most likely because of the recent tax amendment treating both generally alike, while a large number of institutional shareholders prefer share repurchases. The conformity of interests between private and institutional active shareholders ensures the necessary support from fellow shareholders. A partial conformity is likely to influence the demands of active shareholders. The restraints resulting from the different distribution mechanisms on the corporate cash flow and the administration's flexibility increase from share repurchase and special dividend, to dividend payments, and then to supportive corporate leverage. Administrations confronted with corresponding demands are therefore likely to prefer unlevered share repurchases or special dividends to (elevated) dividends or levered share repurchases. Altogether, this may explain the higher success rates of distribution demands under U.S. law.

2) Applied shareholder means

The German regime of shareholder participation in corporate decisions about share repurchases, special dividends, regular dividends, and levered distributions is more complex than the U.S. regime. It demonstrates the attempt of the German legislator to balance the interests of shareholders and the administration. The restriction of shareholder-authorized share repurchases to 10 percent and the internal character of the authorization not granting shareholders a mandatory initiation right causes them to use general formal

2390 DAI/McKinsey, Investorendialog im Umbruch, 2009, 25 et seq.

2391 Brav et al., *Hedge Fund Activism, Corporate Governance, and Firm Performance* 42, www.ssrn.com/abstract=948907 (2008).

2392 Bratton, 95 Geo. L.J. 1375, 1416 (2007).

2393 Böhm/Grothe, Hedgefonds-Aktivismus in Deutschland, BVAI Newsletter IV 2009, 14 (16), www.bvai.de/newsletter (choose BAI Newsletter IV/2009).

and informal means to change an administrative financial decision. The annual financial statements, as determined and approved by the administration, bind the net profit available for distribution via regular or special dividends. In practice, it may determine that more than half of the annual surplus will be put into corporate reserves. Shareholders need to use the mentioned means to augment the distributable net profit before it is fixed in the annual financial statements. Finally, the corporate decision to increase leverage, despite the shareholder meeting's approval requirements for special obligation types, is an exclusive management task. Despite the complex distribution regime, active shareholders under German corporate law have no useful special formal means, an exception applying to the shareholder right to decide against the administrative proposal about the use of the annual net profit.

Despite the lack of special shareholder means under U.S. law, evidence from U.S. financial activism proves that it is more successful than German financial activism. The exercise of pressure on the administration is the most efficient means for active shareholders to have their distribution demands fulfilled. Due to the lack of comprehensive data regarding financial activism in German corporations[2394] and absent special formal shareholder means to impact the corporate distribution decisions, with one exception, these results may be carefully transferred to the German financial activism.

3) Concerns and limitations

Finally, evidence concerning both markets does not sustain the charges that active shareholders exploit targeted corporations to pursue short-term orientated distributions or distributions putting their fellow shareholders at a disadvantage. As in U.S. corporations, active investors in German corporations invest comparably with intermediate investors. More importantly, more recent U.S. evidence confirms that the engagement of active shareholders, especially of hedge funds, results in positive market reactions for the targeted firms around the filing date. In addition, available, though not uncontroversial, data sustain the strong likelihood that the long-term performance and corporate governance of these firms is positively (or at least not negatively) impacted while agency costs resulting from free cash flow are reduced. The concern about their detrimental impact on the long-term performance of targeted firms is therefore unjustified, which is consistent with theoretical and practical considerations. In contrast, data sustaining the myopia of the capital market or the short-termism of active shareholders have not yet been provided. U.S. evidence complements these results also regarding greenmail-like repurchase deals according to which they are not pursued by active shareholders.

2394 Dai/McKinsey, Investorendialog im Umbruch, 2009, 31: referring solely to the frequency of the communication means used by active shareholders, but not to their effectiveness with regard to the different demands; Böhm/Grothe, Hedgefonds-Aktivismus in Deutschland, BVAI Newsletter, IV 2009, 14 (16), www.bvai.de/newsletter (choose BAI Newsletter IV/2009): 25 percent of the hedge fund events resulted in distributions.–Both together only allow the careful assumption that in about 50 percent of hedge fund activism adminstrations have been confronted with financial demands, of which about 50 percent are assumed to have been successful.

Newer statutory provisions under German law further mitigate remaining concerns regarding short-termism. The variable compensation of administrative members, especially the management board, needs to support sustainable corporate development and depend on several years' basis. Consequently, even generally applicable potential short-term incentives of the members of the administration would be diminished.

German corporate law provides a broad regime of limitations relevant in the context of financial activism. Besides the limitation of authorized share repurchases to ten percent of the share capital, the limitation of the dividends to the net profit fixed in the financial statements and an efficient capital maintenance regime protect targeted corporations from overly generous distributions. As expected due to the traditional German blockholder structure, a widely applicable equal treatment regime and practical considerations efficiently protect fellow investors from selected distributions to active shareholders. The traditionally low capital requirements under U.S. law provide comparably less reliable protection for the long-term value of targeted corporations. Even though the fraudulent transfer regime is effective, the level of protection is lower. The protection of fellow shareholders through administrative fiduciary duty obligations applies only to scenarios involving conflicts of interest. Contrary to the initial expectation, the protection of the corporations and its shareholders from overly generous distributions initiated by active shareholders is therefore efficient, but lower than under German law. Moreover, only dividends have to apply equally to all shareholders. Still, both jurisdictions allow greenmailing-like negotiated package repurchases only under exceptional circumstances, which are irrelevant for active shareholders.

As a consequence, based on available evidence, further considerations, and the current legal regimes, the advantages of financial activism for the targeted corporation's corporate governance are not outweighed by their potential disadvantages. The more comprehensive German regime[2395] has proven to be only secondary in this context. It seems therefore unnecessary to adapt the specific limitations under the U.S. regime. Rather, general concerns of short-termism apart from shareholder activism make it worthwhile to consider the implementation of a compensation scheme for administrative members which takes into account the long-term performance of corporations. It would represent an important step in changing the incentives of administrative members and the consciousness of the capital markets toward a focus on the long-term effect of corporate strategy.

2395 Kumpan, AG 2007, 461 (468 et seq.).

F) Conclusion

I) Summary and final thesis

This entire analysis has strongly underscored the importance of the effectiveness of the shareholder franchise as a means to reduce agency conflicts based on the separation of ownership and control in order to increase the shareholder value of corporations. The effectiveness of the accountability mechanism of the shareholder franchise depends, however, mainly on the accountability friendliness of the underlying procedures or the ability of the economic owners to amend them. The analysis demonstrates that U.S. shareholders in particular face nomination and election procedures for the board of directors that do little to enhance accountability. In addition, they did not, at least until recently, have the opportunity to amend them in favor of a more effective shareholder franchise. At least in theory, shareholders of German corporations can, in contrast, use nomination and election procedures of the supervisory board that encourage accountability, partially even in the form of mandatory or default statutory provisions. In practice, de-facto cooptation prevails. However, active shareholders with stronger incentives and capable of overcoming free-rider issues and rational apathy are provided with useful accountability-friendly nomination and election procedures. The analysis has underscored the necessity to continue the path in favor of accountability-friendly nomination and election procedures under U.S. law to mitigate the legal barriers (active) shareholders have been confronted with in holding administrative members accountable.

Despite the legal barriers under U.S. law, active shareholders, especially hedge funds, have in both jurisdictions successfully led campaigns impacting specific management decisions. Their successful impact is usually based on the use of general formal means, especially the threat or the actual use of a proxy contest or the removal of board members. In addition, informal means, especially personal communication with administrative members and, in the United States, mechanisms to circumvent the proxy rules regime, have been applied successfully. During the few constellations of activism involving a direct shareholder vote, the activist efforts focused primarily on overcoming collective action issues (and the legal barriers related to the proxy contest under U.S. law), being equally relevant in constellations using the shareholder franchise.

Successful active shareholders are confronted with several *charges*. Especially in the context of transaction activism, they relate to the *use of (financial) instruments* resulting in the separation of economic interests and administrative shareholder rights. Evidence does not, however, sustain the charge. In addition, through the elaborate general disclosure regime coupled with qualified enforcement mechanisms, the comparably liberal U.S. corporate and securities regime provides a particularly effective regime that prevents active shareholders from pursuing deviating interests to the detriment of their fellow investors. Planned amendments to the disclosure regime should therefore concentrate on the careful amendment of the historic wording of the relevant provisions rather than adopting additional disclosure obligations that could have the opposite effect. The same applies to the discussion about the possible extension of liability provisions to active minority shareholders. Germany provides a less effective disclosure regime as well as practically little relevant liability provisions opportunistically acting active shareholders are subject to. Constellations of hidden ownership, frequently used by active shareholders, are currently subject to the disclosure regime. Empty voting constellations, however, still remain undisclosed. The European legislator had also tackled both issues. However, ESMA's call for evidence did not result in the necessary evidence to regulate empty voting, and the European Commission's proposal of maximum harmonizationization concerning hidden ownership does not require notifications by share lenders. Finally, the limited practical relevance of the in regard of the still insufficient notification regime particularly important liability provisions could be overcome, for instance, by an adaption of the relevant precedent. Other concerns, like *short-termism* to the detriment of the long-term value of the targeted corporation and its shareholders as well as *distributions for the exclusive benefit of the active shareholders*, did not prove to be justified either. Regarding the latter concern, U.S. evidence did not sustain the charges of package deals like repurchases by active shareholders. Neither do U.S. law nor German corporate statute provide relevant exceptions under the rational business purpose test or the equal treatment doctrine. Regarding the sharpest charge against shareholder activism, short-termism, comprehensive evidence proves that active shareholders invest on average for about two years and therefore for intermediate terms. In addition, targeted firms experience significantly rising stock prices not only at the announcement of their engagement in the targeted firms. Rather, recent evidence suggests that even the long-term performance of targeted firms has been improved based on data sets relating to performance after the active shareholders have exited the target. As a consequence, evidence does not sustain concerns about the short-termism of active shareholders to the detriment of long-term value of the targeted firms. Even more important, the evidence suggests that the theory that active shareholders reduce agency costs produced by opportunistically acting administrations as a consequence of the separation of ownership and control, by increasing the targeted corporation's shareholder value, is successfully implemented by the new breed of active shareholders, hedge funds. This makes sense, as active shareholders in using their shareholder franchise to change administrative decisions depend on the support of their fellow, mainly long-term orientated shareholders. Furthermore, their strategies, based on publicly available information, need to target general value-creating changes to prevent unforeseeable consequences. Consequently, the historically low level of capital protection under U.S. law, compared to a stricter German capital maintenance regime, should not be amended. Rather, the implementation of long-term orientated administrative compensation could work against the general short-term alignment of administrative interests.

As a consequence, the question about the benefits and drawbacks of shareholder activism and the corresponding necessary amendments of current statutory provisions should be answered as follows. Available data on the new and more active form of shareholder activism suggest its potential to mitigate the agency costs based on the separation of ownership and control in publicly listed corporations while increasing the shareholder value of the targeted corporations. As a consequence, the corporate governance of publicly listed corporation *benefits* from shareholder activism. Therefore, it should *generally remain unrestricted.* An exception applies only to the rare occasion of abusive shareholder activism impacting a targeted corporation in the pursuit of deviating interests to the detriment of the corporation and fellow shareholders. Improving, as far as necessary, the applicable disclosure regime, can prevent this. Under German law, case law adapting the burden of proof of relevant liability provisions in the for opportunistic activism likely area of transaction activism could fill the gap in the meantime.

To support the beneficial impact of shareholder activism on corporate governance, the shareholder franchise's effectiveness is key. It depends significantly on the *accountability friendliness of the underlying nomination and election procedures*, which need to be *improved* to a certain extent. German corporate law provides an accountability-friendly status quo of nomination and election procedures involving mainly mandatory and default rules. A recommended improvement is the implementation of a mandatory cumulative-voting rule. The relevant U.S. corporate and securities provisions have come and still have a long way to go to match the German provisions. The permissibility of shareholder proposals mandating procedural amendments of the corporate bylaws relevant to the nomination and election procedures was a significant first step. However, the vacation of the SEC-adopted mandatory proxy access rule, despite its comparably restrictive ownership requirements, was a large step backwards with regard to accountability. As a consequence, shareholders will need to continue to use the costly proxy contest or the time-consuming two-step procedure involving private ordering to amend the bylaws then permitting proxy access. The German experience underscores the recommendation to do the second step with regard to this issue and to implement a mandatory proxy access rule with significantly lowered timely ownership requirements. Another step backwards with regard to more accountability concerned the dropping of the Senat's proposal to adopt the majority-voting requirement as a listing requirement through the SEC by the Dodd-Frank Act. Again, despite the finally accepted way of private ordering mandatorily initiated by the shareholders, a mandatory or default majority-voting rule should be the aim. Finally, the implementation of a mandatory cumulative-voting rule, as has historically been the case in most states, would help to increase accountability. It reduces the expense for shareholders with significant minority stakes, like active shareholders, to obtain a board position.

Additional legal provisions to reduce the potential pursuit of deviating interests to the detriment of the targeted corporation and its shareholders are needed only to a limited extent. Most of the concerned areas have already been or are about to be tackled by the relevant legislator. One area that is still in need of attention is the disclosure of empty voting constellations under German capital markets law, while the (financial) instruments used to hide ownership need, at least currently, to be disclosed.

Consequently, the benefits and drawbacks of shareholder activism demand both the amendment of statutory provisions to improve current shareholders means, especially under U.S. law, as well as the adoption of provisions reducing the likelihood of potentially abusive shareholder activism, especially under German law.[2396] Correspondingly, the German experience with accountability friendly nomination and election rules may serve as a model for the amendment of U.S. nomination and election rules. Vice versa, the U.S. disclosure rules may help the European and German legislator in setting up a disclosure regime covering hidden ownership and empty voting constellations.

II) How (active) shareholders should be dealt with

Independent of the needed amendments of statutory provisions to prevent abusive shareholder activism, certain means have proven effective in limiting the potentially disruptive and costly effects for targets of shareholder activism.[2397] They are not only effective for targeted corporations confronted with the demands of active shareholders. To a certain extend, they also tend to prevent these companies from becoming targets in the first place while simultaneously enhancing their general corporate governance.

1) Independent of being targeted

Even without an attempt by active shareholders to contact a corporation, it is recommended that listed corporations regularly observe the investor basis[2398] and trading activities of their own securities. They need to pay attention to large accumulations of stock or extraordinary purchase patterns and to keep updated profiles on all institutional investors with material investments, including publicly available filings and statements about their shareholder activism experience.[2399] Furthermore, it is recommended that the company keep all shareholders informed,[2400] especially regarding corporate accounting

2396 Shortly summarized: United States: proxy access after less than 3 years of ownership, implementation of mandatory majority and cumulative voting standards, reassessment of Regulation FD, court rulings clarifying the need to disclose purely economic positions (§ 13(d) SEA), long-term orientated compensation of administrative members, Germany: development of indicas to shift burden of proof for acting in concert, as it is the case under U.S. law, amendment of disclosure rules to disclose separation of economic interests and administrative shareholder rights beyond constellations of hidden ownership, amendments easing the burden of proof for relevant liability provisions in constellations likely to involve opportunistic transaction activism to increase their practical relevance.

2397 Park & Tonello, *Avoiding Shareholder Activism*, The Conference Board – Executive Action Series, 1, www.scribd.com (search: avoiding shareholder activism) (2009).

2398 DAI/McKiney, Investorendialog im Umbruch, 2009, 36.

2399 Park & Tonello, *Avoiding Shareholder Activism*, The Conference Board – Executive Action Series 1, 7, www.srcibd.com (search "avoiding shareholder activism") (2009).

2400 Arnold, ZCG 2008, 221 (228).

and (potential deviations from) prognoses,[2401] and regularly contact larger shareholders to inform them of the corporate business strategy and efforts to improve shareholder value.[2402] It is necessary to consider measures that are likely to increase corporate profitability, anticipating the potential demands of active shareholders.[2403] Moreover, attendance at shareholder meetings needs to be increased, perhaps through the amendment of the articles of incorporation to allow shareholders to participate online, § 118 (1) sent. 2, (2) AktG. This will help to avoid coincidental majorities and therefore decrease the impact of active shareholders, as the success of their demands would depend on the support of a substantial part of the remaining shareholders.[2404] Targeted CeWe, for instance, raised shareholder attendance in the relevant shareholder meeting from mid-thirty to more than eighty percent. Another recommendation for German corporations concerns the removal of provisions in the articles of incorporation lowering the quorum pursuant to § 103 (1) AktG to remove supervisory board members, as CeWe also did. The statutory default rule requires at least three-fourths of the votes cast to remove supervisory board members without cause.

2) Once targeted by active shareholders

Once corporations have been confronted with the demands of active shareholders, they should seriously consider them. Not only should these demands be discussed internally, but active shareholders should also be involved in the discussion as far as their suggestions appear justified and kept informed about its progress via direct, continuous, and personal contact.[2405] Furthermore, targeted corporations need to intensify their preparation for shareholder meetings, such as by assuring a functioning back office and by clarifying shareholder majorities for the relevant agenda topics, road shows, and analyst or other relevant conferences.[2406]

2401 Carl, Conflicts with active investors? Recommendations for Executive and Supervisory Boards, Finanzplatz 3/09, 13 (14).

2402 Park & Tonello, *Avoiding Shareholder Activism*, The Conference Board – Executive Action Series 1, 10, www.srcibd.com (search "avoiding shareholder activism") (2009).

2403 DAI/McKiney, Investorendialog im Umbruch, 2009, 36.

2404 Arnold, ZCG 2008, 221 (228); Carl, Conflicts with active investors? Recommendations for Executive and Supervisory Boards, Finanzplatz 03/2009, 13 (14); DAI/McKiney, Investorendialog im Umbruch, 2009, 36: noting that about 62 percent of the corporations confronted with active shareholders do so; Schmolke, ZGR 2007, 701 (738 et seq.); Weber, Aktivistische Aktionäre – Handlungsspielraum und Grenzen, 2009, 2, www.whitecase.com (search „Aktivistische Aktionäre").

2405 DAI/McKinsey, Investorendialog im Umbruch, 2009, 21; Robert Weber, *Aktivistische Aktionäre – Handlungsspielraum und Grenzen*, 2009, 3, www.whitecase.com (search „Aktivistische Aktionäre").

2406 DAI/McKinsey, Investorendialog im Umbruch, 2009, 21; Graeff, Reden mit den Rebellen, Shareholder Activism – Herausforderungen für die Kommunikation, Finanzplatz 2/2009, 16 (16).

3) Once active shareholders have decided for confrontation

The direct, continuous, and personal contact with active shareholders via the investor relations department or administrative members must be complemented by a coordinated media strategy. It has to ensure that the corporation speaks with one voice in regarding the strategy pursued by the administration and against possibly unjustified demands or accusations of active shareholders, as CeWe did effectively. In addition, it makes sense for targeted corporation to contact their long-term shareholders holding significant stakes in order to explain the strategy pursued by the administration in more detail to prevent them from selling their shares to the active shareholders.[2407] The search for anchor shareholders has only been pursued by about a quarter of German corporations confronted with demands by active shareholders.[2408] An anchor shareholder may effectively prevent measures demanded by active shareholders from obtaining the necessary support (as done by TUI with Mordaschow). However, the anchor shareholder may also decide to change sides and support the active shareholder (as done by Grenzebach, initially anchor shareholder of KUKA AG, who switched to the side of active shareholder Wyser-Pratte). A switch to named shares,[2409] however, does not seem to be worth the effort (see the case of Deutsche Börse), as the share register does not sufficiently display the actual owners of the shares. They may be held by custodians not obliged to disclose or as pending holdings once sold and not re-registered.[2410] The same applies to shares of U.S. corporations, which may be held by nominees or in the street name.

III) Outlook

Recent U.S. data on the new, more active form of hedge fund shareholder activism suggest that shareholder activism results not only in theory, but also in practice in positive, not only short-term beneficial shareholder value effects for all shareholders of targeted corporations. It permits the expectation that more active forms of shareholder activism will be established as recognized mechanisms to improve the corporate governance of publicly listed corporations by reducing agency issues based on the separation of ownership and control. The acknowledged benefits of shareholder activism may help to overcome the remaining doubts and corresponding legal restrictions applying to shareholder means, especially in the United States, to increase the accountability of the agents, and to remove current limitations on active shareholders. Shareholder activism is expected to have a generally beneficial effect on the corporate governance of public corporations apart from actual confrontations. The preventive enhanced information policies and the increased responsiveness to shareholder interests by anticipatory shareholder value

2407 Graeff, Reden mit den Rebellen, Shareholder Activism – Herausforderungen für die Kommunikation, Finanzplatz 2/2009, 16 (16).

2408 DAI/McKinsey, Investorendialog im Umbruch, 2009, 36 et seq.

2409 Robert Weber, *Aktivistische Aktionäre – Handlungsspielraum und Grenzen*, 2009, 2, www.whitecase.com (search „Aktivistische Aktionäre").

2410 Seifert, Invasion der Heuschrecken, 2006, 26.

increasing measures will reduce current agency conflicts. In comparison to prior mechanisms that intended to overcome the same issue, the strength of shareholder activism is its flexibility based on its different strategies. Therefore, it is generally independent of economic developments, in contrast to LBOs that failed during the financial crises, and of administrative measures, in contrast to takeovers thwarted by poison pills and staggered boards.

Even for shareholder activism in U.S. corporations, additional evidence is needed to remove the last doubts about the beneficial impact of the more active form of shareholder activism. At the same time, it will permit the evaluation of the effects of the expected enhanced impact of shareholders on the nomination and election of directors. The same applies to the expected, legally more certain disclosure regime in preventing the pursuit of deviating interests able to harm targeted corporations and its shareholders. In Germany, the decreased impact of banks and the declining number of blockholders increase the freefloat in corporations and have led to a growing lack of control of the managers. The relevance of shareholder activism in German corporations has and will therefore increase.[2411] This will provide the necessary data to evaluate the long-term effects of shareholder activism in targeted German corporations to determine whether the carefully transferred U.S. data have resulted in the proper assumptions. Furthermore, it will allow a conclusion on the effectiveness of the recently implemented and expected German disclosure provisions in preventing active shareholders from acting to the detriment of targeted corporations and their shareholders.

2411 DAI/McKinsey, Investorendialog im Umbruch, 2009, 40: about 70 percent of the corporations asked assume that the significance of shareholder activism will increase during the following three years.

Schriftenreihe zum Gesellschafts- und Kapitalmarktrecht

Herausgegeben von Lutz Michalski (†),
Axel Jäger und Klaus-Rudolf Wagner

Band 1 Volker Schulenburg: Bankenhaftung bei geschlossenen Immobilienfonds. Zugleich eine Untersuchung der Wissenszurechnung im Konzern. 2002.

Band 2 Jan Wittenberg: Der Bestandsschutz von Arbeitsverhältnissen im Umwandlungsrecht. 2002.

Band 3 Christian A. Eichner: Management-Buy-Out-Gestaltungen beim Konzern-Spin-Off. Unter besonderer Berücksichtigung der Unternehmenssteuerreform. 2002.

Band 4 Thomas Wunsch: Tracking Stocks – Geschäftsbereichsbezogene Gewinnbeteiligungen bei Aktiengesellschaften. Eine systematische gesellschafts- und steuerrechtliche Betrachtung. 2002.

Band 5 Jan Blumentritt: Die privatrechtlich organisierte Börse. Ein Beitrag zur Diskussion um die Neuordnung des Börsenwesens. 2003.

Band 6 Michael Grüner: Die Beendigung von Gewinnabführungs- und Beherrschungsverträgen. 2003.

Band 7 Holger Pittroff: Die Zurechnung von Stimmrechten gemäß § 30 WpÜG. 2004.

Band 8 Wolfgang Höhn: Ausgewählte Probleme bei Lock-up Agreements. 2004.

Band 9 Gunter Reiff: Gesellschaftsrechtliche Aspekte des regulären Delistings. 2004.

Band 10 Christoph Radke: Die Entsprechenserklärung zum Deutschen Corporate Governance Kodex nach § 161 AktG. Grundlagen und Haftungsfragen. 2004.

Band 11 Gordon Geiser: Gesellschaftsorganisation und Gesellschaftsinnenrecht virtueller Unternehmen. 2004.

Band 12 Gero F. Pfeiffer: Die Kommanditgesellschaft auf Aktien als Beteiligte eines Beherrschungsvertrags und einer Eingliederung. Ein Beitrag zum Konzernrecht einer hybriden Rechtsform. 2005.

Band 13 Markus Rasner: Die Pflichten der Zielgesellschaft bei unfreundlichen Übernahmeangeboten nach dem neuen deutschen WpÜG. Unter besonderer Berücksichtigung europäischer und US-amerikanischer Übernahmeregelungen sowie der Konzeption des Gemeinsamen Entwurfs einer EU-Übernahmerichtlinie. 2005.

Band 14 Julia Kraft: Die Europäisierung der deutschen Mitbestimmung durch das SE-Beteiligungsgesetz. Eine europa- und verfassungsrechtliche Analyse der Richtlinienumsetzung 2001/86/EG zur Ergänzung des Statuts der Europäischen Gesellschaft hinsichtlich der Beteiligung der Arbeitnehmer. 2005.

Band 15 Tobias A. Heinrich: Kapitalmarktrechtliche Transparenzbestimmungen und die Offenlegung von Beteiligungsverhältnissen. Eine rechtsvergleichende Untersuchung des europäischen, deutschen, englischen und US-amerikanischen Rechts. 2006.

Band 16 Hendrik Mielke: Die Rechtsstellung der Verfahrensbeteiligten im gesellschaftsrechtlichen Spruchverfahren. 2006.

Band 17 Florian Mahler: Rechtsgeschäftliche Verfügungen über sonder- und sammelverwahrte Wertpapiere des Kapitalmarktes. 2006.

Band 18 Ines Tauscher: Der Anwendungsbereich der §§ 293a–293g Abs. 1, 2 S. 1, Abs. 3 AktG. In einstufigen vertraglichen Unternehmensverbindungen. 2007.

Band 19 Wolfgang Böh: Die Aufklärungspflicht einer Bank bei der Finanzierung einer Beteiligung an einem geschlossenen Immobilienfonds. 2007.

Band 20 Angela Koch: Die Abkehr von der „bilanziellen Betrachtungsweise" und ihre Auswirkungen auf die Existenzvernichtungshaftung. 2007.

Band 21 Markus Käppler: Die Rücknahme von Erwerbs- und Übernahmeangeboten nach dem WpÜG. 2008.

Band 22 Lars M. Laeger: Deutsch-amerikanisches Internationales Gesellschaftsrecht. Festschreibung der Gründungstheorie durch den deutsch-amerikanischen Freundschaftsvertrag? 2008.

Band 23 Wolf Rainer Bussian: Due Diligence bei Pakettransaktionen. Zur Rechtsstellung des Vorstands zwischen Auskunftsanspruch der Aktionäre, Insiderverboten und Datenschutz. 2008.

Band 24 Arne Kießling: Der übernahmerechtliche Squeeze-out gemäß §§ 39a, 39b WpÜG. Analyse eines neuen Instituts zum Ausschluss von Minderheitsaktionären. 2008.

Band 25 Uwe Trafkowski: Kreditderivate und Versicherungsderivate als Risikotransferverträge. 2009.

Band 26 Jörg Christoph Bussian: Die Verantwortung der Organe einer Aktiengesellschaft bei Fehlinformation des Sekundärmarkts. 2009.

Band 27 Dennis A. Lepczyk: Rechtliche Aspekte internationaler Börsenfusionen. Gesellschaftsrecht – Organisationsrecht – Aufsichtsrecht. 2009.

Band 28 Anna Lucia Izzo-Wagner: Kollisionsrecht und Gesellschaftsrecht nach der EuGH-Rechtsprechung und europäischen Normgebung. Konsequenzen für grenzüberschreitende Sitzverlegungen nach Inspire Art und Restrukturierungen von Kapitalgesellschaften nach Sevic, der Verschmelzungsrichtlinie und SEStEG unter Berücksichtigung steuerrechtlicher Aspekte. 2009.

Band 29 Hans-Georg Schulze: Geschäfte der Kapitalgesellschaft mit ihren Organmitgliedern. Ein Rechtsvergleich zwischen Deutschland, England und Frankreich. 2010.

Band 30 Annette Christoph: Insiderhandel unter besonderer Berücksichtigung von M&A-Transaktionen. 2010.

Band 31 Magdalena Boguslawska: Das Verbot des Handels in eigenen Aktien und seine Ausnahmen. 2010.

Band 32 Philipp Storm: Alternative Freiverkehrssegemente im Kapitalmarktrecht. Zugleich ein Beitrag zur rechtsökonomischen Analyse emittentenbezogener Regulierung durch einen Marktveranstalter und zum System der Segmentierung. 2010.

Band 33 Manuel M. Meder: Die persönliche Unabhängigkeit der Aufsichtsratsmitglieder und Directors in börsennotierten Aktiengesellschaften. Eine vergleichende Untersuchung zum deutschen und US-amerikanischen Aktienrecht. 2010.

Band 34 Niko Oertel: Fungibilität von Anteilen an Publikumskommanditgesellschaften. Der Entscheidungsspielraum unter Vinkulierungs- und Erwerbsvorrechtsklauseln. 2010.

Band 35 Henning Blaufuß: Rechtsfähige Wohnungseigentümergemeinschaft und nicht rechtsfähige Gemeinschaft der Wohnungseigentümer. Entstehung der rechtsfähigen Wohnungseigentümergemeinschaft als Folge richterlicher Rechtsumgestaltung und ausgewählte Folgeprobleme. 2010.

Band 36 Christoph R. Wolter: Der Gläubigerschutz bei der grenzüberschreitenden Verschmelzung von Kapitalgesellschaften unter Beteiligung einer GmbH. 2012.

Band 37 Andreas Voth: Beratende Hauptversammlungsbeschlüsse – zugleich eine kritische Betrachtung des § 120 Abs. 4 AktG. 2012.

Band 38 Marcus Jerg: Eine Analyse der Unternehmergesellschaft (haftungsbeschränkt) unter besonderer Berücksichtigung des Gläubigerschutzes. 2013.

Band 39 Dörthe Imberg: Die „Best Execution" im deutschen Wertpapierhandel gemäß § 33a WpHG. Der mit der europäischen MiFID bezweckte Anlegerschutz und seine Berücksichtigung im nationalen Aufsichts- und Haftungsrecht. 2013.

Band 40 Anja Wiedemann: Die GmbH nach ihrer Löschung aus dem Handelsregister. Erfordernis einer „Nach-GmbH"? 2013.

Band 41 Katja Scharkowski: Anlegerschutz durch die Regulierung von Investmentvermögen und Corporate Governance. Eine rechtsvergleichende Studie des deutschen und britischen Investmentrechts. 2013.

Band 42 Marcel Kleemann: Der Leiter der GmbH-Gesellschafterversammlung. 2013.

Band 43 Marion D. Hartmann: Shareholder Activism. Benefits and Drawbacks. 2014.

www.peterlang.com

www.ingramcontent.com/pod-product-compliance
Ingram Content Group UK Ltd.
Pitfield, Milton Keynes, MK11 3LW, UK
UKHW021830100926
8556IPUK00004B/256

9 783631 642931